Microsoft®
Office 97
Professional Edition

Illustrated Millennium Edition

Microsoft®
Office 97
Professional Edition

Illustrated Millennium Edition

Marie L. Swanson
Elizabeth Eisner Reding
David W. Beskeen
Steven M. Johnson
Mary Kemper

COURSE
TECHNOLOGY

ONE MAIN STREET, CAMBRIDGE, MA 02142

an International Thomson Publishing company I(T)P®

Cambridge • Albany • Bonn • Boston • Cincinnati • London • Madrid • Melbourne • Mexico City
New York • Paris • San Francisco • Singapore • Tokyo • Toronto • Washington

Microsoft® Office 97 Professional Edition—Illustrated Millennium Edition is published by Course Technology

Managing Editor:	Nicole Jones Pinard
Senior Product Manager:	Katie Schooling
Product Managers:	Ann Marie Buconjic, Jennifer Thompson
Contributing Authors:	Ann Barron, Joan Carey, Jeff Goding, Chet Lyskawa, Sasha Vodnik
Production Editors:	Christine Spillett, Nancy Shea, Patty Stephan, Melissa Panagos
Developmental Editors:	Rachel Bunin, Kim T. M. Crowley, Meta Chaya Hirschl, Janice Jutras, Katherine T. Pinard, Jennifer Duffy
Composition House:	GEX, Inc.
QA Manuscript Reviewer:	Seth Freeman, Chris Hall, John McCarthy, Brian McCooey, Jessica Sisak, Alex White
Text Designer:	Joseph Lee
Cover Designer:	Joseph Lee
Learning Microsoft Outlook 97 E-mail Programming Team:	David Bacon, Paul Bacon, Richard Bidleman, Istvan Siposs

© 2000 by Course Technology—I(T)P®

For more information contact:

Course Technology
One Main Street
Cambridge, MA 02142

ITP Europe
Berkshire House 168-173
High Holborn
London WCIV 7AA
England

Nelson ITP, Australia
102 Dodds Street
South Melbourne, 3205
Victoria, Australia

ITP Nelson Canada
1120 Birchmount Road
Scarborough, Ontario
Canada M1K 5G4

International Thomson Editores
Seneca, 53
Colonia Polanco
11560 Mexico D.F. Mexico

ITP GmbH
Königswinterer Strasse 418
53227 Bonn
Germany

ITP Asia
60 Albert Street, #15-01
Albert Complex
Singapore 189969

ITP Japan
Hirakawacho Kyowa Building, 3F
2-2-1 Hirakawacho
Chiyoda-ku, Tokyo 102
Japan

Trademarks

Course Technology and the Open Book logo are registered trademarks of Course Technology. Illustrated Projects and the Illustrated Series are trademarks of Course Technology.

I(T)P® The ITP logo is a registered trademark of International Thomson Publishing.

Some of the product names and company names used in this book have been used for identification purposes only and may be trademarks or registered trademarks of their respective manufacturers and sellers.

Disclaimer

Course Technology reserves the right to revise this publication and make changes from time to time in its content without notice.

ISBN 0-7600-6399-0

Printed in the United States of America

1 2 3 4 5 6 7 8 9 BM 03 02 01 00 99

Enhance Any Illustrated Text With These Exciting Products!

Course CBT

Enhance your students' Office 2000 classroom learning experience with self-paced computer-based training (CBT) on CD-ROM. Course CBT engages students with interactive multimedia and hands-on simulations that reinforce and complement the concepts and skills covered in the textbook. All the content is aligned with the MOUS (Microsoft Office User Specialist) program, making it a great preparation tool for the certification exams. Course CBT also includes extensive pre- and post-assessments that test students' mastery of skills. These pre- and post-assessments automatically generate a "custom learning path" through the course that highlights only the topics students need to practice.

Course Assessment

How well do your students *really* know Microsoft Office? Course Assessment is a performance-based testing program that measures students' proficiency in Microsoft Office 2000. Previously known as SAM, Course Assessment is available for Office 2000 in either a live or simulated environment. You can use Course Assessment to place students into or out of courses, monitor their performance throughout a course, and help prepare them for the MOUS certification exams.

Create Your Ideal Course Package with CourseKits™

If one book doesn't offer all the coverage you need, create a course package that does. With Course Technology's CourseKits—our mix-and-match approach to selecting texts—you have the freedom to combine products from more than one series. When you choose any two or more Course Technology products for one course, we'll discount the price and package them together so your students can pick up one convenient bundle at the bookstore.

For more information about any of these offerings or other Course Technology products, contact your sales representative or visit our web site at:

www.course.com

Preface

Welcome to *Microsoft Office 97 – Illustrated Millennium Edition!* This Millennium Edition contains the same great page-for-page content as our Enhanced text with a bonus unit at the end, *What's New in Microsoft Office 2000*. This new unit introduces the newest features of the Office Suite that will help your students successfully transition into an Office 2000 environment. From installation issues to the improved web integration features of the software, this additional *What's New in Microsoft Office 2000* unit gives your students an excellent overview of what's to come. In addition, we've included an appendix on the looming Y2K issue from the perspective of a home computer owner.

► Organization and Coverage

This text is organized into sections, illustrated by the brightly colored tabs on the sides and tops of the pages. Each section covers basic skills for Microsoft Windows 95, Microsoft Word 97, Microsoft Excel 97, Microsoft Access 97, Microsoft PowerPoint 97, Microsoft Outlook 97, Microsoft Internet Explorer 3, Microsoft Internet Explorer 4, an introduction to Microsoft Windows 98 and integrating Office 97 programs. In these units students learn how to work with the different applications to create simple documents, spreadsheets, databases, presentations, publications, Web pages, and email.

► About this Approach

What makes the Illustrated approach so effective at teaching software skills? It's quite simple. Each skill is presented on two facing pages, with the step-by-step instructions on the left page, and large screen illustrations on the right. Students can focus on a single skill without having to turn the page. This unique design makes information extremely accessible and easy to absorb, and provides a great reference for after the course is over. This hands-on approach also makes it ideal for both self-paced or instructor-led classes.

Each lesson, or "information display," contains the following elements:

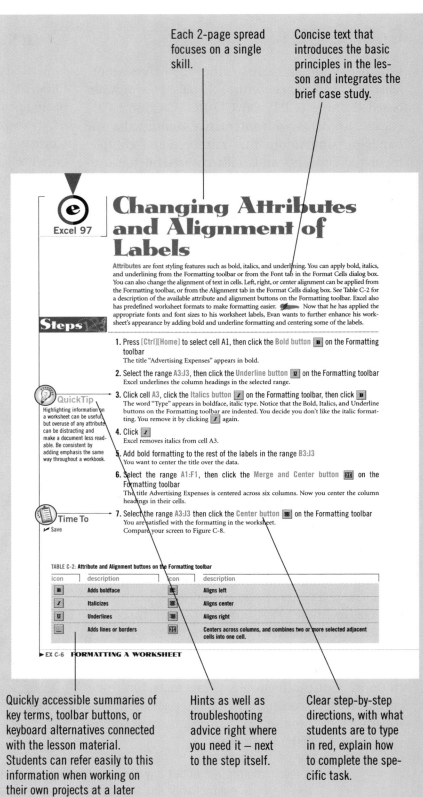

Each 2-page spread focuses on a single skill.

Concise text that introduces the basic principles in the lesson and integrates the brief case study.

Quickly accessible summaries of key terms, toolbar buttons, or keyboard alternatives connected with the lesson material. Students can refer easily to this information when working on their own projects at a later time.

Hints as well as troubleshooting advice right where you need it — next to the step itself.

Clear step-by-step directions, with what students are to type in red, explain how to complete the specific task.

Every lesson features large, full-color representations of what the screen should look like as students complete the numbered steps.

Brightly colored tabs above the program name indicate which section of the book you are in. Useful for finding your place within the book and for referencing information from the index.

Additional Features

The two-page lesson format featured in this book provides the new user with a powerful learning experience. Additionally, this book contains the following features:

▶ **What's New in Microsoft Office 2000 Preview**
The Office 2000 Preview unit offers hands-on exercises that walk students through the major features of Office 2000 and its individual applications: Word, Excel, Access and PowerPoint 2000.

▶ **Preparing for the Year 2000 Appendix**
The Year 2000 Appendix discusses the nature of the Year 2000 Computer Problem in a clear and concise way that is applicable to personal computer users. The Appendix also teaches students how Office 2000 handles the Year 2000 computer problem.

▶ **Windows 95 Overview**
The Microsoft Windows 95 section provides an overview so students can begin working in the Windows environment right away.

▶ **Real-World Case**
The case study used throughout the textbook, a fictitious company called Nomad Ltd, is designed to be "real-world" in nature and introduces the kinds of activities that students will encounter when working with Microsoft Office. With a real-world case, the process of solving problems will be more meaningful to students.

▶ **Internet Explorer Units**
This book has two units on Internet Explorer 3 and two on Internet Explorer 4. The first unit of each teaches basic browser skills and the second unit teaches how to create Web pages using the Office 97 programs.

▶ **Integration Units**
The three integration units provide hands-on instruction and meaningful examples for using Word, Excel, Access, and PowerPoint together. These integration units also reinforce the skills and concepts learned in the program sections.

FIGURE C-8: Worksheet with formatting attributes applied

Title centered across columns

Buttons indented

Center button

Column headings centered, bold, and underlined

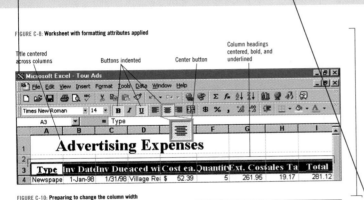

FIGURE C-10: Preparing to change the column width

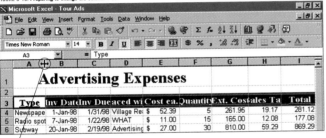

Resize pointer between columns A and B

Using AutoFormat
Excel provides 16 preset formats called AutoFormats, which allow instant formatting of large amounts of data. AutoFormats are designed for worksheets with labels in the left column and top rows and totals in the bottom row or right column. To use AutoFormatting, select the data to be formatted—or place your mouse pointer anywhere within the range to be selected—click Format on the menu bar, click AutoFormat, then select a format from the Table Format list box, as shown in Figure C-9.

FIGURE C-9: AutoFormat dialog box

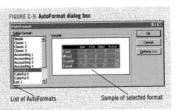

List of AutoFormats

Sample of selected format

FORMATTING A WORKSHEET EX C-7 ◀

Excel 97

Clues to Use Boxes provide concise information that either expands on the major lesson skill or describes an independent task that in some way relates to the major lesson skill.

The page numbers are designed like a road map. EX indicates the Excel section, C indicates the third unit, and 7 indicates the page within the unit.

About this Enhanced Edition

This special Enhanced Edition contains the exact content from the First Edition plus additional material and tools to give your students the best learning experience possible. The enhancements we've added since the First Edition are as follows:

Microsoft Internet Explorer 4   At the end of this book, you'll find two units on Internet Explorer 4, updated from the Internet Explorer 3 units which appear in the main content of the book. The first unit introduces students to the Internet Explorer 4 suite and browser, and teaches basic browser skills. The second unit teaches how to create Web pages using the Office 97 programs and FrontPage Express, a component of the Internet Explorer 4 suite. No matter what version of the software you're using, teaching the Internet is easy!

Microsoft Windows 98 Walking Tour   entitled "Comparing Microsoft Windows 95 and Windows 98," this unit covers all of the new features of Windows 98, such as the Active Desktop, the Quick Launch toolbar, and using Windows Explorer to browse the Web.

Student Offline Companion   New to this Edition is an innovative Student Offline Companion that lets students complete the Web Work exercises without accessing the Internet. Cached files are provided to the instructor on CD-ROM. To use the Offline Companion, a Web browser is required.

SAM (Skills Assessment Manager)   This ground-breaking new assessment tool tests students' ability to perform real-world tasks "live" in the Microsoft Office 97 applications. Designed to be administered over a network, SAM tracks every action students perform in Microsoft Office 97 as they work through an exam. Upon completion of an exam, SAM assesses not only the *results* of students' work, but also the *way* students arrived at each answer and *how efficiently* they worked. Instructors may use SAM to create their own custom exams, or they may select from a library of pre-made exams, including exams that map to the content in this text as well as the Microsoft Office User Specialist certification program. SAM is available to test students who have purchased this text. Instructors interested in using SAM to test students out of a course, or to place them into a course, should contact their Course Technology sales representative.

Instructor's Resource Kit

The Instructor's Resource Kit is Course Technology's way of putting the resources and information needed to teach and learn effectively into your hands. With an integrated array of teaching and learning tools that offer you and your students a broad range of technology-based instructional options, we believe this kit represents the highest quality and most cutting edge resources available to instructors today. Many of these resources are available at www.course.com. The resources available with this book are:

CourseHelp 97 CourseHelp 97 is a student reinforcement tool offering online annotated tutorials that are accessible directly from the Start menu in Windows 95. These on-screen "slide shows" help students understand the most difficult concepts in a specific program. Students are encouraged to view a CourseHelp 97 slide show before completing that lesson. This text includes the following CourseHelp 97 slide shows:

- Moving and Copying Data
- Creating and Formatting Sections
- Moving and Copying Text
- Relative versus Absolute Cell Referencing
- Choosing a Chart Type
- Planning a Database
- Sorting Records
- Filtering Records
- Aligning, Grouping, and Stacking Objects
- Slide Show Special Effects
- Object Linking and Embedding

Learning Microsoft Outlook 97 E-mail Learning Microsoft Outlook 97 E-mail is a simulation program designed to mimic the experience of using the mail capabilities of Microsoft Outlook 97. Using Learning Microsoft Outlook 97 E-mail, your students will learn to send, receive, forward, and reply to messages, as well as to manage a mailbox. To complete the Microsoft Outlook 97 unit, your students must use a computer that has the Learning Microsoft Outlook 97 E-mail program installed from either the Review Pack or the Instructor's Resource Kit. Adopters of this text are granted the right to install Learning Microsoft Outlook 97 E-mail on any standalone computer or network.

Student Online and Student Offline Companions Also featured with this text are the Student Online Companion and the Student Offline Companion, which are used to complete the Web Work exercises in each unit. The innovative Online Companion enhances and augments the printed page by bringing students onto the Web for a dynamic and continually updated learning experience. The Offline Companion allows students to complete the Web Work exercises without Internet access. Instructions for installation of the Offline Companion are in the Readme file that accompanies the Offline Companion files.

Course Test Manager Designed by Course Technology, this cutting-edge Windows-based testing software helps instructors design, administer, and print tests and pre-tests. A full-featured program, Course Test Manager also has an online testing component that allows students to take tests at the computer and have their exams automatically graded.

Instructor's Manual Quality assurance tested and includes:

- Solutions to all lessons and end-of-unit material
- Detailed lecture topics for each unit with teaching tips
- Extra Independent Challenges
- Task References
- Transparency Masters
- Student Files
- CourseHelp 97
- Student Online Companion
- Student Offline Companion
- Learning Microsoft Outlook 97 E-mail

www.course.com We encourage students and instructors to visit our web site at www.course.com to find articles about current teaching and software trends, featured texts, interviews with authors, demos of Course Technology's software, Frequently Asked Questions about our products, and much more. This site is also where you can gain access to the Faculty Online Companion or Student Online Companion for this text – see below for more information.

Course Faculty Online Companion Available at www.course.com, this World Wide Web site offers Course Technology customers a password-protected Faculty Lounge where you can find everything you need to prepare for class including the Instructor's Manual in an electronic Portable Document Format (PDF) fileformat (Portable Document Format) and Adobe Acrobat Reader software. Periodically updated items include any updates and revisions to the text and Instructor's Manual, links to other Web sites, and access to student and solution files. This site will continue to evolve throughout the semester. Contact your Customer Service Representative for the site address and password.

Course Student Online Companion This book features its own Student Online Companion available at www.course.com, where students can go to obtain any information regarding the text, and to gain access to Web sites that will help them complete the Web Work Independent Challenges. These links are updated on a regular basis.

Student Files To use this book students must have the Student Files. See the inside front or inside back cover for more information on the Student Files. Adopters of this text are granted the right to post the Student Files on any stand-alone computer or network.

Brief Contents

Exciting New Illustrated Projects V

Preface VI

Windows 95	Getting Started with Windows 95	W A-1
	Managing Files, Folders, and Shortcuts	W B-1
Office 97	Introducing Microsoft Office 97 Professional	OF A-1
Internet	Getting Started with the Internet Explorer 3	IE A-1
Word 97	Getting Started with Microsoft Word 97	WD A-1
	Editing and Proofing Documents	WD B-1
	Formatting a Document	WD C-1
	Working with Tables	WD D-1
Excel 97	Getting Started with Excel 97	EX A-1
	Building and Editing Worksheets	EX B-1
	Formatting a Worksheet	EX C-1
	Working with Charts	EX D-1
Integration	Integrating Word and Excel	IN A-1
Access 97	Getting Started with Microsoft Access 97	AC A-1
	Creating and Managing Data	AC B-1
	Creating a Form	AC C-1
	Creating a Report	AC D-1
Integration	Integrating Word, Excel, and Access	IN B-1
PowerPoint 97	Getting Started with PowerPoint 97	PP A-1
	Creating a Presentation	PP B-1
	Modifying a Presentation	PP C-1
	Enhancing a Presentation	PP D-1
Integration	Integrating Word, Excel, Access, and PowerPoint	IN C-1
Internet	Creating a Web Publication	IE B-1
Outlook	Getting Started with Microsoft Outlook	OL A-1
Internet	Getting Started with Internet Explorer 4	IE4 A-1
	Creating a Web Publication	IE4 B-1
Windows 98 Preview	Comparing Microsoft Windows 95 and Windows 98	W98 1

Glossary 1

Index 17

Contents

Exciting New Illustrated Products   V
Preface   VI

 ▶ | Windows 95 |

Getting Started with Windows 95   W A-1
Starting Windows and Viewing the Desktop ....W A-2
   More about operating systems....................................W A-3
Using the Mouse..W A-4
Starting a Program ....W A-6
Resizing a Window ....W A-8
   More about sizing windows ....W A-9
Using Menus and Toolbars ....W A-10
Using Dialog Boxes..W A-12
Using Scroll Bars...W A-14
Getting Help ....W A-16
   More about Help....................................W A-17
Choosing a Program and Shutting Down Windows ....W A-18
   Closing programs and files with the Close button ....W A-19
Concepts Review ....W A-20
Skills Review ....W A-21
Independent Challenges..W A-22

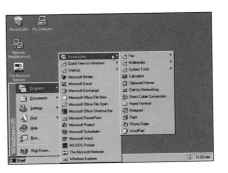

Managing Files, Folders, and Shortcuts   W B-1
Formatting a Disk ....W B-2
Creating a Paint File..W B-4
   Reversing actions....................................W B-5
Saving a Paint File ....W B-6
Working with Multiple Programs ....W B-8
Understanding File Management ....W B-10
Viewing Files and Creating Folders with My Computer ....W B-12
Moving and Copying Files Using My Computer ....W B-14
   Using Edit commands to copy and move files ....W B-15
Viewing Files and Renaming Folders with Windows Explorer ....W B-16
   Quick View ....W B-17
Deleting and Restoring Files ....W B-18
   Important note about deleting files on a floppy disk ....W B-19
Managing Files on the Desktop..W B-20
   Adding shortcuts to the Start menu ....W B-21
Concepts Review ....W B-22
Skills Review ....W B-23
Independent Challenges..W B-24

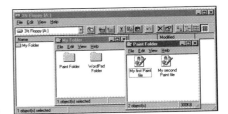

Contents

Office 97

Introducing Microsoft Office 97 Professional — OF A-1

Understanding Office 97 components .... OF A-2

Understanding the docucentric environment .... OF A-3

Create documents with Word 97 .... OF A-4

Build worksheets with Excel 97 .... OF A-6

Managing data with Access 97 .... OF A-8

Designing presentations using PowerPoint 97 .... OF A-10

Managing Office 97 Tasks Using Outlook .... OF A-12

Browsing the World Wide Web with Internet Explorer 3 .... OF A-14

Concepts Review .... OF A-16

Internet Explorer 3

Getting Started with Internet Explorer 3 — IE A-1

Understanding Web Browsers .... IE A-2

The history of the Internet and the World Wide Web .... IE A-3

Starting Internet Explorer 3.0 .... IE A-4

Exploring the Browser Window .... IE A-6

Opening and Saving a URL .... IE A-8

Choosing favorites .... IE A-9

Following Links on a Web Page .... IE A-10

Selecting a home page .... IE A-11

Getting Help .... IE A-12

Getting Help using the right mouse button .... IE A-13

Printing a Web Page .... IE A-14

Printer properties .... IE A-15

Searching for Information on the Internet .... IE A-16

Search engines .... IE A-17

Exiting Internet Explorer .... IE A-18

Saving or sending a Web page .... IE A-19

Concepts Review .... IE A-20

Skills Review .... IE A-22

Independent Challenges .... IE A-23

Word 97

Getting Started with Word 97 — WD A-1

Defining Word Processing Software .... WD A-2
Launching Word 97 .... WD A-4
   Creating Shortcuts .... WD A-4
Viewing the Word Program Window .... WD A-6
   Customize ScreenTips .... WD A-7
Entering and Saving Text in a Document.. WD A-8
   Working with Automatic Corrections .... WD A-9
Inserting and Deleting Text .... WD A-10
   Inserting Built-in AutoText Entries .... WD A-11
Selecting and Replacing Text .... WD A-12
Getting Help with the Office Assistant .... WD A-14
   More about using help .... WD A-15
Previewing, Printing, Closing a Document, and Exiting Word ...... WD A-16
Concepts Review .... WD A-18
Skills Review .... WD A-19
Independent Challenges .... WD A-21
Visual Workshop .... WD A-24

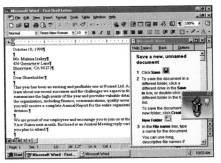

Editing and Proofing Documents — WD B-1

Planning a Document .... WD B-2
   Creating new documents using wizards and templates .... WD B-3
Opening a Document and Saving it with a New Name .... WD B-4
Copying Text .... WD B-6
Moving Text .... WD B-8
   Viewing CourseHelp .... WD B-9
Correcting Spelling and Grammar Errors .... WD B-10
   Using the Thesaurus .... WD B-11
Finding and Replacing Text.. WD B-12
   Using the Find command .... WD B-12
Previewing a Document .... WD B-14
Printing a Document.. WD B-16
Concepts Review .... WD B-18
Skills Review... WD B-20
Independent Challenges .... WD B-21
Visual Workshop .... WD B-24

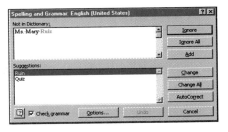

Formatting a Document — WD C-1

Applying Font Effects Using the Toolbar .... WD C-2
   Serif vs. sans serif fonts... WD C-3
Applying Special Font Effects .... WD C-4
   *Applying special effects using the Character Spacing and
   Animation tabs* .... WD C-5
Aligning Text with Tabs .... WD C-6
Changing Paragraph Alignment .... WD C-8

Contents

Indenting Paragraphs ....WD C-10

   Using Hanging Indent paragraph formatting ....WD C-11

Changing Paragraph Spacing ....WD C-12

Creating Bulleted and Numbered Lists ....WD C-14

Applying Borders and Shading ....WD C-16

   Creating borders with the Borders and Shading command ....WD C-17

Concepts Review ....WD C-18

Skills Review...WD C-20

Independent Challenges ....WD C-22

Visual Workshop ....WD C-24

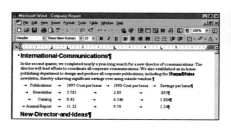

Working with Tables   WD D-1

Creating a New Table..WD D-2

Converting Text to a Table....................................WD D-4

   Adjusting row height ....WD D-5

Inserting and Deleting Rows and Columns ....WD D-6

   Using the selection bar in tables ....WD D-7

Calculating Data in a Table ....WD D-8

   Creating your own calculations ....WD D-9

Sorting Information in a Table ....WD D-10

   Sorting by more than one column ....WD D-11

Formatting a Table..WD D-12

Using the Draw Table Button ....WD D-14

Modifying a Table with the Tables and Borders Toolbar.............WD D-16

Concepts Review ....WD D-18

Skills Review...WD D-20

Independent Challenges ....WD D-22

Visual Workshop ....WD D-24

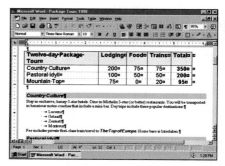

Excel 97

Getting Started with Excel 97   EX A-1

Defining Spreadsheet Software ....EX A-2

Starting Excel 97 ....EX A-4

Viewing the Excel Window ....EX A-6

Opening and Saving an Existing Workbook ....EX A-8

Entering Labels and Values..................................EX A-10

   Navigating the worksheet ....EX A-11

Previewing and Printing a Worksheet ....EX A-12

   Using Zoom in Print Preview ....EX A-13

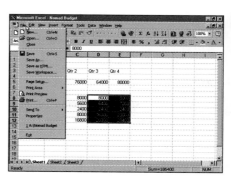

Getting Help ....EX A-14
 Changing the Office Assistant ....EX A-14
Closing a Workbook and Exiting Excel ....EX A-16
Concepts Review ....EX A-18
Skills Review ....EX A-20
Independent Challenges ....EX A-21
Visual Workshop ....EX A-24

Building and Editing Worksheets   EX B-1

Planning, Designing, and Creating a Worksheet..............EX B-2
Editing Cell Entries and Working with Ranges................EX B-4
 Using range names in a workbook............................EX B-5
Entering Formulas..EX B-6
 Order of precedence in Excel formulas ....EX B-7
Introducing Excel Functions ....EX B-8
 Introducing the Paste Function ....EX B-9
Copying and Moving Cell Entries ....EX B-10
Copying Formulas with Relative Cell References ....EX B-12
Copying Formulas with Absolute Cell References ....EX B-14
 Project a What-If Analysis....................................EX B-15
Naming and Moving a Sheet ....EX B-16
Concepts Review ....EX B-18
Skills Review ....EX B-19
Independent Challenges ....EX B-21
Visual Workshop..EX B-24

Formatting a Worksheet   EX C-1

Formatting Values ....EX C-2
 Using the Format Painter......................................EX C-3
Selecting Fonts and Point Sizes ....EX C-4
 Using the Formatting toolbar to change fonts and sizes ...EX C-5
Changing Attributes and Alignment of Labels ....EX C-6
 Using AutoFormat ....EX C-7
Adjusting Column Widths ....EX C-8
 Specifying row height...EX C-9
Inserting and Deleting Rows and Columns..................EX C-10
 Using dummy columns and rows.............................EX C-11
Applying Colors, Patterns, and Borders......................EX C-12
 Using color to organize a worksheet ....EX C-13
Using Conditional Formatting ....EX C-14
 Deleting conditional formatting ....EX C-15
Checking Spelling ....EX C-16
 Modifying the spell checker ....EX C-17

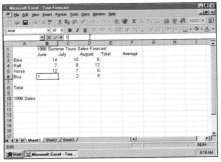

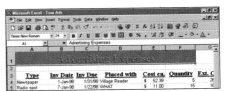

Contents

Concepts Review .... EX C-18
Skills Review .... EX C-19
Independent Challenges .... EX C-21
Visual Workshop .... EX C-24

Working with Charts   EX D-1

Planning and Designing a Chart .... EX D-2
Creating a Chart .... EX D-4
Moving and Resizing a Chart and Its Objects................... EX D-6
   Viewing multiple worksheets .... EX D-7
Editing a Chart .... EX D-8
   Rotating a chart .... EX D-9
Changing the Appearance of a Chart .... EX D-10
Enhancing a Chart .... EX D-12
   Changing text font and alignment in charts .... EX D-13
Adding Text Annotations and Arrows to a Chart .... EX D-14
   Pulling out a pie slice .... EX D-15
Previewing and Printing a Chart .... EX D-16
Concepts Review .... EX D-18
Skills Review .... EX D-19
Independent Challenges .... EX D-21
Visual Workshop .... EX D-24

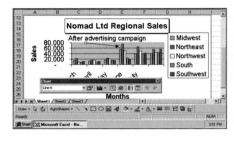

(i) ▶ Integration

Integrating Word and Excel   IN A-1

Opening Multiple Programs .... IN A-2
   Using shortcut keys to switch between open programs......... IN A-3
Copying Word Data into Excel .... IN A-4
Creating a Dynamic Link (DDE) between Excel and Word .... IN A-6
   Breaking links .... IN A-7
Independent Challenges .... IN A-8

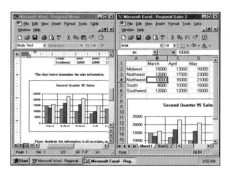

(a) ▶ Access 97

Getting Started with Access 97   AC A-1

Defining Database Software .... AC A-2
Starting Access 97 .... AC A-4
Viewing the Access Window.. AC A-6
   Finding out about Buttons and Menu commands .... AC A-6
Opening a Database Table .... AC A-8
Entering and Editing Records .... AC A-10
   Moving table columns .... AC A-10

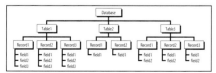

Previewing and Printing a Datasheet...AC A-12
Getting Help ....AC A-14
   Changing the Office Assistant ....AC A-14
Closing a Database and Exiting Access ....AC A-16
Concepts Review ....AC A-18
Skills Review ....AC A-20
Independent Challenges ....AC A-21
Visual Workshop ....AC A-24

Creating and Managing Data

                                                              AC B-1
Planning a Database ....AC B-2
   Creating a backup ....AC B-3
Creating a Table ....AC B-4
   Creating a table manually..AC B-5
Modifying a Table ....AC B-6
Finding Records ....AC B-8
   Using Wildcards in Find ....AC B-9
Sorting a Table ....AC B-10
   Using the Menu Bar to Sort ....AC B-11
Filtering a Table..AC B-12
   When to use a Filter ....AC B-12
Creating a Simple Query ....AC B-14
Creating a Complex Query ....AC B-16
   Using And and Or to affect query results ....AC B-17
Concepts Review...AC B-18
Skills Review ....AC B-19
Independent Challenges ....AC B-22
Visual Workshop...AC B-24

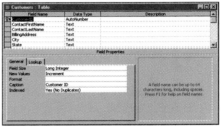

Creating a Form

                                                           AC C-1
Creating a Form ....AC C-2
   Using AutoForm...AC C-3
Modifying a Form Layout ....AC C-4
Changing the Tab Order...AC C-6
Using the Expression Builder AC-C-8
Formatting Controls ....AC C-10
Adding a Field to a Form ....AC C-12
Adding a Graphic Image to a Form ....AC C-14
Using a Form to Add a Record ....AC C-16
Concepts Review ....AC C-18
Skills Review ....AC C-19
Independent Challenges ....AC C-24
Visual Workshop...AC C-24

Contents

Creating a Report — AC D-1

Creating a Report .... AC D-2
   Using Auto Report .... AC D-3
Grouping Records in a Report .... AC D-4
Aligning Fields .... AC D-6
Resizing a Control .... AC D-8
Adding an Expression to a Report .... AC D-10
   Adding a Field to a Report .... AC D-10
Creating a Report From a Query .... AC D-12
Saving a Form as a Report .... AC D-14
Creating Labels .... AC D-16
Concepts Review .... AC D-18
Skills Review .... AC D-20
Independent Challenges .... AC D-22
Visual Workshop .... AC D-24

Integration

Integrating Word, Excel, and Access — IN B-1

Merging Data Between Access and Word .... IN B-2
Using Mail Merge to Create a Form Letter .... IN B-4
Exporting an Access Table to Excel .... IN B-6
   Exporting an Access table to Word .... IN B-7
Independent Challenges .... IN B-8

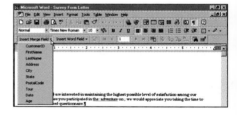

PowerPoint 97

Getting Started with PowerPoint 97 — PP A-1

Defining Presentation Software .... PP A-2
Starting PowerPoint 97 .... PP A-4
   Moving the PowerPoint shortcut to the desktop .... PP A-5
Using the AutoContent Wizard .... PP A-6
Viewing the PowerPoint Window .... PP A-8
   Using the scroll bars .... PP A-9
Viewing Your Presentation .... PP A-10
Saving Your Presentation .... PP A-12
   Filenames and extensions .... PP A-13
Getting Help .... PP A-14
Printing and Closing the File, and Exiting PowerPoint .... PP A-16
   Viewing your presentation in black and white ...... PP A-17
Concepts Review .... PP A-18
Skills Review .... PP A-20
Independent Challenges .... PP A-22

Creating a Presentation — PP B-1

Planning an Effective Presentation .... PP B-2
Choosing a Look for a Presentation .... PP B-4
   Presentation templates versus presentation design templates .... PP B-4
Entering Slide Text .... PP B-6
Creating a New Slide .... PP B-8
Working in Outline View .... PP B-10
Entering Text in Notes Page View .... PP B-12
   Adding slide footers and headers .... PP B-13
Checking Spelling in the Presentation .... PP B-14
   Checking spelling as you type .... PP B-15
Evaluating Your Presentation .... PP B-16
   Creating your own design templates .... PP B-17
Concepts Review .... PP B-18
Skills Review .... PP B-19
Independent Challenges .... PP B-21
Visual Workshop .... PP B-24

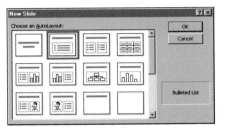

Modifying a Presentation — PP C-1

Opening an Existing Presentation .... PP C-2
   Searching for a file by properties .... PP C-3
Drawing and Modifying Objects .... PP C-4
Editing Drawing Objects .... PP C-6
   More ways to change objects .... PP C-7
Aligning and Grouping Objects .... PP C-8
   Object stacking order .... PP C-9
Adding and Arranging Text .... PP C-10
   Adding comments .... PP C-11
Formatting Text .... PP C-12
   Replacing text and attributes .... PP C-13
Changing the Color Scheme and Background .... PP C-14
Correcting Text Automatically .... PP C-16
Concepts Review .... PP C-18
Skills Review .... PP C-19
Independent Challenges .... PP C-21
Visual Workshop .... PP C-24

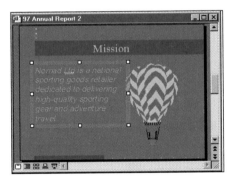

Enhancing a Presentation — PP D-1

Inserting Clip Art .... PP D-2
   More about Clip Gallery .... PP D-3
Inserting and Cropping a Picture .... PP D-4
   Graphics in PowerPoint .... PP D-5
Embedding a Chart .... PP D-6
Entering and Editing Data in the Datasheet .... PP D-8
   Series in Rows vs. Series in Columns .... PP D-9
Formatting a Chart .... PP D-10
   Customizing Charts .... PP D-11

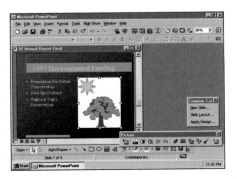

Contents

Using Slide Show Commands ....PP D-12

    Showing slide shows on other computers ....PP D-13

Setting Slide Show Timings and Transitions.......................PP D-14

    Rehearsing slide show timing ....PP D-15

Setting Slide Animation Effects ....PP D-16

    Presentation Checklist ....PP D-17

Concepts Review...PP D-18

Skills Review ....PP D-19

Independent Challenges ....PP D-21

Visual Workshop...PP D-24

 ► Integration

Integrating Word, Excel, Access, and PowerPoint

                                                      IN C-1

Inserting a Word Outline into a PowerPoint Presentation ....IN C-2

Embedding a Word Table into a PowerPoint Slide ....IN C-4

Embedding an Excel Chart into a PowerPoint Slide ....IN C-6

    Embedding objects using Paste Special........................IN C-7

Linking an Excel Worksheet to a PowerPoint Slide....................IN C-8

Updating a Linked Excel Worksheet in PowerPoint ....IN C-10

    Updating links ....IN C-11

Exporting a PowerPoint Presentation to Word ....IN C-12

Independent Challenges ....IN C-14

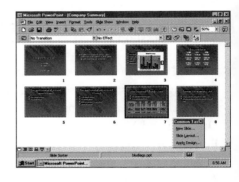

 ► Internet Explorer 3

Creating A Web Document

                                                      IE B-1

Planning Web Publication Content ....IE B-2

Creating a Web Page Document ....IE B-4

    Choosing Web page content and style ....IE B-5

Formatting a Web Page ....IE B-6

Creating a Web Page from a Word Document.......................IE B-8

    Web browsers and web page appearance ....IE B-9

Creating a Web Page from an Access Object ....IE B-10

Creating a Web Page from an Excel Workbook ....IE B-12

Creating Web Pages from a PowerPoint Presentation ....IE B-14

    Using frames...IE B-15

Adding Hyperlinks..IE B-16

    Publishing your Web publication ....IE B-17

Concepts Review ....IE B-18

Skills Review...IE B-20

Independent Challenges ....IE B-23

Visual Workshop ....IE B-24

Outlook

Getting Started with Microsoft Outlook   OL A-1

Understanding Electronic Mail .... OL A-2
    Electronic mail etiquette .... OL A-3
Starting Learning Outlook .... OL A-4
    Keeping your password secure .... OL A-5
Viewing the Learning Outlook Window .... OL A-6
Replying to Messages .... OL A-8
    Emoticons .... OL A-9
Creating and Sending New Messages .... OL A-10
    Options when sending messages .... OL A-11
Forwarding Messages .... OL A-12
    Using Tracking Options when sending messages .... OL A-13
Managing Your Inbox .... OL A-14
    Using folders to manage your inbox .... OL A-15
Creating a Personal Distribution List .... OL A-16
    Adding names to the Personal Address Book .... OL A-17
Sending Mail to a Personal Distribution List .... OL A-18
Concepts Review .... OL A-20
Skills Review .... OL A-21
Independent Challenges .... OL A-23

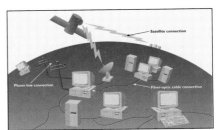

Internet Explorer 4

Getting Started with Internet Explorer 4   IE4 A-1

Understanding Web Browsers IE4 A-2
Starting Internet Explorer 4 .... IE4 A-4
    History of the Internet and the World Wide Web IE4 A-4
Exploring the Browser Window IE4 A-6
Opening and Saving a URL IE4 A-8
    Choosing Favorites IE4 A-9
Navigating Web Pages IE4 A-10
    Selecting a Home page IE4 A-10
Getting Help IE4 A-12
Printing a Web Page IE4 A-14
    Printer properties IE4 A-15
Searching for Information on the Internet IE4 A-16
    Search engines IE4 A-16
Exiting Internet Explorer IE4 A-18
    Saving or sending a Web page IE4 A-19
Concepts Review IE4 A-20
Skills Review IE4 A-22
Independent Challenges IE4 A-23
Visual Workshop IE4 A-24

Contents

Creating a Web Publication · IE4 B-1

Planning Web Publication Content IE4 B-2
Creating a Web Page Document IE4 B-4
  Choosing Web page content and style IE4 B-5
Formatting a Web Page IE4 B-6
Creating a Web Page from a Word Document IE4 B-8
  Web browsers and Web page appearance IE4 B-9
Creating a Web Page from an Access Object IE4 B-10
  Static and dynamic pages IE4 B-11
Creating a Web Page from an Excel File IE4 B-12
Creating Web Pages with PowerPoint IE4 B-14
  Using frames IE4 B-15
Adding Hyperlinks IE4 B-16
  Publishing your Web publication IE4 B-17
Concepts Review IE4 B-18
Skills Review IE4 B-19
Independent Challenges IE4 B-22
Visual Workshop IE4 A-24

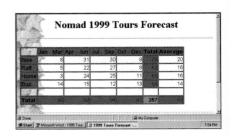

Windows 98 Preview

Comparing Microsoft Windows 95 and Windows 98 — W98 1

Upgrading to a New Operating System W98 2
The Windows 98 Desktop W98 2
   Underlined Icon Names W98 4
   The Quick Launch Toolbar W98 5
The Start Menu W98 7
Mouse Operation W98 7
Active Desktop W98 8
   Using a Web Page as Background Wallpaper W98 8
   Web Components on the Desktop W98 10
Web View in Explorer Windows W98 11
   Web View Toolbars W98 13
   Using Windows Explorer to Browse the Web W98 14
Additional Windows 98 Features W98 14
Independent Challenges W98 16

Previewing Microsoft Office 2000 Professional — OF B-1

Installing Microsoft Office 2000 .... OF B-2
Using Personalized Menus .... OF B-4
Using Personalized Toolbars .... OF B-6
   To turn off personalized toolbars .... OF B-6
Using Multiple Languages in Office 2000 .... OF B-8
Exploring Changes to Dialog Boxes .... OF B-10
Exploring Changes to Switching Between Open Files .... OF B-12
Exploring Changes to Other Commonly Used Features .... OF B-14
Examining New Online Features .... OF B-16
   Office 2000 Web Folders .... OF B-17
Exploring the New Features of Microsoft Word .... OF B-18
Exploring the New Features of Microsoft Excel .... OF B-20
Exploring the New Features of Microsoft Access .... OF B-22
Exploring the New Features of Microsoft PowerPoint .... OF B-24

Glossary — 1
Index — 17

Getting
Started with Microsoft Windows 95

Objectives

- ► **Start Windows and view the desktop**
- ► **Use the mouse**
- ► **Start a program**
- ► **Resize a window**
- ► **Use menus and toolbars**
- ► **Use dialog boxes**
- ► **Use scroll bars**
- ► **Get Help**
- ► **Close a program and shut down Windows**

Microsoft Windows 95 is an operating system that controls the basic operation of your computer and the programs you run on it. Windows has a graphical user interface (GUI) which means you can use pictures (called icons) in addition to words to carry out tasks and operations. Windows 95 also helps you organize the results of your work (saved as files) and coordinates the flow of information among the programs, files, printers, storage devices, and other components of your computer system. ✐ This unit introduces you to basic skills that you can use in all Windows programs.

Starting Windows and Viewing the Desktop

Microsoft Windows 95 is an operating system designed to help you get the most out of your computer. You can use Windows 95 to run **programs**, also known as **applications**, which are software tools you use to accomplish tasks. When you first start Windows, you see the **desktop**, which is the area on your screen where you organize your computer work. See Figure A-1. The small pictures you see on the desktop are called icons. Icons represent a program you use to carry out a task, or a document, or a set of files or documents. The **My Computer** icon represents a program you use to organize the files on your computer. The **Recycle Bin** icon represents a storage area for deleted files. Below the desktop is the taskbar, which shows you the programs that are running (at the moment, none are running). At the left end of the taskbar is the **Start button**, which you use to start programs, find files, access Windows Help and more. Use Table A-1 to identify the icons and other key elements you see on your desktop. ➤ If Windows 95 is not currently running, follow the steps below to start it now.

- -

1. Turn on your computer and monitor

Windows automatically starts, and the desktop appears as shown in Figure A-1. If you are working on a network at school or at an office, you might see a password dialog box. If so, continue to step 2.

2. Type your password, then press **[Enter]**

If you don't know your password, see your instructor. Once the password is accepted, the Windows desktop appears on your screen, as shown in Figure A-1.

▶ W A-2   GETTING STARTED WITH MICROSOFT WINDOWS 95

FIGURE A-1: **Windows desktop**

Icons ——

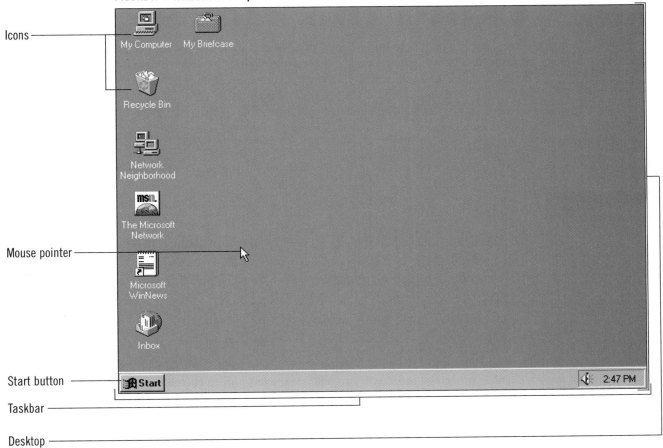

Mouse pointer ——

Start button ——

Taskbar ——

Desktop ——

More about operating systems

Windows95 is one of several operating systems. The operating system you use depends to some degree on the kind of computer you are using. For example, the Apple Macintosh computer uses an operating system that only runs on Macintosh computers. Other computers might run other operating systems such as UNIX and OS/2. Each operating system has its own unique features and benefits, causing different user communites to prefer one over the other based on their computing needs. Before Windows, many personal computers ran an operating system called MS-DOS. This character-based operating system required that you enter commands very carefully when you used the computer. With the development of Windows (and more powerful computers), personal computers can now run programs that take advantage of a graphical user interface. As a result computers have become easier to use.

TABLE A-1: **Elements of the Windows desktop**

desktop element	description
Icon	Picture representing a task you can carry out, a program you can run, or a document
Mouse pointer	Arrow indicating the current location of the mouse on the desktop
Taskbar	Area that identifies any programs currently open (that is, running); by default, the taskbar is always visible
Start button	Provides main access to all Windows operations and programs available on the computer

Windows 95

Using the Mouse

The mouse is a handheld input device that you roll on a smooth surface (such as your desk or a mousepad) to position the mouse pointer on the Windows desktop. When you move the mouse, the mouse pointer on the screen moves in the same direction. The buttons on the mouse, shown in Figure A-2, are used to select icons and commands. You also use the mouse to select options and identify the work to be done in programs. Table A-2 shows some common mouse pointer shapes. Table A-3 lists the five basic mouse actions. ◀▬▬ Begin by experimenting with the mouse now.

Steps

1. **Locate the mouse pointer** ▯ **on the Windows desktop and then move the mouse across your desk**
   Watch how the mouse pointer moves on the desktop in response to your movements. Practice moving the mouse pointer in circles, and then back and forth in straight lines.

2. **Position the mouse pointer over the My Computer icon**
   Positioning the mouse pointer over an icon is called **pointing**.

3. **With the pointer over the My Computer icon, press and release the left mouse button**
   Unless otherwise indicated, you will use the left mouse button to perform all mouse operations. Pressing and releasing the mouse button is called **clicking**. When you position the mouse pointer over an icon and then click, you **select** the icon. When an icon is selected, both it and its title are highlighted. Practice moving an icon by **dragging** it with the mouse.

4. **With the icon selected, press and hold down the left mouse button, then move the mouse down and to the right and release the mouse button**
   The icon becomes dimmed and moves with the mouse pointer. When you release the mouse button, the icon relocates on the desktop. Next, you will use the mouse to display a pop-up menu.

5. **Position the mouse pointer over the My Computer icon, then press and release the right mouse button**
   Clicking the right mouse button is known as **right-clicking**. Right-clicking an item on the desktop displays a **pop-up menu**, as shown in Figure A-3. This menu displays the commands most commonly used for the item you have clicked.

6. **Click anywhere outside the menu to close the pop-up menu**
   Now use the mouse to open a window.

7. **Position the mouse pointer over the My Computer icon, then press and release the left mouse button twice quickly**
   Clicking the mouse button twice quickly is known as **double-clicking**. Double-clicking this icon opens a window. The My Computer window displays additional icons that represent the drives and system components that are installed on your computer.

8. **Click the Close button ☒ in the upper-right corner of the My Computer window**

FIGURE A-2: The mouse

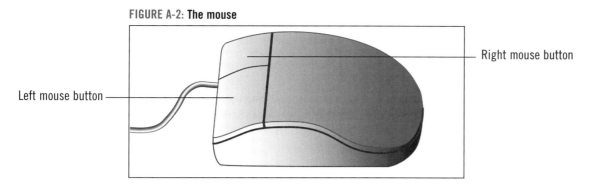

Right mouse button

Left mouse button

FIGURE A-3: Displaying a pop-up menu

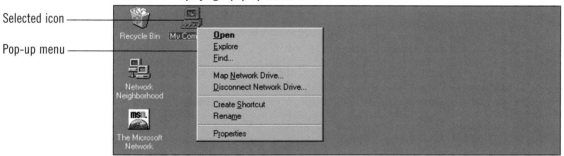

Selected icon

Pop-up menu

TABLE A-2: Common mouse pointer shapes

shape	used to
⇖	Select items, choose commands, start programs, and work in programs
I	Position mouse pointer for editing or inserting text; called the insertion point or cursor
⧖	Indicate Windows is busy processing a command
↔	Change the size of a window; appears when mouse pointer is on the border of a window

TABLE A-3: Basic mouse techniques

technique	what to do
Pointing	Move the mouse to position the mouse pointer over an item on the desktop
Clicking	Press and release the left mouse button
Double-clicking	Press and release the left mouse button twice quickly
Dragging	Point to an item, press and hold the left mouse button, move the mouse to a new location, then release the mouse button
Right-clicking	Point to an item, then press the right mouse button

Windows 95

Starting a Program

Clicking the Start button on the taskbar displays the all-important Start menu. You use the Start menu to start a program, find a file, or display help information. Table A-4 describes the **default** categories of items available on this menu that are installed with Windows 95. As you become more familiar with Windows you might want to customize the Start menu to include additional items that you use most often. ✎ Begin by starting the **WordPad** program, an Accessory that comes with Windows 95. You can use WordPad to create and edit simple documents. See Table A-5 for a description of other popular Windows Accessories.

Steps

1. Position the mouse pointer over the Start button on the taskbar, then click
The Start menu appears. Next, you need to open the Programs submenu.

2. Point to Programs
An arrow next to a menu item indicates a **cascading menu**. Pointing at the arrow displays a submenu from which you can choose additional commands, as shown in Figure A-4.

3. Point to Accessories
This is the Accessories menu, containing several programs to help you complete day-to-day tasks. You want to Start WordPad, which should be at the bottom of the list.

4. Click WordPad
The WordPad program opens and a blank document window appears, as shown in Figure A-5. WordPad is a simple word processor provided with Windows 95 that you can use to write and edit documents. Note that when a program is open, a program button appears on the taskbar indicating that it is open. An indented button indicates the program that is currently active. Leave the WordPad window open for now, and continue to the next lesson.

TABLE A-4: Start menu categories

category	description
Programs	Opens programs included on the Start menu
Documents	Opens documents most recently opened and saved
Settings	Allows user preferences for system settings, including control panels, printers, Start menu, and taskbar
Find	Locates programs, files, and folders not included on the Start menu
Help	Displays Windows Help information by topic, alphabetical index, or search criteria
Run	Opens a program or file based on a location and filename that you type or select
Shut Down	Provides options to shut down the computer, restart the computer in Windows mode, restart the computer in MS-DOS mode, or log on to the system as a different user

FIGURE A-4: Cascading menus

Arrow indicates cascading menu will open

Cascading menus

WordPad program

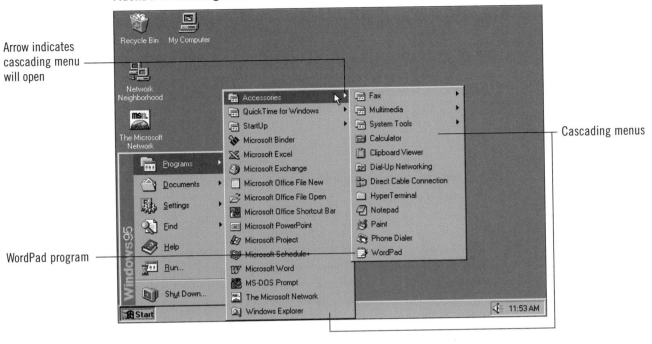

FIGURE A-5: WordPad document window

Indented program button indicates active program

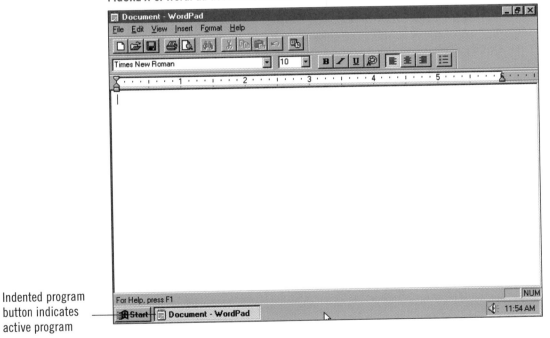

TABLE A-5: Common Windows Accessories

accessory	description
Calculator	Use to add, subtract, divide, and multiply numbers
Paint	Use to draw and edit graphic images
WordPad	Use to create and edit documents

Windows 95

Resizing a Window

The Windows desktop can quickly get cluttered with icons and windows. One of the ways to keep your desktop organized is by changing the size of the windows. Each window is surrounded by a standard border and sizing buttons that allow you to change the size of windows by minimizing, maximizing, and restoring windows as needed. You can also drag a window's border to size it. See the related topic "More about sizing windows" for more information. ◢▬▬▬ Practice sizing the WordPad window now.

Steps 1234

1. **In the WordPad window, click the Maximize button ⬜, if the WordPad window does not already fill the screen**
   When a window is maximized, it takes up the whole screen.

2. **Click the Restore button ⧉ in the WordPad window**
   The Restore button returns a window to its previous size, as shown in Figure A-6. The Restore button only appears when a window is maximized. In addition to minimizing, maximizing, and restoring windows, you can also change the dimensions of any window. Next, experiment with changing the dimensions of the WordPad window.

3. **Position the pointer on the right edge of the WordPad window until the pointer changes to ↔, then drag it to the right**
   The width of the window increases. You can size the height and width of a window by dragging any of the four sides individually. You can also size the height and width of the window simultaneously by dragging the corner of the window.

4. **Position the pointer in the lower-right corner of the WordPad window, as indicated in Figure A-6, then drag down and to the right**
   The height and width of the window are increased at the same time. You can also position a restored window wherever you wish on the desktop by dragging its title bar.

5. **Click the title bar on the WordPad window and drag up and to the left**
   The window is repositioned on the desktop. At times, you might wish to close a program's window, yet keep the program running and easily accessible. You can accomplish this by minimizing a window.

6. **In the WordPad window, click the Minimize button ⬜**
   When you minimize a window, it shrinks to a program button on the taskbar, as shown in Figure A-7. The WordPad program is still open and running; however, it is not active.

7. **Click the WordPad program button on the taskbar to restore the window to its previous size**
   The WordPad program is now active; this means that any actions you perform will take place in this window. Next, return the window to its full size.

8. **Click the Maximize button ⬜ in the upper-right corner of the WordPad window**
   The window fills the screen. Leave the WordPad window maximized and continue with the next lesson.

FIGURE A-6: Restored WordPad window

Title bar ⎯⎯⎯⎯⎯⎯

Sizing buttons

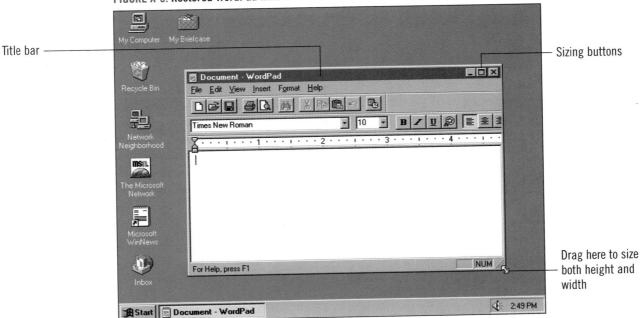

Drag here to size both height and width

FIGURE A-7: Minimized WordPad window

Indicates program is running but not active

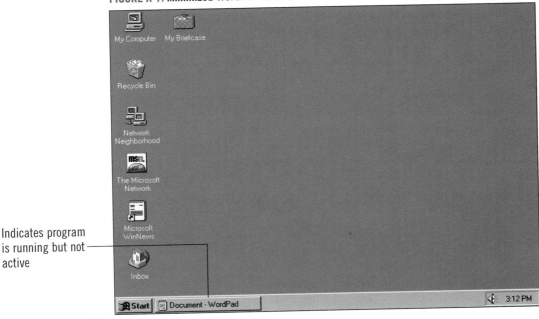

More about sizing windows

More programs contain two sets of sizing buttons: one that controls the file which can be a document, spreadsheet, database, or presentation window within the program. The program sizing buttons are located in the title bar; the file sizing buttons are located below them in the menu bar. See Figure 1-8. When you minimize a file window within a program, the file window is reduced to an icon in the lower-left coner of

program window. The size of the program window remains intact.

Program window sizing buttons

FIGURE A-8: Program and file window sizing buttons

File window sizing buttons

Using Menus and Toolbars

A **menu** is a list of commands that you use to accomplish certain tasks. You've already used the Start menu to start WordPad. Each Windows program also has its own set of menus, which are located on the **menu bar** along the top of the program window. The menus organize commands into groups of related operations. See Table A-6 for examples of what you might see on a typical menu. Some of the commands found on a menu can also be carried out by clicking a button on a **toolbar**. Toolbar buttons provide you with convenient shortcuts for completing tasks. Open the Control Panel program, then use a menu and toolbar button to change how the window's contents are displayed.

Steps 1 2 3 4

1. **Click the Start button on the taskbar, point to Settings, then click Control Panel**
   The Control Panel window contains icons for various programs that allow you to specify your preferences for how your computer environment looks and performs.

2. **Click View on the menu bar**
   The View menu appears, displaying the View commands, as shown in Figure A-9. When you click a menu name, a general description of the commands available on that menu appears in the status bar. On a menu, a check mark identifies a feature that is currently selected (that is, the feature is enabled). To disable the feature, you click the command again to remove the check mark. A bullet mark can also indicate that an option is enabled. To disable this option, however, you must select another option in its place. In the next step, you will select a command.

3. **On the View menu, click Small Icons**
   The icons are now smaller than they were before, taking up less room in the window. You can also use the keyboard to access menu commands. Next, open the View menu by pressing [Alt] on the keyboard and then the underlined letter of the menu on the menu bar.

4. **Press and hold [Alt], then press [V] to open the View menu, then release both keys**
   The View menu appears. Notice that a letter in each command is underlined. You can select these commands by pressing the underlined letter. Now, select a command using the keyboard.

5. **Press [T] to select the Toolbar command**
   The Control Panel toolbar appears below the menu bar. This toolbar includes buttons for the commands that you use most frequently while you are in the Control Panel program. When you position the mouse pointer over a button, the name of the button – called a ToolTip – is displayed. Pressing a button displays a description of the button in the status bar. Use the ToolTip feature to explore a button on the toolbar.

Trouble?

If you cannot see the Details button on the toolbar, you can resize the Control Panel window by dragging the right border to the right until the button is visible.

6. **On the Control Panel toolbar, position the pointer over the Details button 🔲 as shown in Figure A-10, then click**
   The Details view includes a description of each Control Panel program. If you were to click the View menu now, you would see that the Details command is now checked.

FIGURE A-9: View menu on Control Panel menu bar

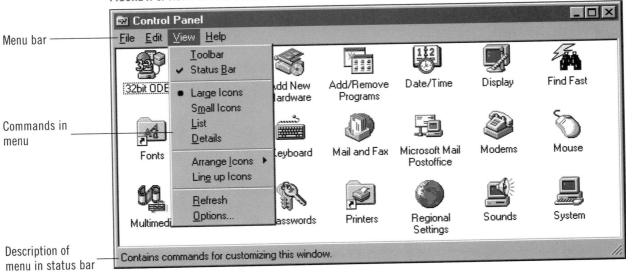

Menu bar

Commands in menu

Description of menu in status bar

FIGURE A-10: Control Panel toolbar

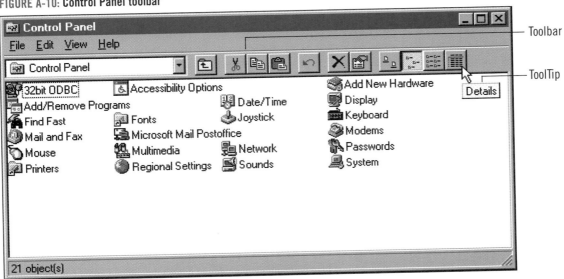

Toolbar

ToolTip

TABLE A-6: Typical items on a menu

item	description
Dimmed command	A menu command that is not currently available
Ellipsis	Choosing this menu command opens a dialog box that allows you to select different or additional options
Triangle	Choosing this menu command opens a cascading menu containing an additional list of menu commands
Keyboard shortcut	A keyboard alternative for executing a menu command
Underlined letter	Pressing the underlined letter executes the menu command

Windows 95

Using Dialog Boxes

A command from a menu that is followed by an ellipsis (…) requires more information before it can complete its task. When you select this type of command a **dialog box** opens for you to specify the options you want. See Figure A-11 and Table A-7 for some of the typical elements of a dialog box. ✎ Practice using a dialog box to control your mouse settings.

Steps

1. **In the Control Panel window, double-click the Mouse icon (you might need to resize the Control Panel window to find this icon)**
   The Mouse Properties dialog box opens, as shown in Figure A-12. The options in this dialog box allow you to control the way the mouse buttons are configured, select the types of pointers that are displayed, choose the speed of the mouse movement on the screen, and specify what type of mouse you are using. **Tabs** at the top of the dialog box separate these options into related categories.

2. **Click the Buttons tab if it is not the frontmost tab, then in the Button configuration area, click the Left-handed radio button to select it**
   If the Left-handed radio button is already selected, click the Right-handed radio button. Use this option to specify which button is primary (controls the normal operations) and which is secondary (controls the special functions, such as context-sensitive pop-up menus). Next, select an option which shows pointer trails when you move the mouse.

3. **Click the Motion tab, then in the Pointer trail area click the Show pointer trails check box to select it**
   This option makes the mouse pointer easier to see on certain types of computer screens such as laptop computers. The slider feature, located below the check box, lets you specify the degree to which the option is in effect, in this case, the length of the pointer trail.

4. **Drag the slider below the check box all the way to the right**
   As you move the mouse, notice the longer pointer trails.

5. **Click the other tabs in the Mouse Properties dialog box and experiment with the options that are available in each category**
   Finally, you need to select a command button to carry out the options you've selected. The two most common command buttons are OK and Cancel. Clicking OK accepts your changes and closes the dialog box; clicking Cancel leaves the settings intact and closes the dialog box. The third command button in this dialog box is Apply. Clicking the Apply button accepts the changes you've made and keeps the dialog box open so that you can select additional options. Because you might share this computer with others, it's important to return the dialog box options back to the original settings.

6. **Click Cancel to leave the original settings intact and close the dialog box**

FIGURE A-11: Dialog box elements

Spin box

Radio button

Check box

List box

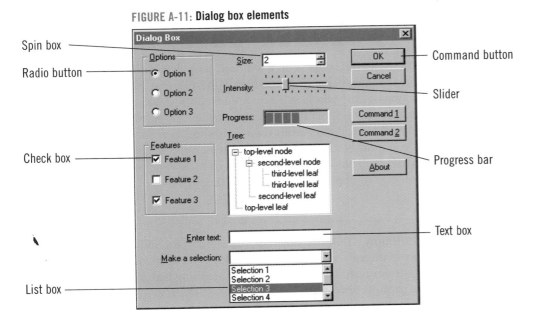

Command button

Slider

Progress bar

Text box

FIGURE A-12: Mouse Properties dialog box

Tabs

Button configuration area

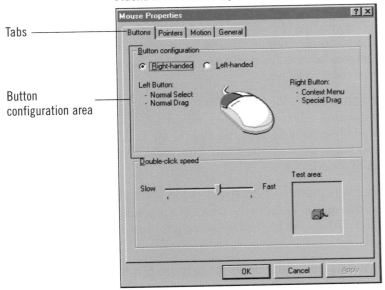

TABLE A-7: Typical items in a dialog box

item	description	item	description
Check box	Clicking this square box turns a dialog box option on or off	**List box**	A box containing a list of items; to choose an item, click the list arrow, then click the desired item
Text box	A box in which you type text	**Spin box**	Allows you to scroll or type numerical increments
Radio button	Clicking this small circle selects a single dialog box option	**Slider**	Allows you to set the degree to which an option is in effect
Command button	Clicking this button carries out a command in a dialog box	**Progress bar**	Indicates how much of a task is completed

Using Scroll Bars

When you cannot see all of the items available in a window, scroll bars will appear on the right and/or bottom edges of the window. Using the scroll bars, you can move around in a window to display the additional contents of the window. There are several ways you can scroll in a window. When you need to scroll only a short distance, you can use the scroll arrows. Clicking in the scroll bar above or below the scroll box scrolls the window in larger increments, while dragging the scroll bar moves you quickly to a new part of the window. See Table A-8 for a summary of the different ways to use scroll bars. ➤ With the Control Panel window in the Details view, you can use the scroll bars to view all of the items in this window.

Steps

1. **In the Control Panel window, click the down scroll arrow, as shown in Figure A-13**
   Clicking this arrow moves the view down one line. Clicking the up arrow moves the view up one line at a time. So that you can better explore other scrolling features in this lesson, you will resize the window to show fewer items.

2. **Drag the bottom border of the Control Panel window up so that only 6 or 7 items appear in the window**
   Notice that the scroll box appears smaller than in the previous step. The size of the scroll box changes to reflect the amount of items available, but not displayed in a window. For example, a larger scroll box indicates that a relatively small amount of the window's contents is not currently visible; therefore you need to scroll only a short distance to see the remaining items. A smaller scroll box indicates that a relatively large amount of information is currently not visible. To see the additional contents of the resized window, you can click in the area below the scroll box in the vertical scroll bar.

3. **Click the area below the scroll box in the vertical scroll bar**
   The view moves down one window full of information; for example, you see another 6 or 7 items further down in the window. Similarly, you can click in the scroll bar above the scroll box to move up one window full of information. Next, you will display the information that appears at the very bottom of the window.

4. **Drag the scroll box all the way down to the bottom of the vertical scroll bar**
   The view displays the items that appear at the very bottom of the window. Similarly, you can drag the scroll box to the top of the scroll bar to display the information that appears at the top of the window.

5. **Drag the scroll box all the way up to the top of the vertical scroll bar**
   This view displays the items that appear at the top of the window. Next, you will explore the horizontal scroll bar, so you can see all of the icons near the right edge of the window.

6. **Click the area to the right of the scroll box in the horizontal scroll bar**
   The far right edge of the window comes into view. Next, you will redisplay the left edge of the window.

7. **Click the area to the left of the scroll box in the horizontal scroll bar**

8. **Resize the Control Panel window so that the scroll bars no longer appear**

Trouble?

If you cannot see both the vertical and horizontal scroll bars, make the window smaller (both shorter and narrower) until both scroll bars appear.

FIGURE A-13: **Control Panel window in Details view**

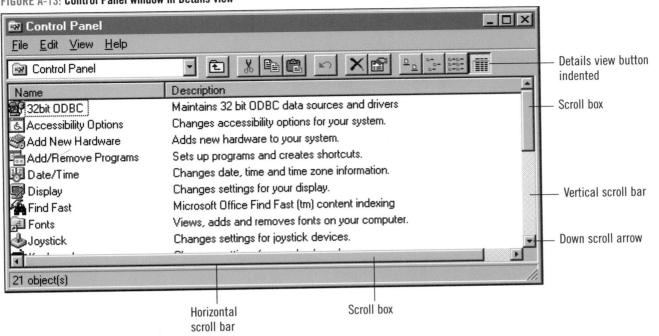

Details view button indented

Scroll box

Vertical scroll bar

Down scroll arrow

Horizontal scroll bar

Scroll box

TABLE A-8: **Using scroll bars in a window**

to	do this
Move down one line	Click the down arrow at the bottom of the vertical scroll bar
Move up one line	Click the up arrow at the top of the vertical scroll bar
Move down one window	Click in the area below the scroll box in the vertical scroll bar
Move up one window	Click in the area above the scroll box in the vertical scroll bar
Move up a greater distance in the window	Drag the scroll box up in the vertical scroll bar
Move down a greater distance in the window	Drag the scroll box down in the vertical scroll bar
Move a short distance side to side in a window	Click the left or right arrows in the horizontal scroll bar
Move to the right one screenful	Click in the area to the right of scroll box in the horizontal scroll bar
Move to the left one screenful	Click in the area to the left of the scroll box in the horizontal scroll bar
Move left or right a greater distance in the window	Drag the scroll box in the horizontal scroll bar

Windows 95

Getting Help

Windows 95 comes with a powerful online Help system that allows you to obtain help information in several ways, depending on your current needs. The Help system provides guidance on many Windows features, including detailed steps for completing a procedure, definitions of terms, lists of related topics, and search capabilities. You can also receive assistance in a dialog box; see the related topic "More about Help" for more information. ◆━━━ In this lesson, you'll get Help on how to start a program. You'll also get information on the taskbar. You start the online Help system from the Start menu.

Steps 1234

1. Click the **Start button** on the taskbar, then click **Help**
   The Help Topics dialog box opens, as shown in Figure A-14. Verify that the Contents tab is selected.

2. Click the **Contents tab** if it isn't the frontmost tab, double-click **How To** in the list box, then double-click **Run Programs**
   The Help window displays a selection of topics related to running programs.

3. Click **Starting a program**, then click **Display**
   A Windows Help window opens. At the bottom of the window, you can click the Related Topics button to display a list of topics that may also be of interest. Some help topics also allow you to display additional information about important words; these words are identified with a dotted underline.

4. Click the dotted underlined word **taskbar**
   A pop-up window appears with a definition of the underlined word.

5. Read the definition, then click anywhere outside the pop-up window to close it

6. Click the **Help Topics button** to return to the Help Topics window
   You can use the Find tab to search for a specific word or phrase for which you want to display help topics. As you type the word or phrase in the first list box, any available words that match appear in the second list box. In the next step, search for help topics on the word "taskbar."

7. Click the **Find tab**, then in the first list box, type **taskbar**
   Two word matches are displayed in the second list box, as shown in Figure A-15. The third list box displays help topics related to the selected word.

8. In the third list box, click **Customizing the taskbar or Start menu**, then click **Display**
   The Help window that appears lists the steps for completing this task. Close the Windows Help window for now.

9. In the Windows Help window, click the **Close button** ☒ in the upper-right corner of the window
   Clicking the Close button closes the active window.

FIGURE A-14: Help Topics dialog box

Click this tab to display an alphabetical index of Help topics

Click this tab to search for words and phrases in the Help topics

Prints contents of help topic on a printer connected to your computer

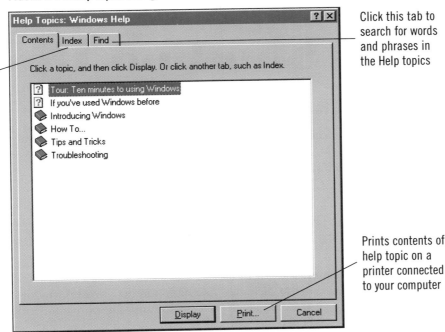

FIGURE A-15: Find tab in Help Topics dialog box

Type the word you are searching for here

List word matches

Lists the help topics for word matches

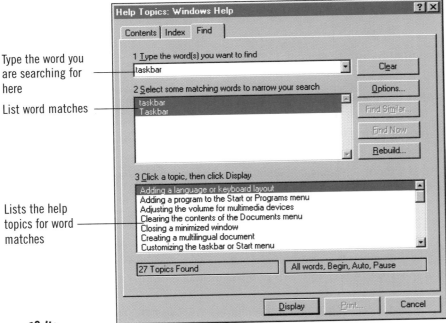

More about Help

To receive online help in a dialog box, click the Help button ⓘ in the upper-right corner of the dialog box. The mouse pointer changes to ⓚ. Click the Help pointer on the item for which you need additional information. A pop-up window provides a brief explanation of the selected feature. You can also click the right-mouse button on an item in a dialog box. Then click the What's This? button to display the help explanation. In addition, when you click the right mouse button in a help topic window, you can choose commands to annotate, copy, and print the contents of the topic window. From the Help pop-up menu, you can also choose to have topic windows always appear on top of the currently active window, so you can see help topics while you work.

Windows 95

Closing a Program and Shutting Down Windows

When you are finished working with Windows, close all the open programs and windows, and then exit Windows using the Shut Down command on the Start menu. Do not turn off the computer while Windows is running; you could lose important data if you turn off your computer too soon. ✏️ Close all your active programs and exit Windows.

1. Click the **WordPad program button** on the taskbar to make the WordPad program active

To close a program and any of its currently open files, you select the Exit command on the File menu. You can also click the Close button in the program window. See the related topic "Closing programs and files with the Close button" for more information. If you have made any changes to the open files, you will be prompted to save your changes before the program quits. Some programs also give you the option of choosing the Close command on the File menu. This command closes the active file but leaves the program open, so you can continue to work in it. In the next step, you will quit the WordPad program and return to the Windows desktop.

QuickTip

Some programs allow you to close multiple files simultaneously by pressing [Shift], then clicking File on the menu bar. Click Close All to close all open files at once.

2. Click **File** on the menu bar, then click **Exit**

3. If you see a message asking you to save changes to the document, click **No**

4. In the Control Panel window, click the **Close button** ☒ in the upper-right corner of the window

The Control Panel window closes. *Complete the remaining steps to shut down Windows and your computer only if you have been told to do so by your instructor.*

5. Click the **Start button** on the taskbar, then click **Shut Down**

The Shut Down Windows dialog box opens, as shown in Figure A-16. In this dialog box, you have the option to shut down the computer, restart the computer in Windows mode, restart the computer in MS-DOS mode, or log on to the computer as another user.

6. Verify that the first option, "Shut down the computer?," is selected

7. If you are working in a lab click **No**; if you are working on your own machine or if your instructor told you to shut down Windows, click **Yes** to exit Windows and shut down the computer

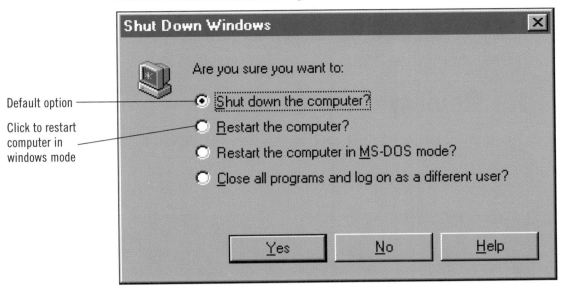

Default option ——

Click to restart
computer in
windows mode

CLUES TO USE

Closing programs and files with the Close button

You can also close a program and its open files by
clicking the Close button ⊠ on the title bar in the
upper-right corner of the program window. If there is
a second set of sizing buttons in the window, the
Close button that is located on the menu bar will
close the active file only, leaving the program open
for continued use.

Practice

► Concepts Review

Without referring to the unit material, identify each of the items in Figure A-17.

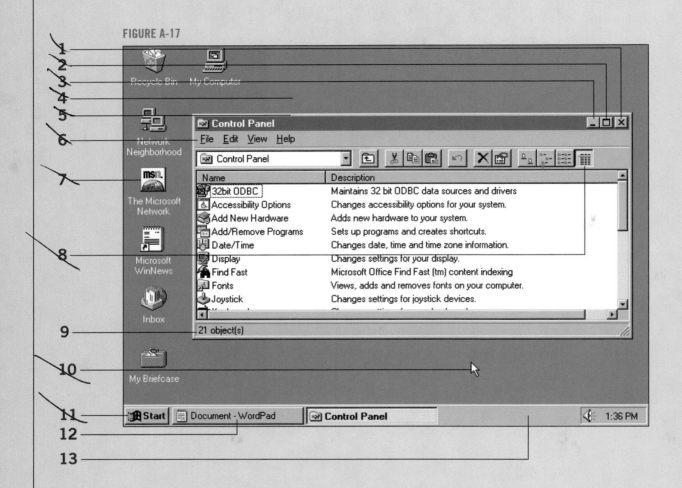

FIGURE A-17

Match each of the statements with the term it describes.

14. **Start button**
15. **Dialog box**
16. **Taskbar**
17. **Mouse**
18. **Title bar**
19. **Minimize button**
20. **Icon**

a. Shrinks a window to a button on the taskbar
b. Displays the name of the window or program
c. Displays list of programs you can run
d. Requests more information that you supply before carrying out command
e. Displays Start button and currently open programs
f. Lets you point to and make selections
g. Graphic representation of program you can run

► Skills Review

1. **Start Windows and identify items on the screen.**
   a. Turn on the computer, if necessary.
   b. After Windows loads, try to identify as many items on the desktop as you can, without referring to the lesson material. Then compare your results with Figure A-1.

2. **Practice dragging, maximizing, restoring, sizing, and minimizing windows.**
   a. Drag the Recycle Bin icon to the bottom of the desktop.
   b. Double-click the My Computer icon to open the My Computer window.
   c. Maximize the window, if it is not already maximized.
   d. Restore the window to its previous size.
   e. Size the window by dragging the window borders until you see both horizontal and vertical scroll bars.
   f. Size the window until the horizontal scroll bar no longer appears.
   g. Click the Minimize button. Now try restoring the window.

3. **Run a program.**
   a. Click the Start button on the taskbar, then point to Programs.
   b. Point to Accessories, then click Calculator.
   c. Minimize the Calculator program.

4. **Practice working with menus and dialog boxes.**
   a. Click the Start button on the taskbar, then point to Settings, then click Control Panel.
   b. Click View on the menu bar, then click Toolbar twice to practice hiding and displaying the toolbar.
   c. Double-click the Display icon.
   d. Click the Appearance tab.
   e. Write down the current settings you see in this dialog box.
   f. Try out different selections in this dialog box to change the colors on your desktop and click the Apply button.
   g. Return the options to their original settings and click OK to close the dialog box.

5. **Use online Help to learn more about Windows.**
   a. Click the Start button on the taskbar, then click Help.
   b. Click the Contents tab.
   c. Double-click Introducing Windows.
   d. Double-click each of the following topics (click Help Topics to return to the Contents window after reading each topic):
      Welcome, then A List of What's New, then A new look and feel
      Getting Your Work Done, then The basics
      Keyboard Shortcuts, then General Windows keys
      Using Windows Accessories, then For General Use
      Using Windows Accessories, then For Writing and Drawing

6. **Close all open windows.**
   a. Click the Close button to close the Help topic window.
   b. Click File on the menu bar, then click Exit to close the Control Panel window.
   c. Click Calculator in the taskbar to restore the window.
   d. Click the Close button in the Calculator window to close the Calculator program.
   e. Click the Close button in the My Computer window to close the window.
   f. If you are instructed to do so by your instructor, use the Shut Down command on the Start menu to exit Windows. Otherwise, be sure all windows and programs are closed and you have returned the desktop to its original appearance as it appeared before you began this unit.

▶ Independent Challenges

1. Microsoft Windows 95 provides an extensive help system designed to help you learn how to use Windows effectively. In addition to step-by-step instructions, there are also tips that you can try to gain even greater confidence as you become acquainted with Windows features. In this challenge, you start Help, double-click Tips and Tricks, then double-click Tips of the Day. Read each of the following topics (click Help Topics to return to the Contents window after reading each topic):

> Getting your work done
> Personalizing Windows
> Becoming an expert
> Optional: If you have a printer connected to your computer, click the Print button to print the tips described in each Help topic window.
> Close all the Help topic windows and return to the desktop.

2. Use the skills you have learned in this unit to create a desktop that looks like the desktop in Figure A-18. It's OK if your desktop contains more items than in this figure.

FIGURE A-18: **Shut Down Windows dialog box**

Be sure to return your settings and desktop back to their original arrangement when you complete this challenge.

Windows 95

Managing
Files, Folders, and Shortcuts

Objectives

- ► **Format a disk**
- ► **Create a Paint file**
- ► **Save a Paint file**
- ► **Work with multiple programs**
- ► **Understand file management**
- ► **View files and create folders with My Computer**
- ► **Move and copy files using My Computer**
- ► **View files and rename folders with Windows Explorer**
- ► **Delete and restore files**
- ► **Manage files on the desktop**

In this unit, you will explore the file management features of Windows 95. In this unit you will learn how to format a floppy disk, so that you can permanently store your work. You will then create and save files using a drawing program called Paint. Next, you will learn how to use the Clipboard to copy and paste your work from one program to another. Then, you will learn two methods for managing the files you create: using My Computer and Windows Explorer. Finally, you will learn how to work more efficiently by managing files directly on your desktop.

Windows 95

Formatting a Disk

When you use a program, your work is temporarily stored in your computer's random access memory (RAM). When you turn off your computer, the contents of RAM are erased. To store your work permanently, you must save your work as a file on a disk. You can save files either on an internal **hard disk** (which is built into your computer, usually drive C) or on a removable 3.5 or 5.25 inch **floppy disk** (which you insert into a drive on your computer, usually drive A or B). Before you can save a file on a floppy disk, you must prepare the disk to receive your file by first **formatting** the disk. ✒ To complete the steps below, you need a blank disk or a disk containing data you no longer need. Formatting erases all data on a disk, so be careful which disk you use.

Steps 1 2 3 4

1. **Place a blank, unformatted disk in drive A:**
   If your disk does not fit in the drive A, try drive B and substitute drive B wherever you see drive A.

2. **Double-click the My Computer icon on the desktop**
   The My Computer window appears, as shown in Figure B-1. This window displays all the drives and printers that you can use on your computer; depending on your computer system, your window might look different. You can use My Computer for managing your files as well as for formatting your disk. You will learn more about My Computer later in this unit. For now, locate the drive that contains the disk you want to format in the My Computer window.

3. **Right-click the 3½ Floppy (A:) icon**
   This icon is usually the first icon in the upper-left corner of the window. Clicking with the right mouse button displays a pop-up menu of commands that apply to using drive A, including the Format command.

4. **Click Format on the pop-up menu**
   The Format dialog box opens, as shown in Figure B-2. In this dialog box, you specify the capacity of the disk you are formatting and the kind of formatting you want to do. See Table B-1 for a description of formatting options.

5. **Click the Full radio button, then click Start**
   Windows is now formatting your disk. By selecting the Full option, you ensure that the disk can be read by your computer. Once a disk is formatted you will not need to format it again. After the formatting is complete, you see a summary about the size of the disk. Now that the disk is formatted, you are ready to save files on it. From now on, we will refer to this disk as your **Work Disk**. Before you continue with this unit, close each of the open dialog boxes.

6. **Click Close in the Format Results dialog box, then click Close in the Format dialog box**
   You can keep the My Computer window open for now; you will return to it later in this unit.

Trouble?

Windows cannot format a disk if it is write-protected, therefore, you need to remove (on a 5.25 disk) or move (on a 3.5 disk) the write-protect tab to continue. See Figure B-3 to locate the write-protect tab on your disk.

FIGURE B-1: My Computer window

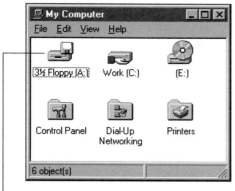

Drive containing
disk

FIGURE B-2: Format dialog box

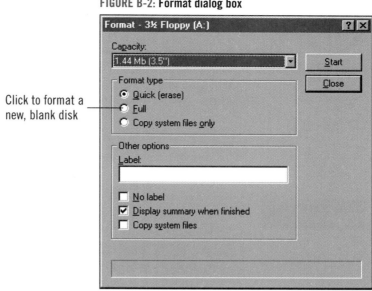

Click to format a
new, blank disk

FIGURE B-3: Write-protect tabs

Write-protected tabs

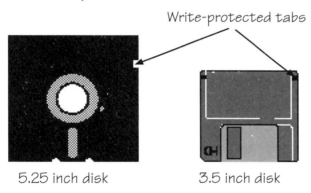

5.25 inch disk   3.5 inch disk

TABLE B-1: Formatting options

Option	Description
Capacity	Click the Capacity list arrow to specify the amount of information your disk is made to hold; for a high-density disk, choose 1.44 Mb, for double-density disks, choose 720Kb
Quick (erase)	Choose this option if your disk contains files that you want to erase; it takes less time than the Full option
Full	Choose this option if you are using a new, blank disk; this option initializes, as well as formats, the disk, requiring more time to complete than the Quick option
Copy System	Use this option when you want to make the disk you are formatting bootable; this means you will be able to start Files Only
Label	Choose this option to give your disk a name; this will help you keep track of the files you save on a disk

Creating a Paint File

Most of your work on a computer involves creating files in programs. When you use a program, you can use many of the Windows skills you have already learned. In this lesson, you'll work with **Paint**, a drawing program located on the Accessories submenu that you use to create simple graphics. 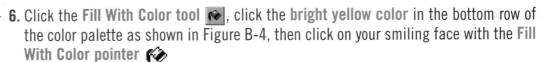 Launch Paint and create the drawing shown in Figure B-4.

Steps

1. Click the **Start button** on the taskbar, point to **Programs**, point to **Accessories**, then click **Paint**

   The Paint program window opens. Notice the title and menu bars across the top of the screen. Along the left side of the window is the Toolbox. The white rectangular area, called the **drawing area**, is where you draw. The **color palette**, which contains the colors you use to paint with, is at the bottom of the window.

2. Click the **maximize button**, if necessary, to maximize the window, then click the **Brush tool**

   A Linesize box appears under the Toolbox where you choose the line size of the brush stroke you want. The Brush tool is a freehand drawing tool that you will control with your mouse. See Table B-2 for description of each of the Paint tools.

3. In the Linesize box, click the **thickest line width**, then move the mouse pointer on the drawing area of the Paint window

   Your pointer changes to ▪ and you are now ready to create a simple picture.

4. Press and hold the **left mouse button**, drag the mouse in a large circle, then release the mouse button

5. Add eyes and a mouth inside the circle to create a smiling face

   Next, you will add color to the image.

Trouble?

If you make a mistake while painting, choose Undo from the Edit menu.

6. Click the **Fill With Color tool** , click the **bright yellow color** in the bottom row of the color palette as shown in Figure B-4, then click on your smiling face with the **Fill With Color pointer**

   The Fill With Color tool fills the area with the currently selected color and your drawing is complete; compare it to Figure B-4. Don't worry if your file looks slightly different. In the next lesson, you will save your work.

FIGURE B-4: Paint window with graphic

Toolbox

Fill with color pointer

Color palette

TABLE B-2: Paint Toolbox tools

tool	description	tool	description
Free-Form Select	Selects a free-form section of the picture to move, copy, or edit	Airbrush	Produces a circular spray of dots
Select	Selects a rectangular section of the picture to move, copy, or edit	Text	Inserts text in to the picture
Eraser/Color Eraser	Erases a portion of the picture using the selected eraser size and foreground color	Line	Draws a straight line with the selected width and foreground color
Fill With Color	Fills closed shape or area with the current drawing color	Curve	Draws a wavy line with the selected width and foreground color
Pick Color	Picks up a color off the picture to use for drawing	Rectangle	Draws a rectangle with the selected fill style; also used to draw squares by holding down [Shift] while drawing
Magnifier	Changes the magnification; displays list of magnifications under the toolbar	Polygon	Draws polygons from connected straight-line segments
Pencil	Draws a free-form line one pixel wide	Ellipse	Draws an ellipse with the selected fill style; also used to draw circles by holding down [Shift] while drawing
Brush	Draws using a brush with the selected shape and size	Rounded Rectangle	Draws rectangles with rounded corners using the selected fill style; also used to draw rounded squares by holding down [Shift] while drawing

CLUES TO USE

Reversing actions

With the Undo feature (available in most Windows applications), you can reverse the result of the last action. For example, if you are creating a drawing in Paint and you draw a rectangle when you intended to draw a straight line, you can click Edit on the menu bar and then click Undo. In this case, this command will remove the rectangle from the graphic, so you can click a new tool and try again.

Saving a Paint File

Much of your work with Windows will involve saving different types of files. The files you create using a computer are stored in the computer's random access memory (RAM). **RAM** is a temporary storage space that is erased when the computer is turned off. To store a file permanently, you need to save it to a disk. You can save your work to a 3.5 inch disk, also know as a **floppy disk**, which you insert into the drive of your computer (i.e., drive A or B), or a hard disk, which is built into your computer (usually drive C). Now, save the Paint file you created in the last lesson in two different forms.

Steps 1234

1. Click File on the menu bar, then click Save As, as shown in Figure B-5
   The Save As dialog box opens, as shown in Figure B-6. In this dialog box, you give your work a file name and specify where you want the file saved. Specify the location first.

2. Click the Save In list arrow, click 3½ Floppy (A:) (or whichever drive contains your Work Disk), then click the Save as type list arrow and click 16 color Bitmap
   The drive containing your Work Disk is now active. This means that the file you save will be saved on the disk in this drive.

3. Double-click the text in the File Name box, type My first Paint file, then click Save
   Your drawing is now saved as a Paint file with the name "My first Paint file" on your Work Disk in drive A. When you name a file, you can type up to 255 characters (including spaces and punctuation) in the File Name box. You can also use both upper and lowercase. Next, you will modify the Paint file and save the changed file with a new name.

4. Click a light blue color on the color palette, then click on the smiling face
   The face is now filled with the light blue color. To save this modified drawing in a new file (so you can keep the original unchanged), you can use the Save As command. If you wanted to save a change in the original file, you could use the Save command.

5. Click File on the menu bar, then click Save As
   The Save As dialog box opens, as shown in Figure B-7. Because Windows "remembers" where you last saved a file, you do not need to specify a location this time. Enter a new file-name to create a new file.

6. With the text in the File Name box selected, type My second Paint file, then click Save
   Your revised drawing is now saved as a new Paint file with the name "My second Paint file" on your Work Disk. The original file closes automatically when you use the Save As command. There are now two Paint files on your Work Disk.

FIGURE B-5: The Save As command

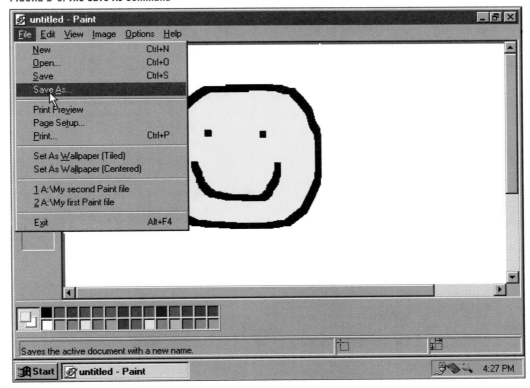

FIGURE B-6: Save As dialog box

Click to select a new location for a file

Existing files (if any) appear in list

Enter filename

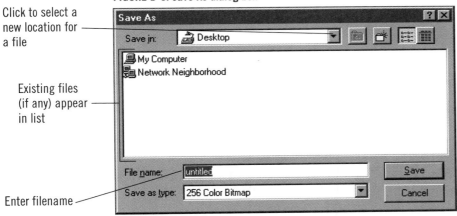

FIGURE B-7: Save As dialog box for saving your second Paint file

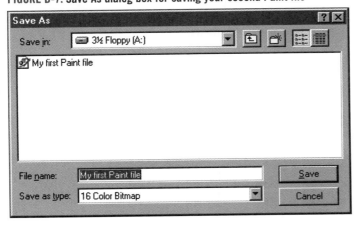

Windows 95

Working with Multiple Programs

Occasionally, you might want to work with more than one program at a time. For example, perhaps you have created a graphic file that you want to include with text in a document file. With Windows 95 you can copy objects onto the Clipboard. The Clipboard is a temporary area in your computer's memory for storing text or graphics. Once you place something on the Clipboard, you can paste it into other locations. Using the taskbar or keyboard, you can switch to another program quickly so that you can paste the contents of the Clipboard into another file without closing the original program. ➤ Next, you will copy the logo graphic you created in the previous lesson into a WordPad document.

Steps 1 2 3 4

1. **Click the Start button on the taskbar, point to Programs, point to Accessories, then click WordPad**
   The WordPad program window opens. If the WordPad program window does not fill your screen, click the Maximize button. The blinking insertion point, also called the cursor, indicates where the text you type will appear.

2. **In the WordPad window, type This is the new logo I created for our company brochure., then press [Enter] twice**
   Pressing [Enter] once places the insertion point at the beginning of the next line. Pressing [Enter] again creates a blank line between the first line of text and the graphic you will copy from the Paint program.

3. **Click the Paint program button on the taskbar**
   The Paint program becomes the active program in the window. Next, you will select the logo graphic in the Paint window.

4. **Click the Select tool ▢, then drag a rectangle around the entire graphic**
   When you release the mouse button, the dotted rectangle indicates the contents of the selection. The next action you take will affect the entire selection.

5. **Click Edit on the menu bar, then click Copy**
   The selected logo graphic is copied to the Clipboard. When you copy an object onto the Clipboard, the object remains in its original location, and is also available to be pasted into another location. Now you will switch to the WordPad window using the keyboard.

6. **Press and hold down [Alt], press [Tab] once, then release [Alt]**
   A box appears, as shown in Figure B-8, indicating which program will become active when you release the Alt key. If you have more than two programs open, you press the Tab key (while holding down [Alt]) until the program you want is selected. The WordPad program becomes the active program in the window.

7. **Click Edit on the menu bar, then click Paste**
   The contents of the Clipboard, in this case the Paint graphic, are pasted into the WordPad window at the location of the insertion point.

8. **Click File on the menu bar, then click Save As, and save the file to your Work Disk with the name My WordPad file**
   Be sure to select the Work Disk in the Save In box before naming the file.

9. **Click the Close buttons in both the WordPad and Paint programs to close the open files and exit the programs**
   You return to the desktop and the My Computer window.

Trouble?

If you make the wrong program active, hold down [Alt] and press [Tab] to redisplay the box. Then (while holding down [Alt]), press [Tab] to move the selection box from program to program. When the program you want to make active is selected, then release both keys.

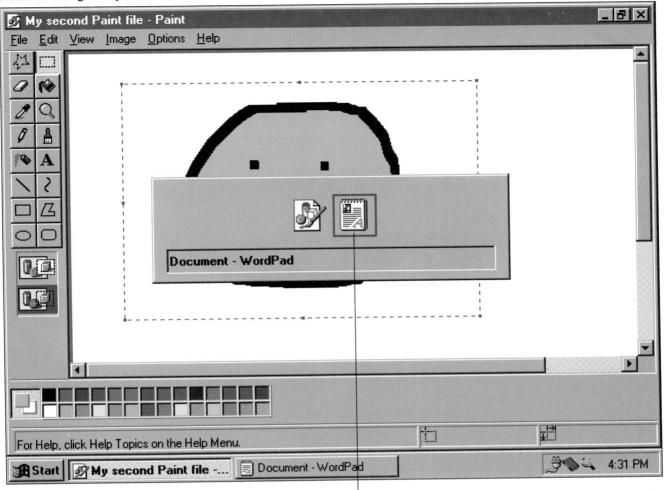

Indicates which
program will
become active

Understanding File Management

After you have created and saved numerous files while working in various programs, it can be a challenge to keep track of all of your files. Fortunately, Windows 95 provides the tools you need to keep everything organized so you can quickly locate the files you need. There are two main tools for managing your files: My Computer (which you have already opened when you formatted your Work Disk) and Windows Explorer. You'll learn more about Windows Explorer later in this unit. No matter which tool you use, Windows 95 gives you the ability to:

Details

Create folders in which you can save your files
Folders are areas on your disk (either a floppy disk or a hard disk) in which you can save files. For example, you might create a folder for your documents and another folder for your graphics. Folders can also contain additional folders, so you can create a more complicated structure of folders and files, called a hierarchy. See Figure B-9 for an example of your Work Disk hierarchy.

Examine the hierarchy of files and folders
When you want to see the overall structure of your folders and files, you can use either My Computer or Windows Explorer. By examining your file hierarchy with these tools, you can better organize your files by adding new folders, renaming folders, deleting folders, and adjusting the hierarchy to meet your needs. Figures B-10 and B-11 illustrate sample hierarchies for your Work Disk, one using My Computer and the other using Windows Explorer.

Copy, move, delete, and rename files
For example, if you decide that a file belongs in a different folder, you can move the file to another folder. You can also rename a file if you decide a new name is more descriptive. If you want to keep a copy of a file in more than one folder, you can copy files to new folders. With the same files in two different folders, you can keep track of previous versions of files, so that they are available in the event of data loss. You can also delete files you no longer need, as well as restore files you delete accidentally.

Locate files quickly with the Windows 95 Find feature
With Find you can quickly locate files by providing only partial names or by other factors, such as by file type (for example, a WordPad document, a Paint graphic, or a program) or by the date the file was created or modified.

Preview the contents of a file without opening the file in its program
For example, if after locating a particular file, you want to verify that it is the file you want, you can use the Preview feature to quickly look at the file. The Preview feature saves you time because you do not need to wait for the program to open the file. Other options help you get additional information about your files so you can better organize your work.

FIGURE B-9: Sketch of Work Disk hierarchy

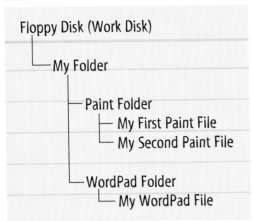

Floppy Disk (Work Disk)

— My Folder

— Paint Folder
— My First Paint File
— My Second Paint File

— WordPad Folder
— My WordPad File

FIGURE B-10: Sample hierarchy in My Computer

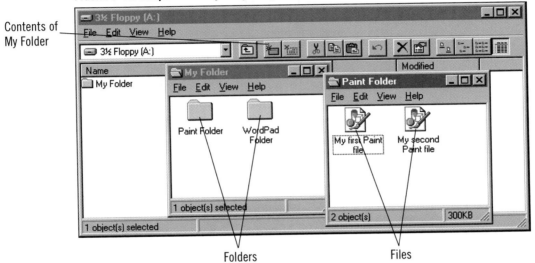

Contents of My Folder

Folders

Files

FIGURE B-11: Sample hierarchy in Windows Explorer

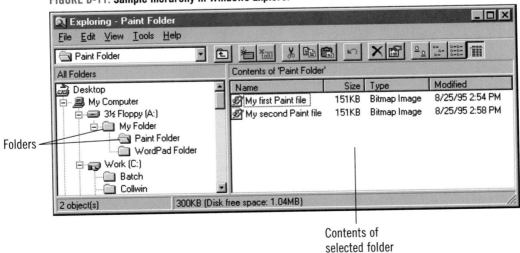

Folders

Contents of selected folder

Viewing Files and Creating Folders with My Computer

The My Computer window displays the contents of the selected drive or folder. When you double-click a drive or folder, its contents appear in a new window. ◄▬▬ Begin by using My Computer to move around in the system's file management hierarchy and then create a new folder on your Work Disk that will contain the files you create. First, you need to turn on the My Computer toolbar if it is not currently displayed. See Figure B-12 if you're not sure what the toolbar looks like.

Steps

1. Click the **Maximize button** in the My Computer window, if My Computer does not already fill the screen
   If your toolbar is visible, skip Step 2 and continue with Step 3.

2. Click **View** on the menu bar, then click **Toolbar**

3. Click the **drive list arrow**, then click the drive icon for your hard disk
   Now you are ready to view the hierarchy of your hard drive. You can do this using any one of the four view buttons on the My Computer toolbar.

4. Click the **Details button** 📧 on the My Computer toolbar
   In addition to the drive and folder icons, Details view also displays the type of drive or folder, the amount of total available space on the hard disk, and the remaining free space, as shown in Figure B-12. The List button provides a slightly smaller amount of information, but still mostly text-based. Let's try viewing the files and folders using a more graphical view.

5. Click the **Large Icons button** 📧 on the My Computer toolbar
   This view offers less information but provides a large, clear view of the contents of the disk.

6. Click the **Small Icons button** 📧 on the My Computer toolbar
   This view provides the same amount of information as the large icons except that the icons are smaller and take up less space in the window. Next, you want to display the contents of My Computer again, so that you can choose another drive.

7. Click the **Up One Level button** 📧 on the My Computer toolbar
   Clicking the Up One Level button displays the next level up the file hierarchy, in this case My Computer. Now, you are ready to create a folder on your Work Disk so you need to select the drive that contains your Work Disk.

8. Double-click the **3½ Floppy (A:) icon** (or B if that drive contains your Work Disk)
   You can now create a folder that will contain the files you create in this unit.

9. Click **File** on the menu bar, point to **New**, then click **Folder**
   A new folder is created on your Work Disk. Finally, give the folder a unique name.

10. Type **My Folder**, then press **[Enter]**
    Verify that the contents contained in the window are the same as those shown in Figure B-13. Depending on the selections used by the previous user, your window might not match the one in the illustration. If you wish, you can match the illustration by resizing the window, displaying the toolbar, and clicking the Details button.

FIGURE B-12: Using Details view to examine the hard disk

Toolbar

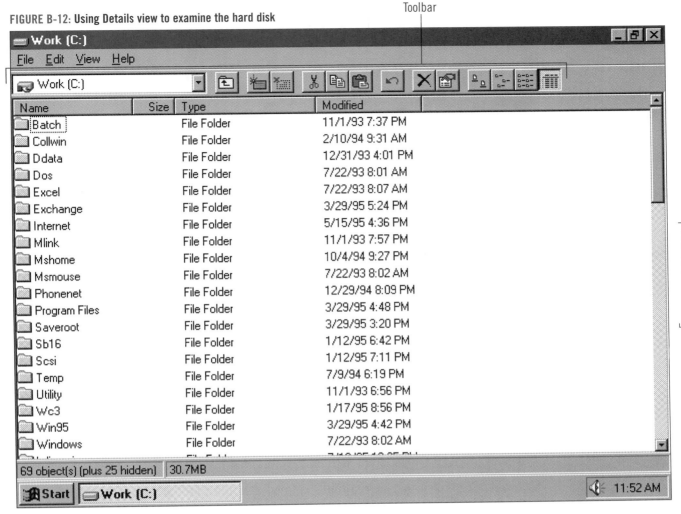

FIGURE B-13: New folder in A: window

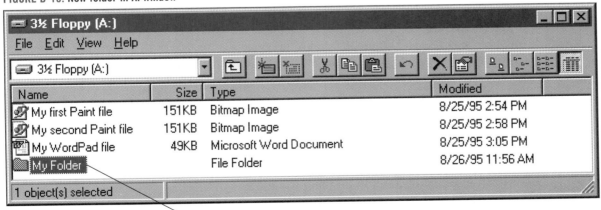

New folder

Moving and Copying Files Using My Computer

At times you might want to change the hierarchy of your files within a particular drive. For example, to better organize your files, you might decide to place files in a folder whose name reflects the name of a project or the program in which the file was created. My Computer allows you to quickly move or copy files and folders to another location. ⬤⬤⬤ In this lesson you will create two folders within the folder you created in the previous lesson. Then you will move the appropriate files into these new folders.

Steps

1. Double-click the **My Folder** to open it
The My Folder window opens. Before you can create a folder, you have to make sure you are creating it in the right place—in this case within the My Folder. Now you will create two folders, one named Paint Folder and the other named WordPad Folder.

2. Right-click in an empty area of the My Folder window (away from files, folder, and buttons)

3. Point to **New** in the pop-up menu, then click **Folder**
A new folder appears in the My Folder window. Next, you'll name it.

4. Type **Paint Folder**, then press **[Enter]**
Now you need to repeat these steps to create another folder.

5. Repeat Steps 2-4 to create a folder named **WordPad Folder**
Compare your My Folder window to Figure B-14. Next, you will move the Paint files to the Paint Folder, removing them from the original location at the root of drive A:.

6. In the 3½ Floppy (A:) window, click **My first Paint file**, then press **[Shift]** and click **My second Paint file**, then drag both files on top of the Paint Folder icon in the My Folder window
Windows displays the Moving window which shows the names of the files being moved and how much of the move operation is complete. See Table B-3 for a description of the different file selection techniques. Instead of dragging files or folders to a new location, you can use the cut, copy, and paste commands on the Edit menu or the Cut, Copy, and Paste toolbar buttons. Next, you will move the WordPad file to the WordPad folder.

QuickTip

To cut a selected file, you can press [Ctrl] [X]. To copy a selected file, you can press [Ctrl] [C]. To paste a selected file, you can press [Ctrl] [V].

7. Click **My WordPad file** to select it, then drag the file over the **WordPad Folder** icon and release the mouse button
The My WordPad file is moved to the WordPad Folder. Next, you will close all of the open windows including the 3½ Floppy (A:) window.

8. Click the **Close buttons** in all open windows
All open windows are closed and you return to the Windows desktop.

FIGURE B-14: Contents of My Folder

Newly created folder

Newly created folder

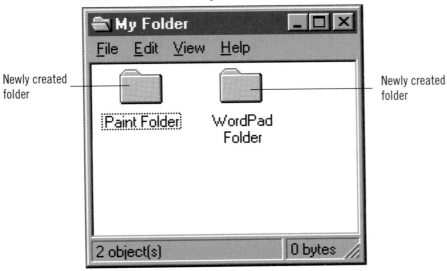

TABLE B-3: File/folder selection techniques

To Select This	Use This Technique
Individual objects not grouped together	Click the first object you want to select, then press [Ctrl] as you click each additional object you want to add to the selection
Objects grouped together	Click the first object you want to select, then press [Shift] as you click the last object in the list of objects you want to select; all the objects listed between the first and last objects are selected

Using Edit commands to copy and move files

An alternative to dragging files is to use the Cut, Copy, or Paste commands on the Edit menu or the Cut, Copy and Paste buttons on the toolbar. The Cut and Copy commands or Cut and Copy buttons place the selected files on the Clipboard.

Once on the Clipboard, the files can be pasted into the destination folder with the Paste command or Paste button. Be sure to select the destination folder before you paste your files. You can also use keyboard shortcuts to cut, copy, and paste files.

Viewing Files and Renaming Folders with Windows Explorer

You've seen how to view, copy, and move files and create folders with My Computer. Windows 95 also provides another tool, Windows Explorer, that is particularly useful when you need to establish a hierarchy or move and copy files between multiple drives. You can also use Windows Explorer to view files without opening them. In this lesson, you will copy a folder from your Work Disk onto the hard drive, and then rename it.

Steps

1. **Click the Start button, point to Programs, click Windows Explorer, then click the Maximize button in the Windows Explorer window**
   The Windows Explorer window appears, as shown in Figure B-15. You can see right away that unlike My Computer, the window is divided into two sides called panes. The left pane displays the drives and folders on your computer. The right pane displays the contents of the drive or folder selected in the left pane. A plus sign next to a folder in the left pane indicates there are additional files or folders located within a drive or folder. A minus sign indicates that all folders of the next level of hierarchy are displayed.

2. **In the left pane, right-click the hard drive icon, then click Properties on the pop-up menu**
   The Properties dialog box opens with the General tab the frontmost tab. Here, you see the capacity of your hard drive and how much free space you have available. After you've examined the properties of your hard drive you can close this window.

3. **Click the Close button in the Properties dialog box**
   Next, you will use Windows Explorer to examine your Work Disk.

4. **In the left pane double-click the 3½ Floppy (A:) icon**
   The contents of your Work Disk are displayed in the right pane as shown in Figure B-16. The plus sign next to My Folder indicates that it contains additional folders. Try expanding My Folder in the next step.

5. **In the left pane, click the plus sign next to My Folder**
   The folders contained within the My Folder now appear in the left pane.

6. **In the left pane, click the WordPad folder**
   The contents of the WordPad folder appear in the right pane of Windows Explorer. In the next step, you'll copy the WordPad folder to the hard drive in order to have a backup copy for safe keeping.

7. **In the left pane, drag the WordPad folder on top of the icon for the hard drive, then release the mouse button**
   The WordPad folder and the file in it are copied to the hard disk. Check to see if the copy of this folder is on the hard drive.

8. **In the left pane, click the icon representing your hard drive**
   The WordPad Folder should now appear in the list of folders in the right pane. You might have to scroll to find it. Now let's rename the folder so you can tell the original folder from the backup.

9. **Right-click the WordPad folder in the right pane, click Rename in the pop-up menu, then type Backup WordPad Folder and press [Enter]**
   Leave the Windows Explorer window open and continue with the next lesson.

FIGURE B-15: Windows Explorer window

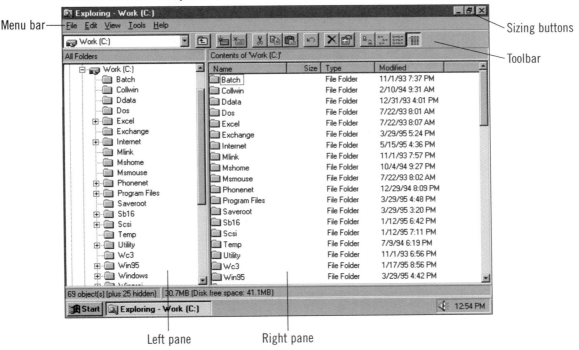

FIGURE B-16: Contents of your Work Disk

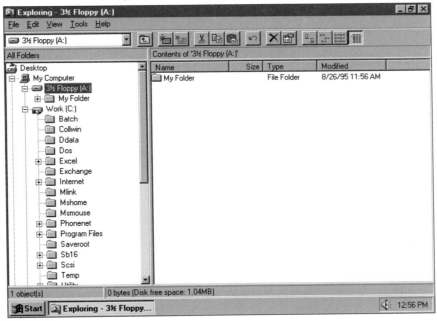

CLUES TO USE

Quick View

At times you might want to preview a document to get an idea of what is in the file before opening it. It is much faster to preview the document using either My Computer or Windows Explorer than opening the program in which the file was created, then opening the file. To preview the file, simply right-click the selected file, then click Quick View on the pop-up menu. A preview of the file appears in the Quick View box. If the Quick View command does not appear on the pop-up menu, it means that this feature was not installed on your computer; see your instructor or technical support person for additional information.

Windows 95

Deleting and Restoring Files

To save disk space and to manage your files more effectively, you should delete files you no longer need. Because all files deleted from your hard drive are stored in the Recycle Bin (until you remove them permanently), you can restore files you might have deleted accidentally. There are many ways to delete files in Windows 95. In this lesson, you'll use two different methods for removing files you no longer need. Then you will learn how to restore a deleted file.

1. Click the **Restore button** on the Windows Explorer title bar

Now you should be able to see the Recycle Bin icon on your desktop. If you can't see it, resize or move the Windows Explorer window until it is visible.

2. Drag the folder called **Backup WordPad Folder** from the right pane to the **Recycle Bin** on the desktop

The folder no longer appears in the Windows Explorer window because you have moved it to the Recycle Bin. The Recycle Bin looks as if it contains paper. If you see an "Are you sure you want to delete" confirmation box, click No and see the Trouble? on the next page. Next, you will examine the contents of the Recycle Bin.

3. Double-click the **Recycle Bin** icon on the desktop

The Recycle Bin window appears, as shown in Figure B-17. Depending upon the number of files already deleted on your computer, your window might look different. The folder doesn't appear in the Recycle Bin window but the file does. Use the scroll bar if you can't see it. Next, you'll try restoring a deleted folder.

4. Click **Edit** on the Recycle Bin menu bar, then click **Undo Delete**

The Backup WordPad folder is restored and should now appear in the Windows Explorer window. You might need to move or resize your Recycle Bin window if it blocks your view of the Windows Explorer window. Next, you can delete the Backup WordPad folder for good using a Windows Explorer toolbar button.

5. Click the **Backup WordPad Folder** in the left pane, then click the **Delete button** ☒ on the Windows Explorer toolbar

The Confirm Folder Delete dialog box opens as shown in Figure B-18.

6. Click **Yes**

When you are sure you will no longer need files you've moved into the Recycle Bin, you can empty the Recycle Bin. You won't do this now, in case you are working on a computer that you share with other people. But, when you're working on your own machine, simply right-click the Recycle Bin icon, then click Empty Recycle Bin in the pop-up menu.

Leave both the Recycle Bin and the Windows Explorer windows open and continue to the next lesson.

Trouble?

If you are unable to recycle a file, it might be because your Recycle Bin is full, or too small, or the properties have been changed so that files are not stored in the Recycle Bin, they are deleted right away. Right-click the Recycle Bin icon, then click Properties on the pop-up menu to change the settings for storage and capacity.

FIGURE B-17: Contents of Recycle Bin

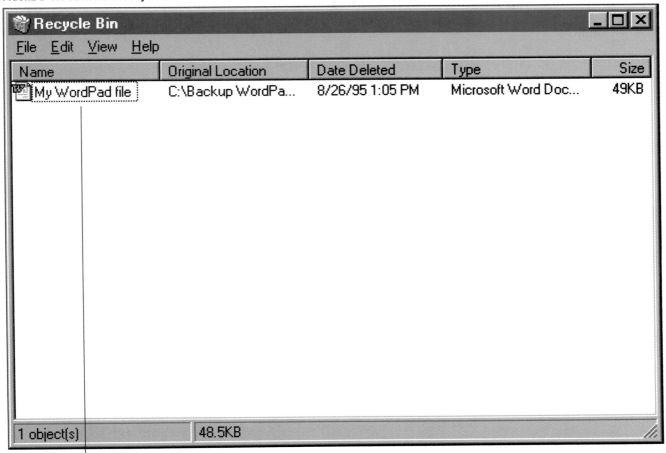

File you just
deleted

FIGURE B-18: Confirm Folder Delete dialog box

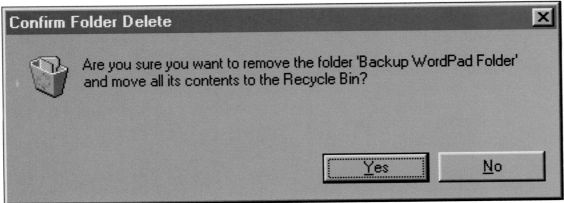

CLUES TO USE

Important note about deleting files on a floppy disk

You cannot restore files deleted from a floppy disk.
Once a file on a floppy disk is sent to the Recycle Bin,
it is permanently removed from the floppy disk and
cannot be retrieved.

Windows 95

Managing Files on the Desktop

You've now learned two different tools for managing files in Windows 95: My Computer and Windows Explorer. There is yet another Windows 95 feature you can use to make it easier to access files, folders, or programs you frequently use. A pop-up menu on the Windows desktop allows you to create folders and shortcuts on the desktop itself. **Shortcuts** are icons that point to an object that is actually stored elsewhere in a drive or folder. When you double-click a shortcut, you open the object without having to find its actual location. ◀━━ In this lesson, you will create a shortcut to the My WordPad file. Creating shortcuts to files you use frequently and placing them on the desktop allows you to work more efficiently.

QuickTip

Windows 95 enables you to customize your desktop to suit your work habits. For example, you can create a folder on the desktop that you can use to store all of your shortcuts. You can even create a shortcut folder on the desktop.

1. **In the left pane of the Windows Explorer window, click the WordPad folder**
   You need to select the file you want to create a shortcut to, first.

2. **In the right pane, right-click the My WordPad file**
   A pop-up menu appears as shown in Figure B-19.

3. **Click Create Shortcut in the pop-up menu**
   The file named Shortcut to My WordPad file appears in the right pane. Now you need to move it to the desktop so it will be at your fingertips whenever you need it. If you drag it using the left mouse button you will copy it to the desktop. If you drag it using the right mouse button you will have the option to copy or move it. Let's try dragging it using the right mouse button.

4. **Right-drag the Shortcut to My WordPad file to an empty area of the desktop**
   When you release the mouse button a pop-up menu appears.

5. **Click Move Here in the pop-up menu**
   A shortcut to the My WordPad file now appears on the desktop as shown in Figure B-20. When you double-click this shortcut icon, you will open both WordPad and the My WordPad file document. Now let's delete the shortcut icon in case you are working in a lab and share the computer with others. Deleting a shortcut does not delete the original file or folder to which it points.

6. **On the desktop, click the Shortcut to My WordPad file, then press [Delete]; click Yes to confirm the deletion**
   The shortcut is removed from the desktop and now appears in the Recycle Bin; however, the file itself remains intact in the WordPad folder. (See the Windows Explorer window to make sure it's still there.)

7. **Close all open windows**

FIGURE B-19: **Pop-up menu**

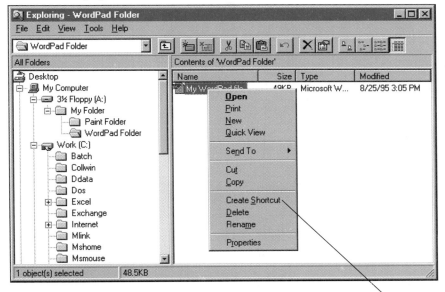

Click to create a
shortcut to the file

FIGURE B-20: **Shortcut on desktop**

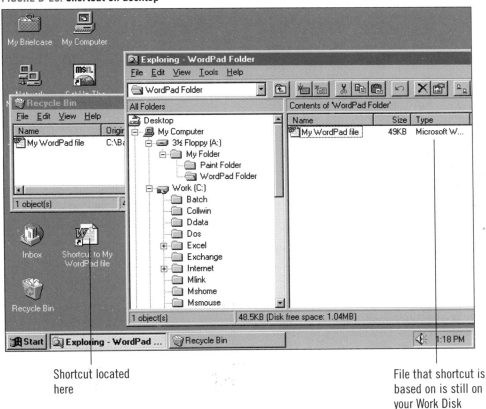

Shortcut located
here

File that shortcut is
based on is still on
your Work Disk

CLUES TO USE

Adding shortcuts to the Start menu

If you do not want your desktop to get cluttered with icons, but you would still like easy access to certain files, programs, and folders, you can create a shortcut on the Start menu or any of its cascading menus.

Drag the file, program, or folder that you want to add to the Start menu from the Windows Explorer window to the Start button. The file, program, or folder will appear on the first level of the Start menu.

Practice

► Concepts Review

Label each of the elements of the Windows Explorer window shown in Figure B-21.

FIGURE B-21

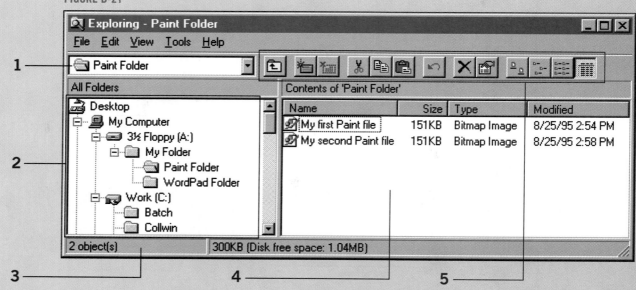

1
2
3
4
5

Match each of the descriptions with the correct term.

6. RAM
7. Folders
8. Files
9. Hierarchy
10. Clipboard

a. Permanent storage of your work in programs
b. Temporary location of your work as you use a program
c. Temporary location of information you wish to paste into another program
d. Storage area for organizing files or folders by type, project, or whatever you wish
e. Structure of files and folders revealing organization of a disk

Select the best answer from the list of choices.

11. To prepare a floppy disk to receive your files, you must first do which of the following?
   a. Copy work files to the disk
   b. Format the disk
   c. Erase all the files that might be on the disk
   d. Place the files on the Clipboard

12. To view the contents of a folder, you can use which of the following tools?
   a. The desktop   b. Windows Explorer   c. My Computer   d. Either b or c

13. You can use the My Computer program to:
   a. Create a drawing of your computer.
   b. View the contents of a folder.
   c. Customize the Start menu.
   d. Determine what programs begin automatically when you start Windows.

14. While you are working in a program, where is your work stored?
   a. On a hard drive   b. In RAM   c. In the monitor   d. On the Clipboard

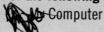
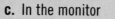

15. **What is the correct sequence for starting the Paint program?**
   a. Double-click the Paint shortcut on the desktop
   b. Click Start, Programs, Accessories, Paint
   c. Click Start, Programs, Paint
   d. Click Start, Accessories, Paint

16. **Which of the following best describes the WordPad program?**
   a. A program for pasting in graphics
   b. A program for performing complex financial analysis
   c. A program that is a simple text editor for creating basic documents
   d. A program for creating graphics

17. **For most Windows programs, the Save As command is located on which menu?**
   a. File
   b. Edit
   c. Help
   d. Save

18. **Which of the following is NOT a way to move files from one folder to another?**
   a. Opening the file and using the Save As command to save the file in a new location.
   b. In My Computer or the Windows Explorer, drag the selected to the new folder.
   c. Use the Cut and Paste commands on the Edit menu while in the My Computer or the Windows Explorer windows.
   d. Use the [Ctrl] [X] and [Ctrl] [V] keyboard shortcuts while in the My Computer or the Windows Explorer windows.

19. **Which of the following is a way to rename the selected file in either the My Computer window or the Windows Explorer window?**
   a. Click Edit on the menu bar, then click Rename.
   b. Click File on the menu bar, then click Rename.
   c. Click the Rename button on the toolbar.
   d. You can only rename files in the program in which the file was created.

20. **In which of the following can you view the hierarchy of drives, folder, and files in a split pane window?**
   a. The Windows Explorer window
   b. The Programs window
   c. The My Computer window
   d. The WordPad window

▶ Skills Review

1. **Format a disk.**
   a. Insert a new blank disk in a drive.
   b. Open My Computer and use the right mouse button to click on the drive.
   c. Format the disk using the Format command on the pop-up menu. Check that the capacity and format type are correct.

2. **Create a WordPad file.**
   a. Launch WordPad.
   b. Type a short description of your artistic abilities and press [Enter] several times to create extra space between the text and the graphic you are about to create.
   c. Insert your Work Disk in the appropriate disk drive, then save the document as My New Document to the My Folder on your Work Disk.
   d. Minimize the WordPad program.

3. **Create and save a Paint file.**
   a. Launch Paint.
   b. Create your own unique, colorful design using several colors. Use a variety of tools. For example, create a filled circle and then place a filled square inside the circle. Use the Text button to create a text box in which you type your name.
   c. Save the picture as My Art to the My Folder on your Work Disk.
   d. Select the entire graphic and copy it onto the Clipboard.

   e. Switch to the WordPad program.

   f. Place the insertion point below the text and paste the graphic into your document.

   g. Save the changes to your WordPad document.

   h. Switch to the Paint program.

   i. Using the Fill With Color button, change the color of a filled area of your graphic.

   j. Save the revised graphic with a new name, My Art2 to the My Folder on your Work Disk.

   k. Select the entire graphic and copy it to the Clipboard.

   l. Switch to the WordPad program and above the picture type "This is an improved graphic."

   m. Select the old graphic by clicking the picture, then paste the new contents of the Clipboard. The new graphic replaces the old graphic that was selected.

   n. Save the changed WordPad document with a new name, My Second Document to the My Folder on your Work Disk.

   o. Exit the Paint and WordPad programs.

4. Manage files and folders with My Computer.

   a. Open My Computer.

   b. Be sure your Work Disk is in either drive A or drive B.

   c. Double-click the drive icon that contains your Work Disk to prepare for the next step.

5. Create new folders on the Work Disk and on the hard drive.

   a. Create a folder called My Review Folder on your Work Disk by clicking File, New, then clicking Folder.

   b. Open the folder to display its contents in a separate window.

   c. Create another folder (at the root of C on the hard drive) called My Temporary Folder.

   d. In the My Review Folder window, click File, New, then click Folder. Create two new subfolders (under My Review Folder), one called Documents and the other called ArtWork.

   e. In the My Computer window, double-click the drive C icon to display the contents of your hard drive in a new window.

6. Move files to the new folders in the My Review Folder.

   a. Open the ArtWork folder on your Work Disk.

   b. From the root of the Work Disk, drag the two Paint files into the ArtWork folder window on your Work Disk. Close the ArtWork folder window.

   c. Open the Documents folder on your Work Disk.

   d. From the root of the Work Disk, drag the two WordPad files into the Documents folder window on your Work Disk. Close the Documents folder window.

   e. Close all of the open windows in My Computer.

7. Copy files to the My Temporary Folder on the hard drive.

   a. Open the Windows Explorer.

   b. Copy the four WordPad and Paint files from the folders on the Work Disk to the My Temporary Folder.

8. Delete files and folders.

   a. Drag the My Temporary Folder to the Recycle Bin icon.

   b. Click the My Review Folder and press [Del]. Then confirm that you want to delete the file.

   c. Double-click the Recycle Bin icon and restore the My Temporary Folder and its files. Delete the folder again.

9. Create a shortcut that opens Windows Explorer.

   a. Use Windows Explorer to locate the Windows folder on your hard drive. In the right side of the window, scroll through the list of objects until you see a file called Explorer.

   b. Drag the Explorer file to the desktop.

   c. Close the Windows Explorer.

   d. Double-click the new shortcut to test the shortcut for starting Windows Explorer. Then close the Explorer again.

   e. Delete the shortcut for Windows Explorer. Then use the Start button to verify that the Windows Explorer program is still available on the Programs menu.

▶ Independent Challenges

1. It is important to develop a sound, organized plan when you manage files and folders. Practice your skills by organizing the following list of names into a coherent and logical hierarchy. Begin by identifying folders. In each folder, identify the files you could expect to find in them. Sketch a hierarchical structure like the one you would see in the right side of a Windows Explorer window.

- Projects
- My Resume
- Recommendation letter
- First Qtr Bulletin
- Marketing
- Finance
- Sales 95
- Sales 96
- Personal
- Employee Profile article
- Sales 94
- Project Plan Second Qtr
- Project Plan First Qtr
- Sales Summary
- Performance Review 1996

2. It is important to develop a sound, organized plan when you manage files and folders. Practice your skills by organizing the following list of names into a coherent and logical hierarchy. Begin by identifying folders. Then in each folder, identify the files you could expect to find in them. Sketch the series of windows containing the folders and files you would display using My Computer. For example, one of the windows might represent the contents of a folder designated for non-work related files.

- Projects
- My Resume
- Recommendation letter
- First Qtr Bulletin
- Marketing
- Finance
- Sales 95
- Sales 96
- Personal
- Employee Profile article
- Sales 94
- Project Plan Second Qtr
- Project Plan First Qtr
- Sales Summary
- Performance Review 1996

3. On your computer's hard drive (at the root of C:), create a folder called My Review Folder. Then using the files on your Work Disk, create the file hierarchy indicated below. Follow these guidelines to create the files you need to place in the correct folders.

1. Create a new file using WordPad that contains a simple list of things to do. Save the file as To Do List.
2. Create two copies of any WordPad files and rename them New WordPad Article and Copy of Article.
3. Copy any Paint file and rename the copy Sample Logo.
4. Copy the To Do List, and rename the copy Important.

After you have placed the files in their correct folders, copy the My Review Folder (and its contents) to your Work Disk. Then on your hard drive, delete the My Review Folder. Using the Recycle Bin icon, restore the file called Important. To remove all your work on the hard drive, delete this file again.

4. To make working with files on a floppy disk easier, create a shortcut to a Windows Explorer window that displays the contents of a disk in the drive that currently contains your Work Disk. (*Hint:* Open Windows Explorer as shown in Figure B-23 and drag the icon representing your floppy drive to the desktop). Next, capture a picture of your desktop (with the new shortcut) onto the Clipboard by pressing the [Prnt Scrn] key (located on the upper-right side of your keyboard). With the picture on the Clipboard, open the Paint program and paste the contents of the Clipboard into the drawing window as shown in Figure B-24. Save the Paint file as My Desktop Picture on your Work Disk. Finally, delete the shortcut.

FIGURE B-22

```
My Review Folder
  ➥Projects
        ➥To Do List
      ➥Communications (folder)
            ➥New WordPad Article
          ➥Copy of Article
  ➥Graphics (folder)
        ➥Sample Logo
      ➥CTI Important
```

Introducing
Microsoft Office 97 Professional

Objectives

▶ **Understand Office 97 components**
▶ **Create documents with Word 97**
▶ **Build worksheets with Excel 97**
▶ **Manage data with Access 97**
▶ **Design presentations with PowerPoint 97**
▶ **Manage office tasks with Outlook**
▶ **Browse the World Wide Web with Internet Explorer 3**

Microsoft Office 97 Professional is a collection of programs designed to take advantage of the Windows 95 interface and improve your computer efficiency. When programs are grouped together, as in Microsoft Office, this collection is called a **suite**, and all its components have similar icons, functions, and commands. ▰▰▰ This unit will introduce you to Nomad Ltd, a tour and sporting goods company with five regional offices. Nomad Ltd organizes guided outdoor tours for activities like hiking, rafting, and biking. The company also sells the equipment needed to do these activities. By exploring how Nomad Ltd uses Microsoft Office components, you will learn how each program can be used in a business environment.

Understanding Office 97 Components

Microsoft Office contains all the programs commonly used in businesses. The documents created with Office programs can be opened without opening the program itself by using a button on the **Office Shortcut bar.** These buttons, listed in Table A-1, let you create new files, open existing files, use **Outlook,** a personal information manager, and travel the World Wide Web using Microsoft's web browser **Internet Explorer 3.0.** Since use of the Shortcut Bar is optional, it will not be covered in this book. The Microsoft Windows taskbar, located at the bottom of the screen, lets you switch between programs simply by clicking the program button. Office 97 is available in two arrangements: Professional and Standard. Office 97 Professional contains Access, the database program; Office 97 Standard does not. Nomad Ltd employees began using Office 97 Professional when the five regional offices switched from manual functions to networked personal computers. Figure A-1 is Nomad's organizational chart. Below are some of the ways the company uses Office 97 to create its Annual Report.

Details

Create text documents using Word
Word is the word processor in Office. You use a **word processor** to create documents, such as descriptions of Nomad's financial condition and projected expansion reports.

Analyze sales figures using Excel
Excel is the spreadsheet in Office. You use a **spreadsheet** to analyze data and perform calculations. You can also use a spreadsheet to create charts to give a visual representation of the data.

Track product inventory using Access
Access is the database management system in Office. A **database** is a collection of related information like a list of employees and their social security numbers, salaries, and vacation time. A **database management system** organizes databases and allows you to cross-check information in them.

Create presentation graphics using PowerPoint
PowerPoint is the presentation graphics program in Office. You use **presentation graphics** to develop materials to enhance written reports and slides for visual presentations. Figure A-1 was created using PowerPoint.

Share or link text and graphics among programs to increase accuracy
Information in one program can be **dynamically linked** or **embedded** to another program. Using dynamic links or embedding techniques data in one file can be updated in other files. This means that an Excel chart linked to a PowerPoint slide will be automatically updated if a worksheet value changes. A company logo can be made available to all regional offices and placed in Word, Excel, Access, and PowerPoint files.

Schedule appointments, maintain a task list, record customer contact information with Outlook, and send electronic mail
This personal information manager has all the features of a hardcopy appointment book, and information can be shared with other Office programs. It's also a tool to send electronic mail.

Discover the ever-changing World Wide Web using Internet Explorer
The Internet Explorer lets you travel the World Wide Web, allowing you to access current information and global resources.

Nomad Ltd

Headquarters
Boston, MA

| Northeast | South | Midwest | Southwest | Northwest |

Retail Outlets (Northeast)
Retail Outlets (South)
Retail Outlets (Midwest)
Retail Outlets (Southwest)
Retail Outlets (Northwest)

Understanding the docucentric environment

Office documents that were previously created can be opened using the Shortcut bar buttons or by clicking the filename in the Documents listing on the Start menu. This **docucentric** environment shifts the focus to completing document-related tasks rather than using the programs themselves.

TABLE A-1: Microsoft Office 97 Shortcut bar buttons

button	name	function
	Office	Add or remove Office programs and customize the Shortcut bar
	New Office Document	Create a document in any of the installed Office programs
	Open Office Document	Open a document in any of the installed Office programs
	New Message	Launch Microsoft Exchange, an electronic mail program
	New Appointment	Create any appointment using Outlook
	New Contact	Add a contact to the Outlook address book
	Create Microsoft Outlook Task	Add a task to the Outlook To Do list

Office 97

Creating Documents with Word 97

All of Nomad's regional offices use Word while gathering data for the Annual Report. Word allows you to create and edit text documents, such as a newsletter or correspondence. Using Word, you can compose a document, then easily modify it. The result is a professional-looking document. The actual Annual Report is created using Word. Below are some of the benefits of using Word.

Details

Enter text quickly and easily

Word makes it easy to enter text, and then edit it later. Rather than having to retype a document, the text can be rearranged or revised.

Create error-free copy

You use Word's spell checker after you finish typing. It compares each word in a document to a built-in dictionary and notifies you if it does not recognize a word. Word's AutoCorrect feature automatically corrects words as you type them. Word provides several entries for commonly misspelled words, but you can add your own.

Combine text and graphics

Using Word, you can combine text and graphics easily. Figure A-2 shows the Word document containing text and graphics as it looks on the screen; Figure A-3 shows the completed sample memo.

Add special effects

Word gives you the ability to create columnar documents, drop caps (capital letters that take up two or three lines), and WordArt (text you customize by changing its appearance to become 3-dimensional or shadowed), adding a professional quality to your documents.

FIGURE A-2: Microsoft Word containing memo

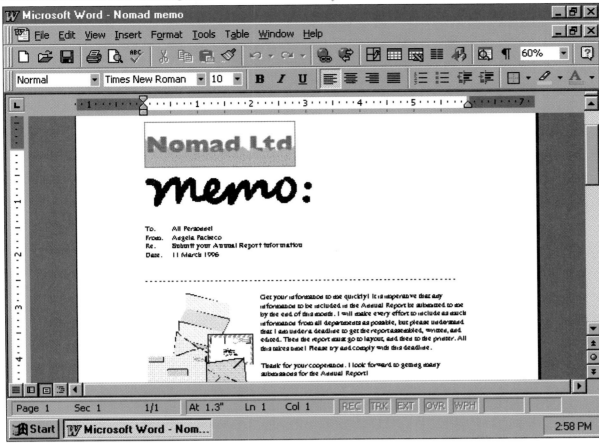

FIGURE A-3: Memo created in Word

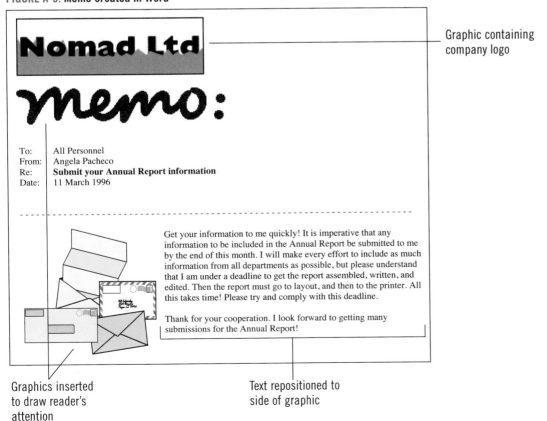

Graphic containing
company logo

Graphics inserted
to draw reader's
attention

Text repositioned to
side of graphic

Building Worksheets with Excel 97

The Excel program performs numeric calculations rapidly and accurately. Like traditional paper-based spreadsheets, an electronic spreadsheet contains a **worksheet** area that is divided into columns and rows which form individual **cells**. Cells can contain text, numbers, formulas, or a combination of all three. Sales and revenue data collected by Nomad's employees is stored and manipulated using Excel and then used in the Annual Report. What follows are some of the benefits of using Excel.

Details

Calculate results quickly and accurately
Using Excel, you enter only data and formulas and then Excel calculates the results.

Recalculate easily
Excel recalculates any results based on a changed entry automatically.

Speculate outcomes using what-if analysis
Because equations are automatically recalculated, this lets you say "what-if" and create a variety of scenarios. For example, you could anticipate and avoid a revenue shortfall if expenses were to rise 15%.

Complete complex mathematical equations
Using Excel's Paste Function, you can easily complete complicated math computations using built-in equations. The Paste Function tells you what data is needed and you fill-in-the-blanks. This saves you valuable time.

Create charts
Excel makes it easy to create charts based on information in a worksheet. With Excel, charts are automatically updated as data changes. The worksheet in Figure A-4 shows a column chart that graphically shows the distribution of sales for each of Nomad's regional offices.

Create attractive output
Printouts of numeric data can be made more attractive using charts, graphics, and text formatting such as bolding and italicizing, as shown in Figure A-5.

FIGURE A-4: Microsoft Excel containing worksheet

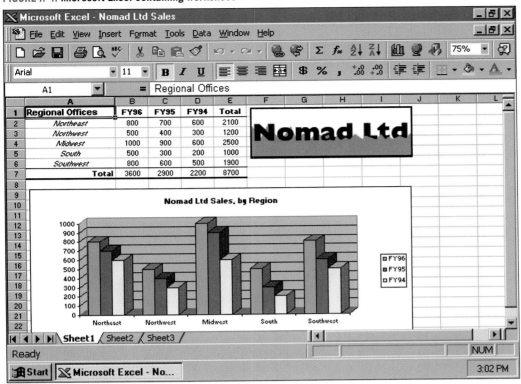

FIGURE A-5: Sales summary and chart created in Excel

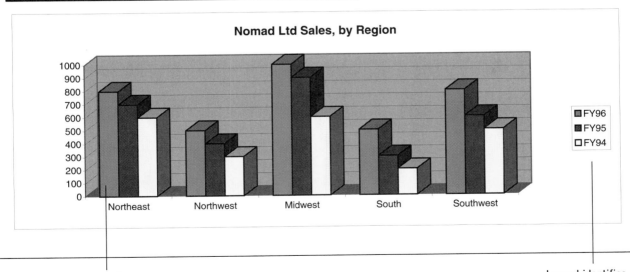

Sales Summary

Regional Offices	FY96	FY95	FY94	Total
Northeast	800	700	600	2100
Northwest	500	400	300	1200
Midwest	1000	900	600	2500
South	500	300	200	1000
Southwest	800	600	500	1900
Total	3600	2900	2200	8700

Corresponds to
Northeast sales
data for FY96

Legend identifies
colors used in chart

Managing Data with Access 97

In addition to Word and Excel, Office 97 includes Access, a database manager. Access is used to arrange large amounts of data in various groups or **databases**, such as an inventory of products. The information in the databases can be retrieved in a variety of ways. For example, a database like an inventory list might be arranged alphabetically, by stocking location, or by the number of units on order. A powerful database, such as Access, lets you look up information quickly, easily, and in a wide variety of ways. ◆━━━ Once the Annual Report is completed, the database containing stockholders names and address will be used to generate mailing labels so the report can be distributed. Below are some of the benefits of using Access.

Details

Enter data easily

Employees enter inventory items in whatever order they are received. Because Access organizes the data for you, the order in which items are entered is not a concern.

Retrieve data easily

Access makes it easy for you to specify criteria, or conditions, and then produce a list of all data that conforms to that criteria. You might want to see a list of products by supplier or a list of discontinued products. Figure A-6 shows a list of bicycle products sold at Nomad's retail stores sorted by product name then by the supplier ID number.

Create professional-looking forms

You can enter data into an on-screen form that you create in Access. This makes entering data more efficient, and you'll be less prone to making errors. Figure A-7 shows a screen form which can be used for data entry.

Add graphics to printed screen forms and reports

Forms and reports can contain graphic images, text formatting, and special effects, such as WordArt to make them look more professional. Beautifully designed screen forms can contain graphics and can be printed, as seen in Figure A-8.

FIGURE A-6: List of bicycle inventory containing selected table files

Product ID	Product Name	Supplier ID	Units In Stock	Unit Price
11162	Look PP166 pedals	94	45	$45.00
11162	Look PP166 pedals	91	45	$45.00
11162	Look PP166 pedals	63	45	$45.75
11162	Look PP166 pedals	63	45	$45.00
11162	Look PP166 pedals	63	45	$45.00
11162	Look PP166 pedals - adv	63	45	$45.00
11162	Look PP168 pedals	63	45	$45.00
76662	Nomad Aerospoke Wheels	56	30	$200.00
76662	Nomad Aerospoke Wheels	56	30	$200.00
76662	Nomad Aerospoke Wheels	56	30	$200.00
76662	Nomad Aerospoke Wheels	56	30	$200.00
76662	Nomad Aerospoke Wheels	56	30	$200.00
32323	Nomad Beauty Handlebar	10	27	$3.00
32323	Nomad Beauty Handlebar	10	27	$2.00

Items first sorted alphabetically by product name

Consecutive entry numbers rearranged by sort orders

Items then sorted in descending order by Supplier ID

FIGURE A-7: Microsoft Access containing form

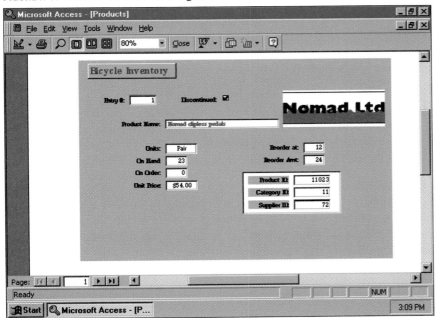

FIGURE A-8: Inventory screen form created in Access

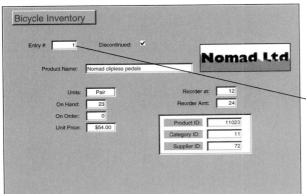

Field number automatically advances to the next number with each new entry

Designing Presentations Using PowerPoint 97

In PowerPoint, a **slide** is the work area in which handouts, outlines, speakers' notes and 35mm slides are produced. You can also create an online slide show in which flowing images appear on a PC monitor and are viewed by a group of people. Usually the computer is hooked up to a projector so a roomful of many people can see the demonstration. ▰▱ The Annual Report is presented at the Annual Meeting using a variety of materials created in PowerPoint. The following are benefits of using PowerPoint.

Details

Create and edit easily on a slide
Text can be written directly on a PowerPoint slide, enabling you to see if your slide looks cluttered. Editing is accomplished using the same methods as in Word. Text can be cut, copied, pasted, and moved simply and easily.

Combine information from Office 97 programs
Data created in Word, Excel, and Access can all be utilized in slides. This means that information created in Excel, for example, can be used on a slide, without having to be retyped.

Add graphics
Graphic images, such as clip art, an Excel chart, or a corporate logo, further enhance any presentation materials. PowerPoint accepts the most commonly available graphic file formats and comes with more than 1,000 clip art images. PowerPoint also allows you to create your own shapes and design your own text. Figure A-9 shows a slide containing an Excel chart.

Print a variety of presentation materials
In addition to being able to print out a slide, as seen in Figure A-10, you can also create many other types of printed materials. Speakers Notes—containing hints and reminders helpful to whomever delivers the presentation—are invaluable. Handouts for presentation attendees contain a reduced image of each slide and a place for handwritten notes.

Special effects
Add special effects, such as transitions from one slide to the next, text and graphics builds within slides, sounds and videos all serve to make your presentation look professional.

FIGURE A-9: Microsoft PowerPoint containing slide

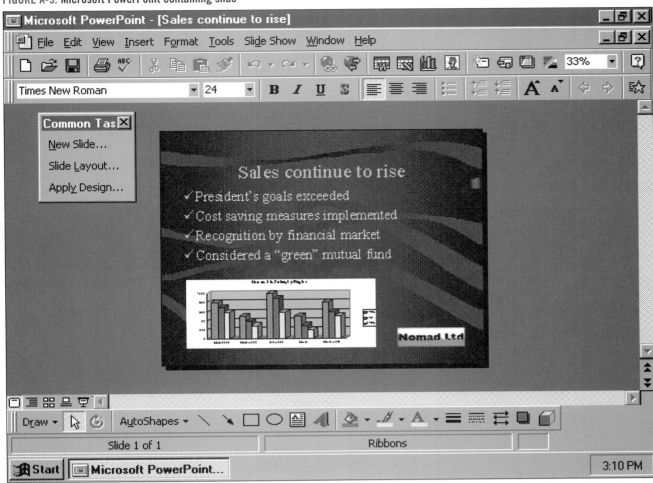

FIGURE A-10: Slide with Excel chart created in PowerPoint

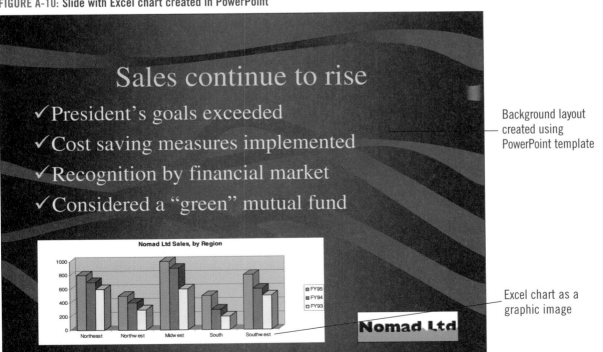

Background layout created using PowerPoint template

Excel chart as a graphic image

Office 97

Managing Office 97 Tasks Using Outlook

There's more to office work than creating documents, worksheets, databases, and presentations. Outlook is a personal information manager that lets you better manage all the items that occur during a typical day. For example, you can send electronic mail—or **e-mail**—to anyone with an Internet address using the Inbox. ✎ Nomad employees work more efficiently using Outlook to send messages, schedule appointments, and keep track of deadlines.

Details

Process mail

Use the Inbox to read, forward, reply, and create e-mail. The Inbox, shown in Figure A-11, displays the first few lines of each unread message, so you can see if you want to read it now or wait until later. In addition to the actual content of a message, individual files can also be attached. This means you can send a colleague a document created in Excel, for example, along with an explanatory message.

Create and maintain appointments

Just like an appointment that sits on your desk, Calendar lets you make appointments with others, plan meetings, and keep track of events such as seminars, hire dates, birthdays, and anniversaries. The task pad always displays, giving you an overview of items in your Task list.

Manage tasks

Tasks lets you keep track of pending jobs, and allows you to set priorities that evaluate the relative importance of one job over another, assign due dates, and express completion expectations. You can also use the Task Request lets you assign a task to another person. This section allows you to monitor the relative status of the many tasks you manager.

Keep track of business contacts

Its impossible to remember every persons name, address, and telephone number. Contacts lets you record vital information such as name, address, and phone number, but also includes space for e-mail addresses and web sites, as shown in Figure A-12.

Maintain a journal

Outlook's Journal is a time management tool that lets you track project phases and record activities with ease. Icons of files related to specific activities can be embedded into the Journal so you'll always be able to return to them.

Create reminders using Notes

Since it's difficult to remember all the things you have to do, use Notes—just like sticky yellow papers attached to items on folders—to leave messages for yourself. These electronic notes serve as reminders of important information that might otherwise get lost on your desk.

FIGURE A-11: Microsoft Outlook Inbox

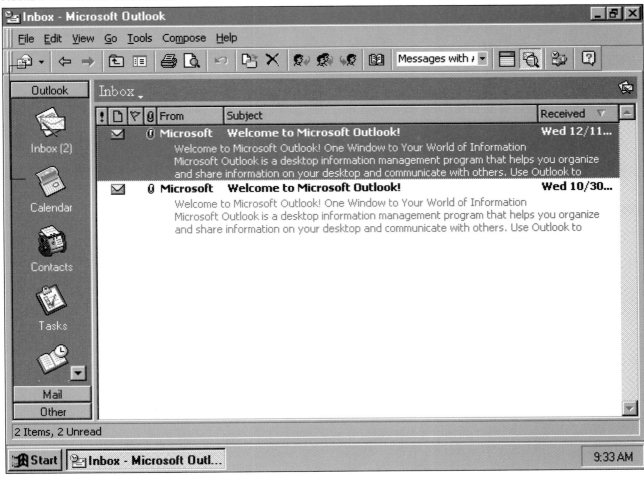

FIGURE A-12: Contact dialog box in Outlook

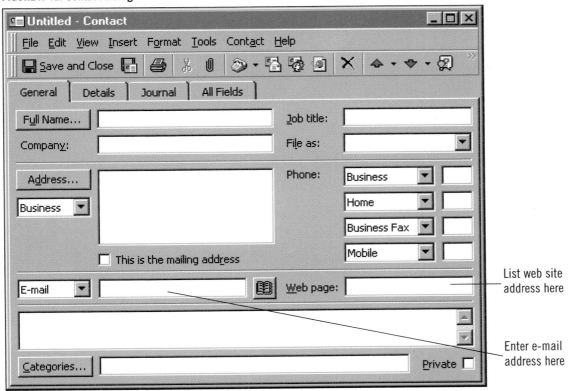

List web site address here

Enter e-mail address here

Office 97

Browsing the World Wide Web with Internet Explorer 3

The World Wide Web—also know as the **Web**—is an element of the Internet that brings global information to your desktop in a graphical format. Internet Explorer 3 is a **browser**, software designed to view the graphic images and multimedia data on the Web. Many Web sites let you move to other sites with the click of your mouse using **links**, instructions that take you to different web site addresses. You can also quickly jump to Web sites entered in any Outlook's Contact. Nomad employees keep informed and up-to-date on the latest trends using Internet Explorer.

Details

Display Web sites
Once you're connected to the Internet, you can view interesting and informative Web pages from all around the globe.

Jump to a Web site listed in Contacts
If you've entered a web site in Contacts as shown in Figure A-13, you can quickly access that site by clicking that Contact, then clicking the Explore Web Page button.

Move from one Web site to another
Links found within a Web page let you effortlessly move from site to site. This lets you easily find information related to the topic you're interested in.

Save your favorite site locations
Once you've located interesting Web sites, you'll want to save their addresses so you can return to them. Internet Explorer makes it easy to compile a list of your favorite locations.

Use multimedia
Video and audio clips are commonly found within Web pages, and you can take advantage of the depth they add by using a browser that's multimedia-capable, such as Internet Explorer.

Print Web pages
As you travel the Web, you may want to print the information you find. You can easily print an active Web page—including text and graphics.

FIGURE A-13: Browsing with Internet Explorer

Practice

► Concepts Review

Label each of the elements in Figure A-14.

FIGURE A-14

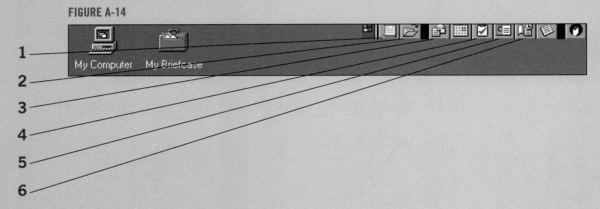

1
2
3
4
5
6

Match each program with the correct icon.

7. **Microsoft PowerPoint**   a.
8. **Microsoft Outlook**   b.
9. **Microsoft Excel**   c.
10. **Microsoft Word**   d.
11. **Microsoft Access**   e.

Select the best answer from the list of choices.

12. **Excel can be used for all of the following tasks, except:**
    a. Entering columns or rows of numbers
    b. Creating charts
    c. Creating columnar text
    d. Recalculating numeric data

13. **Which of the following is not a feature found in Word?**
    a. AutoCorrect
    b. Drop cap
    c. Slide
    d. Columnar documents

14. **Text in a Word document can:**
    a. Be easily modified and rearranged
    b. Contain graphics
    c. Be in a columnar format
    d. Contain all these effects

15. **You can create an on-line slide show containing graphics and text using:**
    a. Word
    b. PowerPoint
    c. Excel
    d. Access

16. **You can enter data easily in Access using:**
    a. Slides
    b. Charts
    c. On-screen forms
    d. Formulas

17. **PowerPoint can create all of the following, except:**
    a. Handouts
    b. Slides
    c. Outlines
    d. Data entry screen forms

Getting
Started with Internet Explorer 3

Objectives

▶ **Understand Web browsers**
▶ **Start Internet Explorer 3**
▶ **Explore the browser window**
▶ **Open and save a URL**
▶ **Navigate Web pages**
▶ **Get Help**
▶ **Print a Web page**
▶ **Search for information on the Internet**
▶ **Exit Internet Explorer 3**

In this unit, you will learn about the benefits of the World Wide Web (WWW), examine the basic features of Internet Explorer 3, and access Web pages. You need a connection to the Internet to complete this unit. If your computer is not connected to the Internet, check with your instructor or technical support person to get connected, or, if necessary, simply read the lessons without completing the steps to learn about using Internet Explorer. Nomad Ltd is a cutting-edge business. Natasha Seyb, a new marketing assistant, wants to learn about bikes to see if Nomad should expand into that area. She uses Internet Explorer to find information about other cycle shops in the country and to check on possible new sources for bike parts.

Understanding Web Browsers

A computer **network** consists of two or more computers that can share information. The **Internet** is a worldwide communications system that connects computer networks from all over the world. Over 40 million computers are currently connected to the Internet through telephone lines, cables, satellites, and other telecommunications media, as depicted in Figure A-1. Through the Internet, these computers can share many types of information, including text, graphics, sounds, videos, and computer programs. Anyone who has access to a computer and a link to the Internet through a computer network or modem can tap into this rich source of information. The **World Wide Web** (also known as the Web or WWW) is a part of the Internet that contains **Web pages** or **Web documents** that are linked together. Web pages contain highlighted words, phrases, and graphics called **hyperlinks**, or simply **links**, that open other Web pages when you click them. Figure A-2 shows a sample Web page. In addition to displaying other Web pages, a page's links may open graphic files, or they may play sound or video files. Web browsers are software programs that are used to access and display Web pages. **Web browsers**, such as Microsoft Internet Explorer 3 and Netscape Navigator, make the Web easy to navigate by providing a graphical, point-and-click environment. This unit features **Internet Explorer 3**, a popular browser from Microsoft that comes with Microsoft Office 97. Natasha realizes that there are many applications for the Internet Explorer in her company.

She can:

 Display Web pages from all over the world

Natasha can look at Web pages for business purposes, such as checking the pages of other bike shops to see how they are marketing their products.

 Use links to move from one Web page to another

Natasha also uses the Web to see the results of some of the European bike races she is following. She found that on some pages, simply by clicking on links she could investigate each of the listed bikers, their equipment, and their records.

 Play audio and video clips

One of the links that Natasha likes to use is the one that provides short video clips of the bike races. She can also hear interviews with the winners of the races.

 Search the Web for information

Natasha can click a search button on her Web browser to access a list of search programs. These search programs allow her to look for information about any topic, on computers throughout the world.

 Save a list of her favorite Web pages

Through the Internet Explorer browser, Natasha can save a list of her favorite Web pages. By adding a page to her list of favorites, it is easy for her to return to the page at a later time.

 Print the text and graphics on Web pages

If Natasha finds some information or images that she would like to print, she can easily print the entire Web page, including the graphics.

FIGURE A-1: Structure of the Internet

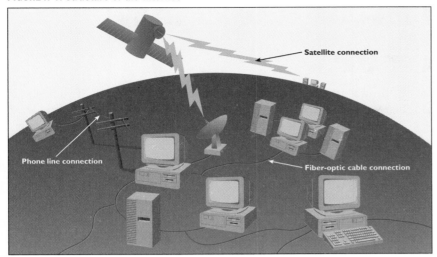

Satellite connection

Phone line connection

Fiber-optic cable connection

FIGURE A-2: Sample WWW page

Graphic hyperlinks

Text hyperlinks

The history of the Internet and the World Wide Web

The Internet has its roots in the United States Department of Defense Advanced Research Projects Agency Network (ARPANET), which was started in 1969. In 1986, the National Science Foundation formed NSFNET, which replaced ARPANET. NSFNET expanded the foundation of the U.S. portion of the Internet with high speed, long-distanced lines. In 1991, the U.S. Congress expanded the capacity and speed of the Internet further and opened it up to commercial use. The Internet is now accessible in over 200 countries.

The World Wide Web was first created in Switzerland in 1991 to allow links between documents on the Internet. In other words, while you are reading a document, it may display words or images that you can click to take you to another document or file. Software programs designed to access the Web (called Web browsers) use common "point-and-click" interfaces. The first graphical Web browser, Mosaic, was introduced at the University of Illinois in 1993. Recently, Netscape Navigator and Microsoft Internet Explorer have become the two most popular Web browsers.

Internet

Starting Internet Explorer

Internet Explorer is a Web browser that can connect you to the World Wide Web if you have an Internet connection. When you install Office 97, an icon for Internet Explorer will appear on your system's desktop. The exact location of the Internet Explorer icon may vary on different computers. See your instructor or technical support person for help if you are unable to locate the Internet Explorer icon or if you do not have an Internet connection. ◢ Before Natasha can take advantage of the many features of the Web, she must start Internet Explorer.

1. **If you connect to the Internet by telephone, follow your normal procedure or your instructor's directions to establish your connection**

2. **Locate the Internet Explorer icon on your desktop**
   The icon should appear on the left side of your screen, as shown in Figure A-3. If the icon is not on your desktop, you can click the Start button on the Taskbar, point to Programs on the Start menu, then click the Internet Explorer icon. Skip step 3.

3. **Double-click the Internet Explorer icon**
   The Internet Explorer opens and displays a Web page, as shown in Figure A-4. (The Web page displayed on your computer may be different.) Continue with the next lesson to view the various elements of the browser window.

Trouble?

It's okay if the Web page on your screen is not the same as the one shown in Figure A-4. Later in this unit, your will learn how to change the page that is displayed when you first launch Internet Explorer.

FIGURE A-3: Internet Explorer icon on the desktop

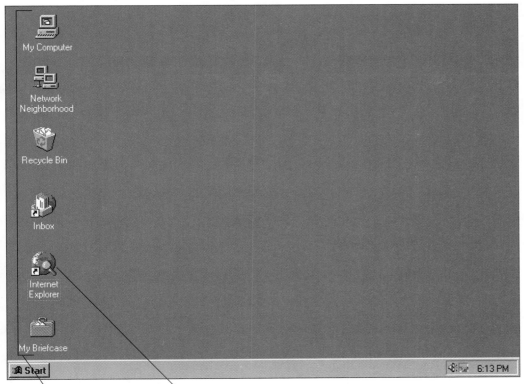

Your desktop icons
might be different

Internet Explorer
shortcut

FIGURE A-4: Web page featuring the Microsoft Corporation

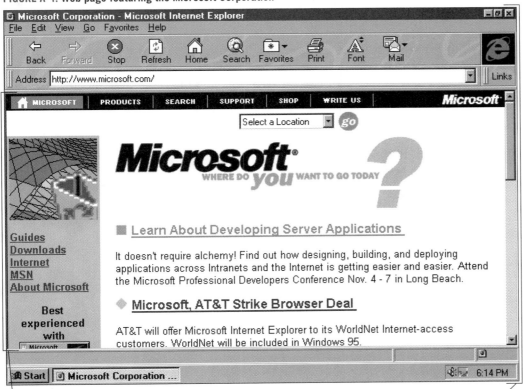

Current Web page
displayed (yours
may be different)

Internet Explorer
window

Exploring the Browser Window

The elements of the Internet Explorer program window, shown in Figure A-5, allow you to view, print, and search for information. Before exploring, or **surfing** the Web, Natasha decides to familiarize herself with the components of the browser window.

Details

She notes the following features:

 The **title bar** at the top of the page generally displays the name of the Web page.

 The **menu bar** provides access to most of the browser's features through a variety of commands, much like other Windows NT programs.

 The **toolbar** provides icons for many options, such as changing the text size on the screen, moving from one Web page to another, printing Web pages, and searching for information on the Internet. These options are explained in Table A-1. Many of the most commonly used commands that are available on menus are more readily available as buttons on the toolbar.

 The **address bar** displays the address of the current Web page. The **Web address** is also referred to as the **URL**, which stands for Uniform Resource Locator.

 The **status indicator** (the Internet Explorer logo) animates while a new Web page is loading.

 The **document window** displays the current Web page. You may need to scroll down the page to view the entire contents.

 The **vertical scroll bar** allows you to move up or down the current Web page. The **scroll box** indicates your relative position within the Web page.

 The **status bar** displays information about your connection progress with new Web pages that you open, including notification that you have connected to another site and the percentage of information that has been transferred. The bar also displays the functions of the links in the document window as you move your mouse pointer over them.

FIGURE A-5: Elements of the Internet Explorer program window

Address bar   Toolbar   Menu bar   Title bar   Status indicator

Status bar   Document window   Vertical scroll bar

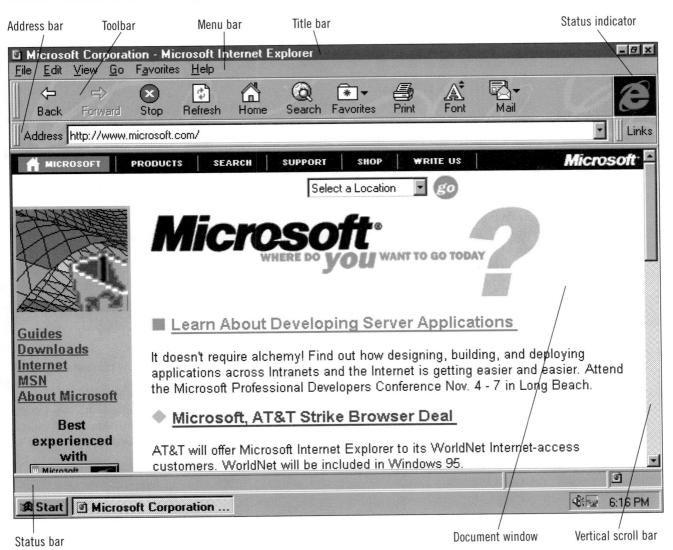

TABLE A-1: Toolbar buttons

button	descripton	button	description
Back	Opens the previous page	Search	Opens the Search page
Forward	Opens the next page	Favorites	Opens the Favorites list
Stop	Stops loading the page	Print	Prints the current Web page
Refresh	Refreshes the contents of the current page	Font	Increases or decreases the font size
Home	Opens the Home page	Mail	Displays options for working with Mail and News

Opening and Saving a URL

The address for a Web page is referred to as a URL. Each Web page has a unique URL that begins with "http" (HyperText Transfer Protocol) followed by a colon, two slashes, and the name of the Web site. At the end of the Web site name, another slash may appear, followed by one or more directories and a filename. For example, in the address, http://www2.coursetools.com/cti/Illustrated/chet/chet.html, the name of the Web site is *www2.coursetools.com*; a directory at that site is called *cti/Illustrated/chet*; and within the chet directory is a file called chet.*html*. Internet Explorer has a feature called **Favorites** that allows you to create a list of Web pages you view often. To add a Web page to your Favorites list, simply click the Favorites button when the page is displayed in your document window, and click Add to Favorites. After you add a Web page to your Favorites list, you can automatically access that page by clicking and selecting its name. Natasha wants to investigate the Web page for a competitor, Chet's Cycles. She knows that the URL for Chet's Web page is http://www2.coursetools.com/cti/Illustrated/chet/chet.html. Natasha wants to access the Web page and add it to her list of favorites so that she can return later without typing in the URL.

1. Click anywhere in the address bar
The current address is highlighted and any text you type will replace the current address.

2. Type http://www2.coursetools.com/cti/Illustrated/chet/chet.html, then press [Enter]
Be sure to type the address exactly as it appears. The status bar displays the connection process. After a few seconds, the Web page for Chet's Cycles appears in the document window, as shown in Figure A-6. (If you receive an error message, enter one of the URLs listed in Table A-2 instead.)

3. Click the Favorites button on the toolbar, click Add to Favorites and type Chet's Cycles (or another appropriate name), then click OK
The name and URL for Chet's Cycles are added to Natasha's list of favorite pages. By adding ther page to the Favorites list, it will be much easier for Natasha to visit the page again in the future — she can simply click and click the name, Chet's Cycles.

4. Click Go on the menu bar, then click Back
The previous Web page appears in the document window. In many cases, the options on the toolbar are easier to locate and use than the selections on the menu bar. You also can use the Back button on the toolbar to return to the previous page.

Trouble?

URLs may be case-sensitive, meaning that you must type them exactly as they appear, using uppercase and lower-case letters.

FIGURE A-6: Web page for Chet's Cycles

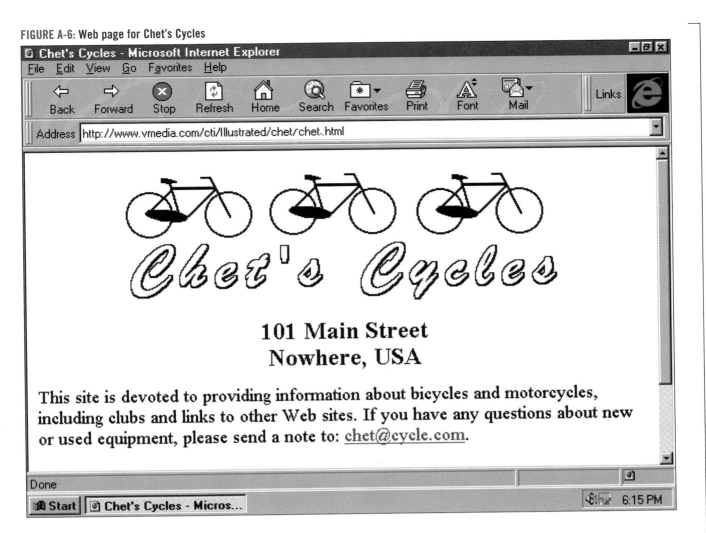

TABLE A-2: URLs of Web sites dealing with bicycles

name of company	url
Bicycle Trader	http://www.bicycletrader.com/
Cyberider Cycling WWW Site	http://blueridge.infomkt.ibm.com/bikes/
McBride Cycle	http://www.mcb-ride.com/

Choosing Favorites

When you add a Web page to your list of favorites, it is much easier to return to the page at a future time or date. To keep your Favorites list a reasonable length, you should only add pages that you will expect to visit several times.

If your list of favorites gets long, you can organize the names into folders. To add a folder in your Favorites list, click Favorites on the menu bar, click Organize Favorites, then click the Create New Folder button.

Following Links on a Web Page

Web pages can be connected to each other through links, as shown in Figure A-7. By clicking a link, you can jump to another location on the same Web page or open a different Web page altogether. You can follow these links to obtain more information about a topic. To follow a link, simply click the highlighted word or phrase. If you change your mind, or the page takes too long to load, you can click the Stop button 🛑. When Natasha was viewing the Web page for Chet's Cycles, she decided to investigate the Cycle Clubs link.

Steps

1. Click the Favorites button 📁 on the toolbar

2. Click Chet's Cycles (or the name you entered in the previous lesson) on the menu,

3. If necessary, click the scroll bar to move down the Web page until you reach the link Cycle Clubs

   When you move the mouse pointer over an active link, the mouse pointer changes to 👆. This is an indication that the text or graphic is a link.

4. Click the link Cycle Clubs

   The status indicator animates as the new Web page is accessed and displayed (see Figure A-8). If you receive an error message, click a different link on the page.

5. Click the Home button 🏠.

   The Home button returns you to the initial Web page.

FIGURE A-7: Hyperlinks on Chet's Cycles Web page

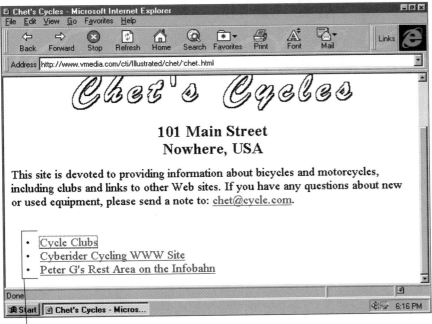

Hyperlinks

FIGURE A-8: Web page for Cycle Clubs

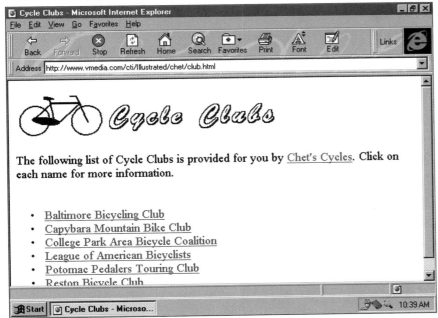

Selecting a Home page

When you click the Home button 🏠, the page that is specified as "home" appears in your document window. When you first install Internet Explorer, the default Home page is a page at the Microsoft Web site. If you want a different page to appear each time you start Internet Explorer and whenever you click the Home button, open that page in the document window, click View on the menu bar, click Options, click the Navigation tab, then click Use Current to specify the current page as the Home page.

Internet

Internet

Getting Help

Internet Explorer provides a Help option on the Menu bar with information and instructions on the features and commands. As she was exploring the Web pages for the cycle clubs, Natasha found a page with very small type. She decided to access the Help option to find instructions on increasing the font size of the type.

Steps

1. **Click Help on the menu bar**
   The Help menu appears.

2. **Click Help Topics**
   The Help Topics: Internet Explorer Help dialog box opens as shown in Figure A-9, with the Contents tab displayed as the front-most tab. Don't worry if you have a different tab in the front. Each of the three tabs will provide a different way to access information and each is explained in Table A-3.

2. **Click the Find tab**
   The Find tab allows you to search for a specific word or phrase. (Note if this is the first time that you have used the Find feature, you will need to click **Next** and **Finish** so that Internet Explorer can create a list of words from your help file.) The Find dialog box will appear.

3. **Type font sizes in the "Type the word(s) you want to find" text area**
   As you enter the words, a list of relevant topics appears in the Topics area of the Find dialog box (see Figure A-10).

4. **Double-click on Displaying text larger or smaller**
   A window opens as shown in Figure A-11 that provides information on how to change the size of the font.

5. **Click the Close button** ⊠ **in the Internet Explorer Help window**
   The Help window closes.

TABLE A-3: Help options

tab	function
Contents	Lists the categories available in Help
Index	Lists the Help topics in alphabetical order and allows you to locate specific topics
Find	Helps you locate the topic you need when you enter a key word or phrase

Click here for a list
of contents

Click here for a list
of topics

Click here for help on
finding information
about Help topics

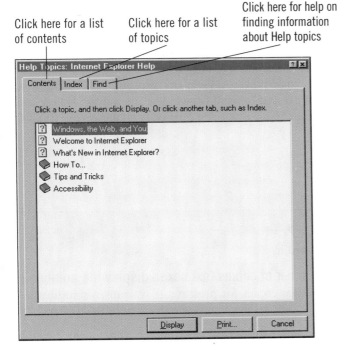

FIGURE A-10: **Find dialog box**

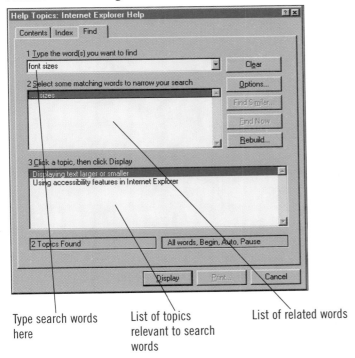

Type search words
here

List of topics
relevant to search
words

List of related words

FIGURE A-11: **Specific Help on a topic**

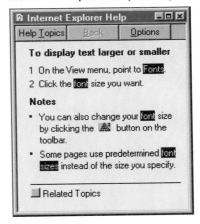

Getting Help using the right mouse button

When the Help topic is open, you can get a menu of
different commands to use with Help by right-clicking
on the Help window. For example, you can annotate a
Help item and add your own notes and ideas about

how a particular feature might be useful to you. You
also can print out the Help topic, copy the information, or change the size of the text to appear in a small,
normal, or large font size.

Internet

Internet

Printing a Web Page

You can print the Web page that is currently displayed in the document window by clicking on the Print button on the toolbar. When the print dialog box appears, you will be able to specify the number of copies and the page ranges to print (see Figure A-12). When you print a Web page, the graphics will print along with the text on the page. Table A-4 explains printing options. When Natasha was viewing a Web page, she decided to print two copies. She wanted to keep one hardcopy in her files and give one to give to her boss when he returned from a business trip.

Steps 123 4

QuickTip

To open the Print dialog box quickly, press [Ctrl][P]. You also can click the Print icon 🖨 on the Toolbar to open the dialog box.

Trouble?

If you are not connected to a printer, or if you see an error message, contact your technical support person or instructor for assistance.

1. Click **File** on the menu bar, then click **Print**
The Print dialog box appears, as illustrated in Figure A-12.

2. Click once on the **up arrow** in the Number of copies text box to display the number 2.
The Copies text box changes to display two copies for printing. If your display indicates a number other than two, click the up or down arrows until the correct number appears.

3. Make sure your computer is connected to a printer that is turned on and contains paper

4. Click **OK**
The print dialog box closes and two copies of the current Web page prints.

FIGURE A-12: Print dialog box

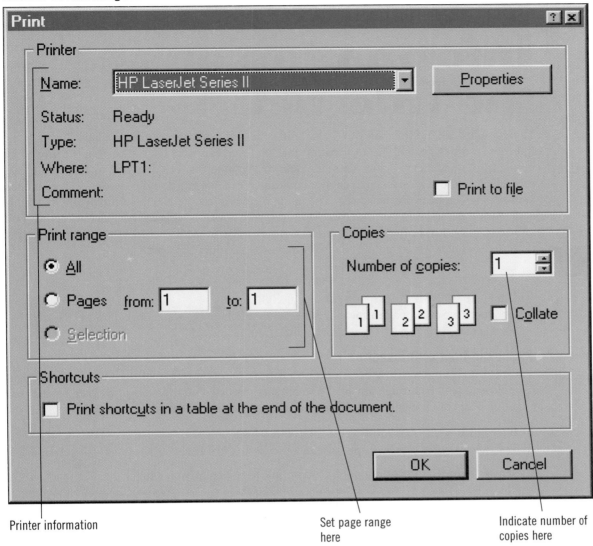

Printer information

Set page range here

Indicate number of copies here

TABLE A-4: Printing options

options	description
Printer	Displays information about the name, status and location of the active printer
Print range	Indicates which pages to print. You can select all or specify a range.
Copies	Indicates the number of copies of each page to print and the sequence of the pages.
Shortcuts	Prints shortcuts in a table at the end of the document

CLUES TO USE

Printer properties

If you select Properties from the Print dialog box, can specify the paper size, paper source, orientation, you and other parameters.

Internet

Searching for Information on the Internet

There are literally millions of Web pages and other information sources available through the Internet. At times, finding the information that you want can seem like looking for the proverbial needle in the haystack. Luckily, there are **search engines** that are designed to help you locate useful information. With a search engine, you can enter a **key word** or phrase, and a list of related Web sites will appear on the screen. The name of each Web site is a hyperlink; you can simply click on the name and go to the corresponding Web address. ▰▰▰ Natasha wanted to find information on a specific type of motorcycle, called the moped. She decided to use one of the powerful, popular search engines, called Infoseek, to conduct her search.

Steps

1. **Click the Search button** ▣ **on the toolbar**
   An Internet Search page appears with several search engines (see Figure A-13). Notice that your screen may appear slightly different.

2. **Click in front of Infoseek**
   One search engine must be selected each time you conduct an Internet search. You can choose to search through any of the search engines listed on this page at no cost. Notice that a different search engine may be selected each time you access this page.

3. **Type moped in the Search area, then click Search**
   The Infoseek Web page will appear with a list of "hits" (related Web sites) on your search word.

4. **Scroll down the list and select a hyperlink to a site of your choice**
   The Infoseek search engine will display a list of Web sites that match your search criteria as shown in Figure A-14. You can click on any of the hyperlinks to access more information.

FIGURE A-13: Internet Search page

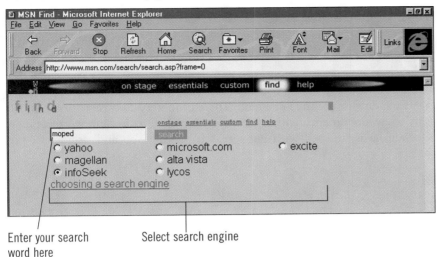

Enter your search word here

Select search engine

FIGURE A-14: Web sites related to mopeds

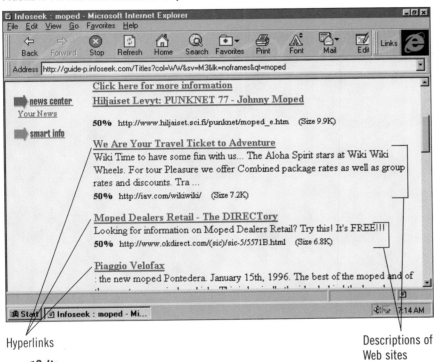

Hyperlinks

Descriptions of Web sites

CLUES TO USE

Search engines

A number of search engines can help you locate information on the Internet (such as Yahoo, Infoseek, Lycos, WebCrawler, and Excite). These search engines routinely use software programs to "crawl" through the entire Internet and create huge databases with links to the Web pages and their URLs. When you enter a key word or phrase, the search engine looks through the index of the database for relevant information (referred to as "hits") and displays a list of Web sites.

Each search engine differs slightly in the way it formats the information, the amount of Internet sites and text it records in the database, and the frequency that it updates the database. As you practice searching for information on the Internet, it is best to try several different search engines. Soon you will develop personal favorites and learn which engine works best in various situations.

Internet

Internet

Exiting Internet Explorer

When you are ready to exit Internet Explorer, you can click the Close button in the upper-right corner of the document window or use the File menu. There is no need to save before you exit, because you can only view documents within Internet Explorer; you cannot create new documents. 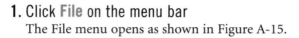 Natasha is finished with her research on the Web and decides to exit Internet Explorer.

1. **Click File on the menu bar**
   The File menu opens as shown in Figure A-15.

QuickTip

You can also exit from Internet Explorer by clicking the **Close button** ☒ in the upper-right corner of the browser window.

2. **Click Close on the File menu**
   The Internet Explorer window closes.

3. **If you connected to the Internet by telephone, follow your normal procedure or your instructor's directions to close your connection**

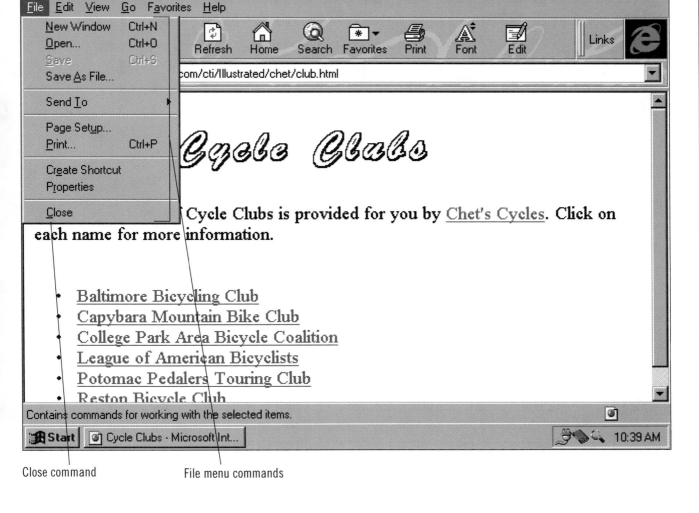

Close command

File menu commands

Saving or sending a Web page

Before you exit from Internet Explorer, you may want to save a copy of the current page or send a copy to someone else. By selecting **Save as File** on the File menu, you can save the text from the page to a file on your computer (the graphics will not be saved). Later, you can open the page in a word processor such as WordPad. If you want to send the page to someone, point to **Send To** on the File menu, then click **Mail Recipient**. Type the address of the person you would like to receive the page.

Internet

Practice

► Concepts Review

Label each of the World Web screen elements indicated in Figure A-16

FIGURE A-16

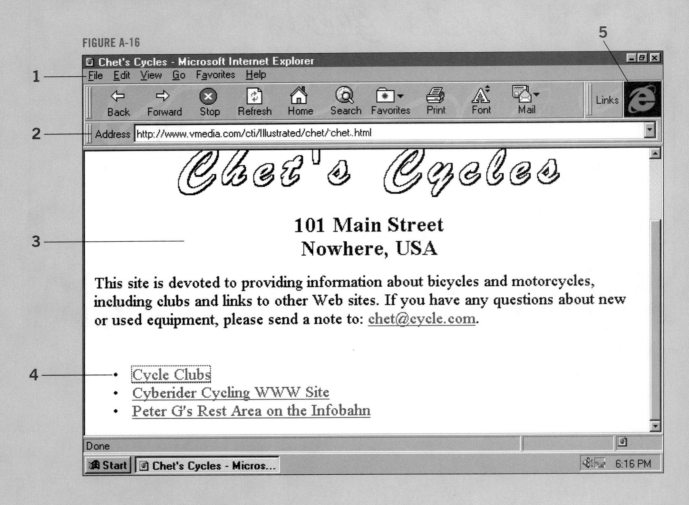

Match each of the terms with the statement that describes its function.

6. Address bar
7. Toolbar
8. Favorites button
9. Status indicator
10. Back button

a. Animates when Internet Explorer is loading a page
b. Displays the URL for the current page
c. Provides shortcuts for options on the menu bar
d. Displays a list of selected Web pages
e. Displays the previously viewed page

Select the best answer from the list of choices.

11. **Software programs that are used to access and display Web pages are called:**
    a. Web sites
    b. Web wackers
    c. Web documents
    d. Web browsers

12. **If you want to save the name and URL of a file and return to it later, you can add it to a list called:**
    a. Favorites
    b. Bookmarks
    c. Home Pages
    d. Preferences

13. **An international telecommunications network that consists of hyperlinked documents is called the:**
    a. NSFNET
    b. Netscape Navigator
    c. Internet Explorer
    d. World Wide Web

14. **Where are the icons that perform many of the common functions, such as printing, in Internet Explorer located?**
    a. Address bar
    b. Toolbar
    c. Status bar
    d. Menu bar

15. **Most Web pages are longer than the document window. What feature must you use to view the entire page?**
    a. Scroll bar
    b. Status bar
    c. Forward button
    d. Home button

16. **Which of the following is a valid URL?**
    a. http://www.usf.edu/
    b. htp://www.usf.edu/
    c. http:/www.usf.edu/
    d. http//www.usf.edu/

17. **Which icon should you click if you want to stop a Web page that is currently loading on your computer?**
    a.
    b.
    c.
    d.

18. **Highlighted or underlined words that have a URL embedded in them to branch to another location are called:**
    a. Explorers
    b. Favorites
    c. Web browsers
    d. Hyperlinks

19. **The URL of the current Web page will be displayed in the:**
    a. Titlebar
    b. Document window
    c. Address bar
    d. Status bar

20. **To locate information on a specific topic on the Internet, you can use a:**
    a. URL locator
    b. Web browser
    c. Favorites list
    d. Search engine

Internet

Skills Review

1. **Start Internet Explorer and explore the browser window.**
   a. Make sure your computer is connected to the Internet.
   b. Double-click the Internet Explorer icon.
   c. Identify the toolbar, menu bar, address bar, status bar, status indicator, URL, document window, and scroll bars.
   d. In the toolbar, identify the icons for printing, searching, viewing favorites, changing the font size, and moving to the previous page.

2. **Open a URL.**
   a. Click the Address bar, then type http://www.cnet.com/ and press [Enter].
   b. Explore the site by using the scroll bars, toolbar, and hyperlinks.

3. **Save a URL.**
   a. Click the Address bar, then type http://www.loc.gov/ and press [Enter].
   b. Click the Favorites button, click Add to Favorites, then click OK.
   c. Click the Home button.
   d. Click the Favorites button.
   e. Click "Library of Congress" to return to that page.

4. **Follow links on a Web page.**
   a. Click in the Address bar, type http://www.sportsline.com/ and press [Enter].
   b. Follow the links to investigate the content.
   c. Click the Home button.

5. **Get Help.**
   a. Click the Help on the menu bar.
   b. Click Help Topics.
   c. Click Index.
   d. Type search.
   e. Double-click "Searching the Internet" in the bottom half of the Index window.

6. **Search for information on the Internet.**
   a. Click the Search button.
   b. Select a search engine.
   c. Type a key word or phrase.
   d. Click Search.

7. **Print a Web page and exit Internet Explorer.**
   a. Click in the Address bar, type http://www.whitehouse.gov/ and press [Enter].
   b. Print the page.
   c. When you are finished, click the Close button to exit Internet Explorer.

► Independent Challenges

1. You will soon graduate from college with a degree in Business Management. Prior to entering the workforce, you want to make sure that you are up to date on all of the advances in the field. You decide that checking on the Web would provide the most current information. In addition, you can look for potential companies for employment opportunities.

Use the Internet Explorer to the All Business Network at http://www.all-biz.com/. Select a promising site and click the Print icon to print the page.

2. You are leaving tomorrow for a business trip in France. You want to make sure that you take the right clothes for the weather, and decide that the best place to check might be the Web. Access one or two of the following weather sites to find out what the weather is like in Paris. Click on the Print icon to print the weather report.

the Weather Channel	http://www.weather.com/
World Weather Guide	http://www.world-travel-net.co.uk/weather/
CNN Weather	http://www.cnn.com/WEATHER/index.html

3. Your boss at the newspaper company where you work wants to buy a new desktop computer. She assigns you the task of investigating the options. You decide that it would be more expedient to look at the options on the Web than to visit the area computer. Visit the following computer company Web sites and print a page from the one or two that you think offers the best deal for your boss.

IBM	http://www.ibm.com/
Apple	http://www.apple.com/
Dell	http://www.dell.com/

4. A recent newspaper article you read mentioned a search engine (HotBot) that was unfamiliar to you. To see how it compares with some of the other search engines, create a chart showing the results of searching for the word "floptical." List the search engine and the number of hits in your chart. You should compare HotBot with the following search engines: Yahoo, Infoseek, Lycos, and Excite.

Internet

▶ Visual Workshop

A ten page paper is due for your History class. You decide to research the Holocaust as a topic for your paper. Using your favorite Web search engine, find the Web site pictured in Figure 7-17. (*Hint*: add quotations marks to your to your search string, for example: "A Teacher's Guide to the Holocaust".)

FIGURE 7-17

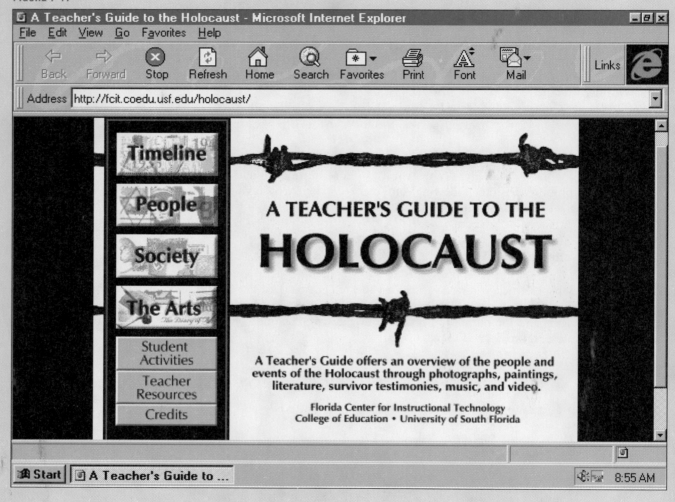

Getting
Started with Word 97

Objectives

► **Define word processing software**
► **Launch Word 97**
► **View the Word program window**
► **Enter and save text in a document**
► **Insert and delete text**
► **Select and replace text**
► **Get Help and with the Office Assistant**
► **Preview, print, close a document, and exit Word**

Welcome to Microsoft Word 97. Microsoft Word is a powerful computer program that helps you create documents that communicate your ideas clearly and effectively. More than an automated typewriter, it provides graphics, sophisticated formatting, proofing tools, and charts, to name just a few of its features. The lessons in this unit introduce you to the basic features of Word and familiarize you with the Word environment as you create a new document. ✐ Angela Pacheco is the marketing manager at Nomad Ltd, an outdoor sporting gear and adventure travel company. Angela's responsibilities include communicating with new and current customers about the company. To make her job easier, she'll be using Word to create attractive and professional-looking documents. She'll begin by exploring the Word environment while creating a letter to her shareholders.

Word 97

Defining Word Processing Software

Microsoft Word is a full-featured **word processing** program that allows you to create attractive and professional-looking documents quickly and easily. You'll find that word processing offers many advantages over typing. Because the information you enter in a word processing document is stored electronically by your computer, it is easy to revise and reuse text in documents that you (or others) have already created. In addition, you can enhance your documents by giving text a special appearance, adding lines, shading, and creating tables. Figure A-1 illustrates the kinds of features you can use in your documents. ◄■■■■ Angela is eager to learn about some of the benefits she can expect by using Word. Table A-1 describes additional features she will use as she learns about working in Word.

Details

Locate and correct spelling mistakes and grammatical errors
As you use Word to create documents use Word's proofreading tools to identify errors and correct them. The AutoCorrect feature even corrects many typing mistakes as you make them.

Copy and move text without retyping
You can save time by copying text from other documents and using it again in the current document. Within the same document, you can easily reorganize and edit text.

Enhance the appearance of documents by adding formatting
By applying different types of formatting (including shading and borders) to important parts of documents, you can create documents that convey your message effectively to your readers. Word features, such as the Formatting toolbar, styles, and AutoFormat, help you do this quickly.

Align text in rows and columns using tables
Although you can use another program such as Microsoft Excel, for complex financial analysis, you can also use tables in Word to present small amounts of financial information in an easy-to-read format. You can also format the tables to emphasize important points.

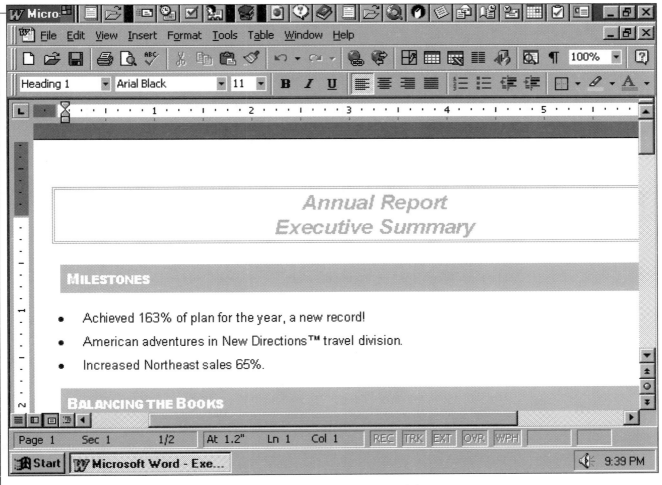

If you had a previous installation of Office on your computer, your screen may contain the Office 97 shortcut bar. Click the Close button on the shortcut bar.

TABLE A-1: Additional Word Features

feature	description	example
AutoSummarize	Allows you to see important ideas in a document	When you use the AutoSummarize command, Word highlights important words, phrases, sentences in the document. This feature helps you learn about the main ideas without requiring you to read the entire document.
Templates and Wizards	Provides the ability to create standard business documents using professionally designed formats	Word provides a number of preformatted business documents that help you quickly create the documents you need, including memos, letters, and faxes. You can even create your own templates for customized company documents.
AutoComplete	After you type a few characters of a word you use often, Word suggests the word it expects you to insert	This feature can save you a lot of time. As you work in Word, it keeps track of words and phrases you use often. Then when you type just a few characters, Word displays a word it expects you to type. When you press [Enter] Word inserts the remaining text.
AutoText	Allows you to store and insert frequently used words and phrases for fast document creation	By storing frequently used words and phrases as AutoText entries, such as a standard closing to letters, you can work faster and with fewer errors.
Document Map	Combines Outline view with Normal view	In a large document, use the Document Map to view the overall structure of the document and quickly locate headings and text you want to edit.

Launching Word 97

To launch Word 97, you must first launch Windows by turning on your computer. You get to the Word program by clicking Start and then choosing Word from the Programs menu. The Programs menu displays the list of programs installed on your computer, including Microsoft Word. You can launch all programs this way. You can also create a shortcut on your desktop that launches Word without opening the Start and Programs menus. A **shortcut** is a faster way to open a program or a document. Because each computer system can have a different setup (depending on the hardware and software installed on it), your procedure for launching Word might be different from the one described below, especially if your computer is part of a network. See your instructor or technical support person for additional instructions.   The marketing department at Nomad has installed Word 97 on all their computers, including Angela's. Angela's first step in learning to use Word 97 is to launch the program.

1. **Make sure the Windows desktop is open, then click the Start button**  **on the taskbar**
   The Start menu appears on the desktop.

2. **On the Start menu, point to Programs**
   Each menu remains open as you point, as shown in Figure A-2. Depending on the programs installed on your computer, the programs you see on the Programs menu might be different from the ones shown in the figure.

3. **On the Programs menu, click Microsoft Word**
   The Word program window appears, as shown in Figure A-3. The blinking vertical line, called the **insertion point**, | in the program window, indicates where text will appear when you begin typing. When you first launch Word, by default you can begin entering text and creating a new document right away. In the next lessons, you will continue to explore basic Word features.

Trouble?

If you have installed Microsoft Office on your computer, you might need to click Microsoft Office on the Programs menu, before you click Microsoft Word.

CLUES TO USE

Creating Shortcuts

You can create a shortcut on the desktop to launch Word without going through all the menus. You just double-click a shortcut, and the program starts. To create a shortcut on the desktop, use either My Computer or Windows Explorer to locate the Program Files folder. In this folder, open the Winword folder, and locate the application file called Winword. Drag this file out of the window and onto the desktop. To eliminate the shortcut, just drag the shortcut to the Recycle Bin and confirm that you want to remove the shortcut from the desktop. Note: If you are working on a network or you share your computer with others, get permission from your instructor or technical support person before creating shortcuts on the desktop.

FIGURE A-2: Menus on the Windows desktop

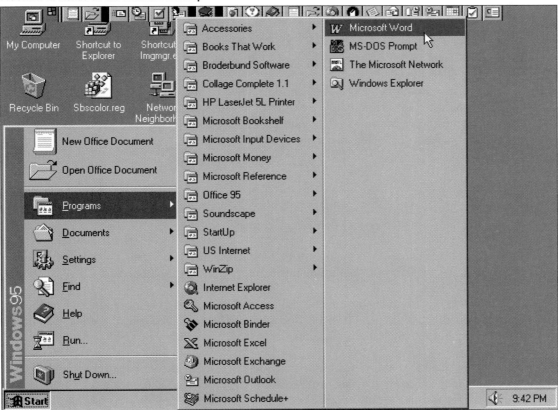

FIGURE A-3: Word program window

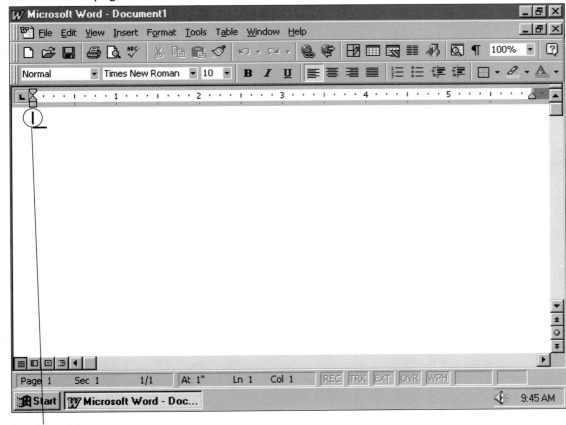

Insertion point

Viewing the Word Program Window

Word 97

Now that you are in the Word **program window**, you can see some of the key features of Word. Word provides different views that allow you to see your document in different ways. In default view (called normal view), you see the features described below. On your computer, locate each of the elements described below using Figure A-4 for reference.

Details

Trouble?

If your document window is not maximized, click the document window Maximize button ⬜. If the Page Layout View button 🔳 in the horizontal scroll bar appears indented, indicating it is selected, the document window is in page layout view. To work in normal view, click the Normal View button ▤ in the horizontal scroll bar.

 The title bar displays the name of the program and the document. Until you save the document and give it a name, the temporary name is Document1.

 The menu bar lists the names of the menus that contain Word commands. Clicking a menu name on the menu bar displays a list of commands from which you can choose.

 The Standard toolbar contains buttons for the most frequently used commands, such as the commands for opening, saving, and printing documents. This toolbar is one of the two default toolbars. Clicking buttons on a toolbar is often faster than using the menu bar.

 The Formatting toolbar contains buttons for the most frequently used formatting commands, such as applying bold to text or aligning text. This toolbar is the other default toolbar. Other toolbars related to other features are also available.

 The horizontal ruler displays tab settings, left and right paragraph margins, and document margins.

 The document window displays the work area for typing text and working with your document. The blinking insertion point is the location where your text appears when you type. When the mouse pointer is in the text area of the document window, the pointer changes to an **I-beam**, Ⅰ. You can have as many document windows open as your computer's memory will hold. You can minimize, maximize, and resize each window. When only one document is open, maximize the document window so that you see more of the document.

 The vertical and horizontal scroll bars display the relative position of the currently displayed text in the document. You use the scroll bars and **scroll boxes** to view different parts of your document.

 The view buttons, which appear in the horizontal scroll bar, allow you to display the document in one of four views: normal, online layout, page layout, and outline. Each view offers features that are useful in the different phases of working with a document.

 The status bar displays the current page and section numbers, the total number of pages, and the position of the insertion point (in inches and in lines from the upper-left corner of the document).

When you position the pointer over a button, a ScreenTip appears showing the name of the button. You can customize the ScreenTips to display keyboard shortcuts. You also have the option to hide the ScreenTips.

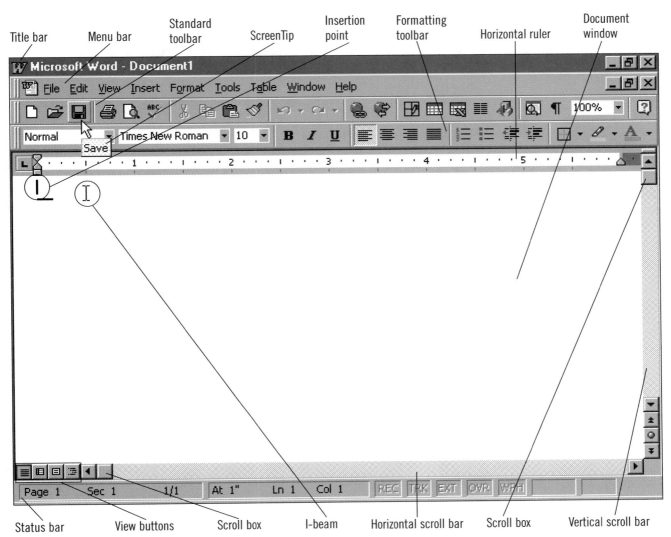

Title bar | Menu bar | Standard toolbar | ScreenTip | Insertion point | Formatting toolbar | Horizontal ruler | Document window

Status bar | View buttons | Scroll box | I-beam | Horizontal scroll bar | Scroll box | Vertical scroll bar

Customizing ScreenTips

To display or hide ScreenTips, click Toolbars on the View menu, click Customize, click the Options tab, then select or clear the Show ScreenTips on toolbars check box. You can also hide or display keyboard shortcuts as part of the ScreenTip by deselecting the Show shortcut keys in ScreenTips check box.

Word 97

Entering and Saving Text in a Document

When you launch Word, the program opens a document window in which you can create a new document. You can begin by simply typing text at the insertion point. When you reach the end of a line as you type, Word automatically moves the insertion point to the next line. This feature is called **word-wrap**. To insert a new line or start a new paragraph simply press [Enter]. It is also a good idea to save your work shortly after writing your first paragraph and every 10 or 15 minutes and before printing. You can save a document using the Save button on the Standard toolbar, or the Save or Save As commands on the File menu. ◆ Angela begins by typing the first two paragraphs in the body of her letter to Nomad Ltd's shareholders.

Steps 1 2 3 4

1. At the insertion point, type the following paragraph:
The year has been an exciting and profitable year, at Nomad Ltd. As a shareholder, you will be interested to learn about our recent successes and the challenges we expect in the coming year and beyond. This letter includes the high points of the year and provides valuable details about our work in individual areas of the organization, including finance, communications, quality assurance, and travel. In the next few days you will receive a complete Annual Report for the entire organization and detailed profiles for each division.
Do not press [Enter] when you reach the end of a line. Just keep typing.

2. Insert your Student Disk in drive A, then click the **Save button** 🖫 on the Standard toolbar
The Save As dialog box opens, as shown in Figure A-5. In this dialog box, you need to assign a name to the document you are creating, replacing the default filename supplied by Word.

3. In the File name text box, type **First Draft Letter**
Next, you need to instruct Word to save the file to your Student Disk. The name of the currently active drive or folder appears in the Save in list box.

4. Click the **Save in list arrow**, then click **3½ Floppy (A:)**, and then click **Save.**
These lessons assume your Student Disk is in drive A. If you are using a different drive or storing your practice files on a network, click the appropriate drive.

5. Press **[Enter]** twice
The first time you press [Enter], the insertion point moves to the start of the next line. The next time you press [Enter], you create a blank line before the text you type next.

6. Type the following paragraph:
We are proud of our employees and encourage you to join us at the Annual Meeting to be held at the Ocean View Suites next month. Enclosed please find an Annual Meeting reply card, which you can return to let us know if you plan to attend.

7. At the end of the second paragraph, press **[Enter]** once
Don't be concerned about making typing mistakes. Also, don't be concerned if your text wraps differently from the text shown in the figure. How text wraps depends on your monitor or printer. Next display the number of spaces between words and paragraphs, by displaying non-printing characters.

8. Click the Show/Hide button ¶ on the Standard toolbar
The spaces between words appear as dots. New lines are represented by ¶ at the end of a paragraph. Compare your screen to Figure A-6 then click Save.

9. Click 🖫
The document is saved with the name First Draft Letter on your Student Disk.

FIGURE A-5: Save As dialog box

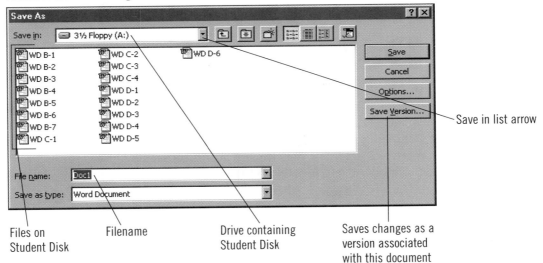

Files on Student Disk

Filename

Drive containing Student Disk

Saves changes as a version associated with this document

Save in list arrow

FIGURE A-6: Text in a Word document

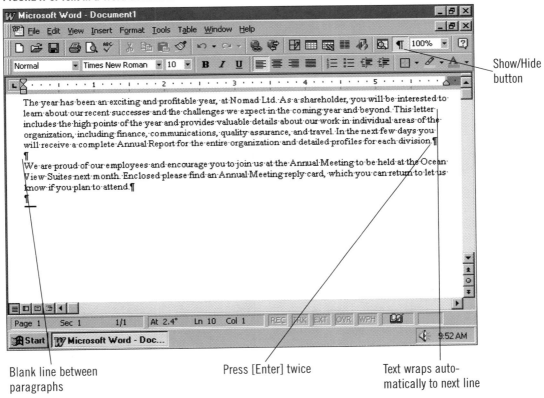

Show/Hide button

Blank line between paragraphs

Press [Enter] twice

Text wraps automatically to next line

CLUES TO USE

Working with Automatic Corrections

If you make certain kinds of spelling or typographical errors, you might notice that Word automatically makes the necessary corrections as you type. This feature is called AutoCorrect. For example, some common spelling mistakes (such as typing 'adn' instead of 'and') are corrected as soon as you type the first space after the word. Similarly, if you type two capitalized letters in a row, Word automatically changes the sec-

ond character to lower case as you continue typing (except in a state's abbreviation, such as 'WA'). If you misspell a word that is not corrected right away, Word underlines the word with a red, wavy underline. If you make a potential grammatical error, Word underlines the error with a green, wavy underline. After you finish typing, click the right mouse button on the word to display a pop-up menu of correction options.

Inserting and Deleting Text

After typing text, you often need to edit it by inserting new text or deleting text you want to remove. To insert text, place the insertion point where you want the new text to appear, then start typing. You can delete text to the left or the right of the insertion point. Word also offers commonly used AutoText entries that can be inserted in your documents for more information. Whenever you insert or delete text, Word adjusts the spacing of the existing text. First, Angela adds the inside address to her letter, then she'll make a few corrections by removing individual characters.

1. Press **[Ctrl][Home]** to place the insertion point at the beginning of the document and type the following address, pressing **[Enter]** after each line:
   Ms. Malena Jeskey [Enter]
   456 Greenview Lane [Enter]
   Shoreview, CA 90272 [Enter]
   Notice that a wavy, red underline appears under the word "Malena" and other proper names. This means that these words are not in Word's dictionary.

2. Press **[Enter]** again to insert a blank line and type **Dear Shareholder:** and press **[Enter]** twice

3. If the Office Assistant appears asking if you want to create a letter using a wizard, click **Cancel** in the Office Assistant balloon-shaped dialog box
   If you create a letter using the Letter Wizard, you simply respond to a series of dialog boxes. So that you can learn a lot more about using Word, for now type this letter without the aid of the wizard. Next, you want to change the word "The" in the first sentence to "This."

4. Place the insertion point after the word **The** (but before the space) in the first sentence, press **[Backspace]**, then type **is**
   This removes the "e" and inserts "i" and "s." Next, you will delete an unnecessary comma.

5. Place the insertion point after the second occurrence of the word **year** (but before the comma) in the first sentence, then press **[Delete]**
   This removes the comma. Next, you will add today's date to the beginning of the letter. First, move to the beginning of the document.

6. Press **[Ctrl][Home]**
   With the insertion point at the beginning of the document, you can insert the date.

7. Click **Insert** on the menu bar, then click **Date and Time**
   The Date and Time dialog box opens. Word displays the date based on your computer's system clock. Before you proceed, verify that the Update Automatically check box is cleared, so that the date is not updated each time you save or print the document. For formatting dates in letters and other business correspondence, choose the third option in the list.

8. In the dialog box, click the third option in the list, then click **OK**
   Today's date automatically appears in the document.

9. Press **[Enter]** twice
   Compare your document to Figure A-7. The date you see might be different.

FIGURE A-7: Letter after inserting and deleting text

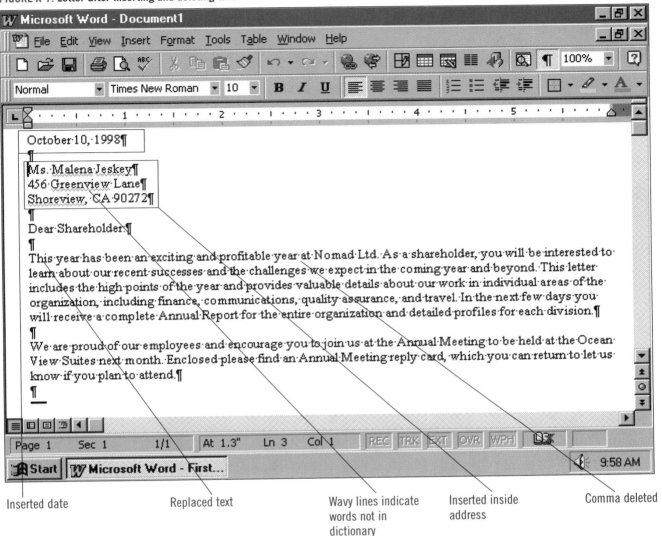

Inserted date

Replaced text

Wavy lines indicate words not in dictionary

Inserted inside address

Comma deleted

CLUES TO USE

Inserting built-in AutoText entries

AutoText entries are words or phrases that are frequently used, such as company names or greetings and closings in letters. Word includes various built-in AutoText entries which are arranged by subject, such as closings and salutations. To insert a built-in AutoText entry, point to AutoText on the Insert menu, click the desired subject, then click the desired AutoText entry as shown in Figure A-8. The AutoText entry is inserted at the place of the insertion point.

FIGURE A-8: Built-in AutoText entries on the Insert menu

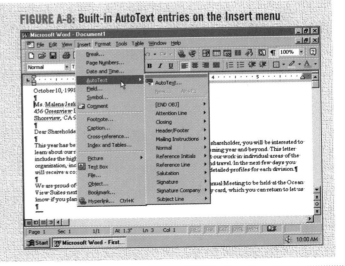

Word 97

Selecting and Replacing Text

In addition to editing characters one at a time, you can also edit multiple characters, words, paragraphs, or the entire document. Most Word editing techniques require that you first select the text you want to edit. For example, to delete existing text and replace it with new text, you first select the text you want to remove, then type the new text. This feature is called **Typing Replaces Selection**. Table A-2 describes the different ways to select text with a mouse. You can also change your mind about the revisions you make with the Undo and Redo features. ✍️ Next, Angela uses various techniques to select and replace text.

Trouble?

If text you type does not replace selected text, click Tools, click Options, click the Edit tab, then click to select the Typing Replaces Selection check box. Click OK to return to the document.

1. Place the insertion point in front of the second occurrence of the word **year** in the first sentence and drag across the word

The highlighting indicates that the word is selected. You want to replace the selection so that the word "year" is not used twice in the same sentence.

2. Type **one**

The word "one" replaces the selected word. Now you will replace several words with one word.

3. Place the insertion point in front of the word **please** in the last sentence and drag across it and the next word, **find**, then release the mouse button and type **is**

Both words and the spaces that follow the words are selected. If you drag across too many words, drag back over the text to deselect it. The word "is" replaces the selected text. Word inserts the correct spacing and reformats the text after the insertion point. You will replace the word "includes" in the third sentence.

4. Double-click the word **includes** in the third sentence, then type **summarizes**

The word "summarizes" replaces the selected text, along with the correct spacing. If you change your mind about a change, you can reverse it. You will reinsert the word "includes."

5. Click the **Undo Typing button** ⟲ on the Standard toolbar

The word "includes" replaces the word "summarizes." Clicking the Undo Typing button reverses the most recent action. The arrow next to the Undo Typing button displays a list of all the changes you've made since opening the document, so you can undo one or more changes. You can also reverse a change you have undone.

6. Click the **Redo Typing button** ⟳ on the Standard toolbar

The word "summarizes" reappears. As with the Undo Typing feature, the arrow next to the Redo Typing button displays a list of changes you can redo.

7. Position the pointer to the far left of the first line of the body of the letter until the pointer changes to ⟋, then click the mouse button

Clicking next to the line in the selection bar selects the text. The **selection bar** is the area to the left of the text in your document, as shown in Figure A-9.

8. Click anywhere in the document to deselect the text

The first line is no longer selected. Whenever you want to deselect text, simply click in the document window. Compare your screen to Figure A-10.

9. Click the **Save button** 💾 on the Standard toolbar.

Your document is now saved.

c

FIGURE A-9: Selected text and selection bar

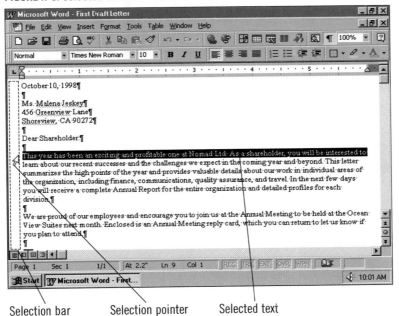

Selection bar   Selection pointer   Selected text

FIGURE A-10: Completed document

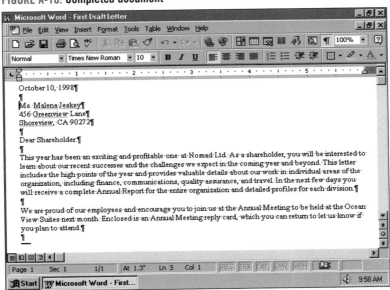

TABLE A-2: Mouse selection techniques

to select text with the mouse	do this
A word	Double-click the word
A sentence	Press and hold [Ctrl] and click in the sentence
A paragraph	Triple-click in the paragraph, or double-click in the selection bar next to the paragraph
A line of text	Click in the selection bar next to the line
An entire document	Press and hold [Ctrl] and click anywhere in the selection bar, or triple-click in the selection bar
A vertical block of text	Press and hold [Alt] and drag through the text
A large amount of text	Place the insertion point at the beginning of the text, move to the end of the desired selection, then press and hold [Shift] and click

Getting Help with the Office Assistant

The Word program includes an online Help system that provides information and instructions on Word features and commands while you are using Word. You can get as little or as much information as you want, from quick definitions to detailed procedures. The **Office Assistant** is just one way to find help while working in Word. Using this animated assistant is an easy way to display Help windows and discover new features. Other Help commands are on the Help menu. ▶ In the next lesson, Angela will save, print, and close the document. Before she does this, she will use the Office Assistant to learn more about saving a document.

Steps 1 2 3 4

1. **Click the Office Assistant button 🔲 on the Standard toolbar**
   The Office Assistant appears, as shown in Figure A-11. Your animated assistant may look different depending on which assistant is selected on your computer. If this is the first time the Office Assistant has been used on your computer, you will see the message "preparing Help file for first use."

2. **Type saving documents under Type your question here, and then click Search**
   In this area you can type key words or whole questions for which you would like more information.

3. **Click Search**
   The Office Assistant offers various topics related to saving documents from which you can choose.

4. **Click the Save a document option button**
   A Help window opens detailing various save features.

5. **Scroll through the Help window and read about saving documents**
   At the bottom of the Help window you will find a list of related topics from which you can choose. These topics will give detailed instructions on performing certain operations.

6. **Position the pointer over the topic Save a new, unnamed document, until the pointer changes to 👆 and click**
   A new Help window opens displaying the steps necessary for saving a document. When the pointer changes to 👆 once you've placed the pointer over a word or button, you can click to display more information.

7. **Click the Save button 🔲 in the Help window**
   A message appears describing the function of this button.

8. **Click outside of the Help window in the letter document**
   The Save button message is hidden, but the Help window is still visible. The letter document is active again. A window is active when the title bar is highlighted. An inactive window will have a dimmed title bar. Compare your screen to Figure A-12.

9. **Click the Close button ✖ in the Help window, and then click the Close button in the Office Assistant window**

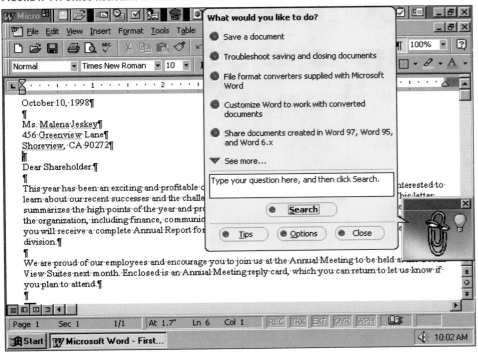

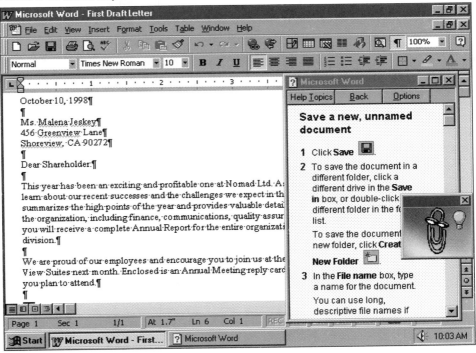

More about using Help

You can also use commands on the Help menu when searching for Help information. Click Help on the menu bar, then click Contents and Index. The Help Topics dialog box will open. You can use the Contents tab to choose from various Help topics or you can use the Find and Index tabs to search for key words that

you provide. You can also use the What's This pointer ☞ to find information. Click What's This on the Help menu, then click the What's This pointer over buttons, formatting, and features. To turn off the pointer, click What's This on the Help menu again.

Previewing, Printing, Closing a Document, and Exiting Word

Once you have saved your document, you can print one copy of the document using the Print button on the Standard toolbar. After you have finished working in a document and it has been saved and printed, you can close the document and exit Word. Angela has finished working with her letter for now. She would like to save, print, and close the document before exiting Word. Angela will use the directions in the Help window to save her document.

Steps 1 2 3 4

1. **Click the Print Preview button on the Standard toolbar**
   The document appears in the Preview window, as shown in Figure A-13. The size of the page you see depends on the number and size of pages displayed the last time the Print Preview command was issued.

2. **Click the Close button on the Print Preview toolbar to return to your document**

3. **Click the Save button on the Standard toolbar to save your document**

4. **Click the Print button on the Standard toolbar**
   The Print button prints the current document to the default printer connected to your computer. If you are not connected to a printer, ask your technical support person or instructor for assistance. You are now ready to close your document.

5. **Click File on the menu bar, then click Close**
   When you close a document that has changes you have not saved, Word asks if you want to save your changes. If you get a message asking if you want to save changes, click Yes. The documents closes.

6. **Click File on the menu bar, then click Exit**
   The Exit command closes the Word program and returns you to the Windows desktop.

QuickTip

Clicking the Close button on the right end of the menu bar closes the document. Clicking the Close button on the right end of the title bar exits the program.

FIGURE A-13: **Document in Print Preview**

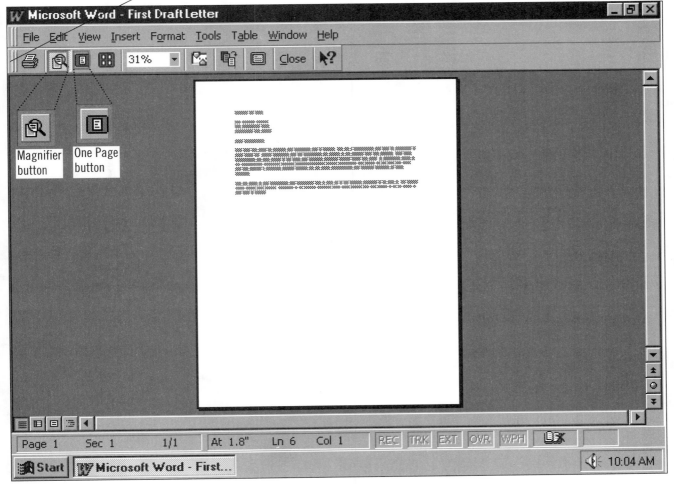

Print Preview
toolbar

Magnifier
button

One Page
button

Practice

► Concepts Review

Label each option in the Save As dialog box shown in Figure A-14.

FIGURE A-14

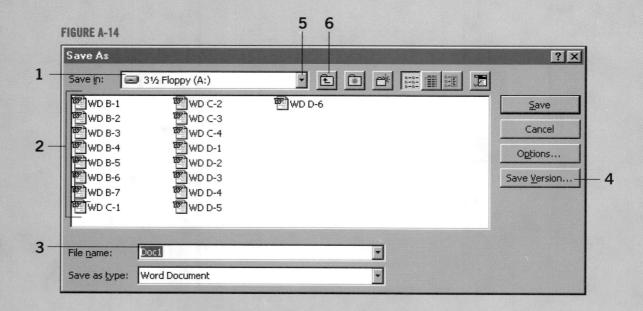

Match each of the following terms with the statement that best describes its function.

7. **Standard toolbar**
8. **Formatting toolbar**
9. **Document window**
10. **Ruler**
11. **Status bar**
12. **Deleting**
13. **Inserting**
14. **AutoText**

a. Displays area in which you enter text
b. Identifies location of insertion point and command status
c. Contains buttons for easy access to general commands such as Open and Print
d. Removing the text to the right or left of the insertion point
e. Displays tab settings, paragraph and document margins
f. Typing text between existing text
g. Contains buttons for easy access to commands that affect the appearance of text in a document
h. Standard text and expressions you can insert instead of typing

Select the best answer from the list of choices.

15. Word processing is most similar to:
- **a.** Performing financial analysis
- **b.** Filling in forms
- **c.** Typing
- **d.** Forecasting mortgage payments

16. To display another part of a document, you:
- **a.** Click in the Moving toolbar
- **b.** Scroll with a scroll bar
- **c.** Drag the ruler
- **d.** Select the Close box

17. You can get Help in any of the following ways, except:
- **a.** Clicking the Help box in a dialog box
- **b.** Double-clicking anywhere in the document window
- **c.** Clicking the Help button on the Standard toolbar
- **d.** Clicking Help on the menu bar

18. What keys do you press to move the insertion point to the first character in a document?
- **a.** [Ctrl][Home]
- **b.** [Home]
- **c.** [Alt][PgUp]
- **d.** [Shift][Tab]

19. The Close command on the File menu:
- **a.** Closes Word without saving any changes
- **b.** Closes the current document and, if you have made any changes, asks if you want to save them
- **c.** Closes all currently open Word documents
- **d.** Closes the current document without saving changes

20. To leave the Word program window, you must:
- **a.** Close all open documents or lose your work when you close Word
- **b.** Click the Exit button on the Standard toolbar
- **c.** Click the Close command on the File menu, which closes documents and closes Word
- **d.** Click the Exit command on the File menu, which closes documents and closes Word

21. Which of the following methods is not a way to select text?
- **a.** Clicking in the selection bar
- **b.** Dragging across the text
- **c.** Double-clicking a word with the left mouse button
- **d.** Dragging text to the selection bar

22. Which key do you press to remove text to the left of the insertion point?
- **a.** [Backspace]
- **b.** [Delete]
- **c.** [Cut]
- **d.** [Overtype]

► Skills Review

1. Launch Word, then identify the parts of the window.
- **a.** Click the Start button on the Windows desktop taskbar.
- **b.** Point to Programs.
- **c.** Click Microsoft Word.
- **d.** Identify as many elements of the Word window as you can without referring to the unit material.

2. Explore the Word program window.

　　a. Click each of the menus and drag the mouse button through all the commands on each menu. To close a menu without making a selection, drag the mouse away from the menu, then release the mouse button.

　　b. Point to each of the buttons on the toolbars, and read the ScreenTips and descriptions.

　　c. Click Tools, then click Options. In the Options dialog box, click the Edit tab and make sure that the first three options are selected. Click any of these three check boxes that are not selected.

　　d. Click OK to close the dialog box.

3. Enter and save text in a new document.

　　a. At the insertion point, type a short letter to a local business describing your interest in learning more about the company.

　　b. Don't type the inside address or a closing yet. For a greeting, type "To Whom It May Concern:". (If the Office Assistant appears offering Help in writing your letter, click Cancel.)

　　c. Be sure to state that you are looking for a position in the company.

　　d. Mention that you have been encouraged to investigate opportunities at the company by counselors, instructors, and alumni.

　　e. Request a copy of the company's annual report to understand the scope of the company's business. For a closing, type "Sincerly," then press [Enter] twice. Notice that Word corrects your typing for you.

　　f. Save the document on your Student Disk as Information Letter.

4. Insert and delete text.

　　a. Place the insertion point at the beginning of the document.

　　b. Insert today's date and press [Enter] twice.

　　c. Type the name of the company contact and press [Enter]. Use whatever contact name you want.

　　d. Type the company name and press [Enter]. Use whatever company name you want.

　　e. Type the company address and press [Enter].

　　f. Type the city, state, and postal code, then press [Enter].

　　g. Press [Enter] twice, then type your name and press [Enter].

　　h. Type your street address and press [Enter].

　　i. Type your city, state, and postal code and press [Enter] again.

　　j. Type your phone number.

　　k. Use [Backspace] to delete your phone number. Press [Enter] once more.

5. Select and replace text.

　　a. Select the text "To Whom It May Concern:", then type "Dear" followed by the name of the recipient of the letter; for example, Mr. Martin.

　　b. Select the last word of the document, then press [Delete] to delete the entire word.

　　c. Click the Undo button to restore the original text.

　　d. Use selecting and replacing techniques to correct any mistakes in your letter.

6. Explore Word Help.

a. Click the Office Assistant button on the Standard toolbar.

b. Type "Print" under What would you like to do?.

c. Click Search.

d. Click the option button next to Print a document.

e. Click Print a range of pages.

f. Click Options, Print Topic.

g. Click the What's This? button, then click Properties.

h. Click Cancel.

i. Click the Close button in the Help window.

j. Click the Close button in the Office Assistant window to close this Help option.

7. Print and close the document and exit Word.

a. Save the document, and then click the Print button on the Standard toolbar.

b. Click File on the menu bar, then click Close.

c. Click No if you see a message asking if you want to save your changes.

d. Click File on the menu bar, then click Exit.

► Independent Challenges

1. Using the Contents and Index command on the Help menu, learn more about Keyboard shortcuts. Use the Show Me button in the Help windows to see an animated demonstration of the features. Print the Help windows as you go using the Print Topic command on the Options menu. Figure A-15 displays an example of one of the windows that you can print.

FIGURE A-15

Keys for working with documents	
To	**Press**
Create a new document	CTRL+N
Open a document	CTRL+O
Close a document	CTRL+W
Split a document	ALT+CTRL+S
Save a document	CTRL+S
Quit Word	ALT+F4
To	**Press**
Find text, formatting, and special items	CTRL+F
Repeat find	ALT+CTRL+Y
Replace text, specific formatting, and special items	CTRL+H
Go to a page, bookmark, footnote, table, comment, graphic, or other location	CTRL+G
Go back to a page, bookmark, footnote, table, comment, graphic, or other location	ALT+CTRL+Z
Browse a document	ALT+CTRL+HOME
To	**Press**
Cancel an action	ESC
Undo an action	CTRL+Z
Redo or repeat an action	CTRL+Y
To	**Press**
Switch to page layout view	ALT+CTRL+P
Switch to outline view	ALT+CTRL+O
Switch to normal view	ALT+CTRL+N
Move between a master document and its subdocuments	CTRL+\

2. As a co-chair for the Lake City High School 1993 class reunion planning committee, you are responsible for recruiting classmates to help with reunion activities. Using Figure A-16 as a guide, draft a letter to the 1993 graduates asking for volunteers to aid the four reunion committees: entertainment, hospitality, meals, and transportation. For the inside address, use any name and address you wish. Save this document as "1993 Letter". Be sure to insert today's date and salutation. (If the Office Assistant appears offering Help in writing your letter, click Cancel.)

FIGURE A-16

June 25, 1998

Ms. Sandy Carter
8899 Lakeshore Boulevard
Minneapolis, MN 56789

Dear Sandy:

As a member of the Lake City High School class of 1993, I often think of the people who made our school such a rewarding experience for me. Of course, there are the close friends I made and kept throughout the years, but also I think about the people I somehow lost track of since graduation. The instructors, students, and administrative staff all contribute to the richness of the memories.

Now is your opportunity to play an important role in helping bring Lake City High School memories alive not only for yourself, but for your fellow classmates as well. As the co-chair of the 1998 Reunion planning committee, I am looking for ambitious, organized alumni who are interested in working on various reunion activities.

We need people for the following areas: meeting coordination for all committees, computer consulting to help us use technology to work efficiently, meals and entertainment planning for the three-day event, and logistics coordination for getting everyone to Lake City and lodging them once they return to campus. All committees need as many volunteers as possible, so you are sure to be able to work in any area you choose.

If you are interested and available to work five hours a month for the next 10 months, please let me know. You can leave me a message at (555)555-4321. I look forward to hearing from you soon.

[your name]
Lake City High School Reunion 1993
Co-Chair

3. As a recent graduate, you are scouring the planet for job opportunities. Log on to the Internet and use your browser to go to http://www.course.com. From there, click Student On Line Companions, and then click the Microsoft Office 97 Professional Edition—Illustrated: A First Course page, then click on the Word link for Unit A. Click on the link that takes you to a list of employment opportunities. After downloading a file of interesting positions, create a cover letter that describes your qualifications or the qualifications such a position would require. Use Figure A-17 as a guide for the content of this letter. Save the document as "Job Letter". Be sure to insert today's date and an inside address and salutation. (If the Office Assistant appears offering Help in writing your letter, click Cancel.)

FIGURE A-17

June 7, 1998

Ms. Kelly Grand
Hewlett Packard
HP Circle W406
Cupertino, CA 98007

Dear Ms. Grand:

I am interested in working as a Senior Programmer for your organization. I am an expert programmer with over 10 years of experience to offer you. I enclose my resume as a first step in exploring the poossibilities of employment with Hewlett Packard.

My most recent experience was designing an automated billing system for a trade magazine publisher. I was responsible for the overall product design, including the user interface. In addition, I developed the first draft of the operator's guide.

As a Senior Programmer with your organization, I would bring a focus on quality and ease of use to your system development. Furthermore, I work well with others, and I am experienced in project management.

I would appreciate your keeping this inquiry confidential. I will call you in a few days to arrange an interview at a convenient time for you. Thank you for your consideration.

Sincerely,

[your name]

4. As a co-chair for the Lake City High School class of 1993 planning committee, you have received a telephone message from a classmate volunteering to serve on the entertainment committee. Use the Letter Wizard, which appears after you type a salutation and press [Enter], to create a thank you letter to this volunteer that provides details about the entertainment committee members, meeting place, and schedule. Enter your letter preferences in each of the Letter Wizard dialog boxes. For the inside address, use any name and address you wish. Save the document with the name "Thank You Letter". Be sure to insert today's date and an inside address and salutation. Compare your letter to the one shown in Figure A-18.

FIGURE A-18

September 15, 1996

Mr. Oliver Randall
Vice President/Marketing
InterSysData Corp.
4440 Pacific Boulevard
San Francisco, CA 94104

Dear Mr. Randall:

Thank you for volunteering to participate on the entertainment committee for the Lake City High School 1990 class reunion. We are looking forward to working with you on these events.

So that you can arrange your time accordingly, please block out the first Thursday of each month for the next six months for planning meetings. All meetings will take place at 7:30 p.m. at the Comfort Corner Coffee Shop in Middleburg (on Highway 95, next to the Burger Palace drive-in). Our first meeting will be next month; please come prepared to discuss your ideas for entertainment events at the reunion.

Please let me know by noon on the meeting date if you are unable to attend any of these meetings.

[your name]
Lake City High School Reunion 1990
Co-Chair

Visual Workshop

You are currently planning an International Communications conference and have been contacting independent consultants to deliver short presentations. Type a thank you letter to a consultant who has agreed to demonstrate new online features to conference attendees. Be sure to misspell some words so you can observe the automatic corrections provided by Word. You can view AutoCorrect entries with the AutoCorrect command on the Tools menu. Try to use as many inserting, selecting, and replacing techniques as possible. Save the document as "International Voices". Compare your document to Figure A-19. You can either use the Letter Wizard or create your own letter from scratch.

FIGURE A-19

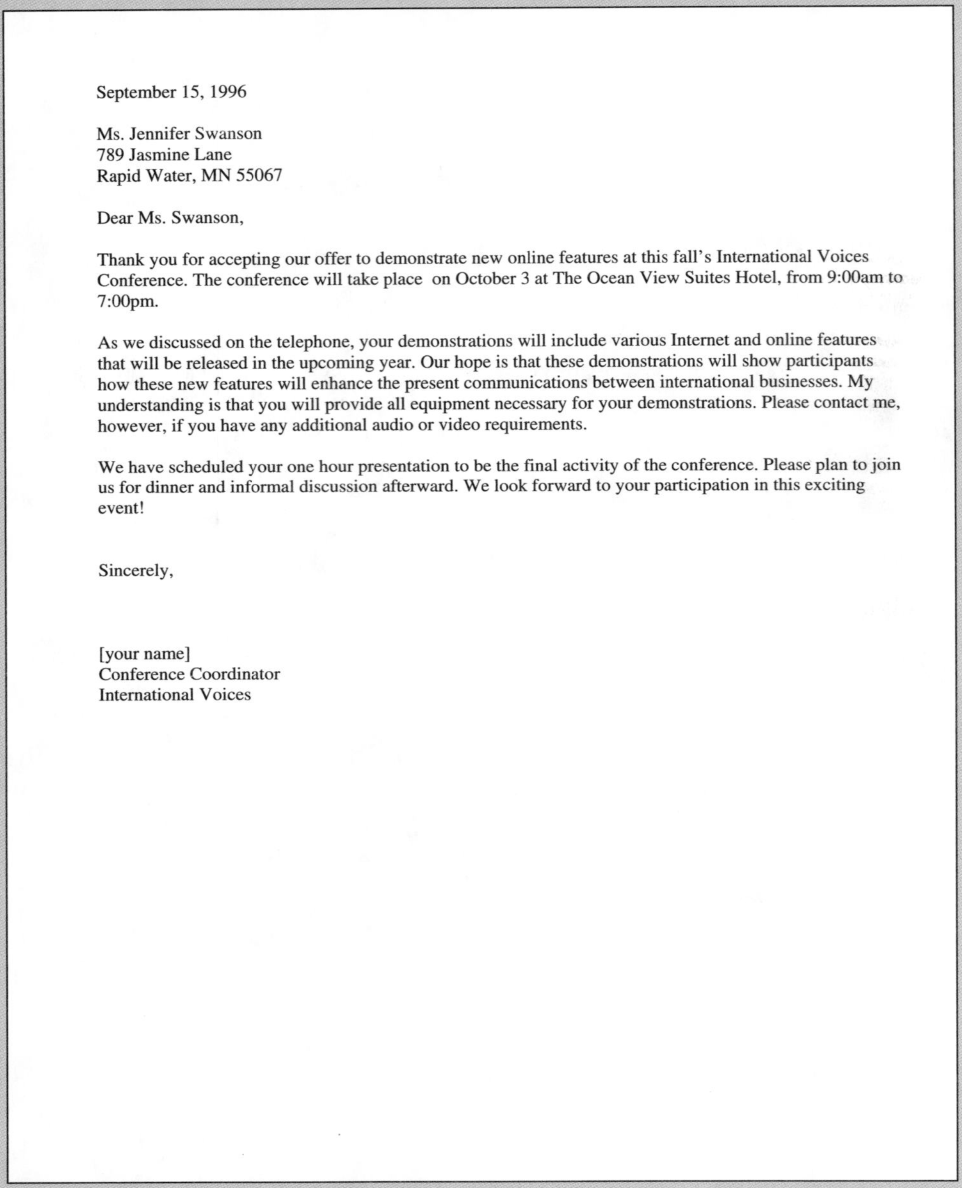

September 15, 1996

Ms. Jennifer Swanson
789 Jasmine Lane
Rapid Water, MN 55067

Dear Ms. Swanson,

Thank you for accepting our offer to demonstrate new online features at this fall's International Voices Conference. The conference will take place on October 3 at The Ocean View Suites Hotel, from 9:00am to 7:00pm.

As we discussed on the telephone, your demonstrations will include various Internet and online features that will be released in the upcoming year. Our hope is that these demonstrations will show participants how these new features will enhance the present communications between international businesses. My understanding is that you will provide all equipment necessary for your demonstrations. Please contact me, however, if you have any additional audio or video requirements.

We have scheduled your one hour presentation to be the final activity of the conference. Please plan to join us for dinner and informal discussion afterward. We look forward to your participation in this exciting event!

Sincerely,

[your name]
Conference Coordinator
International Voices

Editing
and Proofing Documents

Objectives

► **Plan a document**
► **Open a document and save it with a new name**
► **Copy text**
► **Move text**
► **Correct spelling and grammatical errors**
► **Find and replace text**
► **Preview a document**
► **Print a document**

In this unit, you will save a document with a new name so that the original document is unchanged. Using a variety of copying and moving techniques, you will learn how to make fast work of reusing and rearranging text in a document. You will also use Word's proofing tools to find and correct misspelled words and grammatical errors. In addition, Word's find and replace capabilities enable you to locate specific occurrences of text and replace each instance consistently throughout a document. After proofreading a document, you can preview it, make any necessary adjustments, then print it. At Nomad Ltd, Angela drafted a letter to Nomad shareholders that will serve as a cover letter to the annual report. Angela would like to copy text from another document to add to the letter and proof this letter before printing it.

Planning a Document

Although Word makes it easy to modify documents after you have created them, it is always a good idea to plan the document. Planning involves identifying the audience and purpose, developing the content and organization, and then matching the tone to all these elements. After identifying the audience and the purpose of the document, which form the foundation of the plan, determine what you want to say. Once you have listed the main ideas of the document, it's important to organize these ideas into a logical sequence. When you begin writing, use a tone that matches the audience, purpose, content and organization. For example, the tone in an announcement to a company picnic will be different from a business letter requesting payment for an overdue invoice. Finally, make the document visually appealing, by using formatting that emphasizes the ideas presented. If you are working on a document for someone else, it is a good idea to verify your plan with your supervisor before you continue. ◣ Angela wants to inform shareholders of an upcoming Annual Meeting and provide an overview of the year's highlights.

Steps

1. Identify the intended audience and purpose of the document

Jot down general ideas for each of these elements, as shown in Figure B-1.

2. Choose the information and important points you want to cover in the document

You write down your ideas for the document.

3. Decide how the information will be organized

Because the information about the meeting is most important, you decide to present it first. The company highlights are included next. Later, if you decide to rearrange the structure of the document, you can use Word's editing features to move, copy, and cut text as needed.

4. Choose the tone of the document

Because the document is being sent to corporate shareholders, you will use a businesslike tone. In addition, it has been a good year at Nomad Ltd, so you will also use a positive, enthusiastic tone intended to encourage shareholders to feel good about their investments in the company. You can edit the document as needed until you achieve exactly the tone you want.

5. Think about how you want the document to look

To best communicate this information to your readers, you plan to use a straightforward business letter format for the document. The letter will include lists, directions, and a signature block. Each part will require special formatting to distinguish it from the rest of the letter. If you change your mind about the format of the document, you can make adjustments later.

6. After you have completed the planning you'll want to verify the document plan with your supervisor.

You can save much time later and avoid confusion about key elements before you begin the document. Be sure to clarify any elements you are unsure about. The planning stage is a good point at which to clarify your plan.

FIGURE B-1: A possible document plan

Audience   Businesslike tone for business meeting

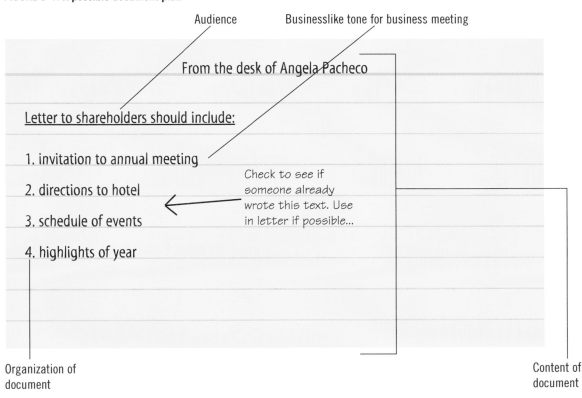

From the desk of Angela Pacheco

Letter to shareholders should include:

1. invitation to annual meeting

2. directions to hotel

3. schedule of events

4. highlights of year

Check to see if
someone already
wrote this text. Use
in letter if possible...

Organization of
document

Content of
document

Creating new documents using wizards and templates

You can use Word's document wizards and templates to create a variety of professionally-designed business documents, including resumes, memos, faxes, and business letters. These wizards and templates take into account the planning techniques described above to create documents that are consistent in tone, purpose, and formatting. All you do is provide the text. To create such a document, click the New command on the File menu, and double-click the icon for the type of document you want to create. You can use either a wizard (which guides you through a series of dialog boxes regarding your preferences for the document) or you can use a template in which you replace placeholder text with your own text. Either method gives you a great head start in developing attractive and effective documents.

Word 97

Opening a Document and Saving it with a New Name

Using text from existing documents saves you time and energy. To prevent any changes to the original document, you can open it and save it with a new name. This creates a copy of the document, leaving the original unchanged. ✎ Earlier Angela reviewed a document created by a colleague at Nomad Ltd. This document contains additional text Angela wants to use in the shareholder letter she created earlier. So that she does not alter the original documents, Angela opens the documents and saves both with new names.

Time To

✔ Start Word 97

1. **Click the Open button** 🖿 **on the Standard toolbar**
   Word displays the Open dialog box, as shown in Figure B-2. The Look in list box displays the name of the drive or folder you accessed the last time you saved or opened a file. Table B-1 describes the buttons in this dialog box.

2. **Click the Up One Level button** 🗁 **until you see the drive where you save your files for this book**
   The name of the drive containing your Student Disk appears in the large box.

3. **Double-click the drive to display its contents**
   The Look in box displays the drive containing your Student Disk and the lesson files appear in the large box.

4. **Click the document named WD B-1 in the file list box, then click Open**
   The document WD B-1 appears in the document window. To keep this original file intact, you will save it with a new name, Shareholder Letter.

5. **Click File on the menu bar, then click Save As**
   The Save As dialog box opens, in which you can enter a new name for the document. Make sure the Save in list box displays the drive where you want to save your files.

6. **In the File name text box, type Shareholder Letter, then click Save**
   The document is saved with the new name, and the original document is closed. You can now safely use Shareholder Letter without changing the original document. You now need to open and save another document before beginning revisions.

7. **Repeat steps 1–6, opening the document WD B-2 and saving the document as Report**
   The document is saved with the new name, as shown in Figure B-3, and the original document is closed. The Shareholder Letter is still open in a document window behind the newly saved Report document.

QuickTip

You can double-click a filename in the Open dialog box to open the document. This is faster than clicking the filename then clicking Open.

FIGURE B-2: Open dialog box

Look in list box

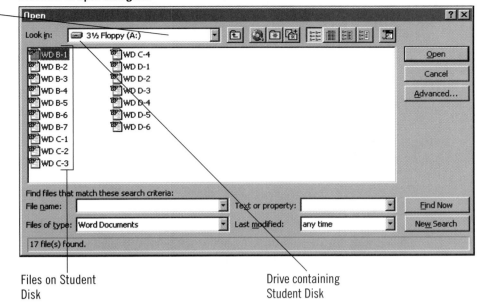

Files on Student
Disk

Drive containing
Student Disk

FIGURE B-3: Saved document

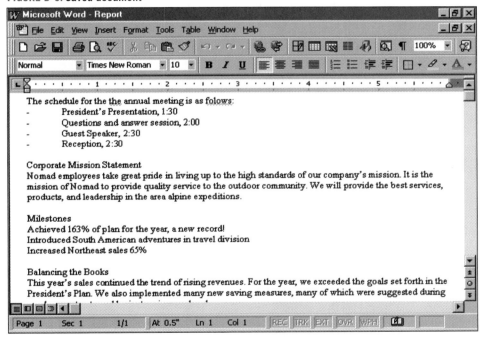

TABLE B-1: Open dialog box buttons

button	description
	Moves up one folder (the folder that contains the current folder)
	Displays icon and document name in a list
	Displays detailed information about the document, including its name, its size, its type (folder or type of file), and the date it was last modified
	Displays additional document details, including the author's name, the date created, who last saved the document, the program in which the document was created, the number of revisions, and the number of pages and words
	Displays a small picture of the document's contents to help you identify the document

Word 97

Copying Text

You can copy existing text that you want to reuse in a document. You can use the Copy command or Copy button to copy text to the Clipboard so that the text is available to be pasted in other locations in the document. The Clipboard (available in any Windows program) is a temporary storage area in computer memory for text and graphics. You can also drag selected text to a new location using the mouse. Dragging is a great way to copy text when both the text and its new location are visible in the window at the same time. ◢▬▬ Next Angela will copy text from her colleague's document to her shareholder letter. Angela displays both documents at once, in separate windows, so that she can work in both documents at the same time.

Steps

QuickTip

Display paragraph marks by clicking the Show/Hide button ¶ on the Standard toolbar.

1. **Click Window on the menu bar, then click Arrange All**
   Both documents appear in the program window, as shown in Figure B-4. You want to copy all the text from the Report document to the Shareholder Letter.

2. **With the pointer in the selection bar of the Report document, triple-click the left mouse button**
   Triple-clicking in the selection bar selects the entire document.

CourseHelp

The camera icon indicates there is a CourseHelp available with this lesson. Click the Start button, point to programs, point to CourseHelp, then click Word 97 Illustrated. Choose the CourseHelp that corresponds to this lesson.

3. **Click the Copy button 🖹 on the Standard toolbar**
   The selected text is copied to the Clipboard. By placing text on the Clipboard (with either the Cut or Copy command), you can insert the text as many times as you want. You want to place this text before the last sentence in the Shareholder Letter.

4. **Click in the Shareholder Letter document window to make it active, then place the insertion point in front of the first sentence in the paragraph before the signature block**

5. **Click the Paste button 🖺 on the Standard toolbar**
   The copied text is inserted. It remains on the Clipboard until you copy or cut new text. To make it easier to work in the document, maximize the Shareholder Letter document window.

Time To

✔ Save

6. **In the Shareholder Letter document window, click the Maximize button, 🔲 then scroll to the top of the document**
   You can see more of the document at once with the window maximized. Compare your document to Figure B-5.

FIGURE B-4: **Two open documents in the Word program window**

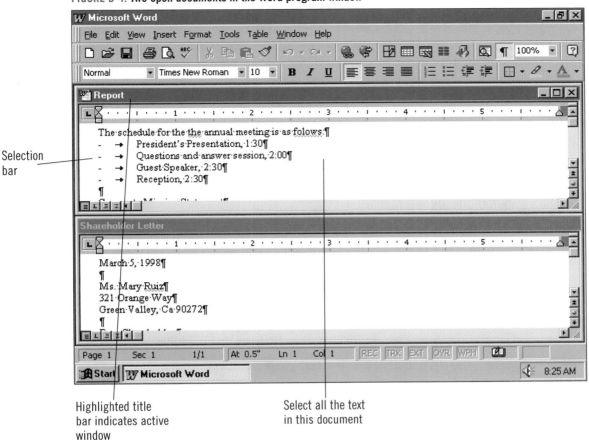

Selection bar

Highlighted title bar indicates active window

Select all the text in this document

FIGURE B-5: **Completed document**

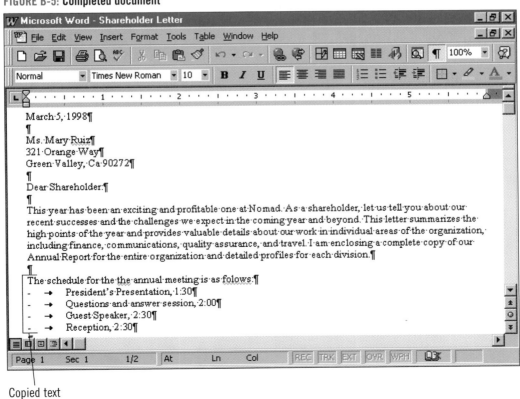

Copied text

Moving Text

You can also move text from its current location and place it in new locations, even in other documents. You can use the Clipboard by cutting the text in one location and pasting it in new locations. You can also drag selected text to a new location using the mouse. Be sure to view the CourseHelp for this lesson before completing the steps. ◣▬▬ Next Angela will move text to a new location within her Shareholder Letter, using the cut and paste method. She will also move text by dragging it to a new location.

1. In the Shareholder Letter document, scroll to the end and select the last two sentences before the signature block

CourseHelp

The camera icon indicates there is a CourseHelp available with this lesson. Click the Start button, point to programs, point to CourseHelp, then click Word 97 Illustrated. Choose the CourseHelp that corresponds to this lesson.

2. Click the **Cut button** ✂ on the Standard toolbar
   The cut text is removed from the document and placed on the Clipboard.

3. Scroll through the document until you see the schedule for the annual meeting, and then place the insertion point in the first line below the last event (Reception, 2:30)

4. Click the **Paste button** 📋 on the Standard toolbar
   The sentences are inserted. Next use the dragging method to move text to the new location.

5. Select the first sentence of the text you just moved

QuickTip

If you want to copy selected text rather than move it when you drag, press and hold [Ctrl] first. The pointer changes to the Copy pointer ▷ when you copy text by dragging.

6. Press and hold the mouse button over the selected text until the pointer changes from ◁ to ▷, *do not release the mouse button*

7. Drag the mouse up, placing the vertical bar of the pointer in the first line of text above the schedule

8. Release the mouse button
   The sentence is inserted.

9. Click anywhere in the window to deselect the highlighted text
   Compare your document to Figure B-6. The sentence has been moved.

10. Click the **Save button** 💾 on the Standard toolbar

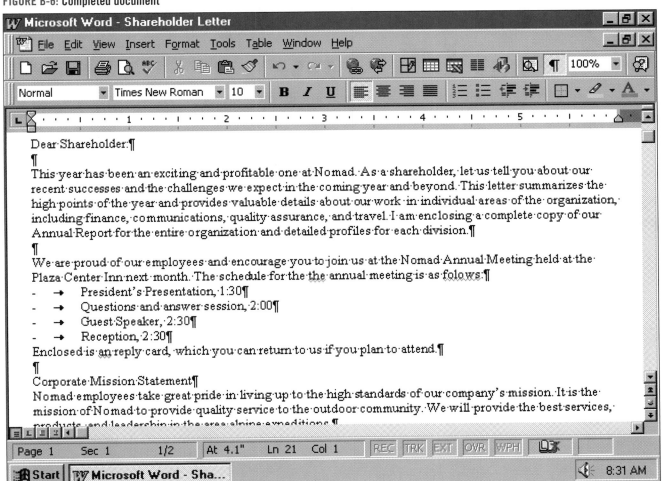

Viewing CourseHelp

The camera icon on the opposite page indicates there is a CourseHelp available for this lesson. CourseHelps are on-screen "movies" that bring difficult concepts to life, to help you understand the material in this book. Your instructor received a CourseHelp disk and should have installed it on the machine you are using.

Because CourseHelp runs in a separate window, you can start and view a movie even if you're in the middle of completing a lesson. Once the movie is finished, you can click the Word program button on the taskbar and continue with the lessons, right where you left off.

Correcting Spelling and Grammar Errors

Word's Spelling and Grammar command identifies and corrects spelling mistakes and repeated words (such as "the the"). When you use this command, Word highlights any word that is not in its standard dictionary and displays suggested spellings from which you can choose. This command also allows you to review your document for grammatical errors such as mistakes in punctuation, sentence fragments, or agreement errors. Angela will proofread her Shareholder Letter using the Spelling and Grammar command to correct any spelling or grammatical errors.

1. Press **[Ctrl][Home]** to move to the top of the document, then click the **Spelling and Grammar button** on the Standard toolbar
Clicking this button is the same as choosing Spelling and Grammar from the Tools menu. The Spelling and Grammar dialog box opens, as shown in Figure B-7. The dialog box identifies the word "Ruiz" as a possible misspelling. The highlighted word is a proper noun, so you can ignore this occurrence.

2. Click **Ignore** in the Spelling and Grammar dialog box
Next, the dialog box indicates that "the" word the is repeated.

3. Click **Delete** to delete the second occurrence of the word **the**
The Spelling command next identifies "folows" as a misspelled word. Suggested spellings appear in the Suggestions list. The spelling that most closely resembles the misspelled word is highlighted in the Suggestions list. You can choose any one of the suggested spellings.

4. Click **Change** in the Spelling dialog box
The highlighted text in the Suggestions list replaces the misspelled word. Next, the Spelling and Grammar dialog box suggests using the word "a" in place of "an." To learn more about the error, you view an explanation.

5. Click the **Office Assistant button** in the Spelling and Grammar dialog box
The Office Assistant displays an explanation of the rule that applies to this error.

6. After reading the explanation, click the **Close box** in the right corner of the Office Assistant window
According to the information in the explanation, you decide that a change is necessary.

7. Click **Change**
The word "a" is substituted for the incorrect word "an." The Spelling and Grammar command finishes searching for errors.

8. Click **OK**
The message box closes. Compare your corrected document to Figure B-8.

9. Save your work

> **QuickTip**
>
> The buttons in the Spelling and Grammar dialog box change depending on the type of error.

FIGURE B-7: Spelling and Grammar dialog box

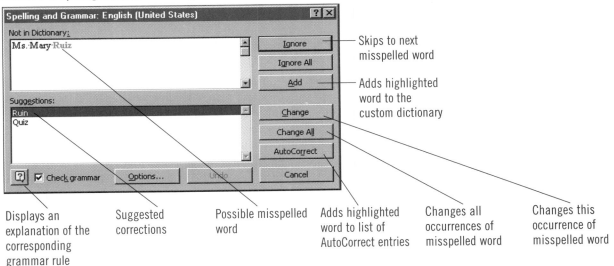

Skips to next
misspelled word

Adds highlighted
word to the
custom dictionary

Displays an
explanation of the
corresponding
grammar rule

Suggested
corrections

Possible misspelled
word

Adds highlighted
word to list of
AutoCorrect entries

Changes all
occurrences of
misspelled word

Changes this
occurrence of
misspelled word

FIGURE B-8: Proofed document

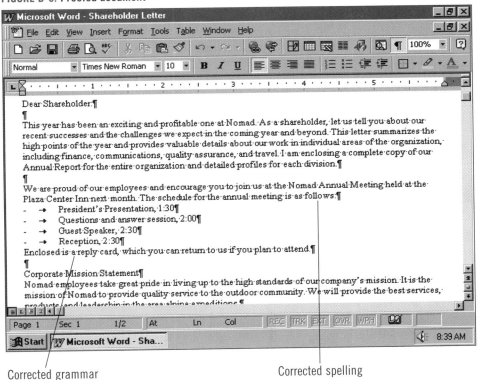

Corrected grammar

Corrected spelling

CLUES TO USE

Using the Thesaurus

You can use the Thesaurus to look up synonyms of overused or awkward words in your document. Select the overused word, click Tools on the menu bar, point to Language, then click Thesaurus. The Thesaurus dialog box opens, listing synonyms of the selected word. This dialog box also displays antonyms for appropriate words. Choose a desired word in the Replace with Synonym list and click Replace to replace the selected word in your document.

FIGURE B-9: Thesaurus dialog box

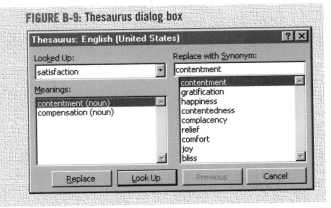

Word 97

Finding and replacing text

Sometimes you need to find and replace text throughout a document. For example, you might need to make a product name change, company name change, or change an abbreviation to a full name. In a long document, doing this manually would be time-consuming and prone to error. Word's Replace command automates this process, locating each occurrence of the text you want to replace. You can replace all occurrences at once or choose to replace specific occurrences individually. Word's Find command is also a useful searching tool. Angela's letter refers to the company name as simply Nomad. However, Angela believes the letter will sound more professional if she uses the company's full name, Nomad Limited. She'll use the Replace command to correct all instances of the company name at one time.

QuickTip

Click the More button in the Find and Replace dialog box to include formatting in your searches.

1. If necessary, press **[Ctrl][Home]** to move to the top of the document, then click **Edit** on the menu bar, then click **Replace**

The Find and Replace dialog box opens with the Replace tab selected, as shown in Figure B-10. There are many ways to specify the text for which you want to search. See Table B-2 for a summary of search and replace options that are available when you click More. Unless you click the More button, you will not see these additional options.

2. In the Find what box, type **Nomad**

You need to replace all occurrences of "Nomad" with "Nomad Limited" so that the correct company name will appear in the letter.

3. Press **[Tab]** to move to the Replace with box, then type **Nomad Limited**

4. Click **Replace All**

Word changes all occurrences of "Nomad" to "Nomad Limited" in the document. A message appears telling you the number of occurrences (6) of the text in the document that were changed.

5. Click **OK**

The message box closes and you return to the Find and Replace dialog box.

6. Click **Close**

The dialog box closes and you return to the document. Compare your document to Figure B-11.

7. Save your work

Using the Find command

The Find command on the Edit menu allows you to locate specified text. If after finding the text, you decide you want to replace this and other occurrences, you can click the Replace tab. If you want to choose the individual occurrences of text to change, click Find Next in the Replace dialog box to locate the next occurrence. Then click Replace to change it or click Find Next again to skip to the next occurrence.

FIGURE B-10: Find and Replace dialog box

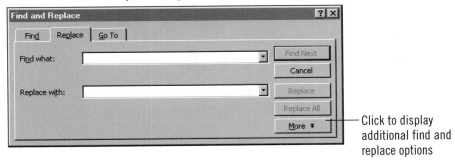

Click to display additional find and replace options

FIGURE B-11: Document after changes

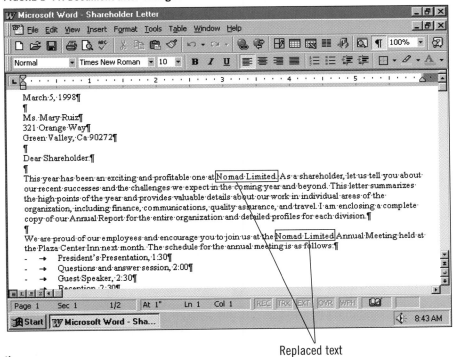

Replaced text

TABLE B-2: Replace options

replace option	description
Find What	Identifies the text to be replaced
Replace With	Identifies the text to use as a replacement
Search	Specifies the direction of the search from the current position of the insertion point: Down, Up, All (default)
Match Case	Locates only text with uppercase and lowercase letters that match exactly the entry in the Find what box
Find Whole Words Only	Locates only words that are complete and are not included as part of a larger word
Use Pattern Matching	Searches for a group of characters located at the beginning of specified text, at the end of specified text, or within specified text
Sounds Like	Locates words that sound like the text in the Find what box, but have different spellings
Find All Word Forms	Replaces all forms of a word. For example, specifying "find" in the Find what box locates "find," "finds," "found," and "finding" and replaces each with the comparable form of the replacement word.
No Formatting	Removes any formatting specifications noted in the Find what or Replace with box
Format	Displays a list of formatting specifications to find and replace
Special	Allows you to search for and replace special characters, such as a tab character or a paragraph mark

Previewing a Document

After proofreading and correcting your document, you can print it. Before you do, it is a good idea to display the document using the Print Preview command. In print preview, you can easily check the overall appearance of your document. You can also get a close-up view of the page and make final changes before printing. Next, Angela previews the document before printing it.

Steps

QuickTip

The keyboard shortcut for the Print Preview command is [Ctrl][F2].

1. **Click the Print Preview button on the Standard toolbar**
   The document appears in the Preview window. The size of the page you see depends on the number and size of pages displayed the last time the Print Preview command was issued. You want to see both pages of the document.

2. **Click the Multiple Pages button on the Print Preview toolbar and drag to show two pages, as shown in Figure B-12**
   As you view the document, you notice that something is missing in the signature block. Get a close-up view of this part of the letter to examine it more carefully.

3. **Move the pointer over the page until it changes to ⊕ , then click near the signature block of the letter**
   The document is magnified, allowing you to read and edit the text. For example, you can change the abbreviation "VP" to a more official title, "Vice President." You can make this change without first returning to the document window.

4. **If necessary, click the Magnifier button on the Print Preview toolbar**
   The Magnifier pointer changes to Ι. Now you can edit the text.

5. **Select the text VP, then type Vice President**
   While you are near the end of the document, you add some additional text.

6. **Place the insertion point in the line just above the text "Sincerely" and press [Enter] to create a new blank line**

QuickTip

Although it is convenient to edit in Print Preview, unlike page layout view, print preview does not display non-printing characters. Therefore, do not use print preview when you are doing a lot of editing that requires rearranging text.

7. **Type the following sentence, then press [Enter]**
   We hope to see you at the upcoming Annual Meeting.
   You can see that the letter spills only a few lines onto the second page. You would like the letter to fit on one page, which is a change you can make in Print Preview.

8. **Click the Shrink to Fit button on the Print Preview toolbar**
   The text is adjusted to fit on one page. Next, you display the full page of the document.

9. **Click the One Page button on the Print Preview toolbar to see the full page of the document and compare your document to Figure B-13**
   With the document complete, you can now save the document and print it without returning to the document window.

10. **Save your document.**

FIGURE B-12: **Two pages in Print Preview**

Print Preview toolbar

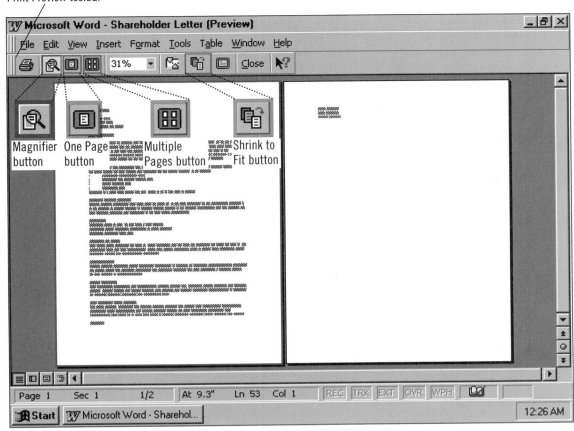

FIGURE B-13: **Document fit to one page**

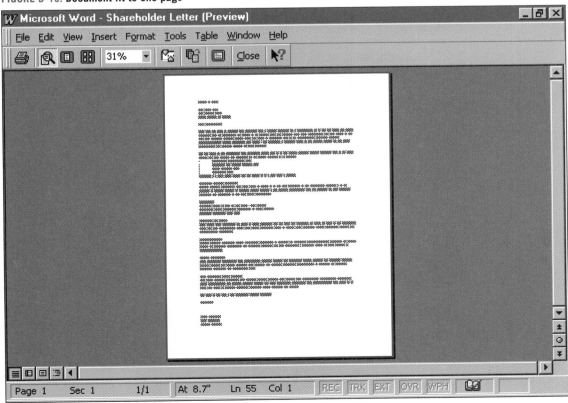

Word 97

Printing a Document

After proofreading and correcting a document, you're ready to print it. Printing a document is as simple as clicking the Print button on the Print Preview toolbar or the Standard toolbar. However, to take advantage of many printing options, use the Print command on the File menu. See Table B-3 to learn more about printing options. ▰▰▰▰ Angela uses the Print command to print two copies of her letter. In general, it is a good practice to save your document before printing it (to prevent loss of work if there are printer problems, for example). However, Angela saved her work at the end of the previous lesson, so she can continue without saving.

Steps

1. Click File on the menu bar, then click Print

The Print dialog box opens, as shown in Figure B-14. In this dialog box, you can specify the print options you want to use when you print your document. The name of the printer and the options you have available might be different, depending on the kind of printer you have set up with your computer.

2. In the Number of copies box, type 2

If applicable, you can submit the second copy of the document to your instructor. In general, avoid using the printer as a copier to produce multiple copies of larger documents.

3. Click OK

The Print dialog box closes and Word prints your document. You may notice a printer icon at the bottom of the screen while the document prints. Compare your document to Figure B-15.

Trouble?

If you are not connected to a printer, ask your technical support person or instructor for assistance.

4. Click the Close button on the Preview toolbar

You leave Print Preview and return to the document window.

5. Press and hold down [Shift], click File on the menu bar, then click Close All

Your document no longer appears in your document window and the other document that was open closes as well.

6. If you see a message box asking if you want to save changes, you can click Yes

7. Click File on the menu bar, then click Exit to close the Word

TABLE B-3: Printing options

print options	description
Name	Displays the name of the selected printer
Properties	Displays dialog box which specifies other options that vary based on the features available with your printer, such as the size or type of paper loaded in the printer, and the resolution of the graphics in the document (if any).
Print to File	Prints a document to a new file instead of a printer
Page Range	All: prints the complete document Current page: prints the page with the insertion point or the selected page Selection: prints selected text only Pages: prints user-specified pages (separate single pages with a comma, a range of pages with a hyphen)
Number of Copies	Specifies the number of copies to print
Collate	Prints all pages of the first copy before printing subsequent copies, (not available on all printers)
Print What	Prints the document (default), or only comments, annotations, styles, or other text associated with the document
Print	Specifies the print order for the page range: All Pages in Range, Odd Pages, Even Pages

FIGURE B-14: **Print dialog box**

Click to select a
new printer

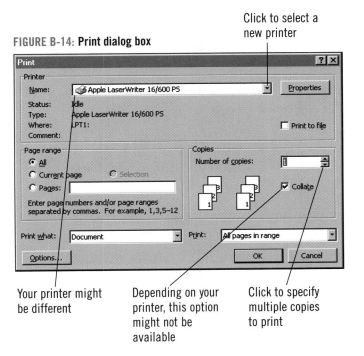

Your printer might
be different

Depending on your
printer, this option
might not be
available

Click to specify
multiple copies
to print

FIGURE B-15: **Shareholder Letter**

March 5, 1998

Ms. Mary Ruiz
321 Orange Way
Green Valley, Ca 90272

Dear Shareholder:

This year has been an exciting and profitable one at Nomad Limited. As a shareholder, let us tell you about our recent
successes and the challenges we expect in the coming year and beyond. This letter summarizes the high points of the
year and provides valuable details about our work in individual areas of the organization, including finance,
communications, quality assurance, and travel. I am enclosing a complete copy of our Annual Report for the entire
organization and detailed profiles for each division.

We are proud of our employees and encourage you to join us at the Nomad Limited Annual Meeting held at the Plaza
Center Inn next month. The schedule for the annual meeting is as follows:
-        Presidentís Presentation, 1:30
-        Questions and answer session, 2:00
-        Guest Speaker, 2:30
-        Reception, 2:30
Enclosed is a reply card, which you can return to us if you plan to attend.

Corporate Mission Statement
Nomad Limited employees take great pride in living up to the high standards of our companyís mission. It is the
mission of Nomad Limited to provide quality service to the outdoor community. We will provide the best services,
products, and leadership in the area alpine expeditions.

Milestones
Achieved 163% of plan for the year, a new record!
Introduced South American adventures in travel division
Increased Northeast sales 65%

Balancing the Books
This yearís sales continued the trend of rising revenues. For the year, we exceeded the goals set forth in the Presidentís
Plan. We also implemented many new saving measures, many of which were suggested during employee retreats and
brainstorming weekends.

Communications
Nomad Limited developed office publishing department to produce all corporate communications including the annual
report, the corporate newsletter, and corporate catalogs. We also completed a yearlong search for new director of
communications.

Quality Assurance
This department normalized and implemented Product Testing and Standards review process. QA installed Product
Testing Center. QA started working with guiding and outdoor leadership organizations to field-test all products
including outerwear and recreational gear.

New Directions Travel Division
The travel division purchased two national guiding services and another with international connections. Combined,
these organizations will deliver services through the New Directions subsidiary. This diversification will allow us to
offer new tours in exciting locations, including South America and Africa.

We hope to see you at the upcoming Annual Meeting.

Sincerely,

Chris Peterson
Vice President
Nomad Limited

Practice

► Concepts Review

Label each of the elements of the Spelling and Grammar dialog box in Figure B-16.

FIGURE B-16

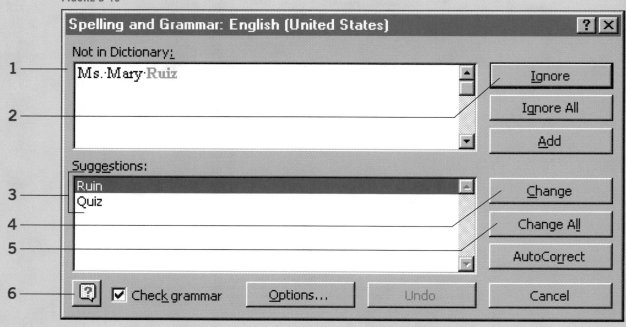

Match each of the following commands or features with the statement that best describes its function.

7. Copy command
8. Paste command
9. Spelling and Grammar command
10. Thesaurus command
11. Cut command
12. Replace command
13. Find command

a. Locates each occurrence of specified text

b. Reviews a document for correct spelling, punctuation, and usage errors

c. Lists synonyms and antonyms

d. Removes text from the document and places it on the Clipboard

e. Copies text to the Clipboard

f. Locates each occurrence of specified text and replaces all occurrences or those occurrences you specify

g. Copies text from the Clipboard into a document

14. To place text on the Clipboard, you must first
    a. Click the Copy button
    b. Click the Cut button
    c. Click the Paste button
    d. Select the text

15. To display two open documents at once, you use which menu and command?
    a. Click Window on the menu bar, then click Arrange All
    b. Click Window on the menu bar, then click Split
    c. Click Window on the menu bar, then click New Window
    d. Click File on the menu bar, click Print Preview, then click Multiple Pages

16. Which option is NOT available in the Spelling and Grammar dialog box when a spelling error is identified?
    a. Add the word to the dictionary
    b. Add an AutoCorrect entry
    c. Select a synonym for the word
    d. Choose a suggested spelling

17. Which statement does not describe the Spelling and Grammar command?
    a. Provides a way to learn about a grammatical error
    b. Suggests revisions to make a sentence correct
    c. Revises your document based on the style of the document
    d. Checks for spelling errors

18. Which tool will identify as misspelled the word "your" when the word "you're" should be the correct word?
    a. The Spelling and Grammar command
    b. The Preview command
    c. The Thesaurus command
    d. The AutoCorrect command

19. Using the Find and Replace command you can do all of the following EXCEPT:
    a. Check for all usages of the passive voice in your document.
    b. Search the document for specified text in a certain direction only.
    c. Replace all occurrences of a word or words with another word.
    d. Find all of the different forms of a word.

20. In print preview, how do you get a close-up view of a page?
    a. Click the Print Preview button.
    b. Click the Close button.
    c. Click the page with the Magnifier pointer.
    d. Click the One Page button.

21. Which of the following is NOT true about printing?
   a. You can choose to print only the current page of a document.
   b. You can print a range of pages in a document.
   c. You can print all the open documents from the Print dialog box.
   d. The Print button automatically prints your document without displaying the Print dialog box.

▶ Skills Review

1. Open a new document and save it with a new name.
   a. Open the document named WD B-3, then save it as "Road Map."
   b. Insert today's date at the top of the document.
   c. Add an extra line after the date.
   d. Edit the signature block to contain your name.

2. Copy and move text.
   a. Using the mouse, copy the text "Open Roads, Inc." from the first sentence to the last line in the signature block.
   b. Using the Clipboard, move the last two sentences of the first body paragraph to the paragraph mark under the text "How does it work?"

3. Correct spelling and grammatical errors.
   a. Click the Spelling and Grammar button on the Standard toolbar.
   b. Correct any spelling and grammatical errors.
   c. Click OK after Word has finished searching for spelling and grammar errors.
   d. Save your changes.

4. Find and replace text.
   a. Click Edit, then click Replace.
   b. Type "Inc." in the Find what box.
   c. Type "Intl." in the Replace with box.
   d. Click Replace All to substitute the new company name.
   e. Click OK, then click Close.
   f. Save your changes.

5. Preview a document.
   a. Click the Print Preview button on the Standard toolbar.
   b. Click the One Page button.
   c. Click the page near the signature.
   d. Click the Magnifier button on the Print Preview toolbar.
   e. Select Account Representative, then type "Corporate Sales."
   f. Click the One Page button on the Print Preview toolbar.
   g. Click Close to return to normal view.

6. Print a document.

   a. Save your document.

   b. Click File, then click Print.

   c. In the copies box, type "2."

   d. Click OK.

   e. Click File, then click Close.

   f. Click File, then click Exit.

▶ Independent Challenges

1. As the co-chair for the Lake City High School class of 1993 reunion planning committee, you are responsible for recruiting classmates to help with reunion activities. Open the draft letter WD B-4 and save it as "Lake City Reunion Letter". Using Figure B-17 as your guide, use Word's proofing tools to make the following changes to the letter. To complete this independent challenge:

1. Use the Find command to locate the word "ambitious," and then use the Thesaurus to substitute another word of your choice.
2. Preview the document and edit the signature block to display your name.
3. Check the spelling and grammar in the document. Ignore your name if Word identifies it as a possible misspelled word.
4. In Print Preview, modify the title in the signature block.
5. Save your changes and print the document.

FIGURE B-17

September 17, 1998

Mr. Chris Randall
Randall and Associates
4440 Pacific Boulevard
San Francisco, CA 94104

Dear Chris:

As a member of the Lake City High School class of 1993, I often think of the people that made our school such a rewarding experience for me. Of course, there are the close friends I made and kept throughout the years, but also I think about the people that I somehow lost track of since graduation. The instructors, students, and administrative staff all contribute to the richness of the memories.

Now is your opportunity to play a important role in helping bring Lake City High memories alive not only for yourself, but for your fellow classmates as well. As the co-chair of the Lake City High Reunion 1998 planning committee,

I am looking for resourceful, organized alums that are interested in working on various reunion activities. We need people for the following areas: meeting coordination for all committees, computer consulting to help us use technology to work efficiently, meals and entertainment planning for the three-day event, and logistics coordination for handling getting everyone to Lake City and lodging them once they return to campus. All committees need as many volunteers as they can get, so you are sure to get to work in any area you choose.

If you are interested and available to work five hours a month for the next 10 months, please let me know. You can leave me a message at (555) 555-4321. I look forward to hearing from you soon.

Angela Pacheco
Lake City High Reunion 1998
Co-Chair

2. As an account representative for Lease For Less, a company that leases various office equipment such as fax machines and large copiers, you previously drafted a proposal describing the corporate discount program to a current customer. Open the document named WD B-5 and save it as "Discount Proposal." Using Figure B-18 as your guide, use Word's proofing tools to make the following changes to the letter. To complete this independent challenge:

1. Check the spelling and grammar in the document.
2. Use the Find command to locate the word "sequential."
3. Use the Thesaurus to look up an alternative word for "sequential" and replace it with a word of your choice.
4. Add the company before the text "Discount Proposal" at the top of the document.
5. Preview the document and edit the "From" line to display your name, followed by your title "Account Representative".
6. Save your changes and print the document.

3. You are the fund-raising coordinator for a nonprofit organization called Companies for Kids. In response to a potential corporate sponsor, you have previously drafted a short letter describing the benefits of being a sponsor. Open the document named WD B-6 and save it as "Kids Fund Raising." Using Figure B-19 as your guide, use Word's proofing tools to make the following changes to the letter. To complete this independent challenge:

1. Move the last sentence of the first paragraph to the start of the second paragraph.
2. Check the spelling and grammar in the document. Insert spaces between periods and the start of the next sentence as needed.
3. Use the Replace command to locate all occurrences of the word "valuable" and replace it with "important" throughout.
4. Preview the document and edit the signature block to display your name. Also, add the title "Companies for Kids" and your title to the signature block.

FIGURE B-18

LEASE FOR LESS DISCOUNT PROPOSAL

TO: MS. SANDY YOUNGQUIST
FROM: KIM LEE, ACCOUNT REPRESENTATIVE
SUBJECT: DISCOUNT PRICING
DATE: SEPTEMBER 17, 1998
CC: MARION WEST, SALES DIRECTOR

Thank you for your inquiry about a corporate discount for our temporary office services company. Enclosed is the information you requested. In addition, I have also include the premier issue of *EasyLeasing*, our exclusive newsletter.

You must use our services for at least 100 days each year, for two consecutive years to be eligible for the corporate discount. As a corporate customer, you will receive a 20% discount on general office temps and a 30% discount for our professional personnel. As your account representative, I would be pleased to discuss your temporary requirements with you. I will call you to arrange a time when we can meet.

FIGURE B-19

Companies for Kids Needs Your Help!

September 17, 1998

Celia Warden
Goff Associates
567 Ash Lane
Spring Lake, MN 55667

Dear Ms. Ward:

To complete our mission of collecting toys, clothing, and various necessary materials for children in local shelters, we would like to request your important assistance.

We depend largely on local businesses to help fund our efforts. Your company's time, services, and donations will benefit children in need. You can choose to donate time and services. Each weekend *Companies for Kids* sends out a number of teams to collect clothing and toys from the community. We desperately need organized teams to help us in this effort. Your company may also choose to make monthly donations, which will be put towards furnishing the shelters and paying various staff members that touch the lives of these children daily.

No matter how your company decides to participate in this program, you will no doubt benefit the lives of all the children who enter these shelters. I hope we can look forward to Goff Associates's participation in this important community program.

Sincerely,

Daniel Montreux
Companies for Kids
Fund Raising Coordinator

5. Save your changes and print the document.

6. Log on to the Internet and use your browser to go to http://www.course.com. From there, click Student On Line Companions, and then click the link to go to the Microsoft Office 97 Professional Edition—Illustrated: A First Course page, then click on the Word link for Unit B and locate the United Way home page. After reviewing the text and tone of a few pages, insert into your letter a few phrases or sentences that you think are especially effective and then paste them into the document. Edit the text as required to reflect the name of the Companies for Kids organization.

4. As a co-chair for the Lake City High School class of 1993 planning committee, you have received a telephone message from a classmate volunteering to serve on the entertainment committee. Open the thank you memo named WD B-7 and save it as "Volunteer Thanks Memo." Using Figure B-20 as your guide, use Word's proofing tools to make the following changes to the letter. To complete this independent challenge:

1. Move the last sentence of the second paragraph to the start of the second paragraph.

2. Check the spelling and grammar in the document.

3. Ignore the classmate's name if Word identifies it as a possible misspelled word.

4. Use the Replace command to replace all occurrences of the year "1980" with "1993."

5. Preview the document and edit the "From:" line to display your name and title.

6. Save your changes and print the document.

FIGURE B-20

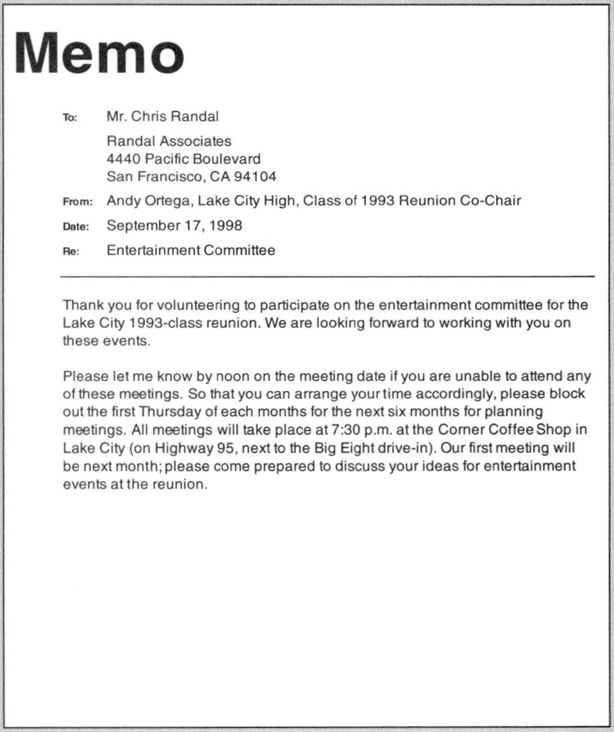

Memo

To: Mr. Chris Randal

         Randal Associates
         4440 Pacific Boulevard
         San Francisco, CA 94104

From: Andy Ortega, Lake City High, Class of 1993 Reunion Co-Chair

Date: September 17, 1998

Re: Entertainment Committee

Thank you for volunteering to participate on the entertainment committee for the Lake City 1993-class reunion. We are looking forward to working with you on these events.

Please let me know by noon on the meeting date if you are unable to attend any of these meetings. So that you can arrange your time accordingly, please block out the first Thursday of each months for the next six months for planning meetings. All meetings will take place at 7:30 p.m. at the Corner Coffee Shop in Lake City (on Highway 95, next to the Big Eight drive-in). Our first meeting will be next month; please come prepared to discuss your ideas for entertainment events at the reunion.

► Visual Workshop

As the conference coordinator for International Voices' upcoming conference, you are in charge of organizing the details for the informal dinner that will complete the Communications Conference. Use the Letter Wizard to type a letter to the banquet caterer at the conference site. Use Figure B-21 as a guide when selecting options in the wizard dialog boxes to decide how the banquet letter should look. Save the document with the name "Conference Dinner." Use the Spelling and Grammar command to identify any errors you may have made. Experiment with the Thesaurus. Try moving and copying text to arrange the letter more logically. Preview the document and make required edits. Finally, print the document, then close it and exit Word.

FIGURE B-21

October 24, 1998

Ms. Leslie Ryden
Banquet Caterer
Lakeside Center
North Bay, MN 55509

Dear Ms. Ryden:

I would like to take this opportunity to reaffirm how delighted we are to be conducting this fall's Communications Conference at the Lakeside Center on January 4. We at International Voices believe it is the perfect setting for our conference objectives.

As you requested, here are my ideas for the informal dinner that will wrap-up the day's events. I would be interested in having a low-fat, healthful cuisine for this meal. Since we will not be serving any alcoholic beverages, perhaps we could offer an array of fruit juices and sparkling mineral waters. Regarding floral decorations, I particularly liked your idea of international flags drawn by children. I believe this finishing touch will contribute to a wonderful, relaxing environment.

I hope these general guidelines will be helpful to you as you develop your menu and price proposal. I look forward to confirming our plans by late October.

Sincerely,

[your name]
[title]
[company name]

Formatting

a Document

- ► **Apply font effects using the toolbar**
- ► **Apply special font effects**
- ► **Align text with tabs**
- ► **Change paragraph alignment**
- ► **Indent paragraphs**
- ► **Change paragraph spacing**
- ► **Create bulleted and numbered lists**
- ► **Apply borders and shading**

Using Microsoft Word's formatting capabilities, you can change the appearance of text on the page to emphasize important points and make the text easier to read. You can change the appearance of characters and words by applying **font formatting**, and you can change the appearance of entire paragraphs to improve the appearance of your documents. **Paragraph formatting** refers to the spacing, indentation, and alignment of text in paragraphs. ✐ Angela needs to format a Company Report of accomplishments to Nomad Ltd shareholders. Using a variety of methods, she will change the character and paragraph formatting to emphasize the important topics and ideas.

Applying Font Effects Using the Toolbar

You can emphasize words and ideas in a document by applying special effects to text, such as making text darker (called **bold**), slanted (called *italics*), or underlined. These options are available on the Formatting toolbar. See Figure C-1 for the buttons on the Formatting toolbar that you can use to format text.  Angela wants to draw attention to the name of a newsletter described in the Company Report and to the headings, so she applies special formatting to these words.

Steps

1. Start Word

2. Open the document named WD C-1 and save it as **Company Report**
   First locate the text you want to emphasize.

3. In the first body paragraph, select the text **NomadNotes**, then click the **Italic button** *I* on the Formatting toolbar
   Deselect the text to see that it now appears italicized. To give special emphasis to the headings for each topic, apply bold formatting to them.

4. Select the first line in the document, **International Communications**, click the **Bold button** **B** on the Formatting toolbar, and then deselect the text
   The text now appears in bold. You decide to emphasize this text even more using a sans serif font.

5. Select the text again, click the **Font list arrow** on the Formatting toolbar, then scroll to and click **Arial**
   The text appears in the Arial font. The fonts available in the Font list box depend on the fonts installed on your computer. Next, increase the font size of the heading.

6. With the same text still selected, click the **Font Size list arrow** on the Formatting toolbar, then click **14**
   The physical size of the text is measured in points (pts). A point is 1/72". The bigger the number of points, the larger the font size. The selected text appears in 14 point type. Because you want all headings to be formatted this way, copy the formatting to the other occurrences.

QuickTip

With the Format Painter pointer you can drag across or double-click to copy formatting. If you move the pointer into the selection bar, the pointer changes to a selection pointer. With the Format Painter button still active, you can also click with this pointer in the selection bar to copy formatting.

7. With the same words still selected, double-click the **Format Painter button** on the Standard toolbar
   Double-clicking this button allows you to copy the same formatting multiple times. You can also click the Format Painter button once to copy formatting only once. Notice that the pointer changes to ▲I.

8. Drag the ▲I across each of the remaining five headings in the document: New Director and Ideas, In-House Publishing, Newsletter Update, Catalog Redesigned, Shareholder Meeting
   The font effects of the formatted text are copied to the text you select. Scroll toward the top of the screen and compare your document to Figure C-2.

9. Click to deactivate the Format Painter, then save the document
   Notice that the Format Painter button is no longer indented.

FIGURE C-1: Text formatting buttons on the Formatting toolbar

Font   Font list arrow   Bold   Underline

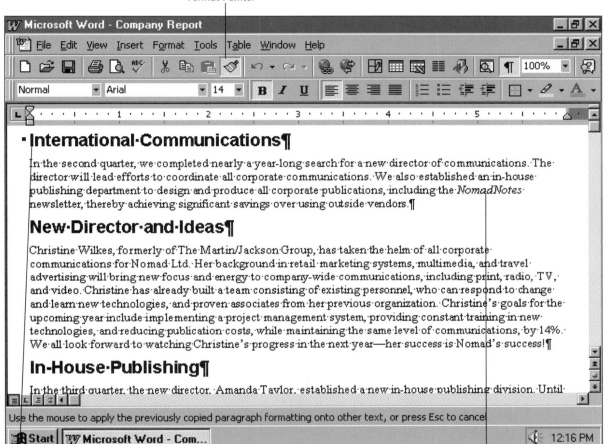

Font size box   Font size list arrow   Italic

FIGURE C-2: Formatted document

Format Painter

International Communications¶

In the second quarter, we completed nearly a year-long search for a new director of communications. The director will lead efforts to coordinate all corporate communications. We also established an in-house publishing department to design and produce all corporate publications, including the *NomadNotes* newsletter, thereby achieving significant savings over using outside vendors.¶

New Director and Ideas¶

Christine Wilkes, formerly of The Martin/Jackson Group, has taken the helm of all corporate communications for Nomad Ltd. Her background in retail marketing systems, multimedia, and travel advertising will bring new focus and energy to company-wide communications, including print, radio, TV, and video. Christine has already built a team consisting of existing personnel, who can respond to change and learn new technologies, and proven associates from her previous organization. Christine's goals for the upcoming year include implementing a project management system, providing constant training in new technologies, and reducing publication costs, while maintaining the same level of communications, by 14%. We all look forward to watching Christine's progress in the next year—her success is Nomad's success!¶

In-House Publishing¶

In the third quarter, the new director, Amanda Taylor, established a new in-house publishing division. Until

Use the mouse to apply the previously copied paragraph formatting onto other text, or press Esc to cancel

Bold, Arial, 14 pt   Italic

CLUES TO USE

Serif vs. sans serif fonts

Serifs are the small strokes at the ends of a character, as shown in Figure C-3. A **serif font**, such as Times New Roman, has a small stroke at the ends of its characters. Simple fonts without serifs, such as Arial, are known as **sans serif fonts**. Typically, sans serif fonts are used for headings in a document, and serif fonts are used for the body text.

FIGURE C-3: Serif vs. sans serif fonts

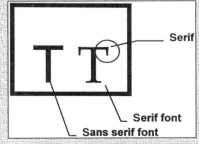

Serif

Serif font

Sans serif font

Applying Special Font Effects

Font formatting options are also available with the Font command. For example, you can apply several different kinds of underlining, as well as format text to appear in all capital letters. The Font tab in the Font dialog box also includes special options such as applying shadow, engraved, or outline effects to text. The Animation tab provides additional font effects that can be used to emphasize text when viewed on screen. ▰▰▰ Angela wants to apply formatting to the name of the newsletter to draw even more attention to this new offering. She will use the options with the Font command to accomplish this.

Steps 1234

1. **In the first body paragraph, double-click the text NomadNotes to select it**
   With the text selected, you can format it.

2. **Click Format on the menu bar, then click Font**
   The Font dialog box opens, as shown in Figure C-4. Distinguish the name of the newsletter from the surrounding text by having it appear in a larger font.

3. **In the Size list, select 11**
   The name of the newsletter appears in 11 point type. In the Preview area of the dialog box, you can see a sample of the font formatting changes. Next, experiment with other font effects.

4. **In the Effects section, click the Engrave check box**
   Notice in the Preview area that this option formats the text so the text has an engraved appearance. However, the text does not show up clearly, so change the color.

5. **Click the Color list arrow, then select Black**
   The text appears in black in the Preview area. Try the Outline effect.

6. **In the Effects section, click Outline**
   The text now appears outlined in the Preview area. With the Outline formatting, your text no longer needs to be italicized.

7. **In the Font style list, click Regular**
   The text is no longer italicized. Now close the dialog box.

Time To

✔ Save

8. **Click OK, then deselect the text**
   View the formatting applied in the document, as shown in Figure C-5.

Applying special effects using the Character Spacing and Animation tabs

To adjust character spacing, click Font on the Format menu and choose the desired option on the Character Spacing tab. You can adjust the spacing between the individual characters. For example, you can create dramatic text effects by expanding the space between characters with the Expanded option. On this same tab, you can adjust the width of individual characters, making the characters themselves narrower or wider as needed to achieve the effect you want. You can also draw attention to text using animated text effects— text that moves or flashes—for documents that will be read online. You can highlight the headline using animated font effects such as a blinking background or red dotted lines moving around the selected text. The animated effects can only be seen online and do not appear in the printed document. Click the Animation tab in the Font dialog box to see the animation effects you can use in an online document.

FIGURE C-4: Font dialog box

Currently selected font

Fonts available on your computer

Font style options

Font Size options

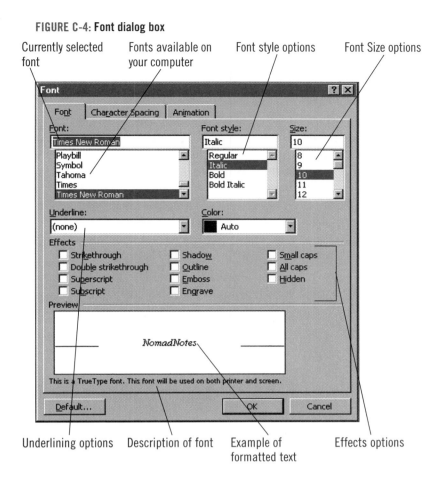

Underlining options   Description of font   Example of formatted text   Effects options

FIGURE C-5: Font formatting

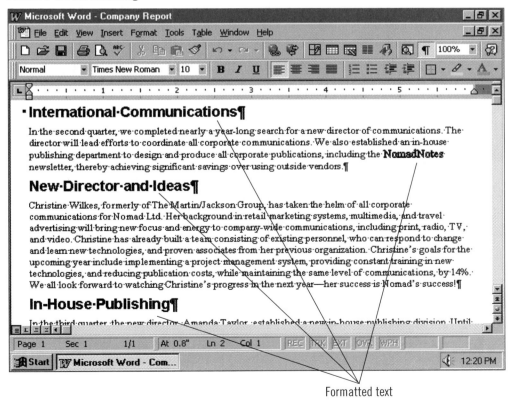

Formatted text

Aligning Text with Tabs

Numerical information (such as tables of financial results) are often easier to read when you align the text with tabs. Use tabs rather than the spacebar to align your text because tab settings are faster, more accurate, and easier to change. When you press the Tab key, the insertion point moves to the next tab stop. By default, tab stops are located at every half inch, but you can use the horizontal ruler to create and modify tab stops. Table C-1 describes the four different types of tabs. In her document, Angela wants to add a list identifying estimated cost savings.

1. **Place the insertion point after the period that follows the word vendors at the end of the first body paragraph, then press [Enter]**
   Pressing [Enter] creates a new blank line. This line will contain the column headings in the cost savings list. Next type the heading for the first column.

2. **Press [Tab], then type Publications, and press [Tab] again**
   A tab character appears before and after the word and the insertion point moves to the right to the 1½" mark on the ruler, as shown in Figure C-6. Next type the remaining headings, separating each one by pressing [Tab].

3. **Type 1997 Cost per Issue, press [Tab], type 1998 Cost per Issue, press [Tab], then type Savings per Issue**
   Currently, the headings are aligned with the default tab stops located every half inch on the horizontal ruler. To space the headings evenly, create new tab stops on the ruler.

Trouble?

You can remove a tab stop by dragging it off the ruler.

4. **With the insertion point in the line of column headings, click the tab alignment indicator at the left end of the ruler until you see the right-aligned tab marker ⌐, then click the 1" mark on the ruler**
   The right edge of the word "Publications" is now aligned with the new tab stop. Format the remaining columns to be left-aligned.

Trouble?

If you see no change in the alignment of the column headings, it means that the text was already aligned at the default tab stop. Placing a tab stop there anyway ensures the proper alignment, even if the amount of text in the line changes.

5. **With the insertion point still in the line of column headings, click the tab alignment indicator until you see the left-aligned tab marker ∟, then click the 1½", 3", and 4¼" marks on the ruler**
   Left-aligned tab stops appear at the locations you clicked. To adjust a tab stop, just drag it with the mouse. Next add additional lines.

6. **Press [End] to place the insertion point at the end of the line, then press [Enter]**
   The tab stops you created for the previous paragraph are still in effect in the new paragraph. Now you can enter additional text for your list.

7. **Type the following information in the document, press [Tab] as indicated, and remember to press [Enter] at the end of each line except after the last line**

   [Tab] Newsletter   [Tab] 3.785   [Tab] 2.89   [Tab] .895 [Enter]
   [Tab] Catalog   [Tab] 8.43   [Tab] 6.546   [Tab] 1.884 [Enter]
   [Tab] Annual Report [Tab] 11.32   [Tab] 9.78   [Tab] 1.54

Time To

✔ Save

8. **Select all the text in the columns, drag the last left tab stop (currently at 4¼" on the horizontal ruler) to the 4½" mark, then deselect the text**
   All the text aligned with this stop is moved. Compare your screen to Figure C-7.

FIGURE C-6: Working with tabs

Tab alignment indicator

Default tab stops

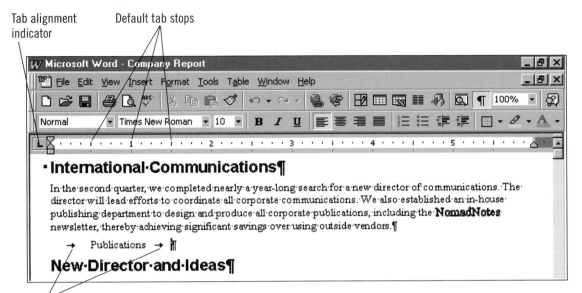

Nonprinting tab marks

FIGURE C-7: Using tabs

Right-aligned tab stop

Left-aligned tab stop

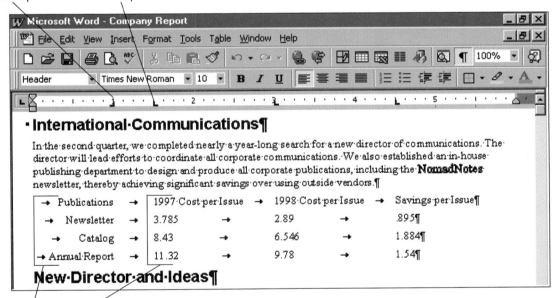

Text aligned with right-aligned tabs

Text aligned with left-aligned tabs

TABLE C-1: Different types of tabs

alignment	description	Button
Left	Text aligns at the left and extends to the right of the tab stop	⌊L⌋
Center	Text aligns at the middle of the tab stop, extending an equal distance to the left and right of the stop	⌊⊥⌋
Right	Text aligns at the right and extends to the left of the tab stop	⌊⌟⌋
Decimal	Text aligns at the decimal point. Text before the decimal extends to the left; the text after the decimal extends to the right	⌊⊥⌋

Changing Paragraph Alignment

Another way to change the appearance of text in a document is to change the alignment of paragraphs. By default your text is left-aligned. However, you can center a paragraph (usually done in a title, or in menus or invitations), or you can right-align a paragraph so that its right edge is even with the right margin (usually seen in dates and signatures of letters). You can also justify a paragraph so that both the left and right edges are even with both margins (as in reports or textbooks). All these alignment options are available on the Formatting toolbar or with the Paragraph command on the Format menu, as shown in Figure C-8. Angela wants the title to stand out, as well as to convey that the document is a first draft. She will use the buttons on the Formatting toolbar to improve the appearance of the document by changing the alignment of specific paragraphs.

Steps

QuickTip

You can also press **[Ctrl] [E]** to center text.

1. Place the insertion point in the first line, **International Communications**, then click the **Center button** on the Formatting toolbar
The first line is centered evenly between the left and right margins of the page. Note that you do not need to select the text in a paragraph to apply paragraph formatting. Next, add a second line of text to the title.

2. Press **[End]** to place the insertion point at the end of the current line, then press **[Enter]**
This inserts a new blank line that is centered between the left and right margins. When you press [Enter], the new paragraph "inherits" the paragraph and font formatting from the previous paragraph.

3. Type **First Draft**
The text is centered automatically as you type. Next, use justified formatting to give the report a more formal appearance.

QuickTip

You can also press **[Ctrl] [J]** to justify text.

4. Place the insertion point in the first body paragraph and click the **Justify button** on the Formatting toolbar
This formatting creates even left and right edges of the paragraph. Continue formatting each of the remaining body paragraphs.

5. Repeat step 4 in each of the remaining five body paragraphs
Compare your document to Figure C-9. Next align the closing text at the end of the document so that it is aligned at the right margin.

QuickTip

You can also press **[Ctrl] [R]** to right align text.

6. Press **[Ctrl] [End]** to place the insertion point at the end of the document, then click the **Align Right button** on the Formatting toolbar
This formatting places the right edge of the text "Nomad Ltd" at the right margin. Include the month and year as part of the closing.

7. Press **[Enter]** and type **Sept**, press **[Enter]**, press **[Spacebar]** and then type **1998**
The AutoComplete feature allows you to type the first few characters of a word and a tag above the text displays the word that Word will insert if you press [Enter]. Notice that the text in the new line remains right-aligned. Compare the end of your document to Figure C-10.

8. Save the document

FIGURE C-8: Paragraph dialog box

Click here to
display paragraph
alignment options

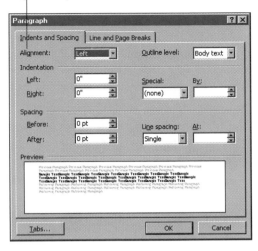

FIGURE C-9: Paragraph formatting changes

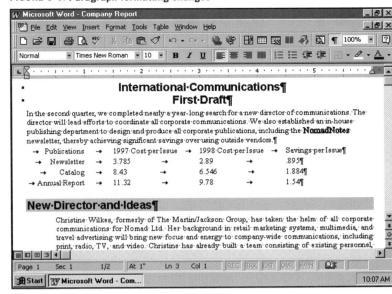

FIGURE C-10: Additional formatting changes

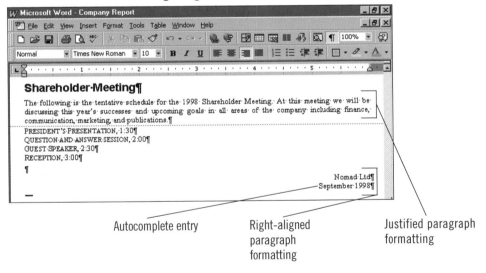

Autocomplete entry

Right-aligned
paragraph
formatting

Justified paragraph
formatting

Indenting Paragraphs

One way to add structure to the appearance of a document is to increase the white space by changing the indentation of individual paragraphs. When you indent a paragraph you are changing the width of each line in the paragraph. You can modify the indentation from the right or left edge of the document, or both. You can indent paragraphs using three methods: with the buttons on the Formatting toolbar, the Paragraph command on the Format menu, and the horizontal ruler. Angela would like to indent several paragraphs in her document to reflect the structure of her document. For example, she wants subtopics to be indented under main ideas.

Steps 1234

1. **Place the insertion point in the paragraph under the heading New Director and Ideas and click the Increase Indent button 📑 on the Formatting toolbar**
   Clicking the Increase Indent button indents the left edge of the paragraph to the first tab stop. To give your document structure, make the "In-House Publishing" heading a subtopic under the heading "New Director and Ideas."

2. **Place the insertion point in the heading In-House Publishing and click 📑**
   Next change the left and right indentation of the next heading and two body paragraphs using the Paragraph command.

3. **Select the body paragraph under the heading In-House Publishing through the body paragraph under Newsletter Update, click Format on the menu bar, and then click Paragraph**
   The Paragraph dialog box appears. Make sure the Indents and Spacing tab appears foremost in the dialog box.

4. **In the Indentation area, click the up arrow in the Left box until you see 1" and in the Right box click the up arrow until you see 0.5"**

5. **Click OK, then deselect the text**
   Word changes the left and right indentation for these paragraphs, as shown in Figure C-11.

6. **Select the heading Catalog Re-designed and the body paragraph that follows, drag the First Line Indent marker ▽ on the ruler to the half-inch mark** Dragging the first line indent marker indents only the first line of text in a paragraph. To have all the lines in the paragraph be indented the same amount, adjust the indentation for the remaining lines of the paragraph.

7. **Drag the Hanging Indent marker △ to the half-inch mark**
   Dragging the hanging indent marker indents the remaining lines of the paragraph (the first line of the paragraph does not move). Although this formatting indents all the lines in these paragraphs in the same way, they are not indented enough to identify the text as a subtopic.

8. **Drag the Left Indent marker ▣ to the 1" mark**
   Dragging this marker indents all the lines of the paragraph at once. The next heading, body paragraph, and list should also be indented.

9. **Select the heading Shareholder Meeting through the end of the list, and then drag the Left Indent marker ▣ to the half-inch mark**

10. **Select all the text from Catalog Re-designed through the last body paragraph, and drag the Right Indent marker △ to the 5.5" mark, then deselect the text**
    You have completed changing the indentation of the paragraphs in the document. Compare your document to Figure C-12.

Trouble?

Word hides settings in a dialog box when you have selected text that includes different format settings for the same feature.

Time To
✔ Save

FIGURE C-11: Indented paragraphs

First Line Indent marker

Hanging Indent marker

Left Indent marker

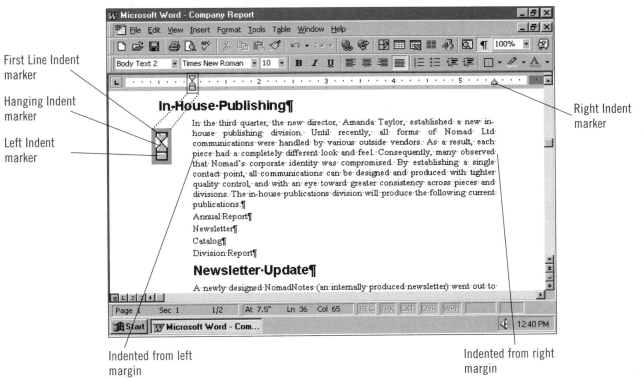

Right Indent marker

Indented from left margin

Indented from right margin

FIGURE C-12: More indented paragraphs

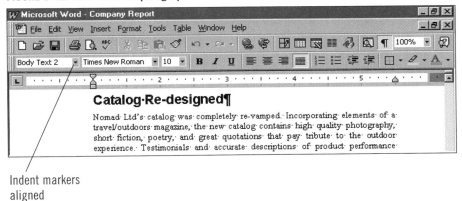

Indent markers aligned

Using Hanging Indent Paragraph Formatting

Sometimes you want a paragraph formatted so that the first line of paragraph is not indented as much as the text in the remaining lines. This formatting is known as a **hanging indent**, as shown in Figure C-13. Hanging indent formatting is usually seen in product or features lists or in glossaries. Notice the arrangement of the indent markers on the horizontal ruler and the indentation of the first and remaining lines of the paragraph. You can create a hanging indent by dragging the hanging indent marker on the horizontal ruler.

FIGURE C-13: Hanging indent

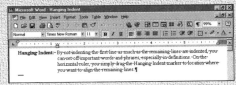

Changing Paragraph Spacing

Another way to make a document easier to read is to increase the amount of spacing between lines. For example, increase the line spacing in documents where you expect readers to add written comments (as in thesis papers or draft versions of a document). Line spacing options are available with the Paragraph command on the Format menu. You can also increase the amount of space between paragraphs to better separate ideas in paragraphs. ✎ Angela would like to provide space in this draft document for comments from her colleagues in the Marketing Department. She'll increase the line spacing and the spacing before and after the list of publications for written feedback.

1. Select the entire document by pressing **[Ctrl][A]**

2. Click **Format** on the menu bar, then click **Paragraph**
   The Paragraph dialog box opens where you can change the line spacing from the default single spacing.

3. Click the **Line spacing list arrow**, click **1.5 lines**, then click **OK**
   The dialog box closes and the paragraphs appear with 1.5 line spacing between the lines. So that the list below the "In-House Publishing" heading is easier to read, you can increase the space after the list.

4. Place the insertion point in the line **Annual Report**, right-click the mouse, click **Paragraph** in the pop-up menu, and then click the **Indents and Spacing tab**
   Using the right mouse button is a handy way to format paragraphs.

5. Click the **up arrow** next to the **Spacing After box** three times until you see **18 pt** in the box
   Each time you click the arrow, the value in the box increases by 6 points. As you click, notice that the Preview area of the dialog box displays the effect of your changes.

6. Click **OK**
   The space between the list and the following body paragraph increases. Next increase the space before the tabbed list.

7. Place the insertion point in the first line of the tabbed list, click **Format** on the menu bar, then click **Paragraph**

Time To

✔ Save

8. Click the **up arrow** next to the **Spacing Before box** twice until you see **12 pt** in the box and click **OK**
   Compare your screen to Figure C-14. You have finished adjusting paragraph spacing for now.

FIGURE C-14: Increased spacing in a document

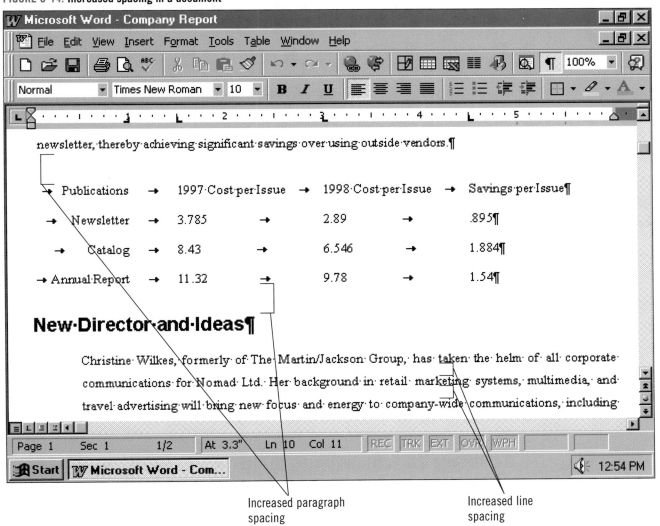

Increased paragraph
spacing

Increased line
spacing

Word 97

Creating Bulleted and Numbered Lists

When you group paragraphs in a list, you can create a bulleted list. In a bulleted list, each paragraph in the list is preceded by a **bullet**, a small symbol such as a circle or square. With the Bullets button on the Formatting toolbar, you can insert a bullet in front of each item in a list. When you want to show items in a sequence, a numbered list best reflects the order or priority of the items. To create a simple numbered list (starting with the numeral "1"), you can use the Numbering button on the Formatting toolbar. You can also use the Bullets and Numbering command on the Format menu to specify additional bullet and numbering formatting options. Angela decides to draw attention to the lists in her document by formatting them with bullets and numbering.

1. Select the list of four publications starting with **Annual Report**, click the **Bullets button** ⊞ on the Formatting toolbar, and then deselect the text
A bullet character appears in front of each item in the list as shown in Figure C-15. Next change the type of bullet shape.

2. Select the four items in the list, click **Format** on the menu bar, then click **Bullets and Numbering**
The Bullets and Numbering dialog box opens, as shown in Figure C-16. In this dialog box, you can choose from seven different bullet styles. You can also change any of the seven styles to use whatever shape you prefer. Change to the arrow style.

3. Click the third box in the second row and click **OK**
The list appears as a bulleted list with a small arrow in front of each line.

4. Click the **Increase Indent button** ⊞ on the Formatting toolbar until the bullets are aligned with the text in the previous paragraph
Next add numbering to the schedule at the end of the document.

5. Select the four items in the meeting schedule at the end of the document, then click the **Numbering button** ⊞ on the Formatting toolbar
The schedule is now a numbered list. Because you would like to view alternate numbering formats, use the Bullets and Numbering command available on a pop-up menu.

6. If necessary, select the four lines of the schedule, then right-click the selected text
A pop-up menu appears, from which you can select the Bullets and Numbering command.

7. Click **Bullets and Numbering** on the pop-up menu, then click the **Numbered tab**, if necessary, in the dialog box
The Numbered tab in the Bullets and Numbering dialog box displays additional numbering options. To impart a more formal tone to the text, choose a Roman numeral format.

8. In the first row, click the **Roman numeral** (the fourth) option and click **OK**
The bullets in the list change to Roman numerals.

9. Click the **Increase Indent button** ⊞ until the numbers are aligned with the text in the previous paragraph, then deselect the text
Compare your document to Figure C-17.

QuickTip

If you right-click a paragraph in a bulleted or numbered list, the pop-up menu provides paragraph formatting options, including the Bullets and Numbering command.

Time To

✔ Save

FIGURE C-15: Bulleted list

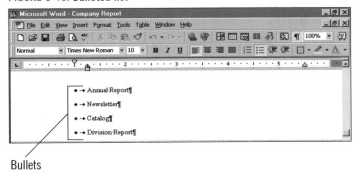

Bullets

FIGURE C-16: Bulleted tab in Bullets and Numbering dialog box

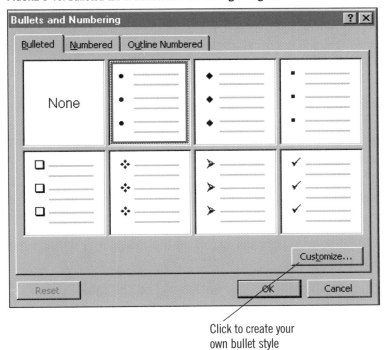

Click to create your
own bullet style

FIGURE C-17: Numbered list

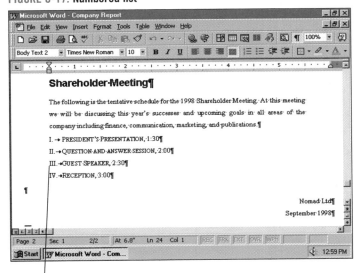

Roman numerals

Applying Borders and Shading

Borders add visual interest to paragraphs of text. **Borders** are lines you can add to the top, bottom, or sides of paragraphs. Preset border settings make it easy to create a box around a paragraph. You can also use shading to offer even more visual interest to paragraphs of text. **Shading** is a background color or pattern you add behind the text of a paragraph. With the Tables and Borders toolbar you can apply borders and shading options you use most often, or you can use the Borders and Shading command to select from additional border and shading options. 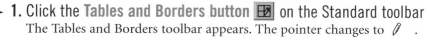 Angela wants to use borders and shading to emphasize the title and main topics in the document. First, she'll add a double-lined box around the title to give the document a more formal appearance.

Trouble?

If you see the Office Assistant, click the Cancel button in the Office Assistant window to work without the Office Assistant.

1. Click the **Tables and Borders button** ⊞ on the Standard toolbar
The Tables and Borders toolbar appears. The pointer changes to ✏ .

2. Click the **Draw Table button** ✏ on the Tables and Borders toolbar to deactivate the Draw Table feature for now
You can move the toolbar anywhere you want by dragging it to a new location. The document now appears in Page Layout view, as shown in Figure C-18. Now you can select the text you want to format.

3. Select the first two lines (the title) of the document
Next select the style of border you want to apply.

4. Click the **Line Style list arrow** on the Tables and Borders toolbar and scroll to select the **double line**

QuickTip

You can quickly remove a border for a selected paragraph by verifying that the line style matches the border you want to remove and then clicking the button that corresponds to the line you want to remove.

5. Click the **Outside Border button** ▣ on the Tables and Borders toolbar
A double-line box border surrounds the text, spanning the width of the margins. Next emphasize the main headings in the document by adding shading.

6. Select the **New Director and Ideas heading** and the **paragraph mark**, then click the **Shading Color list arrow**
Change the shaded background to gray.

7. Click **Gray 25%** (the third option in the second row)
The text appears with a gray background. To apply the same shading to the other main headings in the document, repeat the last command to selected text.

8. For each of the remaining four headings, select the heading and its paragraph mark and click **Edit on the menu bar**, and then click **Repeat Shading Color**
The other main headings are formatted with shading. You have finished formatting your document for now, so hide the Tables and Borders toolbar.

QuickTip

A fast way to repeat the previous command is to press [F4].

9. Click the **Close button** ☒ on the Tables and Borders toolbar
The Tables and Borders toolbar is no longer displayed. Compare your document to Figure C-19.

10. Save your work, then close and exit Word.

FIGURE C-18: Tables and Borders toolbar

Tables and
Borders toolbar

Line Style list
arrow

Shading Color
list arrow

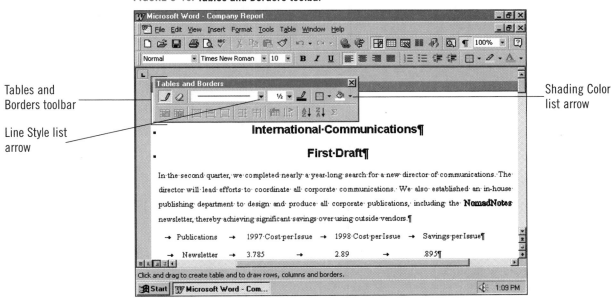

FIGURE C-19: Gray shading in a document

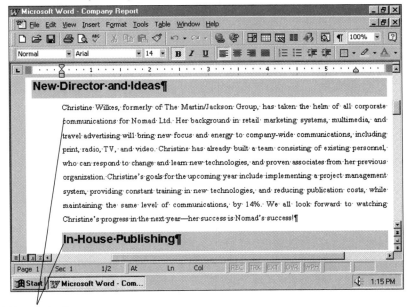

Light gray shading
applied

Creating borders with the Borders and Shading command

The Tables and Borders toolbar provides the most frequently used border and shading options. However, even more border and shading options are available with the Borders and Shading command on the Format menu. This command displays the Borders and Shading dialog box. On the Borders tab, you can select box and shadowed box preset borders, as well as specify the color of the border. You can also indicate how far away from the text the border should appear. On the Shading tab, you can specify the color of both the foreground and background of the shaded area. This feature allows you to customize the intensity of the shading you apply to text.

Practice

► Concepts Review

Label each of the formatting elements shown in Figure C-20

FIGURE C-20

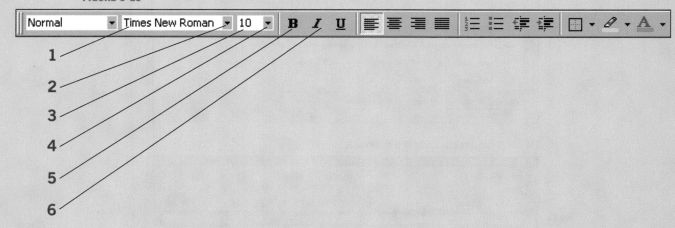

Match each of the following terms with the statement that best describes it or its function.

7. **Font**
8. **Bold**
9. **Font effect**
10. **Bullets**
11. **Numbering**
12. **Borders**
13. **Paragraph formatting**

a. Character formatting such as hidden text and small caps
b. The design set of characters
c. Text which appears darker
d. Used to reflect a sequence of events or importance in a list
e. Symbols or graphics preceding items in a list
f. Lines added to paragraphs of text
g. Changes the line spacing, alignment, and space between paragraphs

Select the best answer from the list of choices.

14. **Which paragraph formatting feature is not available on the Formatting toolbar?**
   a. Paragraph alignment
   b. Line spacing
   c. Decrease indentation
   d. Increase indentation

15. **To add a specific amount of space between paragraphs, the best solution is to:**
   a. Press [Enter] until you get the amount of space you want
   b. Use the Spacing Before and After options in the Paragraph dialog box
   c. Adjust the top margin for each paragraph
   d. Use the Line Spacing options in the Paragraph dialog box

16. **Which of the following automatically adds a bullet to selected text?**
   a. Right-clicking in a bulleted list
   b. Clicking Format on the menu bar, then clicking Bullets and Numbering
   c. Clicking the Bullets button on the Formatting toolbar
   d. Pressing [Ctrl][B] on the keyboard

17. A hanging indent refers to formatting in which:
a. The text in the first line is not indented as much as the remaining lines of a paragraph
b. All lines of a paragraph are indented more than the paragraph above it
c. All lines of a paragraph are aligned under the same tab stop
d. The text in the first line is indented more than the remaining lines of a paragraph

18. You can choose alternative bullet graphics from which of the following dialog boxes?
a. Bullets and Numbering
b. Change Bullets
c. WingDings
d. Symbol

19. Which button do you click when you want to apply shading to text?
a. Borders
b. Tables and Borders
c. Borders and Shading
d. Shading

20. You can access the shading feature by
a. Clicking Format on the menu bar, then clicking Paragraph
b. Clicking the Border button on the Formatting toolbar
c. Clicking the right mouse button in a paragraph
d. Clicking Format on the menu bar, then clicking Borders and Shading

▶ Skills Review

1. Apply font effects using the toolbar.
a. Launch Word.
b. Open the document named WD C-2, then save the document as "Shipping Letter".
c. Select the text "RoadMap" and click the Italic button on the Formatting toolbar.
d. With the text still selected, click the Underline button. Then click the Italic button to remove the italic formatting.
e. With the text still selected, click the Font list arrow and choose Arial.
f. Click the Font Size box on the Formatting toolbar and type "10.5" and press Enter.
g. Repeat Steps c-f for the second occurrence of the word RoadMap.

2. Apply special font effects using the Font command.
a. Select the first occurrence of "Open Roads, Inc."
b. Click Font on the Format menu, choose Arial, then 12 pts, then Bold.
c. In the Effects area, click the Outline box and All caps box, then click OK.
d. With the text still selected, double-click the Format Painter button on the Standard toolbar. With the Format Painter pointer, select each occurrence of the company name, "Open Roads, Inc." in the document.
e. Click the Format Painter button on the Standard toolbar.

3. Align text with tabs

   a. Place the insertion point in the blank line above "Our Promise to You…" and press [Enter].

   b. Press [Tab] then type "Weight"; press [Tab] then type "Cost", then press [Enter] to create a new blank line.

   c. Press [Tab] then type "Under 1 lb"; press [Tab] then type "5.25", then press [Enter] to create a new blank line.

   d. Press [Tab] then type "1 - 10 lbs"; press [Tab] then type "10.75".

   e. Select all three lines of the list and place a left-aligned tab stop at the 2" mark.

   f. With the same three lines selected, click the tab alignment indicator at the left end of the ruler until you see the decimal tab marker.

   g. Place a decimal-aligned tab stop at the 4.5" mark.

   h. Press [End] to place the insertion point at the end of the last item, then press [Enter].

   i. Press [Tab] and type "More than 10 lbs", press [Tab] and type "14.50", save your changes.

4. Apply paragraph formatting

   a. Press [Ctrl][Home] to place the insertion point at the beginning of the document.

   b. Type today's date and press [Enter].

   c. Place the insertion point in the date line, then click the Center button on the Formatting toolbar.

   d. Select the text of the signature block. Click Format on the menu bar, then click Paragraph. In the Indentation area, scroll the Left up arrow until you see 4.5". Click OK to return to your document.

   e. Select all of the body paragraphs (including the list).

   f. Click Format on the menu bar, then click Paragraph.

   g. In the Line Spacing area, choose 1.5 lines, then click OK.

   h. Select the "Generate pre-printed. . . ." line, and then click Paragraph on the Format menu.

   i. In the After box, click the up arrow until you see 12, then click OK.

   j. Select the three body paragraphs, from "Thank you. . ." to ". . . you have."

   k. Click the Justify button on the Formatting toolbar.

   l. Be sure to select the placeholder "[Your Name]" and replace it with your name.

   m. Save your changes.

5. Create bulleted and numbered lists

   a. Select the list of three items starting with "track the location. . ." and ending with "generate pre-printed. . . . "

   b. Click the Numbers button on the Formatting toolbar, then click to deselect the text.

   c. Select the same three lines of text and right-click the selected text.

   d. Click the Bullets and Numbering command on the pop-up menu, then click the Bulleted tab.

   e. Choose a bullet pattern you like, then click OK.

6. Apply borders and shading

   a. Click Toolbars on the View menu, then choose Tables and Borders.

   b. With the insertion point in the line containing the date, choose the $1\frac{1}{2}$ pt line from the Line Style box on the Tables and Borders toolbar.

   c. Click the Bottom Border button on the Tables and Borders toolbar.

   d. Select the list of shipping prices, starting with the line containing "Weight" and "Cost."

   e. Choose the $\frac{3}{4}$ pt line from the Line Style box on the Borders toolbar.

   f. Click the Outside Border button on the Tables and Borders toolbar.

   g. Select the first line of the list and choose the $1\frac{1}{2}$ pt line from the Line Style box on the Borders toolbar.

h. Click the Bottom Border button on the Tables and Borders toolbar.
i. Select the paragraph under the heading in the middle of the document, and choose 25% shading from the Shading box on the Tables and Borders toolbar.
j. Click Toolbars on the View menu, then choose Tables and Borders to hide the Tables and Borders toolbar.
k. Save your changes to the document, print the document, and exit Word.

Independent Challenges

1. As a committee member assigned to plan the Carson Associates Family Weekend, you have been asked to design the announcement for the Carson Classic golf tournament. Another committee member has begun the document by entering some of the tournament information. Open the document WD C-3 and save it as "Golf Classic". Using Figure C-22 as your guide, enhance the appearance of the document using font and paragraph formatting.

To complete this Independent Challenge:

1. Center the title of the document, and change the font to Arial, Bold, Italics, 18 pt.
2. Add 25% Gray shading to the title.
3. Center the paragraph after the title.
4. Add the information about time and location in a list in the center of the document using tabs. Press [Tab] before and after the word "Where".
5. Place a right tab stop at the 1½" mark and a left tab stop at the 2" mark for the tournament information.
6. Center the heading "Schedule". Format this heading in Bold, Arial.
7. Add numbers to the schedule of events. Left align this list.
8. Place a 1½ pt line above the line "Complete and send the attached…"
9. Preview the document and click the Shrink to Fit button if the document does not appear on one page.
10. Save, and print the memo, then close it.

FIGURE C-21

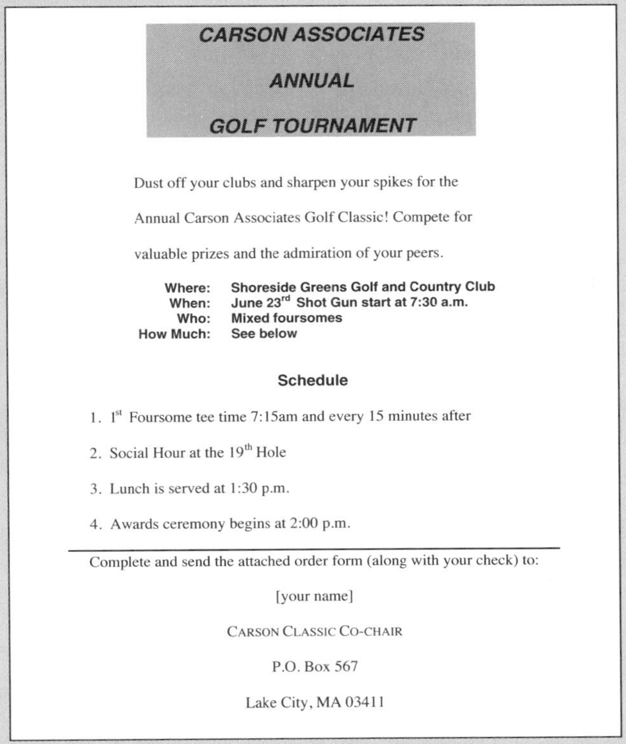

CARSON ASSOCIATES

ANNUAL

GOLF TOURNAMENT

Dust off your clubs and sharpen your spikes for the Annual Carson Associates Golf Classic! Compete for valuable prizes and the admiration of your peers.

Where: Shoreside Greens Golf and Country Club
When: June 23rd Shot Gun start at 7:30 a.m.
Who: Mixed foursomes
How Much: See below

Schedule

1. 1st Foursome tee time 7:15am and every 15 minutes after
2. Social Hour at the 19th Hole
3. Lunch is served at 1:30 p.m.
4. Awards ceremony begins at 2:00 p.m.

Complete and send the attached order form (along with your check) to:

[your name]

CARSON CLASSIC CO-CHAIR

P.O. Box 567

Lake City, MA 03411

2. As coordinator for the Carson Associates Golf Classic, you have been asked to create a certificate to be awarded to the golfer with the longest drive. Open the document WD C-4 and save it as "Golf Certificate". Enhance the appearance of the certificate using font and paragraph formatting. After completing the certificate, access the World Wide Web to plan a golfing vacation in Arizona.

To complete this Independent Challenge:

1. Center all the text.
2. Format the title with 36 pt, bold, italicized, Comic Sans Ms font. In the Font dialog box, apply the shadow effect.
3. Use 1.5 line spacing in all paragraphs.
4. Use 24 pt font on all the text except the title and the text "Longest Drive". Use 36 pt font on this text.
5. Use 12 pt line spacing before and after the date and before the line "for the." Use 12 pt line spacing before and after the line "Presented".
6. Place a 1½ pt line under the line "Recipient" for writing the winner's name.
7. Type your name and title at the bottom of the award. Right align this text and Format it at 24points.
8. Place a ½ pt border above your name for your signature.
9. Drag the Indent marker to the 2" mark.
10. Preview, save, and print the certificate, then close it.
11. Log on to the Internet and use your browser to go to http://course.com. From there, click Student On Line Companions, and then click the link to go to the Microsoft Office 97 Professional Edition-Illustrated: A First Course page, then click on the word link for Unit C.

3. As co-chair for the Lake City High School class of 1993 reunion, you need to draft a memo to the planning committee members informing them of the place and times of committee meetings. Since you are unsure of how to format this memo, you will use the Memo Wizard which will request information about your memo and will format it for you. After the memo is created, you can adjust the formatting to your own preferences. You will save this memo as "Reunion Memo".

To complete this Independent Challenge:

1. Create a new document using the Memo Wizard on the Memo tab in the New dialog box. Choose the Professional memo style.
2. After you answer the questions on each page of the Wizard dialog boxes, then click Next.
3. Enter "Reunion Memo" for the Title.
4. Enter the date, your name, and the topic "Meeting dates". Clear the CC check box.
5. Clear all boxes except Writer's initials and page numbers on the next two pages. Click Finished on the last page.
6. Format the title with Arial, Bold, 14 pt font. Underline the title with a 1½ pt line.
7. Center the title.
8. Create appropriate paragraph text and meeting dates and times.
9. Format the document attractively with borders, shading, bullets, and paragraph formatting a double-line 1½ pt border and 20% gray shading and 6 pt After paragraph formatting.
10. Preview, save, and print the memo, then close it.

4. As an account representative for Lease For Less, a company that rents various office equipment such as fax machines and large copiers, you need to draft a letter explaining the corporate discount program to a current customer. Instead of formatting your letter from scratch, you can use one of Word's letter templates to automatically format parts of the letter for you. You can modify the formatting after the letter is complete. Save this document as "Discount Letter". Use Figure C-22 as a guide to complete the letter.

To complete this Independent Challenge:

1. Use the Professional Letter Template on the Letter tab in the New dialog box.
2. Type the company name and format it with 100% Black shading.
3. Type the return address. Format the Font Size to 9 pt.
4. Type the customer name, address, and body of the letter.
5. Add the bulleted list at the bottom of the letter. Choose any bulleted style you like. Then indent the bulleted list to the 1" mark.
6. Format the Bulleted list to have 6 pt spacing after each line. (Hint: Select all lines at one time.)
7. Add the company name to the signature.
8. Format the letter and company name font in Bold and Shadowed.
9. If you are asked to save changes to the wizard, click No.
10. Preview, save, and print the document, then close it.

FIGURE C-22

Lease for Less	7809 South Washington Drive
	Suite 13B
	Sandy Hills, MN 56789

September 25, 1998

Ms. Louise Rand
River Industries
1 Main St.
Upton, NY 54005

Dear Ms. Rand:

Thank you for your inquiry about a corporate discount for our copier rentals. Enclosed is the information you requested. In addition, I have also included the premier issue of **WorkADay**, our newsletter.

To be eligible for a corporate discount, you must contact to rent 2 or more of our fax or copier machines for at least six months. Of course all of our machines come with unlimited service by our highly trained technicians. As a corporate customer, you will receive a 10% discount on general office rentals and a 15% discount for our industrial copiers including color copy machines. As your account representative, I would be pleased to discuss your office requirements with you. I will call you to arrange a time when we can meet.

With a corporate discount you can rent any of the following office machines:

- Industrial copy machines with correlating, automatic feed, and stapling features.
- Basic copy machines
- Color copiers
- Fax machines
- Binders
- Laminating machines

Sincerely,

[your name]
Lease for Less
Account Representative

Visual Workshop

As fundraising coordinator for Companies for Kids, you have been asked to create a letter to local company owners asking for donations of money and time. Use the Letter Wizard and choose the Elegant letter style to create your letter. After entering text, modify the formatting to improve the appearance of the letter even further. Save the document as "Elegant Kids Letter". Using Figure C-23 as a guide, complete the formatting for the document. Preview, save, and print your document before closing it.

FIGURE C-23

COMPANIES FOR KIDS

October 24, 1998

Jake Wilson
Wilson Jewelers
1014 Farmington Drive
Hillside, CA 92407

Dear Mr. Wilson:

Thank you for your recent inquiry into the COMPANIES FOR KIDS corporate sponsorship program. We are a non-profit community program that attempts to collect toys clothing, and various necessary materials for children in local shelters. We depend largely on local businesses to help fund our efforts.

Your company's time, services, and donations will benefit children in need. You may choose to donate time and services. Each weekend COMPANIES FOR KIDS sends out a number of teams to collect clothing and toys from the community. We are desperately in need of organized teams to help us in this effort. Your company may also choose to help our children in need in any or all of the following ways:

- Monetary donation.

- Teams of company workers to sort or collect clothing and toys.

- Time spent with children in local shelters

I hope we can look forward to your company's support participation in this valuable community program.

Sincerely,

[your name]
COMPANIES FOR KIDS
Fundraising Coordinator

[STREET ADDRESS] • [CITY/STATE] • [ZIP/POSTAL CODE]
PHONE: [PHONE NUMBER] • FAX: [FAX NUMBER]

Working
with Tables

► **Create a new table**
► **Convert text to a table**
► **Insert and delete rows and columns**
► **Calculate data in a table**
► **Sort information in a table**
► **Format a table**
► **Use the Draw Table button**
► **Modify a table with the Tables and Borders toolbar**

In this unit you'll learn how to format text in a table. A **table** is text arranged in a grid of rows and columns. With Word, you can add or delete information in a table without having to manually reformat the entire table. You can sort and calculate information that appears in a table and quickly make attractive tables using preset table formats. You can also customize your tables to fit your exact needs by drawing rows and columns exactly where you would like them. Tables are an excellent tool for displaying data normally found in lists or columns. Nomad Ltd has acquired an adventure travel company called Alpine Adventures. With the acquisition, Angela would like to improve the appearance of Alpine's newsletter. Because the newsletter includes pricing information, Angela uses tables to present this information to readers.

Creating a New Table

To create a blank table, you can use the Insert Table button on the Standard toolbar. Or you can use the Insert Table command on the Table menu. Angela thinks it might help potential customers decide which tour to take if they know the number of participants and general age group for each tour. She will present this information in a table.

Steps

1. Launch Word

2. Open the document named WD D-1 and save it as **Package Tours 1998**
   Begin by placing the insertion point near the end of the document.

3. Scroll to the end of the document and place the insertion point in front of the paragraph mark above the heading **Time to Leave?**
   Now you can create your table.

4. Click the **Insert Table button** on the Standard toolbar, then drag in the grid to select three rows and five columns, as shown in Figure D-1, and then click the mouse
   A blank table appears in the document. To see the entire width of the table, you might need to adjust the magnification.

5. Click in the **Zoom box** on the Standard toolbar, type **95** and then press **[Enter]**
   Compare your table to Figure D-2. A **cell** is the intersection of a row and column. Inside each cell is a **cell marker**, which identifies the end of the contents in the cell. The end of each row is identified with an **end-of-row marker**. **Borders** surround each cell so you can see the structure of the table. Neither the cell markers nor the end-of-row markers appear when you print the document. Next, you enter the information you want in the table.

6. In the first cell, type **Tour**, then press **[Tab]**
   Pressing [Tab] selects the next cell in a table. Pressing [Shift][Tab] selects the previous cell. You continue entering text in the table.

7. Type **Under 20**, press **[Tab]**, type **20-34**, press **[Tab]**, type **35-50**, press **[Tab]**, type **Over 50** and press **[Tab]**
   Pressing [Tab] at the end of a row selects the first cell in the next row. You continue entering text in the table, pressing [Tab] after each cell.

8. Type the following text in the table as indicated below (for now, *do not press [Tab] at the end of the last row*)

Country Culture	15	20	25	45
Pastoral Idyll	20	35	30	15

   At the end of the last row, you decide to add a new row to the bottom of the table.

Time To

✔ Save

9. Press **[Tab]** to create a new row, and type the following text in the table as indicated below (*do not press [Tab] at the end of the last row*)

Mountain Top	45	35	15	5

   Compare your table to Figure D-3.

FIGURE D-1: Dragging to specify rows and columns

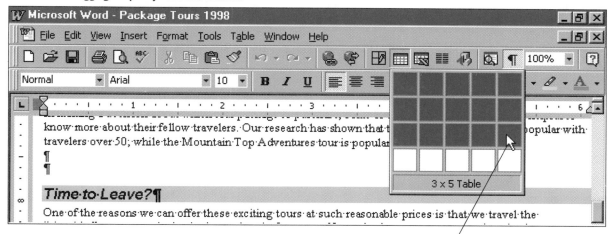

Drag to specify
rows and columns

FIGURE D-2: New table in a document

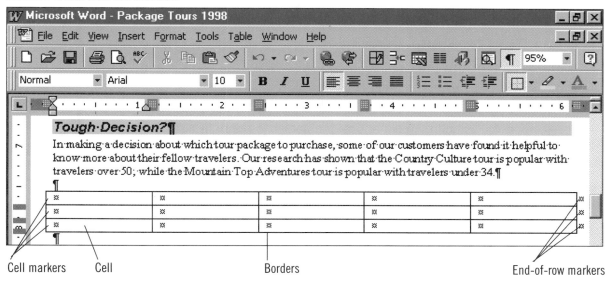

Cell markers   Cell   Borders   End-of-row markers

FIGURE D-3: Completed table

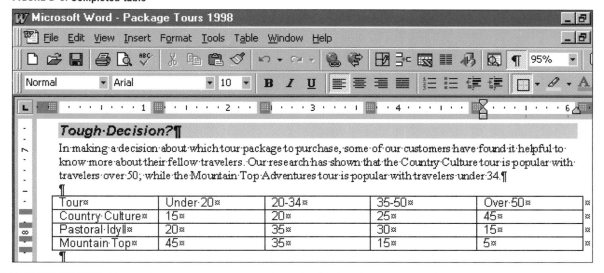

Tour	Under 20	20-34	35-50	Over 50	
Country Culture	15	20	25	45	
Pastoral Idyll	20	35	30	15	
Mountain Top	45	35	15	5	

Converting Text to a Table

You can convert existing text into a table by selecting the text and then using the Insert Table button on the Standard toolbar. The text you are converting to a table must be formatted with tabs, commas, or paragraph marks so that Word can interpret the formatting and create the table. ◢▬▬ Angela wants to convert the text about tour prices to a table so that readers will be able to quickly identify pricing information.

1. **Scroll to the top of the document, and select the four lines that begin with Tour and end with Country Culture**
   Because this text is already formatted with tabs, you can convert it to a table.

2. **Click the Insert Table button ▦ on the Standard toolbar**
   Clicking this button is the same as choosing Insert Table from the Table menu or the Convert Text to Table command on the Table menu.

3. **Deselect the highlighted table**
   The selected text appears in a table format, as shown in Figure D-4. Because one column is too narrow for the text to fit appropriately, you need to adjust the column width.

4. **Position the pointer over the border to the right of the column heading Lodging until the pointer changes to ◀▮▶, then drag to the right slightly so that the heading appears on one line**
   Notice how the height of the row automatically adjusts to accommodate the amount of text that is in the tallest cell in the row. You can also customize the size of the row to a specific height.

5. **Select the text Tour in the first cell of the first row, then type Twelve-day Package Tour**
   The row height adjusts to accommodate the text you type, but notice that the column width does not adjust automatically.

6. **Place the insertion point in the empty cell below Trains and type 50**
   The last price in this column is also missing, so you move to the last cell and enter the new price.

7. **Press [Alt][PgDn] to move to the last cell in the fourth column, then type 75**
   This keyboard shortcut moves you quickly to the last cell in a column. Your table is revised, as shown in Figure D-5, so you save your work.

Trouble?

If the width of only one cell in the column changes when you adjust the column width, deselect the cell, then click the Undo button ↶ on the Standard toolbar. You must deselect the cell before adjusting the column width, if you want to adjust the width of the entire column.

Time To

✔ Save

FIGURE D-4: Text converted to a table

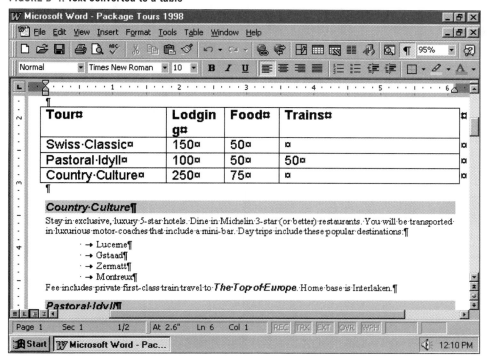

FIGURE D-5: Completed table

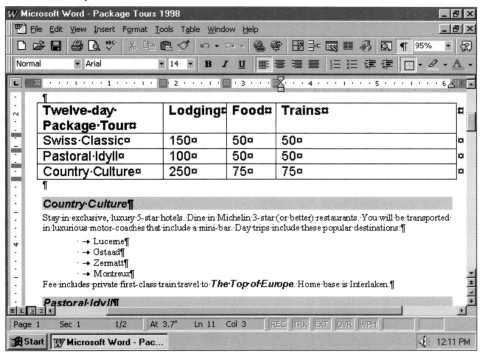

Adjusting row height

To establish a specific row height you can use the Cell Height and Width command on the Table menu. This command displays a dialog box in which you can specify a fixed height for rows. Use this feature when you want to make all the rows in a table the same height. You may also use the Cell Height and Width command to make all columns in a table the same width.

Inserting and Deleting Rows and Columns

You often need to change the number of rows or columns so that you can add or remove information. You can quickly add or delete rows and columns using the commands on the Table menu or use the commands on the pop-up menu for tables.  Nomad Ltd has determined that Alpine Adventures should discontinue the Swiss Classic tour and add a new budget-oriented tour. Angela will delete the row containing the Swiss Classic information, add a row for the new tour, and also add a Total column that displays the total price of each tour.

Steps

1. **Place the insertion point in the Swiss Classic row of the first table, then click the right mouse button**
   The pop-up menu for tables appears. This menu contains the commands you are most likely to use when working in a table.

2. **Click Delete Cells...**
   The Delete Cells dialog box opens. In this dialog box, you can specify the cells you want to remove from the table. Delete the row for the discontinued tour.

3. **Click Delete Entire Row, then click OK**
   This command deletes the row containing the insertion point. Now, add a new row.

4. **Click the Insert Rows button [icon] on the Standard toolbar**
   Notice that the Insert Table button and name changes based on what is currently selected. Next enter the information for the new tour.

5. **Type Mountain Top, press [Tab], then type the following numbers in the cells in the new row: 75   0   20**
   Before adding a new column to the end of the table, you must adjust the width of the last column so that the new column will fit on the page.

6. **Position the pointer over the border to the right of the last column until the pointer changes to ◄‖►, drag to the left to the 5" mark on the horizontal ruler**
   Next, you create a new column at the end of the table for the total price of each tour. To do so, you must first select the end-of-row markers to the right of the last column in the table.

7. **At the top-right of the table, position the pointer above the end-of-row marker, and when the pointer changes to ↓, click the left mouse button as shown in Figure D-6**
   This selects the column of end-of-row markers.

8. **Click Table on the menu bar, then click Insert Columns**
   A new blank column appears at the right end of the table. You can also click the Insert Columns button [icon] on the Standard toolbar to insert a new column (again the Insert Table button will change based on what is selected). Word places the insertion point in the first cell of the new column when you begin typing.

9. **Leaving the column selected, type Total**
   Compare your document to Figure D-7.

FIGURE D-6: Adding a column to the end of the table

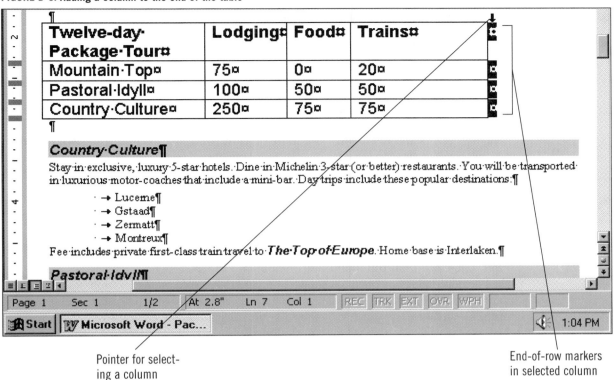

Pointer for select-
ing a column

End-of-row markers
in selected column

FIGURE D-7: Completed table

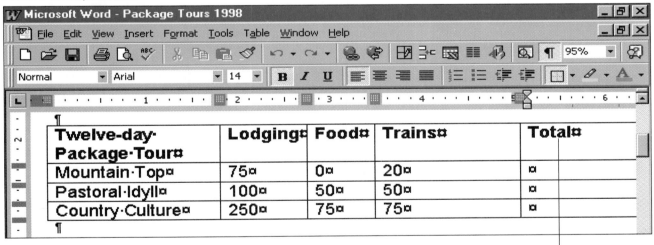

New column and text

Using the selection bar in tables

The area to the left of each row in a table contains the selection bar. Clicking in the selection bar to the left of a row selects that row in the same way clicking in the selection bar to the left of a line of text selects the entire line. In addition, each cell in the table contains its own selection bar. You can click the selection bar to the left of text in a cell to select an individual cell.

Calculating Data in a Table

Your table can include calculations based on the numbers in rows and columns. The Formula command allows you to perform calculations on data in a table. Built-in formulas make it easy to quickly perform standard calculations (such as totals or averages). Using formulas prevents mathematical errors and helps you work more quickly. You can also enter your own formulas. In addition, you can also change data in a table and update calculations. To provide the tour price for each tour, Angela uses the Formula command and a built-in formula to calculate the total cost per day for each tour.

Steps

1. **Place the insertion point in the cell below the Total cell in the first table of the document, click Table on the menu bar, then click Formula**
   The Formula dialog box opens, as shown in Figure D-8. Based on the location of the insertion point in the table, Word suggests a formula in the Formula box—in this case, the built-in SUM formula—and suggests which cells to use in the calculation, the columns to the left. Because these are the values you want to use in this calculation, accept the suggested formula.

2. **Click OK**
   The dialog box closes and the sum of the values in the row appears in the current cell. To calculate the other total values in this column, repeat the last command by pressing [F4].

3. **Press [↓] to move the insertion point to the next cell in the Total column, then press [F4]**
   [F4] is a function key located at the top of your keyboard that repeats the action you just performed. Function keys are used for shortcut commands. After you press [F4], the sum of the values in this row appears in the cell.

4. **Press [↓] to move the insertion point to the last cell in the Total column, then press [F4]**
   The sum of the values in this row appears in the cell. Next, update the cost of lodging for the Country Culture tour to reflect a new lower rate of 200.

5. **Select the last value in the Lodging column, 250, then type 200**
   The new value, 200, replaces the previous value of 250. When you change values used in a calculation, Word does not automatically update the total to reflect a new value, so you need to recalculate the values in the table.

Time To
✔ Save

6. **Select the last value in the Total column, 400, press [F9] and then deselect the cell**
   Word recalculates the total, and "350" appears in the cell, as shown in Figure D-9. Pressing [F9] updates calculations in a table.

FIGURE D-8: Formula dialog box

Formula ? X

Formula:
=SUM(LEFT)

Number format:

Paste function:

Paste bookmark:

OK   Cancel

Suggested formula

FIGURE D-9: Completed table

Microsoft Word - Package Tours 1998

File Edit View Insert Format Tools Table Window Help

Normal   Arial   14   B I U

Twelve-day Package Tour¤	Lodging¤	Food¤	Trains¤	Total¤
Mountain·Top¤	75¤	0¤	20¤	95¤
Pastoral·Idyll¤	100¤	50¤	50¤	200¤
Country·Culture¤	200¤	75¤	75¤	350¤

Recalculated total

Creating your own calculations

To enter your own calculation in the Formula dialog box, you refer to cells in the table using cell references. A cell reference identifies a cell's position in the table. Each cell reference contains a letter (A, B, C and so on) to identify its column and a number (1, 2, 3 and so on) to identify its row. For example, the first cell in the first row is A1, and the second cell in the first row is B1, as you can see in Figure D-10. You can create a formula to multiply, divide, add, and subtract the values of individual cells. Multiplication is represented by an asterisk (*); division is represented by a slash (/). For example, the formula to determine the total price for twelve days of the Country Culture tour would be =E4*12.

FIGURE D-10: Cell references

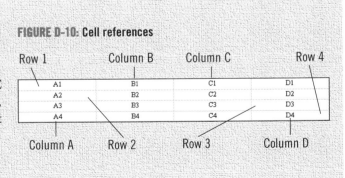

	Column B	Column C	Row 4
Row 1

A1	B1	C1	D1
A2	B2	C2	D2
A3	B3	C3	D3
A4	B4	C4	D4

Column A   Row 2   Row 3   Column D

Sorting Information in a Table

Sometimes the information in a table is easier to interpret if the rows are sorted to appear in a particular order. For example, you might sort a department telephone directory by name, or a project plan by date. You can sort by a single column or by multiple columns. For each column, you can sort in **ascending** or **descending** order. Ascending order (the default) arranges rows from smallest to largest for numbers and from A to Z for text. Descending order arranges rows from largest to smallest for numbers and from Z to A for text. ◢ To arrange the rows in a logical order, Angela sorts the table so that the most expensive tour appears first and the least expensive tour appears last.

Steps

1. **Place the insertion point anywhere in the table**
   You do not need to select the entire table to perform a sort.

2. **Click Table on the menu bar, then click Sort**
   The Sort dialog box opens, as shown in Figure D-11. In this dialog box, you can specify how you want your table sorted. The Sort by list contains the headings for all the columns in the table and displays the heading for the first column by default. Instead, sort the table by the information in the Total column.

3. **Click the Sort by list arrow, then click Total in the list of columns**
   Choose the option to display the tours starting with the most expensive and ending with the least expensive.

4. **Click the Descending radio button in the Sort by section**
   This button sorts rows from the largest value to the smallest value. Next, indicate that you do not want the first row (the column headings) included in the sort.

5. **In the My list has section, make sure the Header row option button is selected**
   This button ensures that the first row of the table (containing the column headings) is not sorted along with the other rows in the table.

6. **Click OK**
   The dialog box closes, and the table is sorted based on the values in the Total column. Deselect the text and compare your document to Figure D-12.

7. **Save the document**

FIGURE D-11: Sort dialog box

First column
heading appears by
default

Click to display list
of column headings
in table

Sorts information
from smallest to
largest value

Sorts information
from largest to
smallest value

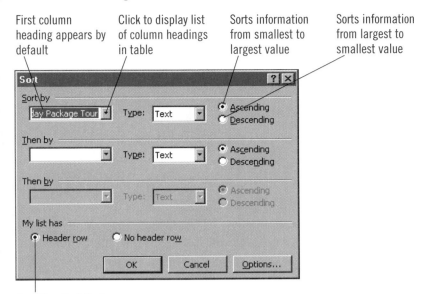

Specifies that first
row is not included
in the sort

FIGURE D-12: Sorted table

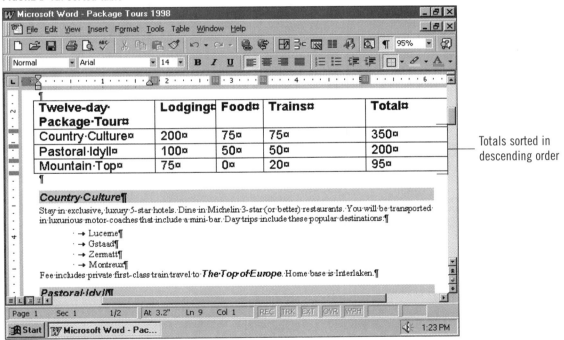

Totals sorted in
descending order

Sorting by more than one column

By sorting your table by more than one column, you can better organize information. For example, if you sort a table by a column containing last names, the rows containing the same last name are grouped together. To sort the rows within each group, select a second column by which to sort, such as one containing first names. You can sort by values in up to three different columns using the Sort by box and the two Then by boxes.

Formatting a Table

In the same way you can add borders and shading to paragraphs, you can improve the appearance of a table by adding borders and shading to rows and columns. Although you can use the buttons on the Tables and Borders toolbar to apply shading and borders to individual rows and columns, Word's Table AutoFormat command provides a variety of preset table formats from which you can choose. ◆━━━ Now Angela will use the Table AutoFormat command to apply attractive borders and shading to the table she created.

QuickTip

For best results, you should always sort a table before formatting it with Table AutoFormat because the borders applied to a row also move when the position of a row changes after sorting. This could cause the table to be formatted inappropriately.

1. With the insertion point in the table, click **Table** on the menu bar, then click **Table AutoFormat**
The Table AutoFormat dialog box opens, as shown in Figure D-13. In this dialog box, you can preview different preset table format settings. You can also identify the parts of the table to which you want to apply specific formatting. For example, use a simple grid format for your table.

2. In the Formats list, scroll the list of formats, then click **Grid 3**
The Preview box shows how the Grid 3 option formats a table. To emphasize the information in the Total column, apply special formatting to the last column.

3. In the Apply special formats to section, click the **Last Column check box**
In the Preview box, notice that the last column of the sample table appears in bold.

4. Click **OK**
The dialog box closes and the table appears with new formatting. Notice that the Table AutoFormat command also adjusted the columns so that the table fits attractively between the margins. Next, you would like to emphasize the column headings.

5. Select the first row (the column headings), then click the **Bold button** $\boxed{\text{B}}$ on the Formatting toolbar
The column headings appear in bold. Next, center the numbers in the table for easier reading.

6. Select the cells that contain numbers, then click the **Center button** $\boxed{\equiv}$ on the Formatting toolbar
The numbers in these cells appear centered in the columns.

7. Deselect the table, then save the document
Compare your table to Figure D-14.

FIGURE D-13: Table AutoFormat dialog box

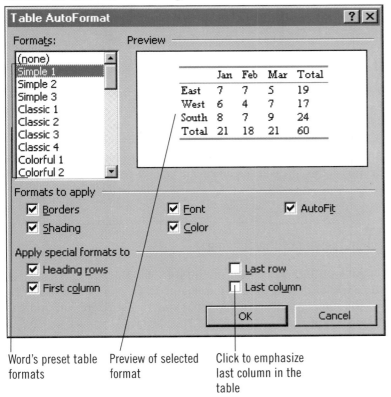

Word's preset table formats

Preview of selected format

Click to emphasize last column in the table

FIGURE D-14: Completed table

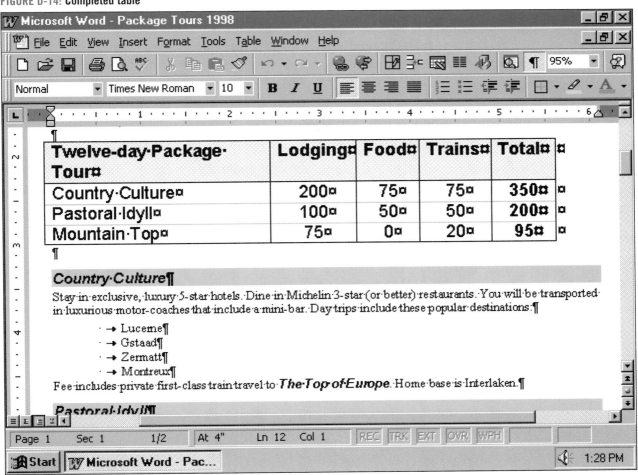

Using the Draw Table Button

Sometimes you may not want a simple table with the same number of cells in each row or column. For example, you might want a table with only one cell in the header row or an extra cell in the last column to display an emphasized total. Word's Draw Table button allows you to customize your tables by drawing the cells exactly where you want them. Angela would like to add a table displaying the best airfares to Switzerland. She would like the top row of the table to contain only the name of the airline. To accomplish this, she will customize her table to contain only one cell in the first row.

Steps

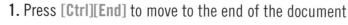

1. Press **[Ctrl][End]** to move to the end of the document

2. Click the **Tables and Borders button** 🔳 on the Standard toolbar
   The Tables and Borders toolbar is displayed, as shown in Figure D-15. Notice that the Draw Table button ✏️ on the Tables and Borders toolbar is automatically depressed and the Draw Table pointer ✏️ is displayed.

3. With the table pointer near the last paragraph mark of the document, click while dragging down and to the right, creating a cell about 4" wide and 1" tall
   Use the rulers as a guide for determining the size of the cell. The first cell you draw using the Draw Table button represents the outside border of the entire table. Next create smaller cells within the first one.

4. Click on the left side of the cell about ¼" below the top line and drag the pointer straight across to the right side of the cell, and then release the mouse
   Notice as you drag the pointer across the table, you can see a dotted line representing a cell border. Next you create a column in the table.

5. Click the bottom of the new line about 1¼" from the left edge of the table and drag down to the bottom line of the table
   Compare your table to Figure D-16. Next, you add more rows to the table.

6. Click on the left side of the table about ¼" under the top cell and then drag across to the right side of the table
   A new row is added to the table. Add another column that divides the right column.

7. Create another line that splits the right column at 2¼", then click the **Draw Table button** ✏️ on the Tables and Borders toolbar
   Clicking the Draw Table button deactivates the table pointer. After customizing your table you are ready to add text.

8. Place the insertion point in the first cell of the table, then type **World Travel Airlines**, as shown in Figure D-17
   In the next lesson, you will modify your table to make it more attractive.

FIGURE D-15: **Tables and Borders toolbar**

Eraser button removes lines between cells

Line Style

Line Weight

Borders

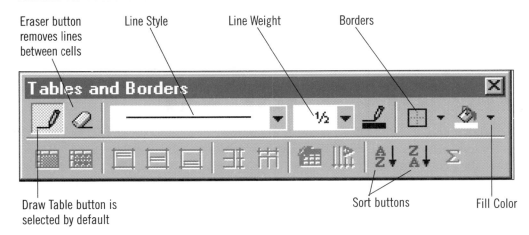

Draw Table button is selected by default

Sort buttons

Fill Color

FIGURE D-16: **Adding a row to a custom table**

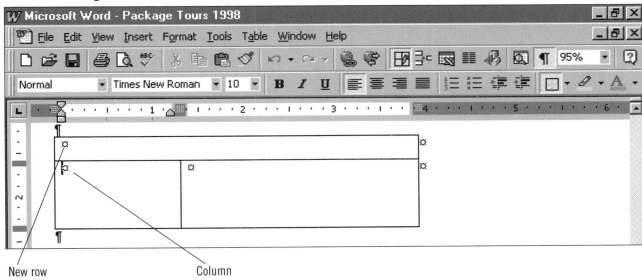

New row

Column

FIGURE D-17: **Completed table**

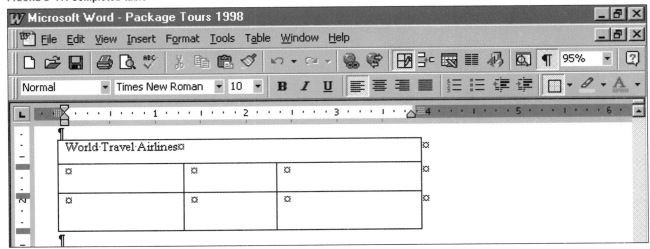

Modifying a Table with the Tables and Borders Toolbar

You can also use the Tables and Borders toolbar to improve the appearance of your tables. This toolbar contains various buttons that can be used to format the table itself or arrange the text within the table. For example, the Distribute Columns button automatically makes selected columns equal widths.  Angela will use the Tables and Borders toolbar to improve the appearance of her table. She will begin by splitting the cells in the table to add another column to the end of the table.

Steps

1. **Select the last column of the second and third rows, and then click the Split Cells button ▦ on the Tables and Borders toolbar**
The Split Cells dialog box opens, as shown in Figure D-18. In this dialog box, you can choose to split the selected cells into additional rows or additional columns or both. In this case, split these cells into 2 rows and 2 columns.

2. **Verify that the Number of rows and Number of columns boxes both display 2, then click OK**
The original cells are divided into 4 smaller cells, as shown in Figure D-19. Next, you make the width of all the columns equal.

3. **Select the entire table, then click the Distribute Columns Evenly button ▦ on the Tables and Borders toolbar**
All the columns are now the same width. Now you are ready to enter text.

4. **In the new cells, type the text shown in Figure D-20 and be sure to press [Tab] at the end of the last row to create a new row of cells**
Next, center the text in the columns.

5. **Select the entire table (do *not* select the end-of-row markers), then click the Center button ▤ on the Formatting toolbar**
To improve the appearance of the table, make all the rows the same height.

6. **Select all the rows in the table, if necessary, and click the Distribute Rows Evenly button ▤ on the Tables and Borders toolbar**
Now all the rows are the same height. Next you can give the table a more elegant appearance.

7. **Click anywhere in the table, click the Table AutoFormat button ▧ on the Tables and Borders toolbar, and then scroll to and double-click the Elegant preset format**

8. **Click Table on the menu bar, and then click Cell Height and Width, and on the Row tab, click the Center option button, and then click OK**
Your table is centered on the page. Compare your table to Figure D-20.

9. **Click the Tables and Borders button ▦ on the Standard toolbar**
The Tables and Borders toolbar is hidden. Angela has finished working with the document for now.

QuickTip
To select the table without selecting the end-of-row markers, select the text in the first row, then drag down and to the right.

Time To

✔ Save
✔ Preview
✔ Print
✔ Exit

FIGURE D-18: Split Cells dialog box

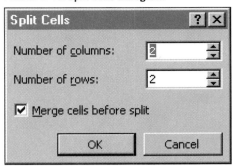

FIGURE D-19: New cells

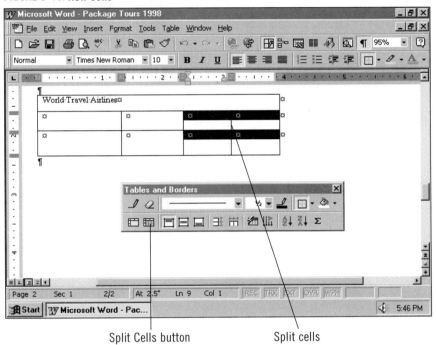

Split Cells button   Split cells

FIGURE D-20: Completed table

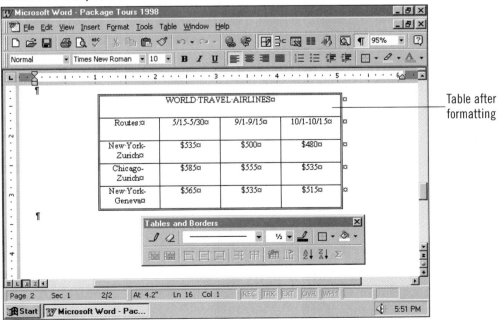

Table after formatting

Practice

► Concepts Review

Label each of the elements in Figure D-21.

FIGURE D-21

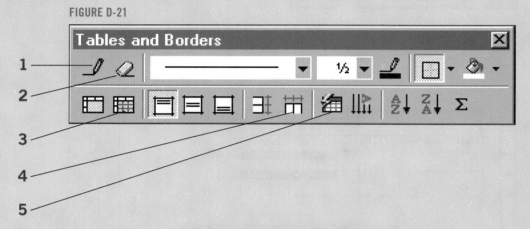

Match the number of each of the following terms with the statement that best describes its function.

6. Insert Table button
7. Table AutoFormat
8. = SUM
9. Gridlines
10. Descending order

a. Sorting from largest to smallest or from Z to A
b. Allows you to choose from preset tables
c. Creates a table from existing text
d. The built-in formula provided by Word in the Formula dialog box
e. Printing lines separating cells in a table

Select the best answer from the list of choices.

11. Which of the following statements is NOT a major benefit of using tables (rather than tabs) to align text in rows and columns?
    a. You can add and delete information without reformatting the entire table.
    b. You can format the table using the Table AutoFormat command.
    c. The status bar displays the cell reference to identify your location in the table.
    d. You can sort and calculate information in a table.

12. Which statement best describes the commands available on the pop-up menu for working in a table?
    a. The pop-up menu contains only the commands found on the Table menu.
    b. The pop-up menu contains the commands you are likely to use most often when working in a table.
    c. The pop-up menu contains Table AutoFormat settings from which you can choose.
    d. The pop-up menu contains the Formula command to insert calculations in a table.

13. Which of the following statements best describes how to delete only the text inside a row?
    a. Select the row, then press [Delete].
    b. With the insertion point in the row, click Table then click Delete Cells. Then click Delete Entire Row.

c. Select the row, then click the Cut button.
d. Select the row, click Edit, then click Cut.

14. To insert a column at the end of a table, you must first:
   a. Select the last column.
   b. Place the insertion point in the last column.
   c. Select the last cell in the table.
   d. Select the end-of-row markers at the right end of the table.

15. To add a new blank row to the bottom of a table, you:
   a. Place the insertion point in the last row, click Table, then click Insert Rows.
   b. Select the last row, click Table, then click Insert Rows.
   c. Place the insertion point in the last cell of the last row, then press [Tab].
   d. Select the end-of-row markers at the right end of the table, then press [Tab].

16. In which one of the following instances does the row height in a table NOT adjust?
   a. When the amount of text in a cell fits on more than one line.
   b. When you click Table, then click Cell Height and Width.
   c. When you drag a horizontal gridline between rows.
   d. When you click Cell Height and Width on the table pop-up menu.

17. When sorting a table, what is the easiest way to ensure that the header row is NOT sorted along with the other rows?
   a. In the Sort dialog box, click the Header row radio button in the My list has section.
   b. Sort the table before adding the header row.
   c. Split the table before sorting it.
   d. Use the Table AutoFormat command first.

18. Which of the following statements is NOT true of the Table AutoFormat command?
   a. You can apply special formatting to the last column.
   b. You can apply special formatting to the last row.
   c. You can see an example of the format in the Table AutoFormat dialog box.
   d. You can see an example of your table with new formatting in the Table AutoFormat dialog box.

19. Which of the following is a valid cell reference for the first cell in the third column?
   a. C1   **c.** 1C
   b. ROW1COL3   **d.** 3A

20. Which of the following is NOT true about sorting rows in a table?
   a. The Sort command always sorts all the rows in a table.
   b. You can sort a table by more than one column.
   c. You can specify not to sort the header row.
   d. You can choose the order in which you want rows sorted.

► Skills Review

1. Create a table and convert text to a table
a. Launch Word, then open the document named WD D-2 and save it as "Travel Expenses".
b. Select all six lines of text.
c. Click the Insert Table button on the Standard toolbar.
d. Select the text "Taxis", then press [Delete].
e. Type "Transportation", then click Bold if necessary.
f. Type "January" in the empty cell in the first row.
g. Click the Save button on the Standard toolbar.

2. Insert and delete rows and columns.
a. With the insertion point in the third row, click Table on the menu bar, then click Delete Cells, click Delete Entire Row, then click OK.
b. Place the insertion point in the last cell of the last row of the table, then press [Tab].
c. Type "Misc.", press [Tab], then type "54.88" [Tab] "73.65" [Tab] "63.49".
d. Select the end-of-row markers at the right end of the table, then click the Insert Columns button on the Standard toolbar.
e. In the first cell of the new column, type "Expense Total".
f. Click the Save button on the Standard toolbar.

3. Calculate data in a table.
a. Place the insertion point in the second cell in the Expense Total column, click Table on the menu bar, click Formula, then click OK.
b. Press [↓] to move the insertion point to the next cell in the Expense Total column and press [F4].
c. Repeat Step 3b for the remaining cells in the Expense Total column.
d. Select the Transportation value in the January column, then type "123.50".
e. Select the Transportation value in the Expense Total column, then press [F9] to update the total.
f. Click the Save button on the Standard toolbar.

4. Sort information in a table.
a. Place the insertion point anywhere in the table.
b. Click Table on the menu bar, then click Sort.
c. In the Sort by section, select Expense Total in the columns list.
d. Click the Descending radio button.
e. In the My list has section, make sure the Header row radio button is selected, then click OK.
f. Click the Save button on the Standard toolbar.

5. Format a table.
a. If the table is not already selected, click Table on the menu bar, then click Select Table.
b. Click the Tables and Borders button on the Standard toolbar.
c. Click the Table AutoFormat button on the Tables and Borders toolbar.
d. In the Formats list, review different formats by selecting each and viewing it in the Preview section.
e. In the Formats list, click Columns 5.
f. In the Apply special formats to section, click the Last column check box, then click OK.
g. Select all the cells that contain numbers and click the Align Right button on the Formatting toolbar.
h. Add "0" to the cents place of any value that is missing the final zero.

i. Click the Save button on the Standard toolbar.

j. Click the Print button on the Standard toolbar, then close the document.

6. Use the Draw Table button.

a. Open a new document and save it as "Agenda".

b. Drag and draw a cell 2" high and 3" wide.

c. Drag a line below the top line of the table creating a cell about .25" high.

d. Repeat Step 6c creating a table with four cells total.

e. Add a vertical line in the middle of the last three cells to make two columns.

f. Enter the text below.

Agenda

8:30   Opening Ceremonies

10:00

12:00   Group Luncheon

g. Click the Save button on the Standard toolbar.

7. Modify a table with the Tables and Borders toolbar.

a. Select the empty cell in the third row.

b. Click the Split Cells button.

c. Be sure that the Number of columns box contains 2, and that the Number of rows box contains 1, then click OK.

d. Enter the text below.

Meeting A for Advisors

Meeting B for Committee Members

e. Select the first column in the table and position the pointer over the border between the first and second columns. Drag the pointer to the left until the column is about ¾" wide.

f. Select the third row and position the pointer over the border between the second and third columns. Drag the pointer to the left until the two cells are about the same size.

g. Select the table, then click the Center button on the Formatting toolbar.

h. Use the Colorful 2 format in Table AutoFormat.

i. Save, print, and close the document. Then hide the Tables and Borders toolbar and exit Word.

Independent Challenges

1. As the director of marketing for ReadersPlus publishing company, you are responsible for sales projections for the new beginners reading series called "Everyone Is A Reader." You have been asked to present these projections at the upcoming sales kickoff meeting. Begin by creating a new document and saving it as "Projected Sales". Then format the document with the following changes, using Figure D-22 as a guide for how the completed document should look.

To complete this independent challenge:

1. Create a table with 5 rows and 5 columns.
2. Enter the following text:

Everyone is a Reader	West	East	Midwest	South
Anthologies Only	5000	7000	5800	7200
Supplements Only	2400	3500	4000	1100
Anthologies with guides	6800	6700	9400	8200
Complete Package	6500	7500	6300	7700

3. Adjust the last column width to be about 1".
4. Add a Total column to the right side of the chart.
5. Calculate the total for each row.
6. Format the table with the Grid 3 preset format.
7. Preview, save, print, then close the document.

FIGURE D-22

Everyone is a Reader	West	East	Midwest	South	Total
Anthologies Only	5000	7000	5800	7200	25000
Supplements Only	2400	3500	4000	1100	11000
Anthologies with guides	6800	6700	9400	8200	31100
Complete Package	6500	7500	6300	7700	28000

2. As the conference coordinator for Educational Consultants, Inc., you are in charge of tracking the costs for an upcoming Creativity Conference. You want to compare this year's conference costs with those of last year's conference. Create a new document and save it as "Conference Costs". Complete the following formatting.

To complete this independent challenge:

1. Create a table with 7 rows and 3 columns.
2. Enter the following text:

Conference Costs	1997	1998
Dinner	740	1300
Audio/video rental	270	425
Presenter fees	300	550
Decorations	500	800
Printing fees	300	420
Hall rental	800	1100

3. Adjust the last column width to be about 1".
4. Add a column to the right side of the chart.
5. Add the column heading "Difference" to the new column.
6. In the Difference column, calculate the difference between 1998 versus 1997 costs for each row. Hint: For the first row, type "=C2-B2" in the Formula dialog box. Using the [F4] key to repeat a command copies the previous formula so you cannot use [F4] to insert formulas with varying cell references.
7. Sort the table by 1997 costs, from highest to lowest.
8. Format the table with the List 5 preset format.
9. Center the columns so that they contain fee values.
10. Preview, save, print, then close the document.

3. Task References are documents which summarize commands, buttons, and keystroke shortcuts for the features you learn about in each unit. Log on to the Internet and use your browser to go to http://www.course.com. From there, click Student On Line Companions, and then click on the link to go to the Microsoft Office 97 Professional Edition-Illustrated: A First Course page, then click on the Word link for Unit D. Download the Unit D Task Reference. Although this document is already formatted as a table, you decide to customize the table. Save the final table as "Table Task Reference".

1. Sort the by the text in the first column.
2. Sort the table again, this time by the text in the third column and the first column.
3. Improve the table's appearance by applying the preset format setting.
4. Preview, save, print, then close the document.

4. As a co-chairman of the entertainment committee for the Lake City 1998 class reunion, you are responsible for calculating attendance fees for the planned events. You want to create a table showing the distribution of attendees among all the events. Another member of the committee has provided you with the number of classmates who have responded for specific events. Open the document named WD D-3 and save it as "Reunion Costs".

To complete this independent challenge:

1. Convert the tabbed text to a table.
2. Add a row to the end of the table, specifying "Variety Show" as the event with 120 attendees at $7 per person.
3. Calculate the total for each row, using a multiplication formula. (Hint: For the first row, type "=B2*C2" in the Formula dialog box. Using the [F4] key to repeat a command copies the previous formula so you cannot use [F4] to insert formulas with varying cell references.)
4. Format the table with the List 8 preset format.
5. Right align the columns that contain numerical values.
6. Preview, save, print, then close the document.

Visual Workshop

As part of your responsibilities as the director of the Extreme Fitness health club, you must prepare a price list for club activities. Use the Draw Table button and other features on the Tables and Borders toolbar to create a table that identifies activities such as basketball, racquetball, aerobics classes, etc., and enter a price for each activity. Use Figure D-23 as a guide for creating your table. Use the Eraser button to delete any border lines you don't want in your table. (Hint: Use the Distribute Columns Evenly button and the Distribute Rows Evenly button to make your columns and rows even.) Format the table in any preset format desired. Save the document as "Activity Prices".

FIGURE D-23

Activity	Price	Sales	Total
Aerobics classes	$15.00	89	$1335.00
Basketball	$7.00	152	$1064.00
Raquetball	$10.00	214	$2140.00
Swimming	$10.00	345	$3450.00
Total for 1997		**800**	**$7989.00**

Getting
Started with Excel 97

Objectives

▶ **Define spreadsheet software**

▶ **Start Excel 97**

▶ **View the Excel window**

▶ **Open and save an existing workbook**

▶ **Enter labels and values**

▶ **Preview and print a worksheet**

▶ **Get Help**

▶ **Close a workbook and exit Excel**

In this unit, you will learn how to start Excel and recognize and use different elements of the Excel window and menus. You will also learn how to open existing files, enter data in a worksheet, and use the extensive online Help system. ◢◣ Evan Brillstein works in the Accounting Department at Nomad Ltd, an outdoor sporting gear and adventure travel company. Evan will use Excel to complete a worksheet that summarizes budget information and create a workbook to track tour sales.

Defining Spreadsheet Software

Excel is an electronic spreadsheet that runs on Windows computers. An **electronic spreadsheet** uses a computer to perform numeric calculations rapidly and accurately. See Table A-1 for common ways spreadsheets are used in business. An electronic spreadsheet is also referred to as a **worksheet**, which is the document that you produce when you use Excel. A worksheet created with Excel allows Evan to work quickly and efficiently, and to update the results accurately and easily. He will be able to produce more professional-looking documents with Excel. Figure A-1 shows a budget worksheet that Evan and his manager created using pencil and paper. Figure A-2 shows the same worksheet that they can create using Excel.

Details

Excel is better than the paper system for the following reasons:

Enter data quickly and accurately

With Excel, Evan can enter information faster and more accurately than he could using the pencil-and-paper method. For example, in the Nomad Ltd. Budget, Evan can use Excel to calculate Total Expenses and Net Income for each quarter by simply supplying the data and formulas, and Excel calculates the rest.

Recalculate easily

Fixing errors using Excel is easy, and any results based on a changed entry are recalculated automatically. If Evan receives updated Expense figures for Qtr 4, he can simply enter the new numbers and Excel will recalculate the spreadsheet.

Perform what-if analysis

One of the most powerful decision-making features of Excel is the ability to change data and then quickly recalculate changed results. Anytime you use a worksheet to answer the question "what if," you are performing a what-if analysis. For instance, if the advertising budget for May were increased to $3,000, Evan could enter the new figure into the spreadsheet and immediately find out the impact on the overall budget.

Change the appearance of information

Excel provides powerful features for enhancing a spreadsheet so that information is visually appealing and easy to understand. Evan can use boldface type and shading to add emphasis to key data in the worksheet.

Create charts

Excel makes it easy to create charts based on information in a worksheet. With Excel, charts are automatically updated as data changes. The worksheet in Figure A-2 includes a pie chart that graphically shows the distribution of Nomad Ltd. expenses for the first quarter.

Share information with other users

Because everyone at Nomad is now using Microsoft Office, it's easy for Evan to share information with his colleagues. If Evan wants to use the data from someone else's worksheet, he accesses their files through the network or by disk. For example, Evan can complete the budget for Nomad Ltd. that his manager started creating in Excel.

Create new worksheets from existing ones quickly

It's easy for Evan to take an existing Excel worksheet and quickly modify it to create a new one. When Evan is ready to create next year's budget, he can use this budget as a starting point.

FIGURE A-1: Traditional paper worksheet

	Qtr 1	Qtr 2	Qtr 3	Qtr 4	Total
Nomad Ltd					
Net Sales	48,000	76,000	64,000	80,000	268,000
Expenses:					
Salary	8,000	8,000	8,000	8,000	32,000
Interest	4,800	5,600	6,400	7,200	24,000
Rent	2,400	2,400	2,400	2,400	9,600
Ads	3,600	8,000	16,000	20,000	47,600
COG	16,000	16,800	20,000	20,400	73,200
Total Exp	34,800	40,800	52,800	58,000	186,400
Net Income	13,200	35,200	11,200	22,000	81,600

FIGURE A-2: Excel worksheet

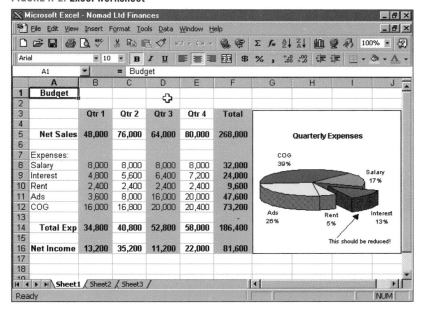

TABLE A-1: Common business spreadsheet uses

use	solution
Maintenance of values	Calculation of figures
Visual representation of values	Chart based on worksheet figures
Create consecutively numbered pages using multiple workbook sheets	Report containing workbook sheets
Organize data	Sort data in ascending or descending order
Analyze data	PivotTable or AutoFilter to create data summaries and short-lists
Create what-if data situations	Scenarios containing data outcomes using variable values

Excel 97

Starting Excel 97

To start Excel, you use the Start Button on the taskbar. Click Programs, then click the Microsoft Excel program icon. A slightly different procedure might be required for computers on a network and those that use utility programs to enhance Windows 95. If you need assistance, ask your instructor or technical support person for help. ✐▬▬ Evan's manager has started creating the Nomad Ltd budget and has asked Evan to finish it. He begins by starting Excel now.

1. **Point to the Start button** 🔲Start **on the taskbar**
   The Start button is on the left side of the taskbar and is used to start, or launch, programs on your computer.

2. **Click** 🔲Start
   Microsoft Excel is located in the Programs group—located at the top of the Start menu, as shown in Figure A-3.

3. **Point to Programs on the Start menu**
   All the programs, or applications, found on your computer can be found in this area of the Start menu.
      You can see the Microsoft Excel icon and other Microsoft programs, as shown in Figure A-4. Your desktop might look different depending on the programs installed on your computer.

4. **Click the Microsoft Excel program icon on the Program menu**
   Excel opens and a blank worksheet appears. In the next lesson, you will familiarize yourself with the elements of the Excel worksheet window.

Trouble?

If you don't see the Microsoft Excel icon, look for a program group called Microsoft Office.

Trouble?

If the Office Assistant appears on your screen, simply choose to start Excel.

FIGURE A-3: Start menu

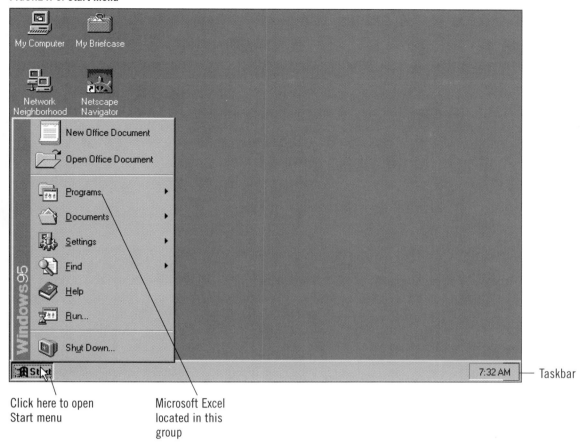

Click here to open
Start menu

Microsoft Excel
located in this
group

Taskbar

FIGURE A-4: Programs available on your computer

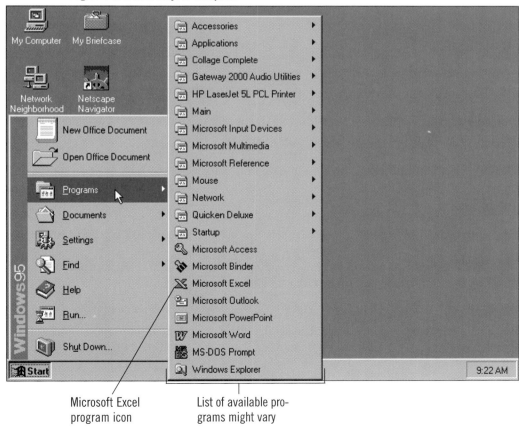

Microsoft Excel
program icon

List of available pro-
grams might vary

Viewing the Excel Window

When you start Excel, the computer displays the **worksheet window**, the area where you enter data, and the window elements that enable you to create and work with worksheets. Evan needs to familiarize himself with the Excel worksheet window and its elements before he starts working with the budget worksheet. Compare the descriptions below to Figure A-5.

Details

Trouble?

If your worksheet does not fill the screen as shown in Figure A-5, click the Maximize button in the worksheet window.

 The **worksheet window** contains a grid of columns and rows. Columns are labeled alphabetically (A, B, C, etc.) and rows are labeled numerically (1, 2, 3, etc.). The worksheet window displays only a tiny fraction of the whole worksheet, which has a total of 256 columns and 65,533 rows. The intersection of a column and a row is a **cell**. Cells can contain text, numbers, formulas, or a combination of all three. Every cell has its own unique location or **cell address**, which is identified by the coordinates of the intersecting column and row. For example, the cell address of the cell in the upper-left corner of a worksheet is A1.

 The **cell pointer** is a dark rectangle that highlights the cell you are working in, or the **active cell**. In Figure A-5, the cell pointer is located at A1, so A1 is the active cell. To make another cell active, click any other cell or press the arrow keys on your keyboard to move the cell pointer to another cell in the worksheet.

 The **title bar** displays the program name (Microsoft Excel) and the filename of the open worksheet (in this case, Book1). The title bar also contains a control menu box, a Close button, and resizing buttons.

 The **menu bar** contains menus from which you choose Excel commands. As with all Windows programs, you can choose a menu command by clicking it with the mouse or by pressing [Alt] plus the underlined letter in the menu name, referred to as the command's **shortcut key**.

 The **name box** displays the active cell address. In Figure A-5, "A1" appears in the name box, indicating that A1 is the active cell.

 The **formula bar** allows you to enter or edit data in the worksheet.

 The **toolbars** contain buttons for the most frequently used Excel commands. The **Standard** toolbar is located just below the menu bar and contains buttons corresponding to the most frequently used Excel features. The **Formatting** toolbar contains buttons for the most common commands used for improving the worksheet's appearance. To choose a button, simply click it with the left mouse button. The face of any button has a graphic representation of its function; for instance, the Printing button has a printer on its face.

 Sheet tabs below the worksheet grid enable you to keep your work in collections called **workbooks**. Each workbook contains 3 worksheets by default and can contain a maximum of 255 sheets. Sheet tabs can be given meaningful names. **Sheet tab scrolling buttons** help you move from one sheet to another.

 The **status bar** is located at the bottom of the Excel window. The left side of the status bar provides a brief description of the active command or task in progress. The right side of the status bar shows the status of important keys, such as the Caps Lock key and the Num Lock key.

FIGURE A-5: Excel worksheet window elements

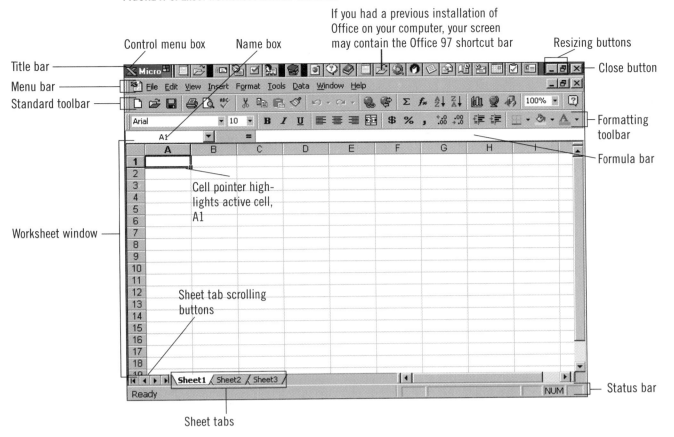

Control menu box Name box

If you had a previous installation of Office on your computer, your screen may contain the Office 97 shortcut bar

Resizing buttons

Title bar

Menu bar

Standard toolbar

Close button

Formatting toolbar

Formula bar

Cell pointer high-lights active cell, A1

Worksheet window

Sheet tab scrolling buttons

Status bar

Sheet tabs

Excel 97

Opening and Saving an Existing Workbook

Sometimes it's more efficient to create a new worksheet by modifying one that already exists. This saves you from having to retype information. Throughout this book, you will be instructed to open a file from your Student Disk, use the Save As command to create a copy of the file with a new name, and then modify the new file by following the lesson steps. Saving the files with new names keeps your original Student Disk files intact in case you have to start the lesson over again or you wish to repeat an exercise. ▟▄▄▄▄ Evan's manager has asked Evan to enter information into the Nomad Ltd budget. Follow along as Evan opens the Budget workbook, then uses the Save As command to create a copy with a new name.

Trouble?

If necessary, you can download your student files from our Web Site at http:\\course.com.

1. **Insert your Student Disk in the appropriate disk drive**

2. **Click the Open button** **on the Standard toolbar**
   The Open dialog box opens. See Figure A-6.

3. **Click the Look in list arrow**
   A list of the available drives appears. Locate the drive that contains your Student Disk.

4. **Click the drive that contains your Student Disk**
   A list of the files on your Student Disk appears in the Look in list box, with the default filename placeholder in the File name text box already selected.

5. **In the File name list box click XL A-1, then click Open**
   The file XL A-1 opens. You could also double-click the filename in the File name list box to open the file. To create and save a copy of this file with a new name, you use the Save As command.

6. **Click File on the menu bar, then click Save As**
   The Save As dialog box opens.

QuickTip

You can also click 🖫 on the Standard Toolbar or use the shortcut key [Ctrl][S] to save.

7. **Make sure the Save in list box displays the drive containing your Student Disk**
   You should save all your files to your Student Disk, unless instructed otherwise.

8. **In the File name text box, double-click the current file name to select it (if necessary), then type Nomad Budget as shown in Figure A-7.**

QuickTip

Use the Save As command to create a new workbook from one that already exists; use the Save command to store any changes on your disk made to an existing file since the last time the file was saved.

9. **Click Save to save the file and close the Save As dialog box, then click OK to close the Summary Info dialog box if necessary**
   The file XL A-1 closes, and a duplicate file named Nomad Budget opens, as shown in Figure A-8. To save the workbook in the future, you can click File on the menu bar, then click Save, or click the Save button on the Standard toolbar.

FIGURE A-6: Open dialog box

Click to display a
list of available
drives

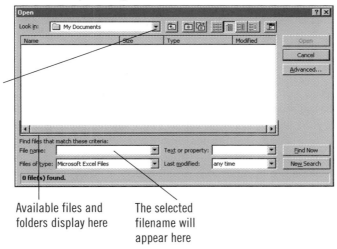

Available files and
folders display here

The selected
filename will
appear here

FIGURE A-7: Save As dialog box

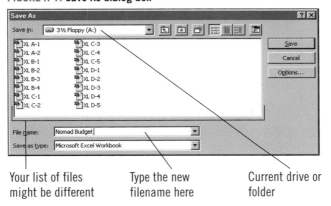

Your list of files
might be different

Type the new
filename here

Current drive or
folder

FIGURE A-8: Nomad Budget workbook

	A	B	C	D	E	F	G	H	I
1	Budget								
2									
3		Qtr 1	Qtr 2	Qtr 3	Qtr 4				
4									
5	Net Sales	48000	76000	64000	80000				
6									
7	Expenses:								
8		8000	8000						
9		4800	5600						
10		2400	2400						
11	Ads	3600	8000						
12	COG	16000	16800						
13									
14									
15									
16									
17									

Entering Labels and Values

Labels are used to identify the data in the rows and columns of a worksheet. They are also used to make your worksheet readable and understandable. For these reasons, you should enter all labels in your worksheet first. Labels can contain text and numerical information not used in calculations, such as dates, times, or addresses. Labels are left-aligned by default. **Values**, which include numbers, formulas, and functions, are used in calculations. Excel recognizes an entry as a value when it is a number or begins with one of these symbols: +, -, =, @, #, or $. All values are right-aligned by default. When a cell contains both text and numbers, Excel recognizes the entry as a label. ▗ Evan needs to enter labels identifying expense categories, and the values for Qtr 3 and Qtr 4 into the Nomad budget worksheet.

1. Click cell A8 to make it the active cell
Notice that the cell address A8 appears in the name box. You will now enter text for the expenses.

2. Type Salary, as shown in Figure A-9, then click the Enter button ☑ **on the formula bar**
You must click ☑ to confirm your entry. You can also confirm a cell entry by pressing [Enter], pressing [Tab], or by pressing one of the arrow keys on your keyboard. If a label does not fit in a cell, Excel displays the remaining characters in the next cell to the right as long as it is empty. Otherwise, the label is **truncated**, or cut off. The contents of A8, the active cell, display in the formula bar.

3. Click cell A9, type Interest, then press [Enter] to complete the entry and move the cell pointer to cell A10; type Rent in cell A10, then press [Enter]
Now you enter the remaining expense values.

4. Drag the mouse over cells D8 through E12
Two or more selected cells is called a **range**. Since these entries cover multiple columns and rows, you can pre-select the range to make the data entry easier.

5. Type 8000, then press [Enter]; type 6400 in cell D9, then press [Enter]; type 2400 in cell D10, then press [Enter]; type 16000 in cell D11, then press [Enter]; type 20000 in cell D12, then press [Enter]
You have entered all the values in the Qtr 3 column. The cell pointer is now in cell E8. Finish entering the expenses in column E.

6. Type the remaining values for cells E8 through E12 using Figure A-10 as a guide

7. Click the Save button 🖫 **on the Standard toolbar**
It is a good idea to save your work often. A good rule of thumb is to save every 15 minutes or so as you modify your worksheet, especially before making significant changes to the worksheet, or before printing.

Trouble?
If you notice a mistake in a cell entry after it has been confirmed, double-click the cell and use [Backspace] or [Delete] to make your corrections, then press [Enter].

QuickTip
To enter a number, such as the year 1997, as a label so it will not be included in a calculation, type an apostrophe (') before the number.

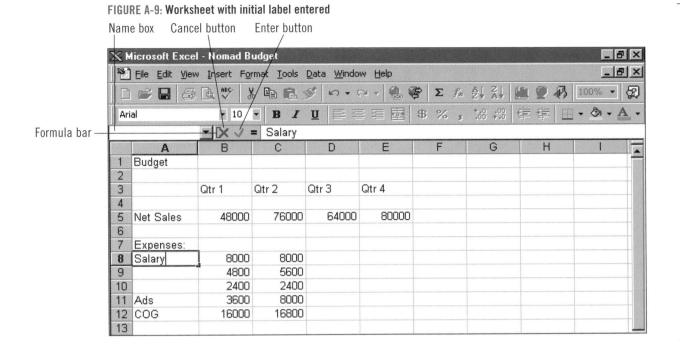

FIGURE A-9: Worksheet with initial label entered

Name box   Cancel button   Enter button

Formula bar

FIGURE A-10: Worksheet with labels and values entered

Labels entered   Values entered   Enter columnar
                                                data by selecting
                                                a range

CLUES TO USE

Navigating the worksheet

With over a billion cells available to you, it is important to know how to move around, or navigate, the worksheet. You can use the pointer-movement keys ([↑], [↓], [←], [→]) to move a cell or two at a time, or the [Page Up] or [Page Down] to move a screenful at a time. You can also simply use your mouse pointer to click the desired cell. If the desired cell is not visible in the worksheet window, you can use the scroll bars, or the Go To command to move the location into view. To return to the top of the worksheet, cell A1, press [Ctrl][Home].

Previewing and Printing a Worksheet

When a worksheet is completed, you print it to have a paper copy to reference, file, or send to others. You can also print a worksheet that is not complete to review it or work on when you are not at a computer. Before you print a worksheet, you should first save it, as you did at the end of the previous lesson. That way, if anything happens to the file as it is being sent to the printer, you will have a clean copy saved to your disk. Then you should preview it to make sure that it will fit on the page the way you want. When you preview a worksheet, you see a copy of the worksheet exactly as it will appear on paper. Table A-2 provides printing tips. ✐ Evan is finished entering the labels and values into the Nomad Ltd budget as his manager asked him to. Before he submits it to her for review, he previews it and then prints a copy.

Steps 1 2 3 4

1. **Make sure the printer is on and contains paper**
   If a file is sent to print and the printer is off, an error message appears. You preview the worksheet to check its overall appearance.

2. **Click the Print Preview button 🔍 on the Standard toolbar**
   You could also click File on the menu bar, then click Print Preview. A miniature version of the worksheet appears on the screen, as shown in Figure A-11. If there was more than one page, you could click Next and Previous to move between pages. You can also enlarge the image by clicking the Zoom button. After verifying that the preview image is correct, print the worksheet.

3. **Click Print**
   The Print dialog box opens, as shown in Figure A-12.

4. **Make sure that the Active Sheet(s) radio button is selected and that 1 appears in the Number of Copies text box**
   Now you are ready to print the worksheet.

5. **Click OK**
   The Printing dialog box appears while the file is sent to the printer. Note that the dialog box contains a Cancel button that you can use to cancel the print job.

TABLE A-2: Worksheet printing tips

before you print	recommendation
Check the printer	Make sure that the printer is turned on and online, that it has paper, and that there are no error messages or warning signals
Preview the worksheet	Check the formatted image for page breaks, page setup (vertical or horizontal), and overall appearance of the worksheet
Check the printer selection	Use the Printer setup command in the Print dialog box to verify that the correct printer is selected

FIGURE A-11: **Print Preview screen**

Move to another page   Enlarge the screen image   Print the worksheet   Change print options   Return to worksheet

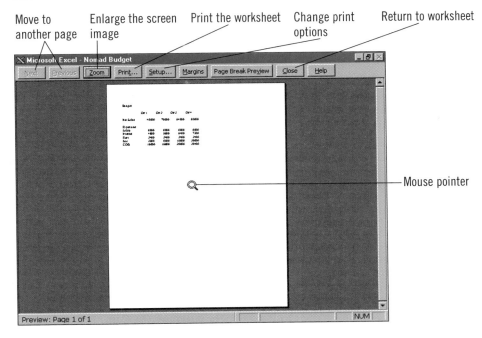

Mouse pointer

FIGURE A-12: **Print dialog box**

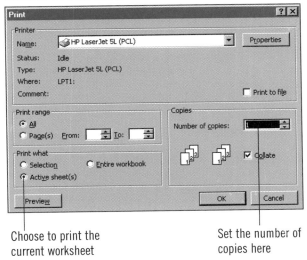

Choose to print the current worksheet

Set the number of copies here

Using Zoom in Print Preview

When you are in the Print Preview window, you can make the image of the page larger by clicking the Zoom button. You can also position the mouse pointer over a specific part of the worksheet page, then click to view that section of the page. While the image is zoomed in, use the scroll bars to view different sections of the page. See Figure A-13.

FIGURE A-13: **Enlarging the view using Zoom**

Excel 97

Getting Help

Excel features an extensive online Help system that gives you immediate access to definitions, explanations, and useful tips. The Office Assistant provides this information using a question and answer format. As you are working, the Office Assistant provides tips—indicated by a light bulb you can click—in response to your own working habits. Help appears in a separate balloon-shaped dialog box that you can resize and refer to as you work. You can press the F1 key at any time to get immediate help. ◢◣ Evan knows the manager will want to know the grand total of the expenses in the budget, and he thinks Excel can perform this type of calculation. He decides to use the animated Office Assistant to learn how to see the sum of a range using the AutoCalculate feature, located in the Status bar.

1. Click the Office Assistant button ◳ on the Standard toolbar
   The Office Assistant helps you find information using a question and answer format.

2. Once the Office Assistant is displayed, click its window to activate the query box
   You want information on calculating the sum of a range.

3. Type How can I calculate a range?
   See Figure A-15. Once you type a question, the Office Assistant can search for relevant topics from the help files in Excel, from which you can choose.

4. Click Search
   The Office Assistant displays several topics related to making quick calculations. See Figure A-16.

5. Click Quick calculations on a worksheet
   The Quick calculations on a worksheet help window opens.

6. Click View the total for a selected range, press [Esc] once you've read the text, then click the Close button on the dialog box title bar
   The Help window closes and you return to your worksheet.

7. Click the Close button in the Office Assistant window

QuickTip

Information in Help can be printed by clicking the Options button, then clicking Print Topic.

QuickTip

You can close the Office Assistant at any time by clicking its Close button.

CLUES TO USE

Changing the Office Assistant

The default Office Assistant is Clippit, but there are eight others from which you can choose. To change the appearance of the Office Assistant, right-click the Office Assistant window, then click Choose Assistant. Click the Gallery tab, click the Back and Next buttons until you find an Assistant you want to use, then click OK. (You may need your Microsoft Office 97 CD-ROM to change Office Assistants.) Each Office Assistant makes its own unique sounds and can be animated by right-clicking its window and clicking Animate! Figure A-16 displays the Office Assistant dialog box.

FIGURE A-14: Office Assistant dialog box

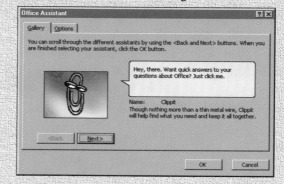

FIGURE A-15: **Office Assistant**

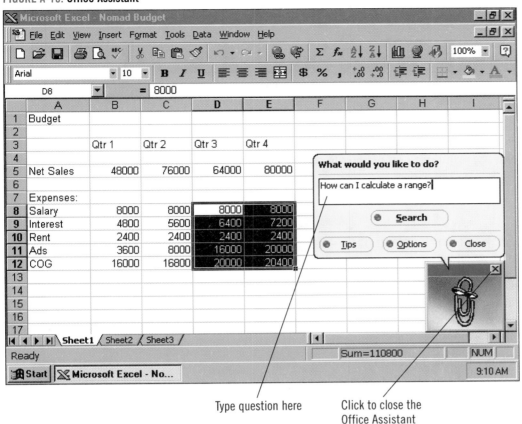

Type question here

Click to close the
Office Assistant

FIGURE A-16: **Relevant Help Assistant topics**

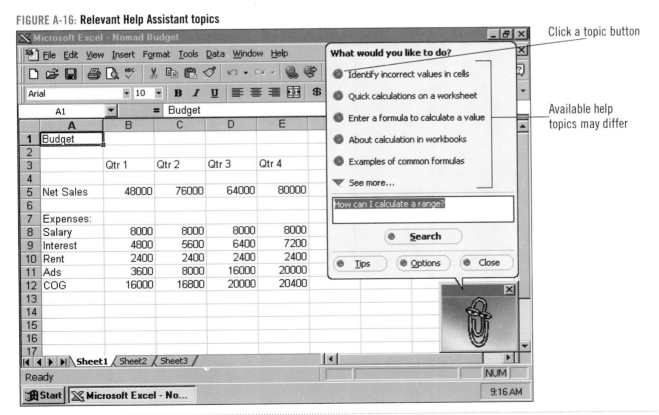

Click a topic button

Available help
topics may differ

Closing a Workbook and Exiting Excel

When you have finished working on a workbook, you need to save the file and close it. Once you have saved a file and are ready to close it, click Close on the File menu. When you have completed all your work in Excel, you need to exit the program. To exit Excel, click Exit on the File menu. ✒ Evan is done adding the information to the Budget worksheet, and he is ready to pass the printout to his manger to review, so he closes the workbook and then exits Excel.

Steps 1 2 3 4

1. Click **File** on the menu bar

The File menu opens as displayed in Figure A-17.

2. Click **Close**

You could also click the workbook Close button instead of choosing File, then Close. Excel closes the workbook and asks you to save your changes; be sure that you do. A blank worksheet window appears.

Trouble?

To exit Excel and close several files at once, choose Exit from the File menu. Excel will prompt you to save changes to each workbook before exiting.

3. Click **File**, then click **Exit**

You could also click the program Close button to exit the program. Excel closes and computer memory is freed up for other computing tasks.

FIGURE A-17: Closing a workbook using the File menu

Program control menu box   Workbook control menu box   Close command

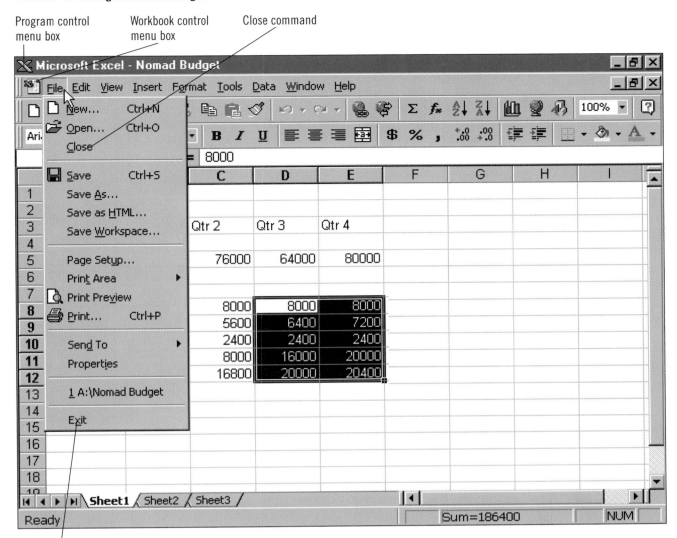

Exit command

Excel 97

Practice

► Concepts Review

Label each of the elements of the Excel worksheet window shown in Figure A-18.

FIGURE A-18

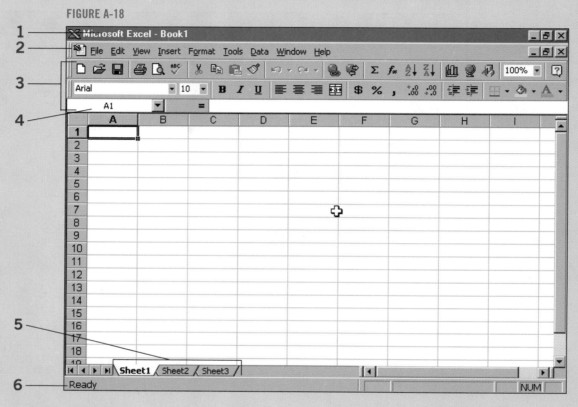

Match each of the terms with the statement that describes its function.

7. Cell pointer
8. Button
9. Worksheet window
10. Name box
11. Cell
12. Workbook

a. Area that contains a grid of columns and rows
b. The intersection of a column and row
c. Graphic symbol that depicts a task or function
d. Collection of worksheets
e. Rectangle that indicates the cell you are currently working in
f. Displays the active cell address

Select the best answer from the list of choices.

13. **An electronic spreadsheet can perform all of the following tasks, *except***
    a. Display information visually
    b. Calculate data accurately
    c. Plan worksheet objectives
    d. Recalculate updated information

14. **Each of the following is true about labels, *except***
    a. They are left-aligned, by default
    b. They are not used in calculations
    c. They are right-aligned, by default
    d. They can include numerical information

15. **Each of the following is true about values, *except***
    a. They can include labels
    b. They are right-aligned, by default
    c. They are used in calculations
    d. They can include formulas

16. **What symbol is typed before a number to make the number a label?**
    a. "
    b. !
    c. '
    d. ;

17. **You can get Excel Help by any of the following ways, *except***
    a. Clicking Help on the menu bar
    b. Pressing [F1]
    c. Clicking the Help button 🔲 on the Standard toolbar
    d. Minimizing the application window

18. **Each key(s) can be used to confirm cell entries, *except***
    a. [Enter]
    b. [Tab]
    c. [Esc]
    d. [Shift][Enter]

19. **Which button is used to preview a worksheet?**
    a. 🔲
    b. 🔲
    c. 🔲
    d. 🔲

20. **Which feature is used to enlarge a print preview view?**
    a. Magnify
    b. Enlarge
    c. Amplify
    d. Zoom

21. **Each of the following is true about the Office Assistant, *except***
    a. It provides tips based on your work habits
    b. It provides help using a question and answer format
    c. You can change the appearance of the Office Assistant
    d. It can complete certain tasks for you

Skills Review

1. Start Excel and identify the elements in the worksheet window.
- **a.** Point to Programs in the Start menu.
- **b.** Click the Microsoft Excel program icon.
- **c.** Try to identify as many elements in the Excel worksheet window as you can without referring to the unit material.

2. Open an existing workbook.
- **a.** Open the workbook XL A-2 by clicking the Open button on the Standard toolbar.
- **b.** Save the workbook as "Country Duds" by clicking File on the menu bar, then clicking Save As.

3. Enter labels and values.
- **a.** Enter labels shown in Figure A-19.
- **b.** Enter values shown in Figure A-19.
- **c.** Save the workbook by clicking the Save button on the Standard toolbar.

FIGURE A-19

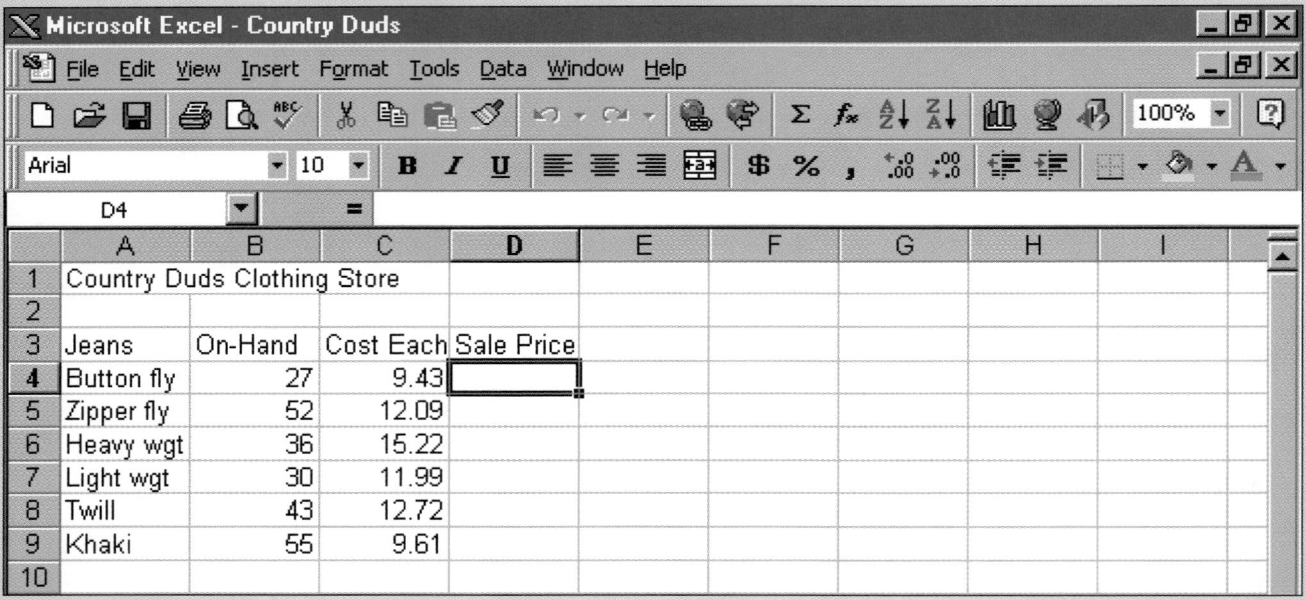

	A	B	C	D	E	F	G	H	I
1	Country Duds Clothing Store								
2									
3	Jeans	On-Hand	Cost Each	Sale Price					
4	Button fly	27	9.43						
5	Zipper fly	52	12.09						
6	Heavy wgt	36	15.22						
7	Light wgt	30	11.99						
8	Twill	43	12.72						
9	Khaki	55	9.61						
10									

4. Previewing and printing a worksheet.
- **a.** Click the Print Preview button on the Standard toolbar.
- **b.** Use the Zoom button to see more of your worksheet.
- **c.** Print one copy of the worksheet.
- **d.** Hand in your printout.

5. Get Help.
- **a.** Click the Office Assistant button on the Standard toolbar if the Assistant is not displayed.
- **b.** Ask the Office Assistant for information about changing the Office Assistant character in Excel.
- **c.** Print information offered by the Office Assistant using the Print topic command on the Options menu.
- **d.** Close the Help window.
- **e.** Hand in your printout.

6. **Close the workbook and exit Excel.**
   a. Click File on the menu bar, then click Close.
   b. If asked if you want to save the worksheet, click No.
   c. If necessary, close any other worksheets you might have opened.
   d. Click File on the menu bar, then click Exit.

▶ Independent Challenges

1. Excel's online Help provides definitions, explanations, procedures, and other helpful information. It also provides examples and demonstrations to show you how Excel features work. Topics include elements such as the active cell, status bar, buttons, and dialog boxes, as well as detailed information about Excel commands and options.
   To complete this independent challenge:

1. Open a new workbook
2. Click the Office Assistant.
3. Type a question that will give you information about opening and saving a worksheet. (Hint: you may have to ask the Office Assistant more than one question.)
4. Print out the information and hand it in.
5. Return to your workbook when you are finished.

Excel 97

2. Spreadsheet software has many uses that can affect the way work is done. Some examples of how Excel can be used are discussed in the beginning of this unit. Use your own personal or business experiences to come up with five examples of how Excel could be used in a business setting.

To complete this independent challenge:

1. Open a new workbook.
2. Think of five business tasks that you could complete more efficiently by using an Excel worksheet.
3. Sketch a sample of each worksheet. See Figure A-20, a sample payroll worksheet.
4. Submit your sketches.

FIGURE A-20

Employee Names	Hours Worked	Hourly Wage	Gross Pay	
Janet Bryce			→	Gross pay=
Anthony Krups			→	Hours worked
Grant Miller			→	times
Barbara Salazar			→	Hourly wage
Total	↓	↓	↓	

3. You are the office manager for Blossoms and Greens, a small greenhouse and garden center. Although the company is just three years old, it is expanding rapidly, and you are continually looking for ways to make your job easier. Last year you began using Excel to manage and maintain data on inventory and sales, which has greatly helped you to track this information accurately and efficiently. However, the job is still overwhelming for just one person. Fortunately, the owner of the company has just approved the hiring of an assistant for you. This person will need to learn how to use Excel. Create a short training document that your new assistant can use as a reference while becoming familiar with Excel.

To complete this independent challenge:

1. Draw a sketch of the Excel worksheet window, and label the key elements, such as toolbars, title bar, formula bar, scroll bars, etc.
2. For each labeled element, write a short description of its use.
3. List the main ways to get Help in Excel. (Hint: use the Office Assistant to learn of all the ways to get help in Excel..)
4. Identify five different ways to use spreadsheets in business.

4. Data on the World Wide Web is current and informative. It is a useful tool that can be used to gather the most up-to-date information which you can use to make smart buying decisions. Imagine that your supervisor has just told you that due to your great work, she has just found money in the budget to buy you a new computer. You can have whatever you want, but she wants you to justify the expense by creating a spreadsheet using data found on the World Wide Web to support your purchase decision.

To complete this independent challenge:

1. Open a new workbook and save it on your Student Disk as "New Computer Data."
2. Decide which features you want your ideal computer to have, and list these features.
3. Log on to the Internet and use your browser to go to the http://www.course.com. From there, click the link Student On Line Companions, then click the Microsoft Office 97 Professional Edition—Illustrated: A First Course page, then click on the Excel link for Unit A.
4. Use any of the following sites to compile your data: IBM [www.ibm.com], Gateway [www.gw2k.com], Dell [www.dell.com], or any other site you can find with related information.
5. Compile data for the components you want.
6. Make sure all components are listed and totaled. Include any tax and shipping costs the manufacturer charges.
7. Indicate on the worksheet your final purchase decision.
8. Save, print, and hand in your work.

▶ **Visual Workshop**

Create a worksheet similar to Figure A-21 using the skills you learned in this unit. Save the workbook as "Bea's Boutique" on your Student Disk. Preview, then print the worksheet.

FIGURE A-21

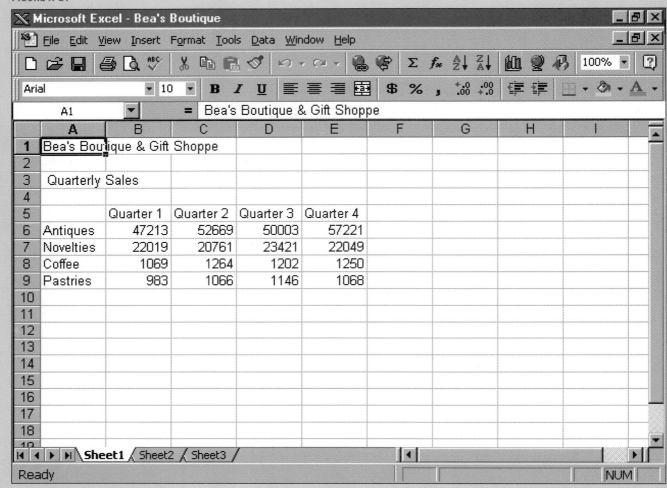

Building
and Editing Worksheets

Objectives

▶ **Plan, design, and create a worksheet**
▶ **Edit cell entries and work with ranges**
▶ **Enter formulas**
▶ **Introduce functions**
▶ **Copy and move cell entries**
▶ **Copy formulas with relative cell references**
▶ **Copy formulas with absolute cell references**
▶ **Name and move a sheet**

You will now plan and build your own worksheets. When you build a worksheet, you enter text, values, and formulas into worksheet cells. Once you create a worksheet, you can save it in a workbook file and then print it. ✐ Evan Brillstein has received a request from the Marketing Department for a forecast of this year's summer tour business, and an estimate of the average tour sales for each type of tour. Marketing hopes that the tour business will increase 20% over last year's figures. Evan needs to create a worksheet that summarizes tour sales for last year and a worksheet that forecasts the summer tour sales for this year.

Planning, Designing, and Creating a Worksheet

Before you start entering data into a worksheet, you need to know the purpose and approximate layout of the worksheet. ✎ Evan wants to forecast Nomad's 1998 summer tour sales. The sales goal, already identified by the Marketing Department, is to increase the 1997 summer sales by 20%. Using Figure B-1 and the planning guidelines below, work with Evan as he plans his worksheet.

Details

Determine the purpose of the worksheet and give it a meaningful title

Evan needs to forecast summer tour sales for 1998. Evan titles the worksheet "1998 Summer Tour Sales Forecast."

Determine your worksheet's desired results, sometimes called output

Evan needs to determine what the 1998 sales totals will be if sales increase by 20% over the 1997 sales totals, as well as the average number of tours per type.

Collect all the information, sometimes called input, that will produce the results you want to see

Evan gathers together the sales data for the 1997 summer tour season. The season ran from June through August. The types of tours sold in these months included Bike, Raft, Horse, and Bus.

Determine the calculations, or formulas, necessary to achieve the desired results

First, Evan needs to total the number of tours sold for each month of the 1997 summer season. Then he needs to add these totals together to determine the grand total of summer tour sales. Finally, the 1997 monthly totals and grand total must be multiplied by 1.2 to calculate a 20% increase for the 1998 summer tour season. He'll use the Paste Function to determine the average number of tours per type.

Sketch on paper how you want the worksheet to look; that is, identify where the labels and values will go

Evan decides to put tour types in rows and the months in columns. He enters the tour sales data in his sketch and indicates where the monthly sales totals and the grand total should go. Below the totals, he writes out the formula for determining a 20% increase in sales for 1997. He also includes a label for the location of the tour averages. Evan's sketch of his worksheet is shown in Figure B-1.

Create the worksheet

Evan enters his labels first to establish the structure of his worksheet. He then enters the values, the sales data into his worksheet. These values will be used to calculate the output Evan needs. The worksheet Evan creates is shown in Figure B-2.

1998 Summer Tours Sales Forecast

	June	July	August	Totals	Average
Bike	14	10	6	3 month total	
Raft	7	8	12		
Horse	12	7	6		
Bus	1	2	9		
Totals	June Total	July Total	August Total	Grand Total for 1997	
1998 Sales	Total X 1.2				

FIGURE B-2: Evan's forecasting worksheet

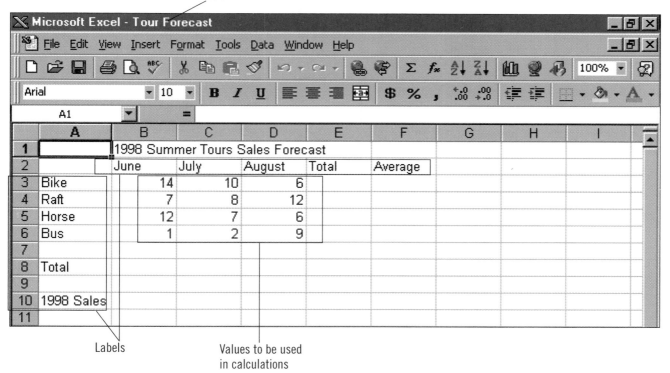

Check title bar for correct title

Labels

Values to be used in calculations

Editing Cell Entries and Working with Ranges

You can change the contents of any cells at any time. To edit the contents of a cell, you first select the cell you want to edit, then click the formula bar, double-click the selected cell, or press [F2]. This puts Excel into Edit mode. To make sure you are in Edit mode, check the **mode indicator** on the far left of the status bar. The mode indicator identifies the current Excel command or operation in progress. ◢◣◤ After planning and creating his worksheet, Evan notices that he entered the wrong value for the June bus tours and forgot to include the canoe tours. He fixes the bus tours figure, and he decides to add the canoe sales data to the raft sales figures.

Steps1 2 3 4

1. Start Excel, open the workbook XL B-1 from your Student Disk, then save it as Tour Forecast

2. Click cell **B6**
   This cell contains June bus tours, which Evan needs to change to 2.

3. Click anywhere in the formula bar
   Excel goes into Edit mode, and the mode indicator displays "Edit." A blinking vertical line, called the **insertion point**, appears in the formula bar, and if you move the mouse pointer to the formula bar, the pointer changes to ⌶ as displayed in Figure B-3.

4. Press [Backspace], type 2, then press [Enter] or click the Enter button ✓ on the formula bar
   Evan now needs to add "/Canoe" to the Raft label.

5. Click cell **A4** then press [F2]
   Excel is in Edit mode again, but this time, the insertion point is in the cell.

6. Type /Canoe then press [Enter]
   The label changes to Raft/Canoe.

7. Double-click cell **B4**
   Double-clicking a cell also puts Excel into Edit mode with the insertion point in the cell.

8. Press [Delete], then type 9
   See Figure B-4.

9. Click ✓ to confirm the entry

FIGURE B-3: Worksheet in Edit mode

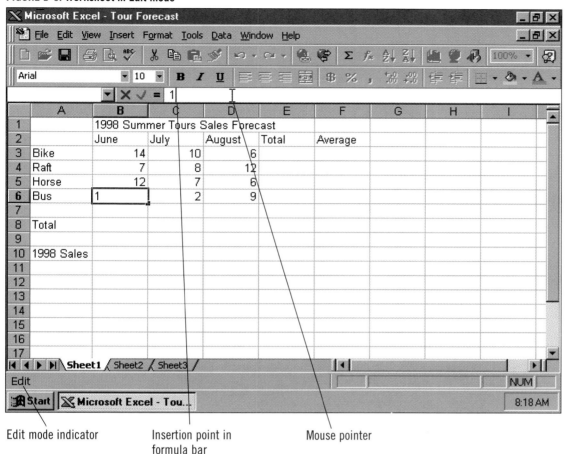

Edit mode indicator

Insertion point in formula bar

Mouse pointer

FIGURE B-4: Edited worksheet

Insertion point in cell

Using range names in a workbook

Any group of cells (two or more) is called a range. To select a range, click the first cell and drag to the last cell you want included in the range. The range address is defined by noting the first and last cells in the range. Give a meaningful name to a range by selecting cells, clicking the name box, and then typing a name. Range names—meaningful English names that Evan uses in this worksheet—are usually easier to remember than cell addresses, they can be used in formulas, and they also help you move around the workbook quickly. Click the name box list arrow, then click the name of the range you want to go to. The cell pointer moves immediately to that range.

Entering Formulas

Formulas are used to perform numeric calculations such as adding, multiplying, and averaging. Formulas in an Excel worksheet start with the formula prefix—the equal sign (=). All formulas use one or more **arithmetic operators** to perform calculations. See Table B-1 for a list of Excel operators. Formulas often contain cell addresses and range names. Using a cell address or range name in a formula is called **cell referencing**. Using cell references keeps your worksheet up-to-date and accurate. If you change a value in a cell, any formula containing that cell reference will be automatically recalculated using the new value. In formulas using more than one arithmetic operator, Excel decides which operation to perform first. ⬤▬▬ Evan needs to add the monthly tour totals for June, July, and August, and calculate a 20% increase in sales. He can perform these calculations using formulas.

Steps 1 2 3 4

1. Click cell **B8**

   This is the cell where you want to put the calculation that will total the June sales.

2. Type = (the equal sign)

   Placing an equal sign at the beginning of an entry tells Excel that a formula is about to be entered rather than a label or a value. The total June sales is equal to the sum of the values in cells B3, B4, B5, and B6.

3. Type **b3+b4+b5+b6**, then click the **Enter button** ☑ on the formula bar

   The result of 37 appears in cell B8, and the formula appears in the formula bar. See Figure B-5. Next, you add the number of tours in July and August.

> **Trouble?**
>
> If the formula instead of the result appears in the cell after you click ☑, make sure you began the formula with = (the equal sign).

4. Click cell **C8**, type **=c3+c4+c5+c6**, then press **[Tab]**; in cell **D8**, type **=d3+d4+d5+d6**, then press **[Enter]**

   The total tour sales for July, 27, and for August, 33, appear in cells C8 and D8 respectively.

5. Click cell **B10**, type **=B8*1.2**, then click ☑ on the formula bar

   To calculate the 20% increase, you multiply the total by 1.2. This formula calculates the result of multiplying the total monthly tour sales for June, cell B8, by 1.2. The result of 44.4 appears in cell B10.

   Now you need to calculate the 20% increase for July and August. You can use the **pointing method**, by which you specify cell references in a formula by selecting the desired cell with your mouse instead of typing its cell reference into the formula.

> **QuickTip**
>
> It does not matter if you type the column letter in lower case or upper case when entering formulas. Excel is not case-sensitive—B3 and b3 both refer to the same cell.

6. Click cell **C10**, type **=**, click cell **C8**, type ***1.2**, then press **[Tab]**

7. Click cell **D10**, type **=**, click cell **D8**, type ***1.2**, then click ☑

   Compare your results with Figure B-6.

TABLE B-1: Excel arithmetic operators

operator	purpose	example
+	Performs addition	=A5+A7
−	Performs subtraction	=A5-10
*	Performs multiplication	=A5*A7
/	Performs division	=A5/A7

FIGURE B-5: Worksheet showing formula and result

Microsoft Excel - Tour Forecast

File Edit View Insert Format Tools Data Window Help

Arial   10   **B** *I* U

B8   =   =B3+B4+B5+B6

	A	B	C	D	E	F	G	H	I
1		1998 Summer Tours Sales Forecast							
2		June	July	August	Total	Average			
3	Bike	14	10	6					
4	Raft/Canoe	9	8	12					
5	Horse	12	7	6					
6	Bus	2	2	9					
7									
8	Total	37							
9									
10	1998 Sales								
11									

Calculated result
in cell

Formula in formula
bar

FIGURE B-6: Calculated results for 20% increase

Microsoft Excel - Tour Forecast

File Edit View Insert Format Tools Data Window Help

Arial   10   **B** *I* U $ % ,

D10   =   =D8*1.2

	A	B	C	D	E	F	G	H	I
1		1998 Summer Tours Sales Forecast							
2		June	July	August	Total	Average			
3	Bike	14	10	6					
4	Raft/Canoe	9	8	12					
5	Horse	12	7	6					
6	Bus	2	2	9					
7									
8	Total	37	27	33					
9									
10	1998 Sales	44.4	32.4	39.6					
11									

Order of precedence in Excel formulas

A formula can include several operations. When you work with formulas that have more than one operator, the order of precedence is very important. If a formula contains two or more operators, such as 4 + .55/4000 * 25, the computer performs the calculations in a particular sequence based on these rules:

Calculated 1st   Calculation of exponents
Calculated 2nd   Multiplication and division, left to right
Calculated 3rd   Addition and subtraction, left to right

In the example 4 + .55/4000 * 25, Excel performs the arithmetic operations by first dividing 4000 into .55, then multiplying the result by 25, then adding 4. You can change the order of calculations by using parentheses. For example, in the formula (4+.55)/4000 * 25, Excel would first add 4 and .55, then divide that amount by 4000, then finally multiply it by 25. Operations inside parentheses are calculated before any other operations.

Introducing Excel Functions

Functions are predefined worksheet formulas that enable you to do complex calculations easily. Like formulas, functions always begin with the formula prefix = (the equal sign). You can enter functions manually, or you can use the Paste Function. ✎ Evan uses the SUM function to calculate the grand totals in his worksheet, and the AVERAGE function to calculate the average number of tours per type.

Steps 1 2 3 4

1. **Click cell E3**
   This is the cell where you want to display the total of all bike tours for June, July, and August. You use the AutoSum button to create the totals. AutoSum sets up the SUM function to add the values in the cells above the cell pointer. If there are no values in the cells above the cell pointer, AutoSum adds the values in the cells to the left of the cell pointer—in this case, the values in cells B3, C3, and D3.

2. **Click the AutoSum button Σ on the Standard toolbar, then click the Enter button ✓ on the formula bar**
   The formula =SUM(B3:D3) appears in the formula bar. The information inside the parentheses is the **argument**, or the information to be used in calculating a result of the function. An argument can be a value, a range of cells, text, or another function.
   The result appears in cell E3. Next, you calculate the total of raft and canoe tours.

3. **Click cell E4, click Σ, then click ✓**
   Now you calculate the three-month total of the horse tours.

4. **Click cell E5 then click Σ**
   AutoSum sets up a function to sum the two values in the cells above the active cell, which is not what you intended. You need to change the argument.

5. **Click cell B5, then drag to select the range B5:D5, then click ✓ to confirm the entry**
   As you drag, the argument in the SUM function changes to reflect the range being chosen, and a tip box appears telling you the size of the range you are selecting.

6. **Enter the SUM function in cells E6, E8, and E10**
   Make sure you add the values to the left of the active cell, not the values above it. See Figure B-7. Next, you calculate the average number of Bike tours using the Paste Function.

7. **Click cell F3, then click the Paste Function button ƒₓ on the Standard toolbar**
   The Paste Function dialog box opens. See Table B-2 for frequently used functions.
   The function needed to calculate averages—named AVERAGE—is included in the Most Recently Used category.

8. **Click the function name AVERAGE in the Function name list box, click OK, then in the AVERAGE dialog box type B3:D3 in the Number 1 text box, as shown in Figure B-8**

9. **Click OK, then repeat steps 7, 8 and 9 to calculate the Raft/Canoe (cell F4), Horse (cell F5), and Bus tours (cell F6) averages**
   The Time To checklist in the left margin contains Steps for routine actions. Everytime you see a Time To checklist, perform the actions listed.

Time To
✔ Save

FIGURE B-7: Worksheet with SUM functions entered

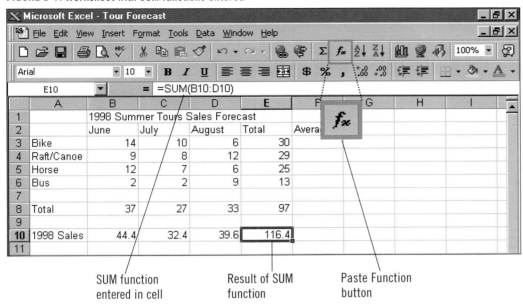

SUM function entered in cell

Result of SUM function

Paste Function button

FIGURE B-8: Using the Paste Function to create a formula

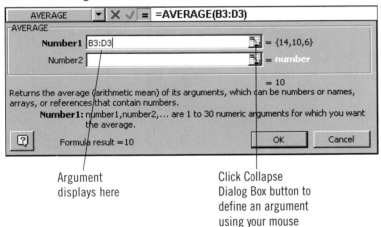

Argument displays here

Click Collapse Dialog Box button to define an argument using your mouse

TABLE B-2: Frequently Used Functions

function	description
SUM(*argument*)	Calculates the sum of the arguments
AVERAGE(*argument*)	Calculates the average of the arguments
MAX(*argument*)	Displays the largest value among the arguments
MIN(*argument*)	Displays the smallest value among the arguments
COUNT(*argument*)	Calculates the number of values in the arguments

CLUES TO USE

Introducing the Paste Function

The Paste Function button *fx* is located to the right of the AutoSum button on the Standard toolbar. To use the Paste Function, click *fx*. In the Paste Function dialog box, click the category containing the function you want, then click the desired function. The function appears in the formula bar. Click OK to fill in values or cell addresses for the arguments, then click OK.

Copying and Moving Cell Entries

Using the Cut, Copy, and Paste buttons or Excel's drag-and-drop feature, you can copy or move information from one cell or range in your worksheet to another. You can also cut, copy, and paste data from one worksheet to another.  Evan included the 1998 forecast for spring and fall tours sales in his Tour Info workbook. He already entered the spring report in Sheet2 and will finish entering the labels and data for the fall report. Using the Copy and Paste buttons and drag-and-drop, Evan copies information from the spring report to the fall report.

Steps 1 2 3 4

CourseHelp

The camera icon indicates there is a CourseHelp available with this lesson. Click the Start button, point to programs, point to CourseHelp, then click Excel 97 Illustrated. Choose the CourseHelp that corresponds to this lesson.

1. Click **Sheet 2** of the Tour Forecast workbook
   First, you copy the labels identifying the types of tours from the Spring report to the Fall report.

2. Select the range **A4:A9**, then click the **Copy button** 📋 on the Standard toolbar
   The selected range (A4:A9) is copied to the **Clipboard**, a temporary storage file that holds all the selected information you copy or cut. The Cut button ✂ removes the selected information from the worksheet and places it on the Clipboard. To copy the contents of the Clipboard to a new location, you click the new cell and then use the Paste command.

3. Click cell **A13**, then click the **Paste button** 📋 on the Standard toolbar
   The contents of the Clipboard are copied into the range A13:A18. When pasting the contents of the Clipboard into the worksheet, you need to specify only the first cell of the range where you want the copied selection to go. Next, you decide to use drag-and-drop to copy the Total label.

4. Click cell **E3**, then position the pointer on any edge of the cell until the pointer changes to ▷

5. While the pointer is ▷, press and hold down **[Ctrl]**
   The pointer changes to ▷.

Trouble?

When you drag-and-drop into occupied cells, Excel asks if you want to replace the existing cells. Click OK to replace the contents with the cells you are moving.

6. While still pressing **[Ctrl]**, press and hold the left mouse button, then drag the cell contents to cell **E12**
   As you drag, an outline of the cell moves with the pointer, as shown in Figure B-9, and a tip box appears tracking the current position of the item as you move it. When you release the mouse button, the Total label appears in cell E12. You now decide to move the worksheet title over to the left. To use drag-and-drop to move data to a new cell without copying it, do not press [Ctrl] while dragging.

7. Click cell **C1**, then position the mouse on the edge of the cell until it changes to ▷, then drag the cell contents to **A1**
   You now enter fall sales data into the range B13:D16.

8. Using the information shown in Figure B-10, enter the sales data for the fall tours into the range **B13:D16**
   Compare your worksheet to Figure B-10.

FIGURE B-9: Using drag-and-drop to copy information

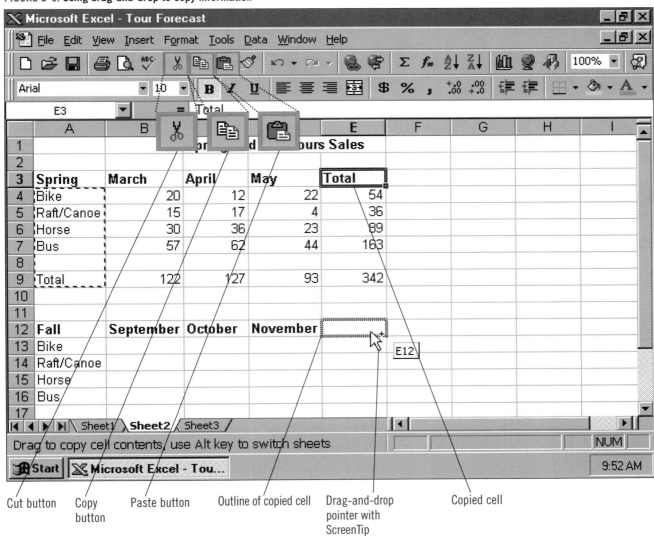

Cut button   Copy   Paste button   Outline of copied cell   Drag-and-drop   Copied cell
              button   pointer with
                                                                ScreenTip

FIGURE B-10: Worksheet with Fall tours data entered

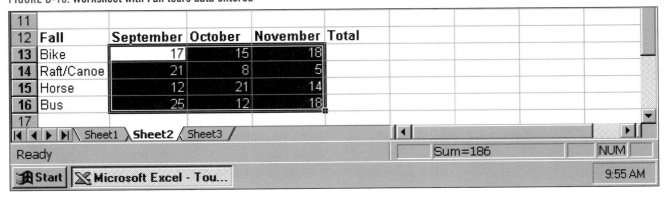

Copying Formulas with Relative Cell References

Copying and moving formulas allows you to reuse formulas you've already created. Copying formulas, rather than retyping them, helps to prevent typing errors. Evan wants to copy from the Spring tours report to the Fall tours report the formulas that total the tours by type and by month. He can use Copy and Paste commands and the Fill right method to copy this information.

Steps

CourseHelp

If you have trouble with the concepts in this lesson, be sure to view the CourseHelp entitled Relative versus Absolute Cell Referencing

1. Click cell **E4**, then click the **Copy button** 📋 on the Standard toolbar
The formula for calculating the total number of spring Bike tours is copied to the Clipboard. Notice that the formula in the formula bar appears as =SUM(B4:D4).

2. Click cell **E13**, then click the **Paste button** 📋 on the Standard toolbar
The formula from cell E4 is copied into cell E13, where the new result of 50 appears. Notice in the formula bar that the cell references have changed, so that the range B13:D13 appears in the formula. Formulas in Excel contain **relative cell references**. A relative cell reference tells Excel to copy the formula to a new cell, but to substitute new cell references so that the relationship of the cells to the formula in its new location remains unchanged. In this case, Excel inserted cells D13, C13, and B13, the three cell references immediately to the left of E13.
Notice that the bottom right corner of the active cell contains a small square, called the **fill handle**. Evan uses the fill handle to copy the formula in cell E13 to cells E14, E15, and E16. You can also use the fill handle to copy labels.

QuickTip

You can fill cells with sequential months, days of the week, years, and text plus a number (Quarter 1, Quarter 2, . . .) by dragging the fill handle. As you drag the fill handle, the contents of the last filled cell appears in the name box.

3. Position the pointer over the fill handle until it changes to ＋, then drag the fill handle to select the range **E13:E16**
See Figure B-11.

4. Release the mouse button
Once you release the mouse button, the fill handle copies the formula from the active cell (E13) and pastes it into each cell of the selected range. Again, because the formula uses relative cell references, cells E14 through E16 correctly display the totals for Raft and Canoe, Horse, and Bus tours

5. Click cell **B9**, click **Edit** on the menu bar, then click **Copy**
The Copy command on the Edit menu has the same effect as clicking the Copy button on the Standard toolbar.

6. Click cell **B18**, click **Edit** on the menu bar, then click **Paste**
See Figure B-12. The formula for calculating the September tours sales appears in the formula bar. Now you use the Fill Right command to copy the formula from cell B18 to cells C18, D18, and E18.

7. Select the range **B18:E18**

QuickTip

Use the Fill Series command on the Edit menu to examine all of Excel's available fill series options.

8. Click **Edit** on the menu bar, point to **Fill**, then click **Right**
The rest of the totals are filled in correctly. Compare your worksheet to Figure B-13.

9. Click the **Save button** 💾 on the Standard toolbar
Your worksheet is now saved.

FIGURE B-11: Selected range using the fill handle

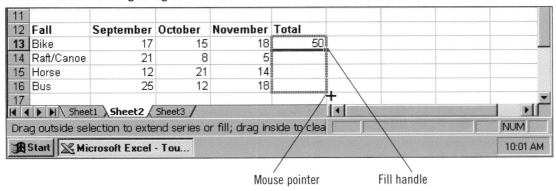

Mouse pointer   Fill handle

FIGURE B-12: Worksheet with copied formula

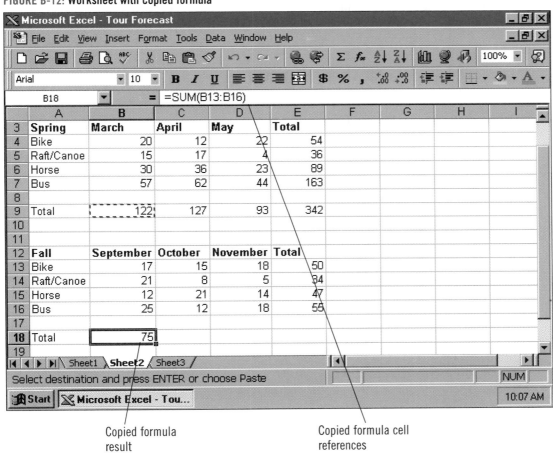

Copied formula
result

Copied formula cell
references

FIGURE B-13: Completed worksheet with all formulas copied

Copying Formulas with Absolute Cell References

Sometimes you might want a cell reference to always refer to a particular cell address. In such an instance, you would use an **absolute cell reference**. An absolute cell reference is a cell reference that always refers to a specific cell address, even if you move the formula to a new location. You identify an absolute reference by placing a dollar sign ($) before the column letter and row number of the address (for example $A$1). Marketing hopes the tour business will increase by 20% over last year's figures. Evan decides to add a column that calculates a possible increase in the number of spring tours in 1998. He wants to do a what-if analysis and recalculate the spreadsheet several times, changing the percentage that the tours might increase each time.

Steps

1. **Click cell G1, type Change, and then press [→]**
   You can store the increase factor that will be used in the what-if analysis in cell H1.

2. **Type 1.1 in cell H1, then press [Enter]**
   This represents a 10% increase in sales.

3. **Click cell F3, type 1998?, then press [Enter]**
   Now, you create a formula that references a specific address: cell H1.

4. **In cell F4, type =E4*H1, then click the Enter button on the formula bar**
   The result of 59.4 appears in cell F4. Now use the fill handle to copy the formula in cell F4 to F5:F7.

5. **Drag the fill handle to select the range F4:F7**
   The resulting values in the range F5:F7 are all zeros. When you look at the formula in cell F5, which is =E5*H2, you realize you need to use an absolute reference to cell H1. You can correct this error by editing cell F4 using [F4], a shortcut key, to change the relative cell reference to an absolute cell reference.

6. **Click cell F4, press [F2] to change to Edit mode, then press [F4]**
   When you pressed [F2], the **range finder** outlined the equations arguments in blue and green. When you pressed [F4], dollar signs appeared, changing the H1 cell reference to an absolute reference. See Figure B-14.

7. **Click the ✓ on the formula bar**
   Now that the formula correctly contains an absolute cell reference, use the fill handle to copy the formula in cell F4 to F5:F7.

8. **Drag the fill handle to select the range F4:F7**
   Now you can complete your what-if analysis by changing the value in cell H1 from 1.1 to 1.25 to indicate a 25% increase in sales.

9. **Click cell H1, type 1.25, then click the ✓ on the formula bar**
   The values in the range F4:F7 change. Compare your worksheet to Figure B-15.

QuickTip

Before you copy or move a formula, check to see if you need to use an absolute cell reference.

CourseHelp

If you have trouble with the concepts in this lesson, be sure to view the CourseHelp entitled Copying Formulas.

FIGURE B-14: Absolute cell reference in cell F4

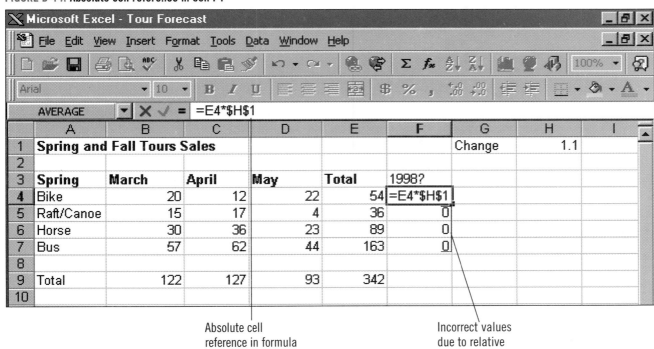

Absolute cell
reference in formula

Incorrect values
due to relative
references

FIGURE B-15: Worksheet with what-if value

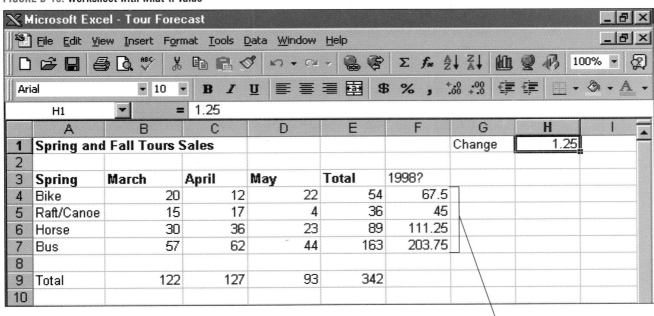

Absolute cell
reference in
formulas

Project a What-If Analysis

The ability to "plug in" values in a worksheet means you can create countless what-if analyses. A what-if analysis occurs when you insert different values into a worksheet model. This type of analysis can help you determine budgetary constraints, and can influence corporate economic decisions.

Naming and Moving a Sheet

Each workbook initially contains three worksheets. When the workbook is opened, the first worksheet is the active sheet. To move from sheet to sheet, click the desired sheet tab located at the bottom of the worksheet window. Sheet tab scrolling buttons, located to the left of the sheet tabs, allow rapid movement among the sheets. To make it easier to identify the sheets in a workbook, you can name each sheet. The name appears on the sheet tab. For instance, sheets within a single workbook could be named for individual sales people to better track performance goals. To better organize a workbook, you can easily rearrange sheets within it. Evan wants to be able to easily identify the Tour Information and the Tour Forecast sheets. He decides to name the two sheets in his workbook, then changes their order.

Steps 1 2 3 4

1. **Click the Sheet1 tab**

   Sheet1 becomes active; this is the worksheet that contains the Fall Tour Forecast information you compiled for the Marketing department. Its tab moves to the front, and the tab for Sheet2 moves to the background.

2. **Click the Sheet2 tab**

   Sheet2, containing last year's Tour Information, becomes active. Now that you have confirmed which sheet is which, rename Sheet1 so it has a name that identifies its contents.

3. **Double-click the Sheet1 tab**

   The Sheet1 text ("Sheet1") is selected. You could also click Format in the menu bar, point to Sheet, then click Rename to select the sheet name.

4. **Type Forecast, then press [Enter]**

   See Figure B-16. The new name automatically replaced the default name on the tab. Worksheet names can have up to 31 characters, including spaces and punctuation.

5. **Double-click the Sheet2 tab, then rename this sheet Information**

   You decide to rearrange the order of the sheets, so that Forecast comes after Information.

6. **Drag the Forecast sheet after the Information sheet**

   As you drag, the pointer changes to a sheet relocation indicator.
   See Figure B-17.

7. **Save and close the workbook, then exit Excel**

FIGURE B-16: Renamed sheet in workbook

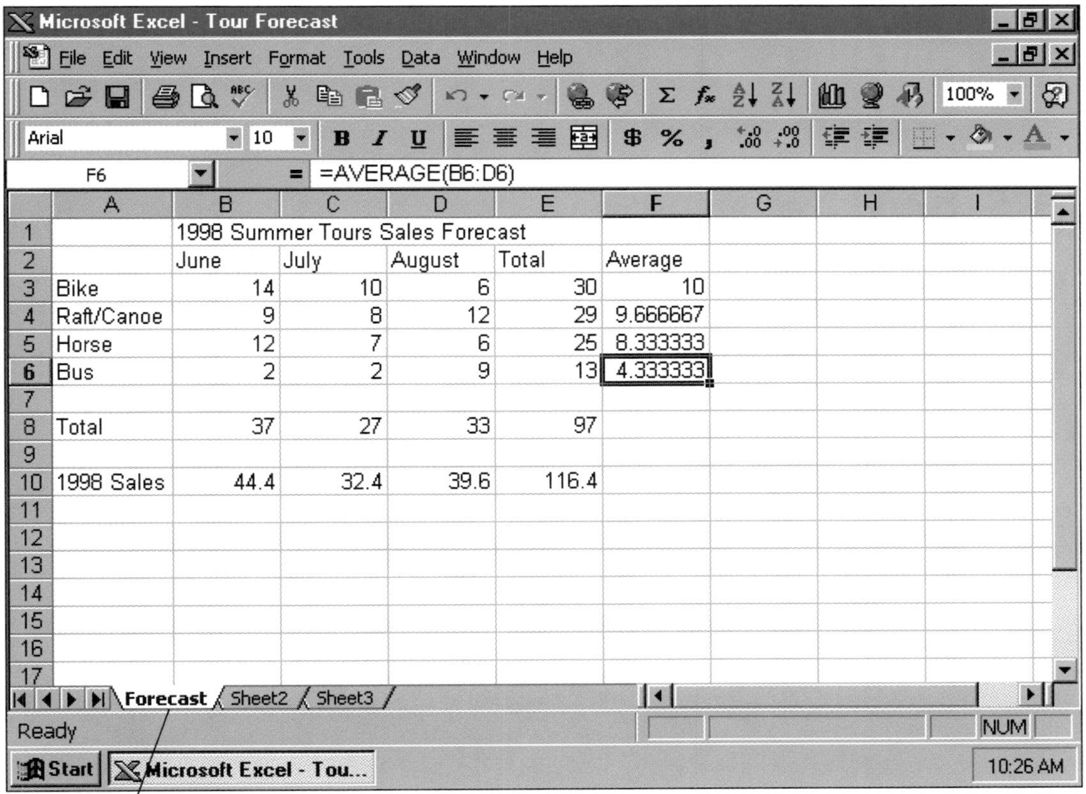

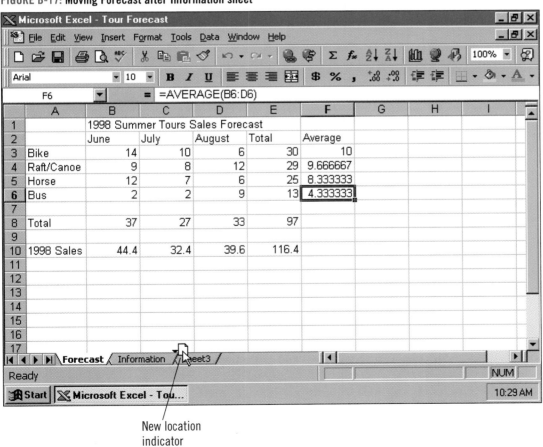

Sheet 1 renamed

FIGURE B-17: Moving Forecast after Information sheet

New location
indicator

Practice

► Concepts Review

Label each of the elements of the Excel worksheet window shown in Figure B-18.

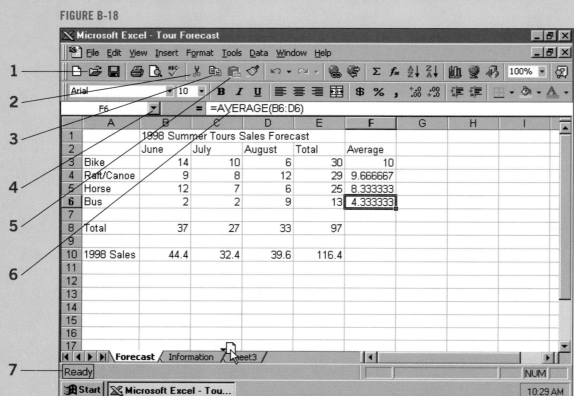

FIGURE B-18

Match each of the terms with the statement that describes its function.

8. Range
9. Function
10. 📋
11. 📄
12. Formula

a. A predefined formula that provides a shortcut for commonly used calculations
b. A cell entry that performs a calculation in an Excel worksheet
c. A specified group of cells, which can include the entire worksheet
d. Used to copy cells
e. Used to paste cells

Select the best answer from the list of choices.

13. What type of cell reference changes when it is copied?
 a. Absolute
 b. Circular
 c. Looping
 d. Relative

14. Which character is used to make a reference absolute?
 a. &
 b. ^
 c. $
 d. @

▶ Skills Review

1 Edit cell entries and work with ranges.
 a. Open workbook XL B-2 and save it as "Mutual Funds" on your Student Disk.
 b. Change the number of Arch shares to 210.
 c. Change the price per share of RST stock to 18.45.
 d. Change the number of United shares to 100.
 e. Name the range B2:B5 "Shares".
 f. Name the range C2:C5 "Price".
 g. Save, preview, and print your worksheet.

2 Enter formulas.
 a. Click cell B6.
 b. Enter the formula B2+B3+B4+B5.
 c. Click cell C6.
 d. Enter the formula C2+C3+C4+C5.
 e. Save your work, then preview and print the data in the Mutual Funds worksheet.

3 Introduce functions.
 a. Click cell C7.
 b. Enter the MIN function for the range C2:C5.
 c. Type the label Min Price in cell A7.
 d. Save your work.
 e. Preview and print this worksheet.

4 Copy and move cell entries.
 a. Select the range A1:E6.
 b. Use drag-and-drop to copy the range to cell A10.
 c. Delete the range B11:C14.
 d. Save your work.
 e. Preview and print this worksheet.

5 Copy formulas with relative cell references.

   a. Click cell D2.

   b. Create a formula that multiplies B2 and C2.

   c. Copy the formula in D2 into cells D3:D5.

   d. Copy the formula in D2 into cells D11:D14.

   e. Save, preview, and print this worksheet.

6 Copy formulas with absolute cell references.

   a. Click cell G2.

   b. Type the value 1.375.

   c. Click cell E2.

   d. Create a formula containing an absolute reference that multiplies D2 and G2.

   e. Copy the formula in E2 into cells E3:E5.

   f. Copy the formula in E2 into cells E11:E14.

   g. Change the amount in cell G2 to 2.873.

   h. Save, preview, and print this worksheet.

7 Name a sheet.

   a. Name the Sheet1 tab "Funds".

   b. Move the Funds sheet so it comes after Sheet3.

   c. Save and close this worksheet.

▶ Independent Challenges

1. You are the box-office manager for Lightwell Players, a regional theater company. Your responsibilities include tracking seasonal ticket sales for the company's main stage productions and anticipating ticket sales for the next season. Lightwell Players sells four types of tickets: reserved seating, general admission, senior citizen tickets, and student tickets. The 1993–94 season included productions of *Hamlet*, *The Cherry Orchard*, *Fires in the Mirror*, *The Shadow Box*, and *Heartbreak House*.

Open a new workbook and save it as "Theater" on your Student Disk. Plan and build a worksheet that tracks the sales of each of the four ticket types for all five of the plays. Calculate the total ticket sales for each play, the total sales for each of the four ticket types, and the total sales for all tickets.

Enter your own sales data, but assume the following: the Lightwell Players sold 800 tickets during the season; reserved seating was the most popular ticket type for all of the shows except for *The Shadow Box*; no play sold more than 10 student tickets. Plan and build a second worksheet in the workbook that reflects a 5% increase in sales of all ticket types.

To complete this independent challenge:

1. Think about the results you want to see, the information you need to build into these worksheets, and what types of calculations must be performed.
2. Sketch sample worksheets on a piece of paper to indicate how the information should be laid out. What information should go in the columns? In the rows?
3. Build the worksheets by entering a title, row labels, column headings, and formulas. Use named ranges to make the worksheet easier to use, and rename the sheet tabs to easily identify the contents of each sheet. (Hint: If your columns are too narrow, position the cell pointer in the column you want to widen. To widen the column, click Format on the menu bar, click Column, click Width, choose a new column width, and then click OK.)
4. Use separate worksheets for existing ticket sales and projected sales showing the 5% increase.
5. Save your work, then preview and print the worksheets.
6. Submit your sketches and printed worksheets.

2. You have been promoted to computer lab manager at your school, and it is your responsibility to make sure there are enough computers for students during scheduled classes. Currently, you have four classrooms: three with IBM PCs and one with Macintoshes. Classes are scheduled Monday, Wednesday, and Friday in two-hour increments from 9 a.m. to 5 p.m. (the lab closes at 7 p.m.), and each room can currently accommodate 20 computers.

Open a new workbook and save it as "Lab Manager" on your Student Disk. Plan and build a worksheet that tracks the number of students who can currently use available computers per two-hour class. Create your enrollment data, but assume that current enrollment averages 85% of each room's daily capacity. Using an additional worksheet, show the impact of an enrollment increase of 25%.

To complete this independent challenge:

1. Think about how to construct these worksheets to create the desired output.
2. Sketch sample paper worksheets, to indicate how the information should be laid out.
3. Build the worksheets by entering a title, row labels, column headings, and formulas. Use named ranges to make the worksheet easier to use, and rename the sheets to identify their contents easily.
4. Use separate sheets for actual enrollment and projected changes.
5. Save your work, then preview and print the worksheets.
6. Submit your sketches and printed worksheets.

3. Nuts and Bolts is a small but growing hardware store that has hired you to organize its accounting records using Excel. The store hopes to track its inventory using Excel once its accounting records are under control. Before you were hired, one of the accounting staff started to enter expenses in a workbook, but the work was never completed. Open the workbook XL B-3 and save it as "Nuts and Bolts Finances" on your Student Disk. Include functions such as the Average, Maximum, and Minimum amounts of each of the expenses in the worksheet.

To complete this independent challenge:

1. Think about what information would be important for the accounting staff to know.
2. Use the existing worksheet to create a paper sketch of the types of functions and formulas you will use and of where they will be located. Indicate where you will have named ranges.
3. Create your sketch using the existing worksheet as a foundation. Your worksheet should use range names in its formulas and functions.
4. Rename Sheet1 "Expenses".
5. Save your work, and then preview and print the worksheet.
6. Submit your sketches and printed worksheets.

4. The immediacy of the World Wide Web allows you to find comparative data on any service or industry of interest to you. Your company is interested in investing in one of any of the most actively traded stocks in the three primary trading houses, and you have been asked to retrieve this information. To complete this independent challenge:

1. Open a new workbook and save it on your Student Disk as Stock Data.
2. Log on to the Internet and use your browser to go to the http://www.course.com. From there, click the link Student On Line Companions, then click the Microsoft Office 97 Professional Edition — Illustrated: A First Course page, then click on the Excel link for Unit B.
3. Use each of the following sites to compile your data: NASDAQ [www.nasdaq.com], the New York Stock Exchange [www.nyse.com], and the American Stock Exchange [www.amex.com].
4. Using one worksheet per exchange, locate data for the 10 most actively traded stocks.
5. Make sure all stocks are identified using their commonly known names.
6. Your company will invest a total of $100,000 and wants to make that investment in only one exchange. Still, they are asking you to research the types of stocks that could be purchased in each exchange.
7. Assume an even distribution of the original investment in the stocks, and total pertinent columns. Determine the total number of shares that will be purchased.
8. Save, print, and hand in a print of your work.

▶ Visual Workshop

Create a worksheet similar to Figure B-19 using the skills you learned in this unit. Save the workbook as "Annual Budget" on your Student Disk. Preview, and then print the worksheet.

FIGURE B-19

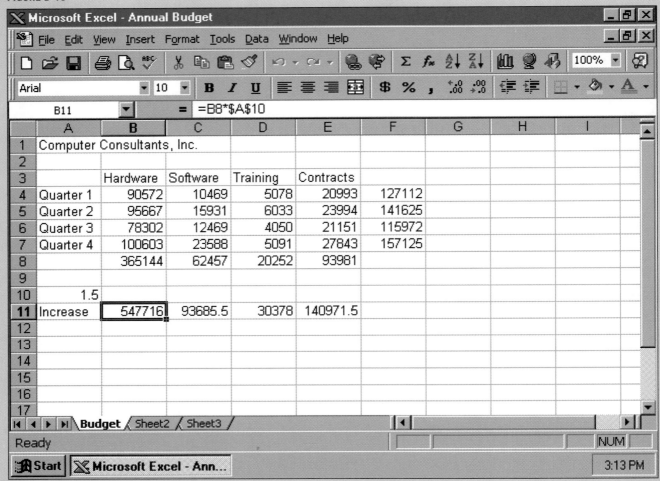

Formatting
a Worksheet

Objectives

► **Format values**
► **Select fonts and point sizes**
► **Change attributes and alignment of labels**
► **Adjust column widths**
► **Insert and delete rows and columns**
► **Apply colors, patterns, and borders**
► **Use conditional formatting**
► **Check spelling**

Now you will learn how to format a worksheet to make it easier to read and to emphasize key data. You do this by formatting cell contents, adjusting column widths, and inserting and deleting columns and rows. The marketing managers at Nomad Ltd have asked Evan Brillstein to create a worksheet that tracks tour advertising expenses. Evan has prepared a worksheet containing this information, and now he needs to use formatting techniques to make the worksheet easier to read and to call attention to important data.

Formatting Values

Formatting is how information appears in cells; it does not alter the data in any way. To format a cell, you select it, then apply the formatting you want. You can also format a range of cells. Cells and ranges can be formatted before or after data is entered. If you enter a value in a cell, and the cell appears to display the data incorrectly, you need to format the cell to display the value correctly. You might also want more than one cell to have the same format. The Marketing Department has requested that Evan track tour advertising expenses. Evan developed a worksheet that tracks invoices for tour advertising. He has entered all the information and now wants to format some of the labels and values in the worksheet. Because some of the format changes he will make to labels and values might also affect column widths, Evan decided to make all his formatting changes before changing the column widths. He formats his values first.

Steps

1. Open the worksheet **XL C-1** from your Student Disk, then save it as **Tour Ads**
The tour advertising worksheet appears in Figure C-1.
You want to format the data in the Cost ea. column so it displays with a dollar sign.

2. Select the range **E4:E32**, then click the **Currency Style button** 💲 on the Formatting toolbar
Excel adds dollar signs and two decimal places to the Cost ea. column data. When the new format is applied, Excel automatically resizes the columns to display all the information. Columns G, H, and I contain dollar values also, but you decide to apply the comma format instead of currency.

3. Select the range **G4:I32**, then click the **Comma Style button** , on the Formatting toolbar
Column J contains percentages.

4. Select the range **J4:J32**, click the **Percent Style button** % on the Formatting toolbar, then click the **Increase Decimal button** .⁰₈ on the Formatting toolbar to show one decimal place
Data in the % of Total column is now formatted in Percent style. Next, you reformat the invoice dates.

5. Select the range **B4:B31**, click **Format** on the menu bar, then click **Cells**
The Format Cells dialog box appears with the Number tab in front and the Date format already selected. See Figure C-2. You can also use this dialog box to format ranges with currency, commas, and percentages.

6. Select the format **4-Mar-97** in the Type list box, then click **OK**
You decide you don't need the year to appear in the Inv Due column.

7. Select the range **C4:C31**, click **Format** on the menu bar, click **Cells**, click **4-Mar** in the Type list box, then click **OK**
Compare your worksheet to Figure C-3.

8. Save your work

FIGURE C-1: **Tour advertising worksheet**

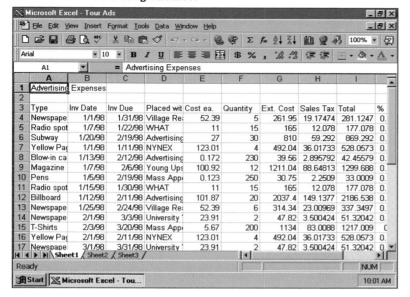

FIGURE C-2: **Format Cells dialog box**

Select a type

Sample of selected type

Select a category

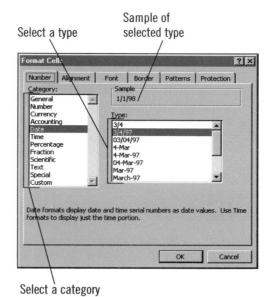

FIGURE C-3: **Worksheet with formatted values**

Currency Style button

Percent Style button

Comma Style button

Increase decimal button

Decrease decimal button

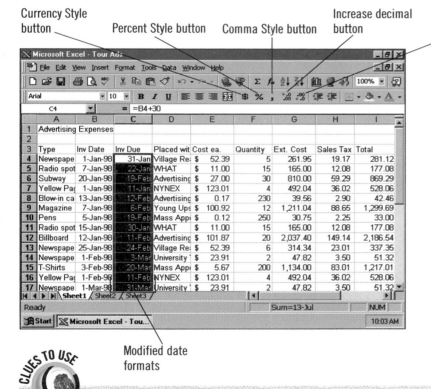

Modified date formats

CLUES TO USE

Using the Format Painter

A cell's format can be "painted" into other cells using the Format Painter button ✍ on the Formatting toolbar. This is similar to using drag-and-drop to copy information, but instead of copying cell contents, you copy only the cell format. Select the cell containing the desired format, then click ✍. The pointer changes to ⊕🖌, as shown in Figure C-4. Use this pointer to select the cell or range you want to contain the painted format.

FIGURE C-4: **Using the Format Painter**

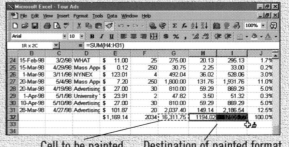

Cell to be painted   Destination of painted format

Selecting Fonts and Point Sizes

A **font** is the name given to a collection of characters (letters, numerals, symbols, and punctuation marks) with a specific design. The **point size** is the physical size of the text, measured in points. The default font in Excel is 10 point Arial. You can change the font, the size, or both of any entry or section in a worksheet by using the Format command on the menu bar or by using the Formatting toolbar. Table C-1 shows several fonts in different sizes. Now that the data is formatted, Evan wants to change the font and size of the labels and the worksheet title so that they stand out.

Steps 1234

QuickTip

You can also open the Format Cells dialog box by right-clicking the mouse after selecting cells, then selecting Format Cells.

Trouble?

If you don't have Times New Roman in your list of fonts, choose another font.

QuickTip

The Format Cells dialog box displays a sample of the selected font. Use the Format Cells command to access the Format Cells dialog box if you're unsure of a font's appearance.

1. Press [Ctrl][Home] to select cell A1

2. Click Format on the menu bar, click Cells, then click the Font tab in the Format Cells dialog box
See Figure C-5.
You decide to change the font of the title from Arial to Times New Roman, and increase the font size to 24.

3. Click Times New Roman in the Font list box, click 24 in the Size list box, then click OK
The title font appears in 24 point Times New Roman, and the Formatting toolbar displays the new font and size information. Next, you make the column headings larger.

4. Select the range A3:J3, click Format on the menu bar, then click Cells
The Font tab should still be the front-most tab in the Format Cells dialog box.

5. Click Times New Roman in the Font list box, click 14 in the Size list box, then click OK
Compare your worksheet to Figure C-6.

6. Save your work

TABLE C-1: **Types of fonts**

font	12 point	24 point
Arial	Excel	Excel
Helvetica	Excel	Excel
Palatino	Excel	Excel
Times	Excel	Excel

FIGURE C-5: Font tab in the Format Cells dialog box

Available fonts on
your computer—
yours may differ

Currently
selected font

Font attribute
options

Type a custom font size
or select from the list

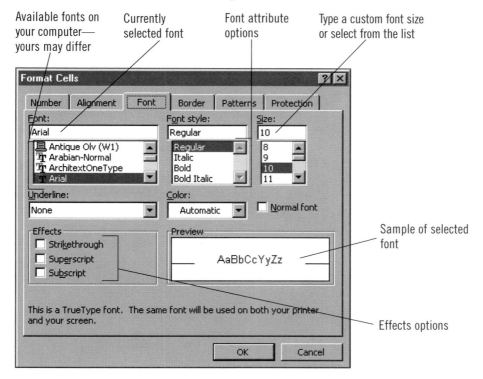

Sample of selected
font

Effects options

FIGURE C-6: Worksheet with enlarged title and labels

Column headings
now 14 point Times
New Roman

Font and size of
active cell

Title after changing
to 24 point Times
New Roman

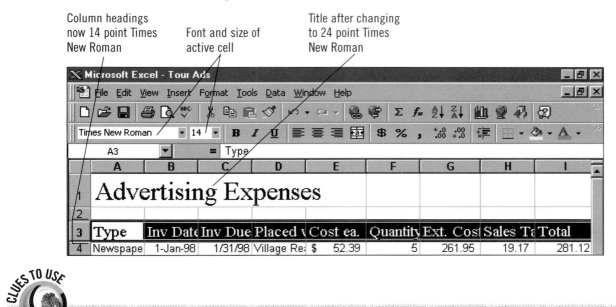

![CLUES TO USE icon]

Using the Formatting toolbar to change fonts and sizes

The font and size of the active cell appear on the
Formatting toolbar. Click the Font list arrow, as
shown in Figure C-7, to see a list of available fonts.
If you want to change the font, first select the cell,
click the Font list arrow, then choose the font you
want. You can change the size of selected text in the
same way, by clicking the Size list arrow on the
Formatting toolbar to display a list of available
point sizes.

FIGURE C-7: Available fonts on the Formatting toolbar

Available fonts
installed on your
computer—yours
may differ

Changing Attributes and Alignment of Labels

Attributes are font styling features such as bold, italics, and underlining. You can apply bold, italics, and underlining from the Formatting toolbar or from the Font tab in the Format Cells dialog box. You can also change the alignment of text in cells. Left, right, or center alignment can be applied from the Formatting toolbar, or from the Alignment tab in the Format Cells dialog box. See Table C-2 for a description of the available attribute and alignment buttons on the Formatting toolbar. Excel also has predefined worksheet formats to make formatting easier. ✎ Now that he has applied the appropriate fonts and font sizes to his worksheet labels, Evan wants to further enhance his worksheet's appearance by adding bold and underline formatting and centering some of the labels.

Steps 123 4

1. Press **[Ctrl][Home]** to select cell A1, then click the **Bold button** **B** on the Formatting toolbar
   The title "Advertising Expenses" appears in bold.

2. Select the range **A3:J3**, then click the **Underline button** **U** on the Formatting toolbar
   Excel underlines the column headings in the selected range.

QuickTip

Highlighting information on a worksheet can be useful, but overuse of any attribute can be distracting and make a document less readable. Be consistent by adding emphasis the same way throughout a workbook.

3. Click cell **A3**, click the **Italics button** **I** on the Formatting toolbar, then click **B**
   The word "Type" appears in boldface, italic type. Notice that the Bold, Italics, and Underline buttons on the Formatting toolbar are indented. You decide you don't like the italic formatting. You remove it by clicking **I** again.

4. Click **I**
   Excel removes italics from cell A3.

5. Add bold formatting to the rest of the labels in the range **B3:J3**
   You want to center the title over the data.

6. Select the range **A1:F1**, then click the **Merge and Center button** 🔲 on the Formatting toolbar
   The title Advertising Expenses is centered across six columns. Now you center the column headings in their cells.

Time To

✔ Save

7. Select the range **A3:J3** then click the **Center button** ☰ on the Formatting toolbar
   You are satisfied with the formatting in the worksheet.
   Compare your screen to Figure C-8.

FIGURE C-8: Worksheet with formatting attributes applied

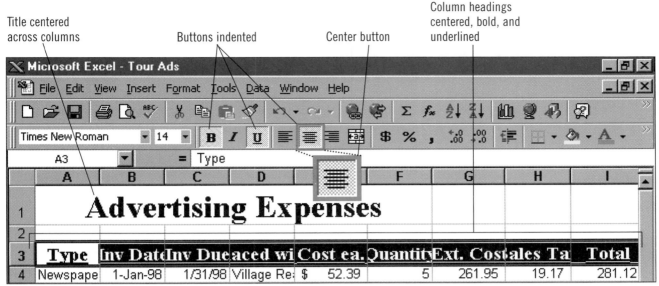

Title centered across columns   Buttons indented   Center button   Column headings centered, bold, and underlined

TABLE C-2: Attribute and Alignment buttons on the Formatting toolbar

icon	description	icon	description
B	Adds boldface	(align left)	Aligns left
I	Italicizes	(align center)	Aligns center
U	Underlines	(align right)	Aligns right
(border)	Adds lines or borders	(center across)	Centers across columns, and combines two or more selected adjacent cells into one cell.

CLUES TO USE

Using AutoFormat

Excel provides 16 preset formats called AutoFormats, which allow instant formatting of large amounts of data. AutoFormats are designed for worksheets with labels in the left column and top rows and totals in the bottom row or right column. To use AutoFormatting, select the data to be formatted—or place your mouse pointer anywhere within the range to be selected—click Format on the menu bar, click AutoFormat, then select a format from the Table Format list box, as shown in Figure C-9.

FIGURE C-9: AutoFormat dialog box

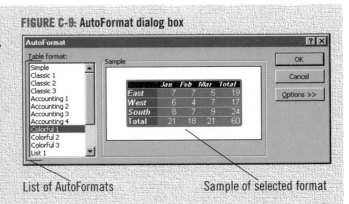

List of AutoFormats   Sample of selected format

Excel 97

Adjusting Column Widths

As you work with a worksheet, you might need to adjust the width of the columns to make your worksheet more usable. The default column width is 8.43 characters wide, a little less than one inch. With Excel, you can adjust the column width for one or more columns using the mouse or the Column command on the Format menu. Table C-3 describes the commands available on the Format Column menu. You can also adjust the height of rows. ✐ Evan notices that some of the labels in column A don't fit in the cells. He decides to adjust the widths of columns so that the labels fit in the cells.

Steps 1234

1. **Position the pointer on the column line between columns A and B in the column header area**
   The pointer changes to ↔, as shown in Figure C-10. You make the column wider.

2. **Drag the line to the right until column A is wide enough to accommodate all of the labels for types of advertising**
   You decide to resize the columns so they automatically accommodate the widest entry in a cell.

3. **Position the pointer on the column line between columns B and C in the column header area until it changes to ↔, then double-click the left mouse button**
   The width of column B is automatically resized to fit the widest entry, in this case, the column head. This feature is called **AutoFit**.

4. **Repeat step 3 to use AutoFit to automatically resize columns C, D, and J**
   You can also use the Column Width command on the Format menu to adjust several columns to the same width.

QuickTip

To reset columns to the default width, select the range of cells, then use the Column Standard Width command on the Format menu. Click OK in the Standard Width dialog box to accept the default width.

5. **Select the range F5:I5**
   Any cells in the columns you want to resize can be selected.

6. **Click Format on the menu bar, point to Column, then click Width**
   The Column Width dialog box appears. Move the dialog box, if necessary, by dragging it by its title bar so you can see the contents of the worksheet.

7. **Type 12 in the Column Width text box, then click OK**
   The column widths change to reflect the new settings. See Figure C-11. You are satisfied and decide to save the worksheet.

8. **Save your work**

TABLE C-3: Format Column commands

command	description
Width	Sets the width to a specific number of characters
AutoFit Selection	Fits the widest entry
Hide	Hide(s) column(s)
Unhide	Unhide(s) column(s)
Standard Width	Resets to default widths

FIGURE C-10: Preparing to change the column width

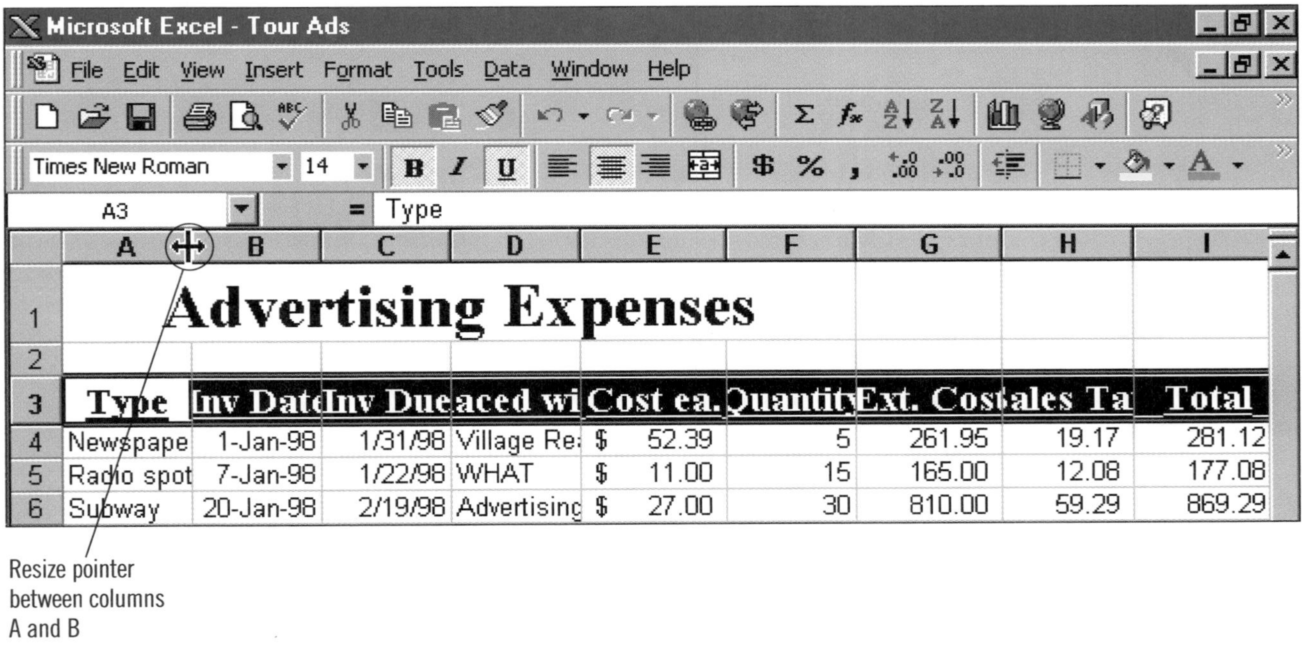

Microsoft Excel - Tour Ads

File Edit View Insert Format Tools Data Window Help

Times New Roman   14   B I U $ % ,

A3   = Type

	A	B	C	D	E	F	G	H	I
1		**Advertising Expenses**							
2									
3	**Type**	**Inv Date**	**Inv Due**	**aced wi**	**Cost ea.**	**Quantity**	**Ext. Cost**	**ales Ta**	**Total**
4	Newspape	1-Jan-98	1/31/98	Village Re:	$ 52.39	5	261.95	19.17	281.12
5	Radio spot	7-Jan-98	1/22/98	WHAT	$ 11.00	15	165.00	12.08	177.08
6	Subway	20-Jan-98	2/19/98	Advertising	$ 27.00	30	810.00	59.29	869.29

Resize pointer
between columns
A and B

FIGURE C-11: Worksheet with column widths adjusted

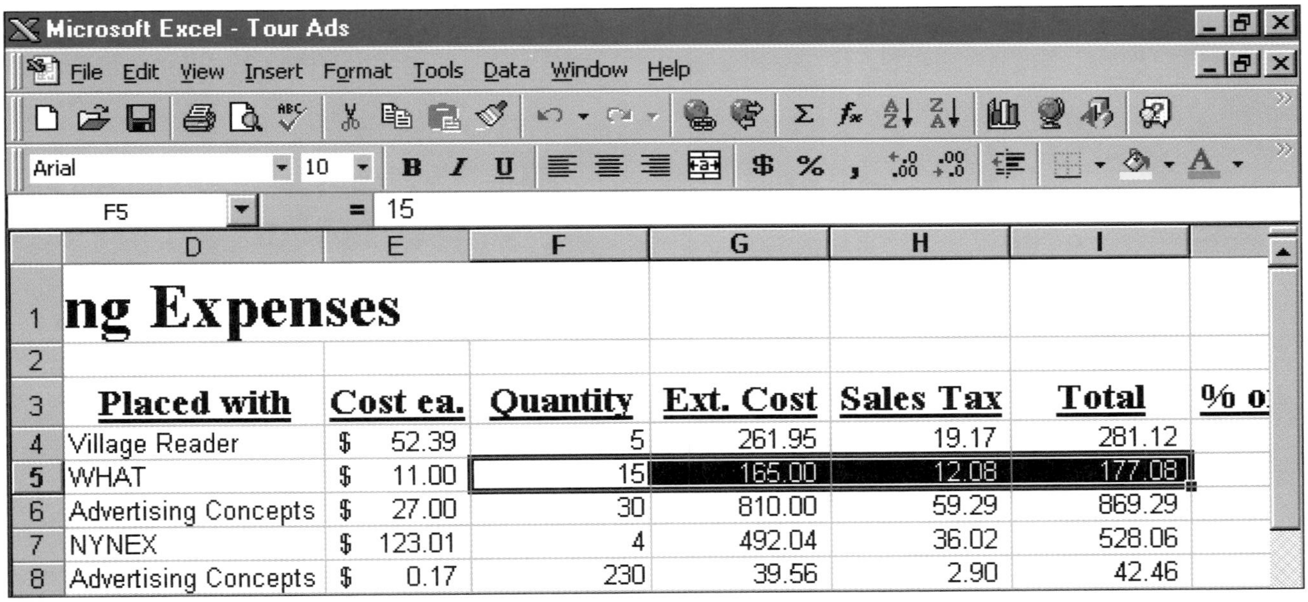

Microsoft Excel - Tour Ads

File Edit View Insert Format Tools Data Window Help

Arial   10   B I U $ % ,

F5   = 15

	D	E	F	G	H	I	
1	**ng Expenses**						
2							
3	**Placed with**	**Cost ea.**	**Quantity**	**Ext. Cost**	**Sales Tax**	**Total**	**% o**
4	Village Reader	$ 52.39	5	261.95	19.17	281.12	
5	WHAT	$ 11.00	15	165.00	12.08	177.08	
6	Advertising Concepts	$ 27.00	30	810.00	59.29	869.29	
7	NYNEX	$ 123.01	4	492.04	36.02	528.06	
8	Advertising Concepts	$ 0.17	230	39.56	2.90	42.46	

CLUES TO USE

Specifying row height

The Row Height command on the Format menu allows you to customize row height to improve readability. Row height is calculated in points, units of measure also used for fonts—one inch equals 72 points. The row height must exceed the size of the font you are using. For example, if you are using a 12 point font, the row height must be more than 12 points. Normally, you don't need to adjust row heights manually. If you format something in a row to be a larger point size, Excel will adjust the row height to fit the largest point size in the row.

Inserting and Deleting Rows and Columns

As you modify a worksheet, you might find it necessary to insert or delete rows and columns. For example, you might need to insert rows to accommodate new inventory products or remove a column of yearly totals that are no longer current. Inserting or deleting rows or columns can help to make your worksheet more readable. ✎ Evan has already improved the appearance of his worksheet by formatting the labels and values in the worksheet. Now he decides to improve the overall appearance of the worksheet by inserting a row between the last row of data and the totals. This will help make the totals stand out more. Evan has also located a row of inaccurate data that should be deleted.

1. **Click cell A32, click Insert on the menu bar, then click Cells**
   The Insert dialog box opens. See Figure C-12. You can choose to insert a column or a row, or you can shift the data in the cells in the active column right or in the active row down. You want to insert a row to add some space between the last row of data and the totals.

QuickTip

Inserting or deleting rows or columns can also cause problems with formulas that reference cells in that area, so be sure to consider this when inserting or deleting rows or columns.

2. **Click the Entire Row radio button, then click OK**
   A blank row is inserted between the title and the month labels. When you insert a new row, the contents of the worksheet shift down from the newly inserted row. When you insert a new column, the contents of the worksheet shift to the right from the point of the new column. Now delete the row containing information about hats, as this information is inaccurate.

3. **Click the row 27 selector button (the gray box containing the row number to the left of the worksheet)**
   All of row 27 is selected as shown in Figure C-13.

4. **Click Edit on the menu bar, then click Delete**
   Excel deletes row 27, and all rows below this shift up one row. You are satisfied with the appearance of the worksheet.

5. **Save your work**

FIGURE C-12: Insert dialog box

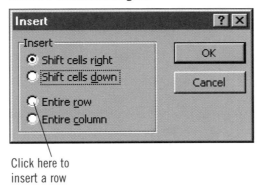

Click here to
insert a row

FIGURE C-13: Worksheet with row 27 selected

25	Pens	15-Mar-98	4/29/98	Mass Appeal, Inc.	$	0.12	250	3
26	Yellow Pages	1-Mar-98	3/11/98	NYNEX	$	123.01	4	49
27	Hats	20-Mar-98	5/4/98	Mass Appeal, Inc.	$	7.20	250	1,80
28	Subway	20-Mar-98	4/19/98	Advertising Concepts	$	27.00	30	81
29	Newspaper	1-Apr-98	5/1/98	University Voice	$	23.91	2	4
30	Subway	10-Apr-98	5/10/98	Advertising Concepts	$	27.00	30	81
31	Billboard	28-Mar-98	4/27/98	Advertising Concepts	$	101.87	20	2,03
32								
33					$1,169.14		2034	16,31
34								
35								

Sheet1 / Sheet2 / Sheet3 /

Ready   Sum=75913.83035   NUM

Start   Microsoft Excel - Tou...   8:26 AM

Row 27 selector   Inserted row
button

Excel 97

Using dummy columns and rows

You use cell references and ranges in formulas. When
you add or delete a column or row within a range used
in a formula, Excel automatically adjusts the formula to
reflect the change. However, when you add a column or
row at the end of a range used in a formula, you must
modify the formula to reflect the additional column or
row. To avoid having to edit the formula, you can
include a dummy column and dummy row within the
range you use for that formula. A dummy column is a
blank column included to the right of but within a
range. A dummy row is a blank row included at the
bottom of but within a range, as shown in Figure C-14.
Then if you add another column or row to the end of
the range, the formula will automatically be modified to
include the new data.

FIGURE C-14: Formula with dummy row

	A	B	C	D	E	F	G
19	Magazine	27-Feb-98	3/29/98	Young Upstart	$ 100.92	12	1,21
20	Subway	22-Feb-98	3/24/98	Advertising Concepts	$ 27.00	30	81
21	Radio spot	1-Feb-98	2/16/98	WHAT	$ 11.00	30	33
22	Newspaper	25-Feb-98	3/27/98	Village Reader	$ 52.39	6	31
23	Blow-in cards	10-Mar-98	4/9/98	Advertising Concepts	$ 0.17	275	4
24	Radio spot	15-Feb-98	3/2/98	WHAT	$ 11.00	25	27
25	Pens	15-Mar-98	4/29/98	Mass Appeal, Inc.	$ 0.12	250	3
26	Yellow Pages	1-Mar-98	3/11/98	NYNEX	$ 123.01	4	49
27	Subway	20-Mar-98	4/19/98	Advertising Concepts	$ 27.00	30	81
28	Newspaper	1-Mar-98	5/1/98	University Voice	$ 27.00	2	4
29	Subway	10-Apr-98	5/10/98	Advertising Concepts	$ 27.00	30	81
30	Billboard	28-Mar-98	4/27/98	Advertising Concepts	$ 101.87	20	2,03
31							
32					$1,161.94	1784	14,51
33							

E32 = =SUM(E4:E31)

Dummy row   Formula with   Rows included
                   dummy row   in formula

Applying Colors, Patterns, and Borders

You can use colors, patterns, and borders to enhance the overall appearance of a worksheet and to improve its readability. You can add these enhancements using the Patterns tab in the Format Cells dialog box or by using the Borders and Color buttons on the Formatting toolbar. When you use the Format Cells dialog box, you can see what your enhanced text will look like in the Sample box. You can apply color to the background of a cell or range or to cell contents. If you do not have a color monitor, the colors appear in shades of gray. You can apply patterns to the background of a cell or range. And, you can apply borders to all the cells in a worksheet or only to selected cells. See Table C-4 for a list of border buttons and their functions. Evan decides to add a pattern, a border, and color to the title of the worksheet. This will give the worksheet a more professional appearance.

Steps

1. Click cell **A1**, then click the **Fill Color button list arrow** ![fill color] on the Formatting toolbar
The color palette appears, as shown in Figure C-15.

> **QuickTip**
>
> Use color sparingly. Excessive use can divert the reader's attention away from the data in the worksheet.

2. Click **Turquoise** (fourth row, fourth color from the right)

3. Click **Format** on the menu bar, then click **Cells**
The Format Cells dialog box opens.

4. Click the **Patterns tab**, as shown in Figure C-16, if it is not already displayed
When choosing a background pattern, consider that the more cell contents contrast with the background, the more readable the contents will be. You choose the diamond pattern.

5. Click the **Pattern list arrow**, click the **thin diagonal crosshatch pattern** (third row, last pattern on the right), then click **OK**
Now you add a border.

6. Click the **Borders button list arrow** ![borders] on the Formatting toolbar, then click the **heavy bottom border** (second row, second border from the left)
Next, you change the font color.

7. Click the **Font Color button list arrow** ![font color] on the Formatting toolbar, then click **blue** (second row, third color from the right)
The text changes color, as shown in Figure C-17.

> **Time To**
>
> ✔ Save

8. Preview and print the first page of the worksheet

TABLE C-4: Border buttons

button	description	button	description
	No border		Thin border around range
	Single underline		Left border
	Double underline		Right border
	Thick bottom, thin top border		Double bottom, single top
	Outline all in range		Thick bottom border
	Thick border around range		

FIGURE C-15: **Fill Color palette**

Choose from
available colors

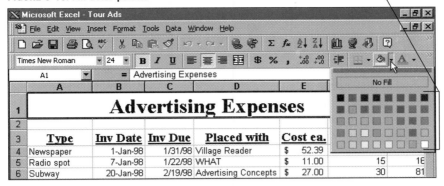

FIGURE C-16: **Patterns tab in the Format Cells dialog box**

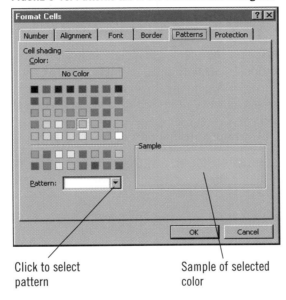

Click to select
pattern

Sample of selected
color

FIGURE C-17: **Worksheet with color, patterns, and border**

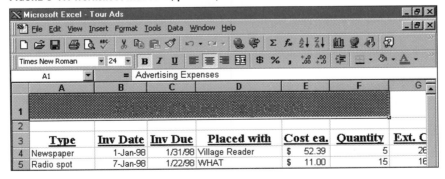

CLUES TO USE

Using color to organize a worksheet

You can use color to give a distinctive look to each part of a worksheet. For example, you might want to apply a light blue to all the rows containing the subway data and a light green to all the rows containing the newspaper data. Be consistent throughout a group of worksheets, and try to avoid colors that are too bright and distracting.

Using Conditional Formatting

Formatting attributes make worksheets look professional, and these same attributes can be applied depending on specific outcomes in cells. Automatically applying formatting attributes based on cell values is called **conditional formatting**. You might, for example, want advertising costs above a certain number to display in red boldface, and lower values to display in blue. Evan wants his worksheet to include conditional formatting so that extended advertising costs greater than $175 display in red boldface. He creates the conditional format in the first cell in the extended cost column.

Steps

1. Click cell **G4**
Use the scroll bars if necessary, to make column G visible.

2. Click **Format** on the menu bar, then click **Conditional Formatting**
The Conditional Formatting dialog box opens, as shown in Figure C-18. The number of input fields varies depending on which operator is selected. You can define up to 3 different conditions that let you determine outcome parameters and then assign formatting attributes to each one.
You begin by defining the first part of the condition.

3. Click the **Operator list arrow**, then click **greater than or equal to**
Next, you define the value in this condition that must be met for the formatting to be applied.

4. Click the **Value text box**, then type **175**
Once the value has been assigned, you define this condition's formatting attributes.

5. Click **Format**, click the **Color list arrow**, click **Red** (third row, first color from the left), click **Bold** in the Font Style list box, click **OK**, then click **OK** again to close the Conditional Formatting dialog box
Next, you copy the formatting to the other cells in the column.

6. Click the **Format Painter button** on the Formatting toolbar, then select the range **G5:G30**
Once the formatting is copied, you reposition the cell pointer to review the results.

7. Click cell **G4**
Compare your results to Figure C-19.

8. Press **[Ctrl][Home]** to move to cell Al

9. Save your work

FIGURE C-18: **Conditional Formatting dialog box**

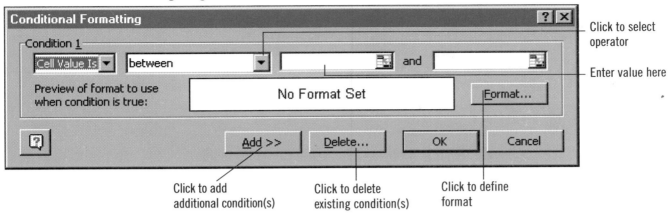

Click to select operator

Enter value here

Click to add additional condition(s)

Click to delete existing condition(s)

Click to define format

FIGURE C-19: **Worksheet with conditional formatting**

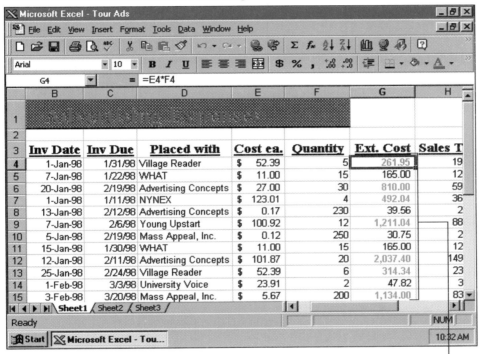

Results of conditional formatting

CLUES TO USE

Deleting conditional formatting

Because its likely that the conditions you define will change, any of the conditional formats defined can be deleted. Select the cell(s) containing conditional formatting, click Format, click Conditional Formatting, then click the Delete button. The Delete Conditional Format dialog box opens, as shown in Figure C-20. Click the checkboxes for any of the conditions you want to delete, then click OK. The previously assigned formatting is deleted—leaving the cell's contents intact.

FIGURE C-20: **Delete Conditional Format dialog box**

Click the existing condition(s) to delete

Excel 97

Checking Spelling

You may think your worksheet is complete, but if you haven't checked for spelling errors, you risk undermining the professional effect of your work. A single misspelled word can ruin your work. The spell checker in Excel is also shared by Word, PowerPoint, and Access, so any words you've added to the dictionary using those programs are also available in Excel. ✎═══ Evan has completed the formatting for his worksheet and is ready to check its spelling.

Steps

1. Click the Spelling button 🔤 on the Standard toolbar

The Spelling dialog opens, as shown in Figure C-21, with the abbreviation Inv selected as the first misspelled word in the worksheet. The spell checker starts from the active cell and compares words in the worksheet to those in its dictionary. Any word not found in the dictionary causes the spell checker to stop. At that point, you can decide to Ignore, Change, or Add the word.

You decide to Ignore All cases of Inv, the abbreviation of invoice.

2. Click Ignore All, then click Ignore All again when the spell checker stops on T-Shirts

The spell checker found the word 'cards' misspelled. You find the correct spelling and fix the error.

3. Scroll through the Suggestions list, click Cards, then click Change

The word 'Concepts' is also misspelled. Make this correction.

4. Click Concepts in the Suggestions list, then click Change

When no more incorrect words are found, Excel displays the message box shown in Figure C-22.

5. Click OK

6. Press [Ctrl][Home] to move to cell A1

7. Save your work

8. Preview and print the worksheet, then close the workbook and exit Excel

FIGURE C-21: **Spelling dialog box**

Misspelled word

Type replacement word here or click a suggestion

Click to add word to dictionary

Click to ignore all occurrences of misspelled word

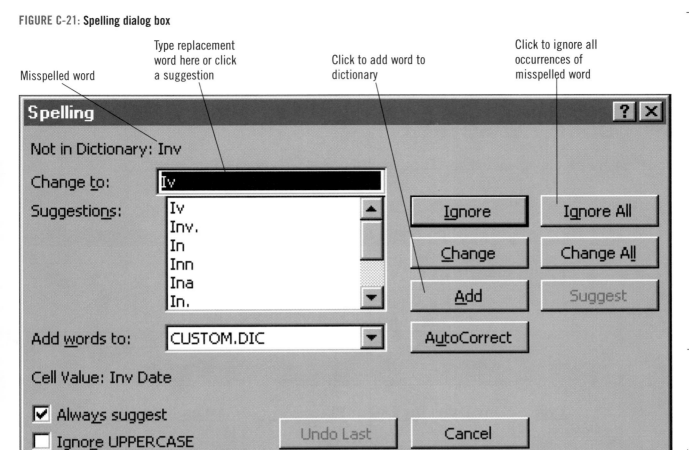

FIGURE C-22: **Spelling completed warning box**

CLUES TO USE

Modifying the spell checker

Each of us use words specific to our profession or task. Because the dictionary supplied with Microsoft Office cannot possibly include all the words that each of us needs, it is possible to add words to the dictionary shared by all the components in the suite.

To customize the Microsoft Office dictionary used by the spell checker, click Add when a word not in the dictionary is found. From then on, that word will no longer be considered misspelled by the spell checker.

Practice

▶ Concepts Review

Label each of the elements of the Excel worksheet window shown in Figure C-23.

FIGURE C-23

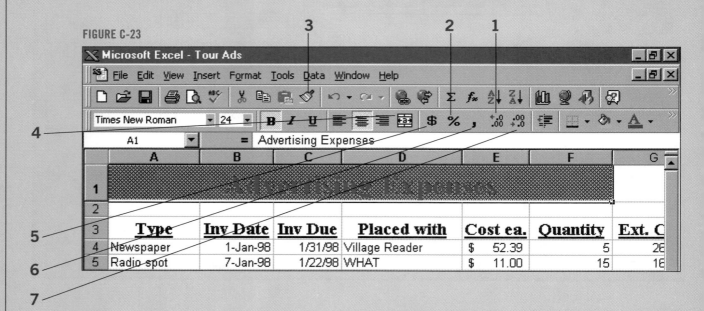

Match each of the statements to the command or button it describes.

8. Format Cells
9. Edit Clear
10. Insert Row/Column
11. 📋
12. $
13. ✓

a. Adds a new row or column
b. Erases the contents of a cell
c. Checks the spelling in a worksheet
d. Changes the point size of selected cells
e. Pastes the contents of the Clipboard in the current cell
f. Changes the format to Currency

Select the best answer from the list of choices.

14. Which button increases the number of decimal places in selected cells?
    a. ⬚   b. ⬚   c. ⬚   d. ⬚

15. Each of the following operators can be used in conditional formatting, *except*
    a. equal to   b. greater than   c. similar to   d. not between

16. How many conditional formats can be created in any cell?
    a. 1   b. 2   c. 3   d. 4

▶ Skills Review

1. **Format values.**
    a. Open a new workbook.
    b. Enter the information from Table C-5 in your worksheet. Make sure you put "Quarterly Sales Sheet" on the next line.
    c. Select the range of values in the Price and Totals columns.
    d. Click the Currency Style button.
    e. Calculate the Totals column by multiplying the price by the number sold.
    f. Save this workbook as Chairs on your Student Disk.

TABLE C-5

Country Oak Chairs, Inc. Quarterly Sales Sheet			
Description	**Price**	**Sold**	**Totals**
Rocker	1299	1104	
Recliner	800	1805	
Bar stool	159	1098	
Dinette	369	1254	

2. **Select fonts and point sizes.**
    a. Select the range of cells containing the column titles.
    b. Change the font of the column titles to Times New Roman.
    c. Increase the point size of the column titles to 14 point.
    d. Resize columns as necessary.
    e. Save your workbook changes.

3. **Change attributes and alignment of labels.**
    a. Select the worksheet title Country Oak Chairs, Inc.
    b. Click the Bold button to apply boldface to the title.
    c. Select the label Quarterly Sales Sheet.
    d. Click the Underline button to apply underlining to the label.
    e. Add the bold attribute to the furniture descriptions, as well as the Totals label.
    f. Make the Price and Sold labels italics.
    g. Select the range of cells containing the column titles.
    h. Click the Center button to center the column titles.
    i. Save your changes, then preview and print the worksheet.

4. **Adjust column widths.**
    a. Change the width of the Price column to 11.
    b. Use the Format menu to make the Description and Sold columns the same size as the Price column.
    c. Save your workbook changes.

5. Insert and delete rows and columns.

   a. Insert a new row between rows 4 and 5.

   b. Add Country Oak Chairs' newest product—a Shaker bench—in the newly inserted row. Enter "239" for the price and "360" for the number sold.

   c. Use the fill handle to copy the formula in cell D4 to D5.

   d. Save your changes, then preview and print the workbook.

6. Apply colors, patterns, and borders.

   a. Add a border around the data entered from Table C-5.

   b. Apply a light green background color to the Descriptions column.

   c. Apply a light pattern to the Descriptions column.

   d. Apply a dark green background to the column labels.

   e. Change the color of the font in the first row of the data to light green.

   f. Save your work.

   g. Preview and print the worksheet, then close the workbook.

7. Use conditional formatting.

   a. Open the file XL C-2 from your Student Disk.

   b. Save it as "Recap" on your Student Disk.

   c. Create conditional formatting that changes values to blue if they are greater than 35000, and changes values to green if they are less than 21000.

   d. Use the Bold button and Center button to format the column headings and row titles.

   e. Autofit the other columns as necessary.

   f. Save your changes.

8. Check spelling.

   a. Open the spell checker.

   b. Check the spelling in the worksheet.

   c. Correct any spelling errors.

   d. Save your changes, then preview and print the workbook.

   e. Close the workbook, then exit Excel.

► Independent Challenges

1. Nuts and Bolts is a small but growing hardware store that has hired you to organize its accounting records using Excel. Now that the Nuts and Bolts hardware store's accounting records are on Excel, they would like you to work on the inventory. Although more items will be added later, enough have been entered in a worksheet for you to begin your modifications.

Open the workbook XL C-3 on your Student Disk, and save it as "NB Inventory."

To complete this independent challenge:

1. Create a formula that calculates the Value of the inventory on-hand for each item.
2. Use an absolute reference to calculate the Sale Price of each item.
3. Use enhancements to make the title, column headings, and row headings more attractive.
4. Make sure all columns are wide enough to see the data.
5. Before printing, preview the file so you know what the worksheet will look like. Adjust any items as needed, check spelling, and print a copy. Save your work before closing the file.
6. Submit your final printout.

2. You recently moved to a small town and joined the Chamber of Commerce. Since the other members are not computer-literate, you volunteered to organize the member organizations in a worksheet. As part of your efforts with the Chamber of Commerce, you need to examine more closely the membership in comparison to the community. To make the existing data more professional-looking and easier to read, you've decided to use attributes and your formatting abilities.

Open the workbook XL C-4 on your Student Disk, and save it as "Community."

To complete this independent challenge:

1. Remove any blank columns.
2. Format the Annual Revenue column using the Currency format.
3. Make all columns wide enough to fit their data.
4. Use formatting enhancements, such as fonts, font sizes, and text attributes, to make the worksheet more attractive.
5. Before printing, preview the file so you know what the worksheet will look like. Adjust any items as needed, check spelling, and print a copy. Save your work before closing the file.
6. Submit your final printout.

3. Write Brothers is a Houston-based company that manufactures high-quality pens and markers. As the finance manager, one of your responsibilities is to analyze the monthly reports from your five district sales offices. Your boss, Joanne Parker, has just told you to prepare a quarterly sales report for an upcoming meeting. Because several top executives will be attending this meeting, Joanne reminds you that the report must look professional. In particular, she asks you to emphasize the company's surge in profits during the last month and to highlight the fact that the Northeastern district continues to outpace the other districts.

Plan and build a worksheet that shows the company's sales during the last three months. Make sure you include:

- The number of pens sold (units sold) and the associated revenues (total sales) for each of the five district sales offices. The five Write Brothers sales districts include: Northeastern, Midwestern, Southeastern, Southern, and Western.
- Calculations that show month-by-month totals and a three-month cumulative total.
- Calculations that show each district's share of sales (percent of units sold).
- Formatting enhancements to emphasize the recent month's sales surge and the Northeastern district's sales leadership.

To complete this independent challenge:

1. Prepare a worksheet plan that states your goal, lists the worksheet data you'll need, and identifies the formulas for the different calculations.
2. Sketch a sample worksheet on a piece of paper, indicating how the information should be organized and formatted. How will you calculate the totals? What formulas can you copy to save time and keystrokes? Do any of these formulas need to use an absolute reference? How will you show dollar amounts? What information should be shown in bold? Do you need to use more than one font? More than one point size?
3. Build the worksheet with your own sales data. Enter the titles and labels first, then enter the numbers and formulas. Save the workbook as Write Brothers on your Student Disk.
4. Make enhancements to the worksheet. Adjust the column widths as necessary. Format labels and values, and change attributes and alignment.
5. Add a column that calculates a 10% increase in sales. Use an absolute cell reference in this calculation.
6. Before printing, preview the file so you know what the worksheet will look like. Adjust any items as needed, check spelling, and print a copy. Save your work before closing the file.
7. Submit your worksheet plan, preliminary sketches, and the final printout.

4. As the manager of your company's computer lab, you've been asked to assemble data on currently available software for use in a business environment. Using the World Wide Web, you can retrieve information about current software and create an attractive worksheet for distribution to department managers. To complete this independent challenge:

1. Open a new workbook and save it on your Student Disk as Software Comparison.
2. Log on to the Internet and use your browser to go to http://www.course.com. From there, click the link Student On Line Companions, then click the Microsoft Office 97 Professional Edition—Illustrated: A First Course page, then click the Excel link for Unit C.
3. Use each of the following sites to compile your data.
   Microsoft Corporation [www.microsoft.com], and Lotus Corporation [www.lotus.com].
4. Retrieve information on word processors, spreadsheets, presentation graphics, and database programs manufactured by both companies. The software must be Windows 95 compatible.
5. Create a worksheet that includes the information in step 4 above, as well as a retail price for each component, and whether all the programs can be purchased as a suite.
6. Use formatting attributes to make this data look attractive.
7. Use conditional formatting so that individual programs that cost over $100 display in red.
8. Save, print, and hand in a print out of your work.

▶ Visual Workshop

Create the following worksheet using the skills you learned in this unit. Open the file XL C-5 on your Student Disk, and save it as January Invoices. Create a conditional format in the Cost ea. column where entries greater than 50 are displayed in red. (Hint: The only additional font used in this exercise is Times New Roman. It is 22 points in row 1, and 14 points in row 3.)

FIGURE C-24

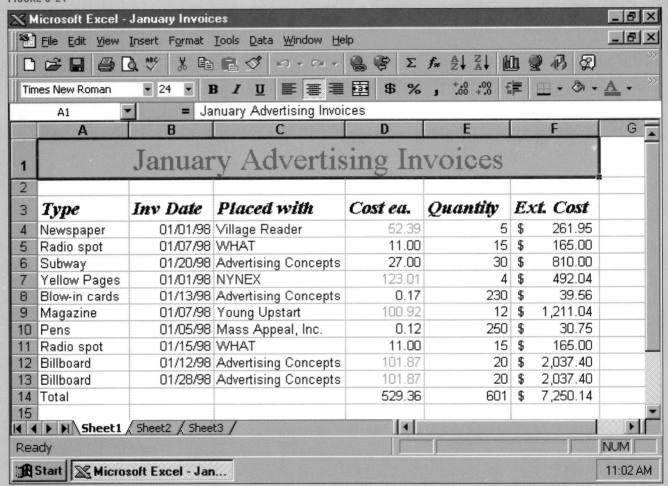

Working
with Charts

Objectives

- ► **Plan and design a chart**
- ► **Create a chart**
- ► **Move and resize a chart and its objects**
- ► **Edit a chart**
- ► **Change the appearance of a chart**
- ► **Enhance a chart**
- ► **Add text annotations and arrows to a chart**
- ► **Preview and print a chart**

Worksheets provide an effective way to organize information, but they are not always the best format for presenting data to others. Information in a selected range or worksheet can be easily converted to the visual format of a chart. Charts quickly communicate the relationships of data in a worksheet. In this unit, you will learn how to create a chart, edit a chart and change the chart type, add text annotations and arrows to a chart, then preview and print it. Evan Brillstein needs to create a chart showing the six-month sales history of Nomad Ltd for the annual meeting. He wants to illustrate the impact of an advertising campaign that started in June.

Excel 97

Planning and Designing a Chart

Before creating a chart, you need to plan what you want your chart to show and how you want it to look. Evan wants to create a chart to be used at the annual meeting. The chart will show the spring and summer sales throughout the Nomad Ltd regions. In early June, the Marketing Department launched a national advertising campaign. The results of the campaign were increased sales for the summer months. Evan wants his chart to illustrate this dramatic sales increase. Evan uses the worksheet shown in Figure D-1 and the following guidelines to plan the chart:

Steps

CourseHelp

The camera icon indicates there is a CourseHelp for this lesson. Click the Start button, point to Programs, then click Excel 97 Illustrated. Choose the CourseHelp that corresponds to this lesson.

1. Determine the purpose of the chart, and identify the data relationships you want to communicate visually
You want to create a chart that shows sales throughout Nomad's regions in the spring and summer months (March through August). In particular, you want to highlight the increase in sales that occurred in the summer months as a result of the advertising campaign.

2. Determine the results you want to see, and decide which chart type is most appropriate to use; Table D-1 describes several different types of charts
Because you want to compare related data (sales in each of the regions) over a time period (the months March through August), you decide to use a column chart.

3. Identify the worksheet data you want the chart to illustrate
You are using data from the worksheet titled "Nomad Ltd Regions, Spring and Summer Sales," as shown in Figure D-1. This worksheet contains the sales data for the five regions from March through August.

4. Sketch the chart, then use your sketch to decide where the chart elements should be placed
You sketch your chart as shown in Figure D-2. You put the months on the horizontal axis (the **X-axis**) and the monthly sales figures on the vertical axis (the **Y-axis**). The **tick marks** on the Y-axis create a scale of measure for each value. Each value in a cell you select for your chart is a **data point**. In any chart, each data point is visually represented by a **data marker**, which in this case is a column. A collection of related data points is a **data series**. In this chart, there are five data series (Midwest, Northeast, Northwest, South, and Southwest), so you have included a **legend** to identify them.

FIGURE D-1: Worksheet containing sales data

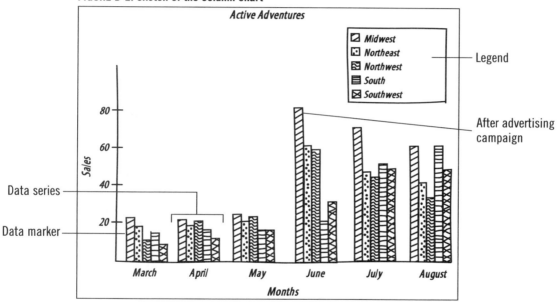

```
Microsoft Excel - Xl d-1                                              _|8|X
 File  Edit  View  Insert  Format  Tools  Data  Window  Help          _|8|X

 D  B  H  B  Q  ABC  X  B  B  ◇  ⌐  ⌐  B  B  Σ  f⋆  A↓ Z↓  B  B  100% ⋆  ?

 Arial          ⋆ 10 ⋆  B  I  U  ≡ ≡ ≡ 图  $ % ,  :8 :8  ≡ ≡  □ ⋆ ◇ ⋆ A ⋆

        A1        ⋆    =
        A        B        C        D        E        F        G        H        I
 1                        Nomad Ltd Regions
 2                        Spring and Summer Sales
 3
 4
 5              March    April    May      June     July     August   Total
 6  Midwest    15,000   13,000   16,000   55,000   40,000   40,000   $257,000
 7  Northeast  22,000   17,000   23,000   75,000   65,000   55,000   $179,000
 8  Northwes   10,000   16,000   21,000   52,000   37,000   30,000   $166,000
 9  South       8,000   10,000   15,000   25,000   40,000   43,000   $158,000
10  Southwes   12,000   12,000   15,000   20,000   42,000   57,000   $141,000
11     Total  $67,000  $68,000  $90,000  $227,000 $224,000 $225,000  $901,000
12
13
14
15
16
 H ◀ ▶ H \ Sheet1 / Sheet2 / Sheet3 /            |◀|                  ▶|
 Ready                                                        NUM
 Start   Microsoft Excel - Xl d-1                            10:02 AM
```

FIGURE D-2: Sketch of the column chart

TABLE D-1: Commonly used chart types

type	button	description
Area		Shows how volume changes over time
Bar		Compares distinct, unrelated objects over time using a horizontal format; sometimes referred to as a horizontal bar chart in other spreadsheet programs
Column		Compares distinct, unrelated objects over time using a vertical format; the Excel default; sometimes referred to as a bar chart in other spreadsheet programs
Line		Compares trends over even time intervals; similar to an area chart
Pie		Compares sizes of pieces as part of a whole; can have slices pulled away from the pie, or "exploded"
XY (scatter)		Compares trends over uneven time or measurement intervals; used in scientific and engineering disciplines for trend spotting and extrapolation
Combination	none	Combines a column and line chart to compare data requiring different scales of measure

Creating a Chart

To create a chart in Excel, you first select the range containing the data you want to chart. Once you've selected a range, you can use Excel's Chart Wizard to lead you through the chart creation process.  Using the worksheet containing the spring and summer sales data for the five regions, Evan will create a chart that shows the monthly sales of each region from March through August.

Steps

1. **Open the workbook XL D-1 from your Student Disk, then save it as Nomad Regions**
   First, you need to select the cells you want to chart. You want to include the monthly sales figures for each of the regions, but not the totals. You also want to include the month and region labels.

2. **Select the range A5:G10, then click the Chart Wizard button 📊 on the Standard toolbar**
   When you click 📊 the Chart Wizard opens. The first Chart Wizard dialog box lets you choose the type of chart you want to create. See Figure D-3. You can see a preview of the chart by clicking the Press and hold to view sample button.

3. **Click Next to accept the default chart type of column**
   The second dialog box lets you choose the data being charted and whether the series are in rows or columns. Currently, the rows are selected as the data series. You could switch this by clicking the Columns radio button located under the Data range. Since you selected the data before clicking the Chart Wizard button, the correct range A5:G10 displays in the Data range text box. Satisfied with the selections, you accept the default choices.

4. **Click Next**
   The third Chart Wizard dialog box shows a sample chart using the data you selected. Notice that the regions (the rows in the selected range) are plotted according to the months (the columns in the selected range), and that the months were added as labels for each data series. Notice also that there is a legend showing each region and its corresponding color on the chart. Here, you can choose to keep the legend, add a chart title, and add axis titles. You add a title.

5. **Click the Chart title text box, then type Nomad Ltd Regional Sales**
   After a moment, the title appears in the Sample Chart box. See Figure D-4.

6. **Click Next**
   In the last Chart Wizard dialog box, you determine the location of the chart. A chart can be displayed on the same sheet as the data, or a separate sheet in the workbook. You decide to display the chart on the current sheet.

7. **Click Finish**
   The column chart appears, as shown in Figure D-5. Your chart might look slightly different. Just as you had hoped, the chart shows the dramatic increase in sales between May and June. The **selection handles**, the small squares at the corners and sides of the chart borders, indicate that the chart is selected. Anytime a chart is selected (as it is now), the Chart toolbar appears. It might be floating, as shown in Figure D-5, or it might be fixed at the top or bottom of the worksheet window.

FIGURE D-3: First Chart Wizard dialog box

Chart types

Chart sub-types

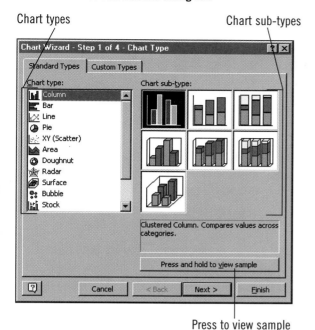

Press to view sample

FIGURE D-4: Third Chart Wizard dialog box

Sample chart   Title added   Legend

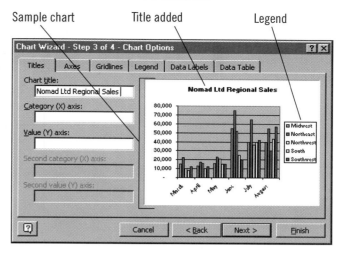

FIGURE D-5: Worksheet with column chart

Floating chart toolbar

Title

Legend

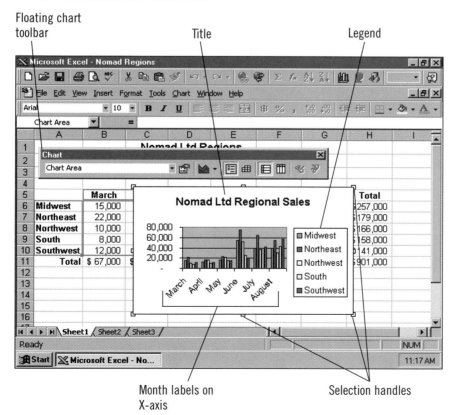

Month labels on X-axis

Selection handles

Moving and Resizing a Chart and its Objects

Charts are graphics, or drawn **objects**, and have no specific cell or range address. You can move charts anywhere on a worksheet without affecting formulas or data in the worksheet. You can even put them on another sheet. You can also easily resize a chart to improve its appearance by dragging the selection handles. Drawn objects such as charts can contain other objects that you can move and resize. To move an object, select it then drag it or cut and copy it to a new location. To resize an object, use the selection handles.  Evan wants to increase the size of the chart and position it below the worksheet data. He also wants to change the position of the legend.

Steps

1. Make sure the chart is still selected. Scroll the worksheet until **row 28** is visible, then position the pointer over the white space around the chart
   The pointer shape ⬉ indicates that you can move the chart or use a selection handle to resize it.

Trouble?

If the Chart toolbar is in the way of the legend, move it out of your way first.

2. Press and hold the mouse button and drag the chart until the lower edge of the chart is in **row 28** and the left edge of the chart is in **column A**, then release the mouse button
   A dotted outline of the chart perimeter appears as the chart is being moved, the pointer changes to ✛, and the chart moves to the new location.

3. Position the pointer over one of the selection handles on the right border until it changes to ↔, then drag the right edge of the chart to the **middle of column I**
   The chart is widened. See Figure D-6.

4. Position the pointer over the top middle selection handle until it changes to ↕, then drag it to the **top of row 12**
   Now, you move the legend up so that it is slightly lower than the chart title.

5. Click the **legend** to select it, then drag it to the upper-right corner of the chart until it is slightly lower than the chart title
   Selection handles appear around the legend when you click it, and a dotted outline of the legend perimeter appears as you drag.

6. Press **[Esc]** to deselect the legend. The legend is now repositioned. See Figure D-7.

7. Save your work

FIGURE D-6: Worksheet with reposition and resized chart

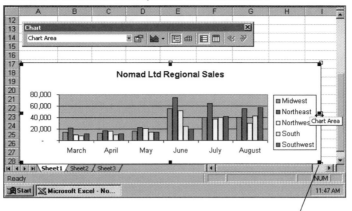

Widened to column I

FIGURE D-7: Worksheet with repositioned legend

Chart menu   Repositioned legend

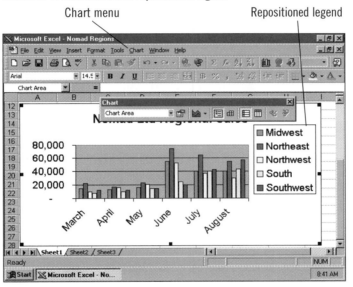

Viewing multiple worksheets

A workbook can be organized with a chart on one sheet and the data on another sheet. With this organization, you can still see the data next to the chart by opening multiple windows of the same workbook. This allows you to see portions of multiple sheets at the same time. Click Window on the menu bar, then click New Window. A new window containing the current workbook opens. To see the windows next to each other, click Window on the menu bar, click Arrange, then choose one of the options in the Arrange Windows dialog box. You can open one worksheet in one window and a different worksheet in the second window. See Figure D-8. To close one window without closing the worksheet, double-click the control menu box on the window you want to close.

FIGURE D-8: Workbook with two windows open

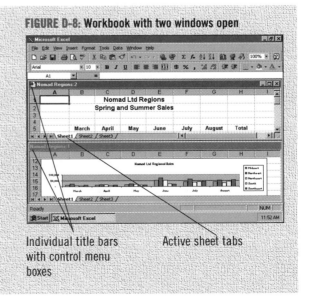

Individual title bars   Active sheet tabs
with control menu
boxes

Editing a Chart

Once you've created a chart, it's easy to modify it. You can change data values in the worksheet, and the chart will automatically be updated to reflect the new data. You can also easily change chart types using the buttons on the Chart toolbar. Table D-2 shows and describes the Chart toolbar buttons. Evan looks over his worksheet and realizes he entered the wrong data for the Northwest region in July and August. After he corrects this data, he wants to find out what percentage of total sales the month of June represents. He will convert the column chart to a pie chart to find this out.

Steps 1234

1. **Scroll the worksheet so that you can see both the chart and row 8, containing the Northwest region's sales figures, at the same time**
   As you enter the correct values, watch the columns for July and August in the chart change.

2. **Click cell F8, type 49000 to correct the July sales figure, press [→], type 45000 in cell G8, then press [Enter]**
   The Northwest columns for July and August reflect the increased sales figures. See Figure D-9.

3. **Select the chart by clicking anywhere within the chart border, then click the Chart Type list arrow 📉▾ on the Chart toolbar**
   The chart type buttons appear, as shown in Figure D-10.

4. **Click the 2-D Pie Chart button 🥧**
   The column chart changes to a pie chart showing total sales by month (the columns in the selected range). See Figure D-11. (You may need to scroll up to see the chart.) You look at the pie chart, takes some notes, and then decide to convert it back to a column chart. You now want to see if the large increase in sales would be better presented with a three-dimensional column chart.

5. **Click 📈▾, then click the 3-D Column Chart button 📊 to change the chart type**
   A three-dimensional column chart appears. You note that the three-dimensional column format is too crowded, so you switch back to the two-dimensional format.

6. **Click 📊▾, then click the 2-D Column Chart button 📊 to change the chart type**

Time To
✓ Save

TABLE D-2: Chart Type buttons

button	description	button	description
📈	Displays 2-D area chart	📉	Displays 3-D area chart
📊	Displays 2-D bar chart	📚	Displays 3-D bar chart
📊	Displays 2-D column chart	📊	Displays 3-D column chart
📉	Displays 2-D line chart	📉	Displays 3-D line chart
🥧	Displays 2-D pie chart	🥧	Displays 3-D pie chart
📊	Displays 2-D scatter chart	📊	Displays 3-D surface chart
🍩	Displays 2-D doughnut chart	🛢	Displays 3-D cylinder chart
🕸	Displays radar chart	🔺	Displays 3-D cone chart

▶ EX D-8 **WORKING WITH CHARTS**

FIGURE D-9: Worksheet with new data entered for the Northwest region

New data

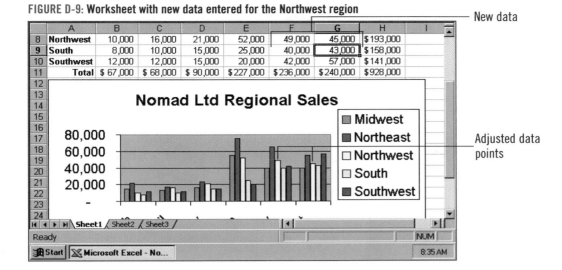

	A	B	C	D	E	F	G	H	I
8	Northwest	10,000	16,000	21,000	52,000	49,000	45,000	$193,000	
9	South	8,000	10,000	15,000	25,000	40,000	43,000	$158,000	
10	Southwest	12,000	12,000	15,000	20,000	42,000	57,000	$141,000	
11	Total	$ 67,000	$ 68,000	$ 90,000	$227,000	$236,000	$240,000	$928,000	

Adjusted data points

FIGURE D-10: Chart Type list box

2-D Column Chart icon

2-D Pie Chart icon

FIGURE D-11: Pie chart

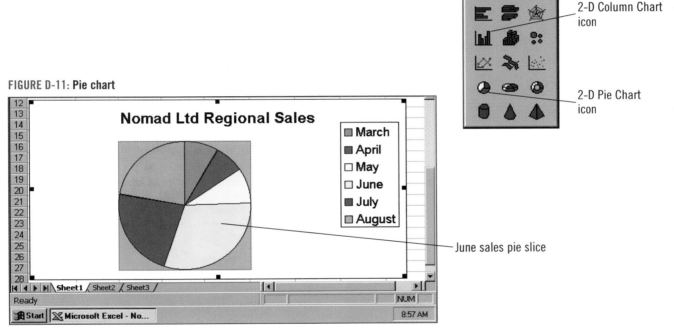

June sales pie slice

Rotating a chart

In a three-dimensional chart, columns or bars can sometimes be obscured by other data series within the same chart. You can rotate the chart until a better view is obtained. Double-click the chart, click the tip of one of its axes, then drag the handles until a more pleasing view of the data series appears. See Figure D-12.

FIGURE D-12: 3-D chart rotated with improved view of data series

Changing the Appearance of a Chart

After you've created a chart using the Chart Wizard, you can modify its appearance by changing the colors of data series and adding or eliminating a legend and gridlines using the Chart toolbar and the Chart menu. **Gridlines** are the horizontal lines in the chart that enable the eye to follow the value on an axis. The corresponding Chart toolbar buttons are listed in Table D-3. Evan wants to make some changes in the appearance of his chart. He wants to see if the chart looks better without gridlines, and he wants to change the color of a data series.

Steps

1. Make sure the chart is still selected

You want to see how the chart looks without gridlines. Gridlines currently appear on the chart.

2. Click Chart on the menu bar, then click Chart Options

QuickTip

Experiment with different formats for your charts until you get just the right look.

3. Click the Gridlines tab in the Chart Options dialog box, then click the Major Gridlines checkbox for the Value (Y) Axis to remove the check and deselect this option

The gridlines disappear from the sample chart in the dialog box, as shown in Figure D-13. You decide that the gridlines are necessary to the chart's readability.

4. Click the Major Gridlines checkbox for the Value (Y) Axis, then click OK

The gridlines reappear. You are not happy with the color of the columns for the South data series and would like the columns to stand out more.

5. With the chart selected, double-click any column in the South data series

Handles appear on all the columns in the South data series, and the Format Data Series dialog box opens, as shown in Figure D-14. Make sure the Patterns tab is the front-most tab.

6. Click the dark green box (in the third row, fourth from the left), then click OK

All the columns in the series are dark green. Compare your finished chart to Figure D-15. You are pleased with the change.

7. Save your work

TABLE D-3: Chart enhancement buttons

button	use	button	use
	Displays formatting dialog box for the selected chart element		Charts data by row
	Selects chart type		Charts data by column
	Adds/Deletes legend		Angles selected text downward
	Creates a data table within the chart		Angles selected text upward

FIGURE D-13: **Chart Options dialog box**

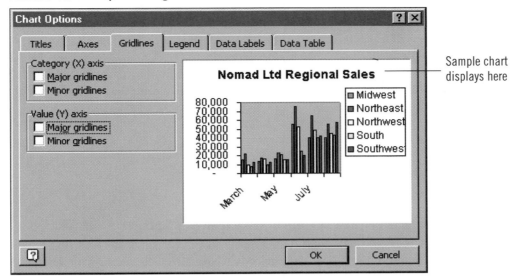

Sample chart
displays here

FIGURE D-14: **Format Data Series dialog box**

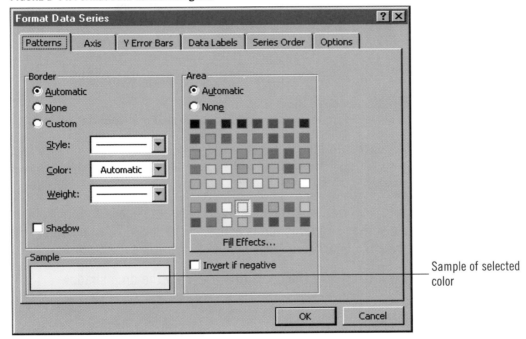

Sample of selected
color

FIGURE D-15: **Chart with formatted data series**

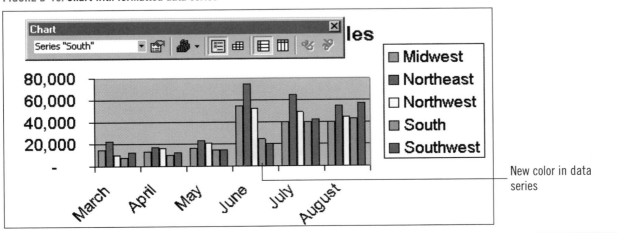

New color in data
series

Enhancing a Chart

There are many ways to enhance a chart to make it easier to read and understand. You can create titles for the X-axis and Y-axis, add graphics, or add background color. You can even format the text you use in a chart. ✐ Evan wants to improve the appearance of his chart by creating titles for the X-axis and Y-axis. He also decides to add a drop shadow to the title.

1. **Make sure the chart is selected**
   You want to add descriptive text to the X-axis.

2. **Click Chart on the menu bar, click Chart Options, click the Titles tab in the Chart Options dialog box, then type Months in the Category (X) Axis text box**
   The word "Months" appears below the month labels in the sample chart, as shown in Figure D-16. You now add text to the Y-axis.

3. **Click the Value (Y) Axis text box, type Sales, then click OK**
   A selected text box containing "Sales" appears to the left of the Y-axis. Once the Chart Options dialog box is closed, you can move the axis title to a new position, by clicking on an edge of the selection and dragging it. If you wanted to edit the axis title, position the pointer over the selected text box until it becomes ⊥ and click, then edit the text.

4. **Press [Esc] to deselect the Y-axis label**
   Next you decide to draw a rectangle with a drop shadow around the title.

5. **Click the chart title to select it**
   If necessary, you may have to move the Chart toolbar. You use the Format button on the Chart toolbar to create a drop shadow.

6. **Click the Format button 🖼 on the Chart toolbar to open the Format Chart Title dialog box, make sure the Patterns tab is active, click the Shadow checkbox, then click OK**
   A drop shadow appears around the title.

7. **Press [Esc] to deselect the chart title and view the drop shadow**
   Compare your chart to Figure D-17.

8. **Save your work**

QuickTip

The Format button 🖼 opens a dialog box with the appropriate formatting options for the selected chart element.

FIGURE D-16: Sample chart with X-axis text

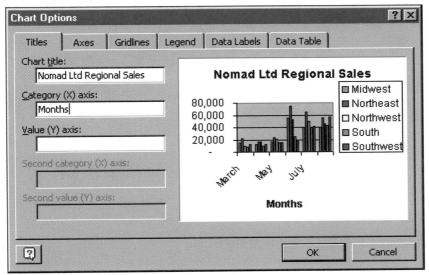

FIGURE D-17: Enhanced chart

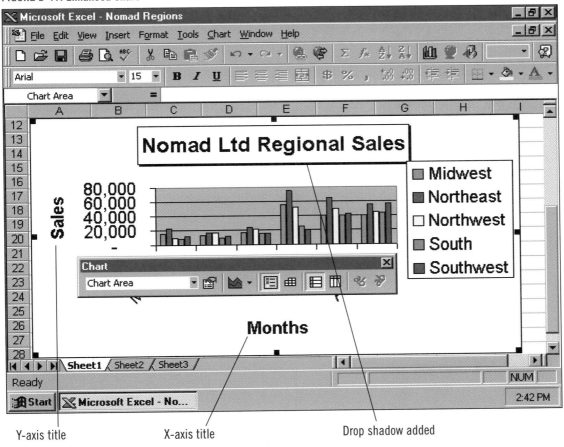

Y-axis title   X-axis title   Drop shadow added

CLUES TO USE

Changing text font and alignment in charts

The font and the alignment of axis text can be modified to make it more readable or to better fit within
the plot area. With a chart selected, double-click the

text to be modified. The Format Axis dialog box
appears. Click the Font or the Alignment tab, make the
desired changes, then click OK.

Excel 97

Adding Text Annotations and Arrows to a Chart

You can add arrows and text annotations to highlight information in your charts. Text annotations are labels that you add to a chart to draw attention to a certain part of it. Evan wants to add a text annotation and an arrow to highlight the June sales increase.

1. **Make sure the chart is selected**
   You want to call attention to the June sales increase by drawing an arrow that points to the top of the June data series with the annotation, "After advertising campaign." To enter the text for an annotation, you simply start typing.

2. **Type After advertising campaign then click the Enter button** ☑ **on the formula bar**
   As you type, the text appears in the formula bar. After you confirm the entry, the text appears in a floating selected text box within the chart window.

3. **Point to an edge of the text box, then press and hold the left mouse button**
   The pointer should be ✥. If the pointer changes to I or ↔, release the mouse button, click outside the text box area to deselect it, then select the text box and repeat Step 3.

4. **Drag the text box above the chart, as shown in Figure D-18, then release the mouse button**
   You are ready to add an arrow.

5. **Click the Drawing button** ✎ **on the Standard toolbar**
   The Drawing toolbar appears.

6. **Click the Arrow button** ↖ **on the Drawing toolbar**
   The pointer changes to +.

QuickTip

You can also insert text and an arrow in the data section of a worksheet by clicking the Text Box button 🖼 on the Drawing toolbar, drawing a text box, typing the text, and then adding the arrow.

7. **Position + under the word "advertising" in the text box, click the left mouse button, drag the line to the June sales, then release the mouse button**
   An arrowhead appears pointing to the June sales. Compare your finished chart to Figure D-19.

8. **Click the Drawing button** ✎ **to close the Drawing toolbar**

9. **Save your work**

FIGURE D-18: Repositioning text annotation

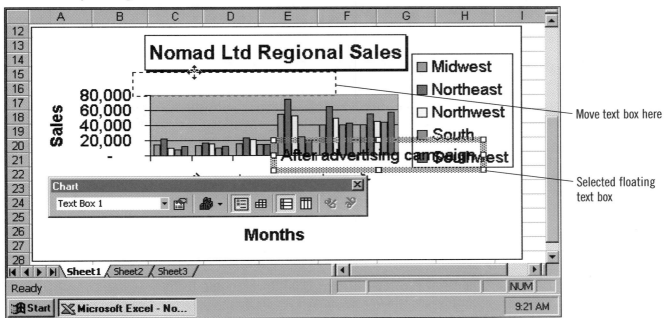

Move text box here

Selected floating text box

FIGURE D-19: Completed chart with text annotation and arrow

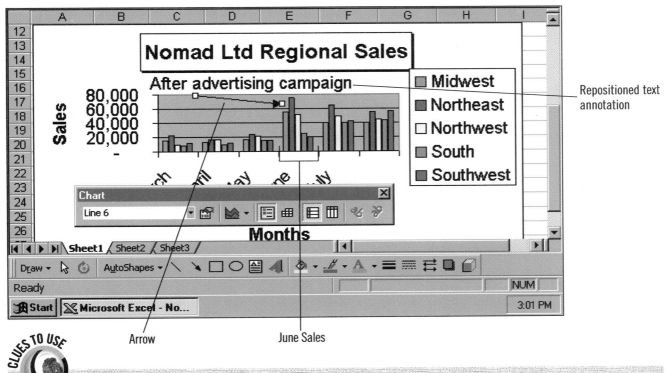

Repositioned text annotation

Arrow

June Sales

Pulling out a pie slice

Just as an arrow can call attention to a data series, you can emphasize a pie slice by exploding it, or pulling it away from, the pie chart. Once the chart is in Edit mode, click the pie to select it, click the desired slice to select only that slice, then drag the slice away from the pie, as shown in Figure D-20.

FIGURE D-20: Exploded pie slice

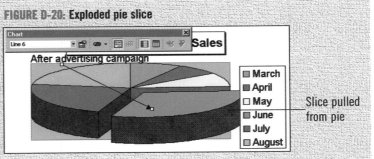

Slice pulled from pie

Excel 97

Previewing and Printing a Chart

After you complete a chart to your satisfaction, you will need to print it. You can print a chart by itself, or as part of the worksheet. Evan is satisfied with the chart and wants to print it for the annual meeting. He will print the worksheet and the chart together, so that the share-holders can see the actual sales numbers for each tour type.

Steps

1. **Press [Esc] twice to deselect the arrow and the chart**
   If you wanted to print only the chart without the data, you would leave the chart selected.

2. **Click the Print Preview button 🔍 on the Standard toolbar**
   The Print Preview window opens. You decide that the chart and data would look better if they were printed in **landscape** orientation—that is, with the page turned sideways. To change the orientation of the page, you must alter the page setup.

3. **Click the Setup button to display the Page Setup dialog box, then click the Page tab**

4. **Click the Landscape radio button in the Orientation section**
   See Figure D-21.
   Because each page has a left default margin of 0.75", the chart and data will print too far over to the left of the page. You change this using the Margins tab.

5. **Click the Margins tab, click the Horizontal checkbox in the Center on Page section, then click OK**
   The print preview of the worksheet appears again. The data and chart are centered on the page that has a landscape orientation, and no gridlines appear. See Figure D-22. You are sat-isfied with the way it looks and print it.

6. **Click Print to display the Print dialog box, then click OK**
   Your printed report should look like the image displayed in the Print Preview window.

7. **Save your work**

8. **Close the workbook and exit Excel**

FIGURE D-21: **Page tab of the Page Setup dialog box**

Landscape selected

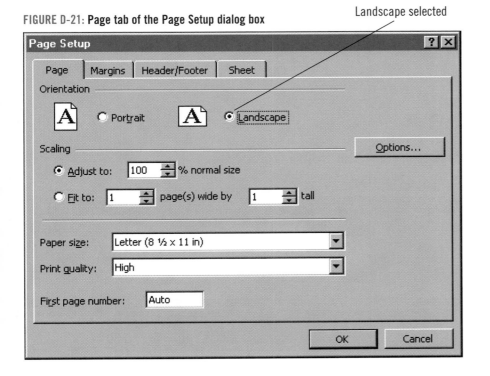

FIGURE D-22: **Chart and data ready to print**

Orientation changed
to landscape

Centered on page

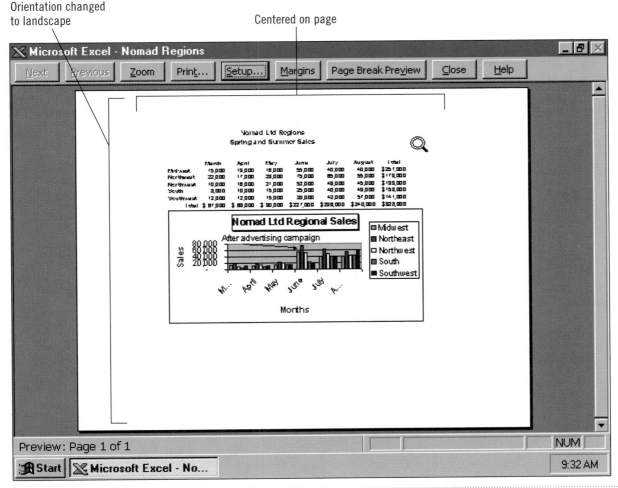

Practice

► Concepts Review

Label each of the elements of the Excel chart shown in Figure D-23.

FIGURE D-23

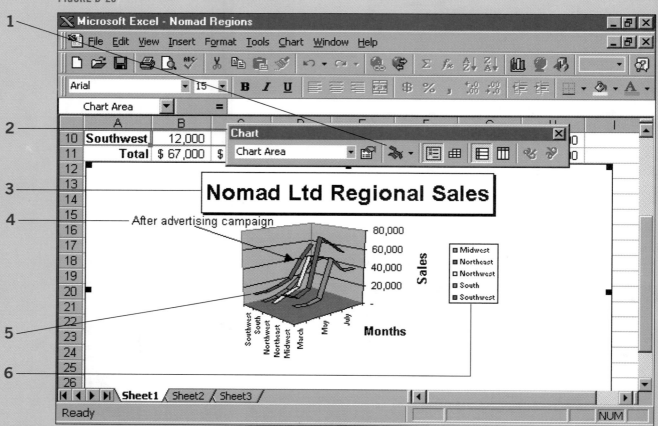

Match each of the statements with its chart type.

7. Column
8. Area
9. Pie
10. Combination
11. Line

a. Shows how volume changes over time
b. Compares data as parts of a whole
c. Displays a column and line chart using different scales of measurement
d. Compares trends over even time intervals
e. Compares data over time—the Excel default

Select the best answer from the list of choices.

12. The box that identifies patterns used for each data series is a
   a. Data point   **b.** Plot   **c.** Legend   **d.** Range

13. What is the term for a row or column on a chart?
   a. Range address   **b.** Axis title   **c.** Chart orientation   **d.** Data series

▶ Skills Review

1. Create a worksheet and plan a chart.
   a. Start Excel, open a new workbook, then save it as Software Used to your Student Disk.
   b. Enter the information from Table D-4 in your worksheet in range A1:E6. Resize columns and rows.
   c. Save your work.
   d. Sketch a chart for a two-dimensional column chart that shows software distribution by department.

TABLE D-4

	Excel	Word	WordPerfect	PageMaker
Accounting	10	1	9	0
Marketing	2	9	0	6
Engineering	12	5	7	1
Personnel	2	2	2	1
Production	6	3	4	0

2. Create a chart.
   a. Select the range you want to chart.
   b. Click the Chart Wizard button.
   c. Complete the Chart Wizard dialog boxes and build a two-dimensional column chart on the same sheet as the data, having a different color bar for each department and with the title "Software Distribution by Department."
   d. Save your work.

3. Move and resize a chart and its objects.
   a. Make sure the chart is still selected.
   b. Move the chart beneath the data.
   c. Drag the chart's selection handles so it fills the range A7:G22.
   d. Click the legend to select it.
   e. Make the legend longer by about ½".
   f. Change the placement of the legend to the bottom right corner of the chart area.
   g. Save your work.

4. Edit a chart.
   a. Change the value in cell B3 to 6.
   b. Click the chart to select it.
   c. Click the Chart Type list arrow on the Chart toolbar.
   d. Click the 3-D Column Chart button in the list.
   e. Rotate the chart to move the data.
   f. Save your work.

5. Change the appearance of a chart.
  a. Change the chart type to 2-D column chart.
  b. Make sure the chart is still selected.
  c. Turn off the displayed gridlines.
  d. Change the X- and Y-axis font to Times New Roman.
  e. Turn the gridlines back on.
  f. Save your work.

6. Enhance a chart.
  a. Make sure the chart is still selected, then click Chart on the menu bar, click Chart Options, then click the Titles tab.
  b. Click the Category (X) axis text box and type "Department."
  c. Click the Value (Y) axis text box, type "Types of Software," and then click OK.
  d. Change the size of the X and Y axes font and the legend font to 8 pt.
  e. Save your work.

7. Adding a text annotation and arrows to a chart.
  a. Select the chart.
  b. Create the text annotation "Need More Computers."
  c. Drag the text annotation about one inch above any of the Personnel bars.
  d. Change the font size of the annotation text to 8 pt.
  e. Click the Arrow button on the Drawing toolbar.
  f. Click below the text annotation, drag down any one of the Personnel bars, then release the mouse button.
  g. Open a second window so you can display the data in the new window and the chart in the original window.
  h. Close the second window.
  i. Save your work.

8. Preview and print a chart.
  a. Deselect the chart, then click the Print Preview button on the Standard toolbar.
  b. Center the data and chart on the page and change the paper orientation to landscape.
  c. Click Print in the Print Preview window.
  d. Save your work, close the workbook, then exit Excel.

▶ Independent Challenges

1. You are the operations manager for the Springfield Recycling Center. The Marketing Department wants you to create charts for a brochure to advertise a new curbside recycling program. The data provided contains percentages of collected recycled goods. You need to create charts that show:

- How much of each type of recycled material Springfield collected in 1995 and what percentage each type represents. The center collects paper, plastics, and glass from business and residential customers.
- The yearly increases in the total amounts of recycled materials the center has collected since its inception three years ago. Springfield has experienced a 30% annual increase in collections.

To complete this independent challenge:

1. Prepare a worksheet plan that states your goal and identifies the formulas for any calculations.
2. Sketch a sample worksheet on a piece of paper describing how you will create the charts. Which type of chart is best suited for the information you need to display? What kind of chart enhancements will be necessary? Will a 3-D effect make your chart easier to understand?
3. Open the workbook XL D-2 on your Student Disk, then save it as Recycling Center.
4. Add a column that calculates the 30% increase in annual collections based on the percentages given.
5. Create at least six different charts to show the distribution of the different types of recycled goods, as well as the distribution by customer type. Use the Chart Wizard to switch the way data is plotted (columns vs. rows and vice versa) and come up with additional charts.
6. After creating the charts, make the appropriate enhancements. Include chart titles, legends, and axes titles.
7. Before printing, preview the file so you know what the charts will look like. Adjust any items as needed.
8. Save your work. Print the charts, then print the entire worksheet. Close the file.
9. Submit your worksheet plan, preliminary sketches, and the final worksheet printouts.

2. One of your responsibilities at the Nuts and Bolts hardware store is to re-create the company's records using Excel. Another is to convince the current staff that Excel can make daily operations easier and more efficient. You've decided to create charts using the previous year's operating expenses. These charts will be used at the next monthly Accounting Department meeting.

Open the workbook XL D-3 on your Student Disk, and save it as Expense Charts.

To complete this independent challenge:

1. Decide which data in the worksheet should be charted. Sketch two sample charts. What type of charts are best suited for the information you need to display? What kind of chart enhancements will be necessary?
2. Create at least six different charts that show the distribution of expenses, either by quarter or expense type.
3. Add annotated text and arrows highlighting data.
4. In one chart, change the colors of the data series, and in another chart, use black-and-white patterns only.
5. Before printing, preview the file so you know what the charts will look like. Adjust any items as needed.
6. Print the charts. Save your work.
7. Submit your sketches and the final worksheet printouts.

3. The Chamber of Commerce is delighted with the way you've organized their membership roster using Excel. The Board of Directors wants to ask the city for additional advertising funds and has asked you to prepare charts that can be used in their presentation.

Open the workbook XL D-4 on your Student Disk, and save it as Chamber Charts. This file contains raw advertising data for the month of January.

To complete this independent challenge:

1. Calculate the annual advertising expenses based on the January summary data.
2. Use the raw data for January shown in the range A16:B24 to create charts.
3. Decide what types of charts would be best suited for this type of data. Sketch two sample charts. What kind of chart enhancements will be necessary?
4. Create at least four different charts that show the distribution of advertising expenses. Show January expenses and projected values in at least two of the charts.
5. Add annotated text and arrows highlighting important data. Change the colors of the data series if you wish.
6. Before printing, preview the file so you know what the charts will look like. Adjust any items as needed.
7. Print the charts. Save your work.
8. Submit your sketches and the final worksheet printouts.

4. Financial information has a greater impact on others if displayed in a chart. Using the World Wide Web you can find out current activity of stocks and create informative charts. Your company has asked you to chart current trading indexes by category.

   To complete this independent challenge:

1. Open a new workbook and save it on your Student Disk as Trading Indexes.
2. Log on to the Internet and use your browser to go to http://www.course.com. From there, click the link Student On Line Companions, then click the Microsoft Office 97 Professional Edition - Illustrated: A First Course page, then click the Excel link for Unit D.
3. Use the following site to compile your data, NASDAQ [www.nasdaq.com].
4. Click the Index Activity button on the NASDAQ home page.
5. Locate Index Value data by category and retrieve this information.
6. Create a chart of the Index Values, by category.
7. Save, print, and hand in a print out of your work.

▶ Visual Workshop

Modify a worksheet using the skills you learned in this unit, using Figure D-24 for reference. Open the file XL D-5 on your Student Disk, and save it as Quarterly Advertising Budget. Create the chart, then change the data to reflect Figure D-24. Preview and print your results, and submit your printout.

FIGURE D-24

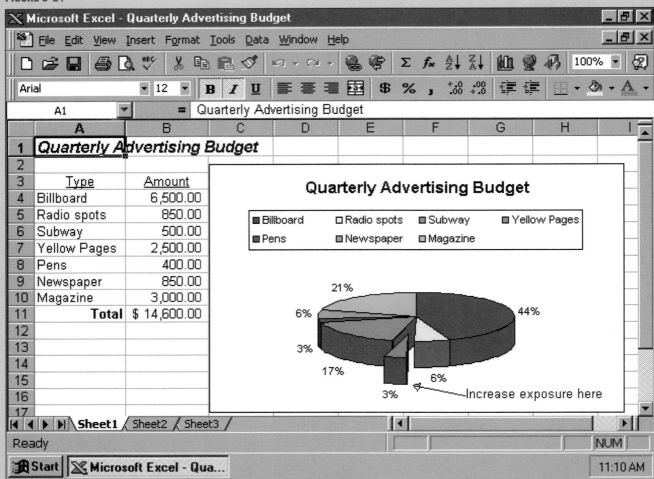

Integrating
Word and Excel

Objectives

► **Open multiple programs**
► **Copy Word data into Excel**
► **Create a dynamic link (DDE) from Excel to Word**

Now that you have experienced the power of Word and Excel, it is time to learn how to integrate the programs. When you integrate programs, you combine information between them without retyping anything.

Andrew Gillespie, the national sales manager for Nomad Ltd, collected the spring quarter sales data for clothing from the five sales regions. He compiled this information in a Word document, and now he wants to add an Excel column chart to his document. Andrew will use simple integration techniques to do this. He will then give the data back to the regional managers so each manager can see how his or his own region compared to the other four regions.

Opening Multiple Programs

When you are integrating information from one program to another, it is helpful to have both files open at the same time. The Windows environment gives you the ability to have more than one program open at a time. This is sometimes called **multitasking**. Before integrating the data, Andrew starts both Word and Excel. To make integrating the data easier, he aligns each program window side by side on the screen.

Steps 1 2 3 4

1. **Click the Start button on the taskbar, then point to Programs**
   The Programs menu opens.

2. **Click Microsoft Word in the Program list**
   The Word program button appears in the taskbar. Minimize the program window.

QuickTip

It is not necessary to minimize a program window before you start another program.

3. **Click the Minimize button in the program window**
   The Word program window appears to shrink into the program button on the taskbar. Next, open the Excel program.

4. **Click the Start button on the taskbar, point to Programs, then click Microsoft Excel**
   A blank Excel workbook appears. You use the taskbar to maximize the Word program and make it active.

5. **Click the Word program button on the taskbar**
   Word maximizes and becomes the active program. Excel is still open, but it is not active, as shown in Figure A-1. Now, arrange the program windows so each occupies half of the screen.

6. **Right-click the taskbar**
   The taskbar pop-up menu appears.

Trouble?

If a dialog box connected to the Office Assistant is showing containing a Tip of the Day, close it by clicking the Close button.

7. **Click Tile Vertically**
   The two program windows each occupy half of the screen. Compare your screen to Figure A-2. The title bars of both windows are gray and both program buttons on the taskbar are raised indicating that neither program window is active.

FIGURE A-1: Word document active and Excel workbook inactive

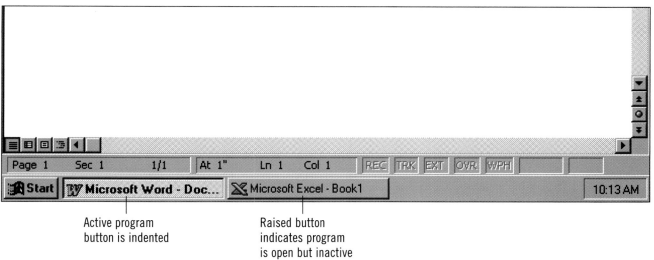

Active program
button is indented

Raised button
indicates program
is open but inactive

Integration

FIGURE A-2: Word window and Excel window on the screen

Each program
displays its own
toolbars

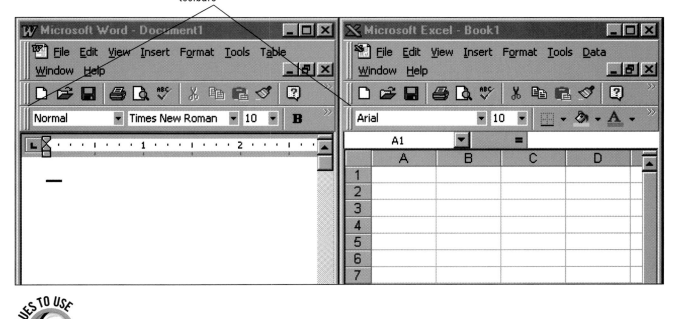

Using shortcut keys to switch between open programs

You can switch between open programs by using the shortcut key combination [Alt][Tab]. Pressing [Alt][Tab] causes the icons and names of open programs (whether or not they are minimized) to appear in the center of the screen, as shown in Figure A-3. To see this on the screen, press and hold [Alt], then press and release [Tab]. If more than one program is open, press and release [Tab] again while still holding down [Alt] to move the selection box to the next icon in the center of the screen. When the program you want to activate is selected, release [Alt].

FIGURE A-3: Word program icon in the center of the Excel worksheet

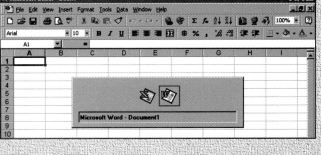

Copying Word Data into Excel

Moving or copying information from one program to another is just like moving or copying information within a single program. You can use the program's Cut, Copy, and Paste commands, buttons on the toolbars, or the drag-and-drop method to move or copy information. Andrew typed a memo to the regional managers that includes a Word table containing the spring quarter sales data from all five regions. He wants to add a column chart to the memo. To create the column chart in Excel, Andrew needs to first copy the data into an Excel workbook.

Steps

1. Click anywhere within the Word program window to make it active
Just like two windows open in the same program, clicking in a window makes that window active. Open your memo.

2. Open the file INT A-1 from your Student Disk
Save this document on your Student Disk.

3. Save this file as Regional Memo on your Student Disk
Regional Memo appears in the Word program window in Page Layout View. To make more of the document visible, reduce the percentage of the document's scale from 100% to 75%.

4. Click View on the menu bar, click Zoom, click the 75% option button, then click OK

5. Scroll down until you can see the table and the body of the memo, then click the right scroll arrow once so you can see the entire table as shown in Figure A-4
The Word document is the **source file**—the file from which the information is copied. The Excel workbook is the **target file**—the file that receives the copied information. You will copy the table containing the spring quarter sales data.

6. Position the pointer in the selection bar next to the top row of the table until the pointer changes to ⇗ , press and hold the mouse button to select the top row of the table, drag the pointer down until all of the rows are selected, then release the mouse button

7. Press and hold [Ctrl], click within the table so the pointer looks like ⇖ , drag the pointer to the Excel worksheet so the destination of the table's outline is in the range A1:D6, as shown in Figure A-5, then release the mouse button and [Ctrl]
The information in the Word table is copied into the Excel worksheet, as shown in Figure A-6. Using drag-and-drop is the easiest way to copy information from a source file to a target file.

8. Click the Save button 🖫 on the Excel Standard toolbar, then save the workbook as Regional Sales 1 on your Student Disk
Now that the data is copied into the Excel worksheet, you can easily create the column chart for the memo.

9. Close the Regional Sales 1 workbook file, but do not exit Excel
Do not close the Regional Memo Word file.

QuickTip

You also can select the Word table, click the Copy button on the Word Standard toolbar, then click the first destination cell in Excel and click the Paste button on the Excel Standard toolbar.

FIGURE A-4: **Regional Memo open**

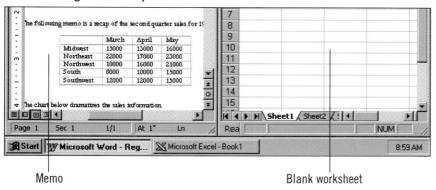

Memo   Blank worksheet

FIGURE A-5: **Drag-and-drop Word text into an Excel worksheet**

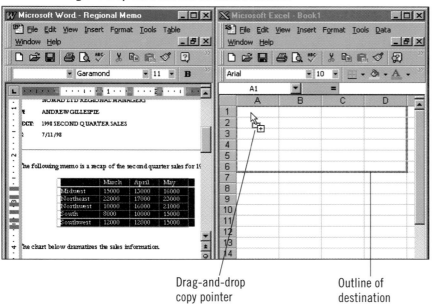

Drag-and-drop   Outline of
copy pointer   destination

FIGURE A-6: **Word table data copied into an Excel worksheet**

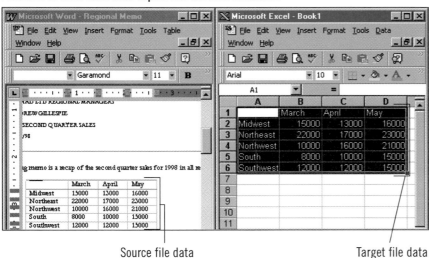

Source file data   Target file data

Creating a Dynamic Link (DDE) between Excel and Word

Sometimes you want the data in two programs to be dynamically linked, not just copied. A **dynamic link**—sometimes called **dynamic data exchange** or **DDE**—means that if the data in the source file is changed, the data in the target file will be automatically updated. Andrew created the column chart in Excel using the data that he had copied from the Word file. Now he wants to paste the chart into his memo. He decides to link it to the document rather than simply copy it, so that the Word memo will always reflect modifications made in the Excel worksheet.

1. In the Excel program window, open the file **INT A-2**, then save it as **Regional Sales 2**
   Regional Sales 2 appears in the Excel worksheet window, as shown in Figure A-7. This file contains the chart created using the data copied from the Word document. You want to copy the chart into the Word document using a dynamic link to the Excel worksheet.

QuickTip

If the Chart toolbar is in the way, drag it by its title bar to a new location.

2. Right-click the **chart** to select it and open the pop-up menu, then click **Copy** on the pop-up menu
   A moving, dotted selection box appears around the chart and the chart is copied to the Clipboard. Now, position the insertion point in the Word document where you want the chart to appear.

3. Click anywhere in the Word program window to make it active, click the **left scroll arrow** once, then click in the blank paragraph below the sentence that begins "The chart below dramatizes…"

4. Click **Edit** on the Word menu bar, click **Paste Special** to open the Paste Special dialog box, click the **Paste link option button**
   The As list box in the Paste Special dialog box changes to list the contents of the Clipboard.

5. Make sure **Microsoft Excel Chart Object** is listed in the As list box, then click **OK**
   The chart is copied into the Word document, and a dynamic link is created between the Word document and the Excel worksheet. Click the scroll buttons to make the chart more visible, if necessary. One of the sales figures is incorrect. The March sales for the Northeast were actually $12,000.

6. Make the Excel worksheet window active, then click cell **B3**

7. Type **12000** then press **[Enter]**
   Watch the chart as the second column, which depicts the Northeast data series, shrinks to reflect the new data. This change occurs in both the Excel worksheet and in the Word document, as shown in Figure A-8.

Time To

✔ Save
✔ Close
✔ Exit Excel

8. Make the Word window active if necessary, click the **Maximize button** in the program window, then click the **Save button** 🔲 on the Word Standard toolbar to save the document

9. Click the **Print Preview button** 🔍 on the Word Standard toolbar, examine your document, click the **Print button** 🖨 on the Print Preview toolbar, and finally close the document and exit Word

FIGURE A-7: Excel worksheet containing chart

Title bar of source
document

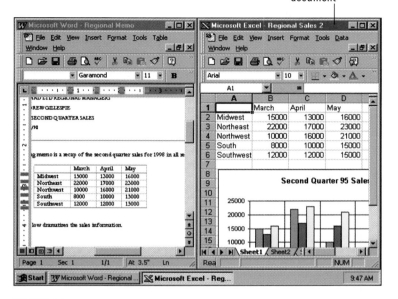

FIGURE A-8: Excel chart linked to Word document

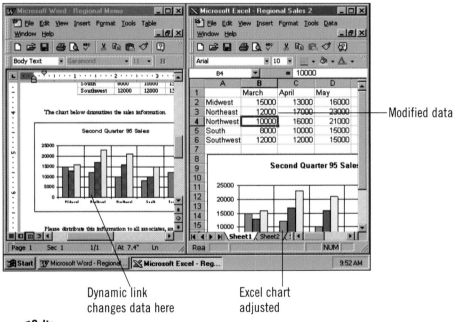

Modified data

Dynamic link
changes data here

Excel chart
adjusted

Breaking links

If you are working with a file containing linked data and you decide that you don't want the linked object to change if the source file changes, you can break the link. In other words, you can change the object from a linked object to a pasted object. In the target file, click the object to select it, click Edit on the menu bar, then click Links to open the Links dialog box, shown in Figure A-9. Click the name of the source file, click Break Link, then click OK. The object in the target file is no longer linked to the source file.

FIGURE A-9: Links dialog box

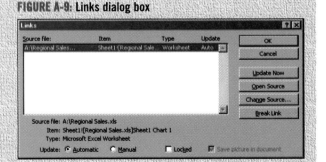

Practice

▶ Independent Challenges

1. The Chamber of Commerce realizes that to improve their advertising coverage, they need to hire an outside consultant. A list of promising consultants is being assembled by other Chamber members. Your job is to create a letter which gives them an overview of the Chamber's advertising efforts.

To complete this independent challenge:

1. Open the Excel file INT A-3 from your Student Disk and save it as Chamber Statistics. Open the Word file INT A-4 from your Student Disk and save it as Chamber Consultants.
2. Examine the chart in the Chamber Statistics workbook. Do you think you can use this chart within a document, or do you need to create other types of charts? What enhancements will need to be added to the charts?
3. Examine the Chamber Consultants file and determine what additions you will need to make to best inform the prospective consultant.
4. Update the date field code in the Chamber Consultants file to reflect the current date.
5. The letter to the Board should contain three charts. Create the additional charts you will need. Add any enhancements, such as text annotations and arrows, which you can call attention to in the letter.
6. Create the document text that will accompany each chart.
7. Paste the charts into the Word document.
8. Preview the Chamber Consultants file. When satisfied it is complete, save it, then print a copy.
9. Submit your printouts.

2. The US Census Bureau maintains a variety of current statistics on the World Wide Web. Using their web site, you can find population projections by state. Use the web site to find populations and projections and then create charts to explain the information.

To complete this independent challenge:

1. Use their web site to find information about state. Use the US Census Bureau's web site to compile your data.
2. Locate download and print the table that shows the Projections of the Total Population of States.
3. Open a new workbook and save it on your Student Disk as Population Projections.
4. Enter data for the United States for the years 1995, 2000, and 2005.
5. Create at least three charts of this data.
6. Open a new Word document and save it on your Student Disk as Population Analysis.
7. Write an description of each of the three Excel charts.
8. Link each of the charts to the Word document above each one's descriptive text.
9. Save, print and hand in print your work.

Getting
Started with Access 97

Objectives

► **Define database software**
► **Start Access 97**
► **View the Access window**
► **Open a database table**
► **Enter and edit records**
► **Preview and print a datasheet**
► **Get Help**
► **Close a database and exit Access**

In this unit, you will learn the basic features of Access, a popular database program, and the various components of a database. You will also learn how to use different elements of the Access window, and how to enter and edit records in a table. Finally, you will learn to use the extensive on-line Help system available in Access. ✎ Michael Belmont is the Travel Division manager at Nomad Ltd, an outdoor gear and adventure travel company. Recently, Nomad switched to Access from a paper-based system for storing and maintaining customer records. Michael will use Access to maintain customer information for Nomad.

Defining Database Software

Access is a database program that runs in the Windows environment. A **database** is a collection of data related to a particular topic or purpose (for example, customer data). Information in a database is organized into **fields**, or categories, such as customer name. A group of related fields, such as all the information on a particular customer, is called a **record**. A collection of related records is called a **table**. A database, specifically a **relational database**, is a collection of one or more related tables that can share information. Figure A-1 shows the structure of a database. Traditionally, businesses kept track of customer information using index cards, as illustrated in Figure A-2. However, with an electronic database, like Access, businesses can store, retrieve, and manipulate data more quickly and easily.

Details

With database software Michael Belmont can:

Enter data quickly and easily

With Access, Michael can enter information on Nomad's customers faster and more accurately than he could using the paper-based method. He can enter data using screen **forms**, which contain **controls** such as check boxes, list boxes, and option buttons, to facilitate data entry. Figure A-3 shows customer information in an Access form.

Organize records in different ways

Michael can review his data sorted by any field, and see records that meet specific criteria by filtering the data. After Michael specifies a sort order, Access automatically keeps records organized, regardless of the order in which they are entered.

Locate specific records quickly

By creating a **query**, a definition of the records he wants to find, Michael can instruct Access to locate the record or records that meet certain conditions. A query can be saved for future use.

Eliminate duplicate data

Access ensures that each record is unique by assigning a **primary key** field to each table. It is not possible for two records in a table to have the same data in their primary key field. Using the paper system, Michael could have duplicate customer records if he forgot that an index card already existed for a particular customer.

Create relationships among tables in a database

Access is a relational database, which allows information within its tables to be shared. This means that Michael needs to enter a customer name only once and it will be referenced in other tables in Nomad's database.

Create reports

Generating professional reports is easy with Access. Michael can produce reports to illustrate different relationships among the data and share these reports with other Nomad employees.

Change the appearance of information

Access provides powerful features for enhancing table data and creating charts so that information is visually appealing and easy to understand.

FIGURE A-1: Structure of a database

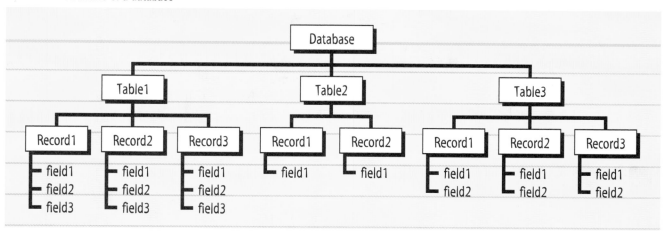

FIGURE A-2: Customer information on an index card

Ginny Braithwaite
3 Which Way, Apt. 2
Salem, MA 01970
(508) 555-7262

Bike tour-Road bike
Loved our ad; thinks Nomad is a wonderfully run company.
She loves our environmentally-friendly attitude!

FIGURE A-3: Customer information in an Access form

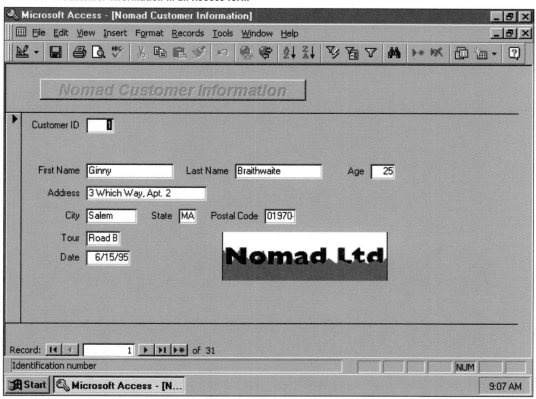

Starting Access 97

To start Access, you use the Windows 95 taskbar. Point to Programs on the Start menu, then click Microsoft Access. A slightly different procedure might be required for computers on a network and those that use utility programs to enhance Windows 95. If you need assistance, ask your instructor or technical support person for help. Michael first needs to start Access so that he can begin to learn how to use it.

Steps 1234

1. **Locate the Start button 🎇 Start on the taskbar**
   The Start button is on the left side of the taskbar and is used to start, or **launch**, programs on your computer.

2. **Click the Start button 🎇 Start**
   Microsoft Access is located in the Programs group—located in the Start menu.

3. **Point to Programs**
   All the programs, or applications, found on your computer can be found in this area of the Start menu.
   Microsoft Access appears in the Program list as shown in Figure A-4.

Trouble?

If you can't locate Microsoft Access in the Programs list, point to Microsoft Office, then click Microsoft Access to start Access.

4. **Click Microsoft Access**
   Access opens and displays the Access window. A Microsoft Access dialog box opens in which you select whether to open a new or existing database. For now, you just want to view the Access window.

5. **Click Cancel**
   The dialog box closes and a blank Access window appears. In the next lesson, you will familiarize yourself with the elements of the Access window.

If you had a previous installation of
Office on your computer, your screen
may contain the Office 97 shortcut bar.

FIGURE A-4: Microsoft Access program selected

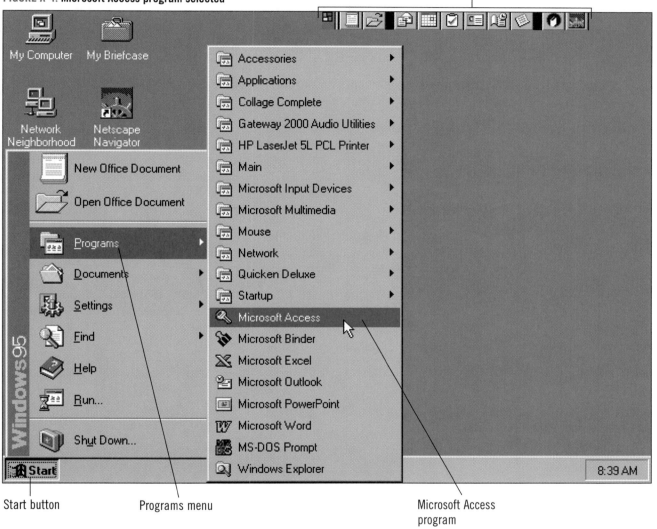

Start button   Programs menu   Microsoft Access
program

Access 97

Viewing the Access Window

Access 97

When you start Access, the screen displays the **startup window**, the area from which you carry out all database operations. The Access window contains many elements that help you enter and manipulate the information in your database. Some of these elements, which are described in Table A-1 and identified in Figure A-5, are common to all Windows programs. ✏ Michael decides to explore the elements of the Access window.

Steps

Trouble?

All lessons from this point on assume you have Access running. If you need help, refer to the previous lesson, "Starting Access 97," or ask your technical support person or instructor for assistance.

1. **Click the Maximize button ▢, if the Access window does not fill the screen**

2. **Look at each of the elements shown in Figure A-5**
   You browse through the commands in the File menu.

3. **Click File on the menu bar**
   The File menu opens, as shown in Figure A-6. The File menu has commands for opening a new or existing database, saving a database in a variety of formats, and printing. At the bottom of the File menu, the four most recently opened databases are listed. Because there are so many components in a database, menu commands vary depending on which database element is currently in use.

4. **Press [Esc] twice to close the File menu**
   Pressing [Esc] once closes the File menu, but File on the menu bar is still highlighted. Pressing [Esc] the second time deselects the menu name.

5. **Review the Database toolbar to see what commands are available**
   Many of the buttons on this toolbar can be found within commands on the File menu, and the remaining buttons can be found in other menu commands.

TABLE A-1: Elements of the Access window

element	description
Menu bar	Contains menus used in Access
Startup window	Area from which database operations take place
Status bar	Displays messages regarding operations and displays descriptions of toolbar buttons
Title bar	Contains program and filename of active database
Database toolbar	Contains buttons for commonly performed tasks

CLUES TO USE

Finding out about buttons and menu commands

If you don't know what a toolbar button does, read its ToolTip—its name—by placing your mouse pointer over its button face. Even though a button is dimmed and not active in a certain window, you can still access its ToolTip.

x

FIGURE A-5: Access window

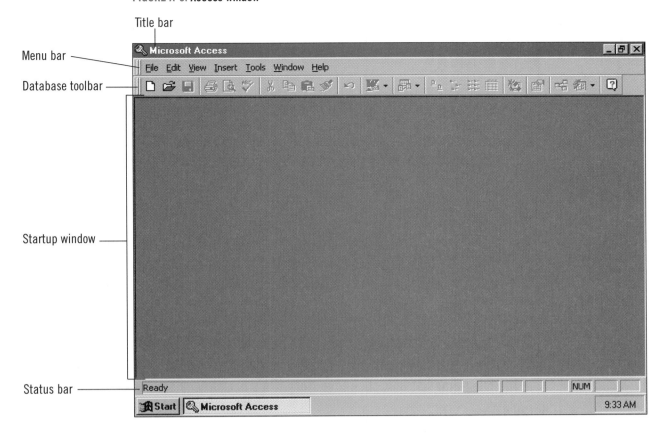

Title bar

Menu bar

Database toolbar

Startup window

Status bar

FIGURE A-6: File menu in startup window

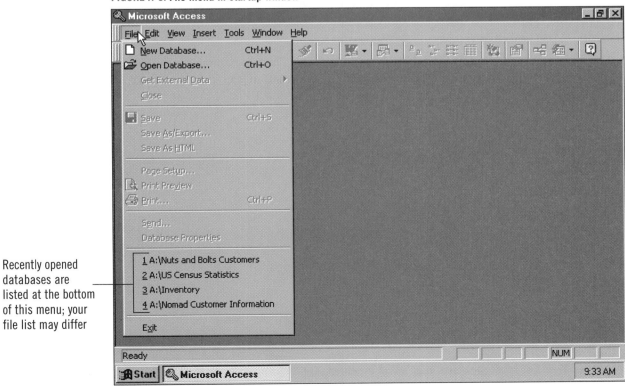

Recently opened databases are listed at the bottom of this menu; your file list may differ

Opening a Database Table

After you open a database, Access displays the database window. The **database window** provides access to all objects in the database. Table A-2 describes the objects—such as tables, forms, and reports—that help you use the information in a database. A database **table** is a collection of related records within a database; a single database can contain multiple tables. Michael wants to open a database and review the table containing information about Nomad's products to see how it is structured.

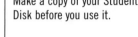

QuickTip

Make a copy of your Student Disk before you use it.

1. Place your Student Disk in the appropriate drive
To complete the units in this book, you need a Student Disk. See your instructor for a copy of the Student Disk, if you do not already have one.

2. Click the Open Database button 🖼 on the Database toolbar
Access displays the Open Database dialog box. Depending on the databases stored on your disk, your dialog box might look slightly different from the one shown in Figure A-7.

3. Click the Look in list arrow, then click the drive that contains your Student Disk
A list of the files on your Student Disk appears in the Look in list box.

4. In the File name list box, click Inventory if it's not already selected

QuickTip

To open a database file quickly, you can double-click the filename in the File name list box of the Open dialog box.

5. Click Open
The Database window for the file Inventory opens, as shown in Figure A-8. The top of the Database window contains the **object buttons** for the Access database objects (which are described in Table A-2). Each object button appears on its own **tab**. The Tables tab is currently the front-most tab in the dialog box. The window lists the tables in the selected database (in this case, the Inventory database contains only one table, Products). The command buttons at the right side of the window allow you to open an existing table, design your own table, or create a new table. You want to open the Products table, which is already selected.

6. Click Open
A window for the Products table opens. The table contains information for 17 Nomad products. Each row is a record and the information is organized by fields arranged in columns.

TABLE A-2: Database objects

object	description
Table	Stores related data in rows (records) and columns (fields)
Query	Asks a question of data in a table; used to find qualifying records
Form	Displays table data in a layout of fields on the screen
Report	Provides printed information from a table, which can include calculations
Macro	Automates database tasks, which can be reduced to a single command
Module	Automates complex tasks using a built-in programming language

FIGURE A-7: **Open dialog box**

Your list of filenames
might be different

Click to display list
of available storage
areas

Open dialog box
toolbar

Click to open
selected file

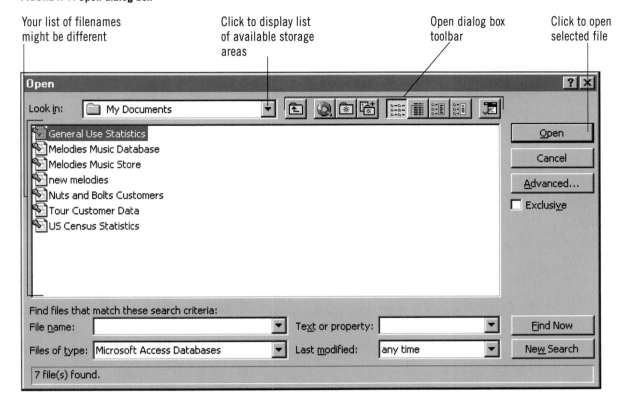

FIGURE A-8: **Database window**

Tables list box

Object button tabs

Command buttons
allow you to open,
design, or create
a table

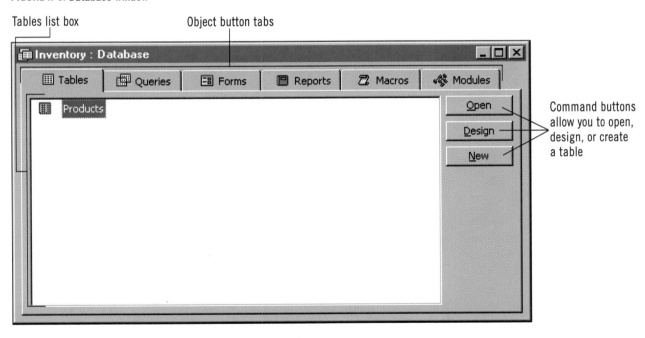

Entering and Editing Records

Data is entered in the datasheet. A **datasheet** is a grid which contains all the records in a table. Each record is contained in a row. Field names are listed as column headings. Careful data entry is vital to obtaining accurate reports from the database. If you enter data carelessly, the results of searches for particular information might be incorrect. You can change the contents of a field at any time. To edit a field, you first click in the field, select the information you want to change, then type the corrections. Table A-3 lists several keyboard shortcuts you can use when editing records.  Michael is now ready to add a new record and edit existing records in the Products table. First, he will maximize the Datasheet window.

1. Click the Maximize button in the Datasheet window title bar

The word "AutoNumber" appears below the last record in the Product ID field, as shown in Figure A-9. This is the primary key assigned by Access for this table. The **AutoNumber field** counts the number of records in the table. Access will increment this field by one to create the primary key data for your new record. The Product Num column contains identification numbers for Nomad's products. Now you are ready to enter the record shown in Figure A-10.

QuickTip

When you are entering data in a table, you can advance to the next field for that record by pressing either [Enter] or [Tab].

2. Click the New Record button ▶* on the Database toolbar, press [Enter] to move to the Product Num field, type 11436, press [Enter], type Shimano Dirt Pirates, press [Enter], type 11, press [Enter], type 27, press [Enter], type 46483, press [Enter], type 24, press [Enter], type 10, press [Enter], type 71.25, press [Enter], type 25, press [Enter], type 15, press [Enter], type Each, then press [Enter]

Record number 18 for the product Shimano Dirt Pirates has been entered.

Next, you'll correct an error in record 12 using a function key to move to the record.

Trouble?

If you cannot see the column in the datasheet window, scroll to the right or left as needed to display the field you need. If you cannot see the row, scroll up or down to display the record you need.

3. Double-click in the Units field for record 12

The contents of the Units field in record 12 is selected. This field should have the same contents as the field above it. You can either type the correct entry in the field, or use a keyboard shortcut that enters the same information for the field as in the previous record.

4. Press [Ctrl][']

The entry changes from 'Pair' to 'Each'. Next, you'll change the Reorder Level in the same record.

5. Press [←] twice, then type 29

Compare your datasheet to Figure A-11. You save the changes made in the table.

QuickTip

When you switch views, from Datasheet to Design View, or when you close the table, any changes to the table are automatically saved.

6. Click the Save button 🖫

When you modify the structure of a table or when you edit records, you need to save the table.

Moving table columns

You can reorganize the columns in a table by moving them from one location to another. To move a column, click its field name so that the entire column is selected, then drag the pointer to the column's new location. As you drag, the mouse pointer changes to ⬚ . A heavy vertical line represents the new location. Release the mouse button when you have correctly positioned the column.

FIGURE A-9: Entering a record in a table

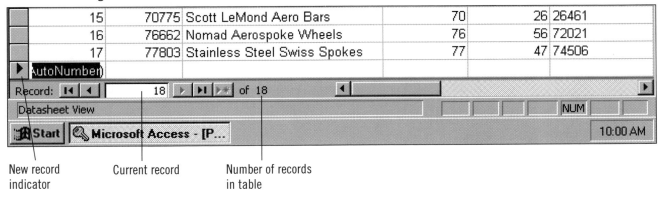

New record indicator | Current record | Number of records in table

FIGURE A-10: Data in record 18

Product ID	Product Num	Product Name	Category ID	Supplier ID	Serial Number	Units in Stock	Units on Order	Unit Price	Reorder Level	Reorder Amount	Units	Disc. Status
18	11436	Shimano Dirt Pirates	11	27	46483	24	10	71.25	25	15	Each	No

TABLE A-3: Keyboard shortcuts in table

shortcut key	action
[F5]	Move to a specific record
[F6]	Move between window sections
[F7]	Open the Spelling dialog box
[Ctrl][']	Insert the value from the same field in the previous record
[Ctrl][;]	Insert the current date
[Ctrl][=]	Move to the first blank record
[Esc]	Undo changes in the current field or record
[Shift][Enter]	Save the current record

FIGURE A-11: Edited record

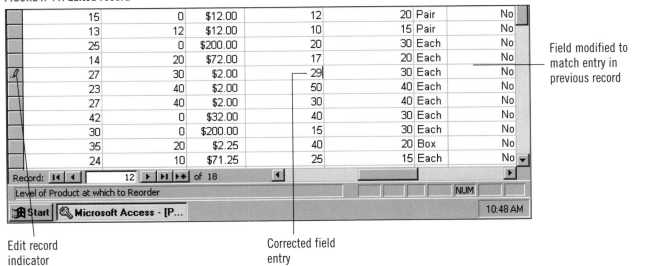

Field modified to match entry in previous record

Edit record indicator | Corrected field entry

Previewing and Printing a Datasheet

After entering and editing the records in a table, you can print the datasheet to obtain a hard copy of the table data. Before printing, it's a good idea to preview the datasheet to see how it will look when printed and, if necessary, to make any adjustments to margins, page orientation, and so on. ✍ Michael is ready to preview and print the datasheet.

Steps 1 2 3 4

1. Click the **Print Preview button** 🔍 on the Database toolbar

The datasheet appears on a miniature page in the Print Preview window, as shown in Figure A-12, and the Print Preview toolbar appears. You decide to use the Magnifier pointer to see how the datasheet looks when magnified.

2. Click the **Magnifier pointer** 🔍 anywhere in the miniature datasheet

A magnified version of the datasheet appears. You notice that most of the fields seem to be cut off the page. You return the datasheet to its original appearance.

3. Click 🔍 anywhere in the magnified datasheet

You decide to print in landscape mode in order to see more fields on each page.

4. Click **File** on the menu bar, then click **Page Setup**

The Page Setup dialog box opens. This dialog box provides options for the way text looks on the page.

5. Click the **Page tab**, click the **Landscape radio button**, as shown in Figure A-13, then click **OK**

Now you can see more of the fields for the table that will print on a page.

6. Click **File** on the menu bar, then click **Print**

The Print dialog box as shown in Figure A-15 opens, giving you several options described in Table A-4. You do not have to make any changes to this dialog box.

7. Click **OK** to print the datasheet, then click **Close** on the Print Preview toolbar to return to the datasheet

With the datasheet printed, you are ready to save the table.

8. Click the **Save button** 💾 on the Standard toolbar

QuickTip

Click the Print button 🖨 to print one copy of the entire datasheet using the default settings without making selections from the Print dialog box.

TABLE A-4: Print dialog box options

option	description
Printer	Displays the name of the selected printer and print connection
Print Range	Specifies all pages, certain pages, a range of pages to print, or selected records
Copies	Specifies the number of copies to print and whether to collate the copies
Print to File	Prints a document to an encapsulated PostScript file instead of a printer
Margins	Adjusts the left, right, top, and bottom margins (available through the Setup option)
Orientation	Specifies Portrait (the default) or Landscape paper (available through the Properties option)

FIGURE A-12: **Datasheet in Print Preview (portrait orientation)**

Close button   Magnifier pointer

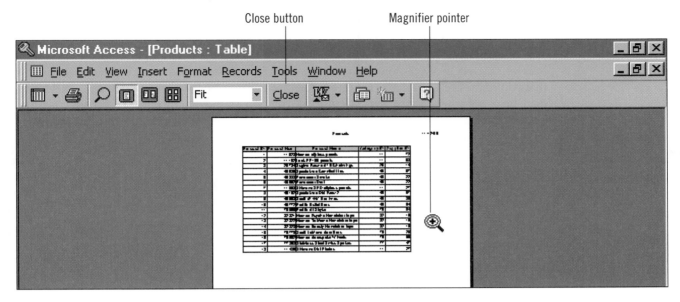

FIGURE A-13: **Page Setup dialog box**

Page tab

Click to display
printout in
Landscape
orientation

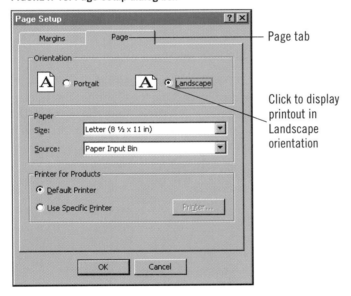

FIGURE A-14: **Print dialog box**

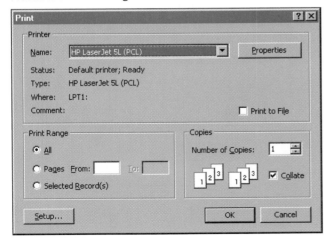

Getting Help

Access provides an extensive on-line Help system that gives you immediate access to definitions, explanations, and useful tips. The **Office Assistant** provides this information using a question and answer format. As you are working, the Office Assistant provides tips—indicated by a light bulb you can click—in response to your own working habits. Help appears in a separate window that you can resize and refer to as you work. You can press the [F1] key at any time to get immediate help.  Michael wants to find information on moving through a database table, and he decides to use the Access Help Assistant to do so. Michael decides to use the animated Office Assistant to learn more about the database window.

1. **If the Office Assistant is not already displayed, click the Office Assistant button** 🔲 **on the Standard toolbar**
   The Office Assistant lets you get information using a question and answer format.

2. **If the Office Assistant is displayed, click its window to activate the query box**
   You want information on how to navigate a datasheet.

3. **Type How do I move between records in a datasheet?**
   See Figure A-16. After you ask a question, the Office Assistant displays relevant topics from which you can choose.

4. **Click Search**
   The Office Assistant displays several topics related to your question, shown in Figure A-17.

5. **Click Moving between records using navigation buttons in Datasheet or Form view**
   The help window, shown in Figure A-18, can be printed by clicking the Options button, then clicking Print Topic. When you point to text that appears as a green underlined topic, the shape of the mouse pointer changes to ⍟. You can click green underlined text to open a dialog box to get more information about that topic.

6. **Click the Close button** ☒ **on the Help dialog box title bar**
   The Help window closes and you return to your worksheet.

QuickTip

You can close the Office Assistant at any time by clicking its Close button ☒.

Changing the Office Assistant

The default Office Assistant is Clippit, but there are 8 others from which you can choose. To change the appearance of the Office Assistant, right-click the Office Assistant window, then select Choose Assistant. Click the Gallery tab, click the Back and Next buttons until you find an Assistant you want to use, then click OK. (You may need your Microsoft Office 97 CD to change Office Assistants.) Each Office Assistant makes its own unique sounds and can be animated by right-clicking its window and selecting Animate! See Figure A-15.

FIGURE A-15: Office Assistant dialog box

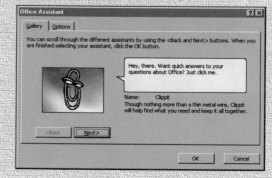

FIGURE A-16: Office Assistant

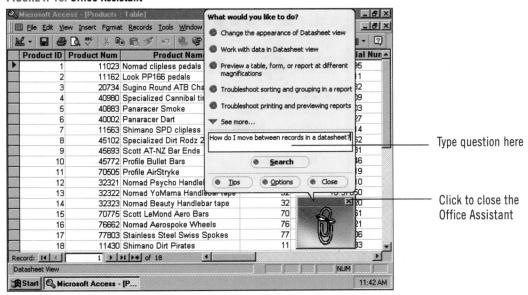

Type question here

Click to close the Office Assistant

FIGURE A-17: Relevant Help Assistant Topics

Click a topic button

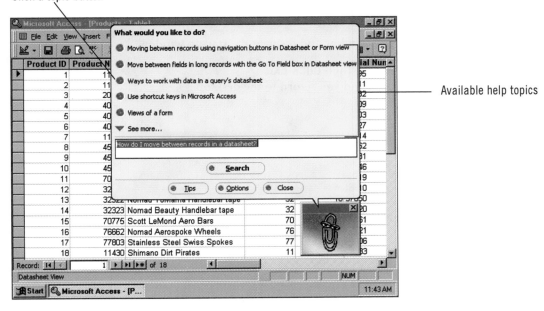

Available help topics

FIGURE A-18: Help window showing navigation buttons

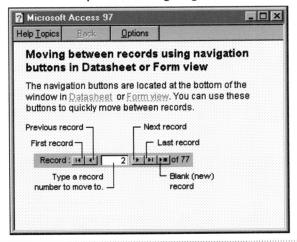

Closing a Database and Exiting Access

When you have finished working in a database, you need to close the object you were working in, such as a table, and then close the database. Unlike other programs you might be familiar with, you don't have to save a table before you close it; Access updates your changes automatically. To close a table, or a database click Close on the File menu. When you have completed all your work in Access, you need to exit the program by clicking Exit on the File menu. Exiting closes all open objects. Table A-5 lists the different ways of exiting Access. ◢▬▬ Michael has finished exploring Access for now. He needs to close the Products table and the Inventory database, then exit Access. Michael begins by closing the Products table.

Steps 1234

1. **Click File on the menu bar, as shown in Figure A-19, then click Close**
Now you need to close the Inventory database.

2. **Click File on the menu bar**
The File menu opens and displays a list of commands. Notice that this Database File menu has different commands than the File menu in the Table window.

3. **Click Close**
Access closes the Database window and displays the startup window.

4. **Click File on the menu bar, then click Exit**
The Access program closes, and you return to the desktop.

QuickTip

Make sure you always properly end your Access session by using the steps in this unit. Improper exit procedures can result in corruption of your data files.

FIGURE A-19:

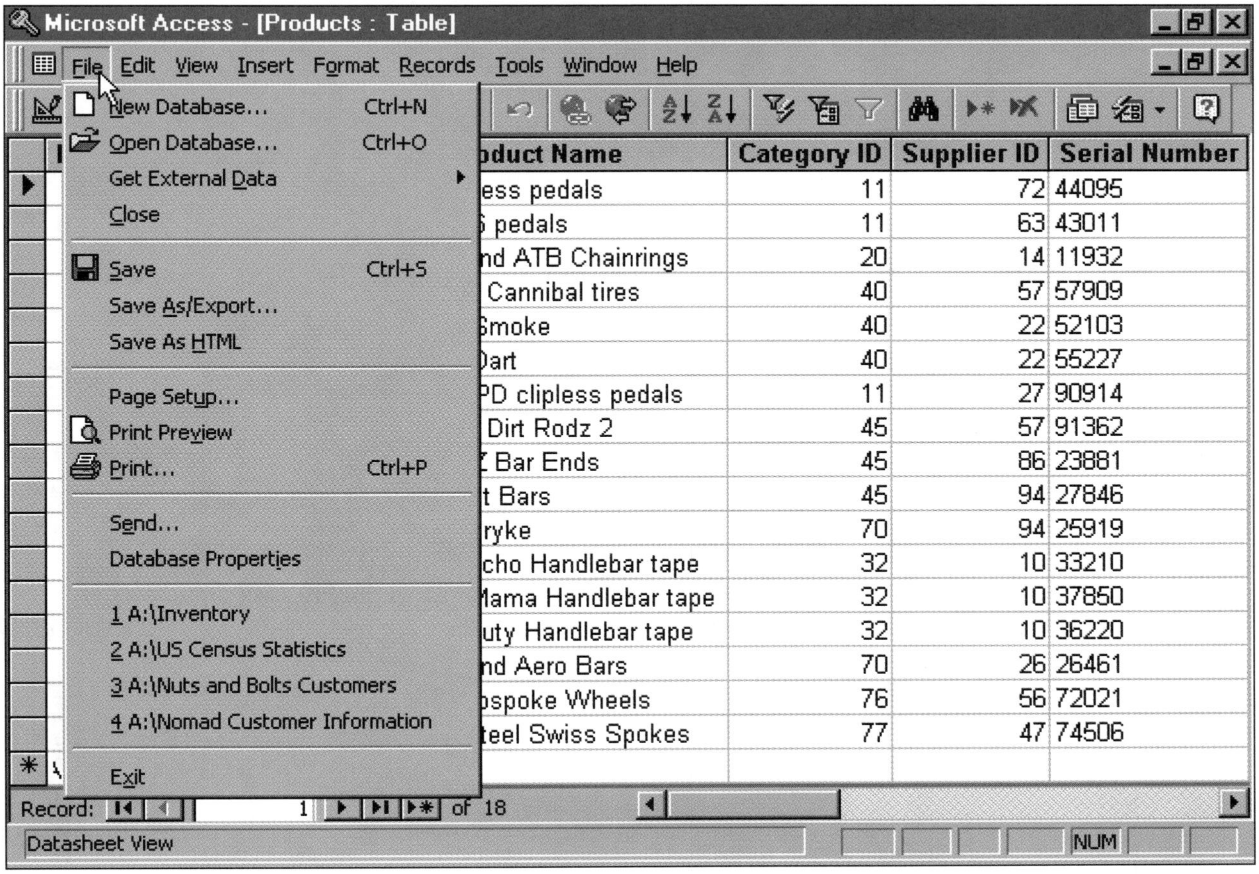

Access 97

TABLE A-5: **Ways to exit Access**

method	key or command
Menu	Choose Exit from the File menu
Keyboard	Press [Alt][F4]
Mouse	Double-click the program control menu box

Practice

► Concepts Review

Label each of the elements of the Access window shown in Figure A-20.

FIGURE A-20

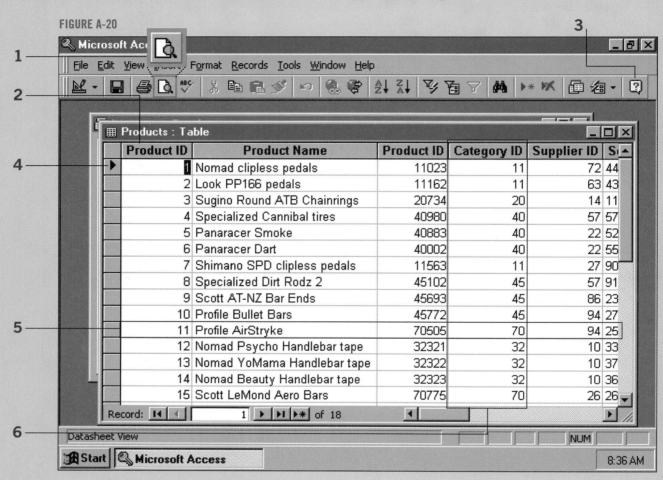

Match each of the following terms with the statement that describes its function.

7. Database window
8. Table
9. Database
10. Office Assistant
11. Shortcut keys

a. A collection of data related to a particular topic or purpose
b. Combination of keys resulting in the execution of a command
c. Area that contains all database objects
d. Stores related data in rows and columns
e. Provides information about Access

Select the best answer from the list of choices.

12. An electronic database can perform all of the following tasks, *except:*
  a. Displaying information visually
  b. Calculating data accurately
  c. Planning database objectives
  d. Recalculating updated information

13. Which of the following is NOT a database?
  a. Customer information
  b. Interoffice memo
  c. Telephone directory
  d. Dictionary

14. Which button opens an existing database?
  a. ✂   **b.** 💾   **c.** 📋   **d.** 📂

15. Which button opens the Office Assistant?
  a. 🔍   **b.** ❓   **c.** 🔍   **d.** ↕

16. You can get Help in any of the following ways, *except:*
  a. Clicking Help on the menu bar
  b. Pressing [F1]
  c. Clicking the Help button ❓
  d. Minimizing the Database window

▶ Skills Review

1. Start Access.
    a. Make sure your computer is on and Windows is running.
    b. Click the Start button, point to Programs, then click Microsoft Access.

2. View the Access Window.
    a. Try to identify as many components of the Access window as you can without referring to the unit material.

3. Open a database table.
    a. Make sure your Student Disk is in the appropriate disk drive.
    b. Click the Open Database button on the Database toolbar.
    c. Open the database named US Census Statistics from your Student Disk.
    d. Click the object tabs in the Database window to see the contents of each object.
    e. Open the Statistical Data table.

4. Enter and edit records.
    a. Click the New Record button.
    b. Enter the following record. State: Virginia, Region: South Atlantic, Year: 1991, Marriages: 68,771.
    c. Change the year in record 6 to 1991.

5. Preview and print a datasheet.
    a. Click the Print Preview button on the Database toolbar to display the datasheet in the Print Preview window.
    b. After viewing the datasheet, click the Print button on the Print Preview toolbar.
    c. After printing, return to the Database window.
    d. Save the table.

6. Get Help.
    a. Click the Office Assistant button on the Database toolbar.
    b. Ask the Office Assistant the following question: "How can I view data?"
    c. Click the topic "Ways to work with data in a table's datasheet."
    d. Click the Options button, click Print Topic, then click OK.
    e. Click the Close button on the Help window.
    f. Click the Close button on the Office Assistant.

7. Close a database and exit Access.
    a. Click File on the menu bar, then click Close to close the "Statistical Data" table.
    b. Click File on the menu bar, then click Close to close the "US Census Statistics" database file.
    c. Click File on the menu bar, then click Exit to exit Access.

▶ Independent Challenges

1. Ten examples of databases are given below. Using each of these examples, write down one sample record for each database and describe the fields you would expect to find in each.

- Telephone directory
- College course offerings
- Restaurant menu
- Cookbook
- Movie listing
- Encyclopedia
- Shopping catalog
- Corporate inventory
- Party guest list
- Members of the House of Representatives

2. Access provides online Help that explains procedures and gives you examples and demos. Help covers such elements as the Database window, the status bar, toolbar buttons, dialog boxes, and Access commands and options. Start Access then explore online Help by clicking the Office Assistant button. Ask the Office Assistant, "What is a database?" Find out about databases—what they are and how they work. Print out information you find on this topic.

FIGURE A-21

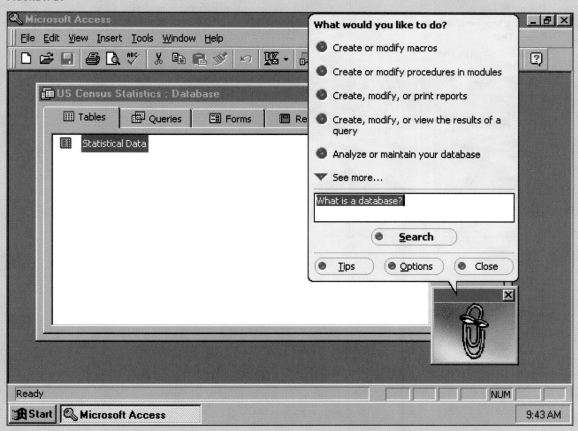

3. To become more accomplished at using databases, you've decided it would be fun to make a list of your favorite films. A database called Favorite Movies has been started. All you need to do is supply information about your favorite films.

   To complete this independent challenge:

1. Open the database called Favorite Movies on your Student Disk.
2. Open the Film Favorites table.
3. Add at least ten entries. The table includes fields for up to 3 co-stars. If you don't know the year the film was released, leave the field blank, or estimate the year.
4. Preview the table, then print it in landscape mode. Submit your finished publication.

FIGURE A-22

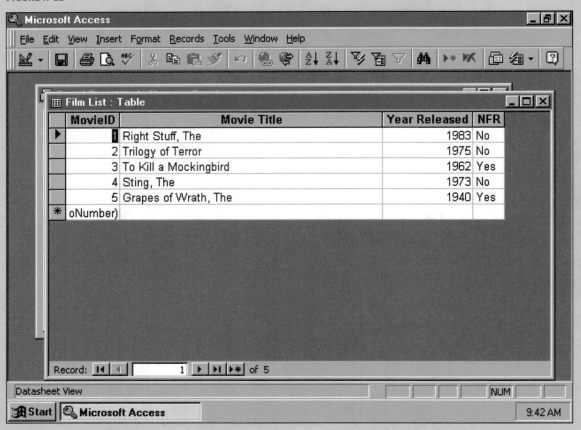

4. Databases on the World Wide Web can be used to retrieve current and historical information. You work for a prestigious socialite who is interested in film preservation. She has purchased The SpeakEasy move theater where she intends to hold many festivals featuring historically important films. Using the World Wide Web, find out about the National Film Registry, which is maintained by the Library of Congress, and begin compiling films for the first festival.

To complete this independent challenge:

1. Log on to the Internet and use your browser to go to http://www.course.com. From there, click the link Student On Line Companions, then click the Microsoft Office 97 Professional Edition—Illustrated: A First Course page, then click the Access link for Unit A.
2. Use the following site to compile your data, The National Film Registry [http://1cweb.loc.gov/film/].
3. Print the National Film Registry's fact sheet.
4. Find out its current membership.
5. Using the list of films, find all the films made in the 1950's.
6. Open the SpeakEasy Movie House database on your Student Disk.
7. Open the Film List table, shown in Figure A-22.
8. Enter these films in the Film List table.
9. Save the table.
10. Preview and print the datasheet.
11. Hand in a printout of your work.

Access 97

▶ Visual Workshop

Modify the existing Customers table in the Corporate Customers database on your Student Disk, then print the datasheet.

FIGURE A-23

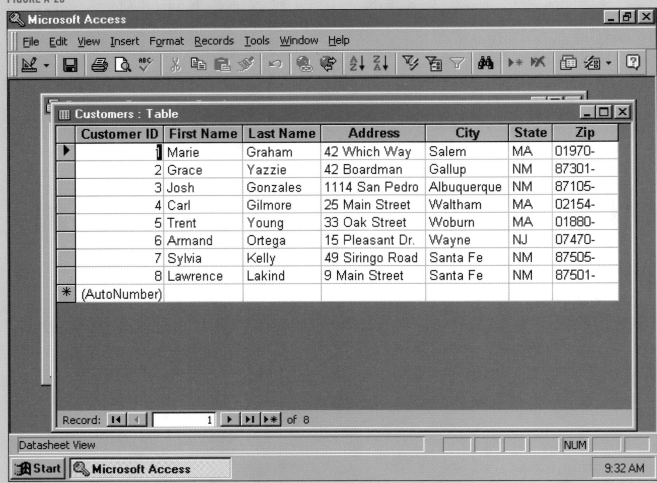

Creating
and Managing Data

Objectives

▶ **Plan a database**
▶ **Create a table**
▶ **Modify a table**
▶ **Find records**
▶ **Sort a table**
▶ **Filter a table**
▶ **Create a simple query**
▶ **Create a complex query**

Now that you are familiar with some of the basic Access features, you are ready to plan and build your own database. When you build a database, you create one or more tables containing the fields that hold the data. After you create a database, you can save, and manage the data within it. In this unit, you will learn how to find and organize data to display the results you want. You will also learn techniques for retrieving information from a table based on specified criteria. ✐━━ Michael wants to build and maintain a database containing information about all Nomad customers who have booked tours since 1991. The information in the database will be useful when Michael budgets for the future, plans new tours, and prepares the company's Annual Report.

Planning a Database

Before you start entering records in the database, you need to identify the goal of the database and plan how you want data stored in it. The planning stage is when you decide how many tables the database will include and what data will be stored in each table. Although you can modify a table at any time, adding a new field after records have been entered means additional work. It's impossible to plan for all potential uses of a database, but any up-front planning makes the process go more smoothly. 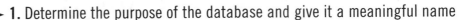 Michael has done some preliminary planning on how the database can be used, but he knows from experience that other Nomad employees might have additional uses for the same customer information. Michael uses the following guidelines to plan his database:

CourseHelp

The camera icon indicates there is CourseHelp available with this lesson. Click the Start button, point to Programs, point to CourseHelp, then click Access 97 Illustrated. Choose the CourseHelp that corresponds to this lesson.

1. Determine the purpose of the database and give it a meaningful name

You need to store information on customers who have taken a Nomad tour. You name the database "Tour Customers," and name the table containing the customer data "Customers." You decide, for now, that the database will contain only one table because all the necessary customer information can be stored there.

2. Determine the results, called **output**, that you want to see, using the information stored in the database

You need to sort the information in a variety of ways: alphabetically by tour name, by tour date to gauge effective scheduling dates, and by postal code for promotional mailings. You will also need to create specialized lists of customers, such as customers who took a bike tour since 1991.

3. Collect all the information, called **input**, that will produce the results you want to see, talking to all the possible database users for additional ideas that might enhance the design

You think the current customer information form, shown in Figure B-1, is a good basis for your database table. The form provides most of the information Nomad wants to store in the database for each customer, making it a good starting point. After talking with the marketing director about targeting tours to specific age groups, you decide to add an Age field to your table.

QuickTip

Multiple database tables can be linked to one another; their information can be shared and queried.

4. Sketch the structure of the table, including each field's **data type**

Using all the information on the original customer information form, you plan each field, the type of data each field contains (such as whether the field contains text or values to be used in calculations), and a brief description of each field's purpose. Figure B-2 is a sketch of the Customers table, which has several new fields not included in the original customer information form.

FIGURE B-1: Original customer information form

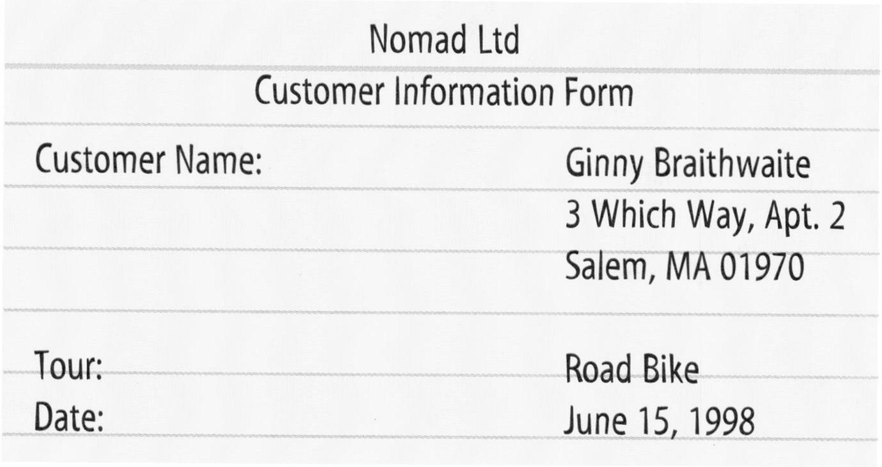

Nomad Ltd

Customer Information Form

Customer Name:	Ginny Braithwaite
	3 Which Way, Apt. 2
	Salem, MA 01970
Tour:	Road Bike
Date:	June 15, 1998

FIGURE B-2: Plan for Customers table

Fields	Data type	Description
CustomerID	Unique number for each record	Identifies each record
FirstName	Text	Customer's first name (+ optional middle initial)
LastName	Text	Customer's last name
Address	Text	Customer's street address
City	Text	Customer's city
State	Text	Customer's state
PostalCode	Text	Customer's zip code
Tour	Text	Type of tour
Date	Date/Time	Starting date of tour
Age	Number	Customer's age

CLUES TO USE

Creating a backup

The information in your database is very important. You should protect your investment of time spent planning the database and entering data in it by creating backup copies of the database file. The database file, which has the extension .MDB, should be copied to a disk or tape on a daily or weekly basis.

Creating a Table

After planning the structure of the database, the next step is to create the database file, which contains all the objects such as tables, forms, reports, and queries that will be used to enter and manipulate the data. When you create a database, you assign it a name. Once the file is created, you are ready to create the table (or tables) in the database. Access offers several methods for creating a table. It is easy to use the Access **Table Wizard**, which guides you through the process of creating a simple table, prompting you to choose the fields and options for your table.
With his plan complete, Michael is ready to create the Tour Customers database file; he uses the Table Wizard to create his Customers table.

Steps

1. **Start Access, click the Blank Database option button in the Create a New Database Using section of the dialog box, then click OK**
   The File New Database dialog box opens.

QuickTip

If Access is already running, you can click the New Database button 🗋 on the Database toolbar to create a database.

2. **Type Tour Customers in the File name text box, insert your Student Disk in the disk drive, click the Save in list arrow, click the appropriate drive, then click Create**
   The Tour Customers database file is saved on your Student Disk. The Database window opens, displaying the new, empty database, as shown in Figure B-3.

3. **In the Tour Customers: Database window, verify that the Tables tab is selected, then click New**
   The New Table dialog box opens. You will use the Table Wizard to create the new table.

4. **Click Table Wizard, then click OK**
   The Table Wizard dialog box opens. The Table Wizard offers 25 business and 20 personal sample tables from which you can select sample fields. You will choose fields from the Customers sample table to include in your Customers table.

5. **Make sure the Business option button is selected, click Customers in the Sample Tables list box, click CustomerID in the Sample Fields list box, then click the Single Field button ▷**
   The CustomerID field is included in the Fields in my new table box. You proceed to add all the necessary fields for the table.

Trouble?

If you inadvertently add the wrong sample field while in the first Table Wizard dialog box, select the field then click the Remove Field button ◁ .

6. **Repeat Step 5 to enter the following fields in the new table: ContactFirstName, ContactLastName, BillingAddress, City, StateOrProvince, and PostalCode**
   Compare your Table Wizard dialog box to Figure B-4. Because you will only be entering states (not provinces) you decide to rename that field.

7. **Click StateOrProvince in the Fields in my new table box, click Rename Field, type State, then click OK**

8. **Click Next**
   The second Table Wizard dialog box opens. You intended to name the table "Customers," which Access suggests in this dialog box. You also want Access to set the **primary key**, a field that qualifies each record as unique. If you do not specify a primary key, Access will assign one for you.

9. **Make sure the "Yes" option button is selected, click Next, click the Modify the table design option button, shown in Figure B-5, then click Finish**
   The table opens in Design view, which allows you to add, delete, or modify the table's structure.

FIGURE B-3: Tour Customers database window

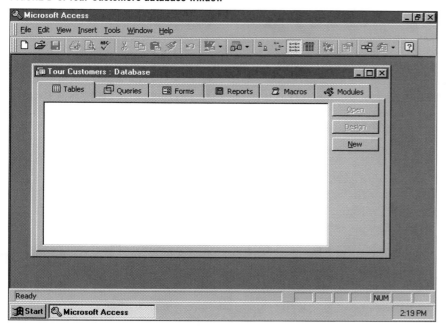

FIGURE B-4: Completed Fields in my new table list

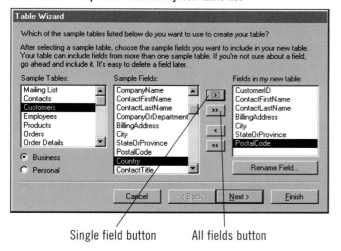

Single field button   All fields button

FIGURE B-5: Third Table Wizard dialog box

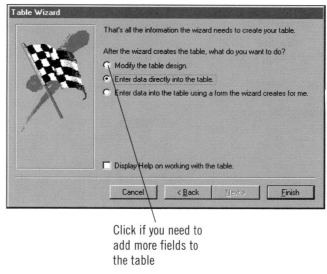

Click if you need to
add more fields to
the table

Creating a table manually

You can create a table manually, without using the Table Wizard, by clicking the Datasheet View or Design View button in the New Table dialog box; you create the field names and their properties as you need them to store your specific data. Field names can contain up to 64 characters including letters, numbers, spaces, and some special characters. You might want to create a table manually if your application is unique or your fields are unusual.

Modifying a Table

After creating a table, you can modify it in **Design view**. Design view allows you to modify the structure of a table by adding and deleting fields, and adding **field descriptions** which clarify the purpose or function of a field and appear in the status bar when you enter data. You can also define other **field properties**, such as the number of decimal places in a number field.  Using the Table Wizard, Michael was able to add all but three of the fields in his table. Now, in Design view, he'll add the three remaining fields, add field descriptions, and modify certain field properties.

Steps

1. Make sure the "Customers" table is open in Design view, as shown in Figure B-6
   Notice the row selectors at the left edge of the table. The selectors can contain **indicators**, such as the primary key indicator. You begin by adding a new field, "Tour," in the first available blank row. This field will identify the type of tour taken by each Nomad customer.

2. Scroll the window until the first blank row is visible, click in the **Field Name box** in this row (under PostalCode), type **Tour**, then press **[Enter]**
   The Data Type field becomes highlighted and displays the word "Text." The Tour field will contain text information, so you accept the suggested data type and enter a description for the field. See Table B-1 for a description of the available data types.

3. Press **[Enter]**, type **Type of tour** in the Description column, then press **[Enter]**
   The next field Michael enters is a date field, which will contain the date the tour was taken. A date field has a data type of Date/Time.

4. Type **Date**, press **[Enter]**, click the **Data Type list arrow**, click **Date/Time**, press **[Enter]**, type **Starting date of tour** in the Description column, then press **[Enter]**
   The last field you must enter is the Age field. This field will contain the age of the tour participant.

5. Type **Age**, press **[Enter]**, click the **Data Type list arrow**, then click **Number**
   By default, number fields are displayed with two decimal places. Because this is not an appropriate format for a person's age, Michael needs to change the format of the number. Use [F6] to move to the Field Properties section of the window.

6. Press **[F6]** to switch panes to the **Field Properties section**
   Currently the Decimal Places box displays the option "Auto," which specifies the default two decimal places. You need to change the number of decimal places so that the ages will appear as whole numbers.

7. Click in the **Decimal Places box**, click the **list arrow**, then click **0** to specify whole numbers
   Next you need to add a description for the Age field you just entered.

8. Press **[F6]** to switch panes, press **[Enter]**, then type **Enter the Customer's age at the time of the tour** in the Description column
   Next you add the descriptions for each of the remaining fields.

Time To

✔ Save
✔ Close

9. Click in the **CustomerID Description box**, type **Identification number**, then click in each of the field name Description boxes and add a description for the six fields as shown in Figure B-7

FIGURE B-6: Customers Table in Design view

Row selectors —

Primary key indicator —

Field Properties section —

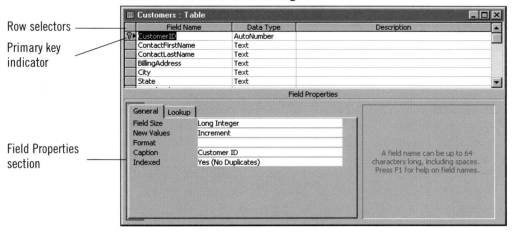

FIGURE B-7: Field descriptions for Customers Table

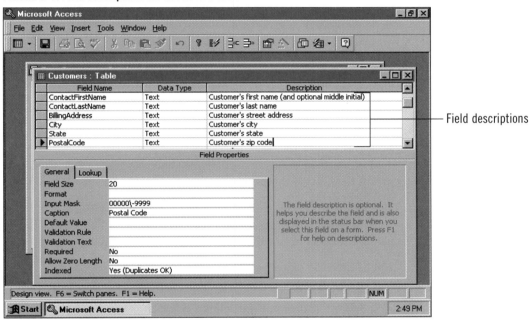

Field descriptions

TABLE B-1: Available Data Types

data type	description	data type shortcuts
Text	Text or a combination of text and numbers that don't require calculations	T
Memo	Lengthy text or a combination of text and numbers	M
Number	Numeric data to be used in calculations	N
Date/Time	Date and time values	D
Currency	Currency values and numeric data used in calculations	C
Yes/No	Fields that can contain only one of two values	Y
OLE object	An object (such as a Word document) that is linked or embedded in an Access table	O
AutoNumber	Unique sequential number that Access assigns to each new record; can't be edited	A
Lookup Wizard	Creates a field that allows you to choose a value from another table or from a list of values	L

Finding Records

Finding records in a table is an important database task. Table B-2 lists a variety of keyboard shortcuts used to navigate a table. In addition, you can locate specific records using the datasheet. ✎ Michael has been busy entering all his data into the Customers table in the database. He also renamed the field names to take up less room on the data sheet. He wants to locate the record for Carol Smith because her name was entered incorrectly; he needs to change the last name to "Smithers." Then he needs to enter a record for a new customer. Michael's work has been saved for you in the Tour Customer Data file on your Student Disk.

Steps

1. Click the **Open Database button** 🖾 on the Database toolbar, click **Tour Customer Data** on your Student Disk, then click **Open**
   Next, open the Customers table and maximize it so it fills the screen.

2. Click the **Tables tab** in the Database window, click **Customers**, click **Open**, then click the **Maximize button** 🔲 to maximize the table window
   Access displays the Customers table, which contains 30 records, as shown in Figure B-8. You will use the Table Datasheet toolbar to change Carol Smith's last name to "Smithers." If the Table Datasheet toolbar is not displayed, continue to Step 3, otherwise skip to Step 4.

3. Click **View** on the menu bar, click **Toolbars** to display the Toolbars dialog box, click **Table Datasheet**, then click **Close**

4. Click any **Last Name field** in the datasheet, then click the **Find button** 🔍 on the Table Datasheet toolbar
   The Find in field dialog box opens, as shown in Figure B-9. By default Access searches the current field, which in this case is Last Name.

5. Type **Smith** in the Find What text box, click **Find Next**, then click **Close**
   Access highlights the name "Smith" in record 11, which is now the current record, for the customer Carol Smith. You can now replace the highlighted name with the correct name.

6. Type **Smithers**
   Next you want to see the last record in the table before you enter the new record.

7. Click **Edit** on the menu bar, click **Go To**, then click **Last**
   The last name of the customer in the last record is selected. Next, you must enter the new record.

Time To
✔ Save

8. Click the **New Record button** ▶* on the Table Datasheet toolbar, press **[Tab]**, then enter the following data in record 31
   Elizabeth Michaels, Mt. Bike, 6/20/98, 57 Beechwood Drive, Wayne, NJ, 07470, 39
   The new record has been added to the table.

TABLE B-2: Keystrokes for navigating a datasheet

keys	actions	keys	actions
[↑], [↓], [←], [→]	Move one field in the direction indicated	[Tab]	Move to next field in current record
[F5]	Move to Record number box on the horizontal scroll bar, then type number of record to go to	[Shift][Tab]	Move to previous field in current record
[Home]	Move to first field in current record	[Ctrl][Home]	Move to first field in first record
[End]	Move to last field in current record	[Ctrl][End]	Move to last field in last record
		[Ctrl][=]	Move to first blank record

FIGURE B-8: Customers table

Table Datasheet toolbar

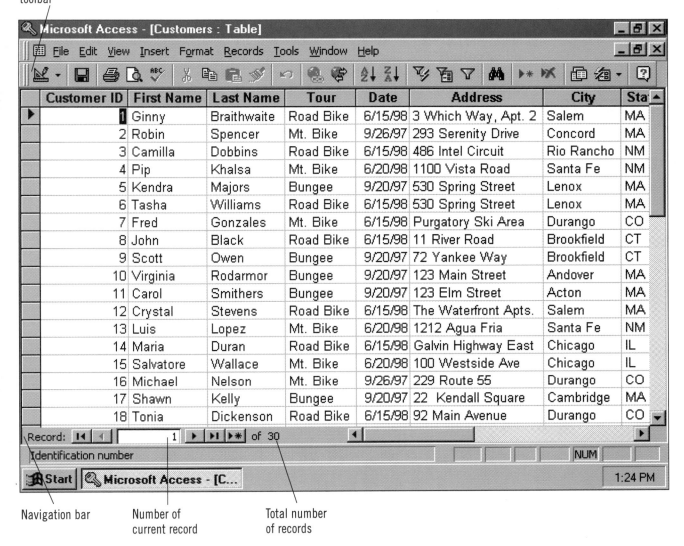

Navigation bar   Number of current record   Total number of records

 Using wildcards in Find

Wildcards are symbols you can use as substitutes for characters in text to find any records matching your entry. Access uses three wildcards: the asterisk (*) represents any group of characters, the question mark (?) stands for any single character, and the pound sign (#) stands for a single number digit. For example, to find any word beginning with S, type "s*" in the Find What text box.

FIGURE B-9: Find in field dialog box

Sorting a Table

The ability to sort information in a table is one of the most powerful features of a database. **Sorting** is an easy way of organizing records according to the contents of a field. For example, you might want to see all records in alphabetical order by last name. You can sort records in **ascending order** (alphabetically from A to Z, numerically from 0 to 9), or in **descending order** (alphabetically from Z to A, numerically from 9 to 0). Michael sorts his table in a variety of ways, depending on the task he needs to perform. His most common tasks require a list sorted in ascending order by tour, and another list sorted in descending order by date.

Steps

CourseHelp

The camera icon indicates that there is a CourseHelp available with this lesson. Click the Start button, point to Programs, point to CourseHelp, then click Access 97 Illustrated. Choose the CourseHelp entitled Sorting records.

1. Position the cursor on the Tour field column head, when the pointer looks like ...↓... , click the Tour field name

The Tour column is selected. The table will be sorted by tour. In addition to clicking the Tour field name to select the field, you can also click any record's Tour field.

2. Click the Sort Ascending button ▲↓ on the Table Datasheet toolbar

The table is sorted alphabetically in ascending order by tour name, as shown in Figure B-10. You decide to print this sorted table for reference using the default settings.

3. Click the Print button 🖨 on the Table Datasheet toolbar

The sorted datasheet prints. You want to return the table to its original order.

4. Click Records on the menu bar, then click Remove Filter/Sort

The table returns to its original order in ascending order by Customer ID. You can also return a table with an AutoNumber field to its original order by sorting that field in ascending order. You decide to sort the records in descending order by the Date field to see the enrollment for each tour.

5. Click the Date field name to select the Date column

6. Click the Sort Descending button ▼↓ on the Table Datasheet toolbar

The records are sorted from most recent to least recent date, as shown in Figure B-11. The sorted list shows that the mid-June bike tour has a higher enrollment than the tour a week later. You want to print the sorted table.

7. Click the Print button 🖨 on the Table Datasheet toolbar

Next you return the table to its original order.

8. Click Records on the menu bar, then click Remove Filter/Sort

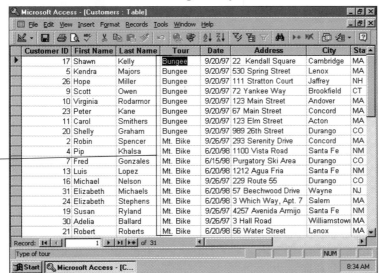

Records sorted by Tour

FIGURE B-11: Table sorted in descending order by Date field

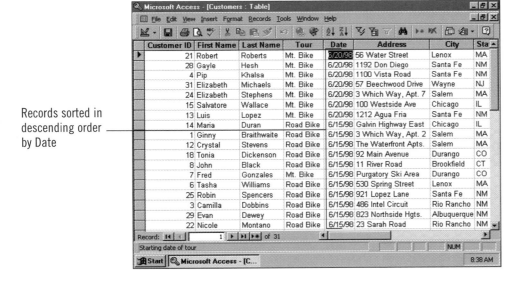

Records sorted in descending order by Date

Using the menu bar to sort

In addition to using buttons on the Table Datasheet toolbar, you can also sort using the menu bar. After you select the field you want to sort, click Records on the menu bar, then click Sort. Click either Ascending or Descending on the Sort menu, shown in Figure B-12.

FIGURE B-12: Sort menu

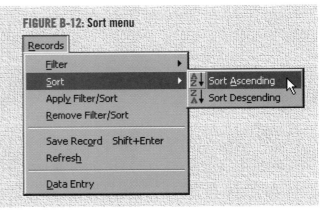

Access 97

Filtering a Table

Sorting allows you to manipulate table records in a simple way and to display them in ascending or descending order. **Filtering** is a more complex method of organizing records, where you define the fields on which the table is sorted. A sort contains all the records in a table, whereas a filter shows only those records that qualify, based on your **criteria**. Qualifying records display in a temporary view that looks and acts like a table. Often, Michael needs a list of customers by a specific tour. He can filter the Customers table to obtain this list.

1. **Make sure the Customers table is open, with all records displayed**
   You want to narrow the number of records displayed so you can see only those records for customers who took a Mt. Bike tour.

Trouble?

If the grid is not cleared of any previous entries, your filter may get erroneous results.

2. **Click Records on the menu bar, click Filter, click Advanced Filter/Sort, then click the Clear Grid button ☒ from the Filter/Sort toolbar to clear the grid of any preexisting criteria**
   The Filter window opens, as shown in Figure B-13. The Filter window consists of two areas: the field list on top, containing all the fields in the table, and the filter grid on the bottom, where you specify the criteria for the filter. The toolbar displayed is the Filter/Sort toolbar. You want to create a filter to show a list of all the customers who took a Mt. Bike tour.

3. **Double-click Tour in the field list**
   Access places the Tour field in the first empty Field cell in the filter grid. Next, you define the criteria for the Tour field.

CourseHelp

If you have trouble with the concepts in this lesson, be sure to view the CourseHelp entitled Filtering Records.

4. **Click the Criteria cell in the Tour column, type Mt. Bike, then press [Enter]**
   Access adds quotation marks around the entry to distinguish text from values. Your completed filter grid should look like Figure B-14.

5. **Click the Apply Filter button ▼ on the Filter/Sort toolbar**
   Only those records containing the Mt. Bike tour appear, as shown in Figure B-15. You can now remove the filter and return the table to its original order.

Time To
✔ Save

6. **Click the Remove Filter button ▼ on the Filter/Sort toolbar to include all the records in the table**

When to use a filter

A filter is temporary and cannot be saved; however, you can print the results of a filter just as you print any datasheet. A filter is best used to narrow the focus of the records temporarily in the current table.

FIGURE B-13: Filter window for the Customers table

Field list   Table name   Field name goes here   Sort order goes here   Filter/Sort toolbar

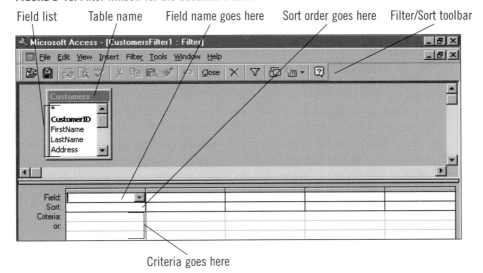

Criteria goes here

FIGURE B-14: Completed filter grid

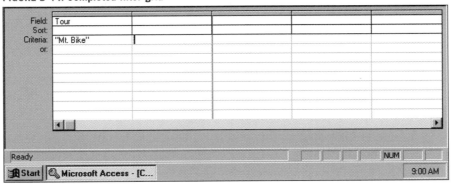

FIGURE B-15: Filtered table records

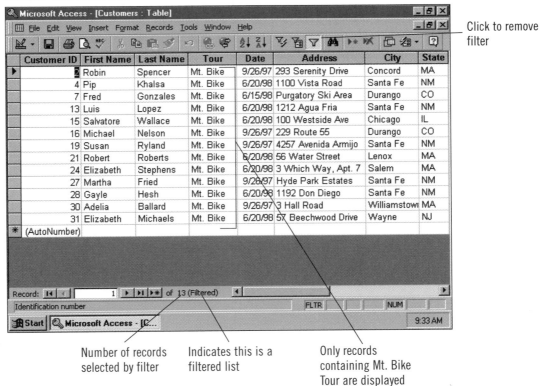

Click to remove filter

Number of records selected by filter

Indicates this is a filtered list

Only records containing Mt. Bike Tour are displayed

Creating a Simple Query

A **query** is a set of restrictions you place on a database table by specifying criteria to retrieve qualifying records. Unlike a filter, which only allows you to manipulate data temporarily, a query can be saved so that you do not have to recreate the fields in the grid. The query results also display only the fields you have specified, rather than showing all table fields. The most commonly used query is the **select query**, in which records are collected, viewed, and can be modified later. The Nomad employee responsible for setting up Road Bike tours often asks Michael for a list of customers who have participated in these tours. Michael needs to create a query that displays only the names of all Road Bike customers in ascending order.

Steps

1. Click the **New Object button list arrow** on the Table Datasheet toolbar, then click **Query** on the pull-down palette
The New Query dialog box opens and displays options for using the Query Wizard. You decide to use the Design View to create a new query.

2. Click **Design View**, then click **OK**
The Select Query window opens, as shown in Figure B-16. The Query Design toolbar provides more buttons than does the Filter/Sort toolbar in the Filter window. You add the first field, sort, and criteria specifications to the Query Design grid. Scroll down the field list to display the **Tour field**.

Trouble?

If you enter a field in the query grid in error, select the field then press [Delete] to delete it.

3. Double-click **Tour** in the field list, then click the checked **Show box** in the grid to turn off the checkmark
The Tour field name appears in the Field cell in the query grid, and the Table field displays the location of the field: the Customers table. The Show box indicates that the field will not be displayed in the query results. Next, specify the criteria for the query.

Trouble?

For a single table query, entries in the grid are not case sensitive: it doesn't matter if you use upper or lower case characters. Field criteria entered in the query grid for linked tables, however, are case sensitive.

4. Click the **Criteria cell** in the Tour column, type **Road Bike**, then press [Enter]
You want the query results to show the last name, in ascending order, of each customer who participated in a Road Bike tour.

5. Double-click **LastName** in the field list, click the **Sort cell** in the LastName column, type **a** (for ascending), then make sure the Show box is selected for the LastName field
Compare your grid to Figure B-17. You want to view the results of the query.

6. Click the **Datasheet View button** on the Query Design toolbar
The results of the query are shown in Figure B-18. The results show the last names of the 10 customers that took Road Bike tours. You return to Design View.

7. Click the **Design View button** on the Query Datasheet toolbar
The query grid is redisplayed. You want to save the query results.

8. Click the **Save button** on the Query Design toolbar, type **Road Bike customers** in the Query Name text box of the Save As dialog box, as shown in Figure B-19, then click **OK**
The query is saved as part of the database file.

FIGURE B-16: **Select Query window**

Query Design toolbar →

Tables used in query display here →

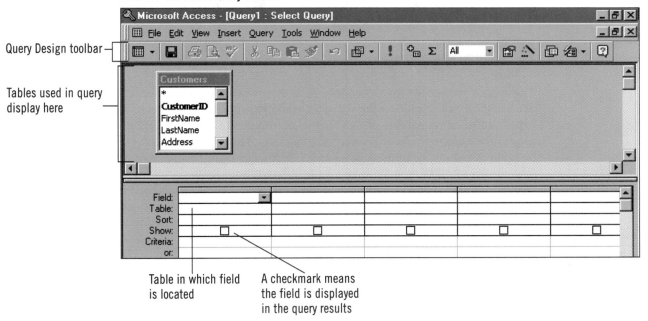

Table in which field is located

A checkmark means the field is displayed in the query results

FIGURE B-17: **Sample query grid**

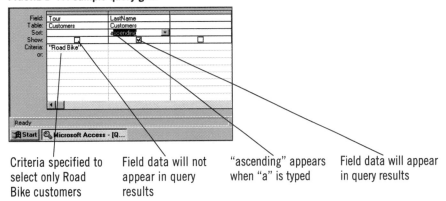

Criteria specified to select only Road Bike customers

Field data will not appear in query results

"ascending" appears when "a" is typed

Field data will appear in query results

FIGURE B-18: **Results of simple query**

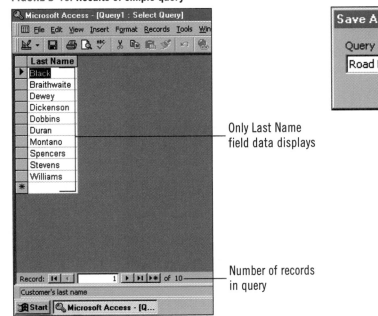

Only Last Name field data displays

Number of records in query

FIGURE B-19: **Save As dialog box for query**

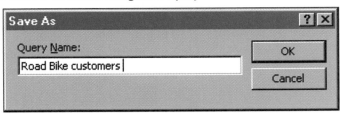

Access 97

Creating a Complex Query

The criteria you specify for a query can be as simple as a list of all customer names, or as complex as a list of all customers over the age of 30, who live in New Mexico and took a tour in June. Using **expressions**, combinations of field names, constant values, and arithmetic operators, you can restrict the number of records returned by a query. The criteria **AND** and **OR** can also be used to broaden or narrow the number of selected records. For example, the result of a query of customers who took a Mt. Bike or Road Bike tour is different from the result of a query of customers who took a Mt. Bike or Road Bike tour and live in New Mexico. Each month, Michael wants to see a list of all customers, in descending order by last name, who took a Mt. Bike or Road Bike tour and who have a postal code greater than 50000. He decides to modify the previous query and save it as a new query.

Steps

1. **Click the Show box for the Tour field**
   You want to display the records of customers who took either a Mt. Bike or Road Bike tour, so you need to display the Tour field. You modify the current entry in the Criteria cell to include the second tour in the "or" field beneath the Criteria cell.

QuickTip

Arithmetic operators used in criteria when creating simple or complex queries are greater than (>), less than (<), equals (=), greater than or equal to (>=), less than or equal to (<=), and not equal to (<>).

2. **Click the Tour field or cell, type Mt. Bike, then press [Enter]**
   The entry "Mt. Bike" appears in the "or" cell. Next, you add the FirstName to the query grid and you want to sort the LastName field in descending order.

3. **Double-click FirstName in the field list, click the LastName field's Sort list arrow, then click Descending**
   The query design changes are specified as shown in Figure B-20. You decide to view the datasheet.

4. **Click the Datasheet View button 🖩 on the Query Design toolbar**
   The results of the query are displayed in the datasheet. Notice that customers who took either a Mt. Bike or Road Bike tour are listed. The last names are sorted in descending order.

5. **Click the Design View button 🖉 on the Query Datasheet toolbar**
   The query grid is redisplayed. You add the PostalCode field and its criteria to the query grid.

6. **Double-click PostalCode in the field list, click its Criteria cell, type >50000, press [↓] to enter the criteria in the "or" criteria cell, type >50000, then press [Enter]**
   If the Tour field scrolls out of view, scroll the window to view the completed query grid. You view the datasheet for the completed query.

7. **Click 🖩**
   Because you wanted to view bike tour customers only with Postal codes above 50000, the query results are narrowed from 23 records to 14, and the query is being sorted by the LastName field, as shown in Figure B-21. Next, you save the modified query within the current database so you can view the results at any time.

QuickTip

You can save a filter as a query by choosing Save As Query from the File menu (while in the Filter window), then name the query and click [OK].

8. **Click File on the menu bar, click Save As/Export, type Bike Tours AND PostalCode >50000 in the New Name text box as shown in Figure B-22, then click OK**
   The new query is saved for future use. You close the query and the table and then exit Access.

9. **Close and exit Access.**

FIGURE B-20: "Or" specification in query grid

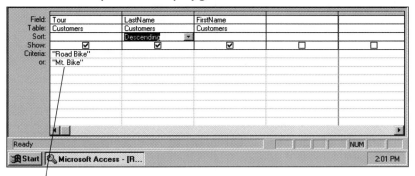

"Or" specification
used in criteria

FIGURE B-21: Results of complex query

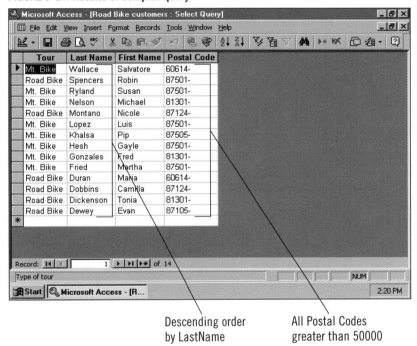

Descending order
by LastName

All Postal Codes
greater than 50000

FIGURE B-22: Save As/Export dialog box

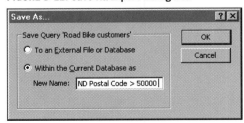

Using And and Or to affect query results

Using the Or criteria generally results in broader query results, as either of the criteria need to be true in order for a record to be selected. The And criteria demands that both criteria be true in order for a record to be selected.

Practice

▶ Concepts Review

Label each of the elements of the select Query window shown in Figure B-23.

FIGURE B-23

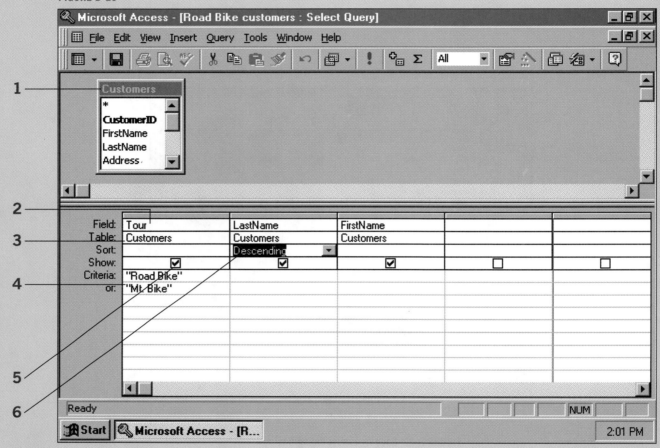

Match each button with its correct description.

7. ▸∗

8. ▦

9. 🗁

10. 🖶

11. 💾

12. 🔍

a. Open Database
b. Print
c. New Record
d. Find
e. Datasheet View
f. Save

Select the best answer from the list of choices.

13. Which button lets you create a new object?

a. ▤▾   b. ▦   c. 📈   d. !

14. The button that sorts a table from A to Z is

a. 🗁   b. ↕   c. ▦   d. Z↓

15. The button used to add a new record to a table is

a. »   b. ▶❙   c. ▸∗   d. ❙◀

16. Each of the following is true about a filter, *except*:

a. It creates a temporary set of records that looks like a table
b. Its contents can be sorted
c. It includes all fields in the table
d. It can be saved for future use

17. Which button is used to clear the filter grid?

a. ▸∗   b. ✕   c. ▤   d. ▽

▶ Skills Review

1. Plan a database.
a. Plan a database that will contain the names and addresses of your business contacts.
b. Based on your own experience, decide which fields you need to include in the database.
c. Write down the necessary fields with names and descriptions for each field.

2. Create a table.
a. Start Access and insert your Student Disk in the disk drive.
b. Use the Blank Database option button to create a new database file.
c. Save the file as "Contacts" on your Student Disk.
d. Click the Tables object tab in the Database window, then click New.
e. Use the Table Wizard to create the new table.
f. In the Sample Tables list box, click Contacts. Make sure the Business option button is selected.
g. In the Sample Fields list box, choose each of the following fields for your table:
> ContactID
> FirstName
> LastName
> Address
> City
> StateOrProvince
> PostalCode
> Birthdate
h. Continue through the Table Wizard. Name the table "Business Contacts."
i. Click the Modify the table design option button in the third Table Wizard dialog box, then click Finish.

3. Modify a table.
a. In the first available blank row, add a new text field called "Other."
b. Click the ContactID field Description box.
c. Type "Unique number for Contact."
d. Add appropriate descriptions for the other fields.

4. Find records.
a. Open the database "Bicycle Parts" from your Student Disk. Open the "Products" table.
b. Use the Find button to locate all records in all fields that match any part of a field and contain the text "bar."
c. Make a note of how many occurrences there are?

5. Sort a table.
a. Sort the Products table in ascending order using the "Product Num field." Print the datasheet.
b. Return the datasheet to its original order.
c. Create and print a list of products in descending order by "UnitsInStock."
d. Return the datasheet to its original order.
e. Create and print a list of products in ascending order by "ProductName."
f. Return the datasheet to its original order.
g. Create and print a list of products in descending order by "SupplierID."
h. Return the datasheet to its original order.

6. Filter a table.

   a. Create a filter that shows all products on order. A product on order has a value larger than 0 in the UnitsOnOrder field. (Hint: Set the criteria in the filter grid to ">0" for Units On Order.)

   b. Print the datasheet.

   c. Return the datasheet to its original order.

   d. Create a filter for all non-discontinued items.

   e. Print the resulting datasheet.

   f. Return the datasheet to its original order.

7. Create a simple query.

   a. Create a query for all the Products On Order that shows only the ProductNum field data and the product name for the items on order. Name this query "Products on Order."

   b. Create a query for all non-discontinued items that shows the ProductName, SupplierID, UnitsInStock, and UnitPrice. Name this query "Non-discontinued Products."

   c. Create another query that lists all products with a unit price greater than $50. Name this query "Products costing >$50." (*Hint:* Do not type the $ in the criteria.)

   d. Use the "Non-discontinued Products" query to create a new query in which the ProductName, ProductNum, UnitsInStock, and UnitPrice field data display. Name this query "Available Products."

   e. Modify the existing "Non-discontinued Products" query for discontinued products. Name this new query "Discontinued Products."

   f. Print out the Discontinued Products query.

8. Create a complex query.

   a. Create a query that shows the ProductName of all products with a DiscoStatus = Yes field AND that are sold by the pair (the Units field). Sort the query in ascending order by units. Name this query "Discoed, by Unit."

   b. Print the datasheet for the query.

   c. Save the Discoed, by Unit query as "Available, by Unit." Change the DiscoStatus = Yes field to DiscoStatus = No.

   d. Print the datasheet for the query.

   e. Modify the "Products on Order" query so that the results are sorted in ascending order by the SupplierID field. Make sure the SupplierID field data is displayed. Save the modified query. Print the query results.

   f. Modify the "Products costing >$50" query to include the following fields: ProductNum, ReorderLevel, and ReorderAmount. Save the modified query. Print the query results.

   g. Modify the "Discoed, by Unit" query so that the results are sorted in descending order by units, and so that the data for the UnitPrice field is displayed. Save the modified query. Print the query results.

   h. Close the file and exit Access.

► Independent Challenges

1. The Melodies Music Store has hired you as the customer service manager. You need to create queries in the store's music database, which is contained in the file "Melodies Music Store" on your Student Disk. The database includes one table, called Available titles.

   To complete this independent challenge:

1. Start Access, open the database file "Melodies Music Store" on your Student Disk.
2. Using the Available titles table, find out how many records are in the Classic group. Should this classification be its own sub-group?
3. Sort the records by CategoryID, then by ProductName. Print the results.
4. Create a filter that examines records with a SerialNumber lower than 400000. Print this list.
5. Because musical categories overlap, group the eight classifications into three subgroups. You might, for example, group Alternative and Metal into a group called New Age; Classic, Pop, and Rock into a group called Rock N Roll; and World Music, Jazz, and Blues into a group called Easy Listening.
6. Create queries for each of the three subgroups. Each query must use an OR specification in the query grid. Name each query for its classification.
7. Query the Available titles table using each query, and print the results of each query.
8. Modify one of the subgroup queries to include a musical classification already included in another subgroup. For example, you could include Pop in Easy Listening as well as Rock N Roll. Print the results of the modified query and submit all printouts.

2. You work in the US Census Office for your city. Using the database "Census Bureau" from your Student Disk, create several queries that examine the data in the Statistical Data table. The records in the Statistical Data table contain marriage information by state.

To complete this independent challenge:

1. Add descriptions for each of the fields in the "Statistical Data" table.
2. Find the states in the same geographical area as your state. For example, if your state is Utah, other states in the Mountain Region are New Mexico, Colorado, Nevada, Montana, Arizona, Idaho, and Wyoming.
3. Create and save a query that selects records in your geographical area and sorts them in ascending order by state. Display the State and Marriages fields.
4. On paper, write down at least three additional queries that would extract meaningful data. Create and save each of these queries. Print a sample of each query's results and submit each of the samples with the hand-written work.

3. Your computer consulting firm has contracted to create a database for a special effects firm called Grand Illusions. Currently, Grand Illusions is working on five films, each having a minimum of three special effects they need to keep track of. Each special effect is created using some combination of computer imaging, prosthetics, multi-media, archived footage, and an in-house tool called Black Midnight.

To complete this independent challenge:

1. Create a database file on your Student Disk called Grand Illusions.
2. Create a table called Special Effects Register.
3. Create records for each special effect used in the five film projects. Each record should include the film name, special effect name, the Director's name, the tools used to create the effect, and the completion date of the effect.
4. Print the results of sorting the records in ascending order by film name.
5. Print the results of sorting the records in ascending order by completion date, then in ascending order by Director's name.
6. Create a query for each film which displays the completion date, Director's name, and the tools used.
7. Save the Query using the film name and Special Effects as the query name.
8. Print out each list and submit all printouts.

4. Proper use of search engines can help you find information about the elected officials in any state. The socialite for whom you work wants to be aware of who is elected to what post, and when their term is up. He has asked you to create a database based on the information you retrieve from the World Wide Web that contains this information.

1. Log on to the Internet and use your browser to go to http://www.course.com. From there click the link Student On Line Companions; then click the link to go to the Microsoft Office 97 Professional Edition—Illustrated: A First Course page, then click the Access link for Unit B.
2. Locate information about your state, and find out about your state's Federal elected officials.
3. Create a new database on your Student Disk called Elected Officials.
4. Include the following information in your table: the official's name, whether they are in the House or Senate, their official title, when their term began, when they're up for reelection, party affiliation, age, and number of years of elected service.
5. Save the table.
6. Create a query that finds Democrats, and one that finds Republicans.
7. Preview and print the datasheet.
8. Hand in a printout of your work.

▶ Visual Workshop

Use the Customers table in the "Tour Customer Data" file on your Student Disk to create the following output using a filter.

FIGURE B-24

Customer ID	First Name	Last Name	Address	City	State	Postal Code	Tour	Date	Age
30	Adelia	Ballard	3 Hall Road	Williamstow	MA	02167-	Mt. Bike	9/26/95	42
13	Luis	Lopez	1212 Agua Fria	Santa Fe	NM	87501-	Mt. Bike	6/20/96	34
31	Elizabeth	Michaels	57 Beechwood Drive	Wayne	NJ	07470-	Mt. Bike	6/20/96	39
16	Michael	Nelson	229 Route 55	Durango	CO	81301-	Mt. Bike	9/26/95	40
2	Robin	Spencer	293 Serenity Drive	Concord	MA	01742-	Mt. Bike	9/26/95	32
24	Elizabeth	Stephens	3 Which Way, Apt. 7	Salem	MA	01970-	Mt. Bike	6/20/96	38

Creating
a Form

Objectives

- ▶ **Create a form**
- ▶ **Modify a form layout**
- ▶ **Change the tab order**
- ▶ **Use the Expression Builder**
- ▶ **Format controls**
- ▶ **Add a field to a form**
- ▶ **Add a graphic image to a form**
- ▶ **Use a form to add a record**

The Datasheet View gives you an overall look at the records in a table. Often, however, the fields you need to view in the table are not all visible unless you scroll left or right. Access allows you to easily create attractive screen forms that let you determine how you view each record's fields and the records in the database. You can design a screen form to match the design of a particular paper form to facilitate data entry. Because Nomad Ltd's Travel Division has been so successful with its bicycle tours, it keeps an inventory of supplies, which it then sells to tour customers. Michael wants to create a form to make it easier to enter inventory data.

Creating a Form

You can create a form from scratch, or you can use the **Form Wizard**. The Form Wizard provides sample form layouts and gives you options for including specific fields in a form. Currently, the Travel Division fills out a paper form for each product in its bicycle inventory. Michael needs to create an Access form for the bicycle inventory data. He wants to design the form so that it looks similar to the original paper form, displays one record at a time, and displays all but one of the table's fields .

Steps

1. Start Access and insert your Student Disk in the appropriate drive

2. Click the Open an Existing Database radio button, then open the database Bike Inventory on your Student Disk
   This database file contains the bicycle inventory data. You want to create a new form for the Bicycle Products table.

3. Click the Forms tab in the Database window, then click New
   The New Form dialog box opens, as shown in Figure C-1. You need to identify the table on which the form will be based, then you can choose the Form Wizard option to create the form.

4. Click the Choose the table or query where the object's data comes from: list arrow, click Bicycle Products, click Form Wizard, then click OK
   A dialog box opens and lists all the fields in the table, as shown in Figure C-2. This dialog box allows you to select which fields you want to include in the form, and to determine the order in which they appear in the form. Instead of selecting each field individually, you decide to select all the fields at one time, and then exclude the one you don't want to appear.

5. Click the All Fields button ⟩⟩ , use the scroll bar in the Selected Fields box to display the top of the list, click ProductNum, then click the Remove Single Field button ⟨
   All the fields except ProductNum appear in the Selected Fields box. You are ready to choose a layout for your form. You decide to accept the default style: a Columnar layout.

6. Click Next > , then click Next > to accept the Columnar layout
   Next, you choose a style for your form. You decide to use the Standard style.

7. Click Standard, then click Next >
   The final dialog box suggests the table name as the title for the form. You accept the title suggestion Bicycle Products and want to see the form with data in it.

8. Click Finish
   The Bicycle Products form opens in Form View, as shown in Figure C-3. The fields are listed in the form organized in columns, and the data for the first record in the table is displayed. The navigation buttons at the bottom of the form allow you to move from record to record. If you can't see all the fields, the vertical scroll bar allows you to move to areas of the form that currently are not visible.

QuickTip

The ⟨ Back button in the Form Wizard dialog boxes allows you to move to the previous dialog box and make changes, as necessary, before completing the form.

▶ AC C-2   **CREATING A FORM**

FIGURE C-1: New Form dialog box

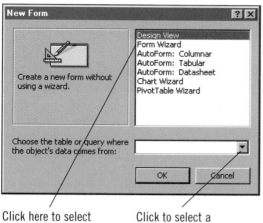

Click here to select
the Form Wizard

Click to select a
table or query on
which to base the
form

FIGURE C-2: Selecting fields in the Form Wizard dialog box

Table that the form
is based on

Places selected
field on form

Places all available
fields on form

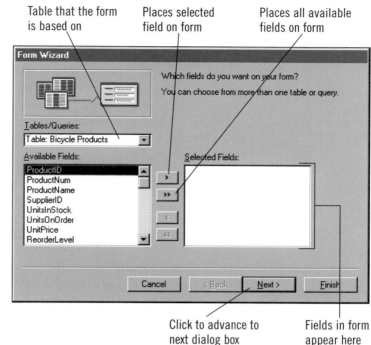

Click to advance to
next dialog box

Fields in form
appear here

FIGURE C-3: Bicycle Products form

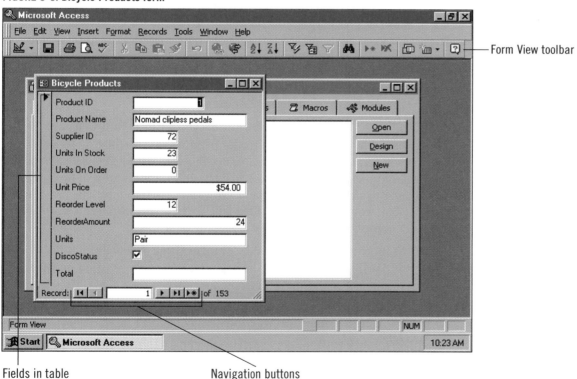

Form View toolbar

Fields in table

Navigation buttons

Using AutoForm

You can create a simple form by clicking the New
Object button [icon] on the Database toolbar, then
clicking AutoForm from the palette. AutoForm offers

no prompts or dialog boxes; it instantly creates a
columnar, tabular, or datasheet form that displays all
the fields in the table or query.

Modifying a Form Layout

After you create a form, you can modify it easily by changing the locations of fields, adding or deleting fields, adding graphics, and changing the color of text and field data. You modify a form in Design View, which is divided into three sections: Form Header, Detail, and Form Footer. The **Form Header** appears at the beginning of each screen form and can contain an additional form title or logo. The **Detail** displays the fields and data for each record. The **Form Footer** appears at the bottom of each screen form and can contain totals, instructions, or command buttons. In Design View, a field is called a control. A **control** consists of the **field label** and the data it contains which is the **field value text box**. There are three types of controls: bound, unbound, and calculated. A **bound control**, such as a field, has a table or query as its information source; an **unbound control**, such as a label or graphic image, has its data source as something other than the database, and a **calculated control** uses an expression as its data source. 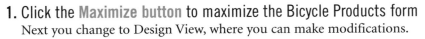 Michael wants to reposition the fields in the form to match the design of the paper form. This will make it easier to enter data from the paper-based forms into the screen form. Figure C-4 shows a completed paper form.

1. Click the Maximize button to maximize the Bicycle Products form
   Next you change to Design View, where you can make modifications.

2. Click the Design View button ![icon] on the Form View toolbar
   The screen changes to Design View, as shown in Figure C-5. The form background changes to a grid, which helps keep fields aligned horizontally and vertically. The **Toolbox toolbar**, which might appear in a different area on your screen, contains buttons you can use to modify the form. The detail section contains the field labels that identify each field; and the field value text boxes, which represent where the actual data for each field will be displayed. Before moving any fields, you want to expand the size of the work area.

QuickTip

If your Toolbox toolbar is in the way, you can drag its title bar to reposition it.

3. Place the pointer on the right edge of the form as shown in Figure C-5, the pointer changes to ↔, then drag the right edge to the 6" mark on the ruler
   You are ready to reposition fields on the form. To do this, you first need to **select** a field by clicking the control for the field. Black squares, called **handles**, appear around the perimeter of a selected control. If you click the field label control you only select the label. If you click the field value text box, you also select the field label. When you work with controls, the pointer assumes different shapes, which are described in Table C-1.

4. Click the ProductName field value text box control, then when the pointer is ✋, drag the control to the right of its current location on the same position on the vertical ruler so the left edge of the label is at 2.5" on the horizontal ruler
   The Product Name label field is now in the middle of its original line, as shown in Figure C-6. You can select multiple controls simultaneously and modify them all together.

5. Click to deselect ProductName, press [Shift] and click each of the remaining controls *except* ProductID, then drag them so the left edge of the labels are at 2" on the horizontal ruler

6. Select the DiscoStatus field value text box control and drag it to the same vertical line as the ProductID control, with the left edge of its label at 2.5" on the horizontal ruler

Time To

✔ Save

7. Drag the Total field value text box control up so the bottom of the controls are at 2.5" on the vertical ruler
   Be sure your form's Design View matches the Design View displayed in Figure C-6. You might need to use the scroll bar to see the remaining controls.

FIGURE C-4: Bicycle Products paper form

Bicycle Products
Product ID:	1	DiscoStatus:	✔
Product Num:	11023	Product Name:	Nomad clipless pedals
Supplier ID:	72		
Units In Stock:	23		
Units On Order:	0		
Unit Price:	$54.00		
Reorder Level:	12		
Reorder Amount:	24		
Units:	Pair		
Total:	$1242.00		

FIGURE C-5: Bicycle Products form in Design View

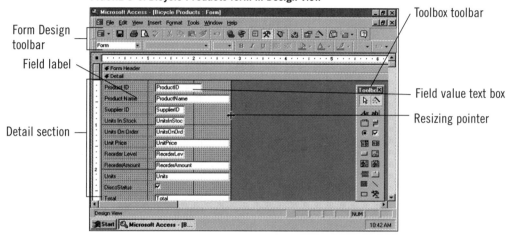

Form Design toolbar

Field label

Detail section

Toolbox toolbar

Field value text box

Resizing pointer

FIGURE C-6: Bicycle Products form with repositioned controls

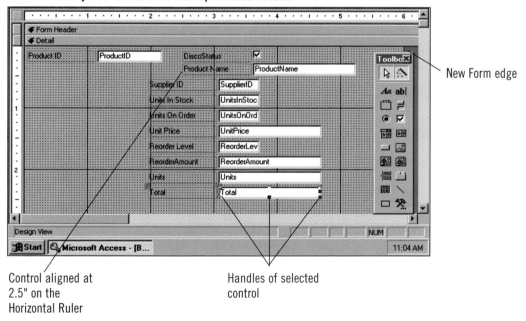

New Form edge

Control aligned at 2.5" on the Horizontal Ruler

Handles of selected control

TABLE C-1: Mouse pointer shapes

shape	action	shape	action
⬚	Selects a control	👆	Moves the control where pointer is currently positioned
✋	Moves all selected controls	↔	Changes a control's size

Access 97

Changing the Tab Order

Once the fields are moved to their new locations, you'll want to change the **tab order**, the order in which you advance from one field to the next when you press [Tab] to enter data in the form. The order of the fields in a table determines the default tab order. Even when controls are repositioned in a form, the tab order remains in the original order of the fields in the table. Michael wants the tab order to reflect the order in which the fields now appear on the form, which matches the paper form, to facilitate data entry from the paper form. He needs to modify the tab order for the form.

Steps

1. **Click View on the menu bar, then click Tab Order**
The Tab Order dialog box opens. In this dialog box you can change the order of fields in any of the three sections on the form. Because fields are usually in the Detail section, this section is automatically selected. The Custom Order list box shows the current tab order, which still reflects the order of the fields in the table. You need to change the tab order so that the DiscoStatus field which indicates whether the product is currently offered or has been discontinued follows the ProductID field.

2. **Click the DiscoStatus row selector in the Custom Order list box**
Now that the DiscoStatus control is selected, you can change its order by dragging its row to a new location.

3. **Drag the DiscoStatus row until it is below ProductID, then release the mouse button, as shown in Figure C-7**
You can also click the Auto Order button in the Tab Order dialog box to rearrange the tab order to left-to-right, top-to-bottom.

4. **Click OK**
Although nothing visibly changes on the form, the tab order changes to reflect the order of the fields on the form. When you use the screen form to enter data from a paper form, the order in which you move from field to field by pressing [Tab] will match the order in the paper form.
You save your work and view the form in Form View.

5. **Click the Form View button 🔳 on the Form Design toolbar**
Compare your form to Figure C-8.

6. **Save your work**

Trouble?

If the pointer changes to an I you will rename the field rather than move it. Click outside the field and try again.

FIGURE C-7: Tab Order dialog box

Indicates form section being displayed

Order in which [Tab] moves from field to field

Row selectors

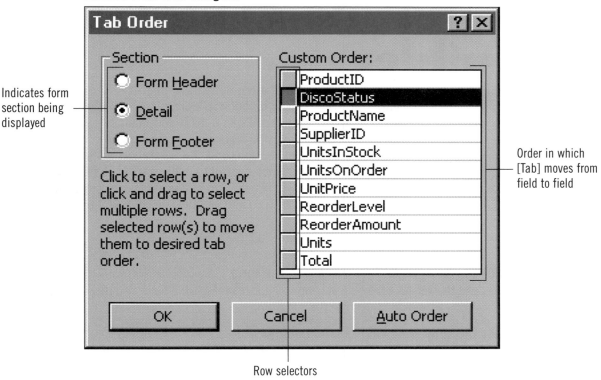

FIGURE C-8: Form displayed in Form View

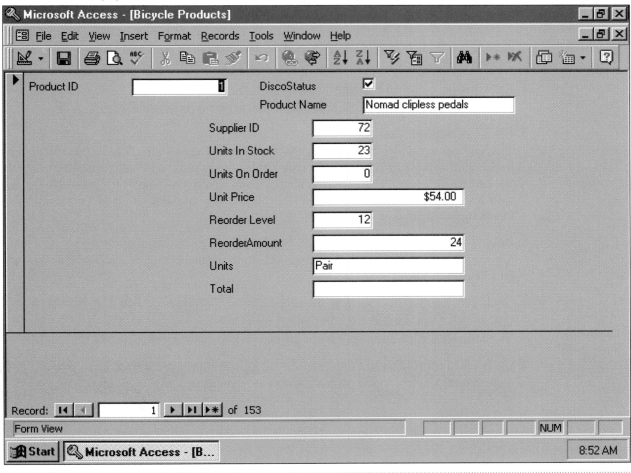

Using the Expression Builder

In addition to repositioning controls, you can also modify the **properties**, or characteristics, of a control to make data entry more efficient. A **calculated control** has a mathematical expression as its data source. The **Expression Builder** displays fields and mathematical symbols you can use to create an expression. By default, all controls occur as text boxes; however, you can create several types of controls, including toggle buttons and check boxes, using the Toolbox toolbar. ▰▰▰ Michael wants to create a calculated control that will display an in-stock value for each item in the inventory. To do this, he will use the Expression Builder to create an equation that multiplies the UnitsInStock field value by the UnitPrice field value. First, Michael returns to Design View.

Steps 1 2 3 4

1. **Click the Design View button** 🔲 **on the Form View toolbar**
   You want the results of the expression to appear in the Total field. You must select the control for this field before creating the equation.

2. **Click the Total field value text box control**
   Handles appear around the field label and the field value text box to indicate that the control is selected. Although you could type an expression directly into the text box, you choose to use the Expression Builder. You access the Expression Builder through the Properties Sheet.

3. **Click the Properties button** 📇 **on the Form Design toolbar**
   The Properties Sheet opens for the Total control. The Properties Sheet shows the control's name and source, the field description, and other relevant information. Because you want to change the Total control to a calculated control, you need to modify the Control Source property.

4. **Click the Data tab in the Total Control's Properties Sheet**
   The Expression Builder's Build button displays, as shown in Figure C-9.

5. **Click the Build button** 📰
   The Expression Builder dialog box opens, as shown in Figure C-10. This dialog box contains a section in which you build the expression, the buttons you use to build the expression, and the control fields and labels selected for the form. The word "Total" appears in the expression text box because that control was selected. Before building the expression, you must delete the word Total.

6. **Double-click Total in the expression list box, then press [Delete]**
   You need to create an expression that will multiply the UnitsInStock field value by the UnitPrice field value.

Trouble?
If you enter the expression incorrectly, modify it using [Backspace], [Delete], and the arrow keys, then enter it again.

7. **Click the Equals button** ▣ **, double-click UnitsInStock, click the Multiplication button** ▣ **, then double-click UnitPrice**
   The completed expression appears in the expression text box. See Figure C-11.

8. **Click OK to return to the Properties Sheet for the Total control**
   Note that the Control Source property shows the expression as the source for the Total control.

FIGURE C-9: Properties Sheet for Total control

Field name and description appear in the Format tab

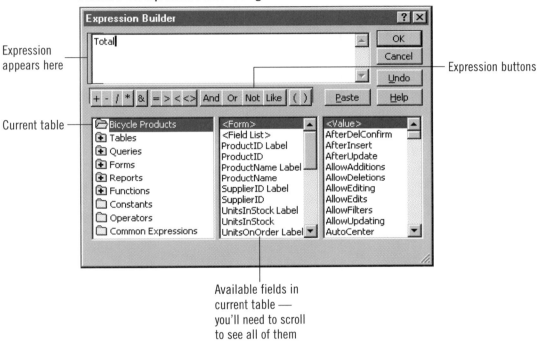

Build button

FIGURE C-10: Expression Builder dialog box

Expression appears here

Expression buttons

Current table

Available fields in current table — you'll need to scroll to see all of them

FIGURE C-11: Completed Expression Builder dialog box

Completed expression

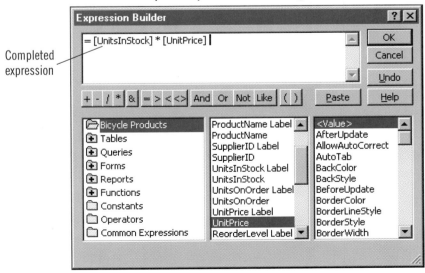

Formatting Controls

Changing the format of a field's control only affects the appearance of the field data in the form; it does not affect how data is stored in the database. Using the Properties Sheet, you can modify numeric formatting, or text attributes such as fonts, font sizes, bolding, or italics. Michael wants the calculated value for the Total to appear extra bold and be displayed with the Currency format, which specifies a dollar sign, two decimal places, and commas separating thousands.

1. Click the Format tab on the Properties Sheet, click the Format list arrow, then click Currency

    The Format property now specifies the Currency format. See Figure C-12. Next, you change the format of this control to bold.

2. Scroll to display Font Weight, click the Font Weight text box, click the Font Weight list arrow, then click Extra Bold

    Now that these changes have been made, you close the Properties Sheet.

3. Click the Close button ☒ on the Properties Sheet window to close it

    The form is displayed in Design View. Note that the equation you created using the Expression Builder appears extra bold in the Total control. You want to view the completed form in Form View.

4. Click the Form View button 🗐 on the Form Design toolbar

    Compare your completed form to Figure C-13. The calculated result of the Total field for the first record appears in Currency format. Don't worry if your controls are spaced differently.

5. Click the Save button 🖫

FIGURE C-12: **Completed Properties Sheet**

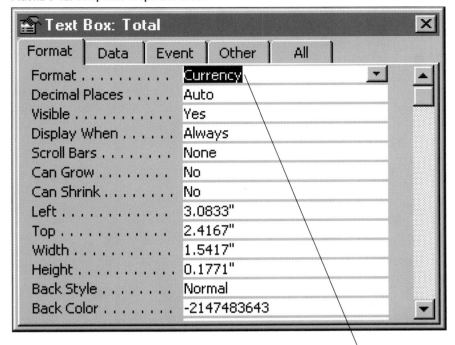

Format changed
to Currency

FIGURE C-13: **Completed form in Form View**

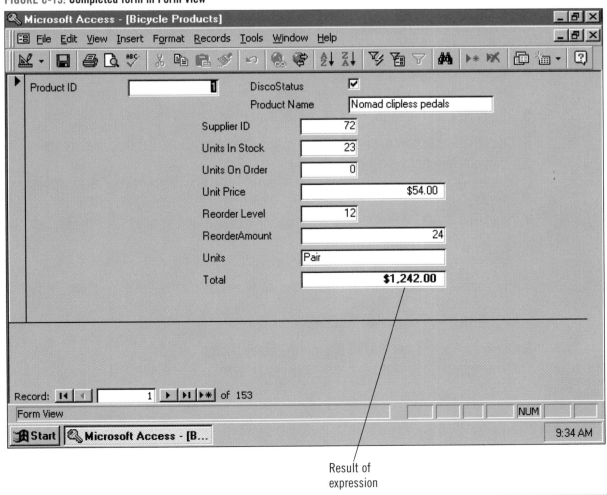

Result of
expression

Access 97

Adding a Field to a Form

Once a form exists, you may find that you want to add a field that had previously been omitted. You can create a form, and then add any missing fields that are needed.  After speaking with the data entry staff at Nomad, Michael learns that Product Number is an important field needed in the form. He returns to the Design View to add the ProductNum field that had not been included originally.

Steps

1. Click the **Design View button**
The field to be added, ProductNum can be selected from the field list and placed on the form. You display the field list.

2. Click the **Field List button** on the Form Design Toolbar
The list of fields in the table display in Figure C-14, although your list may display in a different location. You can drag and drop any field from the field list onto a form.

3. Click the **ProductNum field**, drag it onto the form with the pointer just beneath the currently positioned ProductID field as shown in Figure C-15, then release the mouse button
The field displays directly underneath the existing ProductID field. If necessary, you can reposition the field by moving the control when the pointer looks like 🖐. Satisfied with the addition of this field, you close the Field List.

4. Click the **Field List button**
The addition of this new field means that you have to adjust the Tab Order.

5. Right-click on the form, then click **Tab Order**

6. Click the **ProductNum row selector** in the Customer Order list box, drag it above the ProductName field, then click **OK**
You decide to align the new field's label with the label directly above it using the [Shift] key to select multiple controls and the right-mouse button to change their alignment.

7. Click the **ProductNum label control**, hold down the **[Shift]** key, then click the **ProductID label control**
Selected controls can be aligned to their left, right, top, and bottom edges.

8. Right-click the selected controls, point to **Align**, then click **Left**, as shown in Figure C-16
You decide to view your work in the Form View.

9. Click the **Form View button** on the Form Design toolbar
Compare your form with its newly added and aligned field to Figure C-17.

QuickTip

You can delete a control by selecting it with the mouse, then press [Delete].

Time To

✔ Save the form

FIGURE C-14: Field List displayed

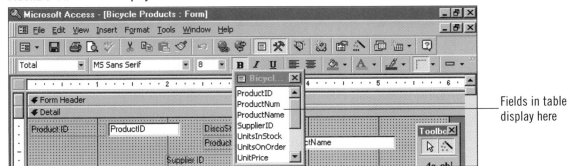

Fields in table display here

FIGURE C-15: Dragging a field to a form

Position of dragged field

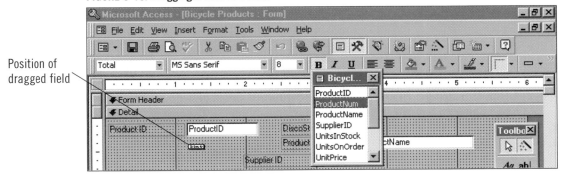

FIGURE C-16: Aligning controls

Selected controls

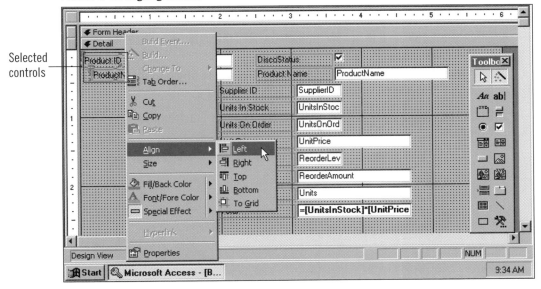

FIGURE C-17: Form with additional field

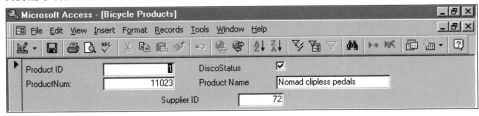

Adding a Graphic Image to a Form

Graphic images add style and a professional look to any form. Using graphic images purchased by your company, or designed by you using any art program can make a form look more appealing. ✎ Michael would like to include Nomad Ltd's logo on his form. He already has the logo in an electronic format and will insert the graphic image using the form's Design View.

Steps 1 2 3 4

QuickTip

You can lock down a toolbox button (so you don't have to keep clicking it for repeated use) by double-clicking it.

QuickTip

Most commonly available graphic image types can be used in a form. These types include .BMP, .PCX, .JPG, and .TIF.

1. **Click the Design View button 📐 on the Form View toolbar**
   A graphic image is inserted onto a form using the Image button on the Toolbox toolbar.

2. **Click the Image button 🖻 on the Toolbox toolbar**
   The pointer changes to ⁺🖻. You use this pointer to define the area where you want the image to be placed.

3. **Drag ⁺🖻 to the right 2" and down from the 1" mark to the 2" mark, as shown in Figure C-18**
   Once the area is defined, the Insert Picture dialog box opens. You supply the name and location of the graphics file to be used. The file you need is on the Student Disk.

4. **Click the Look in list arrow, select the 3½" Floppy (A:), click Nomad.tif, as shown in Figure C-19, then click OK**
   The graphic image displays on the form, surrounded by handles. You decide to look at the form in Form View.

5. **Click the Form View button 📼 on the Design View toolbar**
   Compare your form to Figure C-20.

FIGURE C-18: **Dragging an image's outline**

Outline for new picture

Begin drawing here

End drawing here

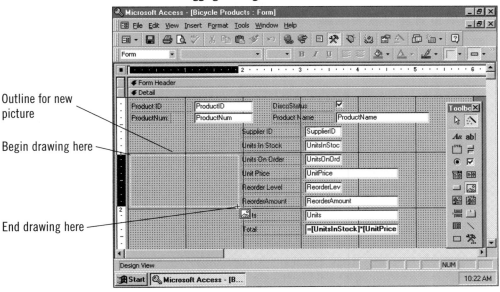

FIGURE C-19: **Insert Picture dialog box**

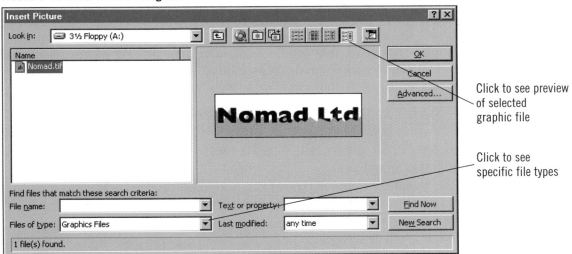

Click to see preview of selected graphic file

Click to see specific file types

FIGURE C-20: **Picture embedded in form**

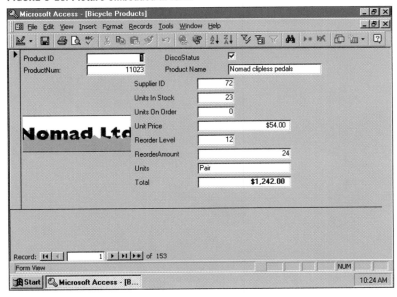

Access 97

Using a Form to Add a Record

After you create a form, you can use it to add records to the database table. To add a record you press [Tab] to move from field to field, entering the appropriate information. You can also print a form to obtain a hard copy for sharing with others. ✐ Michael will use the Bicycle Products form to add a new record to the Bicycle Products table. Then he'll print the form with the data for the new record, and distribute the form to other Nomad employees so that they can see how to use the form to enter data. Because the Bicycle Products table is already selected in the Database window, Michael begins by adding a new record to the open form.

Steps 1234

1. **Click the New Record button ▶* on the Form View toolbar**
   A new, blank record is displayed. The text "(AutoNumber)" appears in the ProductID field. Recall that the first ProductID field is the Counter field for the table. Record 154 of 154 appears in the status bar. See Figure C-21. You begin to enter the data for the new record.

2. **Press [Tab] to advance to the next field**
   The cursor moves to the DiscoStatus field. Remember that when you created the form, you changed the tab order so that DiscoStatus would be the second field moved to in the form. You will leave the DiscoStatus field blank to indicate that the product is currently offered (you would enter a checkmark in this field for a product that is discontinued). You continue to enter the data for the record, pressing [Tab] to move from field to field.

3. **Press [Tab] to advance to the ProductNum field, type 57129, press [Tab], type Nomad FinneganFast Tire, press [Tab], type 22, press [Tab], type 14, press [Tab], type 20, press [Tab], type 15.50, press [Tab], type 15, press [Tab], type 20, press [Tab], type Each, then press [Enter]**
   Compare your completed record to Figure C-22. Notice that the Total field shows the calculated result. The new record is stored in the Bicycle Products table. Next, you want to print the form containing the new record.
   You want to print only this page.

Time To

✔ Save
✔ Close the form
✔ Exit Access

4. **Click File on the menu bar, click Print, click the Selected Record(s) option button, then click OK**
   You close the form and return to the Database window.

FIGURE C-21: Blank form for new record

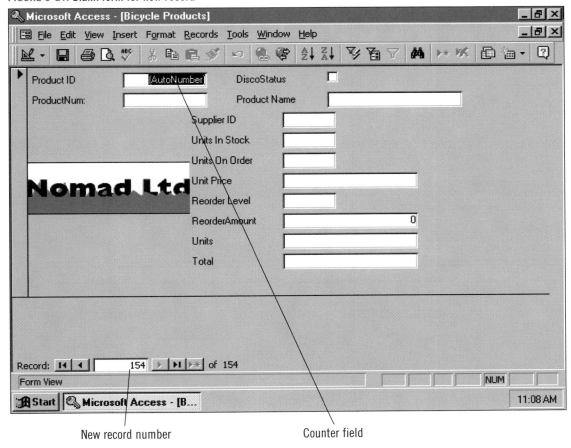

New record number   Counter field

FIGURE C-22: Completed record 154

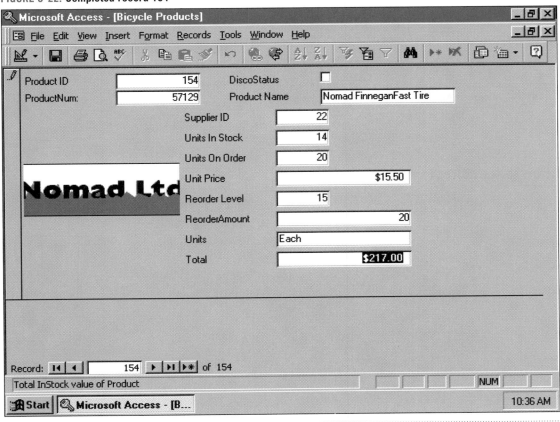

Practice

► Concepts Review

Label each of the elements of the Form Design window shown in Figure C-23.

FIGURE C-23

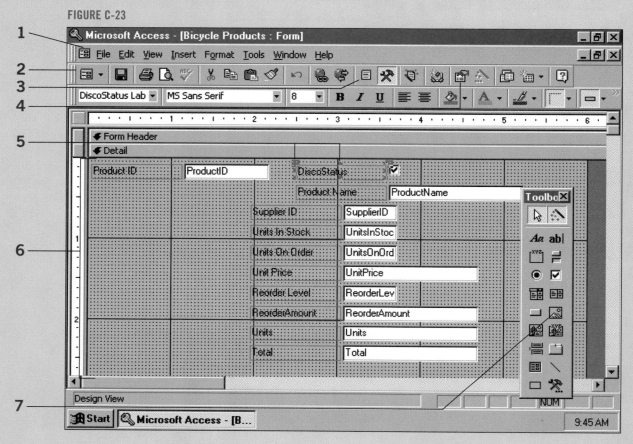

Match each button to its correct description.

8. `<<`

9. `...`

10. ☑️

11. `>`

12. 🔍

13. 🔲

a. Print Preview

b. Add a single field

c. Remove all fields

d. Form View

e. Design View

f. Build an expression

Select the best answer from the list of choices.

14. Objects in a form or report are called
   a. Properties
   b. Controls
   c. Pieces
   d. Handles

15. The pointer used to resize a control is
   a.
   b. ↔
   c.
   d. ⊹

16. A control is considered to be bound when
   a. It is displayed in a form or report
   b. It is used to sort a table
   c. Its data source is found in a table
   d. Its data source is the result of an expression

17. Which button is used to add an existing field to a form?
   a.
   b.
   c. ▸*
   d. ▨

18. Which of the following is used to change the order used to advance from field to field?
   a. Format tab in the Properties Sheet
   b. Data tab in the Properties Sheet
   c. Field List
   d. Tab Order

▶ Skills Review

1. Create a form.
   a. Start Access and make sure your Student Disk is in drive A. Open the file Bike Parts from your Student Disk.
   b. Create a new form for the Products table.
   c. Include all fields except CategoryID in the form.
   d. Use the Form Wizard to create a columnar form.
   e. Use the Stone style.
   f. Use the title Bicycle Parts Database for the form.
   g. Display the form with data.

2. Modify a form layout.
   a. Maximize the Form window and change the form's dimensions so that it is at least 6" wide.
   b. Select controls and position them so that all controls are displayed on the screen in an order you feel makes sense.

3. Change the tab order.
   a. Modify the tab order so that pressing [Tab] moves sequentially through the fields as you have arranged them.
   b. Write down your new tab order, and turn the list in.

4. Use the Expression Builder.

a. Click the text box button in the Toolbox, then create a calculated expression towards the bottom of the form.

b. Calculate the cost of any product reorder. (*Hint*: multiply ReorderAmount by the UnitPrice.)

c. Adjust the Tab Order for the new expression.

d. Save your changes.

5. Format controls.

a. Change the format of the UnitsOnOrder control so that it has one decimal place.

b. Change the number contained in the UnitsInStock field so that it appears in italics.

c. View the changes in Form View.

d. Save your changes.

6. Add a field to a form.

a. Display the Field List.

b. Add the CategoryID field to the form.

c. Modify the Tab Order for the insertion of the new field.

7. Add a graphic image to a form.

a. Use the Image button on the Toolbox toolbar to define an area for a graphic image.

b. Insert the graphic file Nomad.tif, found on your Student Disk.

c. View the form using the Form View.

8. Use a form to add a record.

a. Make sure the form is open in Form View.

b. Enter the following new record: Product Num: 70701, Product Name: Nomad Honey Handlebar tape, Category ID: 32, Supplier ID: 10, Units In Stock: 52, Units On Order: 0, Unit Price: 2, Reorder Level: 30, Reorder Amount: 35, Units: Each, DiscoStatus: No.

c. Save the record.

d. Print the form containing the new record.

▶ Independent Challenges

1. As the Customer Service Manager of the Melodies Music Store, you must continue your work on the music database. Several of the store's employees will be using the database to enter data, and you need to design a form to facilitate this data entry. The employees will be entering data from a paper-based form, shown in Figure C-24. You also need to generate reports for output requests by management as well as customers.

To complete this independent challenge:

1. Open the file "Melodies Music Database" from your Student Disk.
2. Create a single-column form that includes all the fields in the table, then save it as Title Input.
3. The controls should be positioned so that they all fit on the screen. Make sure the tab order reflects any fields that you moved.
4. Use the newly created form to add three new records of your favorite artists.
5. Print the form containing one of the new records.
6. Add an expression that calculates a new field called OnHand that multiplies the UnitsInStock field value by the UnitPrice field value. (*Hint*: Use the text box button on the Toolbox to create a new control.)

FIGURE C-24

Product ID:	Category ID:
Artist:	
Product Name:	
	Serial Number:
Units in Stock:	
Unit Price:	

2. You work in the U.S. Census Office for your city. The records in the Statistical Data table, which is in the database file "Census" on your Student Disk, contain marriage information by state. Each state is assigned a geographical area. Using the Statistical Data table, create a form to facilitate data entry, and create at least two reports showing different groupings of this information.

To complete this independent challenge:

1. Open the database "Census."
2. Create a single-column form containing all the fields in the table.
3. Modify the form by repositioning the controls, then adjusting the tab order.
4. Save the form using a name of your choice.
5. Preview the form after each of your modifications.
6. Create at least two forms based on information in the table. Save each form using a name of your choice.
7. In both forms, make sure the tab order reflects the order of your controls.
8. Use an expression in at least one form, and modify the formatting to include numeric formats and text attributes (bold, italics, or underlining) in both forms.

3. The medical consortium, Allied Surgeons and Physicians, are very satisfied with the database you've created, and would like you to create some customized forms for them.

Using the "Allied Surgeons and Physicians" database created by an employee of the medical group, create forms and reports that will make it easy for patient entries to be made.

To complete this independent challenge:

1. Open the database "Allied Surgeons and Physicians" on your Student Disk.
2. Create a form using the Patient Records table which displays all the fields in the table.
3. Arrange the fields in a way that seems efficient for data entry.
4. Make sure the tab order is updated to reflect the new order of fields.
5. Use the new form to add one new patient for each physician.
6. Print the form containing your new entries.
7. Add an expression that calculates each patient's current age.
8. Include formatting to make the form more attractive.
9. Obtain a graphic image—or create one yourself—and insert it on the form.
10. Submit all printouts.

4. You have been asked to maintain a database of stocks for electronic and other hi-technology firms. Use the World Wide Web to gather this information, then create an attractive form you can use to enter additional records.

To complete this independent challenge:

1. Log on to the Internet and use your browser to go to http://www.course.com. From there, click the link Student On Line Companions, then click the Microsoft Office 97 Professional Edition—Illustrated: A First Course page, then click the Access link for Unit C.

2. Find information for at least 10 hi-tech or electronic company stocks, including a minimum of the stock abbreviation, the name of the parent company, and the price per share. You can add any other fields you feel are necessary.

3. Create a new database file on your Student Disk called Hi-Tech stocks.

4. Use the Table Wizard to create a table.

5. Create a new form you'll use to enter the data into the table.

6. Enter the information you retrieved from the World Wide Web.

7. Preview and print the form.

8. Hand in a printout of your work.

▶ Visual Workshop

Use the Current Product List query in the Bike Inventory database on your Student Disk to create the following form using the skills you learned in this Unit.

FIGURE C-25

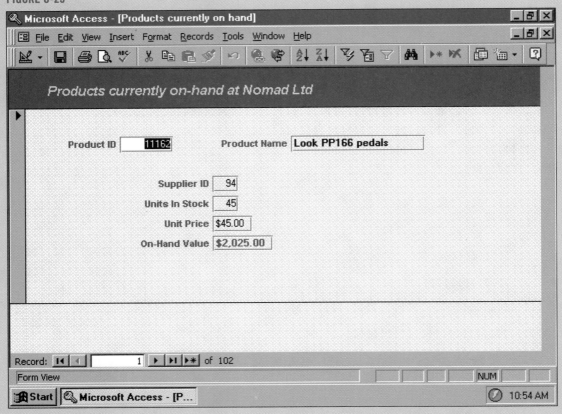

Creating
a report

► **Create a report**
► **Group records in a report**
► **Align fields**
► **Resize a control**
► **Add an expression to a report**
► **Create a report from a query**
► **Save a form as a report**
► **Create labels**

Printed reports are an easy way of distributing information to others. Like information in a datasheet, reports can be based on a table or query, and can contain calculated expressions and sorted data. There are formatting options that let you design appealing reports that present information clearly. ✐ Michael wants to produce reports based on table data that he can distribute to other employees so they will know the status of products carried by Nomad stores.

Creating a Report

The ability to create thoughtful, concise reports enables you to share data with others in meaningful ways. The most significant data can lose its impact if it appears in an unprofessional or poorly laid out report. You can create reports in Access from scratch or you can use the Report Wizard. The **Report Wizard** provides sample report layouts and gives you options for including specific fields in the report. As with a form, the layout of a report includes sections for a Report Header, Detail, and Report Footer. Each report also includes a section for a Page Header and a Page Footer, so you can print information on each report page. ◆ Michael wants to create a report showing all but two fields in the Bicycle Products table. He plans on distributing this report to other Nomad employees and customers.

Steps

1. Start Access, open the Product Inventory database on your Student Disk, click the New Object button list arrow ▭ ▾ on the Database toolbar, then click Report
   The New Report dialog box opens. You could also create a report by clicking the Reports tab in the Database window, then clicking New. You use the Bicycle Products table for this report, which you'll create using the Report Wizard.

2. Click the Choose the table or query where the object's data comes from list arrow, click Bicycle Products, click Report Wizard, then click OK
   The Report Wizard dialog box—which allows you to select which fields appear in the report—opens. You want all fields except the ProductID and Total fields to be included. Rather than individually select all but these two fields, you select all the fields and then remove the two fields you don't want.

3. Click the All Fields button ▭ ▸▸ ▭ in the Report Wizard dialog box
   All the fields move from the Available Fields list to the Selected Fields list. Now you can remove the fields you don't want included in the report.

4. Click Total in the Selected Fields list box, click the Remove Field button ▭ ◂ ▭, click ProductID in the Selected Fields list box, then click ▭ ◂ ▭
   The Report Wizard dialog box on your screen should look like the one in Figure D-1.

5. Click ▭ Next > ▭ to display the next dialog box
   This dialog box, shown in Figure D-2, determines how the data in the report will be grouped.

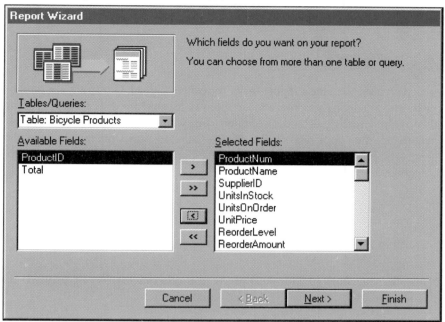

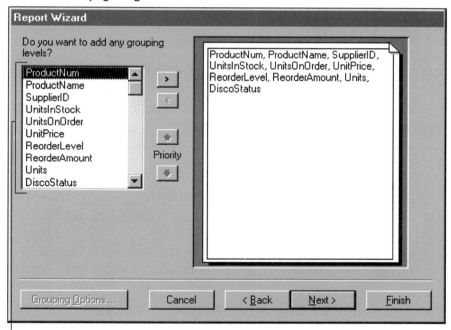

Choose how fields
are grouped using
available fields here

Using AutoReport

You can create a simple report quickly by clicking the New Object button ▣ on the Database toolbar, then clicking AutoReport. AutoReport offers no prompts or dialog boxes; it instantly creates a single-column report that displays all fields in the table or query.

Access 97

Grouping Records in a Report

The grouping of records is used to make a report easier for others to read. **Grouping** is a method of organizing records, just as sorting lets you choose the way records are displayed. For example, if you wanted to see records listed by the supplier from whom they were purchased, you would group the records by the SupplierID field. Michael wants the report to display the inventory in groups by product name so that all of the data for the same products will be listed and totaled together.

1. Click ProductName in the Do you want to add any grouping levels list box, click the Single Field button ▶
The ProductName field appears in blue and above the other fields. When printed, the records with all the same product names will be grouped together.

QuickTip

The Sort Order button in this dialog box is a toggle; click to change from ascending to descending order.

2. Click [Next >]
This dialog box allows you to specify a sort order. You choose to sort by each record's DiscoStatus in ascending order (the default) so that the report will show all currently available items together and all discontinued items together.

3. Click the first list arrow, then click DiscoStatus
Compare your dialog box to Figure D-3. Next, you choose which items will be totaled.

4. Click Summary Options, click to add a checkmark next to each item in the Sum column, as shown in Figure D-4, click OK, then click [Next >]
The next two dialog boxes ask you to select a report style, paper orientation, and report title. You accept the default choices.

5. Click the Landscape radio button, click [Next >], click [Next >] again, type Products by DiscoStatus in the What title do you want for your report text box, then click Finish
Access compiles the report. The report is saved as part of the database file and the Print Preview window is opened. You need to decrease the Zoom factor to see the whole report.

6. Click the Zoom button 🔎 on the Print Preview toolbar
The report appears, as shown in Figure D-5. Notice that the records are grouped by product name. You are satisfied with the report and need to preview and print your work.

Time To

✔ Save

7. Click the Close button on the Print Preview toolbar
You return to Design View. You decide to print just the first page of the report to see how it looks.

8. Click File on the menu bar, click Print, type 1 in the From text box, type 1 in the To text box, then click OK

FIGURE D-3: Choosing the Sort order

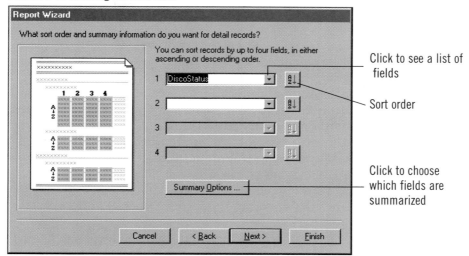

Click to see a list of fields

Sort order

Click to choose which fields are summarized

FIGURE D-4: Summary Options dialog box

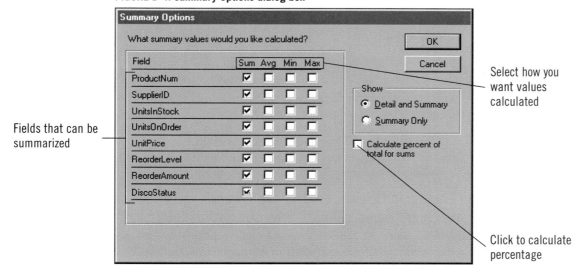

Fields that can be summarized

Select how you want values calculated

Click to calculate percentage

FIGURE D-5: Previewing the report

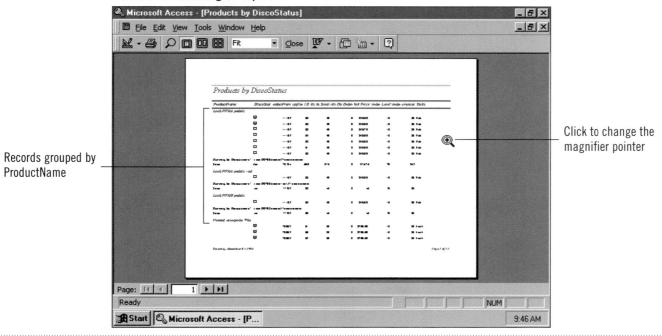

Records grouped by ProductName

Click to change the magnifier pointer

Aligning Fields

You can make modifications to the format of a report, such as bolding column headings or changing the alignment of fields in a column. The Report Design window is divided into seven sections: the **Detail** section, which contains controls and the compiled data from the table, and a Header and Footer section for each of the following: Report, Page, and Group. The **Report Header** and **Report Footer** print only on the first and last page of the report; the **Page Header** and **Page Footer** print on every page. The **Group Header** references the field on which each group is based (in this case, the groups are based on ProductName). Although the Products by DiscoStatus report is adequate, Michael wants to give the report a more professional look. The field headings are not aligned with the data below them, as shown in Figure D-6. Because Michael's screen is already in Design View, he can easily align the field headings with their data to format the report.

Steps

1. Press and hold [Shift], click each of the control headings in the Page Header section, *except* ProductName, then release [Shift]
   You selected nine controls. You can scroll the window and move the Toolbox toolbar to select all the desired controls. Each selected control has handles surrounding it. First you center the selected controls and decrease the font size to make the text less crowded.

2. Click the Center button on the Formatting toolbar, click the Font Size list arrow, then click 8
   Access centers the headings for the selected controls in the Page Header section. See Figure D-7. You want to center align the controls in the Detail section of the report.

3. Select the ProductNum control in the Detail section
   Selecting this control without holding [Shift] deselects the previously selected controls. You continue to make multiple selections in the Detail section.

4. Press and hold [Shift], click each of the controls in the Detail section, *except* the DiscoStatus control, release [Shift], then click on the Formatting toolbar
   Access centers the selected controls in the Detail section. You decide that the current information in the ProductName Footer section is unnecessary and want to delete it, but first you deselect the controls in the Detail section.

5. Click the first control in the ProductName Footer section to select it

6. Press and hold [Shift], click each of the controls in the ProductName Footer section, release [Shift], then press [Delete]
   The report now has a gap in it created by the deleted controls. Later, you will add an expression in this section.

QuickTip

You can select all the controls in a single section by moving the mouse to the left of the section and clicking when the pointer turns to ➡. Press [Shift] and click to deselect individual selected controls.

FIGURE D-6: Unedited Products by DiscoStatus report

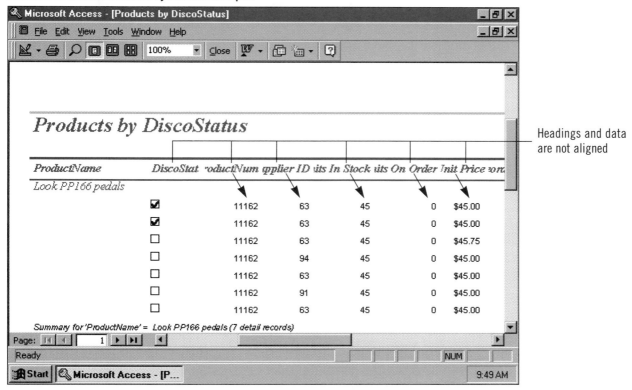

Headings and data are not aligned

FIGURE D-7: Centered controls in the report

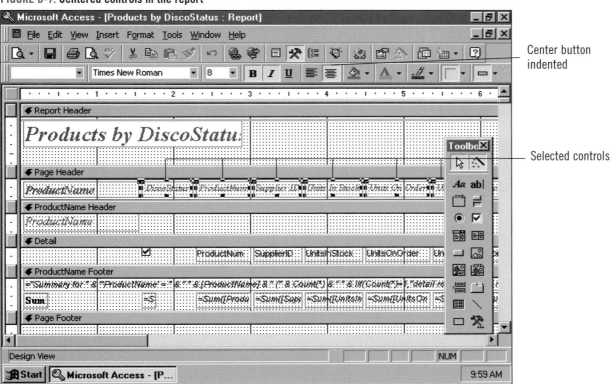

Center button indented

Selected controls

Resizing a Control

The position of controls, as well as their widths, can be changed individually or in groups. If you resize a group of controls it creates a neater, more unified look for your report. Next Michael decides to resize the width of the Units controls in the Detail and Page Header sections because they take up more space than the other controls. By resizing these controls, Michael will be able to tighten up the right side of the report.

Steps 1 2 3 4

1. Click the **Units control** in the Detail section, move the pointer to the right middle handle until the pointer changes to ↔, then drag the handle until it is aligned with 8.25" on the horizontal ruler, as shown in Figure D-8
   Repeat this procedure for the Units control in the Page Header section.

2. Click the **Units control** in the Page Header section, move the pointer to the right middle handle until the pointer changes to ↔, then drag the handle until it is aligned with 8.25" on the horizontal ruler
   The Units controls in the Page Header and Detail sections are now aligned and resized with each other. You want to preview the report and print a sample page.

3. Click the **Print Preview button** 🔍 on the Report Design toolbar
   The controls in the report are aligned, as shown in Figure D-9.

4. Click **File** on the menu bar, click **Print**, type **1** in the From text box, type **1** in the To text box, then click **OK**
   You close the Print Preview window and save the report.

5. Click the **Close button** on the Print Preview toolbar

6. Save your work

Line up the edge of
the control with the
horizontal ruler

FIGURE D-8: **Resizing a control**

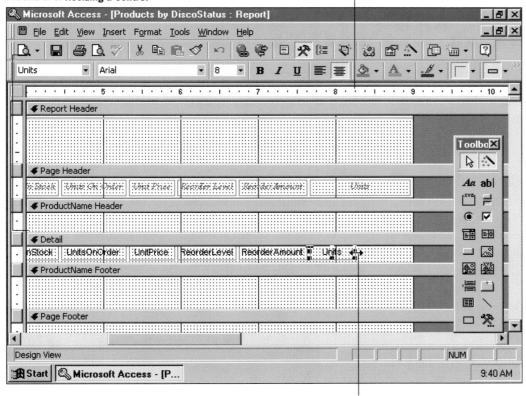

Resizing pointer

FIGURE D-9: **Report in Print Preview**

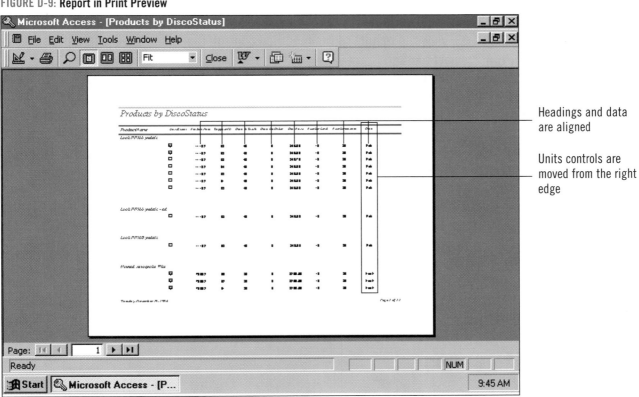

Headings and data
are aligned

Units controls are
moved from the right
edge

Adding an Expression to a Report

You have already seen how an expression can be incorporated in a form. You can also add an expression to a report to perform calculations. The expression can include field names, table names, and functions. A **function** is an easy-to-use preprogrammed mathematical equation. Michael wants to add an expression to the Products by DiscoStatus report. The expression will count the number of products in each group, by product identification number.

Steps

QuickTip

In addition to Count, Access provides many other functions for use in expressions. Ask the Office Assistant how you can use functions in expressions for more information.

1. Click the Text box button |abl| on the Toolbox toolbar, then click in the ProductName Footer section directly under the ProductNum control at the 2¼" mark

This places an unbound control in the ProductName Footer section, where you will type the expression. The expression will include the Count function, which counts the number of occurrences of a specified field in a column.

2. Click inside the unbound control, type =Count([ProductNum]), then press [Enter]

The expression appears in the control, as shown in Figure D-10, although some of its contents might be truncated, or cut off. You want to preview the report to see the results of the expression.

3. Click the Print Preview button 🔍 on the Report Design toolbar, click the Zoom button 🔍 if necessary

The number of records in each group has been counted, although the values need to be aligned with the values in the ProductNum column and it needs a descriptive label.

4. Click the Close button on the Print Preview toolbar, then with the expression still selected, click the Align Left button ▤ on the Report Design toolbar

You decide to preview the report again to check the results of this modification.

5. Click 🔍, view the results of the modified control, then click the Close button on the Print Preview toolbar

When viewing the report in Print Preview, you see the value in the expression is left-aligned in the ProductNum column. Next, add a label to describe what the values represent in the report.

6. Click the unbound label text box control to the left of the expression, double-click the text in the box, type Items in Category, press [Enter], click the Font Size list arrow, click 9

The label is added to the report as shown in Figure D-11. You again preview the report.

7. Click 🔍

Compare your previewed report with Figure D-12. Use Zoom as needed. You print the first page of the report, then close the Print Preview window and save the modifications.

Time To

☑ Save
☑ Close the report

8. Click File on the menu bar, click Print, type 1 in the From text box, type 1 in the To text box, click OK, then click the Close button on the Print Preview toolbar

Adding a field to a report

In addition to adding expressions, you can always add existing fields to a report. Any tables whose fields are available in the table can be dragged to areas within a report by clicking the Field List button 🔳 on the Report Design toolbar, then dragging a field to an area of the report.

FIGURE D-10: Truncated expression in control

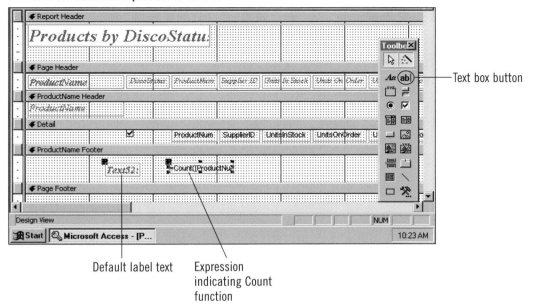

Text box button

Default label text

Expression
indicating Count
function

FIGURE D-11: Descriptive label added to expression

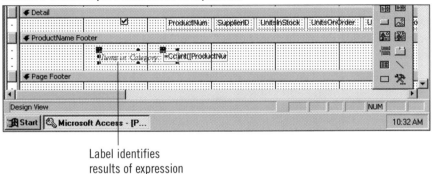

Label identifies
results of expression

FIGURE D-12: Completed report with expression and label

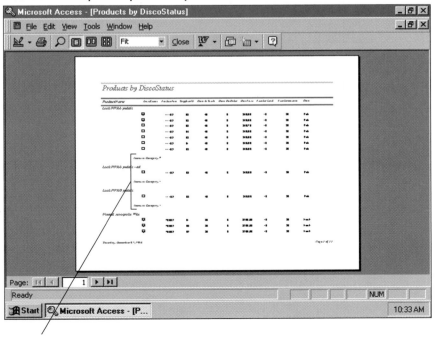

Labels and results
of expression

Creating a Report from a Query

You've seen how to create a report based on the fields in a table. Many times, however, you will want to use a query as the basis for a report to save time since the query may already contain the information you want printed. ✐ Michael has created a query for the Bicycle Products table called Current Product List to display only current products. He wants to use this query as the basis for a new report. Again, he'll use the Report Wizard to create this report.

Steps 1 2 3 4

1. Click the New Object button list arrow ⬚▾ on the Database toolbar, then click Report, click the Choose the table or query where the object's data comes from list box, click the Current Product List then click Report Wizard
   Compare your New Report dialog box with Figure D-13.

2. Click OK
   The Report Wizard dialog box opens, as shown in Figure D-14. The Available Fields list box displays all the available fields in the query (not all the fields in the table). You want to include all these fields in the report.

3. Click the All Fields button ⟩⟩ , then click Next >
   You want the records grouped by ProductName.

4. Click ProductName, then click the Single Field button ⟩
   The records will be grouped by the ProductName field, as shown in Figure D-15. You need to advance to the next dialog box which lets you determine the sort order. You decide that you don't need to sort by any other fields and accept the default.

5. Click Next > , click Next > again
   Next, you decide to accept the default layout and orientation, style, and report title.

6. Click Next > , click Next > , then click Finish
   Access creates the report and displays it in Print Preview.

7. Click the Close button on the Print Preview toolbar
   Satisfied with the report, you decide to print the first page as a sample.

8. Click File on the menu bar, click Print, type 1 in the From text box, type 1 in the To text box, then click OK

9. Save the report using the default report name Current Product List, then close it

QuickTip

When basing a report on a query, give the report the same name as the query name; this will remind you that the report and the query are related.

FIGURE D-13: **New Report dialog box**

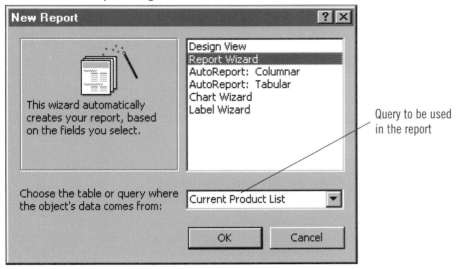

Query to be used
in the report

FIGURE D-14: **Report Wizard dialog box**

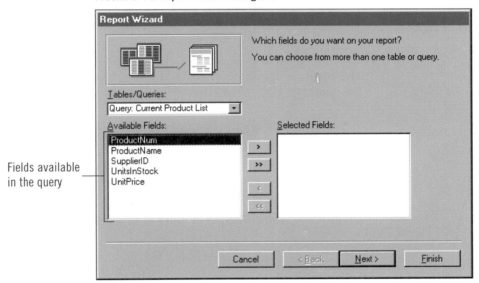

Fields available
in the query

FIGURE D-15: **Grouping records in the Report Wizard dialog box**

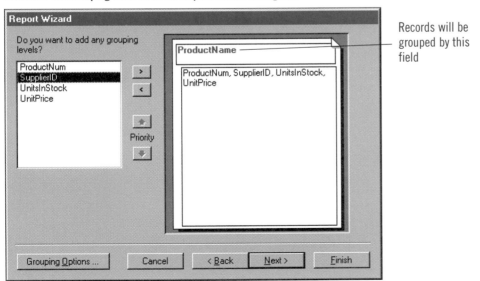

Records will be
grouped by this
field

Saving a Form as a Report

If you already have a form designed that meets your needs, you can work more efficiently by saving a form as a report. This can be an efficient way of creating a familiar-looking report, because your co-workers will already have seen the form. To save a form as a report, open the form in Design View, click File on the menu bar, click Save As Report, then supply a new name for the report. ⬤═══ Michael creates a report from the Bicycle Products form.

Steps 1 2 3 4

1. **Click the Forms tab, then make sure the Bicycle Products form is selected**
   Once the form is selected, you can save it as a report using the context-sensitive pop-up menu.

2. **Right-click the Bicycle Products form**
   The pop-up menu appears, as shown in Figure D-16. You select the Save As Report command.

3. **Click Save As Report**
   You can keep the same name used in the form, but you choose to change the name for the report.

4. **Type Bicycle Products - from Form in the Report Name text box, as shown in Figure D-17, then click OK**
   You decide to preview the report created from the form.

5. **Click the Reports tab, click Bicycle Products - from Form report, then click the Print Preview button on the Database toolbar**

6. **If necessary, click the Maximize button and scroll to see all the records in the report**
   Compare your report to Figure D-18. Satisfied with the new report, you close the Preview window.

7. **Click the Close button on the Print Preview toolbar**

8. **Close the report**

FIGURE D-16: **Pop-up menu**

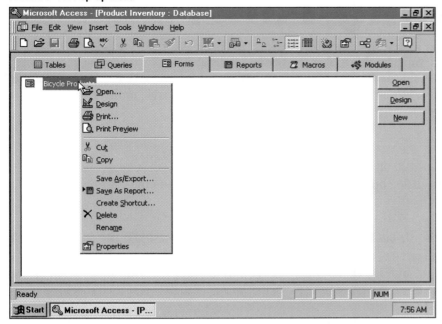

FIGURE D-17: **Save Form As Report dialog box**

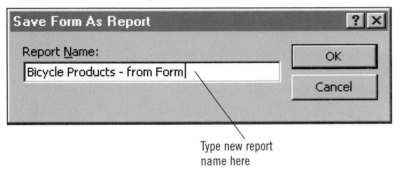

Type new report
name here

FIGURE D-18: **Preview of report created from form**

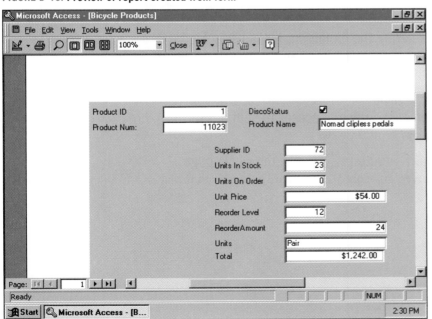

Creating Labels

Labels are a necessity in any office, and they are easy to create using the Access Label Wizard. If you use Avery labels, you'll be able to find the size and style label you currently use, making creating labels based on table or query records a snap. Michael needs to prepare labels for Nomad customers. He'll use the Label Wizard and the Customers table in the Bicycle Supplies database.

Steps 1234

1. Click the New button on the Reports tab

The New Report dialog box opens. You'll create your labels using the Customers table and the Label Wizard.

2. Click Label Wizard, click the Choose the Table or query where the object's data comes from list arrow, click Customers, then click OK

Next, you select the number of the Avery labels on which you will print, as shown in Figure D-19. You decide to use Avery number 5160, that prints 3 labels across each sheet.

3. Click 5160, then click ⬜ Next >

The third dialog box allows you to change the font, font size, and other text attributes. You choose to accept the default values.

4. Click ⬜ Next >

In the next dialog box, you choose which fields you want to include in each label, as well as their placement. Each field is selected from the Available Fields list in the order you want them on the label. Any spaces, punctuation, or hard returns have to be entered using the keyboard.

Enter the information for the first line in the label.

QuickTip

Double-click the field name in the Available Fields list to move it to the Prototype label text box.

5. Click FirstName, click the Single Field button ⬜ > ⬜, press the [Spacebar], click LastName, click ⬜ > ⬜, then press [Enter]

Next, you'll enter the fields for the information containing the address, city, state, and postal code.

6. Repeat step 5 entering the remaining fields using Figure D-20 as a guide

Once the fields in the label are defined, you need to decide how the records should be sorted when they are printed. You want the records sorted by PostalCode, then by LastName.

7. Click ⬜ Next >, click Postal Code, click ⬜ > ⬜, click LastName, click ⬜ > ⬜, click ⬜ Next >, then click Finish to accept the default report name

The labels display in Print Preview.

Time To

✔ Close
✔ Exit

8. Click the magnifier pointer 🔍 to see the whole page

Compare your screen to Figure D-21. You are pleased with the labels and will print them later.

FIGURE D-19: Second Label Wizard dialog box

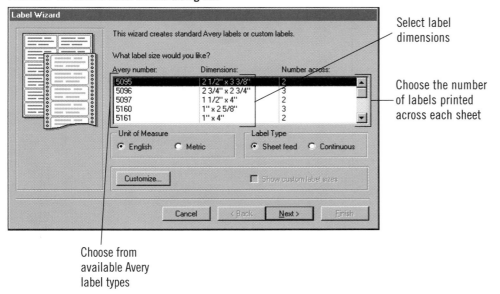

Select label dimensions

Choose the number of labels printed across each sheet

Choose from available Avery label types

FIGURE D-20: Defining fields in a label

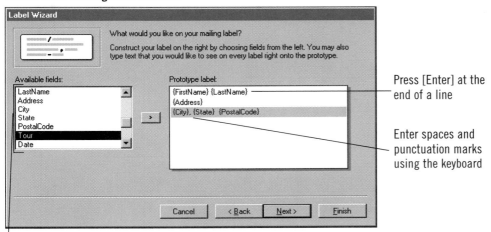

Press [Enter] at the end of a line

Enter spaces and punctuation marks using the keyboard

Fields from the table or query display here

FIGURE D-21: Completed labels

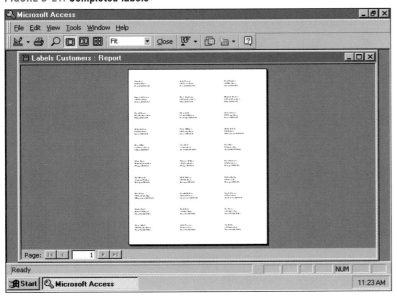

Practice

► Concepts Review

Label each of the elements of the Report Design window shown in Figure D-22.

FIGURE D-22

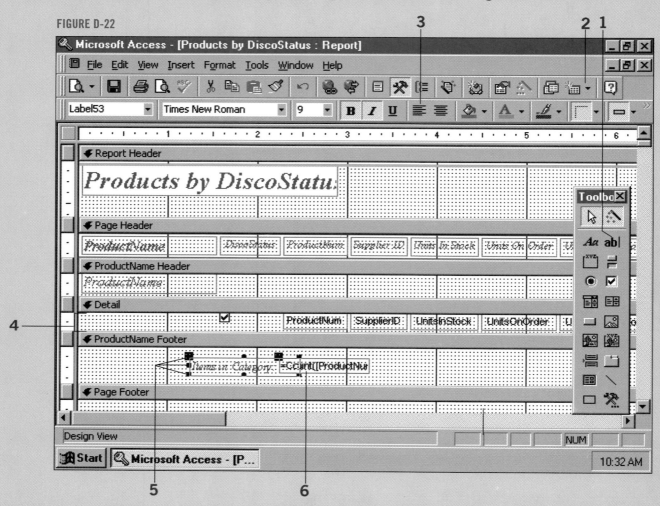

Match each button to its correct description.

7.   **a.** Print Preview
8.   **b.** Zoom
9.   **c.** New Object
10.   **d.** Select field
11.   **e.** Remove field
12.   **f.** Text box

Select the best answer from the list of choices.

13. Which key do you press to select multiple controls?
    a. [Ctrl]   b. [Alt]   c. [Shift]   d. [Tab]

14. The _____ section contains controls and compiles data.
    a. Detail   b. Report Header   c. Group Header   d. Report Footer

15. Which button is used to add an unbound control to a report?
    a. ▤   b. 🖼   c. Aα   d. abl

16. Which of the following is true about report expressions?
    a. They can contain mathematical functions.
    b. In Design View, the contents may appear truncated.
    c. The label text can be customized.
    d. All of the above.

17. How can labels be created?
    a. Click 🔽 , then click Labels
    b. Click Reports from the menu bar, then click Label Wizard
    c. Click New from the Reports tab, then click Label Wizard
    d. Click 🖽 from the Database toolbar

▶ Skills Review

1. **Create a report.**
   a. Open the Parts List database on your Student Disk.
   b. Create a Groups/Totals report based on the Products table using the Report Wizard.
   c. Include all the fields in the report.

2. **Group records in a report.**
   a. Group the report by UnitsinStock.
   b. Sort the report in ascending order by ProductName.
   c. Summarize three fields, get an average for unit price and a sum for the reorder amount and units on order fields.
   d. Accept the default report layout.
   e. Use the Formal style.
   f. Save the report as Products by Units in Stock.
   g. Preview the report with the data in it.
   h. Print the report.

3. **Align fields.**
   a. Align the fields so that the values are centered with the headings above them.
   b. Delete the reorder amount summary which detracts from the report.
   c. Preview and print the report.
   d. Save your changes.

4. **Resize a control.**
   a. Change the font size of the Page Header controls to 8.
   b. Move the ReorderAmount controls closer to the edge of the page.
   c. Resize the ReorderAmount control so it takes up only enough room to display its label.
   d. Save your modifications.
   e. Preview the report.

5. **Add an expression to a report.**
   a. Create an expression in the Detail section under ProductName that subtracts ReorderLevel from UnitsinStock. (*Hint*: Drag the section divider to make room for the new expression)
   b. Add the descriptive label "Reorder if Negative" to the left of the expression.
   c. Adjust the fonts sizes and control locations to create a professional-looking report.
   d. Preview and print the report.
   e. Save your changes.

6. Create a report from a query.

    a. Use the Report Wizard and create a report using the Products sold as "Each" query.

    b. Group the report by UnitsinStock.

    c. Sort the report by ProductName.

    d. Accept the default layout, style, and name for the report.

    e. Preview the report with the data.

    f. Move the controls and align the fields as necessary to create a professional-looking report.

    g. Print the report.

7. Save a form as a report.

    a. Save the Bicycle Parts Database form as a report. Name the new report: Parts List Database - from Form.

    b. Print the first page of the new report.

8. Create labels.

    a. Use the Label Wizard and the Products table to create stock room shelf labels using Avery 5160 labels.

    b. The first line of the label should include the ProductNum and the ProductName.

    c. The second line of the label should include the ReorderLevel and the ReorderAmount.

    d. The third line of the label should include the UnitPrice.

    e. Sort the labels by the ProductName.

    f. Name this report "Shelf Labels."

    g. Save your work.

    h. Print the page of labels.

▶ Independent Challenges

1. You have been using the "Music Store" database for several weeks, and now need to design several reports that can be printed on a weekly basis. Four reports are needed: one that lists all the items in the Available titles table, and one for each of the existing queries.

To complete this independent challenge:

1. Open the file "Music Store" from your Student Disk.
2. Create a report using the Available titles table that displays all the table's fields, grouped by Artist and sorted in descending order by TitleName.
3. The UnitsInStock field should be summed, and the UnitPrice field should be averaged.
4. Use the Outline1 report layout and the Casual style.
5. Name this report Complete titles list.
6. Preview the report.
7. Modify the font size of the heading controls so all the column labels are visible.
8. Save your changes.
9. Preview and print the first page of the report.

▶ Independent Challenges

2. You have determined that shelf labels would make inventory control much more efficient at your music store. On a weekly basis, the inventory is checked against the cash register receipts and the shelves are restocked. Use the Available titles table in the "Music Store" database to design a shelf label.

To complete this independent challenge:

1. Open the file "Music Store" from your Student Disk.
2. Use the Label Wizard and the Available titles table to create shelf labels. Use Avery 5160 labels and red semi-bold, italics text.
3. The first line should say "Artist: ", then display the Artist name, the second line should display the TitleName, and the third line should display the SerialNumber, UnitsInStock, and UnitPrice.
4. Sort the labels by Artist, then by TitleName.
5. Name the report Available Titles Shelf Labels.
6. Save, preview and print report.

▶ Independent Challenges

3. The database you created for the Allied Surgeons and Physicians is very successful. In fact, they would like you to create a report based on the "Patient Records" table.

To complete this independent challenge:

1. Open the file "ASP Database" from your Student Disk.
2. Create a report using the following fields in the Patient Records table: ID, FirstName, LastName, DateofBirth. Gender, Telephone, KnownAllergies, MostRecentVisit, and PhysicianLastName.
3. Group the records by PhysicianLastName.
4. Sort the records by LastName, then FirstName.
5. Use the Outline2 report layout and the Compact style.
6. Name this report All Patients list.
7. Preview the report.
8. Make sure all the column labels are visible.
9. Save your changes.
10. Preview and print the first page of the report.

▶ Independent Challenges

4. Use your knowledge and skills navigating the World Wide Web to create attractive reports of information about colleges and universities. Locate information about institutions that offer programs in computer use, create a database containing this information, then design reports that display this data.

To complete this independent challenge:

1. Create a new database called "Colleges" on your Student Disk. Include any fields you feel are important, but make sure you include the institution's name, state, and whether it is a 4 or 2-year school.
2. Log on to the Internet and use your browser to go to http://www.course.com. From there, click the link Student On Line Companions, then click the Microsoft Office 97 Professional Edition—Illustrated: A First Course page, then click the Access link for Unit D. Search the World Wide Web for schools that offer programs in computer science using any available search engines.
3. Compile a list of at least 15 institutions.
4. Enter the information in your database.
5. Create a report that includes all the fields in the table, and use the default grouping.
6. Sort the records by the state, then by the institution's name.
7. Save, preview and print the report.
8. Hand in a printout of your work.

▶ Visual Workshop

Use the Products table in the Parts List database to create these labels. Use the settings for Avery label 5161. Sort the labels by SupplierID, then by ProductName, and name the report "Warehouse Labels."

FIGURE D-23

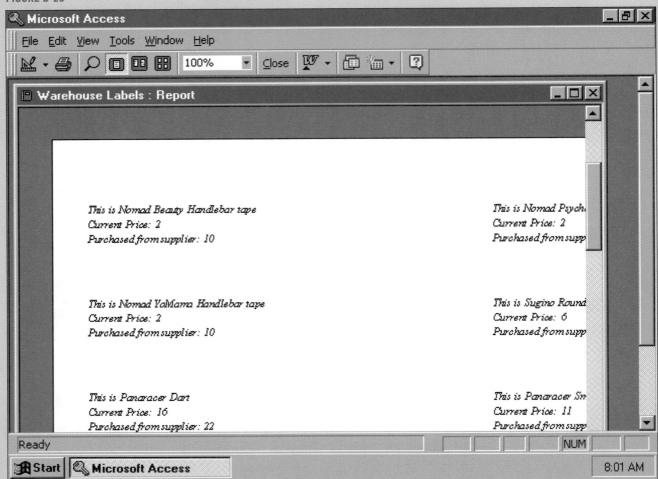

Integrating
Word, Excel, and Access

Objectives

► **Merge data between Access and Word**
► **Use Mail Merge to create a form letter**
► **Export an Access table to Excel**

You have learned how to use Word, Excel, and Access individually to accomplish specific tasks more efficiently. Now you will learn how to integrate files created using these programs so that you can use the best features of each one. ✐ In preparation for the upcoming Annual Report, Andrew Gillespie, the national sales manager for Nomad Ltd, wants to establish a tour customer profile that he can incorporate into the report. To do this, he will mail a survey to Nomad Ltd's tour customers. He also wants to export the Access database of customer names and addresses into an Excel worksheet so that he can create an Excel chart showing from which areas of the country Nomad attracts the most customers.

Merging Data Between Access and Word

Companies often keep a database of customer names and addresses, then send form letters to their customers. With Microsoft Office, you can combine, or **merge**, data from an existing Access table with a Word document to automatically create personalized form letters. ✎ Andrew wants to survey customers who have taken tours with Nomad during the last two years. He wrote a form letter using Word. He wants to merge his form letter with the customer names and addresses that already exist in an Access table.

Steps 1 2 3 4

1. **Start Microsoft Access and open the file Customer Info from your Student Disk**
   The Database window for the file Customer Info opens. Open the Customers table.

QuickTip

To merge the data in the Customers table, you can simply select the table name on the Tables tab, then merge it with the Word document.

2. **Click the Tables tab if necessary, click Customers, then click Open**
   The Customers table is the **data source** for the Mail Merge. To merge the Customers table data with the survey form letter, use the Office Merge It feature.

3. **Click Tools on the menu bar, point to Office Links, then click Merge It with MS Word**
   The Microsoft Word Mail Merge Wizard dialog box appears, as shown in Figure B-1. The Mail Merge Wizard links your data to a Microsoft Word document. The customer survey form letter already exists as a Word document, so accept the default option to link your data to an existing Microsoft Word document.

4. **Click OK**
   The Select Microsoft Word Document dialog box opens.

Trouble?

If a message box appears telling you that there isn't enough memory to open the document file, exit all open programs and try launching Word prior to Step 1.

5. **Select the file INT B-1 from your Student Disk, then click Open**
   Word opens and the document INT B-1 appears in the document window below the Mail Merge toolbar. Table B-1 describes the buttons in the Mail Merge toolbar. The document you just opened is the **main document** for the Mail Merge.

6. **If the Word program window does not fill the screen, click the Word program window Maximize button**
   The Word program window resizes to fill the entire screen. See Figure B-2. Save the document with a new name.

7. **Click File on the menu bar, click Save As, then save the document as Survey Form Letter to your Student Disk**
   In the next lesson, you will continue setting up the mail merge.

TABLE B-1: Mail Merge buttons

name	button	name	button
« » ABC	View Merged Data	☐	Check for Errors
◄	First Record	☐	Merge to New Document
◄	Previous Record	☐	Merge to Printer
1	Go to Record	☐	Mail Merge
►	Next Record	☐	Find Record
►|	Last Record	☐	Edit Data Source
☐	Mail Merge Helper		

FIGURE B-1: Microsoft Mail Merge Wizard dialog box

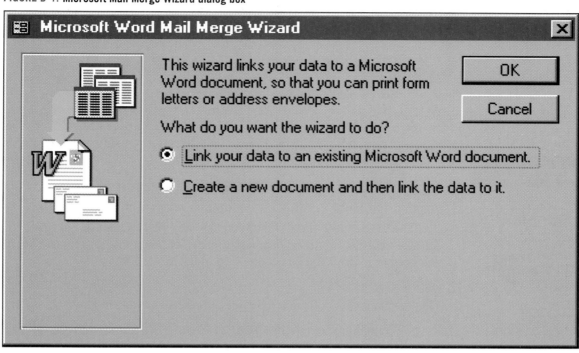

FIGURE B-2: Main document

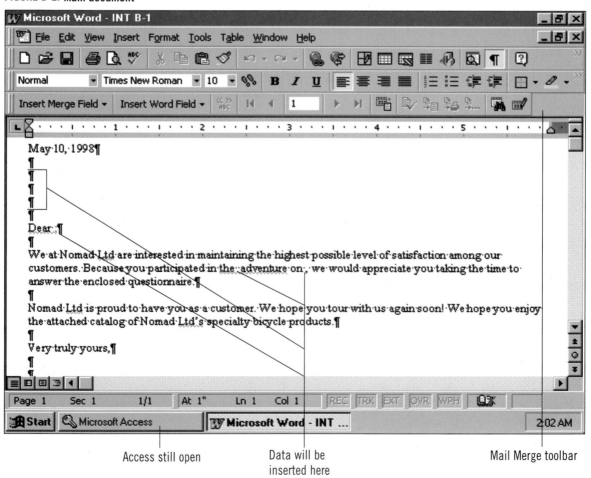

Access still open

Data will be inserted here

Mail Merge toolbar

Integration

Using Mail Merge to Create a Form Letter

Once you have opened and linked the form letter and the Access table, you are ready to insert merge fields into the letter. When you perform the Mail Merge, Access looks for the merge fields in the main document and replaces them with the appropriate field from the data source. After opening the data source and selecting the main document, Andrew needs to insert merge fields into the main document.

Trouble?

If you can't see the paragraph symbols, click the Show/Hide ¶ button ¶ on the Standard toolbar.

1. **Position the pointer in the second empty paragraph below the date, then click the Insert Merge Field menu button on the Mail Merge toolbar**
A list of fields in the Access database appears, as shown in Figure B-3. The first merge field you need to insert is the FirstName field in the inside address.

2. **Click FirstName**
The FirstName field is inserted between brackets in the form letter.

3. **Press [Spacebar], click the Insert Merge Field menu button on the Mail Merge toolbar, click LastName, then press [↓]**

4. **Continue inserting the merge fields and typing the text shown in Figure B-4**
Make sure you insert a comma and a space after the City merge field and a space after the State merge field. After all the merge fields are entered, save the main document.

5. **Click the Save button 🖫 on the Standard toolbar**
Before you merge the data, make sure the merged data appears correctly in the main document.

6. **Click the View Merged Data button 《》 on the Mail Merge toolbar**
The data from the first record (Ginny Braithwaite) appears in the main document as shown in Figure B-5. There are several ways to merge the main document with the data source. If you want to merge the main document with records that meet certain criteria, click the Mail Merge button on the Mail Merge toolbar, then set query options. If you want to merge the files directly to the printer, click the Merge to Printer button on the Mail Merge toolbar. It's a good idea to merge the documents into one new document so that you can examine the final product and make any necessary corrections before you print. Do this now.

7. **Click the Merge to New Document button 🗐 on the Mail Merge toolbar**
"Microsoft Word – Form Letters1" appears in the title bar. You should see the first form letter with Ginny Braithwaite's data on your screen. Save the merged document before printing.

8. **Click 🖫 on the Standard toolbar, then save the document as Survey Letters to your Student Disk**
Now print the document.

9. **Click File on the menu bar, click Print, specify pages 1 through 3 to print only the first three form letters, then click OK**
The first three of the 30 form letters print. Now exit Word.

10. **Click File on the menu bar, click Exit, then click No to save changes to Survey Form Letter**
Word closes and returns you to Access.

FIGURE B-3: List of fields in Access database

Fields in data source

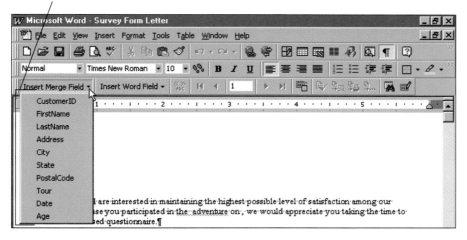

FIGURE B-4: Main document with merge fields inserted

Inserted merge fields

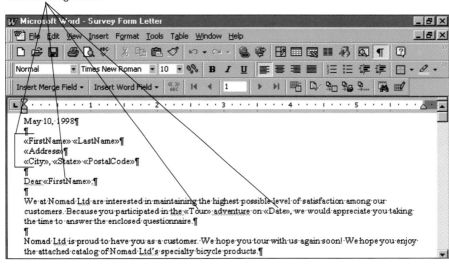

FIGURE B-5: Main document with merged data

Fields from first
record in data source

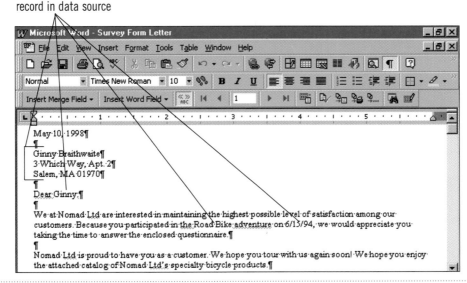

Integration

Exporting an Access Table to Excel

Data in an Access table can be exported to Excel and several other applications. When a table is exported, a copy of the data is created in a format acceptable to the other application, and the original data remains intact. ◆━━ Andrew wants to export the Customer's table in the Customer Info database into Excel so that he can analyze the data. Later he will create a chart that shows the distribution of Nomad's customers by tour type.

Steps

1. Make sure the Customers table is active

2. Click **Tools** on the menu bar, point to **Office Links**, then click **Analyze It with MS Excel**
   The exported data appears in an Excel workbook named Customers that contains only one worksheet, also named Customers. When data is imported into Excel, only one worksheet is supplied, although more can be added. First, maximize the Excel program window if it is not already maximized.

3. If necessary, click the Excel program window **Maximize button**
   Resize the columns so that you can see all the data

4. Select the **A through J column selector buttons**, click **Format** on the menu bar, point to **Column**, click **AutoFit Selection**, then press **[Home]** to return to cell A1
   The column widths resize to fit the data in the worksheet. Sort the table so you can look up customer information faster.

5. Click **Data** on the menu bar, then click **Sort**
   The Sort dialog box appears, as shown in Figure B-6. Notice that the header row option button is selected. This means that the first row in the worksheet will not be sorted. Sort the table by state and then by last name.

6. Click the **list arrow** in the Sort by section, click the **down scroll arrow**, click **State**, click the **list arrow** in the Then by section, click **Last Name**, then click **OK**
   Compare your screen to Figure B-7. Now save and print the worksheet.

7. Click the **Save button** 🖫 on the Standard toolbar, then click the **Print button** 🖨 on the Standard toolbar

Trouble?

If a message appears telling you that the workbook was created in a previous version of Excel, click yes to update it.

8. Click **File** on the menu bar, click **Exit** to exit Excel, then in the Access program window, click **File** on the menu bar and click **Exit** to exit Access

FIGURE B-6: Sort dialog box

Sort on State first   Sort on Last Name second

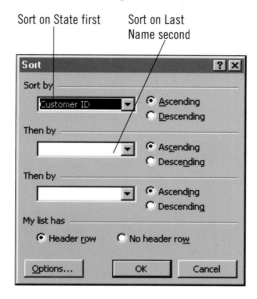

FIGURE B-7: Excel worksheet with sorted data

Sorted on last name second   Sorted on state first

	A	B	C	D	E	F	G	H
1	Customer ID	First Name	Last Name	Address	City	State	Postal Code	Tou
2	18	Tonia	Dickenson	92 Main Avenue	Durango	CO	81301-	Road E
3	7	Fred	Gonzales	Purgatory Ski Area	Durango	CO	81301-	Mt. Bik
4	20	Shelly	Graham	989 26th Street	Durango	CO	81301-	Bunge
5	16	Michael	Nelson	229 Route 55	Durango	CO	81301-	Mt. Bik
6	8	John	Black	11 River Road	Brookfield	CT	06830-	Road E
7	9	Scott	Owen	72 Yankee Way	Brookfield	CT	06830-	Bunge
8	14	Maria	Duran	Galvin Highway East	Chicago	IL	60614-	Road E
9	15	Salvatore	Wallace	100 Westside Ave	Chicago	IL	60614-	Mt. Bik
10	30	Adelia	Ballard	3 Hall Road	Williamstown	MA	02167-	Mt. Bik
11	1	Ginny	Braithwaite	3 Which Way, Apt. 2	Salem	MA	01970-	Road E
12	23	Peter	Kane	67 Main Street	Concord	MA	01742-	Bunge
13	17	Shawn	Kelly	22 Kendall Square	Cambridge	MA	02138-	Bunge
14	5	Kendra	Majors	530 Spring Street	Lenox	MA	02140-	Bunge
15	21	Robert	Roberts	56 Water Street	Lenox	MA	02140-	Mt. Bik
16	10	Virginia	Rodarmor	123 Main Street	Andover	MA	01810-	Bunge

Exporting an Access table to Word

You can export an Access table to Microsoft Word by using the Publish It with MS Word feature. To export a table, open the Access database with the table you want to export, click the table, click **Tools** on the menu bar, point to **Office Links**, then click **Publish It with MS Word.** An Access wizard automatically opens Word, exports the table data, and creates a new table with the database information.

Practice

► Independent Challenges

1. As the administrator for Monroe High School, you want to keep track of student records and generate reports for the principal and school district. You need to create a database containing the current students enrolled in the high school. Once the database table is complete, export the table information to Excel and Word to create reports.

To complete this independent challenge:

1. Decide what fields should be included in the database. Include fields for student's name, address, phone number, gender (male or female), birth date, race, grade level, and cumulative grade point average (GPA).
2. Save the new database file as Student Records then create the student table called Student Info.
3. Create a form to facilitate the entry of your student records, then print one record to show a sample of the form.
4. Add 20 records to your table drawing on names in your local area, then sort the students by last name and then by first name.
5. Export the Student Info table to an Excel worksheet, then resize columns to fit the table.
6. Print out your results, then save the worksheet as Student Profiles to your Student Disk.
7. Export the Student Info table to a Word table, resize columns to fit the table, sort the table by grade level and then by last name, then format the table to make the document more attractive.
8. Save the document as Student Roster to your Student Disk.
9. Submit all printed materials from this challenge.

2. Pleasantown Players, the local theater group that you manage, wants to send a letter to patrons in the database encouraging them to financially support the upcoming session. To maximize your results, you decide to send out the initial mailing to those patrons who have donated more than $500. To complete the task, you need to modify the current Patrons table and create a query to find the appropriate patrons. Once the database query is complete, create a form letter in which you will merge the data stored in the query.

To complete this independent challenge:

1. Create a new database using the Donations Database Wizard.
2. Save the new database file as Pleasantown Players to your Student Disk.
3. Use default settings and include sample data as you step through the Donations Database Wizard.
4. Create a query to find patrons who have donated over $500 called Patrons over $500.
5. Create a main document (form letters) in Word using all the fields you feel are necessary.
6. In the letter, you want to tell patrons how important it is to support local, non-professional theater. Add a paragraph that briefly summarizes the number and location of non-professional theater companies like Pleasantown Players around the country. To find this information, log on to the Internet and use your browser to go to http://www.course.com. From there, click Student On Line Companions, and then click the link to go to the Microsoft Office 97 Professional Edition—Illustrated: A First Course page, then click the Integration link for Unit B. Click the link there to find the number of shows the average non-professional theater company produces per year, and compare Pleasantown Players to that. Use any of the information you find at this Web site to add credibility and interest to your funding request.
7. Save the main document as 5 Star Support Form to your Student Disk.
8. Merge the document 5 Star Support Form and the Patrons over $500 query into a new document named 5 Star Patron Support.
9. Print the first five merged documents in 5 Star Patron Support.

Getting
Started with PowerPoint 97

Objectives

► **Define presentation software**
► **Start PowerPoint 97**
► **Use the AutoContent Wizard**
► **View the PowerPoint window**
► **View your presentation**
► **Save your presentation**
► **Get Help**
► **Print and close the file, and exit PowerPoint**

Microsoft PowerPoint 97 is a presentation graphics program that transforms your ideas into professional, compelling presentations. With PowerPoint, you can create slides to display as an electronic slide show or as 35-mm slides and transparency masters to display on an overhead projector. ✍ Carrie Armstrong is a new executive assistant to the president of Nomad Ltd, an outdoor sporting gear and adventure travel company. She needs to familiarize herself with the basics of PowerPoint and learn how to use PowerPoint to create professional presentations.

Defining Presentation Software

A **presentation graphics program** is a computer program you use to organize and present information. Whether you are giving a sales pitch or explaining your company's goals and accomplishments, a presentation graphics program can help make your presentation effective and professional. You can use PowerPoint to create 35-mm slides, overheads, speaker's notes, audience handouts, outline pages, or on-screen presentations, depending on your specific presentation needs. Table A-1 explains the PowerPoint output capabilities. ◢ Carrie's boss, Lynn Shaw, has asked her to create a brief presentation about Nomad's new initiative to expand its business during the next year as part of Carrie's training. The company president will use the presentation at Nomad Ltd's next company meeting. Carrie is not familiar with PowerPoint so she gets right to work exploring its capabilities. Figure A-1 shows an overhead created using a word processor for the president's most recent presentation. Figure A-2 shows how the same overhead might look in PowerPoint. Carrie can easily complete the following tasks using PowerPoint:

Details

 ### Create slides to display information
With PowerPoint, information is presented on full-color slides with interesting backgrounds, layouts, and clipart. The impact of a full-color slide is more powerful than a traditional black and white overhead.

 ### Enter and edit data easily
Using PowerPoint, you can enter and edit data quickly and efficiently. When you need to change a part of your presentation, you can use the advanced word processing and outlining capabilities of PowerPoint to edit your content rather than re-create your presentation.

 ### Change the appearance of information
By exploring the capabilities of PowerPoint, you will discover how easy it is to change the appearance of your presentation. PowerPoint has many features that can transform the way text, graphics, and slides look.

 ### Organize and arrange information
Once you start using PowerPoint, you won't have to spend a lot of time making sure your information is correct and in the right order. With PowerPoint, you can quickly and easily rearrange and modify any piece of information in your presentation.

 ### Incorporate information from other sources
Often, when you create presentations, you will use information from other people. With PowerPoint, you can import information from a variety of sources, including spreadsheets, graphics, and word-processed files from programs such as Microsoft Excel, Microsoft Access, Microsoft Word, and WordPerfect.

 ### Show a presentation on any Windows 95 computer
PowerPoint has a powerful feature called the PowerPoint Viewer that you can use to show your presentation on computers running Windows 95 that do not have PowerPoint installed. The PowerPoint Viewer displays a presentation as an on-screen slide show.

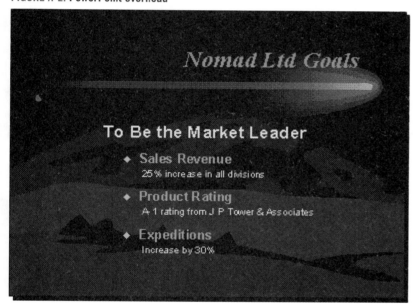

Nomad Ltd Goals

To Be the Market Leader
- Sales Revenue
  - 25% increase in all divisions
- Product Rating
  - A-1 rating from J P Tower & Associates
- Expeditions
  - Increase by 30%

FIGURE A-2: PowerPoint overhead

TABLE A-1: PowerPoint output capabilities

output	method
On-screen presentations	Run a slide show directly from your computer.
35-mm slides	Use a film-processing bureau to convert PowerPoint slides to 35-mm slides.
Black-and-white overheads	Print PowerPoint slides directly to transparencies on your black-and-white printer.
Color overheads	Print PowerPoint slides directly to transparencies on your color printer.
Speaker notes	Print notes that help you remember points about each slide when you speak to a group.
Audience handouts	Print handouts with two, three, or six slides on a page.
Outline pages	Print the outline of your presentation to show the main points.

Starting PowerPoint 97

To start PowerPoint, you must first start Windows, then click Start on the taskbar and point to the Programs folder, which contains the PowerPoint program icon. PowerPoint is usually in the Programs folder, but on your computer it might be in a different location. If you are using a computer on a network, you might need to use a different starting procedure. You also can customize your starting procedure. Carrie starts PowerPoint to familiarize herself with the program.

Steps

1. **Make sure your computer is on and the Windows desktop is visible**
   If any application windows are open, close them.

2. **Click the Start button on the taskbar, then point to Programs**
   The Programs menu opens, displaying icons and names for all your programs, as shown in Figure A-3. Your screen might look different, depending on which programs are installed on your computer.

Trouble?

If you have trouble finding Microsoft PowerPoint on the Programs menu, check with your instructor or technical support person.

3. **Click Microsoft PowerPoint on the Programs menu**
   PowerPoint starts, and the PowerPoint startup dialog box appears, as shown in Figure A-4. This allows you to choose how you want to create your presentation or to open an existing presentation. Don't worry if the animated character, called the Office Assistant, and the small window containing a list of Common Tasks do not appear on your screen. A previous user might have closed them. In the next lesson, you choose the AutoContent Wizard option in the PowerPoint startup dialog box to see how wizards can help you develop a presentation.

4. **If a dialog box connected to the Office Assistant appears, click Close to close it.**

FIGURE A-3: **Programs menu**

Your list of programs
might be different

Microsoft
PowerPoint program

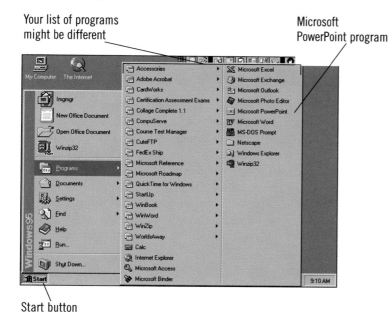

Start button

FIGURE A-4: **Screen after starting PowerPoint**

Common Tasks toolbar

Startup dialog box

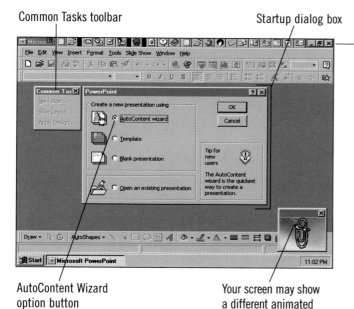

If you had a previous installation
of Office on your computer, your
screen may contain the Office 97
shortcut bar.

AutoContent Wizard
option button

Your screen may show
a different animated
character as the
Office Assistant

Moving the PowerPoint shortcut to the desktop

PowerPoint comes with a shortcut that you can use to start it. To move this shortcut to the desktop, click Start, point to Programs, then click Windows Explorer. In the left section of the Exploring window, click the plus sign next to My Computer. The plus sign changes to a minus sign, and the drives and files on the computer are listed below it. Click the plus sign next to the icon representing the C: drive, then click the plus sign next to the Program Files folder.

(You might need to scroll down to see this folder.) Double-click the Microsoft Office folder. The list of files in the Microsoft Office folder opens in the right section of the window. Drag the PowerPoint shortcut directly to the desktop or to the icon representing the desktop in the left section of the Exploring window. Now you can start PowerPoint by double-clicking the icon on the desktop, without having to navigate through the Programs menu.

PowerPoint 97

Using the AutoContent Wizard

When PowerPoint first starts, the startup dialog box appears. The startup dialog box gives you four options for starting your presentation. See Table A-2 for an explanation of all the options in the PowerPoint startup dialog box. The first option, the AutoContent Wizard, is the quickest way to create a presentation. A **wizard** is a series of steps that guides you through a task (in this case, creating a presentation). Using the AutoContent Wizard, you choose a presentation type from the wizard's list of sample presentations. Then you indicate how the presentation will be used and what type of output you will need. Next, you type the information for the title slide. The AutoContent Wizard then creates a presentation with sample text you can use as a guide to help formulate the major points of your presentation. ✒️ Carrie decides to start her presentation by opening the AutoContent Wizard.

Trouble?

If the Office Assistant dialog box appears asking you if you want help with this feature, click No. If the Office Assistant is in the way, drag it over to the side of the screen.

1. Click the AutoContent Wizard option button to select it, then click OK
The AutoContent Wizard dialog box opens, as shown in Figure A-5. The left section outlines the sections of the AutoContent Wizard and highlights the current screen name, and the text on the right side explains the purpose of the wizard.

2. Click Next
The AutoContent Wizard dialog box opens the Presentation type screen. This screen contains categories and types of presentations. Each presentation type contains suggested text based on that particular use. By default, the category All is selected, and all the presentation types are listed.

3. Click the category Projects, click Project Overview in the list box, then click Next
The Output options screen appears, asking how this presentation will be used.

4. Click the Presentations, informal meetings, handouts option button to select it, then click Next
The Presentation style screen appears, asking you to indicate the type of output you would like.

5. If necessary, click the On-screen presentation option button to select it, click the Yes option button to specify printed handouts, then click Next
The Presentation options screen requests information that will appear on the title slide of the presentation. Enter the presentation title and the president's name.

Trouble?

If the Office Assistant and the Common Tasks are in front of the slide, drag them to the positions shown in Figure A-6. If the Common Tasks commands (New Slide, Slide Layout, and Apply Design) appear in a bar at the bottom of the window, drag the bar up by the double lines on its left side until it becomes a window to the right of the slide.

6. Click and drag the pointer over the text Title goes here to select it, type Nomad Business Expansion Project, press [Tab], type Bill Davidson, press [Tab], type Nomad Ltd, click Next, then click Finish at the bottom of the dialog box
The AutoContent Wizard displays the presentation outline with sample text based on the Project Overview presentation type you chose. Slide 1, containing the title slide information you just entered, is highlighted in the Outline. A reduced color version of Slide 1, called a **slide miniature**, appears on the right side of the screen in a window titled Color. Look at the slide more closely.

7. Right-click the slide miniature, then click Go To Slide View on the pop-up menu
The presentation displays in Slide view, which shows one slide at a time. Finish the lesson by making sure your slide display matches the figures in this book.

8. Click the Restore Window button in the Presentation window (in the menu bar), click the percentage number in the Zoom text box on the Standard toolbar, type 36, then press [Enter]

9. Click Window on the menu bar, then click Fit to Page
Compare your screen with Figure A-6.

FIGURE A-5: AutoContent Wizard opening dialog box

Current screen
name

Click to move to
next screen

FIGURE A-6: Presentation window

Presentation window   Zoom text box

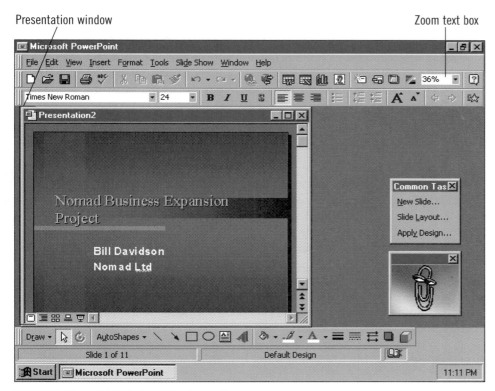

TABLE A-2: PowerPoint startup dialog box options

option	description
AutoContent Wizard	Helps you determine the content and organization of your presentation by creating a title slide and an outline using ready-made text for the category you choose.
Template	Opens the New Presentation dialog box, displaying PowerPoint presentation design templates and preformatted presentations. You can click a template to see a preview of it.
Blank presentation	Opens the New Slide dialog box, allowing you to choose a predesigned slide layout.
Open an existing presentation	Opens the Open dialog box, allowing you to open a previously created presentation. You can see a preview of a selected presentation before you open it.

Viewing the PowerPoint Window

After you make your selection in the PowerPoint startup dialog box, the Presentation window appears within the PowerPoint window, displaying the presentation you just created or opened. You use the toolbars, buttons, and menus in the PowerPoint window to view and develop your presentation. PowerPoint has different **views** that allow you to see your presentation in different forms. You move around in these views by using the scroll bars. You'll learn more about PowerPoint views in the next lesson. Carrie examines the elements of the PowerPoint window. Find and compare the elements described below, using Figure A-7 as a guide.

Details

 The title bar displays the program name and contains a program Control Menu button, resizing buttons, and the program Close button. The Office toolbar appears in the title bar.

 The menu bar contains the names of the menus you use to choose PowerPoint commands. Clicking a menu name on the menu bar displays a list of commands from which you can choose.

 The Standard toolbar contains buttons for the most frequently used commands, such as copying and pasting. Clicking buttons on a toolbar is often faster than using the menu. However, in some cases, using the menu offers additional options not available by clicking a button.

 The Formatting toolbar contains buttons for the most frequently used formatting commands, such as changing font type and size.

 The Presentation window is the "canvas" where you type text, work with lines and shapes, and view your presentation.

 The Common Tasks toolbar displays a menu of three common tasks typically performed in PowerPoint. These three commands have corresponding buttons on the Standard toolbar. The default position for this toolbar is floating, that is, not attached to one side of the window.

 The Office Assistant is an animated character that provides online Help. The character on your screen might be different. You can close the Assistant window, but it will reappear if you use online Help. If another user closed the Assistant, it may not appear on your screen.

 The Drawing toolbar, located below the Presentation window, contains buttons and menus that let you create lines, shapes, and special effects.

 The view buttons, to the left of the horizontal scroll bar, allow you to quickly switch between PowerPoint views.

 The status bar, located at the bottom of the PowerPoint window, displays messages about what you are doing and seeing in PowerPoint, including which slide you are viewing.

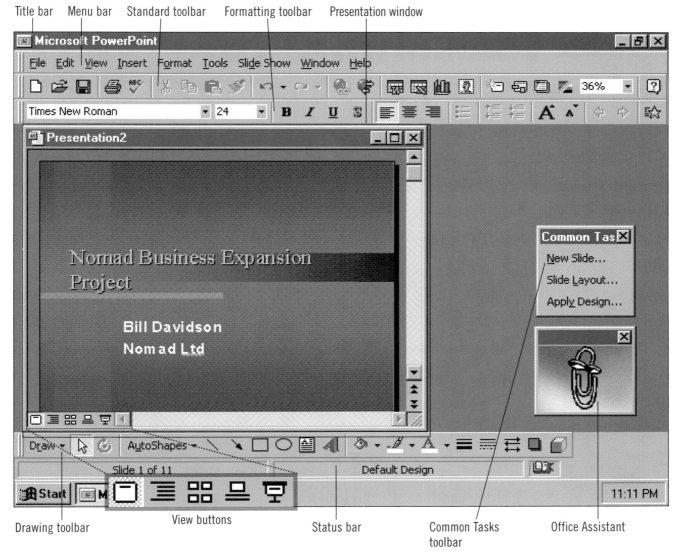

Title bar   Menu bar   Standard toolbar   Formatting toolbar   Presentation window

Drawing toolbar   View buttons   Status bar   Common Tasks toolbar   Office Assistant

Using the scroll bars

If you cannot see an entire slide on the screen, you need to **scroll**, or move, within a window to see more of the window contents. There are three ways to scroll in PowerPoint: click the scroll arrows to move one line at a time; click above or below the vertical scroll box or to the left or right of the horizontal scroll box to move one screen at a time; or drag the scroll boxes to move quickly to any point in the window.

PowerPoint 97

Viewing Your Presentation

This lesson introduces you to the five PowerPoint views: Slide view, Outline view, Slide Sorter view, Notes Page view, and Slide Show view. Each PowerPoint view displays your presentation in a different way and allows you to manipulate your presentation differently. To move easily among the PowerPoint views, you use view buttons located at the bottom of the Presentation window, to the left of the horizontal scroll bar, as shown in Figure A-8. See Table A-3 for a brief description of the PowerPoint views and the view buttons. ◣━━━ Carrie practices scrolling through her presentation and then switches to each PowerPoint view.

1. **Drag the scroll box down the vertical scroll bar until the slide indicator box displays "Slide: 5 of 11, Competitive Analysis, cont.", then release the mouse button**
   See Figure A-8. The **slide indicator box** tells you which slide will appear when you release the mouse button. Now use the Previous Slide button to go to Slide 1.

2. **Click the Previous Slide button ⊼ at the bottom of the vertical scroll bar until Slide 1 appears**
   The scroll box in the vertical scroll bar moves back up the scroll bar. The status bar indicates the view name and the number of the slide you are viewing. As you scroll through the presentation, notice the sample text on each slide created by the AutoContent Wizard.

▶ **QuickTip**
You can also click view on the menu bar, then click the name of the view you want.

3. **Click the Outline View button ▤ to the left of the horizontal scroll bar**
   PowerPoint switches to Outline view, displaying the outline of the presentation with Slide 1 selected. The slide miniature of the selected slide appears in the Color window. Compare your screen with Figure A-9. Notice that the name of the view appears in the status bar. To see the rest of the outline, scroll to the bottom of the outline.

4. **Click the down scroll arrow until you reach the bottom of the outline**
   As you scroll through the presentation, notice that each of the 11 slides in the presentation is identified by a number along the left side of the outline.

5. **Click the Notes Page View button ▣ to the left of the horizontal scroll bar**
   Outline view changes to Notes Page view, showing a reduced image of the title slide above a large box. You can enter text in this box and then print the notes page for your own use to help you remember important points about your presentation.

6. **Click the Slide Sorter View button ▦ to the left of the horizontal scroll bar**
   A miniature image of each slide in the presentation appears in this view. You can examine the flow of your slides and easily move them to change their order.

7. **Click the Slide Show View button ▼ to the left of the horizontal scroll bar**
   The first slide fills the entire screen. In this view, you can practice running through your slides so the presentation can be shown as an electronic slide show.

▶ **QuickTip**
To end a slide show before you reach the last slide, press [Esc] or right-click anywhere on the screen, then click End Show on the pop-up menu.

8. **Click the left mouse button to advance to the next slide**

9. **Press [Spacebar] or [Enter] to advance through the slides one at a time until you return to Slide Sorter view**
   After you view the last slide in Slide Show view, you are automatically returned to Slide Sorter view you were in before you ran the slide show.

FIGURE A-8: Slide view with slide indicator box

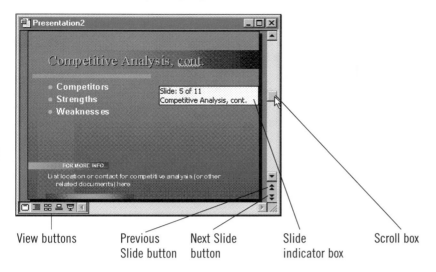

View buttons   Previous   Next Slide   Slide   Scroll box
               Slide button   button   indicator box

FIGURE A-9: Outline view

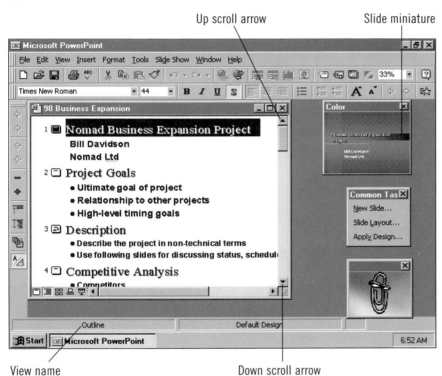

View name   Down scroll arrow

TABLE A-3: View buttons

button	button name	description
▭	**Slide View**	Displays one slide at a time; use this view to modify and enhance a slide's appearance.
☰	**Outline View**	Displays the title and main topics in the form of an outline; use this view to enter and edit the text of your presentation.
🔲	**Slide Sorter View**	Displays a miniature picture of each slide in the order in which they appear in your presentation; use this view to rearrange and add special effects to your slides.
⬜	**Notes Page View**	Displays a reduced slide image and a box to type notes; use this view to take notes on your slides that you can use during your presentation.
▽	**Slide Show View**	Displays your presentation as an electronic slide show.

Saving Your Presentation

To store your presentation permanently, you must save it as a file on a disk. As a general rule, you should save your work about every 10 or 15 minutes and before printing. In this lesson, you will save your presentation to your Student Disk. Carrie saves her presentation as 98 Business Expansion.

1. **Click File on the menu bar, then click Save As**
   The Save As dialog box opens. See Figure A-10.

QuickTip

Make a copy of your Student Disk before you use it.

2. **Make sure your Student Disk is in the appropriate drive, click the Save in list arrow, then click the drive that contains your Student Disk**
   A list of files on your Student Disk appears in the Look in list box, with the default filename placeholder in the Filename text box already selected.

Trouble?

If you see the three-letter extension .PPT on the file-names in the Save As dialog box, don't worry. Windows can be set up to display or not to display the file extensions.

3. **Click in the File name text box to place the blinking insertion point, type 98 Business Expansion, then click Save**
   PowerPoint adds the .PPT extension to the filename, even if it does not appear in the Save As dialog box. The Save As dialog box closes, and the new filename appears in the title bar at the top of the Presentation window. You decide you want to save the presentation in Outline view instead of in Slide Sorter view.

4. **Click the Outline View button** ▤
   The presentation view changes from Slide Sorter view to Outline view.

QuickTip

You also can press the shortcut key combination [Ctrl][S] to save a file quickly.

5. **Click the Save button** 🖫 **on the Standard toolbar**
   The Save command saves any changes you made to the file to the same location you speci-fied when you used the Save As command. Save your file frequently while working with it to protect the presentation.

FIGURE A-10: Save As dialog box

Current drive   Step 2   Save button

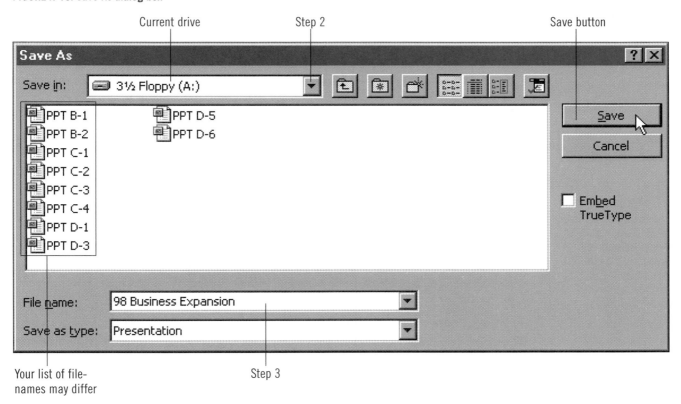

Your list of file-
names may differ   Step 3

Filenames and extensions

When you save a file, PowerPoint automatically adds the extension .PPT to the filename. However, the PowerPoint file extension does not appear in dialog boxes or in Windows Explorer unless you change the DOS file extension setting in the Windows Explorer Options dialog box (on the View menu in the Exploring window). Windows 95 allows you to have filenames up to 255 characters long and permits you to use lower or uppercase letters, symbols, numbers, and spaces.

Getting Help

PowerPoint has an extensive online Help system that gives you immediate access to definitions, reference information, and feature explanations. Help information appears in a separate window that you can move and resize. ✐ Carrie likes the way the AutoContent Wizard helped her create a presentation quickly, and she decides to find out more about it.

Steps 1234

QuickTip

To quickly access the Office Assistant dialog box, click the Assistant animated character, click the Office Assistant button 🔃 on the Standard toolbar, or press [F1].

1. **Click Help on the menu bar, then click Microsoft PowerPoint Help**
   If the Office Assistant wasn't already open, it opens. A balloon-shaped dialog box opens next to the Office Assistant, similar to Figure A-11. At the top of the dialog box, under the question "What would you like to do?" are topics related to what is on-screen and the last few commands you executed. Below the list of topics is a space for you to type a specific question. At the bottom of the dialog box are four buttons. Refer to Table A-4 for a description of these buttons. A lightbulb appears in the Assistant window whenever the Assistant has a context-sensitive tip.

2. **Type AutoContent Wizard, then click Search**
   The dialog box closes and reopens with four topics related to the AutoContent Wizard listed under the head, "What would you like to do?"

3. **Click Create a new presentation**
   A new Help window opens containing information about creating a new presentation. Read the information in the window, using the scroll bar as necessary.

4. **Click Create a presentation based on suggested content and design under the head "What do you want to do?" at the bottom of the window**
   Another Help window opens listing the steps to follow for using the AutoContent Wizard. Read through the steps, scrolling as necessary. See Figure A-12.

5. **Click the Help Topics button**
   The window closes, and a Help Topics dialog box opens. This dialog box contains three tabs: Contents, Index, and Find. The Contents tab contains Help topic organized in outline form. To open a Help window about a topic, double-click it. The Index tab contains an alphabetical list of Help topics. Type the word you want help on, and the list scrolls to that word. On the Find tab, you can search for a key word in all the Help topics. This is similar to how the Office Assistant works.

6. **Click the Close button in the Help Topics dialog box to close it**
   The Help Topics dialog box closes, and you return to your presentation. Now close the Office Assistant window.

QuickTip

You can quickly identify any item on-screen by clicking Help on the menu bar, then clicking What's This? The cursor turns to a help icon ⃗?. The next screen item you click will display a definition of that item.

7. **Click the Close button in the Office Assistant**
   The rest of the figures in this text will not show the Office Assistant.

FIGURE A-11: Office Assistant dialog box

Topics related to
current screen

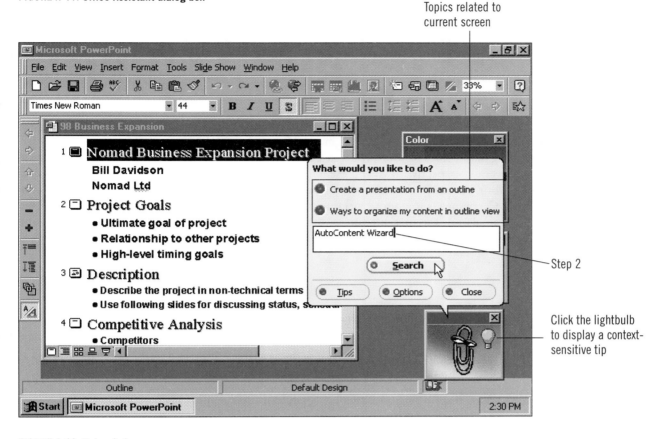

Step 2

Click the lightbulb
to display a context-
sensitive tip

FIGURE A-12: Help window

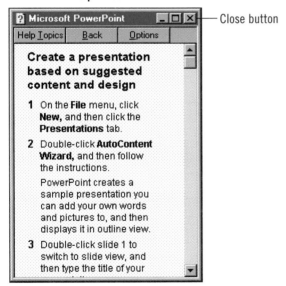

Close button

TABLE A-4: Buttons in the Office Assistant dialog box

button	description
Search	Searches all the PowerPoint Help topics for topics related to the words you type.
Tips	Displays the PowerPoint tips, starting with the Tip of the Day.
Options	Opens a dialog box allowing you to change Office Assistant options or change the animated character.
Close	Closes the Office Assistant dialog box.

Printing and Closing the File, and Exiting PowerPoint

You print your presentation when you have completed it or when you want to review your work. Reviewing hard copies of your presentation at different stages of production is helpful and gives you an overall perspective of your presentation's content and look. When you are finished working on your presentation, close the file containing your presentation and exit PowerPoint. Carrie needs to go to a meeting, so after saving her presentation, she prints the slides and notes pages of the presentation so she can review them later, and then closes the file and exits PowerPoint.

1. Click **File** on the menu bar, then click **Print**

The Print dialog box opens, as shown in Figure A-13. In this dialog box, you can specify which parts of your presentation you want to print (slides, handouts, notes pages, etc.) as well as the number of pages to print and other print options.

2. Make sure the **All option button** is selected in the Print range section

3. Click the **Print what list arrow** and click **Handouts (6 slides per page)**

4. Click the **Black & white check box** to select it

If you have a black and white printer, the presentation will print in black and white, even if you don't check this option; however, checking this option causes PowerPoint to prepare the color slides for black and white output.

5. Click **OK**

The presentation prints on two pages. Now, print the notes pages.

6. Click **File** on the menu bar, then click **Print**

The Print dialog box opens again.

7. Click the **Print what list arrow**, click **Notes Pages**, then click **OK**

The Print dialog box closes, now close the presentation file; the note pages of your presentation prints.

8. Click **File** on the menu bar, then click **Close**

If you have made changes to your presentation, a Microsoft PowerPoint alert box opens asking you if you want to save changes you have made to 98 Business Expansion, as shown in Figure A-14.

9. Click **Yes** to close the alert box

The Presentation window closes. Next, exit the PowerPoint program.

10. Click **File** on the menu bar, then click **Exit**

The PowerPoint program closes, and you return to the Windows desktop.

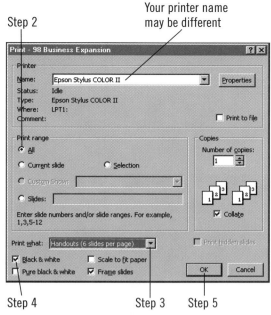

Your printer name
may be different

Step 2

Step 4   Step 3   Step 5

FIGURE A-14: **Save changes alert box**

Presentation window
Close button

PowerPoint window
Close button

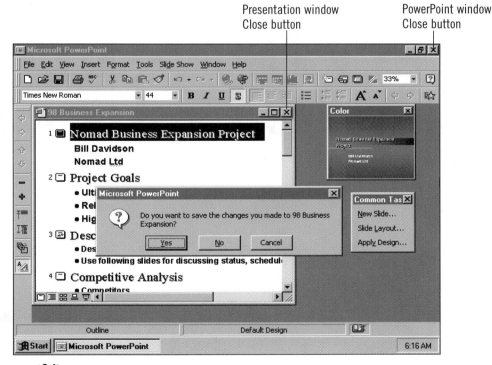

Viewing your presentation in black and white

Viewing your presentation in black and white is very useful when you will be printing a presentation on a black and white or grayscale printer. To see how your color presentation looks in black and white when you are in Outline view, right-click the slide miniature, then click Black and White view on the pop-up menu. In other views, click the Black and White View button

on the Standard toolbar. In Slide view and Notes Pages view, the slide miniature appears in color so you can compare the black and white version with the color version. To remove the slide miniature from the screen, click View, Slide Miniature or click the Close button in the slide miniature window.

PowerPoint 97

Practice

► Concepts Review

Label the PowerPoint window elements shown in Figure A-15.

FIGURE A-15

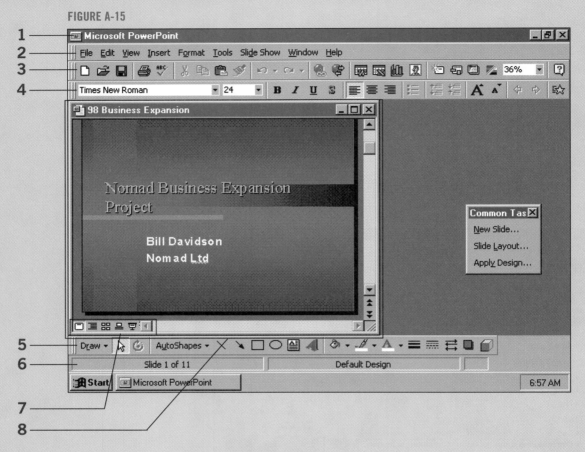

Match each term with the statement that describes its function.

a. AutoContent Wizard
b. Presentation window
c. Zoom box
d. Fit to Page
e. Slide indicator box

9. The area where you work on your presentation.
10. Identifies slide title and number.
11. Series of dialog boxes that guides you through creating a presentation and produces a presentation with suggestions for content.
12. Command that automatically sizes the Presentation window on the screen.
13. Lets you change the magnification of a slide.

Select the best answer from the list of choices.

14. PowerPoint can help you create all of the following, *except:*
   a. 35-mm slides.
   b. Movies.
   c. An on-screen presentation.
   d. Outline pages.

15. The buttons you use to switch between the PowerPoint views are called:
   a. PowerPoint buttons.
   b. View buttons.
   c. Screen buttons.
   d. Toolbar buttons.

16. All of these are PowerPoint views, *except:*
   a. Slide view.
   b. Notes Pages view.
   c. Outline view.
   d. Current Page view.

17. The animated character that appears on the screen when you click the Help button is the:
   a. Office Helper.
   b. Office Assistant.
   c. Assistant Paper Clip.
   d. PowerPoint Assistant.

18. The view that allows you to view your electronic slide show with each slide filling the entire screen is called:
   a. Electronic view.
   b. Slide Sorter view.
   c. Presentation view.
   d. Slide Show view.

19. Which wizard helps you create and outline your presentation?
   a. Pick a Look Wizard
   b. Presentation Wizard
   c. AutoContent Wizard
   d. OrgContent Wizard

20. How do you switch to Slide view?
   a. Click the Slide View button to the left of the horizontal scroll bar.
   b. Click View on the menu bar, then click Slide.
   c. Right-click the slide miniature in Outline view, then click Go To Slide View on the pop-up menu.
   d. All of the above are true.

21. How do you save your presentation after you have saved it for the first time?
   a. Click Save As on the File menu, then assign it a new name.
   b. Click the Save button on the toolbar.
   c. Click Save As on the File menu, then click Save.
   d. Click Save As on the File menu, specify a new location and filename, then click Save.

▶ # Skills Review

1. **Start PowerPoint and use the AutoContent Wizard to create a sample presentation on a topic of your choice.**
   a. Click the Start button on the Taskbar, then point to the Programs folder.
   b. Click Microsoft PowerPoint.
   c. If the Tip of the Day dialog box appears, click Close.
   d. Click the AutoContent Wizard option button, then click OK.
   e. Read the information in the AutoContent Wizard dialog box, then click Next.
   f. Select a presentation category and type, then click Next.
   g. Click the output options of your choice, then click Next.
   h. Click the presentation style of your choice, then click Next.
   i. Enter a presentation title and your name and any additional information you want to appear on the title slide, then click Next.
   j. Click Finish.

2. **View the PowerPoint window and explore the PowerPoint views.**
   a. Click the Slide View button and adjust the Zoom to 36%, click the Restore button in the Presentation window, click Window on the menu bar, then click Fit to Page.
   b. Identify as many elements of the PowerPoint window as you can without referring to the unit material.
   c. Use the Next and Previous Slide buttons to move up and down the slides of your presentation to view its content.
   d. When you are finished, drag the scroll box in the vertical scroll bar up to Slide 1.
   e. Click the Outline View button.
   f. Use the down scroll arrow to view the contents of all your slides.
   g. Click the Notes Page View button, then click the Next Slide button repeatedly to view all your notes pages.
   h. After you finish exploring the presentation, drag the elevator to Slide 1.
   i. Click the Slide Sorter View button, and examine your slides.
   j. Click the Slide Show button. The first slide of your presentation fills the screen. Advance through the slide show by clicking the left mouse button or by pressing [Enter].

3. **Save your presentation.**
   a. Change to the view in which you would like to save your presentation.
   b. Click File on the menu bar, and click Save As.
   c. Make sure your floppy disk is in the correct drive.
   d. Type "Practice Presentation" in the File name text box.
   e. Click Save.
   f. Click a different view button than the one you saved your presentation in.
   g. Click the Save button on the Standard toolbar.

4. Explore PowerPoint Help.

a. If the Office Assistant is open, click it. If it is not on your screen, click the Office Assistant button on the Standard toolbar.

b. Type "Tell me about Help" in the text box and click Search.

c. Click the topic, "Get Help without the Office Assistant."

d. After reading the information in the Help window, click the Help Topics button at the top of the window.

e. Click the Contents tab in the Help Topics dialog box.

f. Double-click any Help topics (identified by book icons) you wish to explore to display the Help subjects (identified by page icons).

g. Double-click the page icons to review the Help information.

h. Click the Help Topics button to return to the main Help Topics dialog box. Explore a number of topics that interest you.

i. When you have finished exploring the Contents tab, click the Index tab.

j. Type a word in the text box with the blinking insertion point.

k. Click a word in the list box if the highlighted word is not the word you want to look up, then click Display.

l. Click the Help Topics button to return to the main Help Topics dialog box. Explore a number of topics that interest you.

m. When you have finished exploring the Index tab, click the Help window Close button.

5. Print your presentation, close the file, and exit PowerPoint.

a. Click File on the menu bar, then click Print.

b. Click the Print what list arrow, and click Handouts (3 slides per page).

c. Make sure the Black & white check box is selected, and click OK.

d. Click File on the menu bar, then click Print.

e. Click the Print what list arrow, and click Outline View.

f. Click OK.

g. Click File on the menu bar, then click Close.

h. Click No if you see a message asking if you want to save the changes.

i. Click File on the menu bar, then click Exit.

PowerPoint 97

▶ Independent Challenges

1. You have just gotten a job as a marketing assistant at Events, Inc., a catering firm specializing in clambakes and barbecues for large company events. John Hudspeth, the marketing manager, has some familiarity with PowerPoint. He has heard that you can print a presentation on a black-and-white printer, but he wants to know just what happens to the text, backgrounds, and so forth when they are converted to black and white.

To complete this independent challenge:

1. If PowerPoint is not already running, start it. When the startup dialog box appears, click Cancel. If PowerPoint is already running, go to Step 2.
2. Use PowerPoint Help to find the answer to John's question.
3. Write down which Help feature you used (Office Assistant, Index, etc.), and the steps you followed.
4. Print the Help window that shows the information you found. (*Hint*: Click the Options button at the top of the Help window, then click Print Topic and click OK in the Print dialog box that appears.)
5. Exit PowerPoint. Turn in the printed Help window and your notes.

2. You are in charge of marketing for ArtWorks, Inc, a medium-sized company that produces all types of art for corporations to enhance their work environment. The company has a regional sales area that includes three neighboring northeastern states. The president of ArtWorks is working on a proposal for American Digital, a national electronics firm, to supply artwork for all their 20 locations. You are given the responsibility of planning and creating the outline of the PowerPoint presentation the president will use to convey his proposal to American Digital.

Create an outline that reflects the major points ArtWorks needs to communicate to American Digital to secure this large contract. Assume the following: ArtWorks needs to promote their company and products to American Digital; ArtWorks supplies all types of artwork, from classic and contemporary posters and reproductions of old masters, to original artwork; and the ArtWorks proposal includes classic posters and art reproductions.

To complete this independent challenge:

1. Start PowerPoint if necessary and choose the AutoContent Wizard option button. (*Hint:* If PowerPoint is already running, click File on the menu bar, click New, click the Presentations tab and double-click AutoContent Wizard.)
2. Choose the Sales/Marketing category, then choose an appropriate presentation type from the list.
3. Scroll through the outline the AutoContent Wizard produced. Does it contain the type of information you thought it would?
4. Plan how you would change and add to the sample text created by the wizard. What information do you need to promote ArtWorks to a large company?
5. Take notes on how you might change the outline text.
6. Switch views. Run through the slide show at least once.
7. Save your presentation to your Student Disk with a meaningful name.
8. Print your presentation as Handouts (3 slides per page).
9. Close and exit PowerPoint. Hand in your notes for promoting ArtWorks along with your presentation.

3. You have recently been promoted to sales manager at Buconjic Industries. Part of your job is to train sales representatives to go to potential customers and give presentations describing your company's products. Your boss wants you to review the Dale Carnegie presentation techniques provided with PowerPoint 97 and describe some of the techniques at the next departmental meeting.

You decide to first review the Dale Carnegie information in PowerPoint Central. PowerPoint Central is a read-only slide show that provides you with extra clip art, templates, and other items available on the Office 97 CD-ROM and the World Wide Web (WWW). Then, you will review the Dale Carnegie information in the AutoContent Wizard.

To complete this independent challenge:

1. Start PowerPoint if necessary.
2. Click Tools on the menu bar, then click PowerPoint Central. Click the Magazine button at the top of the presentation window to open the Dale Carnegie mini-course. Click the right-arrow button at the bottom of the window to move through the slides. See Figure A-16. Take notes as you move through the slide show. When you reach the end of the slide show, click the Close button in the Presentation window.
3. Start the AutoContent Wizard (*Hint:* Click File on the menu bar, click New, click the presentations tab, then double-click AutoContent Wizard.) Choose Carnegie Coach in the Category list on the Presentation type screen, then choose Presentation Guidelines in the list box. Give the presentation an appropriate title, and add your name to the title slide.
4. View the presentation in any view you like, then run through the slide show. Read the guidelines offered and note the graphics on the slides.
5. Write a brief memo to your boss explaining the techniques you think will be most helpful. Print any screens from the presentation you created using the AutoContent Wizard that support your recommendations.
6. Exit PowerPoint without saving the presentation and submit your memo and any printouts.

FIGURE A-16

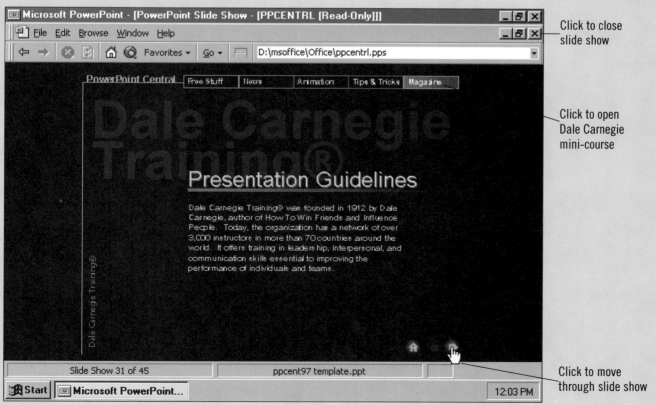

PowerPoint 97

4. You are a marketing assistant for AllCare, a health maintenance organization (HMO) in Memphis, Tennessee. The management of AllCare is interested in expanding its service area to cover areas in the state that are currently underserved by existing health care organizations. The marketing director, Monica Spitz, has heard that you can use PowerPoint 97 to create presentations on the Internet and would like you to learn about it and give her a brief overview of the subject at the next departmental meeting.

You decide to learn the basics from the PowerPoint Office Assistant, then explore the Internet yourself to get a better feel for the subject. Then you will be better able to discuss the topic at the meeting.

To complete this independent challenge:

1. Start PowerPoint if necessary, and use the Office Assistant Search feature. Enter the word "Internet" in the Office Assistant dialog box.
2. When the Assistant displays a list of topics, select the topic, "Presentations on the Internet."
3. Read the information in the Help window that appears, noting how you can open a PowerPoint presentation on the Internet or an intranet, how you can use the Web toolbar and hyperlinks, and how you can publish a presentation on the World Wide Web (WWW).
4. Log on to the Internet and use your browser to go to http://www.course.com. From there, click the link Student On Line Companions, then click the Microsoft Office 97 Professional Edition—Illustrated: A First Course page, then click on the PowerPoint link for Unit A
5. Print the book Web page.
6. Click the Unit A link, and click any link to see what a presentation looks like on the Web. Click any links in the presentation that you want to follow.
7. Log off the Internet, and write a brief memo to Monica, explaining how presentations on the Web and the use of Web features can be useful to AllCare's marketing efforts. Describe the presentation that you saw on the links you followed. Attach any Web page printouts that support your recommendations.
9. Exit PowerPoint and submit your memo and attached printouts.

Creating
a Presentation

▶ **Plan an effective presentation**
▶ **Choose a look for a presentation**
▶ **Enter slide text**
▶ **Create a new slide**
▶ **Work in Outline view**
▶ **Enter text in Notes Page view**
▶ **Check spelling in the presentation**
▶ **Evaluate your presentation**

Now that you are familiar with PowerPoint basics, you are ready to plan and create your own presentation. To do this, you enter and edit text and choose a slide design. PowerPoint helps you accomplish these tasks with the AutoContent Wizard, which supplies sample text for a number of different presentation situations, and with a collection of professionally prepared slide designs, called **presentation design templates**, which can contribute to the look of your presentation. In this unit, you will create a presentation using a presentation design template. ✐⬛ Carrie Armstrong's next assignment is to create the Annual Report the president will present at a shareholders' meeting later in the month. She begins by choosing a design template.

Planning an effective presentation

Before you create a presentation using PowerPoint, you need to plan and outline the message you want to communicate and consider how you want the presentation to look. When preparing the outline, you need to consider where you are giving the presentation and who your primary audience will be. It is also important to know what resources you might need, such as a computer or projection equipment. ▸▸▸ Using Figure B-1 and the planning guidelines below, follow Carrie as she outlines the presentation message.

Details

 Determine the purpose of the presentation and the location and audience
The company president needs to present the highlights of Nomad's Annual Report at a shareholders' meeting in a large hall at the Plaza Center Inn.

 Determine the type of output—black and white (B&W) or color overhead transparencies, on-screen slide show, or 35-mm slides—that best conveys your message, given time constraints and computer hardware availability
Since the president is speaking in a large hall and has access to a computer and projection equipment, an on-screen slide show is the best choice.

 Determine a look for your presentation that will help communicate your message
You can choose one of the professionally designed templates that come with PowerPoint, modify an existing PowerPoint template, or create one of your own. Your template should be appropriate for a corporate audience and should reinforce a message of confidence and accomplishment.

 Determine the message you want to communicate, then give the presentation a meaningful title and outline your message
The president wants to highlight the previous year's accomplishments and set the goals for the coming year. See Figure B-1.

 Determine what other materials will be useful in addition to the presentation
You need to prepare not only the slides themselves, but supplementary materials, including speaker's notes and handouts for the audience. Speaker's notes will allow the president to stay on track and deliver a concise message.

FIGURE B-1: Outline of the text in the presentation

1. Annual Report Executive Summary
   -Bill Davidson
   -June 18, 1998

2. Summary
   -1997 Accomplishments
   -1998 Goals

3. 1997 Accomplishments
   -Product sales up 23.9%
   -Expeditions up 10.4%
   -Environmental funding up 6.4%

4. 1998 Goals
   -Increase product sales 28%
   -Increase expeditions 15%
   -Increase environmental funding 8%

Choosing a look for a presentation

To help you design your presentation, PowerPoint provides over 75 templates so you don't have to spend time creating the right presentation look. A **design template** has borders, colors, text attributes, and other elements arranged in a specific format that is applied to all the slides in your presentation. You can use a design template as is, or you can modify any element to suit your needs. Unless you know something about graphic arts, it is often easier and faster to use or modify one of the templates supplied with PowerPoint. No matter how you create your presentation, you can save it as a template for future use. ✐ Carrie doesn't have a lot of time but wants to create a good-looking presentation, so she uses an existing PowerPoint template.

Steps 1 2 3 4

1. Start PowerPoint, click the Template option button in the PowerPoint startup dialog box, then click OK
The New Presentation dialog box opens, containing four tabs. See Table B-1 for an overview of the tab contents.

2. Click the Presentation Designs tab
This displays 17 of the PowerPoint presentation design templates.

3. Click the Contemporary template icon once
A miniature version of the selected template appears in the Preview box on the right side of the dialog box, as shown in Figure B-2.

4. Click OK
The New Slide dialog box opens, displaying 24 AutoLayouts. An **AutoLayout** is a slide containing placeholders for text and graphics. The first layout is selected, and its name, Title Slide, appears on the right side of the dialog box. Since the first slide of the presentation is the **title slide**, this layout is appropriate.

5. Click OK
A blank title slide, containing placeholders for title and subtitle text, fills the Presentation window. The background of the slide is the Contemporary design template you chose. Notice that the name of the template is in the status bar. Now, restore your window so it will look like the figures in this book.

6. Click the Restore window button on the Presentation window, click the percentage number in the Zoom text box, type 36 and press [Enter], click Window on the menu bar, then click Fit to Page
If the Common Tasks toolbar is on top of the Presentation window, drag it to the right of the screen. Compare your screen with Figure B-3 and make any adjustments necessary, then save the presentation.

7. Click the Save button 🖫 on the Standard toolbar, then save your presentation as 97 Annual Report 1

CLUES TO USE

Presentation templates versus presentation design templates

A **presentation design template** contains a background design, a color scheme, and text placeholders, like the box labeled "Click to add title" in Figure B-3. A **presentation template** contains a background design, a color scheme, and content, sample text for a particular type of presentation. You choose a presentation template when you use the AutoContent Wizard.

FIGURE B-2: **Presentation Designs tab in the New Presentation dialog box**

PowerPoint templates available to supply the look for your presentation

Contemporary template selected

Miniature version of selected template appears here

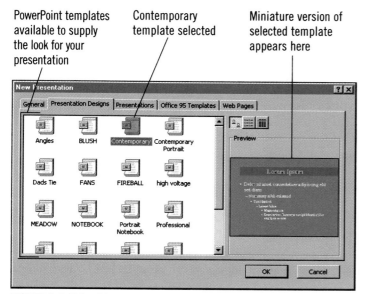

FIGURE B-3: **Title slide with new template design**

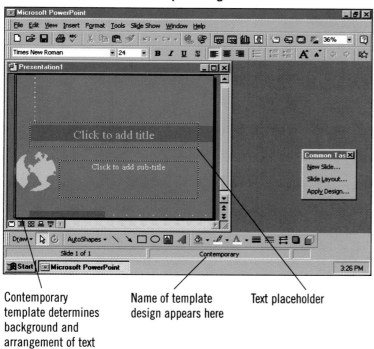

Contemporary template determines background and arrangement of text

Name of template design appears here

Text placeholder

TABLE B-1: **New Presentation dialog box tabs**

tab	contains	use
General	A blank presentation	When you want to create your own presentation, including backgrounds and text formats
Presentation Designs	17 design templates with backgrounds and text formats	When you want to use predesigned templates, so you know the text and graphic design will coordinate well with each other
Presentations	33 design templates that contain suggested content for specific uses. Some templates are available in both a standard version and an Internet version	When you want both a predesigned template design and content guidance
Web Pages	Two Web page banners	When you are designing your own Web page and want a professionally designed banner

Entering slide text

Now that you have applied a template to your presentation, you are ready to enter text into the title slide. The title slide has two **text placeholders**, boxes with dashed line borders where you enter text. Also, the title slide has a **title placeholder** labeled "Click to add title" and a **main text placeholder** labeled "Click to add sub-title" where you enter additional information, such as your company name or department. To enter text in a placeholder, simply click the placeholder and then type your text. After you enter text in a placeholder, the placeholder becomes a text object. An **object** is any item on a slide that can be manipulated. Objects are the building blocks that make up a presentation slide. ✎ ▬▬ Carrie begins working on the president's presentation by entering the title of the presentation in the title placeholder.

Steps 1 2 3 4

1. **Move the pointer over the title placeholder labeled "Click to add title"**
   The pointer changes to ⊥ when you move the pointer over the placeholder. The pointer changes shape, depending on the task you are trying to accomplish. Table B-2 describes the functions of the most common PowerPoint mouse pointer shapes.

2. **Click the title placeholder**
   The **insertion point**, a blinking vertical line, indicates where your text will appear in the title placeholder. A **selection box**, the slanted line border, appears around the title placeholder, indicating that it is selected and ready to accept text. See Figure B-4. Enter the presentation title.

3. **Type Annual Report, press [Enter], then type Executive Summary**
   PowerPoint centers the title text within the title placeholder, now called a text object. Pressing [Enter] in a text object moves the insertion point down to begin a new line of text.

4. **Click the main text placeholder**
   Enter the name and job title of Nomad's president and the meeting date in the main text placeholder.

5. **Type Bill Davidson, press [Enter], type President, press [Enter], then type June 18, 1998**
   Compare your title slide with Figure B-5.

6. **Click outside the main text object in a blank area of the slide**
   Clicking a blank area of the slide deselects all selected objects on the slide.

7. **Click the Save button 🖫 on the Standard toolbar to save your changes**

Trouble?

If you press a wrong key, press [Backspace] to erase the character, then continue to type. If you make a typing error and press [Spacebar] or [Enter], you may see a wavy, red line under the word. This simply means that the automatic spellchecking feature in PowerPoint is active.

TABLE B-2: PowerPoint mouse pointer shapes

shape	description
↖	Appears when you select the Selection tool; use this pointer to select one or more PowerPoint objects
⊥	Appears when you move the pointer over a text object; use this pointer, called the I-beam, to place the insertion point where you want to begin typing or selecting text
✛	Appears when you move the pointer over a bullet, slide icon, or object; use this pointer to select title or paragraph text
+	Appears when you select a drawing tool; use this pointer, called the cross-hair cursor, to draw shapes

FIGURE B-4: Selected title placeholder

Title placeholder   Insertion point   Selection box

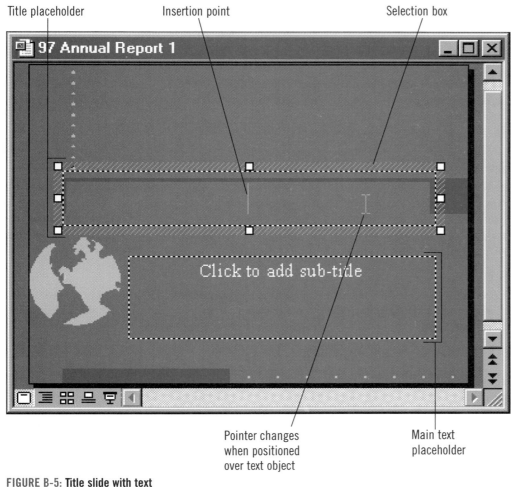

Pointer changes
when positioned
over text object

Main text
placeholder

FIGURE B-5: Title slide with text

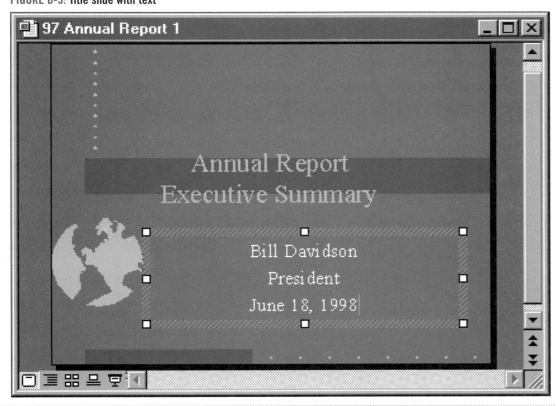

PowerPoint 97

Creating a new slide

To help you create a new slide easily, PowerPoint offers 24 predesigned AutoLayouts, which include a variety of placeholder arrangements for objects including titles, main text, clip art, graphs, charts, and media clips. You have already used the title slide AutoLayout. See Table B-3 for an explanation of the different placeholders you'll find in the AutoLayouts. To continue developing the presentation, Carrie needs to create a slide that displays the topic headings for the president's presentation.

Steps

QuickTip

You also can click the Insert New Slide button on the Standard toolbar.

QuickTip

To add a new slide with the same layout as the current slide, press and hold [Shift], then click New Slide on the Common Tasks toolbar, or click.

1. Click New Slide on the Common Tasks toolbar

The New Slide dialog box opens, displaying the different AutoLayouts. (Click the down scroll arrow to view more.) This is the same dialog box that appeared when you chose the title slide layout. The title for the selected AutoLayout appears in a Preview box to the right of the layouts, as shown in Figure B-6. You can choose the best layout by clicking it. Use the Bulleted List AutoLayout, which is already selected.

2. Click OK

A new slide appears after the current slide in your presentation, displaying a title placeholder and a main text placeholder for the bulleted list. Notice that the status bar displays Slide 2 of 2. Enter a title for this slide.

3. Click the title placeholder, then type Summary

4. Click the main text placeholder

This deselects the title text object. The insertion point appears next to a bullet in the main text placeholder. Enter the first two topic headings for the president's presentation.

5. Type 1997 Accomplishments, then press [Enter]

A new bullet automatically appears when you press [Enter].

6. Type 1998 Goals

7. Click outside the main text object in a blank area of the slide to deselect the main text object

Compare your slide to Figure B-7.

8. Click the Save button on the Standard toolbar

Your changes are saved.

FIGURE B-6: **New Slide dialog box**

Default AutoLayout

Title of selected AutoLayout

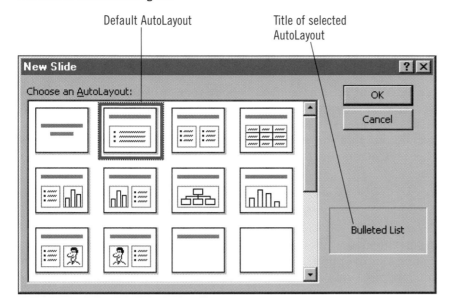

FIGURE B-7: **New slide with bulleted list**

Bulleted list

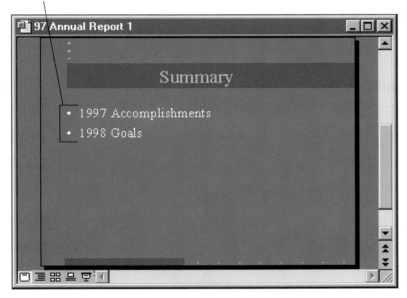

TABLE B-3: **AutoLayout placeholder types**

placeholder	symbol	description
Bulleted List		Displays a short list of related points
Clip Art		Inserts a picture, such as PowerPoint clip art
Chart		Inserts a chart that uses standard Microsoft chart techniques
Organization Chart		Inserts an organizational chart
Table		Inserts a table from Microsoft Word
Media clip		Inserts a music, sound, or video clip
Object		Inserts an external object such as WordArt, an equation, a spreadsheet, or a picture

PowerPoint 97

Working in Outline view

In PowerPoint, you can enter your presentation text in Slide view or in Outline view. **Outline view** displays the titles and main text of all the slides in your presentation. As in a regular outline, the headings, or **titles**, appear first; then under them, the subpoints, or **main text**, appear. The main text appears as one or more lines of bulleted text under a title. Carrie entered the first two slides of her presentation in Slide view. Now, she switches to Outline view to enter text for two more slides.

Steps

1. **Click the Outline View button ▤ to the left of the horizontal scroll bar**
   The outline fills the Presentation window with the title of Slide 2 selected (the slide you just created). The Outlining toolbar appears on the left side of the PowerPoint window, and the Drawing toolbar no longer appears at the bottom of the window. Table B-4 describes the buttons available on the Outlining toolbar. The slide miniature window appears to the right of the outline. Now, enter the text for the third slide. Since the third slide is a bulleted list like the second slide, insert a new slide with the same layout as Slide 2.

2. **Press [Shift] and click New Slide in the Common Task window**
   Pressing [Shift] while clicking New Slide inserts a new slide with the same AutoLayout as the current slide. A symbol called a **slide icon** appears next to the slide number when you add a new slide to the outline. See Figure B-8. Text you enter next to a slide icon becomes the title for that slide.

QuickTip

You can also press [Tab] to indent text one level.

3. **Type 1997 Accomplishments, then press [Enter]**
   A new slide is inserted. You want to enter the main text for the Accomplishments slide; so you need to indent this line.

4. **Click the Demote button ⇨ on the Outlining toolbar**
   The slide icon changes to a bullet and indents one level to the right.

Trouble?

If you accidentally pressed [Enter] after typing the last bullet, press [Backspace], then press [Ctrl][Enter].

5. **Type Product sales up 23.9%, then press [Enter]; type Expeditions up 10.4%, then press [Enter]; type Environmental funding up 6.4%, then press [Ctrl][Enter]**
   Pressing [Ctrl][Enter] while the cursor is in the main text creates a new slide with the same layout as the previous slide.

6. **Type 1998 Goals, then press [Ctrl][Enter]; type Increase product sales 28%, then press [Enter]; type Increase environmental funding 8% then press [Enter]; type Increase expeditions 15%**
   Pressing [Ctrl][Enter] while the cursor is in title text creates a bullet. Two of the bulleted points you just typed for Slide 4 are out of order. Move them into the correct position.

QuickTip

You can also drag slide icons or bullets to a new location.

7. **Position the pointer to the left of the last bullet in Slide 4, then click the mouse button**
   The pointer changes from Ⅰ to ✛. PowerPoint selects the entire line of text.

8. **Click the Move Up button ⬆ on the Outlining toolbar**
   The third bullet point moves up one line and trades places with the second bullet point, as shown in Figure B-9. Now look at the slide you just created in Slide view.

Time To

✓ Save

9. **Double-click the slide icon for Slide 4, then click the Previous Slide button ⬍ below the vertical scroll bar three times to view each slide**
   Double-clicking the slide icon in Outline view switches you to Slide view. When you are finished viewing all the slides, Slide 1 of 4 should appear in the status bar.

FIGURE B-8: **Outline view**

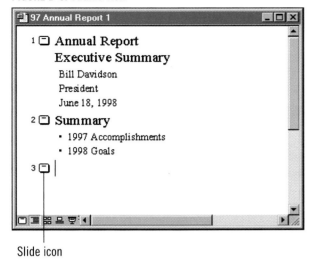

Slide icon

FIGURE B-9: **Bulleted item moved up in Outline view**

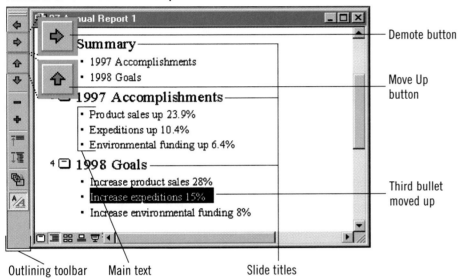

Demote button

Move Up button

Third bullet moved up

Outlining toolbar   Main text   Slide titles

TABLE B-4: **Outlining toolbar commands**

button	button name	description
⬅	**Promote**	Indents selected text one tab to the left
➡	**Demote**	Indents selected text one tab to the right
⬆	**Move Up**	Moves the selection above the previous line
⬇	**Move Down**	Moves the selection below the next line
–	**Collapse**	Displays only the titles of the selected slide
+	**Expand**	Displays all levels of the selected slide
⬆≡	**Collapse All**	Displays only the titles of all slides
⬇≡	**Expand All**	Displays all levels of all slides
▢	**Summary Slide**	Creates a new bulleted slide containing only the titles of selected slides. Good for creating an agenda slide
ᴬ⁄ₐ	**Show Formatting**	Displays or hides all character formatting

Entering text in Notes Page view

To help you give your presentation in front of a group, you can create speaker's notes that accompany your slides so you don't have to rely on your memory. Notes Page view displays a reduced slide image and a text placeholder, where you enter the notes for each slide of your presentation. The notes you enter there do not appear on the slides themselves; they are private notes. You also can print these pages. To make sure the president doesn't forget key points of his presentation, Carrie enters notes for some of the slides.

Steps

1. **Click the Notes Page View button**
   The view of your presentation changes from Slide view to Notes Page view, as shown in Figure B-10.

2. **Click the text placeholder below the slide image**
   The insertion point appears, indicating the placeholder is ready to accept your text. The insertion point is small and difficult to see, so increase the view size.

3. **Click the Zoom list arrow on the Standard toolbar, then click 66%**
   The text placeholder increases in size. Now that the text placeholder is larger and easier to see, enter the notes for Slide 1. In the next step, make sure you type "Welcome" without the "e" as shown.

4. **Type Welcom to the 1997 Annual Report meeting for shareholders and employees.**
   The red, wavy line under the word "Welcom" means that this word is not in the Microsoft Office spellchecker dictionary. In the next step, make sure you misspell the word "Nomd," as shown.

5. **Click the Next Slide button below the vertical scroll bar, click the text placeholder, then type The main purpose of this meeting is to share with you the exciting accomplishments Nomd Ltd has achieved in the last year, as well as our goals for 1998.**
   As you type, text automatically wraps to the next line.

6. **Click to go to the third slide, click the text placeholder, then type Due to our record year in 1996, Nomad's 1997 goals were very aggressive. Let's see how we did. Our award-winning OutBack camping gear series has continued to do well and helped push overall product sales up almost 24%. New Directions, our travel subsidiary, has seen an increase in expeditions of over 10%, and we have increased our support for environmental causes over 6%.**

7. **Click , click the text placeholder, type, As a result of our accomplishments over the last year, we have set even higher goals for 1998. We are confident that we can achieve a sales increase of 28%, increase expeditions 15%, with the help of the incredible marketing and location development strategies of New Directions, and increase our environmental funding 8%.**

8. **Press [Enter], then type I would like to thank you all for your hard work and support, and I look forward to working with you all in 1998.**
   Slide 4 in Notes Page view is shown in Figure B-11.

Time To

✔ Save

FIGURE B-10: Notes Page view

Text placeholder   Reduced slide image

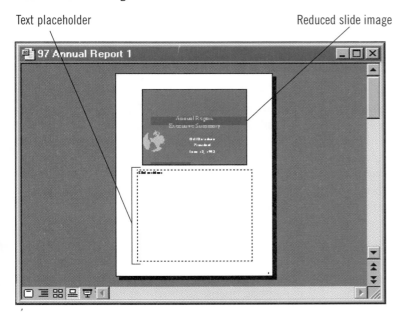

FIGURE B-11: Slide 4 in Notes Page view with text

Speaker's notes

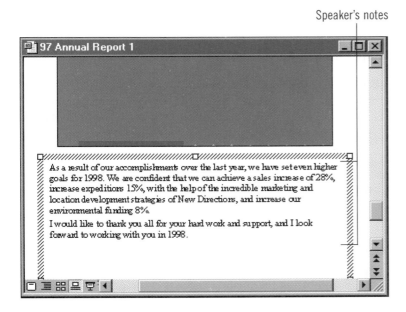

Adding slide footers and headers

To customize your slides, notes pages, or handouts with information, such as your company or product name, the slide number, or the date, you can add headers and footers. To add a header or footer, click View on the menu bar, then click Header and Footer. Each element in the Header and Footer dialog box with a checkmark in the checkbox will be included as part of the header or footer. As you click the check-boxes, watch the Preview box to see where the element will appear. On the Slide tab, you can add only footers. To have the footer appear on only the current slide, click Apply; to have footers appear on all the slides, click Apply to All. On the Notes and Handouts tab, you can choose to add headers and footers, and they will appear on all the pages.

Checking spelling in the presentation

As your work nears completion, you need to review and proofread your presentation thoroughly for errors. You can use the spell-checking feature in PowerPoint to check for and correct spelling errors. The spell-checking feature compares the spelling of all the words in your presentation against the words contained in its electronic dictionary. You still must proofread your presentation for punctuation, grammar, and word-usage errors, however. The spell checker recognizes misspelled words, not misused words. For example, the spell checker would not identify "The Test" as an error even if you had intended to type "The Best." ✐ Carrie has finished adding and changing text in the presentation, so she checks her work.

1. Click the Spelling button 🔤 on the Standard toolbar

PowerPoint begins to check the spelling in your presentation. It will check the spelling in the Notes Pages, even if you are in another view. When PowerPoint finds a misspelled word or a word it doesn't recognize, the Spelling dialog box opens, as shown in Figure B-12. In this case, PowerPoint does not recognize 'Welcom' in the speaker's notes for slide 1. (If you made a typing error, another word might appear in this dialog box.) Fix the spelling by choosing the correction offered by PowerPoint.

2. Click Change

PowerPoint replaces the incorrect word, then continues checking the presentation. The next word the spell checker identifies as an error is the word "Nomd" in the second notes page. Choose the correct spelling from the list of suggestions.

3. Click Nomad in the Suggestions list box, then click Change

Next, the spell checker identifies "Ltd" as misspelled. This word is spelled correctly, so Carrie tells PowerPoint to ignore all instances of this word and continue through the presentation.

4. Click Ignore All

The spell checker ignores all instances of the word "Ltd" throughout the presentation. Next, the spell checker finds the word "OutBack" in the Slide 4 speaker notes. Although the word is not misspelled, PowerPoint detects that the capital B in the middle of the word might be an error. This is the correct spelling, however, so tell PowerPoint to ignore all instances of this word.

5. Click Ignore All

If PowerPoint finds any other words it does not recognize, either change them or ignore them. When the spell checker finishes checking your presentation, the spelling dialog closes and a PowerPoint alert box opens, indicating the spelling check is complete.

6. Click OK

The alert box closes.

7. Click File on the menu bar, then click Print

8. Click the Print what list arrow, click Notes Pages, click the Black & white check box to select it, then click OK

9. Save your presentation, then return to Slide 1 in slide view

Trouble?

If your spell checker doesn't find the word "Ltd," then a previous user probably added it to the custom dictionary. Skip Step 4 and continue with the lesson.

QuickTip

The spell checker does not check the text in pictures or embedded objects. You'll need to spell check text in imported objects, such as charts, Word documents or tables, using their original application.

FIGURE B-12: **Spelling dialog box**

Unrecognized word appears here

Suggested replacement appears here

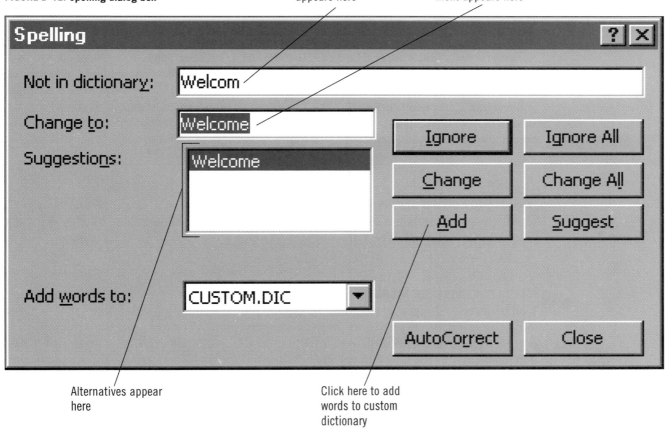

Alternatives appear here

Click here to add words to custom dictionary

Checking spelling as you type

PowerPoint checks your spelling as you type. If you type a word that is not in the electronic dictionary, a red, wavy line appears under it. To correct the error, right-click the misspelled word. A pop-up menu appears with one or more suggestions. You can select a suggestion, add the word you typed to your custom dictionary, or ignore it. To turn off automatic spell checking, click Tools on the menu bar, then click Options to open the Options dialog box. Click the Spelling tab, and in the section Check spelling as you type, click the Spelling check box to deselect it, then click OK. To temporarily hide the red, wavy lines, select the Hide spelling errors check box on the Spelling tab in the Options dialog box. See Figure B-13.

FIGURE B-13: **Spelling tab in the Options dialog box**

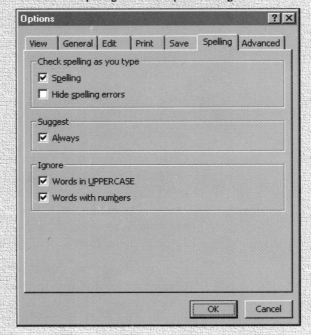

Evaluating your presentation

As you plan and create a presentation, keep in mind that good design involves preparation. An effective presentation is both focused and visually appealing. A planned presentation is easy for the speaker to present and easy for the audience to comprehend. The visual elements (colors, graphics and text) you choose can strongly influence audience attention and interest and can determine the success of your presentation.  Carrie evaluates her presentation's effectiveness. Her final presentation is shown in Figure B-14. For contrast, Figure B-15 shows a poorly designed slide.

Time To

✔ Save

1. Click the Slide Show button
2. Click the mouse button to move through the slide show
3. When you are finished viewing the slide show, click the Slide Sorter button 🔳, click Window on the menu bar, then click Fit to Page
   See Figure B-14.

 Keep your message focused

Don't put everything you are going to say on your presentation slides. Keep the audience anticipating further explanations to the slides' key points. For example, the Annual Report presentation focuses the audience's attention on the sales numbers and projections because you included only the sales percentage increases and the goals for next year. You supplemented the slides with speaker's notes that explain the reasons for the increases.

 Keep the design simple, easy to read, and appropriate to the content

Usually, you will use a predesigned template that uses appropriate fonts, font sizes, and background colors. A design template also makes the presentation consistent. If you design your own layout or alter an existing one, do not add so many elements that the slides look cluttered. Use the same design elements consistently throughout the presentation; otherwise, your audience will get confused. The design template you used for the Annual Report presentation is simple; the horizontal bars on every slide give the presentation a clean, solid, and businesslike look that is appropriate to a Board of Directors meeting.

 Choose attractive colors that make the slide easy to read

Use contrasting colors for slide background and text, so that the slides are easy to read. If you are giving your presentation on a computer, you can use almost any combination of visually appealing colors.

 Keep your text concise

Limit each slide to six words per line and six lines per slide. Use lists and symbols to help prioritize your points visually. Your presentation text provides only the highlights; the president will use the speaker notes to give the background information.

 Choose fonts, typefaces, and styles that are easy to read and emphasize important text

Don't use the same typeface for all your text, and vary typeface weights. As a general rule, use no more than two fonts and three typefaces in a presentation. Use bold and italic selectively. Do not use text smaller than 18 point. In the design template you used, the titles are 44-point Arial and 32-point Times New Roman for the main text.

 Use visuals to help communicate the message of your presentation

Commonly used visuals include clip art, photographs, charts, worksheets, tables, and movies. Whenever possible, replace text with a visual, but be careful not to overcrowd your slides. You will add some visuals in the next two units.

FIGURE B-14: **The final presentation**

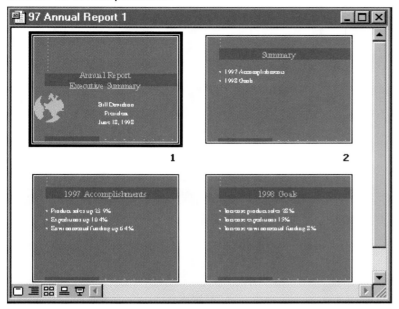

FIGURE B-15: **Poorly designed slide**

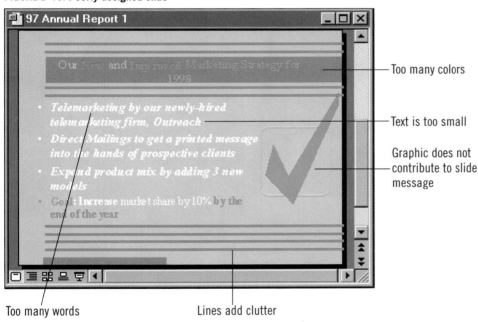

Too many colors

Text is too small

Graphic does not
contribute to slide
message

Too many words

Lines add clutter

CLUES TO USE

Creating your own design templates

You are not limited to the templates in PowerPoint; you can either modify a PowerPoint template or create your own presentation template. For example, you might want to use your company's color as a slide background or incorporate your company's logo on every slide. If you modify an existing template, you can keep, change, or delete any color, graphic, or font. To create a new template, click File then click New, and on the General Tab double-click Blank Presentation, then click the Blank AutoLayout. Add the design elements you want, then use the Save As command on the File menu to name and save your customized design. Click the Save as type list arrow, and choose Presentation templates. PowerPoint will automatically add a .pot file extension to the filename. Then you can use your customized template as a basis for future presentations.

Practice

▶ Concepts Review

Label each of the elements of the PowerPoint window shown in Figure B-16.

FIGURE B-16

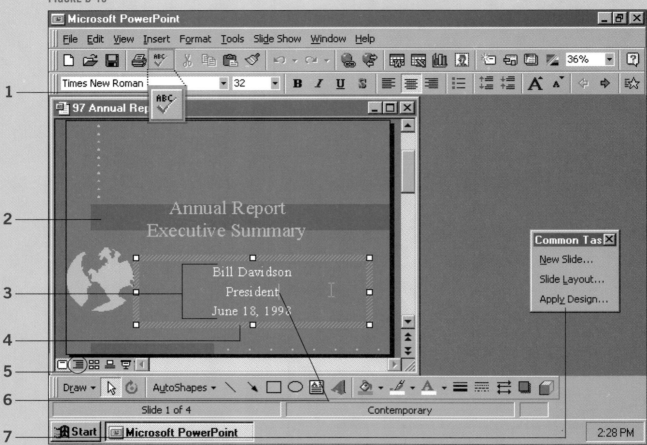

Match each of the terms with the statement that describes its function.

8. **Placeholder**
9. **Insertion point**
10. **Slide icon**
11. **template**

a. A specific design, format, and color scheme that is applied to all the slides in a presentation

b. A blinking vertical line that indicates where your text will appear in a text object

c. A dotted box containing prompt text in which you can enter text

d. In Outline view, the symbol that represents a slide

Select the best answer from the list of choices.

12. The ⌶ pointer shape appears for which one of the following tasks?
  a. Entering text
  b. Switching views
  c. Choosing a new layout
  d. Inserting a new slide

13. To move an item up one line in Outline view:
  a. Click ➡
  b. Click ⬆
  c. Press [Tab]
  d. Click ⬇

14. When the spell checker identifies a word as misspelled, which of the following is *not* a choice?
  a. To ignore this occurrence of the error
  b. To change the misspelled word to the correct spelling
  c. To have the spell checker automatically correct all the errors it finds
  d. To ignore all occurrences in the presentation of the error

15. When you evaluate your presentation, you should make sure it follows which of the following criteria?
  a. The slides should include every piece of information to be presented so the audience can read it.
  b. The slides should use as many colors as possible to hold the audience's attention.
  c. Lots of different typefaces will make the slides more interesting.
  d. The message should be clearly outlined without a lot of extra words.

16. According to the unit, which of the following is *not* a presentation planning guideline?
  a. Determine the purpose of the presentation
  b. Determine what you want to produce when the presentation is finished
  c. Determine which type of output you will need to best convey your message
  d. Determine who else can give the final presentation

17. Which of the following statements is *not* true?
  a. You can customize any PowerPoint template.
  b. The spell-checker will identify "there" as misspelled if the correct word for the context is "their."
  c. The speaker's notes do not appear during the slide show.
  d. PowerPoint has many colorful templates from which to choose.

18. What does a title text placeholder or a main text placeholder become when you type in it?
  a. A text object
  b. A title slide
  c. A text slide
  d. An insertion point

▶ Skills Review

1. Choose a look for your presentation.
  a. If PowerPoint is not running, start PowerPoint, click the Template option button, click OK, then go to Step c.
  b. If PowerPoint is already running, click File on the menu bar, then click New.
  c. Click the Presentation Designs tab.
  d. Review the PowerPoint design templates. Click each template icon to display a picture of the template in the Preview box.

e. When you have finished reviewing the PowerPoint design templates, find and click Contemporary Portrait then click OK. The New Slide dialog box opens.

f. Click OK to choose the Title Slide AutoLayout.

g. Save the presentation as "Weekly Goals" to your Student Disk.

2. **Enter slide text.**
   a. Click the title placeholder.
   b. Type "Product Marketing".
   c. Click the main text placeholder.
   d. Type "Les Bolinger".
   e. Press [Enter], then type "Manager".
   f. Press [Enter], then type "Aug. 2, 1998".
   g. Display and examine the different pointer shapes in PowerPoint. Refer back to Table B-2 to help you display the pointer shapes.
   h. Click in a blank area of the slide.

3. **Create new slides and enter text in Outline view.**
   a. Click New Slide on the Common Tasks toolbar.
   b. Click each of the AutoLayouts in the list. Identify each AutoLayout by its name in the Preview box.
   c. Click the Bulleted List AutoLayout, then click OK.
   d. Enter the text from Table B-5 into the new slide.
   e. Switch to Outline view.
   f. Press [Shift] and click New Slide on the Common Tasks toolbar.
   g. Enter the text from Table B-6 into the new slide.
   h. Press [Ctrl][Enter].
   i. Enter the text from Table B-7 into the new slide.

4. **Enter text in Notes Page view.**
   a. Switch to Notes Page view for Slide 2.
   b. Click the notes placeholder.
   c. Zoom in the view to 66%.
   d. Enter the following speaker's notes:
      — I am interviewing new candidates for the product marketing position.
      — Each of you will interview the candidates who meet initial qualifications the following week.
      — I need all reports for the weekly meeting by Fri.
      — Reminder of the company Profit Sharing party next Fri. Work half day.
      — Open agenda for new division items.
   e. Click the Next Slide button.

TABLE B-5

(Slide title)	Goals for the Week
(Main text object, first indent level)	Les
(Main text object, second indent level)	Interview for new marketing rep
	Discuss new procedures with Pacific Rim marketing reps
	Finish marketing reports--see April by Thurs
	Prepare for weekly division meeting next Mon

TABLE B-6

(Slide title)	Goals for the Week
(Main text object, first indent level)	John
(Main text object, second indent level)	Revise product marketing report
	Set up plan for the annual sales meeting
	Discuss new procedures with U.S. marketing reps
	Thurs--fly to Phoenix for sales meeting planning session

TABLE B-7

(Slide title)	Goals for the Week
(Main text object, first indent level)	April
(Main text object, second indent level)	Complete division advertising plan for next year
	Establish preliminary advertising budget for division VP
	Complete monthly division report--due Fri
	Investigate new advertising agencies for company

f. Enter the following speaker's notes:
  — I need the marketing report by Wed.
  — John: Come by my office later this afternoon to review the sales meeting plan.
  — Open agenda for new division items.
g. Click the Next Slide button.
h. Enter the following speaker's notes:
  — I need to review the advertising company list by Fri.
  — April: See me about weekly division report after this meeting.
  — Status on the advertising budget and next year's advertising plan.
  — Open agenda for new division items.
i. Switch back to Slide view.

5. Check the spelling in the presentation.
  a. Click the Spelling button on the Standard toolbar.
  b. Change any misspelled words. Ignore any words that are correctly spelled but that the spell checker doesn't recognize.
  c. When the spell checker finishes, click OK to close the message box that tells you PowerPoint has finished spell checking.
  d. Save the presentation.

6. Evaluate and print your presentation.
  a. Move to Slide 1, click the Slide Show button, then click the mouse button to move through the slide show.
  b. When the slide show is finished, click the Slide Sorter button.
  c. Evaluate the presentation using the points described in the last lesson as criteria.
  d. Click File on the menu bar, then click Print.
  e. Click the Print what list arrow, then click Notes Pages.
  f. Click the Black & white check box to select it.
  g. Click OK.

► Independent Challenges

1. You have been asked to give a one-day course at a local adult education center. The course is called "Personal Computing for the Slightly Anxious Beginner" and is intended for adults who have never used a computer. One of your responsibilities is to create presentation slides and an outline of the course materials.

Plan and create presentation slides that outline the course material for the students. Create slides for the course introduction, course description, course text and grading, and a detailed syllabus. For each slide, include speaker's notes to help you stay on track during the presentation.

Create your own course material, but assume the following: the school has a computer lab with IBM-compatible computers and Microsoft Windows software; each student has a computer on his or her desk; the prospective students are intimidated by computers but want to learn; and the course is on a Saturday from 9 to 5, with a one-hour lunch.

To complete this independent challenge:

1. Think about the results you want to see, the information you need, and the type of message you want to communicate.
2. Write an outline of your presentation. What content should go on the slides? On the notes pages?
3. Create the presentation by choosing a presentation look, entering the title slide text and the outline text. Remember, you are creating and entering your own presentation material.
4. Create an ending slide that summarizes your presentation.

5. Add speaker's notes to the slides.
6. Check the spelling in the presentation.
7. Save the presentation as Class 1 on your Student Disk.
8. View the slide show, then view the slides in Slide Sorter view. Evaluate your presentation, and adjust it as necessary so that it is focused, clear, concise, and readable.
9. Print the slides and notes pages.
10. Submit your presentation plan, your preliminary sketches, and the final worksheet printout.

2. You are the training director for Events, Inc., which coordinates special events, including corporate functions, weddings, and private parties. Events, Inc. regularly trains groups of temporary employees that they can call on as coordinators, kitchen and wait staff, and coat checkers for specific events. One of your responsibilities is to introduce the monthly training class for new temporary employees. Events, Inc. trains 10 to 15 new workers a month for the peak season between May and September.

Plan and create presentation slides that outline your part of the new employee training. Create slides for the introduction, agenda, company history, dress requirements, principles for interacting successfully with guests, and safety requirements. For each slide, include speaker's notes that you can hand out to the employees.

Create your own presentation and company material, but assume the following: the new employee training class lasts for four hours; the training director's presentation lasts for 15 minutes; and the dress code requires uniforms, supplied by Events, Inc. (white for daytime events, black and white for evening events).

To complete this independent challenge:

1. Think about the results you want to see, the information you need, and the type of message you want to communicate for this presentation.
2. Write a presentation outline. What content should go on the slides? On the notes pages?
3. Create the presentation by choosing a presentation look, entering the title slide text, and the outline text. Remember, you are creating and entering your own presentation material.
4. Create an ending slide that summarizes your presentation.
5. Add speaker's notes to the slides.
6. Check the spelling in the presentation.
7. Save the presentation as Orientation Class on your Student Disk.
8. View the slide show, then view the slides in Slide Sorter view. Evaluate your presentation, and make any changes necessary so that the final version is focused, clear, concise, and readable. Adjust any items as needed.
9. Print the slides and notes pages.
10. Submit your presentation plan and the final worksheet printout.

3. You are an independent distributor of natural foods in Tucson, Arizona. Your business, Harvest Natural Foods, has grown progressively since its inception eight years ago, but sales and profits have plateaued over the last nine months. In an effort to turn your business around, you decide to acquire two major natural food dealers, which would allow Harvest Natural Foods to expand its territory into surrounding states. Use PowerPoint to develop a presentation that you can use to gain more business.

In this independent challenge, you will complete an outline and choose a look for the presentation. Create your own material to complete the slides of the presentation. To begin, open the presentation provided for you on your Student Disk.

To complete this independent challenge:

1. Open a new presentation. Choose the Meadow Presentation design. Add the title "Harvest Natural Foods" as the main title on the title slide.
2. Add five more slides with the following titles: Slide 2–Background; Slide 3–Current Situation; Slide 4–Acquisition Goals; Slide 5–Our Management Team; Slide 6–Funding Required.
3. Think about the results you want, the information you need, and the way you want to communicate your message.

4. Change the sample text in the title and main text placeholders of the slides. Use both Slide and Outline views to enter text.

5. Create a new slide at the end of the presentation. Enter concluding text on the slide, summarizing the presentation's main points.

6. Add speaker's notes to the slides.

7. Check the spelling in the presentation.

8. Save the presentation as Crystal Clear Presentation to your Student Disk.

9. Click the Slide Show button and view the slide show. Evaluate your presentation. If you make any changes, click the Save button to save them.

10. Print the slides as Handouts, 6 per page and including the outline of the presentation.

11. Submit your final printouts.

WEB WORK

4. You are an employee at the Literacy Project of Massachusetts, a nonprofit organization that provides free reading and English-language tutoring for adults across the state. Traditionally, the state government has provided most of the funding for the project. However, due to recent state budget cuts, it has become necessary to solicit private corporations and private trusts for grants. It is your responsibility to develop the outline and basic look for a standard presentation that the president of the Literacy Project can present to various corporate officers and trust fund boards. You want your presentation to emphasize that the English-language tutoring for people from other countries (English as a Second Language, or ESL) is becoming a larger part of the Literacy Project mission.

In this independent challenge, you will complete the outline and choose a look for the funding presentation. Create your own material to complete the slides of the presentation. At least one fact in your presentation should be based on your research on the Internet. To begin, open the presentation provided on your Student Disk.

To complete this independent challenge:

1. Open a new presentation. Choose the Notebook Presentation Design. Add the title "Literary Project on Massachusetts" as the main title on the Title Slide.

2. Add five more slides with the following titles: Slide 2—History of the Literacy Project; Slide 3—Our Accomplishments; Slide 4—Our Mission; Slide 5—Our Goals; Slide 6—Past Funding Sources.

3. Think about the results you want, the information you need, and the way you want to communicate the message. Remember that this presentation should be standardized so the president of the Literacy Project can use it for different audiences.

4. Enter text into the main text placeholders of the slides. Use both Slide and Outline views to enter text.

5. You want to support your argument that there is increased need for funding, based especially on the percentage of people who have limited English language skills. Log on to the Internet and use your browser to go to http://www.course.com. From there, click the link Student On Line Companions, then click Microsoft Office 97 Professional Edition – Illustrated: A First Course page, then click the PowerPoint link for Unit B.

6. Use the Internet to find additional information. Use a search engine (such as http://excite.com or http://www.yahoo.com) to look for information on the 1990 U.S. Census of Population and Housing for the State of Massachusetts. Use the language-skill information you find there (or from any other site) and incorporate it into your presentation.

7. Create a new slide at the end of the presentation. Enter concluding text on the slide, summarizing the financial needs of the Literacy Project.

8. Add speaker's notes to the slides.

9. Spell-check the presentation.

10. Save the presentation as Funding Presentation to your Student Disk.

11. Click the Slide Show button and view the slide show. Evaluate your presentation. If you make any changes, click the Save button to save them.

12. Print the slides and outline of the presentation.

13. Submit your final printouts.

▶ Visual Workshop

Create the marketing presentation shown in Figures B-17 and B-18. Save the presentation as Sales Project 1 on your Student Disk. Review your slides in Slide view, then print your presentation in Slide view and in Outline view.

FIGURE B-17

FIGURE B-18

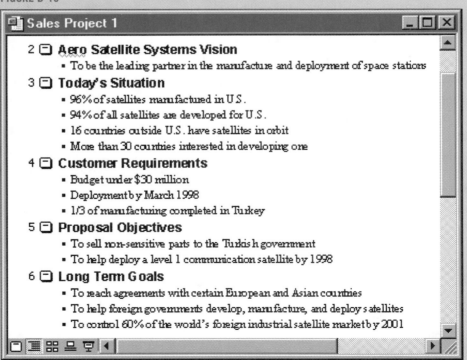

PowerPoint 97

Modifying
a Presentation

Objectives

► **Open an existing presentation**
► **Draw and modify objects**
► **Edit drawing objects**
► **Align and group objects**
► **Add and arrange text**
► **Format text**
► **Change the color scheme and background**
► **Correct text automatically**

After you create the basic outline of your presentation and enter text, you need to add visuals to your slides to communicate your message in the most effective way possible. In this unit, you will open an existing presentation; then draw and modify objects; add, arrange, and format text; change a presentation color scheme; and automatically correct text. After Carrie Armstrong reviews her presentation with her supervisor, Lynn Shaw, Carrie continues to work on the Annual Report Executive Summary presentation for the president of Nomad Ltd. Carrie uses the PowerPoint drawing and text-editing features to bring the presentation closer to a finished look.

Opening an Existing Presentation

Sometimes the easiest way to create a new presentation is by changing an existing one. Revising a presentation saves you from typing duplicate information. You simply open the file you want to change, then use the Save As command to save a copy of the file with a new name. Whenever you open an existing presentation in this book, you will save a copy of it with a new name to your Student Disk, which keeps the original file intact. Saving a copy does not affect the original file. ► To add visuals to her presentation, Carrie opens the presentation she has been working on.

Steps

1. **Start PowerPoint and insert your Student Disk in the appropriate disk drive**

Trouble?

If PowerPoint is already running, click the Open button 🖼 on the Standard toolbar.

2. **Click the Open an existing presentation radio button in the PowerPoint startup dialog box, then click OK**
The Open dialog box opens. See Figure C-1.

3. **Click the Look in list arrow, then locate the drive that contains your Student Disk**
A list of drives opens.

4. **Click the drive that contains your Student Disk**
A list of the files on your Student Disk appears in the Look in list box.

Trouble?

If the Open dialog box on your screen does not show a preview box, click the Preview button 🖼 in the toolbar at the top of the dialog box.

5. **In the Look in list box, click PPT C-1**
The first slide of the selected presentation appears in the preview box on the right side of the dialog box.

6. **Click Open**
The file named PPT C-1 opens. Now save a copy of this file with a new name to your Student Disk, using the Save As command.

7. **Click File on the menu bar, then click Save As**
The Save As dialog box opens. See Figure C-2. The Save As dialog box works just like the Open dialog box.

QuickTip

Ordinarily, when you save copies of files, you may want to use a naming system. Many people use the name of the original file followed by consecutive numbers (1, 2, 3...) or letters (a, b, c...) to designate revisions of the same document or presentation.

8. **Make sure the Save in list box displays the drive containing your Student Disk and the current filename in the File name text box is selected, then type 97 Annual Report 2**
Compare your screen to the Save As dialog box in Figure C-2.

9. **Click Save to close the Save As dialog box**
PowerPoint creates a copy of PPT C-1 with the name 97 Annual Report 2 and closes PPT C-1.

10. **Make sure the percentage in the Zoom text box is 36, click the Restore button on the Presentation window, click Window on the menu bar, then click Fit to page**

FIGURE C-1: Open dialog box

The list of files in
your Look in list box
might be different

Step 3   Step 6

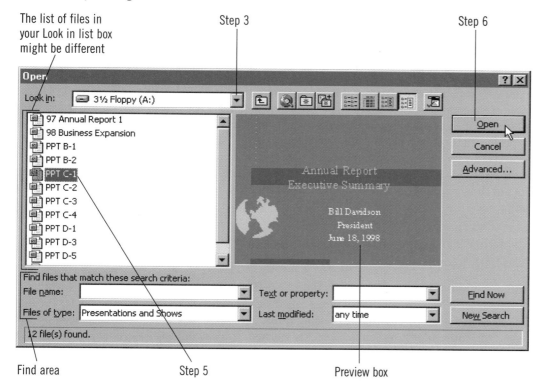

Find area   Step 5   Preview box

FIGURE C-2: Save As dialog box

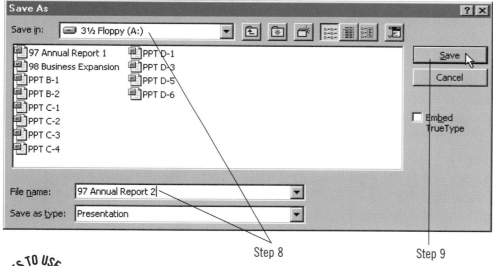

Step 8   Step 9

CLUES TO USE

Searching for a file by properties

If you can't find a file, you can search for it using the
Find area of the Open dialog box. (See Figure C-1.) To
search for a file, click the Open an existing presentation radio button in the PowerPoint startup dialog box
or click the Open button on the Standard toolbar to
display the Open dialog box. Type the name of the presentation file in the File name text box at the bottom
of the dialog box, then click Find Now. PowerPoint
searches for the file in the current drive and directory.

If the file (or a related file) is found, it is displayed in
the Look in list box. You also can type information
into the Text or property text box to help PowerPoint
find a file. For example, if you want to find a presentation that contains the word "investment," type "investment" in the Text or property text box. Then, the Look
in list box lists presentations containing that word (not
just with that word in the title).

Drawing and Modifying Objects

The drawing capabilities of PowerPoint allow you to draw and modify lines, shapes, and pictures to enhance your presentation. Lines and shapes that you create with the PowerPoint drawing tools are objects that you can change and manipulate at any time. These objects have graphic attributes that you can change, such as fill color, line color, line style, shadow, and 3-D effects. To add drawing objects to your slides, you use the buttons on the Drawing toolbar at the bottom of the screen above the status bar. Table C-1 describes some of the Drawing toolbar buttons. Carrie decides to draw an object on Slide 4 of the president of Nomad Ltd's presentation to add impact to her message.

Steps

1. **Click the Next Slide button ▼ three times to move to Slide 4**
   The 1997 Accomplishments slide appears.

2. **Press and hold [Shift], then click the main text object**
   A dotted selection box with small boxes called **sizing handles** appears around the text object. If you click a text object without pressing [Shift], you make the object active, but you do not select the entire object. When an object is selected, you can adjust the size and shape of it or change its attributes. Resize the text object to make room for a drawing object next to it.

Trouble?

If you are not satisfied with the size of the text object, resize it again.

3. **Position the pointer over the right, middle sizing handle, then drag the sizing handle to the left until the text object is about half its original size**
   When you position the pointer over a sizing handle, it changes to ↔ or ┼. It points in different directions depending on which sizing handle it is positioned over. When you drag a text object's sizing handle, the pointer changes to ┼, and a dotted outline representing the size of the text object appears. See Figure C-3. Now, add a shape to the slide.

QuickTip

Position the pointer on top of a button to see its name.

4. **Click the AutoShapes menu button on the Drawing toolbar, point to Stars and Banners, then click the Up Ribbon button 🎗 (third row, first item)**
   After you select a shape in the Stars and Banners menu and move the pointer off the menu, the pointer changes to ┼ again.

QuickTip

To create a circle or square, click the Oval or Rectangle button on the Drawing toolbar and either press [Shift] while dragging the pointer to create a proportional object from the edge of the object or press [Ctrl] while dragging the pointer to create a proportional object from the center of the object.

5. **Position ┼ in the blank area of the slide to the right of the text object, press [Shift], drag down and to the right to create a ribbon object, then release the mouse button and release [Shift]**
   When you release the mouse button, a ribbon object appears on the slide, filled with the default color and outlined with the default line style, as shown in Figure C-4. Pressing [Shift] while you create the object keeps the object's proportions as you change its size.

6. **If your ribbon object is not approximately the same size as the one shown in Figure C-4, press [Shift] and drag one of the sizing handles to resize the object**
   Now change the color of the outline of the ribbon object using the Line Color button.

7. **Click the Line Color list arrow 🖊▾ on the Drawing toolbar, then click the black square**
   PowerPoint applies the color black to the selected object's outline. Next, change the color of the ribbon.

Time To

✔ Save

8. **Click the Fill Color list arrow 🪣▾ on the Drawing toolbar, then click the royal blue square (the second square from the right)**
   PowerPoint fills the ribbon with the royal blue color.

FIGURE C-3: **Resizing the text object**

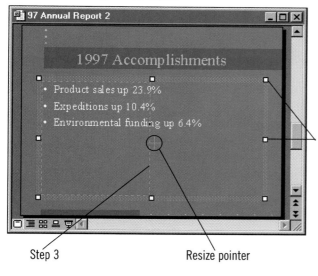

Sizing handles

Step 3   Resize pointer

FIGURE C-4: **Slide showing ribbon object**

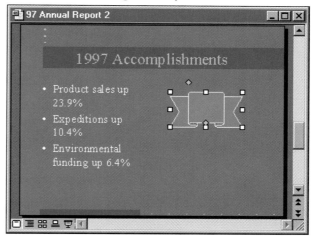

TABLE C-1: **Drawing toolbar buttons**

button	name	use it to
Draw ▾	**Draw menu button**	Choose commands from the Draw menu
AutoShapes ▾	**AutoShapes menu button**	Add one of over 150 shapes
＼	**Line button**	Add lines
↘	**Arrow button**	Add arrows
▢	**Rectangle button**	Add rectangles and squares
○	**Oval button**	Add ovals and circles
▤	**Text Box button**	Add word-processing boxes
◀	**Insert Word Art button**	Open WordArt Galley to apply special text formatting
◇	**Fill Color button**	Add colored fill to any selected object
✎	**Line Color button**	Change the color of any selected line
A	**Font Color button**	Change the color of any selected text
≡	**Line Style button**	Change the thickness of any selected line
▢	**Shadow button**	Apply shadow styles to selected objects
◰	**3-D button**	Apply 3-D styles to selected objects

Editing Drawing Objects

Often, a drawing object does not match the slide or presentation "look" you are trying to achieve. PowerPoint allows you to manipulate the size and shape of objects on your slide. You can change the appearance of all objects by resizing their shape, as you did when you resized the text object in the previous lesson, or by adjusting the objects' dimensions. You also can cut, copy, and paste objects and add text to most PowerPoint shapes. ✐ Carrie changes the shape of the ribbon object, then makes two copies of it to help emphasize each point on the slide.

Steps 1 2 3 4

1. **If the ribbon object is not selected, click it to make the sizing handles appear around the edge of the ribbon object**
   In addition to sizing handles, small diamonds called **adjustment handles** appear above and below the selected object. You drag the adjustment handles to change the appearance of an object, usually its most prominent feature, like the size of an arrow head, or the proportion of a ribbon's center to its "tails." Now, resize the ribbon object.

2. **Drag the bottom right sizing handle up and to the right about ¼" in both directions**
   Next, move the ribbon next to the first bulleted item on the slide.

3. **Position the pointer over the middle of the selected ribbon object**
   The pointer changes to ✛.

Trouble?

If you have trouble aligning the objects with the text, press and hold down [Alt] while dragging the object to turn off the automatic grid.

4. **Drag the ribbon so that the top of the ribbon is aligned with the top of the first bullet**
   A dotted outline appears as you move the ribbon object to help you position it. Compare your screen to Figure C-5, and make any adjustments necessary. Now, make two copies of the ribbon object and place them below the first object.

5. **Position ✛ over the ribbon object, then press and hold [Ctrl]**
   The pointer changes to ▨, indicating that PowerPoint will make a copy of the ribbon object when you drag the mouse.

QuickTip

You can use PowerPoint rulers to help you align objects. To display rulers, position the pointer in a blank area of the slide, right-click, then click Ruler in the pop-up menu or click View on the menu bar and click Ruler.

6. **Drag a copy of the ribbon object down the slide until the dotted lines indicating the position of the copy are aligned with the second bullet, then release the mouse button**
   An exact copy of the first ribbon object appears. Compare your screen to Figure C-6. Next, make a copy of the second ribbon object.

7. **Position the pointer over the second ribbon object, press [Ctrl], then drag a copy of the ribbon object down the slide until it is aligned with the third bullet**
   Compare your screen to Figure C-6. Now add text to the ribbon objects.

8. **Click the top ribbon object, then type 23.9%**
   The text appears in white in the center of the object. The text is now part of the object, so if you move the object, the text will move with it. Now add text to the other two ribbon objects.

Time To

✔ Save

9. **Click the middle ribbon object, type 10.4%; click the bottom ribbon object, type 6.4%, then click a blank area of the slide to deselect the object**
   The graphics you have added reinforce the slide text. The ribbon shape suggests achievement, and the numbers, which are the focus of this slide, are more prominent.

FIGURE C-5: Slide showing resized ribbon object

Adjustment handle

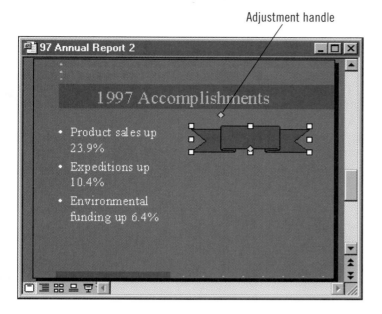

FIGURE C-6: Slide showing duplicated ribbon objects

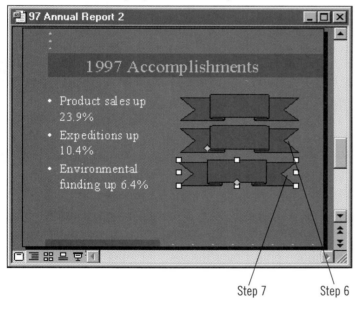

Step 7   Step 6

More ways to change objects

You can change the appearance of an object by
rotating or flipping it, or by making it three-
dimensional. To rotate or flip an object, select it,
click the Draw menu button on the Drawing toolbar,
point to Rotate or Flip, then click one of the available menu commands, as shown in Figure C-7. To
make an object three-dimensional, select it, click the
3-D button, and click one of the options shown on
the 3-D menu in Figure C-8.

FIGURE C-7: Rotate or Flip submenu

FIGURE C-8: 3-D menu

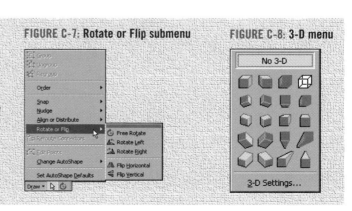

Aligning and Grouping Objects

After you create objects, modify their appearance, edit their size and shape, and position them on the slide, you can align and group them. The Align command aligns objects relative to each other by snapping the selected objects to an invisible grid of evenly spaced vertical and horizontal lines. The Group command groups objects into one object to make editing and moving them much easier. 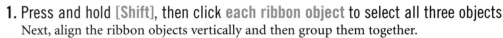 Carrie aligns, groups, and positions the ribbon objects. Then she copies and pastes the grouped ribbon object to the next slide.

1. **Press and hold [Shift], then click each ribbon object to select all three objects**
   Next, align the ribbon objects vertically and then group them together.

2. **Click the Draw menu button on the Drawing toolbar, then point to Align or Distribute**
   A menu of alignment and distribution options appears. The top three options align objects horizontally, whereas the next three options align objects vertically.

3. **Click Align Center**
   The ribbon objects align on their centers, as shown in Figure C-9. Now group the objects together to maintain their exact spacing and position relative to each other.

4. **Click the Draw menu button on the Drawing toolbar, then click Group**
   The ribbon objects group to form one object without losing their individual attributes. Notice the sizing handles now appear around the outer edge of the grouped object, not around each individual object. You can ungroup objects to restore each individual object. Now, move the grouped ribbon object to a specific position on the slide.

5. **Right-click a blank area of the slide, then click Guides in the pop-up menu**
   The PowerPoint guides appear as white dotted lines on the slide. (The dotted lines might be very faint on your screen.) The guides intersect at the center of the slide. Use the guides to position the ribbon object on the slide.

6. **Position the pointer over the vertical guide in a blank area of the slide and press and hold the mouse button until the pointer changes to a guide measurement box, then drag the guide to the right until the guide measurement displays approximately 1.75**
   Now move the grouped ribbon object over the vertical guide until it is centered on the guide.

7. **Press [Shift], drag the grouped ribbon object over the vertical guide until the center sizing handles are approximately centered over the vertical guide**
   Pressing [Shift] while you drag an object constrains the movement to either vertical or horizontal. Next, copy the grouped object to Slide 5.

8. **Right-click the ribbon object, click Copy on the pop-up menu, click the Next Slide button ⬇, then click the Paste button 📋 on the Standard toolbar**
   Slide 5 appears and the ribbon object from Slide 4 is pasted onto Slide 5. Notice that the position of the pasted ribbon object on Slide 5 is the same as it was on Slide 4. Now, hide the guides and ungroup the ribbons so you can change the text in the ribbon objects to match the slide text.

9. **Click the Draw menu button on the Drawing toolbar, click Ungroup, click View on the menu bar, then click Guides**

10. **Triple-click the top ribbon object, then type 28%; triple-click the middle ribbon object, then type 15%; triple-click the bottom ribbon object, type 8%, then click outside the object to deselect it**
    Compare your screen to Figure C-10.

FIGURE C-9: Slide 4 showing aligned ribbon objects

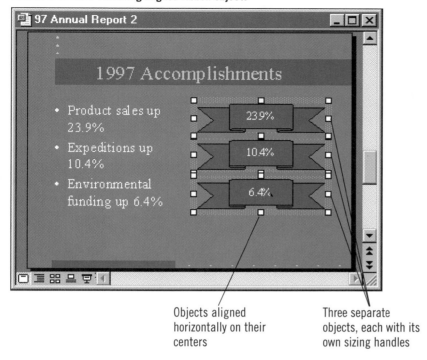

Objects aligned
horizontally on their
centers

Three separate
objects, each with its
own sizing handles

FIGURE C-10: Slide 5 showing pasted ribbon objects

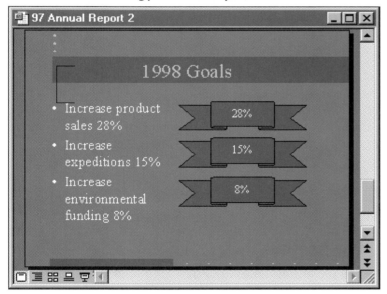

Object stacking order

Stacking order refers to how objects are placed, or layered, on top of one another. The first object you draw is on the bottom of the stack. The last object you draw is on the top of the stack. You can change the order of the stack by right-clicking an object and then clicking Order, or by clicking the Draw menu button on the Drawing toolbar and clicking Order, then choosing the Bring to Front, Send to Back, Bring Forward, or Send Backward command. For example, if you drew a colored box on top of a text object, but you wanted the text to appear on top of the box, you would change the stacking order to bring the text object to the front or send the box object to the back.

Adding and Arranging Text

Using the advanced text editing capabilities of PowerPoint, you can easily add, insert, or rearrange text. On a PowerPoint slide, you either enter text in prearranged text placeholders or use the Text Box button on the Drawing toolbar to create your own text objects when the text placeholders don't provide the flexibility you need. With the Text Box button, you can create two types of text objects: a text label, used for a small phrase inside a box where text doesn't automatically wrap to the next line, and a word processing box, used for a sentence or paragraph where the text wraps inside the boundaries of a box. ✐━━ Carrie already added a slide to contain Nomad Ltd's Mission Statement. Now, she uses the Text Box button to create a word-processing box on Slide 3 to enter the Nomad Ltd mission statement.

1. **Drag the scroll box up the vertical scroll bar until the Slide Indicator box displays Slide 3**
   Now create a word processing box and enter the company mission statement next to the balloon graphic.

2. **Click the Text Box button 📧 on the Drawing toolbar**

3. **Position the pointer about ½" from the left edge of the slide and about even with the top of the balloon graphic already on the slide, then drag the word processing box toward the balloon graphic so that your screen looks like Figure C-11**
   After you click 📧, the pointer changes to ↓. When you begin dragging, the pointer changes to ✛ and an outline of the box appears, indicating how wide a text object you are drawing. After you release the mouse button, an insertion point appears inside the text object, ready to accept text.

QuickTip

To create a text label where text doesn't wrap, click 📧, position ↓ where you want to place the text, then click once and enter the text.

4. **Type Nomad Ltd is a national sporting goods retailer dedicated to delivering high-quality adventure sporting gear and travel.**
   Notice that the word processing box increases in size as your text wraps inside the object. There is a mistake in the mission statement. It should be "adventure travel" not "adventure sporting gear." Correct the error by moving "adventure" to its correct position.

5. **Double-click I on the word adventure to select it**
   When you select a word, the pointer changes from I to ⬉.

QuickTip

You also can use the Cut and Paste buttons on the Standard toolbar and the Cut and Paste commands on the Edit menu to move a word.

6. **Position the pointer on top of the selected word and press and hold the mouse button**
   The pointer changes to ⬉. The dotted insertion line indicates where PowerPoint will place the word when you release the mouse button.

7. **Drag the word "adventure" to the left of the word "travel" in the mission statement, then release the mouse button**

8. **Click a blank area of the slide outside the text object, then save your changes**
   The text object is deselected. Your screen should look similar to Figure C-12.

FIGURE C-11: **Slide showing word processing box ready to accept text**

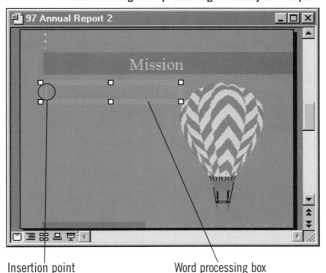

Insertion point   Word processing box

FIGURE C-12: **Slide after adding text to a word processing box**

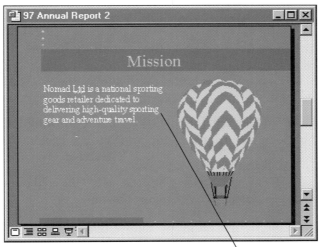

Your text might
wrap differently,
depending on the
size of your word
processing box

Adding comments

The comment feature in PowerPoint allows you to insert comments on a presentation. To insert a comment, click Insert on the menu bar, click Comment, then type your notes. The comment appears in a yellow box in the upper-left corner of the slide, as shown in Figure C-13. Your name as it appears on the General tab of the Options dialog box (on the Tools menu) appears as the first line of the comment. The Reviewing toolbar also appears. To hide or show comments, click View on the menu bar, then click Comments. You also can insert or show a comment by clicking the appropriate button on the Reviewing toolbar .

FIGURE C-13: **Comment on a slide**

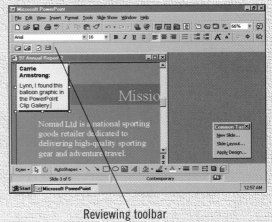
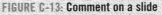

Reviewing toolbar

Formatting Text

Once you have entered and arranged the text in your presentation, you can change and modify the way the text looks to emphasize your message. Important text needs to be highlighted in some way to distinguish it from other text or objects on the slide. For example, if you have two text objects on the same slide, you could draw attention to one text object by changing its color or size. To change the way text looks, you need to select it, and then choose one of the Formatting commands. ▰▰▰ Carrie uses some of the commands on the Formatting and Drawing toolbars to change the way the company mission statement looks.

Steps 1 2 3 4

1. **On Slide 3, press [Shift], then click the main text box**
   The entire text box is selected. Any changes you make will affect all the text in the selected text box. Change the size and appearance of the text to emphasize it on the slide.

2. **Click the Increase Font Size button A** on the Formatting toolbar twice
   The text increases in size to 32 points.

3. **Click the Italic button I on the Formatting toolbar**
   The text changes from normal to italic text. The Italic button, like the Bold button, is a toggle button, which you click to turn the attribute on or off. Next, change the color of the mission statement text.

4. **Click the Font Color list arrow A ▾ on the Drawing toolbar**
   The Font Color menu appears, displaying the eight colors used in the current presentation.

5. **Click the gold box**
   The text in the word-processing box changes to the gold color. Now, put the finishing touch on the mission statement by changing the font.

6. **Click the Font list arrow on the Formatting toolbar**
   A list of available fonts opens, as shown in Figure C-14. The double line at the top of the font list separates the most recent fonts you used from the complete list of available fonts. Choose the Arial font to replace the current font in the text object.

7. **Click the scroll arrows if necessary, then click Arial**
   The Arial font replaces the original font in the text object. Compare your screen to Figure C-15.

Time To
↳ Save

8. **Click a blank area of the slide outside the text object to deselect the text object**

FIGURE C-14: Font list open

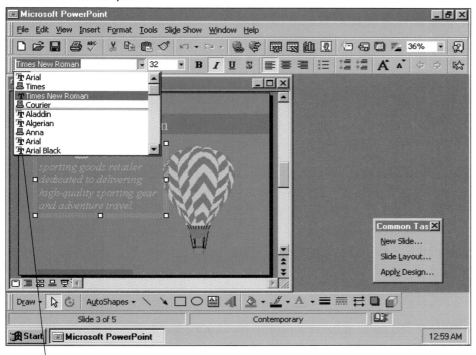

Your list of fonts
may be different

FIGURE C-15: Slide showing formatted text box

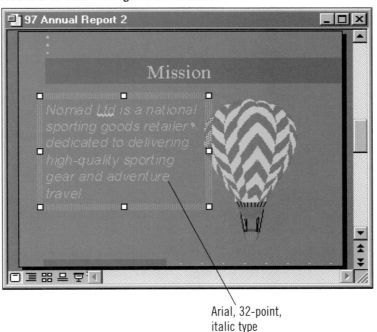

Arial, 32-point,
italic type

CLUES TO USE

Replacing Text and Attributes

As you review your presentation, you may decide to replace certain words or fonts throughout the entire presentation. You can automatically modify words, sentences, fonts, text case, and periods. To replace specific words or sentences, use the Replace command on the Edit menu. To change a font, use the Replace

Fonts command on the Format menu. To automatically add or remove periods from title or body text and to automatically change the case of title or body text, select Style Checker on the Tools menu and click the Options button.

Changing the Color Scheme and Background

Every PowerPoint presentation has a set of eight coordinated colors, called a **color scheme**, that determines the main colors in your presentation for the slide elements: slide background, text and lines, title text, shadows, fills, and accents. See Table C-2 for a description of the slide color scheme elements. The **background** is the area behind the text and graphics. Every design template has a default color scheme and background that you can use, or you can create your own. 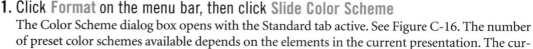 Carrie decides she doesn't like the solid blue color of the presentation background, so she decides to change it.

1. Click Format on the menu bar, then click Slide Color Scheme
   The Color Scheme dialog box opens with the Standard tab active. See Figure C-16. The number of preset color schemes available depends on the elements in the current presentation. The current color scheme is selected with a black border. Replace the current color scheme.

2. Click the bottom-left color scheme with the teal background, then click Apply to All
   The dialog box closes, and the new color scheme is applied to all the slides in the presentation. Now, change the background shading to emphasize the presentation's message.

3. Click Format on the menu bar, then click Background
   The Background dialog box opens.

4. In the Background fill section, click the list arrow below the preview of the slide, click Fill Effects, then click the Gradient tab
   See Figure C-17. Change the background colors to a combination of teal and black.

5. In the Colors section, click the Two colors option button, click the Color 2 list arrow, then click the black box
   The horizontal shading style is selected, as is the first of the four variants, showing that the background is shaded from color 1 (teal) on the top to color 2 (black) on the bottom.

6. In the Shading Styles section, click the Diagonal up option button, click OK, then click Apply to all
   The background is now shaded from teal (upper-left) to black (lower-right), and the text stands out because it is on the lighter color. Next, make the title color brighter.

7. Click Format on the menu bar, click Slide Color Scheme and click the Custom tab
   The eight colors for the selected color scheme appear.

8. In the Scheme colors section, click the Title text color box, then click Change Color
   The Title Text Color dialog box opens with the current Title text color selected.

9. Click the yellow color cell just above and to the left of the current color, as shown in Figure C-18
   The Current color and the New color appear in the box in the lower-right of the dialog box. Now, apply this scheme to the presentation, and save it as a standard scheme for future use.

10. Click OK, click Add As Standard Scheme, then click Apply to All
   PowerPoint updates the color scheme in all your slides, and the title text is changed to the lighter yellow. The next time you open the Color Scheme dialog box in this presentation, your new scheme will appear, along with the existing schemes.

QuickTip

To apply a new color scheme to only selected slides, switch to Slide Sorter view, select the slides you want to change, then click Apply instead of Apply to All in the dialog box.

QuickTip

To see which colors are used in the current color scheme, click a color button on the Drawing toolbar, such as the Font Color button, then move the pointer over each of the eight colors below the Automatic box.

Time To

✓ Save

FIGURE C-16: **Color Scheme dialog box**

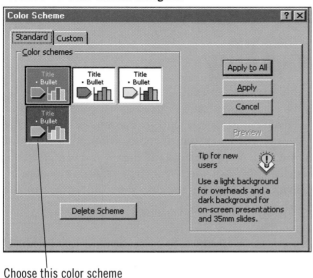

Choose this color scheme

FIGURE C-17: **Gradient tab of Fill Effects dialog box**

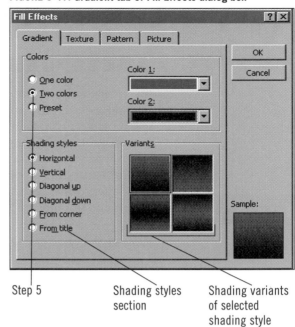

Step 5   Shading styles   Shading variants
             section   of selected
                                    shading style

FIGURE C-18: **Standard tab in the Title Text Color dialog box**

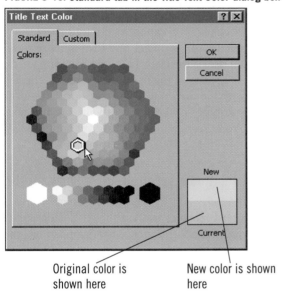

Original color is   New color is shown
shown here   here

TABLE C-2: **Color scheme elements**

scheme element	description
Background color	Color of the slide's canvas, or background
Text and lines color	Used for text and drawn lines; contrasts with the background color
Shadows color	Color of the text's shadow or other object; generally a darker shade of the background color
Title text color	Used for slide title; like the text and line colors, contrasts with the background color
Fills color	Contrasts with both the background and the text and line colors
Accent color	Colors used for other objects on slides, such as bullets
Accent and hyperlink colors	Colors used for accent objects and for hyperlinks you insert
Accent and followed hyperlink	Color used for accent objects and for hyperlinks after they have been clicked

Correcting Text Automatically

As you enter text into your presentation, the AutoCorrect feature in PowerPoint automatically replaces misspelled words and corrects some word-capitalization mistakes, whether on slides or in speaker notes, without bringing up a dialog box or a menu; for example, if you type "THursday" instead of "Thursday," PowerPoint corrects it as soon as you type it. If there is a word you often type incorrectly, for example, if you type "tehm" instead of "them," you can create an AutoCorrect entry that corrects that misspelled word whenever you type it in a presentation.
After reviewing the presentation, Lynn asks Carrie to add one more slide, thanking the employees and stockholders for their support.

Steps 1 2 3 4

1. **Click the Next Slide button** ⬇ **as necessary to move to Slide 5, hold down [Shift] and click New Slide on the Common Tasks toolbar**
   A new bulleted list on Slide 6 appears. First, check the AutoCorrect dialog box to see which options are selected and to have PowerPoint automatically correct a particular word.

2. **Click Tools on the menu bar, then click AutoCorrect**
   The AutoCorrect dialog box opens, as shown in Figure C-19. The top part of the dialog box contains check boxes that have PowerPoint automatically change two capital letters at the beginning of a word to a single capital letter, capitalize the first letter of a sentence and the names of days, and correct capitalization errors caused by accidental use of the Caps Lock key. The fifth check box, Replace text as you type, tells PowerPoint to change any of the mistyped words on the left in the scroll box in the lower part of the dialog box with the correct word on the right. The scroll box contains customized entries. For example, if you type (c), PowerPoint will automatically change it to ©, the copyright symbol. See Table C-3 for a summary of AutoCorrect options.

3. **Click any check boxes that are not selected**

4. **In the Replace text as you type section, click the down scroll arrow to view all the current text replacement entries, then click OK**
   To test the AutoCorrect feature, you decide to enter incorrect text on the fifth slide. First, you'll type text using two capital letters in the word "Thank." Watch what happens to that word when you press [Spacebar].

5. **Click the title placeholder, then type THank You**
   As soon as you pressed [Spacebar] after typing the word "THank," PowerPoint automatically corrected it to read "Thank." Now enter the word "adn," which is currently in the Replace text as you type list.

6. **Click the main text placeholder, type Sales adn Marketing staff, and press [Enter]**
   As soon as you pressed [spacebar] after typing the word "adn," PowerPoint automatically corrected it to read "and." Now, enter the trademark symbol ™ after a product name.

7. **Type OutBack(tm) promotional team, then click outside the main text object**
   As soon as you pressed the spacebar after OutBack(tm), PowerPoint automatically changed the (tm) to the trademark symbol ™.

8. **Click the Slide Sorter View button** ⊞, **click the Maximize button in the Presentation window**
   Compare your screen to Figure C-20. (The Common Tasks toolbar does not appear in the figure.)

9. **Save your presentation, print the slides, then exit PowerPoint**

FIGURE C-19: AutoCorrect dialog box

Automatic
correction options

Type your own
custom AutoCorrect
entries here

Default AutoCorrect
entries

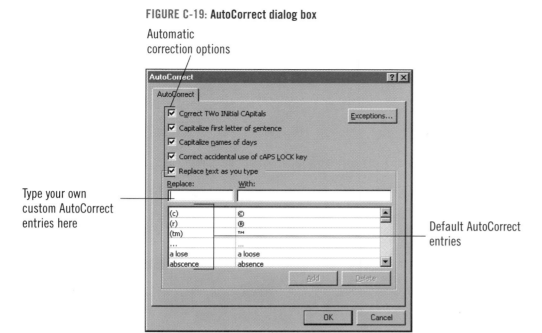

FIGURE C-20: The final presentation

New slide with
corrected text

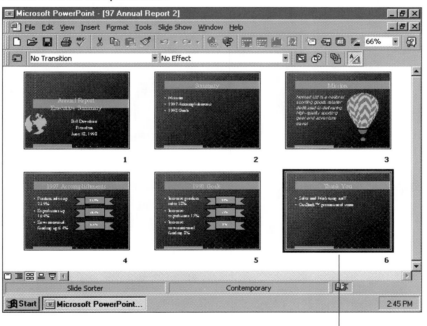

TABLE C-3: AutoCorrect Options

option	action
Turn off AutoCorrect	Click to remove all the check marks in the AutoCorrect dialog box
Edit an AutoCorrect entry	Select the entry in the list, click in the With text box, correct the entry, and click Replace
Delete an AutoCorrect entry	Highlight the entry in the scroll box and click Delete
Rename an AutoCorrect entry	Select the entry in the list, click in the Replace text box, click Delete, type a new name in the Replace box, and click Add

Practice

► Concepts Review

Label each of the elements of the PowerPoint window shown in Figure C-21.

FIGURE C-21

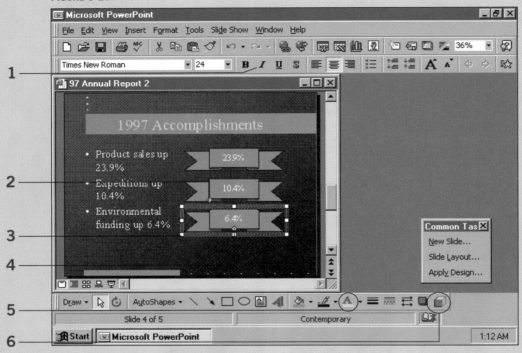

Match each of the terms with the statement that describes its function.

7. **Word processing box**
8. **Text label**
9.
10.
11. **Sizing handles**

a. Button that changes the text color
b. Use this to create a text object on a slide
c. Small boxes that surround an object when it is selected
d. A text object that does not word wrap
e. A text object you create by dragging to create a box after clicking the Text Box button

Select the best answer from the list of choices.

12. **How do you draw or resize an object proportionally?**
    a. Press and hold the spacebar while you draw or resize the object.
    b. Press and hold [Shift] or [Ctrl] while you draw or resize the object.
    c. Very carefully drag sizing handles on each side of the object so the proportions stay the same.
    d. Double-click, then draw or resize the object.

13. **What is the best way to align objects?**
    a. Drag each object to the center of the slide.
    b. Align each object using a reference point on the PowerPoint window.
    c. Select all the objects, then click Group on the Draw menu.
    d. Select all the objects, click Align or Distribute on the Draw menu, then click an alignment option.

14. How do you change the size of a PowerPoint object?

a. Move a sizing handle.

b. Click the Resize button.

c. Move the adjustment handle.

d. You can't change the size of a PowerPoint object.

15. What would you use to position objects at a specific place on a slide?

a. PowerPoint placeholders

b. PowerPoint guides and rulers

c. PowerPoint grid lines

d. PowerPoint anchor lines

▶ Skills Review

1. Open an existing presentation.

a. Start PowerPoint, click the Open an existing presentation radio button in the PowerPoint startup dialog box, then click OK. If PowerPoint is already open, click the Open button on the Standard toolbar.

b. Make sure the drive containing your Student Disk is listed in the Look in list box, type "ppt" in the File name text box at the bottom of the dialog box, then click Find Now to find all the files on your Student Disk that have ppt in the filename and that are presentation or show files.

c. Click PPT C-2 in the Look in list box to select it.

d. Click Open.

e. Click File on the menu bar, then click Save As.

f. Make sure the text in the File name text box is highlighted, type "Series Report", then click Save.

2. Draw and modify an object.

a. Move to Slide 3, then Click the AutoShapes menu button on the Drawing toolbar.

b. Point to Stars and Banners, and click the Explosion 1 button.

c. Position the pointer in the lower-right corner of the slide, press [Shift], then drag up to create an explosion shape about 1½" in diameter, so that it partially covers the text.

d. Click the Line Color button on the Drawing toolbar, then click No Line.

e. Click the Shadow button on the Drawing toolbar, then click the Shadow Style 1 button in the upper left.

f. Click the Draw menu button, point to Order, then click Send to Back, then deselect the object.

g. Click the Save button on the Standard toolbar.

3. Edit drawing objects.

a. Move to Slide 4, and click the arrow object to select it.

b. Drag the right, middle, sizing handle to the left about 1".

c. Make two copies of the arrow object by holding down [Ctrl] and dragging the arrow object. Position the copies approximately as shown in Figure C-22.

d. Click the left arrow object, then type "Teams"; click the middle arrow object, then type "Goals"; click the right arrow object, then type "Resources"; click the cube, type "OutBack," press [Enter], then type "Product."

e. Drag to select the OutBack Product text on the cube, click the Font Color button, and click the black square.

f. Click the Save button on the Standard toolbar.

4. Align and group objects.

a. Select the four objects on Slide 4.

b. Click the Draw menu button, point to Align or Distribute, and click Align Bottom.

c. Click the Font list arrow and click Arial, then click the Italic button on the Standard toolbar.

d. Select only the three arrow objects, click the Draw menu button on the Drawing toolbar, then point to Align or Distribute, and click Distribute Horizontally.

e. Click the Draw menu button on the Drawing toolbar, then click Group.

f. Click the right mouse button in a blank area of the slide, then click Guides on the pop-up menu.

g. Move the vertical guide to the left and stop when you reach the approximate measurement 4.15.

h. Move the horizontal guide down and stop when you reach the measurement 3.00.

i. Click the grouped object, then move the object until the bottom-left corner of the object snaps to the corner where the guides intersect. If your object does not snap to the guides, click the Draw menu button, point to Snap, and make sure the "To Grid" command on the Snap menu is selected (it should look indented).

j. Right-click in an empty area of the slide, then click Guides to hide the guides. Compare your screen to Figure C-22 and make any adjustments necessary.

FIGURE C-22

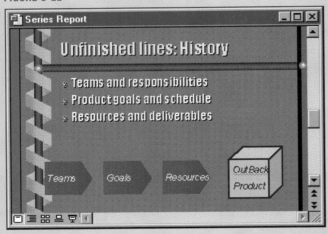

5. Add and arrange text.

a. Move to Slide 2, click the I-beam cursor to place the blinking insertion point at the end of the word "developed" in the main text object.

b. Press [Enter], then type "Consumer response to the series".

c. Click the Text Box button on the Drawing toolbar, position the pointer near the bottom of the slide, below the tree graphic, then drag to create a box about 3" wide.

d. Type "Department product managers have 20 minutes for line reports."

e. Double-click the word "product," then drag it in front of the word "line."

6. Format text.

a. Click in the Presentation window to deselect the word processing box, press [Shift], then click the word processing box you just created again to select it.

b. Click the Font Color list arrow on the Drawing toolbar, then click the black box.

c. Click the Increase Font Size button on the Formatting toolbar.

d. Move the text object so the text is inside the slide border, then deselect the text.

e. Press [Shift], then click the main text object.

f. Click the Bullets button on the Formatting toolbar to add bullets to the list.

g. Click on a blank area of the slide to deselect the text object then save your changes.

7. Change a presentation color scheme and background.

a. Click Format on the menu bar, then click Slide Color Scheme.

b. Click the lower-left color scheme, with the white background and green arrow, then click Apply to All.

c. Click Format on the menu bar, then click Background.

d. Click the list arrow below the slide miniature, click Fill Effects, then click the Gradient tab.

e. Click the Two colors option button, click the Color 2 list arrow, then click the light green square on the far right.

f. In the Shading Styles section, click the Diagonal up option button, click OK, and click Apply to all.

g. Click Format on the menu bar, click Slide Color Scheme, and click the Custom tab.

h. Click the Title text color square, then click Change Color.

i. Click the third gray cell from the left in the bottom row, then click OK.

j. Click Add As Standard Scheme.

k. Click the Standard tab. The new color scheme is added to the available color scheme list.

l. Click Apply to All, then save your changes.

8. Correct text automatically.

a. Go to Slide 5 and press the Caps Lock key.

b. Click the I-beam pointer after the word "report," press [Enter] to add a fourth bullet, and type "Schedules" (it will come out sCHEDULES), but do not press [Enter].

c. Press [Enter] and notice how PowerPoint reverses the capitalization as soon as you press [Enter].

d. Type "All by next thursday" and press [Spacebar]. Notice that PowerPoint automatically capitalizes the word "Thursday" for you.

e. Check the spelling in the presentation and make any changes necessary.

f. Go to Slide 1, view the final slide show, and evaluate your presentation.

g. Save your changes, print the slides and then close the presentation.

▶ Independent Challenges

1. You work for Chicago Language Systems (CLS), a major producer of computer-based language training materials sold in bookstores and computer stores. CLS products include CD-ROMs with accompanying instructional books. Twice a year, the Acquisitions and Product Development departments hold a series of meetings, called Title Meetings, to determine the new title list for the following production term. The meetings, which last an entire day, are also used to decide which current CD titles need to be revised. As the director of acquisitions, you chair the September Title Meeting and present the basic material for discussion. You decide to create a presentation that describes the basic points to be addressed.

To complete this independent challenge:

1. Open the file PPT C-3 on your Student Disk and save it as "Title Meeting 9-98".

2. After you open the presentation, look through it in Slide view and consider the results you want to see on each slide. What slides could you add or delete? Look at the organization of the presentation; you may need to make some adjustments in Outline view. If you reorganize the presentation, be able to support your decision.

3. Add a design template to the presentation.

4. Evaluate the fonts used throughout the presentation. Format the text so that the most important information is the most prominent.

5. Use the drawing tools to add appropriate shapes that amplify the most important parts of the slide content. Format the objects using color and shading. Use the Align and Group commands to organize your shapes.

6. Evaluate the color scheme and the background colors. Make any changes you feel will enhance the presentation.

7. Spell check the presentation, view the final slide show and evaluate your presentation. Make any changes necessary.

8. Save the presentation, print the slides, and submit your final printouts.

2. The Software Learning Company is a Silicon Valley-based corporation dedicated to the design and development of instructional software that helps college students learn software applications. As the company's main graphics designer, you have been asked by the marketing manager to design and develop a standardized set of graphics for the company that all the employees can use for their business presentations. To help promote the company, the marketing group unveiled a new company slogan: "Software is a snap!"

Plan and create standard text and graphical objects for the Software Learning Company that employees can copy and paste into their business presentations. Create five different slides with a company logo, using the AutoShapes toolbar, and a company slogan, using the Text tool. The marketing group will decide which of the five designs looks best. Create your own presentation slides, but assume that: the company colors are blue and green.

To complete this independent challenge:

1. Think about the results you want to see and the information you need to create this presentation.
2. Sketch your logos and slogan designs on a piece of paper. What text and graphics do you need for the slides?
3. Create a new presentation using a design template, and save it as "Software Learning" on your Student Disk. Remember, you are creating and entering your own presentation material. The logo and the marketing slogan should match each other in tone, size, and color, and the logo objects should be grouped together to make it easier for other employees to copy and paste.
4. Change the color scheme and background as necessary.
5. Spell check the presentation, View the final slide show, and evaluate your presentation. Make any changes necessary.
6. Save the presentation and print the slides and notes pages (if any).
7. Submit your presentation plan, preliminary sketches, and the final presentation printout.

3. You work for Scenes, Inc., a firm that designs and builds sets for television shows, and theater, opera, and ballet companies in California. One of your responsibilities is to create a process flow diagram for the new apprentice construction team to follow during the building of a theater set. The process flow diagram describes the construction process from start to finish. Plan and create a construction process flow diagram using PowerPoint text and drawing tools. The diagram should include shapes, lines, and text labels to indicate the flow of information. Assume that the process includes filling out materials requisition forms, getting the requisitions signed by the director, ordering materials, setting the construction schedule, hiring contract workers, building backdrops, platforms and set pieces (statues, pillars, etc.), installation, and finishing work.

To complete this independent challenge:

1. Think about the desired results, the information you need to create this presentation, and the type of message you want to communicate. What text and graphics are needed for the slides?
2. Create a new presentation using a design template. Save it as Construction Process to your Student Disk. Remember, you are creating and entering your own presentation material. Group the diagram objects together to make it easier for other employees to change.
3. You can add explanatory notes using Speaker's notes if this will help the viewer understand your decisions.
4. Evaluate your color scheme and background. Make changes to make the flow diagram the central focus of each slide.
5. Spell check the presentation, view the final slide show and evaluate your presentation. Make any changes necessary.
6. Save your changes and print the slides and notes pages (if any).
7. Submit your presentation plan, preliminary sketches, and the final presentation printout.

4. You are the customer service manager for State Bank, a full-service bank with its home office located in San Diego, California, and six branches located throughout the state. To keep tellers and customer service personnel up to date with new services, procedures, and general bank policy information, State Bank conducts a three-day update seminar once every six months for the entire customer service department at each branch office. It is your job to travel around the state to each of State Bank's regional offices and give the first day of the three-day seminar. Your portion of the seminar covers new services and procedures.

To complete this independent challenge:

1. Open the file PPT C-4 on your Student Disk and save it as "State Training Sept 98".
2. After you open the presentation, look through it in Slide Show view and think about the results you want to see on each slide. What information is provided, and what could you add? How do you want to communicate the message? Look at the organization of the presentation; you may need to make some adjustments. If you decide to reorganize the presentation, be able to support your decision.
3. Apply an appropriate design template to the presentation.
4. Customers have been asking if State Bank will be starting a page on the World Wide Web (WWW). In fact, the vice president asked you to look into the issue and to do some research to help you make suggestions on what the Web page should contain. Create two new slides in your presentation that outline some of the major elements you think the State Bank Web page will have. To get ideas for content, go to the following WWW sites:
   - Log on to the Internet and use your browser to go to http://www.course.com. From there, click the link Student On Line Companions, then click the Microsoft Office 97 Professional Edition—Illustrated: A First Course page, then click the PowerPoint link for Unit C.

   Circle the links there then choose several elements from these web pages that you think would be useful for a State Bank web page, and create a slide that outlines your ideas.
5. Make sure the AutoCorrect options are all selected, then create a new slide titled "Training Seminar Agenda" with the information provided in Table C-4. Put the slide in the proper place so it flows in the presentation.

TABLE C-4

bullet	information
First bullet point	Sept 23rd (morning session) — Bank Policy on minority hiring
Second bullet point	Sept 23rd (afternoon session) — Bank Role in Community Development
Third bullet point	Sept 24th (morning session) — Federal Regulations on FHA loans
Fourth bullet point	Sept 24th (afternoon session) — Federal Regulations on Retirement Allocation advice

6. Add a word-processing box to Slide 3, and add text that describes a two-day turnaround time that anxious first-time buyers will appreciate.
7. Use the drawing tools to add shapes to your slides that help reflect the presentation message and environment. Add text to any shapes you feel would help communicate the message more clearly. Format the objects using color and shading. Use the Align and Group commands to organize your shapes.
8. Change the color scheme and background.
9. Add speaker's notes (at least one sentence) to each slide.
10. Spell check the presentation, view the final slide show and evaluate your presentation.
11. Save your changes and print the Notes Pages and Handouts (6 slides per page) of the presentation.

PowerPoint 97

▶ Visual Workshop

Create a three-slide presentation that looks like the examples shown in Figures C-25, C-26, and C-27. Save the presentation as Bowman Logos to your Student Disk. Spell check the presentation, then save and print the slides in Slide view. (*Hint:* Design 8 uses the 3-D Settings option on the 3-D menu. You can find other effects using the Object command on the Format menu on the menu bar.)

FIGURE C-25

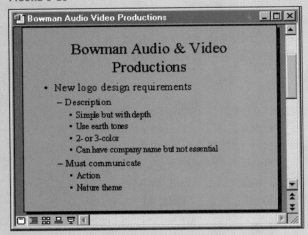

FIGURE C-26

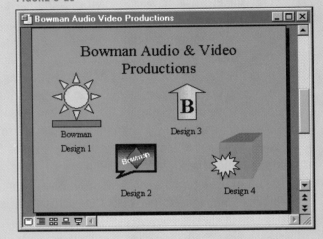

FIGURE C-27

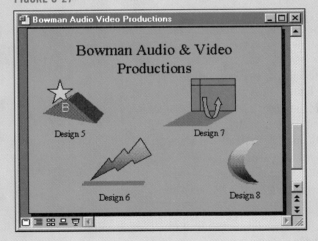

Enhancing
a Presentation

Objectives

- ► **Insert clip art**
- ► **Insert and crop a picture**
- ► **Embed a chart**
- ► **Enter and edit data in the datasheet**
- ► **Format a chart**
- ► **Use slide show commands**
- ► **Set slide show timings and transitions**
- ► **Set slide animation effects**

After completing the content of your presentation, you can enhance it to make it more visually interesting. When you prepare a presentation, it's important to supplement your slide text with clip art or graphics, charts, and other visuals that help communicate your content and keep your slide show interesting. In this unit, you will learn how to insert three of the most common visual enhancements: a clip art image, a picture, and a chart. These objects are created in other programs. After you add the visuals, you will rehearse the slide show and add special effects. Carrie Armstrong has changed the presentation based on feedback from Lynn and the president of Nomad Ltd. Now, she wants to revise the Annual Report Executive Summary presentation to make it easier to understand and more interesting to watch.

Inserting Clip Art

PowerPoint has over 1000 professionally designed images, called **clip art**, that you can place in your presentation. Using clip art is the easiest and fastest way to enhance your presentations. Clip art is stored in a file index system called a **gallery** that sorts the clip art into categories. You can open the Clip Gallery in one of three ways: by double-clicking a clip art placeholder from an AutoLayout; using the Insert Clip Art button 🖼 on the Standard toolbar; or choosing Picture, then Clip Art on the Insert menu. As with drawing objects, you can modify clip art images by changing their shape, size, fill, or shading. Clip art is the most widely used method of enhancing presentations, and it is available from many sources outside Clip Gallery, including the World Wide Web (WWW) and collections on CD-ROMs. ◀▬▬ Carrie wants to add a picture from the Clip Gallery to one of the slides and then adjust its size and placement.

Steps

1. Open the presentation **PPT D-1** from your Student Disk, save it as **97 Annual Report Final** to your Student Disk, make sure it is at 36% zoom, click the **Restore Window** button on the presentation window, click **Window** on the menu bar, then click **Fit to Page**

2. Drag the vertical scroll box to the last slide in the presentation, Slide 9 of 9
   The Thank You slide appears. Change the AutoLayout to a layout that contains a clip art placeholder, so you'll be able to easily add a piece of clip art to the slide.

3. Click **Slide Layout** on the Common Tasks toolbar
   The Slide Layout dialog box opens with the Bulleted List AutoLayout selected. Choose the layout with bulleted text on the left and clip art on the right.

4. Click the **Text & Clip Art AutoLayout** (third row, first column), then click **Apply**
   PowerPoint applies the Text and Clip Art AutoLayout to the slide, which makes the existing text object narrower, and then inserts a clip art placeholder, where the clip art object will be placed on the slide.

5. Double-click the **clip art placeholder**
   The Microsoft Clip Gallery 3.0 dialog box opens, similar to Figure D-1.

6. Make sure the **Clip Art tab** is selected and in the category list on the left, drag the scroll box to the bottom, then click **Transportation**
   If the Transportation category doesn't appear, select a different category. The preview box to the right of the categories displays small previews of the clip art in the Transportation category. Now, select a graphic and import it to Slide 9.

7. In the preview box, click the **down scroll arrow** twice, click the **sailboat** shown in Figure D-1, then click **Insert**
   The picture of the sailboat appears on the right side of the slide, and the Picture toolbar automatically opens. If you don't have a picture of a sailboat in your Clip Gallery, select a similar picture. Now, resize the sailboat picture.

8. Place the pointer over the lower-right sizing handle, hold down [Shift], and drag the handle slightly up and to the left, until the image height is approximately the same as the height of the text box
   Remember, pressing [Shift] while resizing an object causes the object to be resized proportionately. Now, adjust the placement of the clip art and text blocks.

9. With the sailboat object still selected, press the keyboard arrow keys until the sailboat is centered between the text block and the right edge of the slide as shown in Figure D-2, then deselect the picture
   Compare your screen with Figure D-2, and make any necessary corrections.

Trouble?

If this is the first time the Clip Gallery is opened, PowerPoint needs to build the clip art visual index. Click OK to build the index, then click OK when you get a message telling you that the index is complete. If a dialog box appears telling you that additional clips are available on the Microsoft Office 97 CD-ROM disc, click OK to close the dialog box.

Time To

✔Save

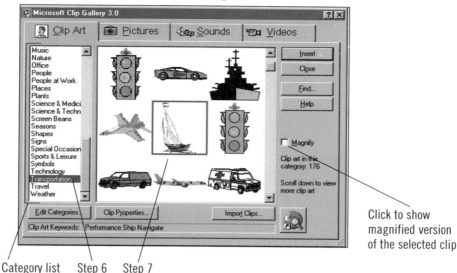

Category list   Step 6   Step 7

Click to show
magnified version
of the selected clip

FIGURE D-2: Last slide with sailboat resized and repositioned

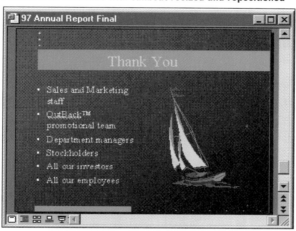

More about Clip Gallery

To add other clip art (or pictures, sounds, or videos) to the Clip Gallery, you must first import them into the Clip Gallery using the Import Clips command button. When you import a clip, Clip Gallery asks you to assign keywords to each one. Keywords are words you use to quickly find the object in the future. Notice in Figure D-1 the keywords Performance, Ship, and Navigate below the preview box have already been assigned to the selected sailboat graphic. To use keywords to find an image, click the Find button in the Clip Gallery dialog box to open the Find Clip dialog box shown in Figure D-3. Type a keyword in the Keyword text box or click the Keyword list arrow and click a keyword, then click Find Now. Clip Gallery places images of all objects that have that keyword assigned to them in the Clip Gallery window and assigns a new category to them called [Results of Last Find].

FIGURE D-3: Find Clip dialog box

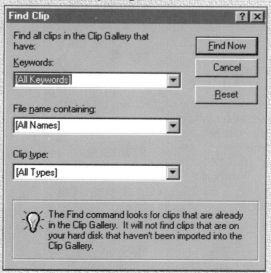

Inserting and Cropping a Picture

A picture in PowerPoint is a scanned photograph, a piece of line art, clip art, or other artwork that is created in another program and inserted into a PowerPoint presentation. You can insert over 20 types of pictures using the Insert Picture command. As with other PowerPoint objects, you can move or crop an inserted picture. **Cropping** a picture means to hide a portion of the picture in cases where you don't want to include all of the original. ◢ Carrie inserts a picture, crops it, and adjusts its background.

Steps

1. Go to Slide 7, titled "1997 Environmental Funding," click Slide Layout on the Common Tasks toolbar, click the Text & Object AutoLayout (fourth row, first column), then click Apply

2. Double-click the object placeholder
   The Insert Object dialog box appears. You will insert a picture that has already been saved in a file.

3. Click the Create from file option button
   The dialog box changes to a text box that lists the filename of the object you will insert.

4. Click Browse, click the Look in list arrow, click the drive containing your Student Disk, click PPT D-2 in the Look in list, click OK, then click OK in the Insert Object dialog box
   The picture appears on the slide, and the Picture toolbar automatically opens. See Figure D-4. Now that the picture is in place, crop out the sun from the top to give the picture more impact.

5. Click the Crop button ⊞ on the Picture toolbar, then place the cursor over the top middle handle of the tree picture
   The pointer changes to ⌐.

6. Drag the top edge downward until the dotted line indicating the top edge of the picture is below the sun image, as shown in Figure D-5
   As you drag with the cropping tool, the pointer changes to ⊥. Now, increase the size of the text and the picture to make better use of the space on the slide.

7. Click twice on a blank area of the slide to deselect the cropping tool and the picture, press [Shift] and click on the main text box, then click the Increase Font Size button A⁺ on the Formatting toolbar

8. Click on the picture to select it, press [Shift], drag the upper-right sizing handle until the right border of the picture is touching the edge of the slide, then release [Shift] and drag the selected picture up and to the left to center it in the space
   The tree would look better without its white background. Make the background transparent.

9. With the image still selected, click the Set Transparent Color button ⃠ on the Picture toolbar, click the white background, and click on a blank area of the slide to deselect the picture
   The white background is no longer visible, and the tree contrasts well with the teal background, as shown in Figure D-6.

10. Save your changes

Trouble?
If the Picture toolbar does not appear, right-click on the picture, then click Show Picture Toolbar on the pop-up menu.

Trouble?
If the Microsoft Paint program becomes active when you click on the picture, click anywhere in the window outside of the picture to return to PowerPoint.

FIGURE D-4: Inserted picture object and Picture toolbar

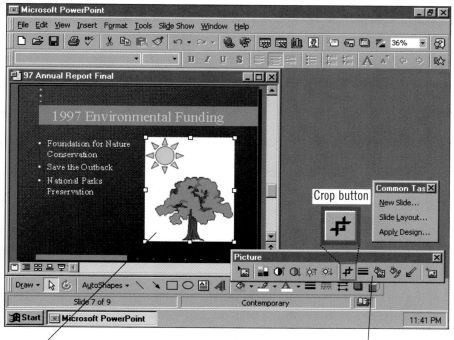

Crop button

Picture toolbar may appear in a different position on your screen

Inserted picture object

FIGURE D-5: Using the cropping pointer to crop out the sun image

Cropping pointer changes shape as you drag

FIGURE D-6: Completed slide with the cropped and resized graphic

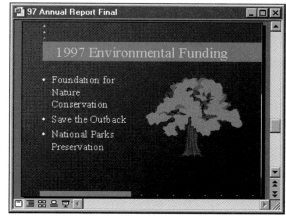

Graphics in PowerPoint

You can insert many different types of pictures with a variety of graphics **formats**, or file types, in PowerPoint. By looking at its file extension, you can see what format a graphic is in. The clip art that comes with PowerPoint is in **.wmf**, or **Windows metafile**, format. A graphic in .wmf format can be ungrouped (using the Ungroup command on the Draw menu) into its separate PowerPoint objects and then edited with PowerPoint drawing tools. **Bitmap** pictures, which have the file extension **.bmp**, cannot be ungrouped. Although you cannot ungroup .bmp files, you can still modify some of their characteristics with PowerPoint drawing tools. The clip art sailboat you inserted in the last lesson is in .wmf format, and the tree picture you inserted in this lesson is in .bmp format.

Embedding a Chart

Often, the best way to communicate information is with a visual aid such as a chart. PowerPoint comes with a program called **Microsoft Graph** (often called **Graph**) that you use to create graph charts for your slides. A **graph object** is made up of two components: a **datasheet**, containing the numbers you want to chart, and a **chart**, which is the graphical representation of the datasheet. Table D-1 lists the Graph chart types. When you insert a graph into PowerPoint, you are actually embedding it. **Embedding** an object means that the object copy becomes part of the PowerPoint file, but you can double-click on the embedded object to display the tools of the program in which the object was created. You can use these tools to modify the object. If you modify the embedded object, the original object file does not change. Carrie wants to embed a Graph object in the slide containing the 1997 Sales Analysis.

Steps

1. **Go to Slide 5, titled "1997 Sales Analysis"**
   Because you are going to place a chart on this slide, change the slide layout to accommodate a chart.

2. **Click Slide Layout on the Common Tasks toolbar**
   The Slide Layout dialog box opens with the Bulleted List AutoLayout selected. Select the Chart AutoLayout to replace the current layout.

3. **Click Chart AutoLayout (second row, far right), then click Apply**
   The Chart AutoLayout, which contains a chart placeholder, appears on the slide. Double-click the chart placeholder to open Microsoft Graph.

4. **Double-click the chart placeholder**
   Microsoft Graph opens and embeds a default datasheet and chart into the slide, as shown in Figure D-7. The Graph datasheet is composed of rows and columns. The intersection of a row and a column is called a **cell**. Cells are referred to by their row and column location; for example, the cell at the intersection of column A and row 1 is called cell A1. Cells along the left column and top row of the datasheet typically display **data labels** that identify the data in a column or row; for example, "East" and "1st Qtr" are data labels. Cells below and to the right of the data labels display the data values that are represented in the Graph chart. Each column and row of data in the datasheet is called a **data series**. Each data series has corresponding **data series markers** in the chart, which are graphical representations such as bars, columns, or pie wedges. The PowerPoint Standard and Formatting toolbars have been replaced with the Microsoft Graph Standard and Formatting toolbars, and the menu bar has changed to include Microsoft Graph commands.

5. **Move the pointer over the datasheet**
   The pointer changes to ✛. Cell A1 is the **active cell**, which means that it is selected. The active cell has a heavy black border around it.

6. **Click cell B3**
   Cell B3 is now the current cell.

7. **Click a blank area of the Presentation window to exit Graph and deselect the chart object**
   Compare your slide to Figure D-8. In the next lesson, you will replace the default information in the chart with Nomad's sales information for 1997.

Trouble?

If the Graph Formatting toolbar doesn't appear, click View on the menu bar, point to Toolbars, and click the Formatting check box.

QuickTip

When the Data and Chart menus are present, you are working in Graph. Clicking outside the Graph object returns you to PowerPoint.

FIGURE D-7: Datasheet and chart open in the PowerPoint window

Graph toolbars   Data labels   Active cell

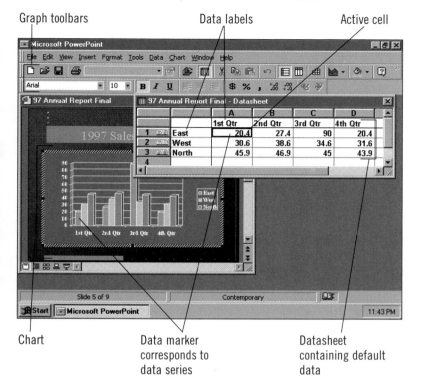

Chart   Data marker   Datasheet
                      corresponds to   containing default
                      data series   data

FIGURE D-8: Chart object on a slide

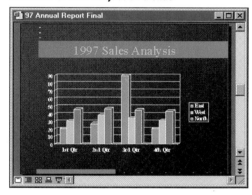

TABLE D-1: Microsoft Graph Chart Types

chart type	use to
Column	Track values over time or across categories
Bar	Compare values in categories or over time
Line	Track values over time
Pie	Compare individual values to the whole
XY (Scatter)	Compare pairs of values
Area	Show contribution of each data series to the total over time
Doughnut	Compare individual values to the whole with multiple series
Radar	Show changes in values in relation to a center point
Surface	Show value trends across two dimensions
Bubble	Indicate relative size of data points
Stock	Show stock market information or scientific data
Cylinder, cone, pyramid	Track values over time or across categories

PowerPoint 97

Entering and Editing Data in the Datasheet

After you embed the default datasheet and chart into your presentation, you need to change the data label and cell information in the sample datasheet to create the chart you need. While you can import information from a spreadsheet, it is often easier to use Graph and type in the information. As you enter data or make changes to the datasheet, the chart automatically changes to reflect your alterations. ◄────── Carrie enters the 1997 quarterly sales figures by product type that Nomad Ltd's president wants to show to the stockholders and employees. She first changes the data labels and then the series information in the cells.

Steps 1234

1. **Double-click the chart**
   The graph is selected and the datasheet appears.

2. **Click the East data label, type Expeditions and press [Enter]**
   After you press [Enter], the first data label changes from East to Expeditions and the data label in row 2, the cell directly below the active cell, becomes selected. Don't worry if the column is not quite wide enough to accommodate the label; you'll fix that after you enter all the column labels.

3. **Type Sporting Gear, press [Enter], type Clothing, and press [Enter]**
   Notice that row 1 has scrolled up behind the column data labels, and there is no automatic label text in row 4.

4. **Type Supplies, press [Tab], then press [↑] three times to display all the rows**
   Pressing [Tab] moves the active cell one column to the right. Notice that in the chart itself, below the datasheet, the data labels you typed are now in the legend to the right of the chart. Now that you have entered all the column data labels, widen the data label column.

5. **Position the pointer on top of the column divider to the left of the letter A so that ⬦ changes to ╫ and double-click**
   The data label column automatically widens to display all the column label text. Now, enter the data series information for each product type by quarter.

6. **With cell A1 selected, type 98, press [Enter], type 50, press [Enter], type 45, press [Enter], type 30 and press [Tab], then press the [↑] three times to move to the top of the second data series column**
   Notice that the heights of the bar chart columns changed to reflect the numbers you typed.

Trouble?

The datasheet window can be manipulated in the same ways other windows are. If you can't see a column or a row, use the scroll bars to move another part of the datasheet into view or resize the datasheet window so you can see all the data.

7. **Enter the rest of the numbers shown in Figure D-9 to complete the datasheet, then navigate using the arrow keys to make cell A1 the active cell**
   The chart bars adjust to reflect the new information. The chart currently shows the bars grouped by quarter (the legend represents the columns in the datasheet). It would be more effective if the bars were grouped by product type (with the legend representing the rows in the datasheet). Change this by using the Series in Columns command on the Data menu.

8. **Click Data on the menu bar, then click Series in Columns**
   The horizontal axis labels now displays Expeditions, Sporting Gear, and so on, instead of the quarters. The groups of data markers (the bars) now represent product types and show sales for each quarter.

Time To

✔Save

9. **Click in the Presentation window outside the chart area and compare your chart to Figure D-10**
   The datasheet closes, allowing you to see your entire chart. This chart layout clearly shows that Expeditions are Nomad's largest revenue source.

FIGURE D-9: Datasheet showing Nomad Ltd's revenue for each quarter

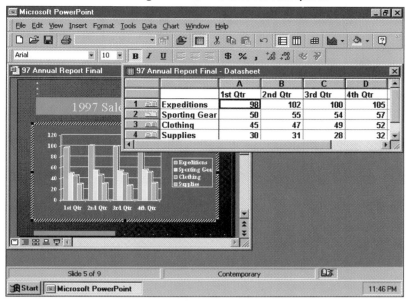

FIGURE D-10: Chart showing data grouped by product type

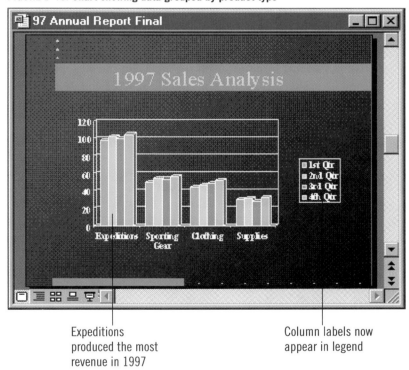

Expeditions
produced the most
revenue in 1997

Column labels now
appear in legend

CLUES TO USE

Series in Rows vs. Series in Columns

If you have difficulty visualizing the difference between the Series in Rows and the Series in Columns commands on the Data menu, think about the legend. **Series in rows** means that the information in the *rows* will become the legend in the chart (and the col-umn labels will be on the horizontal axis). **Series in Columns** means that the information in the *columns* will become the legend in the chart (and the row labels will be on the horizontal axis).

Formatting a Chart

Graph lets you change the appearance of the chart to emphasize certain aspects of the information you are presenting. You can change the chart type, create titles, format the chart labels, move the legend, or add arrows. ✎ Carrie wants to improve the appearance of her chart by formatting the vertical and horizontal axes and by inserting a title.

1. Double-click the **chart** to reopen Microsoft Graph, then click the **Close button** in the Datasheet window to close the datasheet
   Display the vertical axis numbers in currency format with dollar signs ($).

2. Click the **sales numbers** on the vertical axis to select them, then click the **Currency Style button** $ on the Chart Formatting toolbar
   The numbers on the vertical axis appear with dollar signs and two decimal places. You don't need to display the two decimal places, since all the values are whole numbers.

Trouble?

If the Office Assistant appears with a tip in the balloon-shaped dialog box, drag it out of the way or click the Office Assistant Close button.

3. Click the **Decrease Decimal button** on the Chart Formatting toolbar twice
   The numbers on the vertical axis now have dollar signs and show only whole numbers. The product type names on the horizontal axis take up a lot of space, and actually reduce the size of the chart itself. Decrease the font size to improve the fit.

4. Click any of the **product type names** on the horizontal axis, click the **Font Size list arrow** on the Chart Formatting toolbar, and click **14**
   The font size changes from 18 points to 14 points for all the labels on the horizontal axis, and the labels now fit horizontally under each column group. Now, add a title to the chart and labels to the vertical and horizontal axes.

5. Click **Chart** on the menu bar, click **Chart Options**, and click the **Titles tab**
   The Chart Options dialog box opens, in which you can change the chart title, axes, gridlines, legend, data labels, and the table. First, add a title to the chart.

6. Click the **Chart title text box**, then type **Revenue by Product Type**
   The preview box changes to show you the chart with the title.

7. Press **[Tab]** to move the cursor to the **Category (X) axis text box**, type **Product Type**, press **[Tab]** to move the cursor to the **Value (Z) axis text box**, then type **Sales in 000s**
   In the 3-D chart, the vertical axis is called the Z axis and the depth axis, which you don't typically work with, is the Y axis. See Figure D-11 for the completed Titles tab. Now, place the legend below the chart, so the chart itself can be as wide as possible allowing the audience to see the bars clearly.

8. Click the **Legend tab**, click the **bottom option button**, and click **OK**
   Now, turn the vertical axis label 90 degrees to the left, so it takes up less room.

Time To

- ✔ Spell check
- ✔ Return to Slide 1
- ✔ View the slide show
- ✔ Evaluate your presentation
- ✔ Save

9. Make sure the **Value Axis title** "Sales in 000s" label is selected, click **Format** on the menu bar, click **Selected Axis Title** to open the Format Axis Title dialog box, click the **Alignment tab**, drag the **red diamond** in the Orientation section up to a vertical position so the spin box reads 90 degrees, click **OK**, then click a blank area of the Presentation window
   Graph closes and the PowerPoint toolbars and menu bar appear. The completed chart displays as shown in Figure D-12.

FIGURE D-11: Titles tab in the Chart Options dialog box

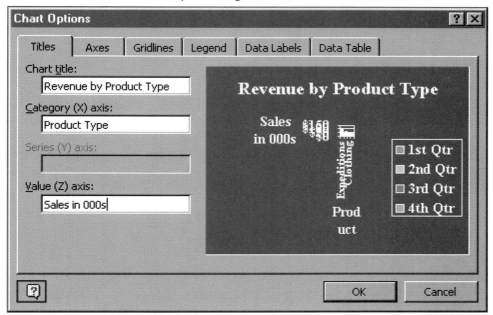

FIGURE D-12: Slide showing formatted chart

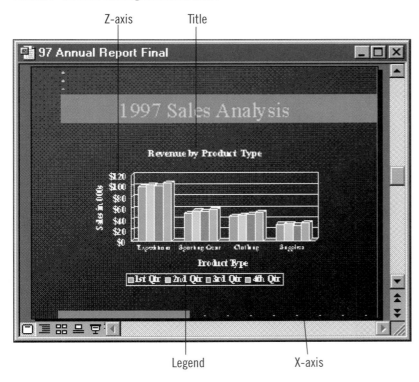

Customizing Charts

You can easily customize the look of any chart in Microsoft Graph. Click the chart to select it, then double-click any data series element (a column, for example) to display the Format Data Series dialog box. Use the tabs to change the element's fill color, border, shape, or data label. You can even use the same fill effects you apply to a presentation background. In 3-D charts, you can change the chart depth as well as the distances between series.

Using Slide Show Commands

With PowerPoint, you can show a presentation on any compatible computer using Slide Show view. As you've seen, Slide Show view fills your computer screen with the slides of your presentation, displaying them one at a time—similar to how a slide projector displays slides. Once your presentation is in Slide Show view, you can use a number of slide show options to tailor the show. For example, you can draw on, or **annotate**, slides or jump to a specific slide. ✎ Carrie runs a slide show of the president's presentation and practices using some of the custom slide show options. Then she can suggest them to Nomad Ltd's president to help make his presentation more effective.

Steps 1 2 3 4

1. Go to Slide 1, then click the **Slide Show button** 🖵
   The first slide of the presentation fills the screen. Advance to the next slide.

2. Press **[Spacebar]**
   Slide 2 appears on the screen. Pressing the spacebar or clicking the left mouse button is the easiest way to move through a slide show. You can also use the keys listed in Table D-2.

3. Move the mouse
   When you move the mouse, the Slide Show menu icon appears in the lower-left corner of the screen. Clicking the Slide Show menu icon or right-clicking anywhere on the screen displays a pop-up menu, which offers several choices for working with an electronic slide show. Sometimes, you will want to use the pop-up menu to go to a specific slide or to make annotations. You can emphasize major points in your presentation by annotating the slide during a slide show using the Pen.

4. Click the **Slide Show menu icon** 🖤◤, then click **Pen**
   The pointer changes to ✎ .

5. Press and hold **[Shift]** and drag ✎ to draw a line under each of the bulleted points on the slide
   Holding down [Shift] constrains the Pen tool to straight horizontal or vertical lines. Compare your screen to Figure D-13. While the annotation pen is visible, mouse clicks do not advance the slide show. However, you can still move to the next slide by pressing the spacebar or [Enter]. Next, erase your annotations.

6. Right-click to display the Slide Show pop-up menu, point to **Screen**, then click **Erase Pen**
   The annotations on Slide 2 are erased. Now, jump to Slide 5.

7. Right-click anywhere on the screen to display the Slide Show pop-up menu, point to **Go**, then click **Slide Navigator**

8. Click **5. 1997 Sales Analysis** in the Slide titles list box, then click **Go To**
   Slide 5 appears. Examine it, then return to Slide 1 and go through the entire presentation in Slide view.

9. Press **[Home]**, then click the mouse, press **[Spacebar]**, or press **[Enter]** to advance through the slide show
   After Slide 9 appears, the next click ends the slide show and returns you to Slide view.

FIGURE D-13: Slide 2 in Slide Show view with annotations

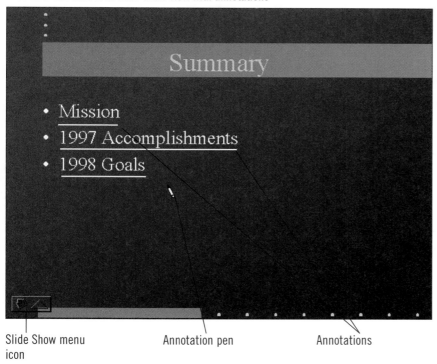

Slide Show menu
icon

Annotation pen

Annotations

TABLE D-2: Slide show keyboard controls

control	description
[E]	Erases the annotation drawing
[Enter], [Spacebar], [→] or [N]	Advances to the next slide
[H]	Displays a hidden slide
[←] or [PgUp]	Returns to the previous slide
[W]	Changes the screen to white; press again to return
[S]	Pauses the slide show; press again to continue
[B]	Changes the screen to black; press again to return
[Ctrl][P]	Changes pointer to ✎
[CTRL][A]	Changes pointer to ⌖
[Esc]	Stops the slide show

CLUES TO USE

Showing slide shows on other computers

You can show a PowerPoint presentation on any compatible computer, even if PowerPoint is not installed on it. To do this, you use a special program called PowerPoint Viewer, which comes with PowerPoint. Put the Viewer on the same disk as your presentation by using the Pack and Go Wizard on the File menu. Then, unpack the Viewer and the presentation together to run the slide show on another computer. You can freely install the PowerPoint Viewer program on any compatible system. If you have access to the World Wide Web (WWW), you can download PowerPoint Viewer by pointing to Microsoft on the Web on the Help menu, and then clicking Free Stuff.

Setting Slide Show Timings and Transitions

In a slide show, you can preset when and how each slide appears on the screen. You can set the **slide timing**, which is the amount of time a slide is visible on the screen. Each slide can have the same or different timing. Setting the right slide timing is important because it determines the amount of time you have to discuss the material on each slide. Also, you can set **slide transitions**, special visual and audio effects you apply to a slide that determine how it moves in and out of view during the slide show. For example, during a slide show you might have one slide fade out while the next one fades in or have another slide uncover slowly across the screen. You make most timing and transition changes in Slide Sorter view. Carrie decides to set her slide timings for 15 seconds per slide and to set the transitions for all slides but the last one to fade to black before the next slide appears.

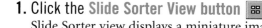

1. Click the Slide Sorter View button 🔡
Slide Sorter view displays a miniature image of the slides in your presentation. The number of slides you see on your screen depends on the current zoom setting. Notice that the Slide Sorter toolbar appears below the Formatting toolbar.

2. Right-click one of the slides, then click Slide Transition
The Slide Transition dialog box, shown in Figure D-14, opens. You want to set the timing between slides to 15 seconds, but you also want to be able to advance to the next slide manually, in case the president finishes talking in less time than that.

3. In the Advance section, make sure the On mouse click check box is selected, click the Automatically after check box to select it, type 15 in the seconds text box, then click Apply to All
The duration you set appears under each slide. When you run the slide show again, each slide will remain on the screen for 15 seconds. If you want to advance more quickly, press [Spacebar] or click the mouse button. Now, set the slide transitions.

4. Right-click one of the slides, click Slide Transition on the pop-up menu, then click the Effect list arrow in the top section
A drop-down menu appears, showing all the transition effects.

5. Scroll down the list, click Fade through black, click Apply to All, then click in a blank area of the Presentation window to deselect the slide
In Slide Sorter view, each slide now has a small transition icon under it, as shown in Figure D-15, indicating there is a transition effect set for the slides. Now, preview the effect.

6. Click the transition icon under any slide
The slide fades and reappears. Apply a different effect to the last slide.

7. Scroll down the Presentation window, right-click the last slide, click Slide Transition, click the Effect list arrow, and click Split Vertical Out
The last slide will now appear with a split from the center of the screen.

8. Click the Sound list arrow, scroll down the list and click Drum Roll or choose another sound effect, then click Apply
Make sure you did not click Apply to All this time. The last slide now has a different visual effect and a drum roll transition applied to it.

9. Press [Home], click the Slide Show View button 🖥 **and watch as the slide show advances with its special effects**
To move more quickly, press the spacebar or [Enter].

QuickTip
You also can click Slide Show on the menu bar, then click Slide Transition.

QuickTip
You also can click Edit on the menu bar, click Select All, then click the Transition list arrow on the Slide Sorter toolbar to apply a transition effect to all the slides.

Time To
✔Save

FIGURE D-14: **Slide Transition dialog box**

Click to set
transition effects

Click to apply
selections to all slides
in the presentation

Set timing
characteristics here

Click to apply
selections only to
selected slides

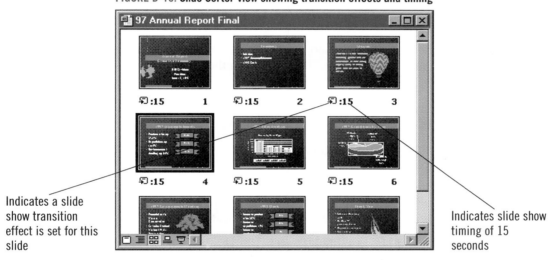

FIGURE D-15: **Slide Sorter view showing transition effects and timing**

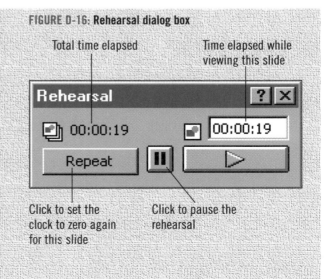

Indicates a slide
show transition
effect is set for this
slide

Indicates slide show
timing of 15
seconds

Rehearsing slide show timing

You can set different slide timings for each slide. For
example, you can have the title slide appear for 20 seconds, the second slide for 3 minutes, and so on. You also
can set timings by clicking the Rehearse Timings button
on the Slide Sorter toolbar or by choosing the Rehearse
Timings command on the Slide Show menu. The
Rehearsal dialog box shown in Figure D-16 appears. It
contains buttons to pause between slides and to
advance to the next slide. Practice giving your presentation while the slide show is running. PowerPoint keeps
track of how long each slide appears and sets the timing
accordingly. You can view your rehearsed timings in
Slide Sorter view. The next time you run the slide show,
you can use the timings you rehearsed.

FIGURE D-16: **Rehearsal dialog box**

Total time elapsed

Time elapsed while
viewing this slide

Click to set the
clock to zero again
for this slide

Click to pause the
rehearsal

PowerPoint 97

Setting Slide Animation Effects

Animation effects let you control how the graphics and main points in your presentation appear on the screen during a slide show. For example, you might want to set the individual slide bullets to "fly in" from the left. You can animate text, images, or even individual chart elements, or you can add sound effects. Keep in mind that the animation effects you choose give a certain "flavor" to your presentation. They can be serious and businesslike or humorous. Choose appropriate effects for your presentation content and audience. ▰▰▰ Carrie wants to animate the text and graphics of several slides in her presentation.

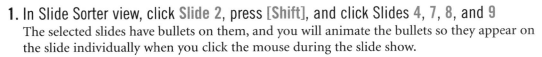

QuickTip

Use the ToolTips to see the names of the toolbar buttons.

QuickTip

If you want a grouped object, like the ribbons on Slides 4 and 8, to fly in individually, then you must ungroup them first.

1. In Slide Sorter view, click Slide 2, press [Shift], and click Slides 4, 7, 8, and 9
   The selected slides have bullets on them, and you will animate the bullets so they appear on the slide individually when you click the mouse during the slide show.

2. On the Slide Sorter toolbar, click the Text Preset Animation list arrow and click Fly From Left
   When you run the slide show, the bullets of the selected slides, instead of appearing all at once, will appear one at a time, "flying" in from the left, each time you click the mouse button.

3. Click Slide 1, then run through the slide show
   The bullets fly in from the left, but the tree and the sailboat do not fly in. To set custom animation effects, the target slide must be in Slide view.

4. Double-click Slide 9 to view it in Slide view, click Slide Show on the menu bar, and click Custom Animation
   The Custom Animation dialog box opens, similar to the one shown in Figure D-17. Objects that are already animated appear in the Animation Order section in the order in which they will be animated. Set the object (the sailboat) to materialize gradually.

5. On the Timing tab, click Object 3 in the text box at the top, then click the Animate option button on the right

6. Click the Effects tab, click the top list arrow in the Entry animation and sound section, scroll down and click Dissolve, click Preview in the upper-right corner of the dialog box to see the new animation effect, then click OK

7. Go to Slide 7 and repeat steps 5 and 6 to change the animation effect for the tree

8. Run the Slide Show again
   The special effects have helped make the presentation easier to understand and more interesting to view.

9. Click the Zoom list arrow, click 33, click Window on the menu bar, then click Fit to Page
   Figure D-18 shows the completed presentation in Slide Sorter view at 33% zoom.

10. Save your presentation, then exit PowerPoint

Text will be
animated first
　
Text and Object have
been animated
　
Preview box
　
Click to preview
special effects

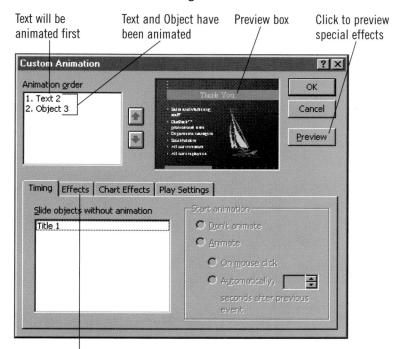

Click here to change
animation effects

FIGURE D-18: **Completed presentation in Slide Sorter view**

Presentation Checklist

You should always rehearse your slide show. If possible, rehearse your presentation in the room and with the computer that you will use. Use the following checklist to prepare for the slide show.

✔ Is **PowerPoint** or **PowerPoint Viewer** installed on the computer?

✔ Is your **presentation file** on the hard drive of the computer you will be using? Try putting a shortcut for the file on the desktop. Do you have a backup copy of your presentation file on a floppy disk?

✔ Is the **projection device** working correctly? Can the slides be seen from the back of the room?

✔ Do you know how to control **room lighting** so that the audience can both see your slides as well as their handouts and notes? You may want to designate someone to control the lights if the controls are not close to you.

✔ Will the **computer** be situated so you can advance and annotate the slides yourself? If not, designate someone to advance them for you.

✔ Do you have enough copies of your **handouts**? Bring extras. Decide when to hand them out, or whether you prefer to have them waiting at the audience members' places when they enter.

Practice

▶ Concepts Review

Label each of the elements of the PowerPoint window shown in Figure D-19.

FIGURE D-19

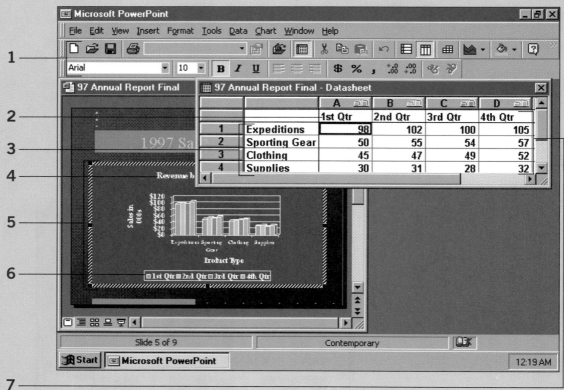

1
2
3
4
5
6
7

Match each of the terms with the statement that describes it.

8. **Chart**
9. **Embedded object**
10. **Animation effect**
11. **Data series markers**
12. **Clip Gallery or Clip art gallery**
13. **Active cell**

a. The selected cell in a datasheet.
b. A graphical representation of a datasheet.
c. Graphical representations of data series.
d. The way bulleted items and images appear on a slide.
e. A copy of an object from which you can access another program's tools.
f. A file index system that organizes images.

Select the best answer from the list of choices.

14. **The PowerPoint clip art is stored in a:**
   a. Folder
   b. Gallery
   c. Card Catalogue
   d. Floppy disk

15. **PowerPoint animation effects let you control:**
    a. the order in which text and objects are animated.
    b. the direction from which animated objects appear.
    c. which text and images are animated.
    d. all of the above.

16. **Which of the following is *not* true of a Microsoft Graph chart?**
    a. A graph is made up of a datasheet and chart.
    b. You can double-click a chart to view its corresponding datasheet.
    c. An active cell has a black selection rectangle around it.
    d. You cannot import data from other programs into a datasheet.

17. **If you annotate in Slide Show view, what are you doing?**
    a. Speaking
    b. Answering questions
    c. Drawing on the slide
    d. Changing the content of the slides

 # Skills Review

1. **Insert clip art.**
    a. Open the presentation PPT D-3 on your Student Disk, save it as "OutBack Report" on your Student Disk.
    b. Click the Next Slide button, then double-click the clip art placeholder on Slide 2.
    c. Click the Clip Art tab, scroll down the category list, then click Maps. If the Maps category doesn't appear, select a different category.
    d. In the preview box, click the 3-D U.S. Map with State Boundaries clip art, then click Insert.
    e. Press and hold [Shift], then drag the lower-right sizing handle to enlarge the map slightly.
    f. Press and hold [Shift] and click to select both the main text block and the map, click the Draw menu button on the Drawing toolbar, point to Align and Distribute, and click Align Top to align the tops of the two objects.

2. **Insert and crop a picture.**
    a. Go to Slide 6, which is the last slide.
    b. Click the Slide Layout button on the Common Tasks toolbar and select the Text & Object layout.
    c. Double-click the Object placeholder, click Create from file, click Browse, and locate the drive containing your Student Disk. Click PPT D-4, then click OK.
    d. Click the Crop button on the Picture toolbar and position the cursor over the left-middle handle of the shuttle image.
    e. Drag the left edge to the right to crop off about ¾" of the steam, then click on a blank area of the slide twice to deselect the cropping pointer and deselect the image.
    f. Press [Shift], click the main text box, click the Increase Font Size button on the Formatting toolbar, then click on a blank area of the slide to deselect the text box.
    g. Press [Shift], then drag the upper-left sizing handle so the image is approximately as large as the main text box.

PowerPoint 97

3. Embed a chart.

  a. Go to Slide 3, OutBack Division Sales.

  b. Click Slide Layout on the Common Tasks toolbar and select the Chart AutoLayout.

  c. Double-click the chart placeholder to start Graph.

4. Enter and edit data in the datasheet.

  a. Click the row 1 label in the datasheet, and type North.

  b. Enter the chart information shown in Table D-3 into the datasheet. Use [Tab], [Return], and the keyboard arrow keys to navigate through the datasheet as you enter data.

  c. Click Data on the menu bar, and click Series in Columns.

  d. Click a blank area of the Presentation window twice to exit Graph.

  e. Click the Save button on the Standard toolbar.

TABLE D-3

	1st Qtr	2nd Qtr	3rd Qtr	4th Qtr
North	36	40	45	43
East	44	50	52	53
South	31	36	40	38
West	54	44	57	59

5. Format a chart.

  a. Double-click the chart object, then click the Close button in the datasheet window.

  b. Click the region names on the X-axis, click the Font Size list arrow on the Formatting toolbar, then click 24.

  c. Click the vertical axis, and click the Currency Style button on the Formatting toolbar.

  d. Click the Decrease Decimal button twice on the Formatting toolbar.

  e. Click Chart on the menu bar, click Chart Options, click the Title tab, click the Chart title text box, and type "1997 OutBack Sales."

  f. Press [Tab] twice to place the insertion point in the Value (Z) Axis text box, type "in 000s," and click OK.

  g. Click Format on the menu bar, click Selected Axis Title, then click the Alignment tab.

  h. In the orientation pane, drag the red diamond up to the 90-degree position, and click OK.

  i. Click the Legend to select it, click Format on the menu bar, and click Selected Legend.

  j. Click the Placement tab, click the Left option button, and click OK.

  k. Click a blank area of the Presentation window to exit Graph.

6. Use slide show commands.

  a. Go to Slide 1, and click the Slide Show button.

  b. Click the mouse button to move to the next slide.

  c. Press [Enter] to advance to Slide 3.

  d. Click the Slide Show menu icon, then click Pen.

  e. Hold down [Shift] and draw two annotation lines under the West axis label on the chart.

  f. Right-click to display the Slide Show pop-up menu, point to Screen, then click Erase Pen.

  g. Open the Slide Show pop-up menu again, point to Go, then click Slide Navigator.

  h. Click 2. OutBack Sales Regions.

  i. Return to Slide 1 by typing the number 1 and pressing [Enter].

  j. Press [End] to move to the last slide, and press [Enter] to return to Slide view.

7. Set slide show timings and transitions.

  a. Click the Slide Sorter View button, and enter 66% in the Zoom text box so all six slides fit on the screen.

  b. Right-click one of the slides, and click Slide Transition from the pop-up menu.

c. In the Advance section of the dialog box, make sure the On Mouse Click is selected, click the Automatically after check box to select it, and type 15 in the seconds text box.

d. In the Effect list box, select Box Out, and click Apply to All.

e. In Slide Sorter view, click the small transition icon under any slide and view the transition effect.

f. Right-click the last slide in the presentation, and click Slide Transition from the pop-up menu.

g. In the Effect List box, select Cover Down, and click Apply.

h. Click View on the menu bar, then click Slide Show to view the transitions.

8. Set slide animation effects.

a. In Slide Sorter view, press [Shift] and click Slides 2, 5, and 6.

b. On the Slide Sorter Toolbar click the Text Preset Animation list box and click Peek From Right.

c. Deselect the slides, then double-click Slide 2 to open it in Slide view.

d. Click Slide Show on the menu bar, and click Custom Animation.

e. In the Animation Order list box, click Object 3, and click the Effects tab.

f. In the Entry animation and sound list box, choose Dissolve, then click Preview.

g. In the Animation Order list box click Text 2.

h. In the After animation list box, click More Colors, click the Standard tab, choose any red color, then click OK.

i. Click Preview, then click OK.

j. Press [Home], then run the slide show.

k. Save, print, and then close the presentation.

▶ Independent Challenges

1. You are a financial management consultant for "Pacific Coast Investments", located in San Jose, California. One of your primary responsibilities is to give financial seminars on different financial investments and how to determine which fund to invest in. In this challenge, you'll need to enhance the look of the slides by adding and formatting objects and adding animations effects and transitions. To begin, open the presentation provided on your Student Disk.

To complete this independent challenge:

1. Open the file PPT D-5 on your Student Disk, and save it as "Fund Seminar" on your Student Disk.

2. Look through the presentation in Slide view and think about how you want each slide to look. What information is provided, and what could you add? How do you want to communicate the message? Look at the presentation organization; you may need to make some adjustments. Is it well done? If you reorganize the presentation, be able to support your decisions.

3. Create a Graph chart, and embed it on Slide 6. Enter the data in Table D-4 into the datasheet.

4. Format the chart. Add titles as necessary.

5. Add clip art to the presentation.

6. Format the objects in the presentation. Use the align and group commands to organize your shapes.

7. Spell check the presentation, then save it.

8. View the slide show and evaluate your presentation. Make changes if necessary.

9. Set animation effects, slide transitions, and slide timings. Your audience includes potential investors who need the information you are presenting to make decisions about where to put their hard-earned money. View the slide show again.

10. Print the slides of the presentation, then show the presentation in Slide Show view. Close the presentation.

TABLE D-4

	1 Yr	3 Yr	5 Yr	10 Yr
Bonds	4.2%	5.2%	7.9%	9.4%
Stocks	7.5%	8.3%	10.8%	12.6%
Mutual Funds	6.1%	6.3%	6.4%	6.1%

2. You are the communications director at Heridia Design, Inc, an international advertising agency. One of your responsibilities is to create an on-screen presentation for a presentation contest at the National Association of Advertising Agencies (NAAA) convention.

Create a presentation using any type of company. The presentation can be aimed to either convince or educate your audience.

To complete this independent challenge:

1. Think about the results you want to see, the information you need to create the slide show presentation, and the message you want to communicate.
2. Plan and create the slide show presentation. Add interesting visuals, and use a color scheme appropriate to the type of business you choose. Use a chart to show how well the company has performed. Evaluate your presentation content.
3. Use slide transitions, animation effects, and slide timings. Remember, your audience consists of a group of advertising executives who create eye-catching ads every day. View the slide show to evaluate the effects you added.
4. Spell-check and save the presentation as "NAAA Presentation" on your Student Disk.
5. Submit your presentation plan and the final slide show presentation.

3. You are the manager of the Markland University Student Employment Office. The office is staffed by work-study students; new, untrained students start work every semester. Create a presentation that you can use to make the training easier. You can create your own content, or use the following: the work-study staff needs to learn about the main features of the office, including its employment database, library of company directories, seminars on employment search strategies, interviewing techniques, and résumé development, as well as its student consulting and bulk mailing services.

To complete this independent challenge:

1. Think about the results you want to see, the information you need to create the slide show presentation, and the message you want to communicate.
2. Plan and create the color slide presentation using Microsoft Clip Gallery. (Check the Business and People categories.)
3. Save the presentation as "Student Employment" on your Student Disk. Before printing, evaluate the contents of your presentation. Preview the file so you know what the presentation will look like. Adjust any items, and then print the slides.
4. Add transitions, build effects and timings to the presentation. Remember, your audience is university students who need to assimilate a lot of information in order to perform well in their new jobs. View the slide show again.
5. Submit your presentation plan and the final slide show presentation.

4. You work for Asset Advisors, a successful investment service company in South Carolina. The company provides a full set of investment opportunities, including stocks, bonds, and mutual funds. Most of the company's clients are individuals who have large estates or who are retired. To generate more business, you've decided that the company needs a standardized presentation promoting the company and its investment principles. John Ricci, president of the company, liked your idea and asked you to develop the presentation.

To complete this independent challenge:

1. Open the file "PPT D-6" from your Student Disk, and save it as Investment Presentation on your Student Disk.
2. After you open the presentation, look through it in Slide view and think about the results you want to see on each slide. What information is provided, and what could you add? How do you want to communicate the message? Look at how the presentation is organized; you may need to make some adjustments. Is it well done? If you reorganize the presentation, be able to support your decision.
3. Create a Graph chart and embed it on Slide 7. Enter the data in Table D-5 into the Graph datasheet.

TABLE D-5

	1 Year	3 Year	5 Year	10 Year
Bonds	8.2	7.5	5.6	2.9
Stocks	17.3	8.9	6.1	3.2
Mutual Funds	15.4	6.1	5.2	4.7

4. Format the chart, then title the chart "Investment Risk Over Time."
5. Make changes to the color scheme. Add the new color scheme to the available color scheme list.
6. Add clip art to the presentation wherever you think it would enhance, but not clutter, the message. Try the Currency, People, and Shapes categories.
7. Format the objects in the presentation. Use the align and group commands to organize your shapes.
8. The president has also asked you to add information about socially responsible investing, a topic many clients have been asking about. You can find information on this topic on the World Wide Web (WWW). Create two new slides in your presentation, one about organizations that promote socially responsible investing, and another about investment funds that invest only in socially responsible organizations. To get ideas for content, log on to the Internet and use your browser to go to http://www.course.com. From there, click the link Student On Line Companions, then click the link to go to the Microsoft Office 97 Professional Edition—Illustrated: A First Course page, then click on the PowerPoint link for Unit D.
http://www.yahoo.com/Business_and_Economy/Markets_and_Investments:Socially_Responsible_Investments(SRI).
9. Fill in the appropriate information on the last two slides in the presentation.
10. Change the slide background to a 2-color background with the gradient of your choice.
11. Spell check the presentation.
12. View the slide show, and evaluate the presentation. Set animations, slide transitions, and slide timings. Keep in mind that your audience is comprised of serious investors, so you'll want to keep any animations or transitions simple, serious, and businesslike, to build trust in your company and keep the audience focused on the presentation content, not the form.
13. View the slide show again to see the animations and transitions you added.
14. Save the presentation.
15. Print the slides of the presentation, then show the presentation in Slide Show view. Close the presentation.

PowerPoint 97

► Visual Workshop

Create two slides that look like the examples in Figures D-20 and D-21. Save the presentation as Sales Presentation to your Student Disk. Save the presentation and print the slides. Submit the final presentation output.

FIGURE D-20

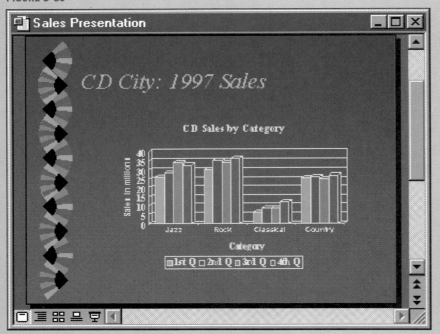

FIGURE D-21

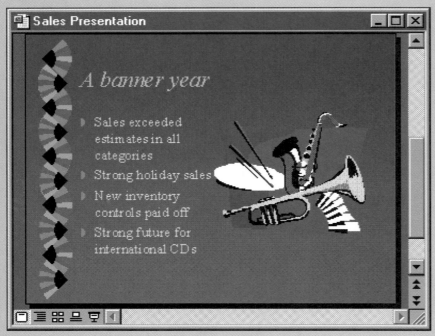

Integrating
Word, Excel, Access, and PowerPoint

Objectives

▶ **Insert a Word outline into a PowerPoint presentation**
▶ **Embed a Word table into a PowerPoint slide**
▶ **Embed an Excel chart into a PowerPoint slide**
▶ **Link an Excel worksheet to a PowerPoint slide**
▶ **Update a linked Excel worksheet in PowerPoint**
▶ **Export a PowerPoint presentation to Word**

PowerPoint, the fourth component of Microsoft Office, can be easily integrated with the other Office programs. For example, to help you develop a PowerPoint presentation, you can insert a document from Word or embed objects like a Word table or an Excel worksheet directly into the slides of your presentation. An embedded object is one that is created in one program, known as a **source program**, and then stored as an independent file in another program, such as your PowerPoint presentation. ✐ In this unit, Lynn Shaw, the executive assistant to the president, creates a small company status presentation that will be used at this year's annual business meeting. To complete the presentation, Lynn gathers some data herself and collects more from various Nomad Ltd divisions. Because everyone at Nomad Ltd uses Microsoft Office, Lynn knows all the files are compatible.

Integration

Inserting a Word Outline into a PowerPoint Presentation

While it is very easy to create an outline in PowerPoint, it is unnecessary if the outline already exists in a Word document. You can easily insert a Word document into PowerPoint to create a presentation outline. When you insert the Word outline, the heading styles in the outline are converted to text levels in PowerPoint. For example, every Word paragraph with the style Heading 1 is converted to a new slide, and every Word paragraph with the style Heading 2 is converted to a subpoint under a slide title. If the outline you are inserting has no styles, the text is converted into an outline based on the structure of the document; each hard return indicates a new slide and each hard return followed by a tab indicates a subpoint. In this lesson, Lynn inserts a Word outline created by Angela Pacheco, Nomad's sales and marketing director. The outline explains Nomad's current company status.

Steps 1 2 3 4

1. **Start PowerPoint and insert your Student Disk into the disk drive**
   The PowerPoint startup dialog box opens.

2. **Click the Open an Existing Presentation option button, then click OK**
   The Open dialog box opens.

3. **Open the file INT C-1 from your Student Disk, then save it as Company Summary to your Student Disk**

4. **Make sure the Zoom text box shows 36%, click the Restore button in the Presentation window, click Window on the menu bar, then click Fit to Page**
   The first slide of the presentation appears as shown in Figure C-1. Switch to Outline view.

5. **Click the Outline View button ▤ to the left of the horizontal scroll bar**
   You can insert a Word document in Slide view or in Outline view. The presentation currently contains two slides. Insert the information from the Word document after the Corporate Mission Statement in Slide 2.

6. **Click the Slide 2 slide icon**
   When you insert the Word document, it will begin with a new slide after the current slide.

7. **Click Insert on the menu bar, then click Slides from Outline**
   The Insert Outline dialog box opens.

8. **Select the file INT C-2 from your Student Disk, click Insert, then scroll down to see the new slides**
   The Word document is inserted as six new slides. See Figure C-2. Once an outline is inserted into a presentation, you can edit it as if it had been created in PowerPoint. Switch to Slide view to see the slides you just inserted.

Time To

✔ Save

9. **Double-click the Slide 3 slide icon to switch to Slide view, then click the Next Slide button ▾ below the vertical scroll bar five times to view the new slides**

FIGURE C-1: Lynn's slide presentation

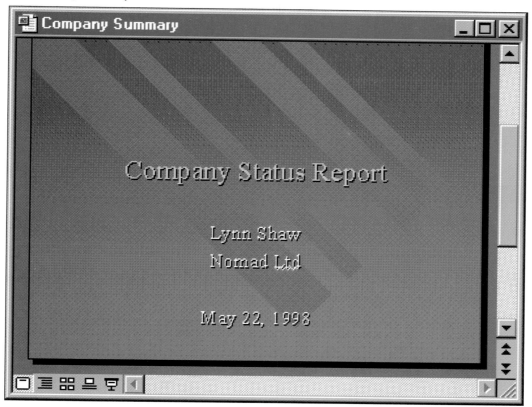

FIGURE C-2: New slides inserted in Outline view

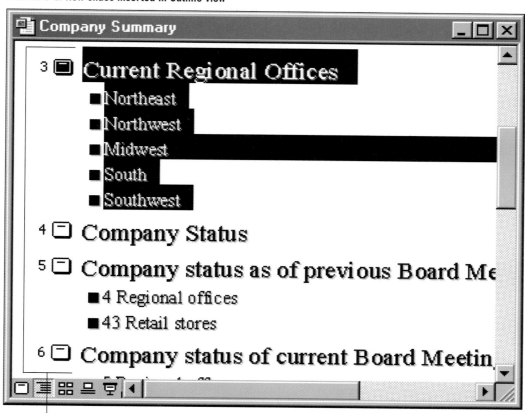

Slides 3 through 6
inserted after Slide 2

Integration

Embedding a Word Table into a PowerPoint Slide

You can create and embed a new Word table in your presentation without leaving PowerPoint. This is similar to using Microsoft Graph to insert a graph into a PowerPoint slide. Make sure to view the CourseHelp for this lesson before completing the steps. ✐ Lynn wants to create a table illustrating the growth of Nomad Ltd over the last two years.

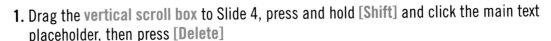

1. Drag the **vertical scroll box** to Slide 4, press and hold **[Shift]** and click the main text placeholder, then press **[Delete]**

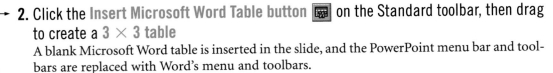
2. Click the **Insert Microsoft Word Table button** 🔲 on the Standard toolbar, then drag to create a **3 × 3 table**
   A blank Microsoft Word table is inserted in the slide, and the PowerPoint menu bar and toolbars are replaced with Word's menu and toolbars.

3. Drag the table down so it is centered between the title text and the bottom of the slide

4. Enter the information in Figure C-3 into your blank table
   Use [Tab] to move from cell to cell in your table. Now format the table using Word's formatting capabilities. First add border lines to the first row in the table.

5. Drag to select the three cells in the top row of the table, click **Format** on the menu bar, then click **Borders and Shading**
   The Borders and Shading dialog box opens with the Borders tab on top.

6. In the Style section, click the **Width list arrow**, click **3 pt**, then click at the **top** and the **bottom** of the Preview diagram as shown in Figure C-4

7. Click **OK**
   A 3 point line appears above and below the first row, although it is difficult to see it while the table is still selected. Now format the column titles.

8. On the Formatting toolbar, click the **Font list arrow**, click **Arial**, click the **Font Size list arrow**, click **36**, then click the **Center button** 🔲 on the Formatting toolbar
   The top row is set apart from the rest of the table, making it easier to read. Now format the bottom two rows.

9. Drag to select the bottom two rows of the table, click the **Outside Border list arrow** on the Formatting toolbar, click the **Bottom Border button** 🔲, click the **Font Size list arrow**, click **28**, then click 🔲
   Because the slide's shaded background is dark blue, make the text in the table white.

10. Drag to select all of the text in the table, click **Format** on the menu bar, click **Font**, click the **Color list arrow**, click **White**, click **OK**, then click a blank area of the Presentation window to deselect the table object
    Compare your screen to Figure C-5.

FIGURE C-3: Microsoft Word table

1996· Status▯	1997· Status▯	1998· Status▯
2·Regional· Offices▯	4·Regional· Offices▯	5·Regional· Offices▯
22·Retail· Stores▯	43·Retail· Stores▯	74·Retail· Stores▯

FIGURE C-4: Borders and Shading dialog box

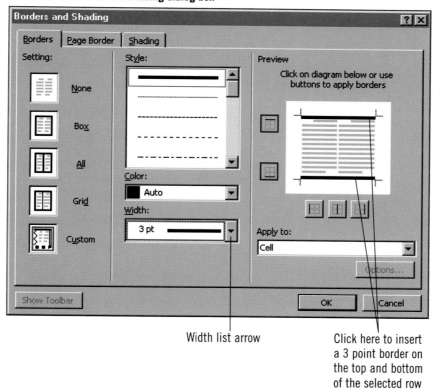

Width list arrow

Click here to insert
a 3 point border on
the top and bottom
of the selected row

FIGURE C-5: Microsoft Word table on slide

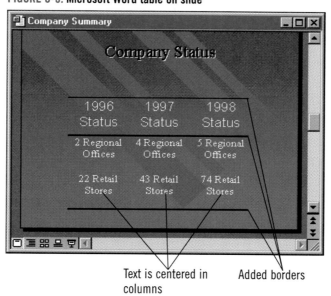

Text is centered in
columns

Added borders

INTEGRATING WORD, EXCEL, ACCESS, AND POWERPOINT

Embedding an Excel Chart into a PowerPoint Slide

A powerful feature of all Microsoft Office programs is their ability to share existing information. For example, you can easily insert information from an existing Word or Excel file into a PowerPoint presentation. The information becomes an **embedded** object in PowerPoint, making it independent from its original source file. If you want to modify an embedded object, you double-click it and the original program in which the file was created opens. ✐ Lynn includes in her presentation an Excel chart that she received from Evan Brillstein in the Accounting division. After she adds the chart to her presentation, Lynn wants to format it, so she decides to embed the chart.

Steps

1. Click the Previous Slide button ⬓ to move to Slide 3, click Slide Layout on the Common Tasks toolbar, click the Text & Object layout (fourth row, first column), then click Apply

2. Double-click the object placeholder
   The Insert Object dialog box opens. You will create an embedded object from an existing file.

3. Click the Create from file option button, click Browse, click the Look in list arrow, click the drive containing your Student Disk, click INT C-3, click OK, then click OK in the Insert Object dialog box
   The Excel chart appears on the slide. Now increase the size of the chart so it is easier to see on the slide.

4. Drag the upper-left sizing handle up and to the left until the dotted line is approximately ¼" below the title text as shown in Figure C-6

5. Click the Fill Color list arrow on the Drawing toolbar, then click the white square
   Next, make the title of the chart larger. To do this, open the chart in Excel.

6. Double-click the worksheet object
   The PowerPoint menu bar and toolbars are replaced with the Excel menu bar and toolbars, and the Excel Chart toolbar appears. If the Chart toolbar does not appear, click View on the menu bar, point to Toolbars, then click Chart.

7. Click the Chart Objects list arrow on the Chart toolbar, click Chart title, click the Font Size list arrow on the Formatting toolbar, and click 36
   The change in the Excel chart is reflected in the embedded object in PowerPoint. Because this is an embedded object, editing the object does not alter the original Excel file.

8. Click in the Presentation window outside the chart object to deselect it and return to PowerPoint

9. Click the text box with the bulleted list to select it, then drag it over to the left so that there is only approximately ¼" space between the bullets and the left side of the slide

10. Click the chart object once to select it, drag the left and bottom resize handles to resize the chart as large as possible as shown in Figure C-8, then click in the Presentation window outside the chart object to deselect it

FIGURE C-6: Resizing the chart object

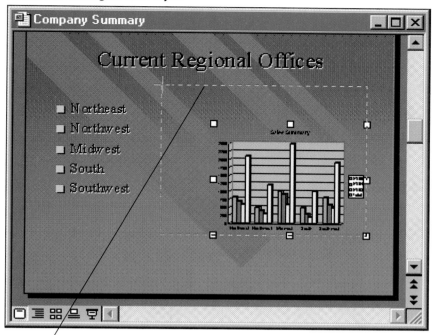

Top border of
resizing box

FIGURE C-7: Excel object embedded in slide

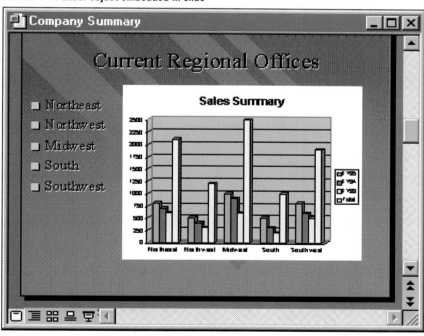

CLUES TO USE

Embedding objects using Paste Special

You can also embed an object or selected information from another Microsoft Office program into PowerPoint by copying and pasting the information. For example, assume you want to embed a worksheet from a Microsoft Excel file. Open the Microsoft Excel file that contains the worksheet, select the worksheet, and copy it to the Clipboard. Open your PowerPoint presentation, click Edit on the menu bar, click Paste Special, then click OK in the Paste Special dialog box.

Linking an Excel Worksheet to a PowerPoint Slide

Objects can also be connected to your presentation by establishing a link between the file that created the object and the PowerPoint presentation that displays the object. Unlike an embedded object which is stored directly in a slide, a linked object is stored in its original file (called the **source file**). When you **link** an object to a PowerPoint slide, a representation, or picture, of the object appears on the slide instead of the actual object, and this representation of the object is connected, or linked, to the original file. Changes made to a linked object's source file are reflected in the linked object. Some of the objects that you can link to PowerPoint include movies, PowerPoint slides from other presentations, and Microsoft Excel worksheets. See Table C-1 for information to help you decide whether to link or embed an object. Lynn needs to insert an Excel worksheet created by Michael Belmont in the New Directions Travel division into her presentation. Michael saved the worksheet to Nomad's company network of computers. Lynn decides to link the worksheet because she knows Michael will have to update the worksheet before the presentation.

Steps

1. Go to Slide 7, click Slide Layout on the Common Tasks toolbar, click the Text over Object layout (fifth row, fourth column), then click Apply

2. Double-click the object placeholder
The Insert Object dialog box opens. You want to create an embedded object from an existing file.

3. Click the Create from file option button, click Browse, click the Look in list arrow, click the drive containing your Student Disk, click New Directions Profit, click OK, then click the Link check box in the Insert Object dialog box
Compare your Insert Object dialog box to Figure C-8.

4. Click OK
The Excel worksheet is linked to the PowerPoint slide. Now format the object to make it easier to read.

5. Drag the corner resize handles and reposition the worksheet object until it is approximately the same size and in the same position as in Figure C-9
Next, change the background color so you can see the type.

6. Click the Fill Color list arrow on the Drawing toolbar, click Automatic, then click in a blank area of the Presentation window to deselect the object
Compare your screen to Figure C-9.

7. Save your work

Trouble?
If Excel opens while you are trying to resize or move the worksheet, click the Close button in the Excel program window.

FIGURE C-8: **Insert Object dialog box**

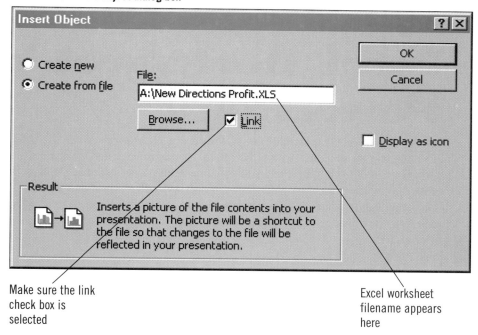

Make sure the link
check box is
selected

Excel worksheet
filename appears
here

FIGURE C-9: **Linked Excel worksheet on slide**

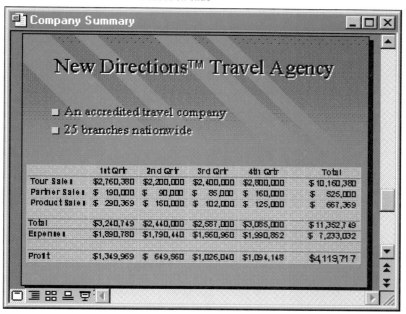

TABLE C-1: **Embedding vs. Linking**

situation	action
When you are the only user of an object and you want the object to be a part of your presentation	Embed
When you want to access the object in its source application, even if the original file is not available	Embed
When you want to update the object manually while working in PowerPoint	Embed
When you always want the latest information in your object	Link
When the object's source file is shared on a network or where other users have access to the file and can change it	Link
When you want to keep your presentation file size small	Link

INTEGRATING WORD, EXCEL, ACCESS, AND POWERPOINT

Updating a Linked Excel Worksheet in PowerPoint

To edit or change the information in a linked object, you must open the object's source file. For example, you must start Microsoft Excel, then open the original worksheet to edit the worksheet you linked to the presentation. You can open the object's source file and the program it was created in by double-clicking the linked object. When you modify a linked object's source file, it is automatically updated in the linked presentation each time you open it. Michael needs to update the linked worksheet because the wrong number was reported for Product Sales for the third quarter.

Steps

QuickTip

To edit or open a linked object in your presentation, the object's source program and source file must be available on your computer or network.

1. Double-click the worksheet object
Microsoft Excel opens in a small window in the middle of the screen, displaying the linked worksheet, and the Excel icon appears on the Taskbar.

2. Double-click cell **D4**, edit the entry to **110000**, click the **Enter button** ✓, click the **Close button** in the Excel program window, then click **Yes** to save the changes
Microsoft Excel closes and the linked Excel worksheet shows the change you made in Excel. Compare your screen to Figure C-10. Now check the spelling in the presentation and save your changes.

3. Click the **Spelling button** on the Standard toolbar and correct any spelling errors in the presentation

4. Click the **Save button** on the Standard toolbar to save the changes you made
Switch to Slide Sorter view.

5. Click the **Slide Sorter View button** to the left of the horizontal scroll bar, click the **Maximize button** in the Presentation window, click the **Zoom list arrow**, then click **50%**
Compare your screen to Figure C-11. Now view the final slide show and evaluate your presentation.

6. Click **Slide 1**, then click the **Slide Show button** to view the final presentation
Now print the slides of your presentation.

7. Click **File** on the menu bar, click **Print**, click the **Black & White check box** to select it, then click **Print** to print the slides

FIGURE C-10: Modifications reflected in linked chart

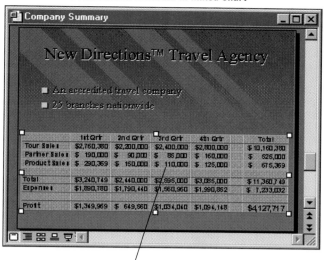

Modified worksheet
data

FIGURE C-11: The final presentation in Slide Sorter view

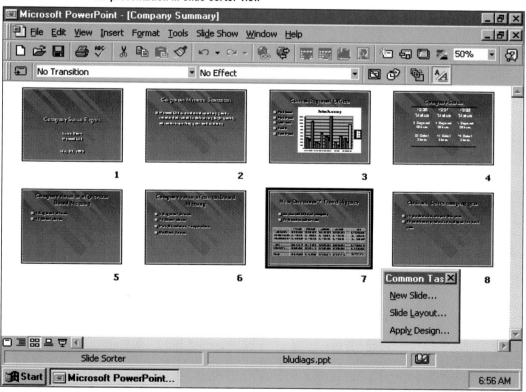

Updating links

If the PowerPoint file is closed when you change the source file, the linked object will still reflect the changes you make to the source file. When you open the file containing the linked object, a dialog box appears reminding you that the file contains links and asking if you want to update the links now. Click OK to update the links or Cancel to leave the linked object unchanged. If you choose Cancel, you can still update the link later. Click Edit on the menu bar, then click Links to open the Links dialog box. Click the file name of the link you want to update, then click Update Now.

Integration

Exporting a PowerPoint Presentation to Word

You can export a PowerPoint presentation to Word. When you choose the Send To Microsoft Word command on the File menu, Word starts and the current PowerPoint presentation's outline exports to Word as a Word document. You can choose one of five layouts for the Word document. Once the PowerPoint outline is in Word, you can save and edit the document. ✐ Lynn wants to create handouts with blank lines so the audience can take notes during the presentation.

Steps

1. Click the **Black and White View button** 🖎 on the Standard toolbar
   The black type does not show up very well on the dark gray background stripes.

2. Click **Format** on the menu bar, click **Background**, click the **Omit background graphics from master check box** to select it, then click **Apply to All**
   Now send the file to Word.

3. Click **File** on the menu bar, point to **Send To**, then click **Microsoft Word**
   The Write-Up dialog box appears. See Figure C-12.

4. Click the **Blank lines next to slides option button**
   Link the presentation in case it changes before you create your handouts.

5. Click the **Paste link option button**

6. Click **OK**
   Microsoft Word opens and the slides appear in a table in a new document. This process may take a little while.

7. Click the **Maximize button** on the Word program window, then scroll up to **page 1**
   See Figure C-13. The slide numbers are in the first column, the slides are in the second column, and blank lines appear next to the slides in the third column. There are three slides per page. Make the slide numbers bold.

8. Select the first column, then click the **Bold button** 🅱 on the Formatting toolbar
   Now save and print the handouts.

9. Save the file as **Handouts for Company Summary** to your Student Disk, then click the **Print button** 🖨 on the Standard toolbar
   The handouts print.

10. Click the **Close button** on the Word program window, then click the **Close button** on the PowerPoint program window without saving any changes
    The programs close. Do not save changes when prompted by the alert box.

FIGURE C-12: Write-Up dialog box

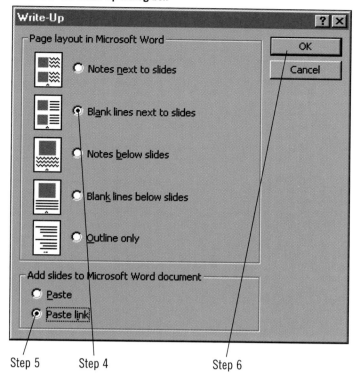

Step 5 Step 4 Step 6

FIGURE C-13: Exported PowerPoint presentation in Word

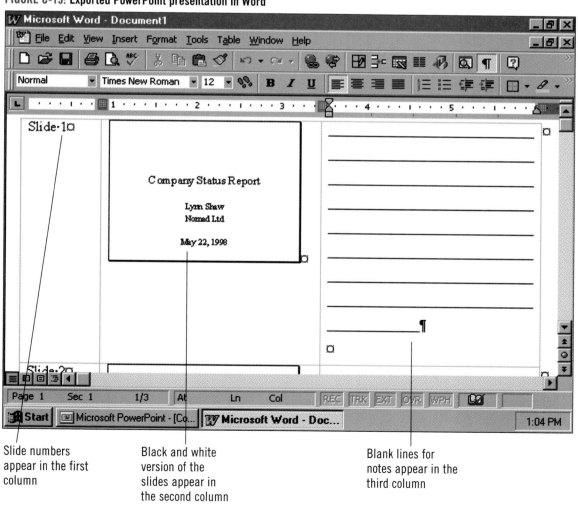

Slide numbers appear in the first column

Black and white version of the slides appear in the second column

Blank lines for notes appear in the third column

INTEGRATING WORD, EXCEL, ACCESS, AND POWERPOINT

Practice

► Independent Challenges

1. You are the person in your company who recommends which software packages should be purchased. You have decided to recommend Microsoft Office. Create a PowerPoint presentation illustrating the advantages of each application in the Microsoft Office suite. Your presentation should contain slides that show how first-time computer users feel about computers and why Microsoft Office is a good choice for them. This information is provided in the file INT C-4 on your Student Disk. Think about what you would like the presentation to say and what graphics you will use. Be prepared to make an on-screen presentation to the class.

To complete this independent challenge:

1. Plan your presentation, determining its purpose and the look you want that will help communicate your message. Sketch on paper how you want the slides to look.
2. Create a PowerPoint presentation and save it as Office Review to your Student Disk.
3. Insert the Word document INT C-4 from your Student Disk into your presentation outline. This file contains information about how first-time computer users feel about computers. Use this outline to help you create your presentation. Your presentation should contain at least 10 slides.
4. Create the title slide for your presentation, then save your work.
5. Add slide show special effects, such as builds and transitions, into the presentation.
6. Check the spelling in your presentation.
7. Run the slide show and evaluate your presentation. Is your message clear? Are the slides visually appealing? Make any changes necessary and save the presentation.
8. Print the slides and outline of your presentation.
9. Submit your presentation plan and printed presentation. Be prepared to present your slide show to the class.

2. To augment the Census Bureau's data on marriage and birth-rate statistics, you have been asked to prepare a PowerPoint presentation that will run continuously at the local census office. Charts on the data need to be linked to PowerPoint slides because data is occasionally updated. Use the data found in the two worksheets in the Excel file INT C-5 on your Student Disk. Create a presentation that explains this data.

To complete this independent challenge:

1. Open the file INT C-5 from your Student Disk, then save it as Statistics to your Student Disk.
2. Create at least four charts using the data in the Marriages worksheet.
3. Create one chart using the data in the Birthrates worksheet.
4. Decide which aspects of the data you want to highlight, and write two to three paragraphs describing how your presentation will illustrate the importance of the data.
5. Create a new Word document containing an outline for your presentation, then save it as Stat Outline to your Student Disk. Print this outline.
6. Open a new PowerPoint presentation. Save it as Bureau on your Student Disk.
7. Create a title slide for the presentation.
8. Insert the Word outline into the presentation.
9. Add slide show special effects, such as builds and transitions, to the slides.
10. Link the four charts in the Marriages worksheet to slides in the presentation.
11. Embed the chart in the Birthrates worksheet in a slide in the presentation.

12. Create handouts in Word so the audience can take notes. Link the presentation in case you make changes. Save this file as Bureau Handouts to your Student Disk.
13. Check the spelling in your presentation, then run the final slide show and evaluate your presentation. Make any changes necessary.
14. Save and print the slides of your presentation.
15. After you have saved the final presentation, go back to Bureau Handouts in Word, update the link, then save and print the document. (*Hint*: To update the link, use the Links command on the Edit menu.)
16. Submit your presentation plan and printed presentation. Be prepared to present your slide show to the class.
17. Close all open applications.

3. You have been hired as an associate in the Marketing Department at Nomad Ltd. Nomad recently completed a big marketing campaign promoting its bicycle tours, but the company neglected its nonbicycle tours. Sales of the bungee jumping tours especially have fallen off. It is your job to develop a marketing strategy to restore the sales levels of non-bicycle tours. The Nomad Board of Directors, concerned about the falling sales, has suggested adding rock climbing and jeep tours to the Nomad tour line to broaden Nomad's customer base.

You decide to send a questionnaire to customers who have taken the bungee jumping tour to ask how this tour can be improved. You also decide to create a PowerPoint presentation that suggests advertising strategies for promoting the new tours. You will need several charts to show the current nonbicycle tour trends and the potential sales for the new tours.

To complete this independent challenge:

1. Start Word and open the file INT C-6 from your Student Disk. Save it as Cover Letter to your Student Disk. This is the cover letter to the questionnaire.
2. Use the Insert Picture command to add the Nomad Ltd logo to the header of the memo. The logo is in the file NOMAD on your Student Disk.
3. Start Access and open the file Customer Data from your Student Disk.
4. Create a query that lists customers who have taken the bungee tour. Save the query as "Bungee Customers".
5. Use Word's Mail Merge feature to merge the cover letter and the Access query you have created. Print the resulting letters.
6. Start Excel and open the file INT C-7 from your Student Disk. Save it as Tour Type to your Student Disk. This worksheet contains data for road bike, mountain bike, and bungee tour sales.
7. Create two charts: one that compares the sales numbers of the tours and the other that shows the tours as a percentage of all tours. Use drawing tools and color, if appropriate, to point out weak sales. Name this worksheet Current.
8. Copy the data from the Current worksheet to a new worksheet. In the new worksheet, add a formula that calculates an increase in the bungee tour sales by 20%, then show this increase in your charts. Use drawing tools and color, if appropriate, to indicate which figures are speculative. Name this worksheet Bungee Increase.
9. Copy the increased bungee tour sales data to another new worksheet, then add two more rows for the rock climbing and jeep tours. Assume their sales equal the sales of the increased bungee tour sales. Create two more charts to show the new tours. Use drawing tools and color, if appropriate, to indicate which figures are speculative and to point out the new tours. Name this worksheet New Tours.
10. Add titles to all three charts to identify them. Use drop shadows and other formatting effects to make them more attractive.
11. Print the data and the charts on all three worksheets.
12. Start PowerPoint and create a new presentation. Save it as Tour Evaluation to your Student Disk. This presentation will illustrate your marketing ideas to increase sales.
13. Create a title slide.

14. Insert the Word outline INT C-8 from your Student Disk after the title slide.

15. Add to the outline your own ideas on how to strengthen bungee tours sales and generate new sales for the new tours. You can suggest additional tours, too.

16. Include the Excel charts on your slides by using the method you feel is best: pasting, linking, or embedding, or a combination of the three.

17. Use templates, clip art, builds, and any other PowerPoint features you want to create an effective and professional-looking presentation.

18. Print the presentation as Handouts (6 slides per page).

19. Submit all your work.

4. One of your jobs at Bolten Industries is to create a presentation on the company's inventory for the yearly report. Bolten Industries produces five specialized aircraft parts for most of the U.S. jet aircraft manufacturers. The annual report needs to show how many parts, or units, were manufactured during the last year and how many were distributed to aircraft manufacturers. The presentation needs to list each aircraft manufacturer, the number of parts they received, and the cost per unit.

You decide to create a 10- to 15-slide presentation that displays all the inventory information for your report. You will need to create all the information for this challenge on your own. To help you create this presentation, assume the following:

- The five aircraft parts Bolten manufactures are the following: (1) 2-stage hydraulic nose gear assembly; (2) door lifter assemblies; (3) wing balance plates; (4) main cargo assembly lifters; (5) hydraulic lifter gears
- Bolten Industries makes parts for the following companies: Boeing, McDonnell Douglas, Lockheed, Cessna, and Learjet

To complete this independent challenge:

1. Create a database in Access using the Inventory Wizard. Enter data in all the database fields using the five aircraft parts listed above. Save the database as Parts Data to your Student Disk.

2. Create an outline in Word that you can insert into PowerPoint to use as your presentation outline. Identify 10 slides and subpoints you want on each slide in the outline and then save the Word outline as Parts Outline.

3. Insert the Word outline into a new PowerPoint presentation. Save the presentation as Bolten Inventory.

4. Create queries from the Parts Data database that list the number of parts manufactured and distributed during the last year, then create at least two Excel worksheets with the information. Embed the worksheets into the Bolten Inventory presentation.

5. Create an Excel worksheet, using your own data and showing revenue data produced by the sale of the company's aircraft parts. Save the workbook as Aircraft Parts Revenue. Link the worksheet to PowerPoint.

6. Use templates, clip art, builds, and any other PowerPoint features you want to create an effective and professional-looking presentation. To find photographs, log on to the Internet and use your browser to go to http://www.course.com. From there, click the link Student OnLine Companions, then click Microsoft Office 97 Professional Edition—Illustrated: A First Course page, then click the Integration link for Unit C. You can download photographs from the links found there.

   Make sure to abide by any terms and conditions for using copyrighted material at the sites. Note that when you include photographs in a presentation, you increase the size of the presentation file significantly.

7. Save and print the presentation.

8. Print out the files you created in Word and Excel.

9. Submit all the files and printouts you created.

Creating
a Web Publication

▶ **Plan Web publication content**

▶ **Create a Web page document**

▶ **Format a Web page**

▶ **Create a Web page from a Word document**

▶ **Create a Web page from an Access object**

▶ **Create a Web page from an Excel file**

▶ **Create Web pages with PowerPoint**

▶ **Add hyperlinks**

Microsoft Office 97 contains features that make it easy for you to create your own Web pages from scratch or by converting existing Office documents to **HTML (Hypertext Markup Language)**. HTML is the language used to describe the content and format of pages on the World Wide Web (WWW). Cleveland Mack works in the Human Resources department at Nomad Ltd. The Human Resources director, Becky Riis, has asked Cleveland to create a set of pages for the company network that will help new Nomad employees learn more about the company. The Human Resources department will then **publish**, or make these pages available, on the Nomad **intranet** — a private network that uses Internet communications technologies — so that all new employees can access them. You'll use Office to help Cleveland create the new Web pages.

Internet

Planning Web Publication Content

As with any other type of document, it is important to plan your Web pages carefully before creating them. This is especially crucial when you are creating a **Web publication**, or a group of associated Web pages around a particular theme or topic. Using a step-by-step process can help you to organize tasks logically and also helps ensure that you thoroughly identify and complete necessary tasks. Cleveland decides to use the following plan to create the Web publication for new employees:

Details

 Sketch outlines of the pages

Draw a sketch of how you want each page to look to make it easier to identify the tasks you need to complete to create your pages. Be sure to indicate the links between pages in your sketch. Cleveland has identified the documents he wants to include in his pages and has sketched the layout, as shown in Figure B-1.

 For each page, perform the following tasks:

Create a new document and enter the page's text, or use a Web page tool to create a page from an existing file.

It is usually easiest to create a page that will contain all new text in a word processor. Word 97's Web Page Wizard simplifies the creation of high-quality Web pages from scratch by providing illustrated templates in which you can place text. Additionally, each Office 97 program contains a tool that can automatically create a Web page from a file in that program's format.

 Format the page's appearance

Word 97 includes special features that facilitate editing any Web page document, including those not created in Word. When you use **Word Web**, Word's Web page editing tool, the Style menu lists acceptable text styles for Web pages. With Word Web, you also can add thematic graphics to your pages easily. To personalize each page further, you may want to add your own images as well. Cleveland will use Word Web's text tools to enhance each page's appearance when he edits it. He also will apply a common visual style to his pages and will insert the Nomad Ltd. company logo at the top of the main page of the Web publication, known as the **home page**.

 View the page and make final corrections

Use a web browser such as Internet Explorer to make sure the page displays as desired. If necessary, use Word to make corrections.

 Format hyperlinks

After you have finalized the text and graphics for all of your pages, add hyperlinks to each page for other pages that are referenced. Cleveland's sketch indicates that he will create a link on his home page to each of the associated pages. He also will create links to other important Nomad pages at the bottom of the home page, as well as add a link back to the home page on each associated page.

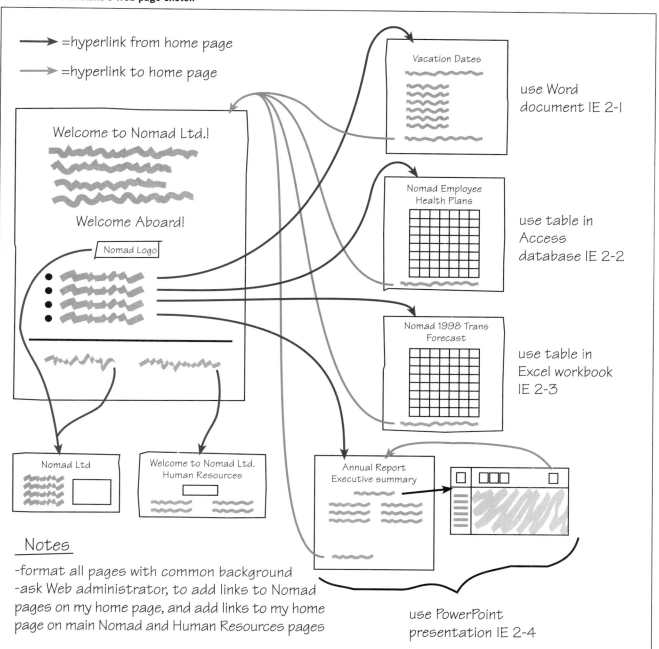

Internet

Creating a Web Page Document

To create a Web page, you create a document that uses HTML formatting. Normally, this involves adding codes, called **tags**, around all the elements of your document, which describe how the elements should be displayed in a Web browser. Microsoft Office's Web tools simplify this process by inserting the codes for you. Additionally, Word's Web Page Wizard includes templates that add thematic formatting and graphics to your Web pages instantly. Cleveland will use Word's Web Page Wizard to create the basic structure of his home page.

Steps 1 2 3 4

1. **Start Word, then make sure the Standard and Formatting toolbars are visible**
   You need to open a new document to begin creating your Web page. You will use the Web Page Wizard to both create and format your new document.

Trouble?

You must have the Web Authoring tools installed in order to do this unit. If you do not, see your instructor or Lab technician for help.

2. **Click File, click New, click the Web Pages tab, then double-click Web Page Wizard**
   The Web Page Wizard dialog box displays a list of templates as shown in Figure B-2. The Simple Layout style previews in the Word document window. Keep in mind that some templates are used for specific types of pages.

3. **Click Simple Layout, then click Next**
   The Web Page Wizard displays a list of visual style options. Choose the ivy and the stones since they fit well with Nomad Ltd.'s company image.

4. **Click on any style names that look interesting, noting the different moods that their layouts and formatting convey; when you are finished browsing, click Outdoors, then click Finish**
   The Simple Layout template opens in the document window with the Outdoors visual style.

5. **Click the Save button 🖫, type Welcome in the File name text box, select the appropriate folder to save your files in the Save in list box, then click Save**
   Notice that Word saves your file in HTML format. This confirms that Word is inserting the HTML tags for you. Begin creating the page by entering your page heading.

6. **Click in the selection bar next to the heading Insert Heading Here to select the line, type Welcome to Nomad Ltd.!, replace the following paragraph with the paragraph shown in Figure B-3, then replace the line "Type some text." with the text Welcome Aboard!**
   Now enter the text for the rest of the page.

Trouble?

To add a bullet, press Enter with the insertion point at the end of a bulleted line.

7. **Highlight the text Add a list item. next to the first stone bullet below the text you just entered, making sure not to select the stone graphic, type List of vacation dates for Nomad employees, then repeat this procedure to enter the text for the remaining bullets shown in Figure B-3**

8. **Press Page Down to move the insertion point to the bottom of the page, then delete the line reading "Type some text" immediately following the bulleted list**
   The text in the last line of the page is blue, indicating hyperlink format. Type the appropriate text for links to two other Nomad pages here; however, you will create the actual links later.

9. **Drag the mouse pointer to select the text Related Page 1, type Nomad Ltd. home page, select the text Related Page 2, type Nomad Human Resources Department home page, select the text Related Page 3 and the vertical line to its left, press Delete, then save your document**
   You have entered all the text for the Welcome page.

FIGURE B-2: Web Page Wizard dialog box

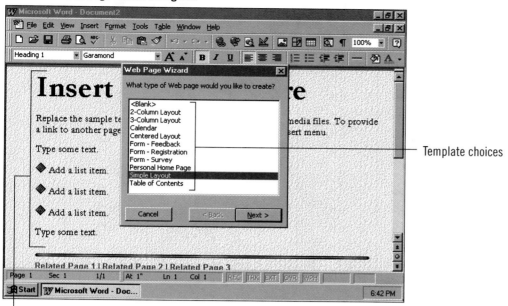

Template choices

Preview of simple
layout template

FIGURE B-3: Text entered for home page

Test to replace
existing line

Heading inserted

Text to replace
existing paragraph

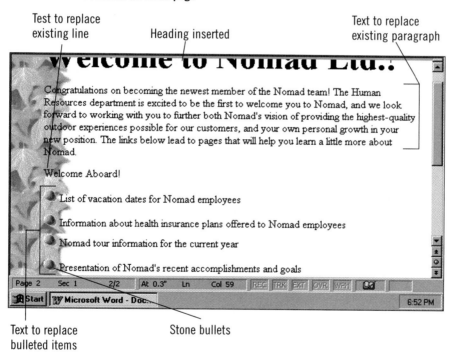

Text to replace
bulleted items

Stone bullets

Choosing Web page content and style

Before deciding how you want your own Web publication to look, look at existing pages on the Web. The styles, layouts, and contents of other people's pages can give you new ideas about how you want to present your own information. By viewing a wide variety of pages, you also may learn about Web page formatting features that have only recently become available. Remember, however, that a Web publication is an expression of your company's or your own identity; rather than simply copying other pages, you should include some personal touches in your pages.

Internet

Formatting a Web Page

Once you have entered the text for a Web page, you can use Word's toolbars and menu options to format it. However, some formatting options available in standard Word documents are not supported by HTML. Word makes these options — such as the Justify button and the Tab key — unavailable when you work with an HTML document, replacing them with useful tools for formatting Web pages. Table B-1 lists the new buttons available on the Formatting and Standard toolbars when working with HTML documents, as well as standard buttons that offer new functions in this mode. Although the template and visual style he selected provided much of the formatting he wanted for his Web page, Cleveland would like to change the format and layout of some of the text and add his own graphic.

Steps

1. Press **[Ctrl][Home]** to move the insertion point to the top of the document
   Make the line of text before the bulleted list a centered heading.

2. Click in the selection bar next to the text "Welcome Aboard!" to select it, click the **Style list arrow**, click **Heading 2**, click the **Center button** ▤, then click anywhere in the text to deselect the heading
   Word Web's Style list contains only styles that are compatible with HTML. Next, indent the list so it stands out from the surrounding text.

3. Use the selection bar to select all four lines of the bulleted list, click the **Increase Indent button** ▣, then click anywhere in the document window to deselect the list
   The list is now indented as shown in Figure B-4. Cleveland's final formatting change is the insertion of the Nomad company logo in the Web page.

4. Move the insertion point to the end of the line containing the text "Welcome Aboard!", then press **[Enter]** to insert a blank paragraph
   This line will serve as the location of the graphic file containing the logo.

5. Click the **Insert Picture button** ▣
   The Insert Picture button is not normally present on Word's Standard toolbar, but is available when you are working in Word Web. The Insert Picture dialog box opens.

6. Select the location of your Student Disk in the Look in text box, click **Nomad** in the file list, and then click **Insert**
   The Nomad logo graphic appears in the blank paragraph. Try centering it to see how it looks.

7. Click the Nomad graphic to select it, click ▤, then click in text to deselect the graphic
   The centered graphic appears as shown in Figure B-5. Clicking a graphic in Word Web adds selection handles and opens the Picture toolbar, just as when you work with graphics in a standard Word document. The final step in the process is to view your page in your Web browser to verify that it appears the way you intended. However, because you are using only simple formatting and layout for your page, and no advanced elements like tables, Word Web displays the page exactly as it would appear in a browser. Therefore, you do not need to open the page in Internet Explorer.

8. If necessary, scroll through the page to see all the elements

9. Save the changes to your Web page, then close the file **Welcome**
   Because you will be creating and editing more pages, leave Word open. Now you are ready to create the associated pages.

FIGURE B-4: Heading and list formatted

Insert Picture button

Text formatted and centered

Bulleted list indented

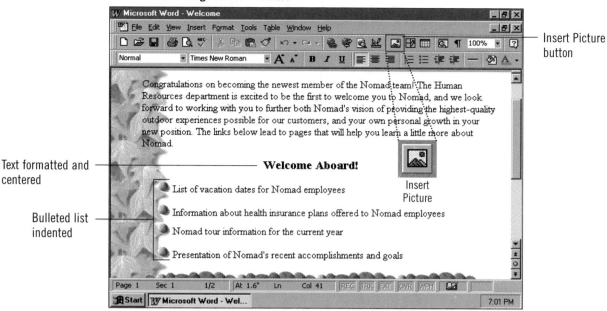

FIGURE B-5: Completed home page

Graphic inserted and centered

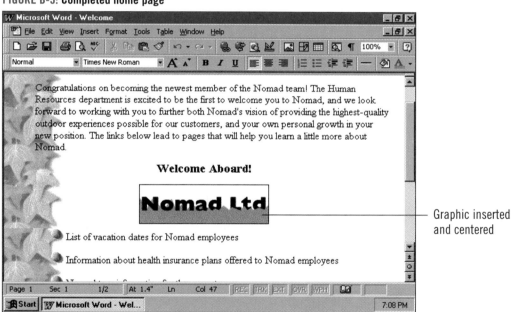

TABLE B-1: Formatting buttons for HTML

button	function
A	Increases font size for selected text to next-highest HTML-standard size
A	Decreases font size for selected text to next-lowest HTML-standard size
—	Creates a horizontal line across the page at the position of the insertion point
	Adds a background color or texture or replaces current background
	Launches a Web browser (if installed) displaying the page currently open in Word Web
	Switches to Forms Design Mode, allowing you to add a form to your Web page
	Inserts an existing picture in the active file at the insertion point

Internet

Creating a Web Page from a Word Document

In addition to offering tools to help you create new Web pages, Microsoft Office 97 makes it easy to create Web pages from existing files. You can use the Web features in Office to convert files from their Office formats to HTML, making them easily viewable on the Web. ✎ As he noted on his original sketch, Cleveland wants to create Web pages using several existing Office documents. He decides to start by creating a Web page from a list of company vacation dates stored in a Word file.

Steps

1. **Open the file IE B-1 from your Student Disk**
   The file contains a list of vacation dates for all employees of Nomad Ltd.

2. **Click File, then click Save as HTML**
   The Save As HTML dialog box opens.

3. **In the File name text box, type Vacation, make sure the drive where you want to save your files displays in the Save in list box, then click Save**
   Word saves a copy of the document in HTML format and switches to Word Web mode. Notice that the formatting toolbar changes to include only tools compatible with HTML, and the document's line spacing is increased to reflect HTML styles. Now you can change some of the page's formatting.

Trouble?

Even though you saved the file as Vacation, the title bar now displays "Vacation dates." This is because Word automatically uses the page heading as the Web page title, which displays in the title bar of a Web browser instead of the filename.

4. **Delete the blank paragraphs before and after the line that begins "The following are…," center the heading Vacation Dates, insert a blank line at the end of the document, type Return to Welcome page, then indent the list of dates**
   Use the last line of text as a link back to the Web publication's home page. Now add a background to match the outdoor theme created on the home page.

5. **Click the Background button 🎨 on the Formatting toolbar**
   Word displays the Background toolbar, as shown in Figure B-6. The Background toolbar contains a palette of colors that you can click to fill the background of the page in the active document window;

6. **Click Fill Effects.**
   The Fill Effects dialog box opens, displaying a selection of patterns that you can select as background for the current page.

Trouble?

If Word Web displays the list of picture files on your Student Disk, use the Look in list arrow to open the folder Microsoft Office\Clipart\Backgrounds on the drive from which Word is running.

7. **Click Other Texture, then, if necessary, click the Preview button 🖼**
   The Select Texture dialog box opens, displaying a list of graphic files that contain other background choices.

8. **Double-click Leaves on the Side, click OK, then, if necessary, scroll through the page to inspect it**
   The border of leaves appears on the left edge of the screen, matching the appearance of the Welcome page you created, as shown in Figure B-7. Save your changes to the Vacation page, then close it. Next, you will convert an Access table to a Web page.

FIGURE B-6: Background toolbar open

Web page title

Background button

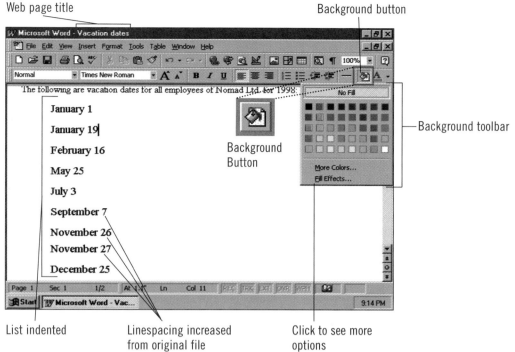

Background toolbar

Background Button

List indented

Linespacing increased from original file

Click to see more options

FIGURE B-7: Completed Vacation page

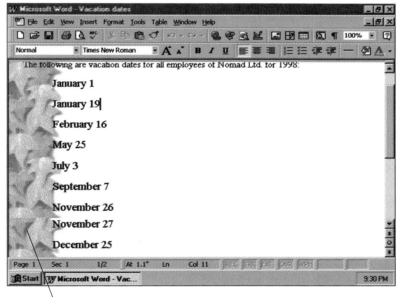

Leaf border added

Web browsers and web page appearance

People use many different browsers to view Web pages, including Lynx (a text-only browser), Netscape Navigator, and Microsoft Internet Explorer. Each browser may display the same Web page differently. Additionally, users can change settings such as always using a certain font or selecting a certain window size, within their personal browsers that affect the way pages display. Using only the limited set of style choices provided by Word Web is one way to help ensure that your Web page displays as consistently as possible on different browsers.

Internet

Creating a Web Page from an Access Object

Like Word, Access offers a tool for converting existing files to Web pages. The Publish to the Web Wizard creates a separate HTML file from each element of a database that you select. You can use Word to format the resulting file like any other HTML file. ◄━━━━ Cleveland wants to create a Web page containing a table that describes the various health insurance plans available to Nomad employees. This information is currently stored in an Access database.

Steps 1 2 3 4

1. Start Access, open the file **IE B-2** from the WWW Access folder on your Student Disk, then open the table **Nomad Employee Health Plans** in Table view

2. Click **File**, click **Save As HTML**, then in the first Publish to the Web Wizard dialog box, make sure the checkbox regarding Web publication profiles is unchecked, then click **Next**
   The next Publish to the Web Wizard dialog box allows you to select the elements of the current database from which you want to create Web pages.

3. Click the **Nomad Employee Health Plans** check box on the Tables tab to check it, then click **Next**
   The Publish to the Web Wizard displays a dialog box for selecting a template.

4. Click **Browse**, click **Stones**, click **Select**, then click **Next**
   The next Publish to the Web Wizard dialog box offers you a choice between different types of HTML code for your new Web page. Because the original file resides on a local computer rather than on the company Web server, you decide to create a static page.

5. Click the **Static HTML option button** to select it, click **Next**, if necessary, click **Browse**, select the main directory of your Student Disk, click **Select**, make sure the **No option button** is selected, then click **Next**
   The next Publish to the Web Wizard dialog box offers you the option of having Access create a home page containing a link to the insurance page you are creating.

6. Make sure the **Yes** check box is not checked, click **Next**, then click **Finish**
   The Publish to the Web Wizard creates a new Web page and saves it on your Student Disk. The Wizard uses the name of the table in the original database as the filename, adding a number to the end in case you create multiple Web pages from the same table. Open your new Web page in Word so that you can make any necessary edits.

7. Close Access, click the **Word program button**, then open the file **Nomad Employee Health Plans_1** from your Student Disk
   The Health Plan Web page opens in Word Web, as shown in Figure B-8. Some of the table text breaks at odd points. Remember, however, that advanced Web page formats such as tables don't always display correctly in Word. Check the table formatting in Internet Explorer after making your changes to the Web page that Access created.

8. Scroll to the bottom of the table, click about an inch below the table on the left side to select an empty graphic frame created by the template, press [Delete] to remove the frame, type **Return to Welcome page**, save your changes to the Web page, click the **Web Page Preview button** 🔲 to open your page in Internet Explorer
   The page appears as shown in Figure B-9. Notice that the table displays in the correct format.

9. Click the **Word program button**, then close the file **Nomad Employee Health Plans_1**

QuickTip

Notice that the Publish to the Web Wizard used the Access object name to create a Web page title, which is displayed in the title bar in place of the filename.

FIGURE B-8: Health Plans Web page in Word Web

Web page title Web Page Preview button

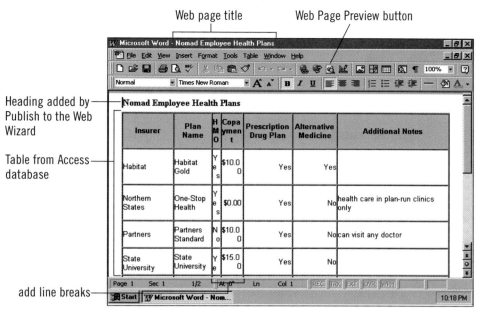

Heading added by Publish to the Web Wizard

Table from Access database

Insurer	Plan Name	HMO	Copayment	Prescription Drug Plan	Alternative Medicine	Additional Notes
Habitat	Habitat Gold	Yes	$10.00	Yes	Yes	
Northern States	One-Stop Health	Yes	$0.00	Yes	No	health care in plan-run clinics only
Partners	Partners Standard	No	$10.00	Yes	No	can visit any doctor
State University	State University	Ye	$15.00	Yes	No	

add line breaks

FIGURE B-9: Health Plans Web page in Internet Explorer

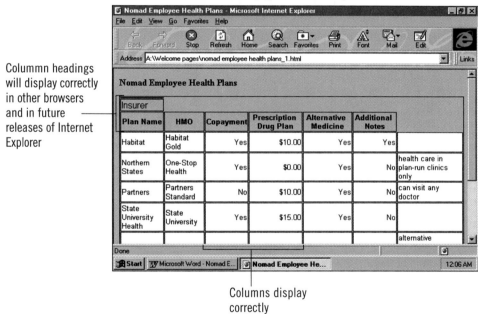

Colummn headings will display correctly in other browsers and in future releases of Internet Explorer

Nomad Employee Health Plans

Insurer						
Plan Name	HMO	Copayment	Prescription Drug Plan	Alternative Medicine	Additional Notes	
Habitat	Habitat Gold	Yes	Yes	$10.00	Yes	Yes
Northern States	One-Stop Health	Yes	Yes	$0.00	Yes	No	health care in plan-run clinics only
Partners	Partners Standard	No	No	$10.00	Yes	No	can visit any doctor
State University Health	State University	Yes	Yes	$15.00	Yes	No
						alternative

Columns display correctly

Static and dynamic pages

The Web Wizard in Access Publish can create both static and dynamic Web pages. When you create a **static HTML page**, the page will contain only the information currently in the table that you are converting. If you choose to create a **dynamic page**, on the other hand, your Web page will be linked to the original database file from which you created it. When you change the original object in the database, the content of a dynamic page will change to reflect your updates, while the contents of a static page will remain unchanged. A dynamic Web page is useful if you expect to make changes to your original Access object often; however, to use this feature, you must locate the database file containing the object on the same file server that contains the dynamic Web page.

Internet

Creating a Web Page from an Excel File

Like Word and Access, Excel includes a Wizard for creating Web pages; however, this feature is tailored to the Excel environment, allowing you to select specific ranges in a worksheet as sources for Web pages. ✏️ Cleveland would like to include pages in the Welcome publication that tell new employees about Nomad's products. A co-worker in the Tours department gave him an Excel workbook that shows a breakdown of the tours planned for 1998 by quarter and tour type. Cleveland will use Excel's Internet Assistant Wizard to create a Web page with this information.

Steps

Trouble?
If the Office Assistant opens, click No to close it.

1. Start Excel, open the file **IE B-3** from your Student Disk, click and drag to select the range **A1...G8**, click **File**, then click **Save as HTML**
The Internet Assistant Wizard — Step 1 of 4 dialog box opens, displaying the address for the range you selected.

2. If necessary, click **Range "$A$1:$G$8"** in the Ranges and charts to convert list to select it, then click **Next**
The next Internet Assistant Wizard dialog box offers you a choice between creating a new HTML file from the selected range or adding this information to an existing Web page file. You will create an independent Web page from this information, so you select the first option.

3. Make sure the option button for the option to create an independent HTML document is selected, click **Next**, make sure the information in the next dialog box matches Figure B-10, then click **Next**
The final Internet Assistant Wizard dialog box contains options for the type and location of the new Web page.

4. If necessary, click the **Save the result as an HTML file** option button to select it, click **Browse**, type **1998 Tours Forecast** in the File name text box, select the appropriate drive in the Save in text box, click **Save**, then click **Finish**
The Internet Assistant Wizard closes after creating and saving your new Web page in the location you specified. Now, view and edit your new file.

5. Close Excel, click **No** if you are asked whether to save changes, click the **Word program button**, then open the file **1998 Tours Forecast** from your Student Disk
The Tours Forecast Web page displays in the Word Web document window, as shown in Figure B-11. You will delete the top row of the table because the heading it contains is duplicated above the table. You also will resize the second column so it is similar in size to the others in the table and add a link to the main Welcome page at the bottom.

6. Right-click in the selection bar next to the top row of the table, click **Delete Rows**, press and hold **[Shift]** while dragging the right border of the second column to the left until it is approximately the same width as the columns for the other quarters, press **[Ctrl][End]**, press **[Enter]**, click the **Italic button** _I_, and then type **Return to Welcome page**
Add the leaf pattern you used on the other Web pages you created in this group.

7. Click the **Background button** 🖼️, click **Fill Effects**, click **Other Texture**, open the folder Microsoft Office\Clipart\Backgrounds, double-click **Leaves on the Side**, then click **OK**

8. Save your changes to the Web page, click the **Web Page Preview button** 🔍, then inspect the Web page
The page appears as shown in Figure B-12.

9. Click the **Word program button**, then close the file **1998 Tours Forecast**

FIGURE B-10: Internet Assistant Wizard – Step 3 of 4 dialog box

Enter text as shown ——

Check both boxes ——

Enter your personal information here

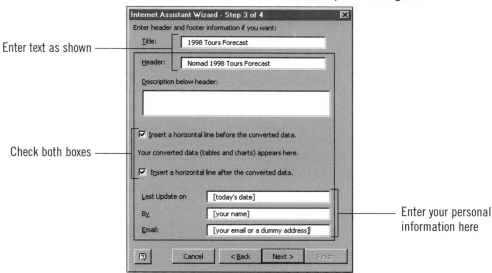

FIGURE B-11: 1998 Tours Forecast In Word Web

Web page title

Heading added by Internet Assistant Wizard

Table from Excel workbook

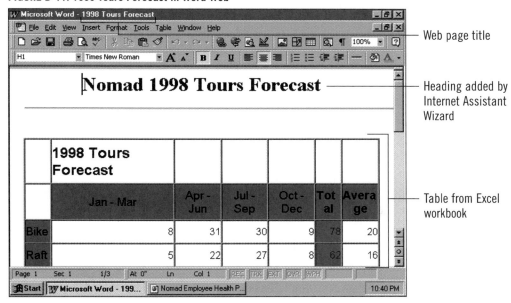

FIGURE B-12: 1998 Tours Forecast in Internet Explorer

Leaf background added

Top row of table deleted

Column resized

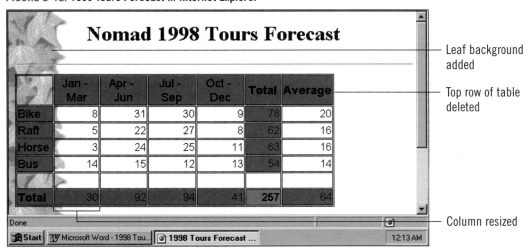

Creating Web Pages with PowerPoint

Unlike other Office files, PowerPoint presentations, however, contain multiple distinct screens of information. The Save as HTML Wizard in PowerPoint addresses this unique situation by creating a separate page for each slide, and grouping the pages together in a folder. People viewing the presentation on the Web can then navigate through it much like they would in PowerPoint. ◆━━━ Cleveland has one final file that he would like to convert to HTML format: a PowerPoint presentation that the company president used at a recent meeting. He will use the Save as HTML Wizard to create a set of Web pages from this presentation.

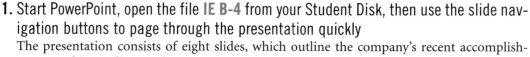

1. Start PowerPoint, open the file **IE B-4** from your Student Disk, then use the slide navigation buttons to page through the presentation quickly
The presentation consists of eight slides, which outline the company's recent accomplishments and immediate goals.

Trouble?

If the Office Assistant opens, click No to close it.

2. Click **File**, click **Save as HTML**, read the opening Wizard screen, click **Next**, make sure the **New layout option button** is selected, then click **Next**
The current Wizard screen provides a choice of Web page styles. You can create a page using the Browser frames format, which takes advantage of the **frames** capability of the newest Web browsers. When a page uses frames, the browser displays different parts the page divided by borders (the frames) to make navigating a group of pages easier for the viewer.

QuickTip

Because the Save as HTML Wizard creates an associated group of Web pages, the Web pages based on this presentation could be considered a publication within your publication.

3. Click the **Browser frames option button**, click **Next**, then complete the remaining Save as HTML dialog boxes, selecting only the following options: **GIF**; **640 by 480**; **3/4 width of screen**; **Use browser colors**; **large square button**; the **Welcome pages directory** on your Student Disk; **Finish**; and **Don't Save**
PowerPoint exports the information in the current presentation in HTML format, creating a title page to serve as a directory to these Web pages. Preview the PowerPoint presentation in your Web browser.

4. Click **OK** to close the PowerPoint dialog box informing you that the Web page creation is complete, close PowerPoint without saving changes, click the **Word program button**, then open the file **index** on your Student Disk
The Presentation title page that the Wizard created displays in the Word Web document window, as shown in Figure B-13. Add the text for the link to your Web publication home page and add the leaf background.

5. Press **[Ctrl][End]**, press **[Enter]**, type **Return to Welcome page**, click the **Background button** ⬛, click **Fill Effects**, click **Other Texture**, open the folder **Microsoft Office\Clipart\Backgrounds**, double-click **Leaves on the Side**, then click **OK**
The title page for the annual report is now formatted similarly to the other pages you have created.

QuickTip

The Forward and Back buttons on the Internet Explorer toolbar do not work within a framed group of pages; to switch between presentation pages, you must use the navigation buttons or the outline.

6. Save your changes to the Web page, click the **Web Page Preview button** 🔍, then click the text **Click here to start** to begin viewing the presentation
Internet Explorer displays the first slide from the presentation, as well as navigation tools for the remaining slides, in frames, as shown in Figure B-14.

7. Experiment with navigating through the slides using both the navigation buttons and the outline, then click the **Index button** 🔲 to return to the title page

8. Click the **Word program button**, then close the file **index**

FIGURE B-13: **Presentation title page in Word Web**

Home Page for
presentation Web
publication

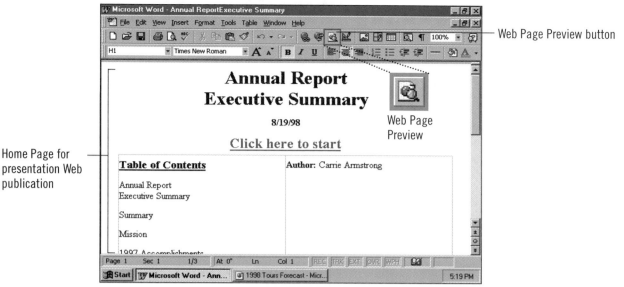

Web Page Preview button

Web Page
Preview

FIGURE B-14: **First slide in frames**

Outline view
buttons

Outline

Navigation buttons

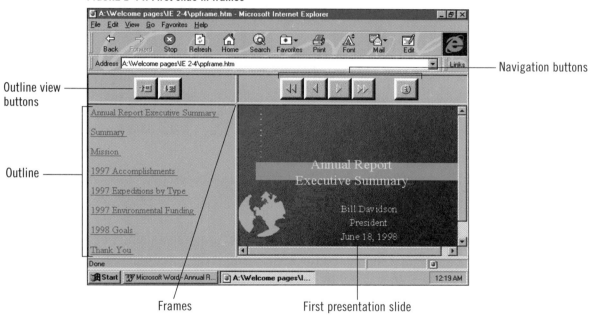

Frames

First presentation slide

Using frames

Frames help you to navigate a group of associated Web pages. Frame formatting is most useful when you want common navigation elements in view for all of the pages. While frames are convenient, keep in mind that they are a relatively new innovation in HTML and not all Web browsers support them. A popular way to address this problem is to create two versions of a publication — one with frames and one without — and to offer a choice between the two on the publication's home page. If you only have the time or resources to create one version, however, use your knowledge of the audience to decide whether or not to use frames. If you were creating a page for a company Intranet and knew that every computer was using the latest version of a graphical browser, adding frames to your publication would make sense. If, however, you were creating a page for publishing on the World Wide Web, for which you wanted the largest possible audience, frames would not work well because some users would be excluded from viewing your document.

Adding Hyperlinks

You have created all the component pages for your Web publication. In order for your pages to take full advantage of the Web once you publish them, you need to add links both between the publication pages and to other pages on the Web. This will help people viewing your publication to locate the information they want more efficiently. ◀▬▬ Cleveland's sketch shows links from the home page to each of the associated pages as well as a link back to the home page from each associated page. His plan also includes links on the home page to take users to other Nomad company pages that they might find useful. Cleveland decides to start by adding the links to his home page.

Steps123⁴

1. **Open the file Welcome from your Student Disk in Word, then if necessary, scroll down so all of the bulleted items are visible in the document window**
   Begin creating the links to the associated pages. Do this by using **relative links**, or links that give another page's address in relation to the current page, rather than **absolute links**, which contain only a fixed address. Once you have created the relative links, you can publish the pages to the Web in their current directory structure, and the links will remain accurate.

2. **Highlight the text next to the first bullet, but not the bullet itself, then click the Insert Hyperlink button** 📇
   The Insert Hyperlink dialog box opens, as shown in Figure B-15.

3. **Click Browse next to the Link to file or URL text box, select the directory containing your Student Disk files in the Look in list box, double-click the file Vacation, make sure a check appears in the Use relative path for hyperlink check box, then click OK**
   The text is now underlined and displays in blue, which is standard format for a hyperlink.

Trouble?

Even though the link address shown contains the full pathname, the link is still relative, as long as you checked the appropriate box when creating it.

4. **Move the mouse pointer over the linked text**
   The mouse pointer changes to 🖑, as the Internet Explorer pointer does when it is over a link. Word Web also displays the address to which an object is linked above it when the pointer is over a linked object.

5. **Repeat Steps 2 and 3 to create relative links for the remaining lines of bulleted text, linking the second line to the file Nomad Employee Health plans_1, the third line to 1998 Tours Forecast, and the fourth line to index (located in the folder IE B-4)**
   Your final tasks are to add a link to the home page at the bottom of each associated page and to check all the links you have inserted.

QuickTip

Links work between unpublished documents as well as published Web pages; you can now use the home page to easily open the remaining documents and add links to them.

6. **Click the text List of vacation dates for Nomad employees**
   The Vacation file opens, without its associated background. Because you have followed a link between files on your computer, Word Web displays the Web toolbar, as shown in Figure B-16.

7. **Press [Ctrl][End], select the text Return to Welcome page, click the Create Hyperlink button** 📇**, create a relative link to the file Welcome on your Student Disk, save the file Vacation, then click the new link to return to the Welcome page**

Trouble?

As in Internet Explorer, clicking a link closes the current file while opening the new one. Thus only the Welcome file is open at the end of this step.

8. **Repeat Steps 6 and 7 to create links to the home page on each of the remaining associated pages, save the Welcome, then close Word and Internet Explorer**
   Now you have successfully created links between the files in your Web publication and have tested the links in Word Web.

FIGURE B-15: Insert Hyperlink dialog box

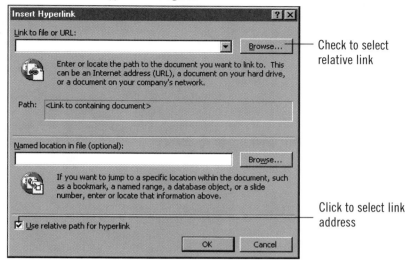

Check to select
relative link

Click to select link
address

FIGURE B-16: Vacation file in World Web window

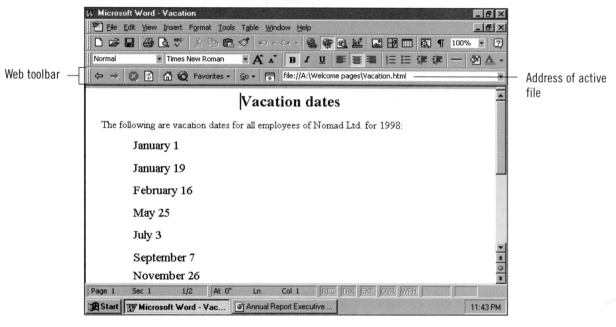

Web toolbar

Address of active
file

Publishing your Web publication

Your Web publication is not available to anyone outside your local computer network or workgroup until you publish it, either by placing a copy on a server for the World Wide Web or an intranet. Keep in mind, though, that whatever links you create on your home page are one-way: they help people viewing your page to find other interesting pages but do not help locate your page in the first place. If you want people to use your WWW publication, you can get the word out by asking friends to create links to your home page on their pages, asking the administrator of your server to add your homepage to the index of the site's Web pages, and e-mailing groups, organizations, and people with Web sites who you think would be interested in your publication. To effectively publish on an intranet, send a memo to employees who you think would be interested in your page, and ask the network administrator and the owners of other relevant pages to add links to your publication on their pages.

Internet

Practice

▶ Concepts Review

Label each of the World Web screen elements indicated in Figure B-17

FIGURE B-17

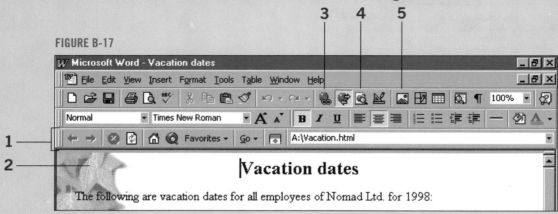

Match each of the terms below with the statement that best describes its function:

6. Frames
7. HTML
8. Home Page
9. Dynamic page
10. Word Web

a. Language for describing Web page contents and format
b. Page linked to original database file
c. Web page editing tool in Word 97
d. Format creating borders between screen elements
e. Main page of a Web publication

Select the best answer from the list of choices.

11. To preview the current Word document in Internet Explorer, click:
    a. 🖶
    b. 🗗
    c. 🔍
    d. 🖼

12. Frames are most useful for:
    a. navigating a group of associated Web pages.
    b. creating hyperlinks.
    c. formatting headings.
    d. creating a home page.

13. Web pages that you create are available to users outside your local network:
    a. when you save them to your hard drive.
    b. after you format them.
    c. when you place a copy on a WWW or intranet server.
    d. only if you use frames.

14. The final step in creating a Web publication is:
    a. viewing a page and making final corrections.
    b. formatting hyperlinks.
    c. creating Web pages based on existing files.
    d. creating a home page.

15. Which of the following Word Web options is not supported by HTML?

- **a.** B
- **b.** ≣
- **c.** A̐
- **d.** All Word Web options are supported by HTML.

16. To add a background to a Web page in Word Web, you:

- **a.** click 🖼, then select an image.
- **b.** click 🖱, then type the address of the image file to use.
- **c.** display the Web toolbar, type the address of the image file to use in the Address text box, then press Enter.
- **d.** click 🖼 then select a style or image.

► Skills Review

1. Plan Web publication content.

- **a.** Sketch an outline of a Web publication for the Nomad Ltd sales department, including a home page, a recent letter sent to past customers, a table of contact information for past customers, a table of the most recent sales figures, and a presentation on Nomad's Outback division.
- **b.** Draw arrows on your sketch indicating hyperlinks between the pages in your publication.

2. Create a Web page document.

- **a.** Start Word, then make sure the Standard and Formatting toolbars are visible.
- **b.** Click File, click New, click the Web Pages tab, then double-click Web Page Wizard.
- **c.** Use the Web Page Wizard to create a new document using the Table of Contents template and the Jazzy visual style, then save the document to your Student Disk as "Nomad Tour Sales Department."
- **d.** Drag to select the heading, then type "Tour Sales Information."
- **e.** Replace the paragraph beneath the heading with "Our company vision:", press Enter, then type, "To provide the highest-quality outdoor experiences possible for our customers."
- **f.** Replace the next line. Type some text with "Use these links to access the latest information about Nomad Tour Sales:."
- **g.** Right-click in the last "Add a Hyperlink" line, then click Insert Rows to add a fourth row to the table.
- **h.** Click and drag across the fourth row of the table to select the row, click the Copy button, click and drag to select, then right-click in the row you just inserted and then right-click and click Paste Cells.
- **i.** Highlight the first line reading "Add a Hyperlink," then type "Letter accompanying survey sent to past customers."
- **j.** Repeat step i to replace the remaining three lines with "Recent tour sales customers," "Most recent sales figures," and "Outback division overview presentation."
- **k.** Replace the text "New!" next to the first line of the table with "Research."
- **l.** Replace the three Related Page hyperlinks at the bottom of the page with "Nomad Ltd home page", "Nomad Sales Dept. ", and "Nomad New Employee Orientation".

3. Format a Web page.

- **a.** Scroll to the top of the document.
- **b.** Apply the Heading 3 style to the text "Our company vision:" and center it, apply the Heading 2 style to the company vision statement and center it, click to the left of the O in the line "Our company vision:," press Enter, then move the insertion point into the blank paragraph you created.
- **c.** Click the Insert Picture button and insert the Nomad graphic from your Student Disk.
- **d.** Save the changes to your Web page, then close the file.

Internet

4. Create a Web page from a Word document.

   a. Open the file IE B-5 from the appropriate directory containing your Student Disk.

   b. Click File, click Save as HTML, then save the file as "Customer Survey Letter".

   c. Delete the three lines for customer address information and the blank paragraph that follows, then delete the text block beginning with "Very truly yours," and ending at the end of the document.

   d. At the end of the document, type "Return to Tour Sales home page".

   e. Apply H2 style to the first line of the document, then center it.

   f. Click the Background button, click Fill Effects, then apply an appropriate background texture or graphic.

   g. Save your changes to the Nomad Customer Survey Letter page, then close it.

5. Create a Web page from an Access table.

   a. Open the file IE B-6 from the appropriate directory on Student Disk, open the table Customers in Table view, click File, then click Save As HTML.

   b. Make sure the checkbox regarding Web publication profiles is unchecked, then click Next.

   c. Click the Customers check box on the Tables tab to check it, then click Next.

   d. Click Browse, select an appropriate template, click Select, then click Next.

   e. Click the Static HTML option button to select it, click Next, select the main directory containing your Student Disk, make sure the No option button is selected, then click Next.

   f. Make sure the Yes check box is not checked, click Next, then click Finish.

   g. Close Access, click the Word program button, and then open the file Customers_1 from your Student Disk.

   h. Scroll to the bottom of the table, click about an inch below the table on the left side to select the empty graphic frame, press Delete, type "Return to Tour Sales home page", then save your changes.

   i. Click the Background button, click Fill Effects, then apply an appropriate background texture or graphic.

   j. Click the Web Page Preview button to open your page in Internet Explorer, then inspect the Web page.

   k. Click the Word program button, then close the file, "Customers_1."

6. Create a Web page from an Excel workbook.

   a. Start Excel, then open the file IE B-7 from the appropriate directory containing your Student Disk.

   b. Click and drag to select the range A1 to H11, click File, then click Save as HTML.

   c. Make sure Range "$A$1:$H$11" in the Ranges and charts to convert list is selected, click Next, make sure the option button for the option to create an independent HTML document is selected, then click Next.

   d. Enter "1998 Summer Tour Sales" in the Title text box, enter "1998 Summer Sales Figures" in the Header text box, click both check boxes to check them, complete the dialog box, then click Next.

   e. Make sure the Save the result as an HTML file option button is selected, click Browse, type 1998 sales, select the location of your Student Disk, click Save, then click Finish. Close Excel without saving changes, click the Word program button, then open the file 1998 sales from the appropriate directory containing your Student Disk. Use the selection bar to select the top four rows of the table, right-click in the selected area, click Delete Rows, move the insertion point to the end of the document, press Enter, click the Italic button to remove italic formatting, then type "Return to Tour Sales home page".

   f. Click the Background button, click Fill Effects, then apply an appropriate background texture or graphic.

   g. Save your changes to the Web page, click the Web Page Preview button, inspect the Web page, use Word to adjust column widths if necessary, then save your changes and click Web Page Preview to inspect them.

   h. Click the Word program button, then close the file 1998 Sales.

7. Create Web pages from a PowerPoint presentation.

a. Start PowerPoint, open the file IE B-8 from your appropriate directory containing your Student Disk, then use the slide navigation buttons to page through the presentation quickly.

b. Click File, click Save as HTML, click Next, make sure the New layout opton button is selected, then click Next.

c. Click the Browser frames option button, click Next, then complete the remaining Save as HTML dialog boxes, selecting only the following options: GIF; 640 by 480; 3/4 width of screen; Use browser colors; circular button; the appropriate directory containing your Student Disk; Finish; and Don't Save.

d. Click OK to close the dialog box informing you that the Web page creation is complete, close PowerPoint without saving changes, click the Word program button, then open the file "index" from the folder IE B-8 in the appropriate directory containing your Student Disk.

e. Move the insertion point to the end of the file, insert a new paragraph, type Return to Tour Sales home page, and then add an appropriate background.

f. Save your changes to the Web page, click the Web Page Preview button, then click the text Click here to start.

g. Navigate through the slides using the navigation buttons or the outline, click the Index button to return to the title page, click the Word program button, then close the file index.

8. Add hyperlinks.

a. Open the file Nomad Tour Sales Department from the appropriate directory containing your Student Disk from Word, then scroll down if necessary so the entire table is visible in the document window.

b. Highlight the text for the first hyperlink, "Letter accompanying ...", then click the Insert Hyperlink button.

c. Select the file Customer Survey Letter from your Student Disk in the Look in list box, make sure Use relative path for hyperlink is checked, then click OK.

d. Repeat Steps b and c to create relative links for the remaining cells in the column, linking the text in the second cell to the file Customers_1, the text in the third cell to 1998 Summer Tour Sales, and the text in the fourth cell to index (located in the folder IE B-8), then save the document.

e. Click the text "Letter accompanying..." Move the insertion point to the end of the file, select the text Return to Tour Sales home page, click the Create Hyperlink button, create a relative link to the file Nomad Tour Sales Department in the appropriate folder on your Student Disk, save the file Customer Survey Letter, then click the new link to return to the Tour Sales home page.

f. Repeat Steps e and f to create links to the home page on each of the remaining associated pages.

g. Print the first page of each of your Web pages using Word Web, then close Word and Internet Explorer.

h. Submit your printouts and sketch to your instructor.

► Independent Challenges

1. You are a volunteer at the Safe Haven Emergency Shelter for families in crisis. Knowing that you are experienced in creating Web publications, the shelter staff members mention that they've wanted to put information about the services and resource requests on the net and ask you to create pages for them using existing files from their printed materials.

To complete this independent challenge, perform the following steps:

1. Draw a sketch of the Safe Haven Web publication. Besides a home page, the publication should include a list of requested items for donation, a table detailing the programs offered at the shelter, a chart showing the income and expenses for last year, and a presentation summarizing the recent activities and immediate goals of the shelter. Be sure to include links between the pages.

Internet

2. Create a home page for Safe Haven using Word's Web Page Wizard. Select the Simple Layout template and the Community visual style. Use "Safe Haven Emergency Shelter" as the heading and create a brief mission statement or summary of the shelter's function (to help families survive homelessness and domestic violence) to replace the sample paragraph. Replace the first "Type some text" line with "More about us:". Create appropriate text for the links to the associated pages, deleting other template text as necessary. Replace the sample text for the "Related page" hyperlinks with the names of national or local organizations with missions similar to that of Safe Haven (search the WWW to find organization names if necessary). Save your home page as "Safe Haven" on your Student Disk.

3. Create a Web page from the Word file IE B-9. Save your file as "Donations" and use the Brick Wall background. Change the appearance of the Web page as necessary, and be sure to insert text at the bottom of the page for a link back to the home page.

4. Create a Web page from the table Programs in the Access database IE B-10. Use the Grayst template, use Static HTML, and save your file to your Student Disk. Use Word Web to add a background and delete the graphic box in the lower-left corner of the page; be sure to insert text for a link to the home page.

5. Create a Web page from the range A1:F20 in the Excel workbook IE B-11. Enter an appropriate title and header, include your name, the creation date, and an e-mail address. Save the page as "Financial Report." Use Word Web to add the Brick Wall background, and format the page as necessary. Make sure the page has only one heading; delete table rows if necessary. Be sure to insert text for a link to the home page.

6. Create a Web page from the PowerPoint presentation IE B-12. Because you want a wide WWW audience for your publication, use the standard page style rather than browser frames. Select GIF, 640 x 480, 3/4 width of screen, Use browser colors, and the button shape and location of your choice. Add the Brick Wall background to the index page in Word Web, and format the page as necessary, being sure to insert text for a link to the home page.

7. Add link addresses to the bulleted list of links on your home page, then test the links in Word Web while adding the return links from each of the associated pages.

8. Print the first page of each of your Web pages using Word Web, then submit the printouts along with your sketch to your instructor.

2. You work in the public relations office at Fox Oil Corporation. In light of questions from the public concern following recent oil spills by other companies, Fox Oil wants to publicize the steps it is taking to guard against oil-tanker spills. Your supervisor has asked you to adapt the documents created for the print and television ad campaigns to create a Web publication to be published on Fox's Internet site.

To complete this independent challenge, perform the following steps:

1. The files for adapting include a press release, a table of Fox's oil-spill-prevention programs, a table summarizing recent oil spills by company, and a presentation detailing Fox's oil spill record and the steps it is taking to ensure that no future spills occur. Sketch how this Web publication should look. Be sure to indicate links between the home page and associated documents.

2. Create a home page for the oil spill publication. Use an appropriate template and visual style. Enter text for the home page, format it, and save it on your Student Disk. Include text for a link to the Fox Oil corporate home page, and add the Fox company logo, located in the file fox.gif on your Student Disk.

3. Convert the Word document IE B-13 to HTML; add, delete, and format the text as necessary; apply a background; and make other necessary changes.

4. Convert the table Prevention Programs in the Access database IE B-14 to HTML. Edit the resulting Web page as necessary, apply a background, and make other changes as appropriate.

5. Convert the table located in the Excel spreadsheet IE B-15 to HTML, using an appropriate template. Edit the resulting Web page as necessary, apply a background, and make other changes as appropriate.

6. Convert the PowerPoint presentation IE B-16 to a set of HTML documents. Edit the resulting index page as necessary, apply a background, and make other changes as appropriate.

7. Format and test the hyperlinks between pages in your Web publication.

8. Print the first page of each of your Web pages, and submit your printouts and your sketch to your instructor.

Visual Workshop

You are an employee at the Shared Harvest restaurant. The manager would like to put information about the restaurant on a local computer network that publishes Web pages for area groups and businesses. Use Word's Web Page Wizard to create the calendar of daily specials shown in Figure B-18. (*Hint*: you can use a Word template to apply the calendar formatting.) Sketch what a publication for this restaurant should look like, then create an appropriate home page to go along with the calendar. Create at least two other associated Web pages by creating files in Office programs, then converting them to HTML and formatting them. Finally, add links between your pages. Print out the first page of each of your Web pages using Word Web, then submit the printouts and your sketch to your instructor.

FIGURE B-18

Shared Harvest Restaurant

June 1998

Daily Specials

Sunday	Monday	Tuesday	Wednesday	Thursday	Friday	Saturday
	1 Shiitake stir-fry	2 Lentil-nut loaf	3 Lasagne	4 Tempeh sloppy joes	5 Tofu scramble	6 Baked tofu with broccoli
7 Vegetable cutlets	8 Lentil-tomato dal	9 Falafel	10 Cashew chili	11 Garlic grilled vegetables	12 Chickpea soufflé	13 Barbecue tempeh burgers
14 Mushroom-barley soup	15 Curried lentils and collards	16 Shiitake stir-fry	17 Lentil-nut loaf	18 Lasagne	19 Tempeh sloppy joes	20 Tofu scramble
21 Baked tofu with broccoli	22 Vegetable cutlets	23 Lentil-tomato dal	24 Falafel	25 Cashew chili	26 Garlic grilled vegetables	27 Chickpea soufflé
28 Barbecue tempeh burgers	29 Mushroom-barley soup	30 Curried lentils and collards				

Join us for lunch or dinner!

Shared Harvest home page

Getting
Started with Microsoft Outlook

Objectives

► **Understand electronic mail**
► **Start Learning Outlook E-mail**
► **View the Learning Outlook E-mail window**
► **Reply to messages**
► **Create and send new messages**
► **Forward messages**
► **Manage your Inbox**
► **Create a Personal Distribution List**
► **Send mail to a Personal Distribution List**

Microsoft Outlook is an integrated desktop information management program that lets you manage your personal and business information and communicate with others. Information such as your electronic messages, appointments, contacts, tasks, and files can all be managed within this exciting new program. In this unit, you will focus on the electronic mail features of Microsoft Outlook, working with a program called "Learning Outlook E-mail" that looks and feels like Microsoft Outlook, but is actually a simulation. Learning Outlook E-mail was specially designed to be used with this book to teach you the basics of sending, receiving, and managing electronic mail messages. You will use Learning Outlook E-mail to communicate with a group of users at Nomad Ltd. The messages you send and receive throughout this unit are not actually being sent to and received by actual users; they are simulations to show you how the real Outlook program works. You will be able to use the skills learned in this unit to work with the actual Microsoft Outlook program.

Outlook

Understanding Electronic Mail

Electronic mail software, popularly known as **e-mail**, is software that lets you send and receive electronic messages over a network. A **network** is a group of computers connected to each other with cables and software. Figure A-1 illustrates how e-mail messages can travel over a network. Because of its speed and ease of use, e-mail is often a very effective way to communicate with co-workers or colleagues. Note that each computer network or workplace could have unique e-mail policies.

 **Steps**

Here are some of the benefits of using electronic mail:

 Provides a convenient and efficient way to communicate

You can send messages whenever you wish; the recipient does not have to be at the computer to receive your message. Other users on your network can also send you electronic messages, even if you are not currently running the mail program. Any new messages sent to you will be waiting when you open your mailbox.

 Lets you send large amounts of information

Your messages can be as long as you wish, so you are not limited to the short time typically allowed on some voice mail systems. You can also attach a file (such as a spreadsheet or word processing document) to a message.

 Lets you communicate with several people at once

You can send (or forward) the same message to multiple individuals at one time (without going to the copy machine first). You can also create your own electronic address book containing the names of the people with whom you frequently communicate.

 Ensures delivery of information

Electronic messages cannot be "lost" so no one can claim not to have received a message you sent. You even have the option to be notified when a recipient has read your message.

 Communicate from a remote place

If you have a modem and communications software, you can connect your computer at home to the computers at your office over the phone lines. This gives you the flexibility to send and receive messages when you are not at the office. You can also join a commercial online service and send e-mail to people on the **Internet**, which is a network that connects millions of computer users around the world.

 Provides a record of communications

You can organize your sent and received messages in a way that best suits your work style. Organizing your saved messages lets you keep a record of communications, which can be very valuable in managing a project or business.

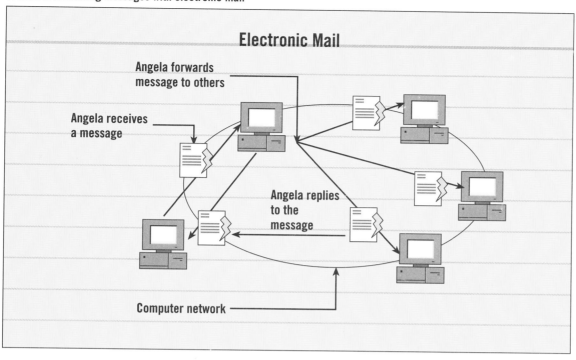

Electronic mail etiquette

It's a good idea to learn whether your company permits sending personal messages. Keep in mind that all messages you send have been legally interpreted as property of the company for which you work, so don't assume that your messages are private. Carefully consider the content of your messages before you send them, and don't send confidential or sensitive material. When you compose a message, take extra care in what you say and how you say it in your messages. The recipient of your message doesn't have the benefit of seeing your body language or hearing the tone of your voice to interpret what you are saying. For example, using all capital letters in the text of a message is the e-mail equivalent of screaming and is not appropriate. Remember, once you send a message, you may not be able to prevent it from being delivered.

Outlook

Starting Learning Outlook E-mail

Before you can read or send messages, you must start Outlook and enter a secret password. In this lesson and throughout this unit, you will work with the Learning Outlook E-mail program, which is installed in the Course Programs program group on the Windows 95 Start menu. (If you were using Microsoft Outlook, it would be installed in a different program group.) You need to complete this unit in one sitting; do not exit Learning Outlook E-mail until instructed.

You will be using the mailbox of Angela Pacheco, who is a marketing manager at Nomad, Ltd. In the steps below, you will start Learning Outlook E-mail and sign in to Angela's mail account using a password.

Steps

1. **Click the Start button on the taskbar, point to Programs, point to Course Programs, then click Learning Outlook E-mail; see Figure A-2.**
   Note that the actual Microsoft Outlook program would be stored in a different program group on your computer.
   You see a message box describing the Learning Outlook E-mail simulation program. Close this message box to continue.

2. **Click Continue**
   The Learning Outlook E-mail program starts, and the Enter Password dialog box appears as shown in Figure A-3. Here you see the user name "Angela Pacheco." Angela is a fictional manager at Nomad, Ltd. You will be using her electronic mailbox to complete the lessons in this unit. You also see a domain name of NOMADLTD. A domain is a collection of computers that the network manager groups together because the computers are used for the same task. NOMADLTD is a fictional domain name. Before you can use Outlook, you must enter a secret password identifying yourself.

3. **Click in the Password box**
   Because you are opening Angela's mailbox, do not change the default mailbox name "Angela Pacheco" or the default domain name "NOMADLTD". If this were your Microsoft account, you would enter a mailbox name and domain name provided by your system administrator. Next, you must enter the password.

4. **In the Password text box, type any password you wish, using up to 19 characters, then press [Enter]**
   In the next lesson, you will examine the Learning Outlook E-mail window.

FIGURE A-2: Course Programs program group

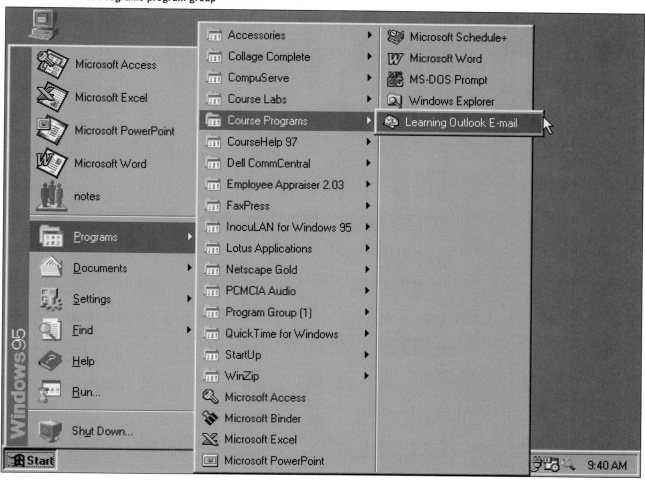

FIGURE A-3: Enter Password dialog box

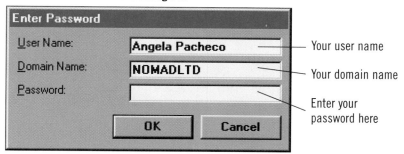

Your user name

Your domain name

Enter your password here

CLUES TO USE

Keeping your password secure

In Learning Outlook E-mail, you can enter any password you wish up to 19 characters. In Microsoft Outlook, however, your system administrator will probably provide you with your own unique and secret password. After you have been assigned a password, you can then change it to one of your own choosing. It is a good idea to change your password every two months, to keep it secure. Make sure you choose a password that is easy for you to remember, but difficult for others to guess. As a security benefit, your password does not appear in the Sign In dialog box as you type it. Instead, you see "*" as you type each letter.

Outlook

Viewing the Learning Outlook E-mail Window

Before you can use Outlook, you need to understand the key parts of the Outlook window. Use the list below and Figure A-4 to learn about each part of the window.

Details

 The messages are shown with the AutoPreview feature enabled, allowing you to read the first line of a message with out actually opening it. In the Learning Outlook E-mail window, you see Angela's **Inbox**, which shows a list of message headers of e-mail she has received. Each **message header** identifies the sender of the message, the subject, and the date and time the message was received.

 Icons to the left of the sender's name identify the attributes of the message. For example, an icon that looks like a closed envelope indicates that the message has not been read. Notice, also, that the message headers of unread messages appear in bold face. See Table A-1 for a description of the icons you might see in the Inbox.

 On the left side of the Learning Outlook E-mail window you see the **Outlook Bar**. To help organize your information, the most frequently used **folders** are arranged into **groups** on the Outlook Bar. The Inbox folder in the Mail group is currently open. To open a different folder or group of folders, you simply click the folder icon or the group name, respectively. The Inbox folder contains all the messages other users have sent you. The Sent Items folder contains messages you have sent. The Outbox folder contains messages you have sent, but which Outlook has not yet delivered. (If your mail server is very quick, you might not see messages in the Outbox at all.) The Deleted Items folder contains messages you have deleted.

 At the top of the window, the **title bar** displays the name of the program, Learning Outlook E-mail. When you are reading messages, the subject of the message appears in the title bar.

 The **menu bar** (as in all Windows programs) contains the names of the menu items. Clicking a menu item on the menu bar displays a list of related commands. For example, you use the commands on the Edit menu to edit the text of your message.

 Under the menu bar, the **toolbar** contains buttons that give you quick access to the most frequently used commands.

 Just below the toolbar, the **folder banner** is the horizontal bar that displays the name of the open folder to the left and the icon of the open folder to the right.

The **status bar** at the bottom of the window indicates the total number of messages that the open folder contains, as well as the number of those messages that have not been read.

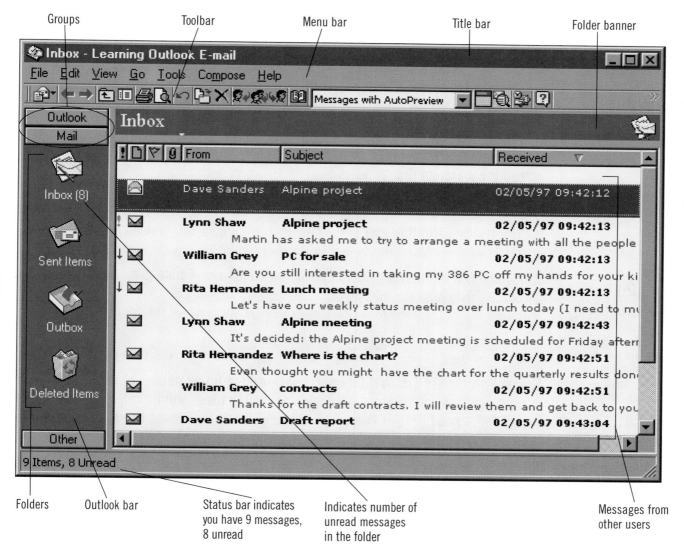

Groups   Toolbar   Menu bar   Title bar   Folder banner

Folders   Outlook bar   Status bar indicates you have 9 messages, 8 unread   Indicates number of unread messages in the folder   Messages from other users

TABLE A-1: Message header icons

icon	description
	High importance message
↓	Low importance message
✉	Unread message
✉	Read message
	Forwarded message
	Replied to message
	Notification of a delivered message
	Notification of a read message
📎	Message has an attachment

Replying to Messages

To read a message in your Inbox, you simply double-click anywhere in the message header. After reading a message, you can delete it or keep it in your Inbox. You can also send a response back to the sender of the message, using the Reply button on the toolbar. The Reply command automatically addresses your comments to the original sender and includes the text of the original sender's message. Angela will read a few messages and send a reply.

Steps

1. **Double-click the message containing Lunch meeting in the Subject column, then read the message that appears**
   The message appears in the message window, as shown in Figure A-5. After reading the message, close this message window.

2. **Click the Close button ✖ in the Lunch meeting message window**
   The message window closes. Now, you can read another message in the Inbox.

3. **Double-click the message from Lynn Shaw containing Alpine project in the Subject column, then read the message**
   You might need to scroll to see the entire message. After reading this message, send a reply.

4. **Click the Reply button 🕮 Reply on the toolbar**
   A new message window appears, as shown in Figure A-6. Next, enter the text of the reply.

5. **Type I prefer the Friday 4:00 time. I am working on an outline of my presentation right now and will send a draft to you soon. Because I will be relying on my assistant for a good part of this project, I think he should be at the meeting as well. What do you think?**
   By default, the text of your reply appears in blue to help distinguish it from the text of the original message. After entering the reply, send the reply back to the original sender.

6. **Click the Send button 🖃 Send in the message window**
   The reply message window closes, and the reply is sent. The original message to which you replied appears, displaying text in the InfoBar recording the date and time that you replied to this message. See Figure A-7. In addition, Outlook stores a copy of the reply in your Sent Items folder. This folder is a permanent log of all of the messages that you have sent; the messages stay in this folder until you delete them. Next, you will reply to a message that has already been read, indicated with an icon that looks like an opened envelope.

7. **Click the ✖ in the Alpine project window**
   The message window closes. In the Inbox, the icon for this message has changed from the Unread message icon ✉ to the Replied to message icon 📬 indicating that Angela has replied to this message.

8. **Select the Alpine project message from Dave Sanders, then click the Reply button 🕮**
   You do not need to open a message to reply to it. The message window appears. Next, enter the text of the reply to the message.

9. **Type I am pleased that you are on the Alpine team. I will research your questions and get back to you.**
   After entering the reply, you can send the reply back to the original sender and close the original sender's message.

10. **Click the 🖃 Send**
    Outlook sends the reply back to the original sender, Dave Sanders, and the message closes.

> **QuickTip**
>
> The Next Item button 🔽 and the Previous Item button 🔼 in the toolbar provide a fast way to scroll through your messages. Clicking the Next Item or Previous Item button closes the currently opened message, and then opens the next or previous message in the Inbox. Clicking the list arrow next to the Next Item or Previous Item button displays options for scrolling to a particular type of message. When you reach the top or bottom of the Inbox, the Next Item or Previous Item buttons respectively appear dimmed.

FIGURE A-5: Message window for reading messages

Message subject appears in titlebar

Sender

Message

Opens and displays next message in Inbox

Opens and displays previous message in Inbox

Date and time message was sent

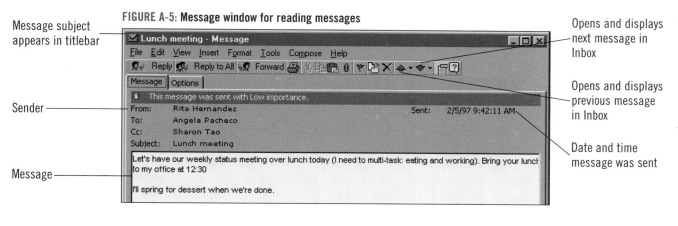

FIGURE A-6: Message window for replying to messages

Original sender of message

Message topic

Enter your reply here

Original text of message

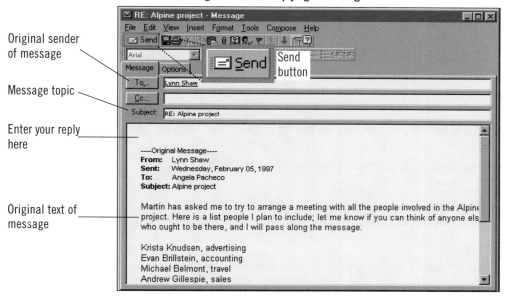

FIGURE A-7: Record of reply in replied to message

InfoBar records the date and time of your most recent reply to this message

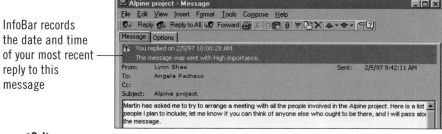

Emoticons

If you see something like this :-) in an e-mail message, you are looking at an emoticon. Emoticons are faces created by simple keyboard characters (in this example the colon, dash, and end parenthesis) to express an emotion or mood. The possibilities are endless and they are a fun way to get your point across.

Outlook

Creating and Sending New Messages

A critical facet of using e-mail is being able to create new messages and send them to other users on your network. When you create a message, you must indicate for whom the message is intended and specify any other recipients who should receive a copy. You also need to enter a meaningful subject for the message. Then you write the text of your message and send it. Angela wants to know if her assistant, Dave Sanders, might be able to complete an assignment earlier than originally planned, so she sends him a message.

1. Click the **New mail message button** 🖃▾ on the toolbar

The new mail message window appears as shown in Figure A-8. In this window, you enter address information and compose your message. Although you could type a name directly in the To box, ensure that you address the message properly by using the Address Book feature to look up the correct name.

QuickTip

In the new message window, clicking the **To... button** or the **Cc... button** is a fast way to open the Select Names dialog box.

2. Click the **Address Book button** 📖 on the new message window toolbar

The Select Names dialog box opens as shown in Figure A-9. In this dialog box, you can view the user names of all the users connected to the mail system. These names belong to an address book (which is simply a collection of names) called the Global Address List. Angela locates her assistant's name from the Global Address List.

3. Click the name **Dave Sanders** to select it, then click the **To button**

The name "Dave Sanders" appears in the To box in the Select Names dialog box. Send a copy of this message to Angela's supervisor, Martin, to let him know she is following up on his request to accelerate the project.

QuickTip

In the Select Names dialog box, double-clicking a name is a fast way to enter a name in the To box.

4. Click the name **Martin C. Danello**, then click the **Cc button**

The name "Martin C. Danello" appears in the Cc box area (for Courtesy Copy).

5. Click **OK**

The new message window appears again. Now, enter the subject of the message.

6. Click in the **Subject box**, then type **New deadline**

The text in the Subject box appears in the recipient's Inbox so that the reader can quickly get an idea about the contents of the message. Next, enter the text of the message to Dave Sanders.

7. Press **[Tab]**, then type **There is an important Alpine project meeting Friday, and I would like to show our ideas at that time. Let me know what I can do to facilitate your work.**

You are now ready to send the message.

8. Click the **Send button** 🖃 Send

Outlook sends the message with the default options in effect. If you would like confirmation that the message has been read, or if you'd like to use other options when you send a message, you can click the Options tab before sending the message.

FIGURE A-8: New message window for sending messages

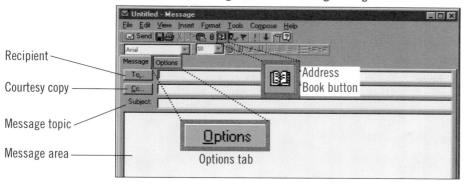

Recipient

Courtesy copy

Message topic

Message area

Address Book button

Options tab

FIGURE A-9: Select Names dialog box

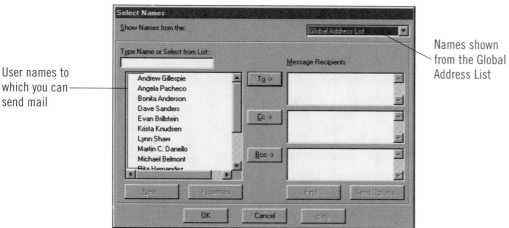

Names shown from the Global Address List

User names to which you can send mail

Options when sending messages

In Microsoft Outlook, there are several options that affect how messages are delivered. In the new mail message window, click the Options tab to display the Options sheet shown in Figure A-10. You can assign a level of importance and a level of sensitivity so that the reader can easily prioritize messages and understand the nature of their contents. You can include voting buttons in a recipient's message to enable the recipient to reply to a question by choosing such options as Approve or Reject. You can specify that replies to your message be sent to another person, such as an assistant. Messages you send are automatically saved in the Sent Items folder. If you prefer to have Outlook delete the messages, disable the Save sent message to check box. By default, messages are sent from the Outbox to their recipients as soon as possible and without expiration dates. Enable the Do not deliver before option to hold messages in the Outbox until a specified date and time,

FIGURE A-10: Options tab sheet

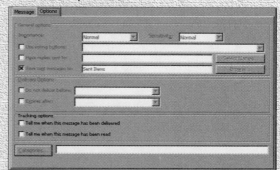

and the Expires after option to specify a date and time after which a time-sensitive message is unavailable. When you want to know when a message has been received or read, you can enable the Tell me when this message has been delivered or the Tell me when this message has been read check boxes, respectively. When the recipient either receives or opens the message, you get a corresponding **report** message in your Inbox.

Outlook

Forwarding Messages

Messages you receive from others might contain information that would be useful to someone else. With Microsoft Outlook, you can forward a message to another user. The recipient of the forwarded message can in turn read and respond to it. Angela has received an agenda for the Alpine project meeting, and would like her assistant to attend the meeting and review the agenda. Angela begins by reading the message containing the agenda.

Steps

1. **In the Inbox window, double-click the message with Agenda in the Subject heading, then click the Forward button on the toolbar**
   The Forward message window appears, as shown in Figure A-11. First, specify to whom you will forward the message.

2. **Click the Address Book button, then double-click the name Dave Sanders**
   The name "Dave Sanders" appears in the To box in the Select Names dialog box.

3. **Click OK**
   You return to the Forward message window. Because the subject is already completed, continue by composing a brief introduction to the message you are forwarding.

4. **Click the insertion point in the message area and type Glad to hear you are making progress. In fact, I think you should attend Friday's meeting. Here is the agenda from Lynn.**
   As in the reply message window, by default, the text in the message area appears in blue to help distinguish it from the text of the original message.
   You have finished writing your message. However, before sending it, tell Outlook to notify Angela when Dave has read the message.

5. **Click the Options tab, then click the Tell me when this message has been read check box**
   The Tracking option is enabled, as shown in Figure A-12. Now, send the message.

7. **Click the Send button**
   The message is now forwarded to Dave Sanders. The original message that you forwarded appears, recording in the InfoBar the most recent date and time that you forwarded this message.

8. **Click the Close button in the Agenda message window**
   After a few moments you see a message indicating the forwarded message was read. Open the Read Report message.

9. **Double-click the message from Dave Sanders with the subject Read: FW: Agenda**
   The Read Report message opens as shown in Figure A-13. The Read Report message displays the details of the message and when it was read.

10. **Click in the message window**
    The message window closes.

FIGURE A-11: Message window for forwarding a message

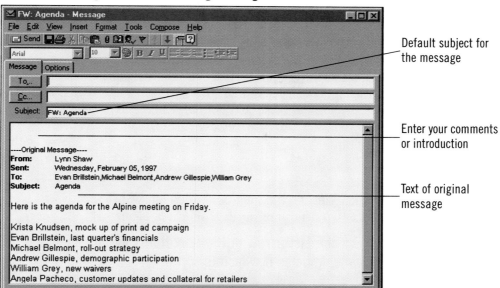

Default subject for the message

Enter your comments or introduction

Text of original message

FIGURE A-12: Send Options sheet

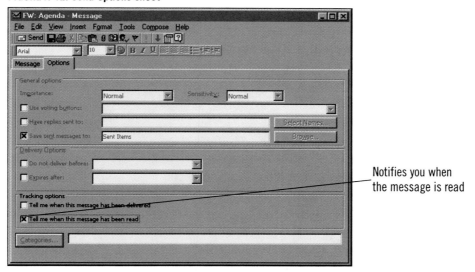

Notifies you when the message is read

FIGURE A-13: Read Report message

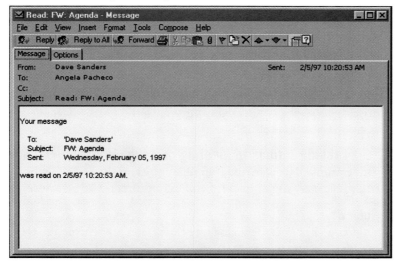

Managing Your Inbox

As you work with Outlook, your Inbox accumulates the messages you receive and read. To keep track of important messages and prevent the Inbox from becoming too big and inefficient, Microsoft Outlook offers several options. For example, you can sort messages to quickly identify the messages you need. You can print messages that you need to keep on paper and you can delete messages you have read and no longer need. Outlook also lets you store messages in folders, which you can create. Currently the messages in the Inbox are sorted by date (the default) with the newest messages appearing at the top of the Inbox. ✐ So that she can identify the topic of each message, Angela sorts the Inbox by subject. Later she will sort the messages by priority.

QuickTip

Clicking a column heading is a fast way to sort messages by a particular heading in the Inbox. Each time you click the column heading, the messages are sorted by that heading in either ascending or descending order.

1. Click **View** on the menu bar, then click **Sort**

The Sort dialog box opens as shown in Figure A-14.

2. Click the **List arrow** in the **Sort Items by box**, then select **Subject** from the list of available fields by which to sort

3. Click **OK**

The messages in the Inbox are sorted alphabetically in ascending order by the subject headings. Next you will delete a message.

4. Click the message that contains **Lunch meeting** in the subject column, then click the **Delete button** ☒ on the toolbar

The message is removed from the Inbox and is now stored in the Deleted Items folder. In Microsoft Outlook if you accidentally delete a message you intended to retain, you can open the Deleted Items folder and retrieve the message. To permanently delete a message, you must delete it from the Deleted Items folder. So that you can quickly locate important messages, sort the Inbox by priority.

5. Click **View** on the menu bar, click **Sort**, select **Priority** in the **Sort Items by box**, then click **OK** and scroll to the top of the Inbox

Messages with the highest priority ⁚ appear in the beginning of the Inbox and messages with the lowest priority ↓ appear at the bottom of the Inbox, as shown in Figure A-15. Delete the lowest priority message.

6. Click the last message displayed in the Inbox (with a priority of ↓), then click ☒

It is a good idea to permanently delete all unwanted messages from the Deleted Items folder since they take up disk storage.

7. Click **Tools** on the menu bar, then click **Empty "Deleted Items" Folder**

A dialog box appears asking you to confirm that you wish to permanently delete all the items and subfolders in the Deleted Items folder.

8. Click **Yes**

All the messages in the Deleted Items folder are permanently deleted. One of the messages displayed provides information Angela would like to have on paper (it contains the directions to Friday's meeting).

9. Select the **directions to meeting message** in the Inbox, click **File**, then click **Print**

This command displays the Print dialog box, as shown in Figure A-16. In Microsoft Outlook, you can specify the number of copies to print and other printing options.

10. Click **OK**

After you click OK, the dialog box closes, you are returned to the Inbox, and Outlook prints the message on your printer.

FIGURE A-14: Sort dialog box

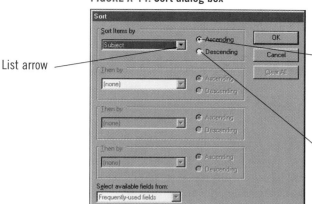

List arrow

Sort messages starting from the first letter of the alphabet, the lowest number, or the earliest date

Sort messages starting from the last letter of the alphabet, the highest number, or the latest date

FIGURE A-15: Messages sorted by priority

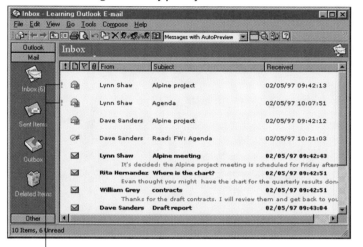

Highest priority messages

FIGURE A-16: Print dialog box

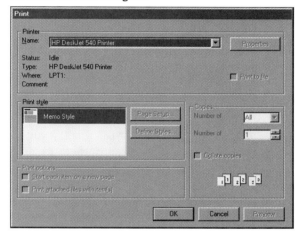

CLUES TO USE

Using folders to manage your inbox

FIGURE A-17: Folders in Microsoft Outlook

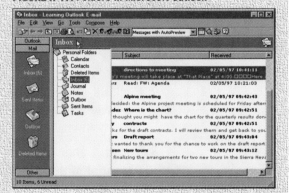

In the actual Microsoft Outlook program you can use folders to organize your messages. On the File menu, you point to New, then click the Folder command to create folders to help you organize your messages. The new folder will automatically appear in the Outlook Bar in the currently open group. To see a list of all available folders, click the Folder List button [ ]. For example, for easy reference you might want to create a folder called "Technical" in which to store messages related to system procedures or using your PC. In addition, you can create folders within folders, allowing you to create a hierarchical structure for your Inbox. For instance, the "Technical" folder could contain the additional folders "Network" and "PC" so that you can further categorize your messages, as shown in Figure A-17. After creating a folder, you simply drag (or use the Cut, Copy, and Paste commands) to place messages in the desired folder. Note that the ability to create folders is not available in the Learning Outlook E-mail program.

Outlook

Creating a Personal Distribution List

When you address a message you must choose a name from the Global Address List. If there are many names in the Global Address List, it can be time consuming to scroll through all the names to select the ones you want. Fortunately, Outlook provides two ways to manage the user names you use most often. You can create a **Personal Distribution List**, which is a collection of names to whom you regularly send the same messages. For example, if you send messages reminding your staff of a weekly meeting, you can create a Personal Distribution List called "Team" that contains the names of your staff. When you want to send a message to everyone on the team, you simply select "Team" from the Select Names dialog box, instead of selecting each user name. You can also create a **personal list** of names, containing only those which you use frequently. Angela finds that she regularly sends the same message to members of her Alpine project team. She will create a Personal Distribution List containing these names.

Steps

1. **Click the Address Book button**
   The Address Book window opens.

2. **Click File on the Address Book menu bar, then click New Entry**
   The New Entry dialog box opens, as shown in Figure A-18. In this dialog box you can select the type of entry you want to make and in which address book the new entry will reside. Currently, there are no Personal Distribution Lists, so you need to create one.

3. **Click Personal Distribution List in the Select the entry type: box, then click OK**
   The New Personal Distribution List Properties dialog box opens, as shown in Figure A-19.

4. **In the Name: box, type Alpine, then click the Add/Remove Members button**
   Outlook displays the list of names from the Global Address List. From this list, select the additional names to include in the Alpine distribution list.

5. **Click the name Andrew Gillespie (if it is not already selected), then press and hold [Ctrl] as you click each of the following names: Dave Sanders, Krista Knudsen, and Steve Nicholas**
   With the names Andrew Gillespie, Dave Sanders, Krista Knudsen, and Steve Nicholas selected, add them to the list.

6. **Click the Members button**
   Verify that all four names appear in the Personal Distribution List area of the dialog box, as shown in Figure A-20.

7. **Click OK**
   The New Personal Distribution List Properties dialog box displays the new Alpine distribution list and its members.

8. **Click OK, then click the List arrow in the Show names from the: list box, then select Personal Address Book.**
   Outlook adds the Alpine distribution list to the Personal Address Book. The Address Book window displays the Personal Address Book contents. Notice that Outlook displays the distribution list names in bold face, with the icon to the left of the name.

9. **Click the Close button X in the Address Book window**

FIGURE A-18: New Entry dialog box

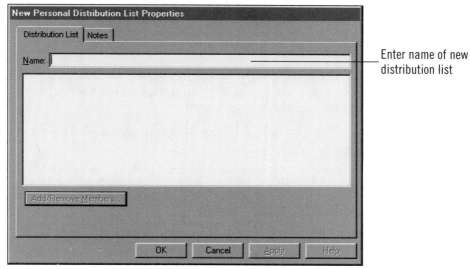

FIGURE A-19: New Personal Distribution List Properties dialog box

Enter name of new distribution list

FIGURE A-20: Edit Members of Alpine dialog box

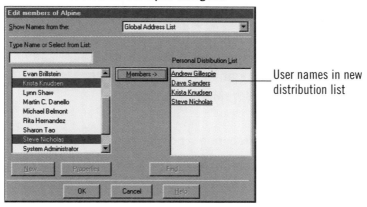

User names in new distribution list

CLUES TO USE

Adding names to the Personal Address Book

In Microsoft Outlook, the names of the people in your Personal Distribution Lists are automatically added to your Personal Address Book, so that you can send messages to individual members without necessarily sending them to all the members of the distribution list. You can also add individual names to your Personal Address

Book without adding them to a distribution list. In the Address Book window, select the names you want to appear in your Personal Address Book, then click the Add to Personal Address Book button 📇. To see the contents of the Personal Address Book, select Personal Address Book in the Show names from the: list box.

Outlook

Sending Mail to a Personal Distribution List

In the same way you can send a message to an individual user, you can send a message to several users at once using a Personal Distribution List. Now that Angela has created a distribution list consisting of her team members, she can send a single message to all of her team using one easy-to-remember distribution list name.

Steps 1 2 3 4

1. Click the New Mail Message button 📧 ▾ on the toolbar
Send a message to all the people on the team.

2. In new mail message window, click the Address Book button
Because you need to send this message to members of a distribution list, switch to the Personal Address Book directory.

3. Click the List arrow in the Show names from the: list box, then select Personal Address Book
The Personal Address Book is displayed in the Select Names dialog box, as shown in Figure A-21.

4. Double-click Alpine from the list

5. Click OK to return to the new mail message window
The To box in the new mail message window contains the name of the Alpine distribution list. Now, enter the subject of the message.

6. In the Subject box, type No team meeting this week
After typing the subject of the message, enter the text of it.

7. In the message area, type Because all of us will be attending the Alpine meeting Friday afternoon, we will not have our usual staff meeting at that time. Instead, let's get together to go over project status at 3:00 Thursday. Let me know if anyone has a problem with that.

8. Click Send
Clicking this button sends the message to all the people in the Alpine distribution list.

9. Click File on the menu bar, then click Exit to exit Learning Outlook E-mail

Names shown from
Personal Address
Book

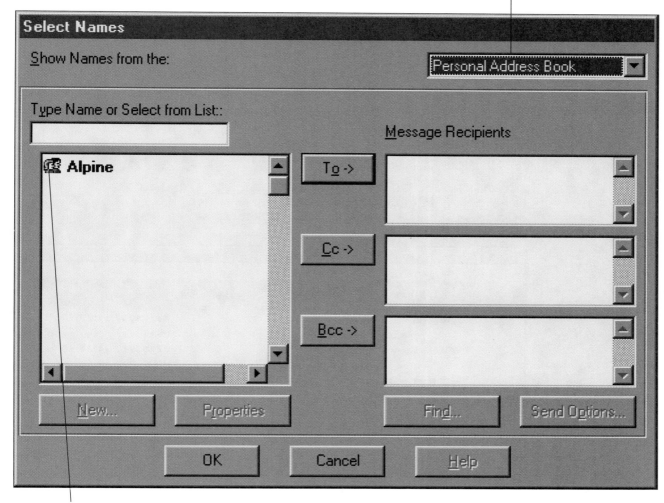

Outlook

New Distribution
List

Practice

► Concepts Review

Label each of the formatting elements

FIGURE A-22

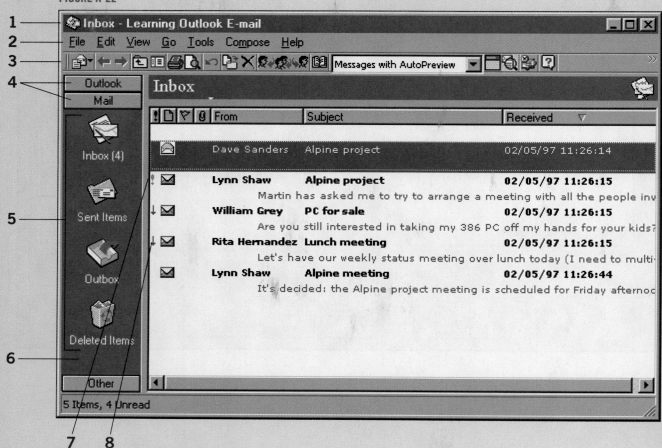

Match each of the following terms with the statement that best describes it.

9. **Electronic mail**
10. **Personal Distribution List**
11. **Global Address List**
12. **Read report**
13. **Inbox**
14. **Message Header**

a. Identifies the sender, subject, and date of the message
b. All of the user names to whom you can send messages
c. A list of users to which you have assigned a name
d. Message you receive when someone reads the message you sent
e. Ability to send and receive messages over a computer network
f. Contains all the messages you have received

15. **Which of the following is the popular abbreviated name for "electronic mail"?**
    a. Mail-net   **b.** Electro-mail   **c.** Learning Mail   **d.** E-mail

16. **After signing into Outlook, you see your messages in the:**
    a. Inbox   **b.** Message window   **c.** Mail window   **d.** Display window

17. **To read a message, you:**
    a. Click View, then click Read
    b. Double-click a message
    c. Click the Read button on the toolbar
    d. Click the Inbox folder

18. **After reading and closing a message:**
    a. The next message opens so you can read it
    b. You can click the Read button to open the next message
    c. An icon in the message header indicates you have read the message
    d. The message is automatically deleted from the Inbox

19. **To forward a selected message to another user, you:**
    a. Click File, then click Forward
    b. Click the Forward button
    c. Click the Send button
    d. Click Tools, then click Forward

20. **To create a new message, you:**
    a. Click the New Mail Message button
    b. Click the Create button
    c. Click the Mail button
    d. Click the Send button

21. **To send the same message to multiple recipients, which of the following is not an option?**
    a. Drag the message to each of the recipient names.
    b. In the Select Names dialog box, you can select multiple names from the Global Address List.
    c. You can enter multiple names in the To box.
    d. Create a personal group containing the names of the users.

▶ Skills Review

If you exited from the Learning Outlook E-mail program before continuing on to this Skills Review, you will need to practice sending and deleting a few messages before you continue. You do not need to perform these steps if you did not exit Learning Outlook E-mail at the end of the unit exercises.

1. Start Learning Outlook E-mail.
2. Send three different messages to any three different users.
3. Delete any two messages from any two users.
4. Send one more message to any user.

After a minute or so, the messages described in the Applications Review exercises will begin to appear, so you can continue.

1. **Read and reply to messages.**
   a. Double-click the message containing "contracts" in the Subject column.
   b. Click the Close button in the message window.
   c. Double-click the message from Krista Knudsen containing "New tours" in the Subject column.
   d. Click the Reply button on the toolbar.
   e. Type "Here are some ideas: Donner Challenge, Tahoe Trails, and Nevada Nirvana. What do you think?"
   f. Click the Send button on the message window toolbar.
   g. Click the Close button in the message window.

2. **Create and send new messages.**
   a. Click the New Mail Message button on the toolbar.
   b. Click the Address Book button on the toolbar.
   c. Click the name "Dave Sanders" to select it, then click the To button.
   d. Click the name "Rita Hernandez," then click the Cc button.
   e. Click OK.
   f. Click in the Subject box, and type "New chart."
   g. Press [Tab] and type "I think the Results chart for Rita should include a pie chart as well as a bar graph."
   h. Click the Send button.

3. **Forward a message.**
   a. In the Inbox window, double-click the message with "Where is the chart?" in the Subject heading, then click the Forward button on the toolbar.
   b. Click the Address Book button, then double-click the name "Dave Sanders."
   c. The name "Dave Sanders" appears in the To box in the Select Names dialog box.
   d. Click OK.
   e. Click the insertion point in the message area and type "Glad to hear you are making progress on the charts. I am passing along a message from Rita. You can respond directly to her."
   f. Click the Options tab and click the Tell me when this message has been read check box.
   g. Click the Send button.
   h. Click the Close Button in the message window.
   i. Double-click the message from Dave Sanders with the subject "Read: FW: Where is the chart?"
   j. Click the Close button in the message window.

4. Manage your Inbox.

a. Click View on the menu bar, then click Sort.

b. Click the List arrow in the Sort Items by box, select From, then click OK.

c. Click the message that contains "Alpine meeting" in the subject column and click the Delete button on the toolbar.

d. Click View on the menu bar, then click Sort.

e. Click the List arrow in the Sort Items by box, select Importance, then click OK.

f. Click the message that contains "Draft report" in the subject column, click File, then click Print.

g. Click OK.

5. Create a Personal Distribution List.

a. Click the Address Book button.

b. Click File on the menu bar, then click New Entry.

c. Click Personal Distribution List in the Select the entry type: box, then click OK.

d. In the Name: box, type Systems Committee, then click the Add/Remove Members button.

e. Click Evan Brillstein, then choose the following names by pressing [Ctrl] as you click each name: Lynn Shaw and William Grey.

f. Click the Members button.

g. Click OK.

h. Click OK.

i. Click the Close button in the Address Book window.

6. Send mail to a Personal Distribution List.

a. Click the New Mail Message button.

b. In the new mail message window, click the Address Book button.

c. Double-click "Systems Committee" from the list.

d. Click OK to return to the new mail message window.

e. In the Subject box, type "Next systems meeting."

f. In the message area, type "For next Thursday's meeting we will review the proposals from the training companies. Please come prepared to defend your preferences."

g. Click Send.

h. If you have been assigned Independent Challenge 1, do not exit the Learning Outlook E-mail program before continuing.

▶ Independent Challenge

1. To help you become more comfortable using the Outlook program, you can start the part of the Learning Outlook E-mail program that is designed to give you the freedom to experiment with Outlook features and procedures. To complete this independent challenge: Send a message (composed of any text) to the user called System Administrator. Shortly after you send a message to the System Administrator, you will receive a number of messages at random over the next few minutes. You can reply to, forward, delete, sort, and print these messages. You can also create and send new messages of your own. Be sure to explore using the different send options described in this unit. When you have finished working with the new messages, you can exit the Learning Outlook E-mail program.

Appendix

Beyond E-mail: Understanding Additional Outlook Features

Objectives

► **Manage your appointments and tasks**
► **Manage your contacts**
► **Track your activities and files**
► **Send mail to a Personal Distribution List**

The lessons in this text focus on teaching you how to send and receive electronic mail messages using the Inbox portion of Microsoft Outlook. However, to effectively use Microsoft Outlook in managing your business and personal information, it is important to know not only how to use Inbox to send and receive electronic messages, but also how to use the additional components in Outlook. Microsoft Outlook integrates several tools, including Inbox, Calendar, Contacts, Tasks, Journal, Notes, and Files to provide you with a uniquely comprehensive information manager. Now that you already know how to manage your electronic messages with Inbox, you will learn how Microsoft Outlook combines e-mail with its other components to create a new class of program: an integrated desktop information manager.

Outlook

Managing Your Appointments and Tasks

The Calendar and Tasks tools in Microsoft Outlook provide convenient, effective means to manage your appointments and tasks. **Calendar** is a robust, electronic equivalent of your day planner book, while **Tasks** is an electronic to-do list. To schedule your activities and appointments, open the Outlook group on the Outlook Bar, then click the Calendar folder. See Figure AP-1. With Calendar, you can schedule an activity such as a meeting, luncheon, or dentist appointment, or all-day and multiple-day events such as birthdays or conferences by simply clicking the New Appointment button on the toolbar. You can specify the subject and location of the appointment, and its start and end times. Also, you can ensure that you do not forget the appointment by having Outlook sound a reminder prior to the start of the appointment. Outlook will notify you if the appointment conflicts with, or is adjacent to, another scheduled activity. You can view any period of time that you desire in Calendar.

Details

Review the following features of Calender and Task:

 To facilitate planning and scheduling your activities, you can choose to view Calendar by day, week, or month, and you can use the **Date Navigator** to quickly select even nonadjacent days. Dates displayed in boldface on the Date Navigator indicate days on which you have scheduled appointments.

 Use the **Meeting Planner** to schedule a meeting by having Outlook compare the free and busy times of all the invitees. Once you have selected a meeting time and location, you can send invitations in meeting requests. If the invitee accepts the invitation, Outlook will post the meeting automatically to the invitee's calendar.

 To manage your business and personal to-do list, open the **Tasks folder** on the Outlook bar. See Figure AP-2.

 Click the **New Task button** to create new tasks. Organize your tasks by grouping them in **categories** such as objectives or project names, and view your tasks in several different ways, including by category, by status, and by timeline. You can mark your progress on tasks by percentage complete, and you can have Outlook create status summary reports in e-mail messages and then send the update to anyone on the update list. Using **task requests**, you can assign tasks to a co-worker or assistant and have Outlook automatically update you on the status of the task completion. To help you coordinate your tasks and your appointments, the task list from Tasks is automatically displayed in the **TaskPad** in Calendar. To schedule time to complete a task, simply drag a task from the TaskPad to a time block in the Calendar. Any changes you make to a task are reflected in both the TaskPad in Calendar and the task list in Tasks.

 If you want to quickly write down an idea or a note concerning an appointment or a task, simply open the Notes folder on the Outlook bar. See Figure AP-3. **Notes** is the electronic version of the popular colored paper sticky notes. Use Notes to store directions to a meeting place, reminders, or any other information you would write in a sticky note. Notes enables you to quickly supplement the information stored in Calendar and Tasks.

FIGURE AP-1: Appointments and tasks displayed in the Calendar window

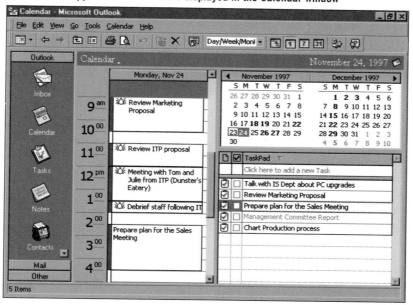

FIGURE AP-2: Tasks list displayed in the Tasks window

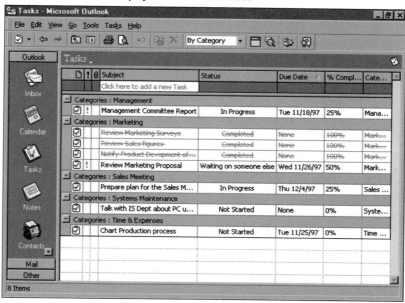

FIGURE AP-3: Notes displayed in the Notes window

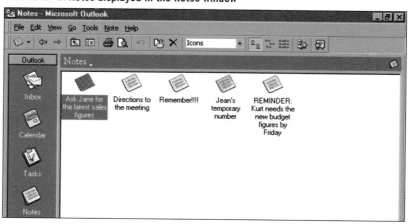

Managing Your Contacts

The **Contacts** tool in Microsoft Outlook enables you to manage all your business and personal contact information. To open Contacts, click the Contacts folder in the Outlook group on the Outlook Bar. See Figure AP-3. Click the New Contact button on the toolbar to enter new contact information and to begin using the Contacts features. With Contacts, you can store each contact's general information such as full name, company, job title, as well as up to three street addresses, three e-mail addresses, and more than a dozen telephone numbers. You also can store each contact's Web page address and quickly go to that Web page simply by clicking the Explore Web Page button on the toolbar.

Review the following Contacts tools:

 Using **AutoName**, you can quickly enter the full name for the contact, and Outlook will automatically separate the first, middle, and last names into different fields, enabling you to easily sort and group your contacts by any part of their names.

Similar to AutoName, **AutoAddress** facilitates entering an address for a contact by automatically separating the street, city, state, and postal code into distinct fields. Click the Details tab on the new contact window to store each contact's detailed information, including the department or office in which he or she works, the assistant's or manager's name, the contact's birthday, anniversary, or even the contact's nickname. In addition, to facilitate finding a contact quickly, Outlook allows you to file each contact under any name that you choose, including under a first name, a last name, a company name, or any word such as "architect" or "caterer." Outlook will automatically present you with several naming options under which to file each contact, but you are free to choose any word you like. Once you have entered your contacts' information, you can view your contacts in a variety of ways, including as detailed address cards, as a phone list, or by company, category, or location.

If you have a modem, use **AutoDial** to quickly dial a contact telephone number. Select a contact, then click the AutoDialer button on the Contacts toolbar. After Outlook has dialed the phone number, pick up the phone handset and click Talk.

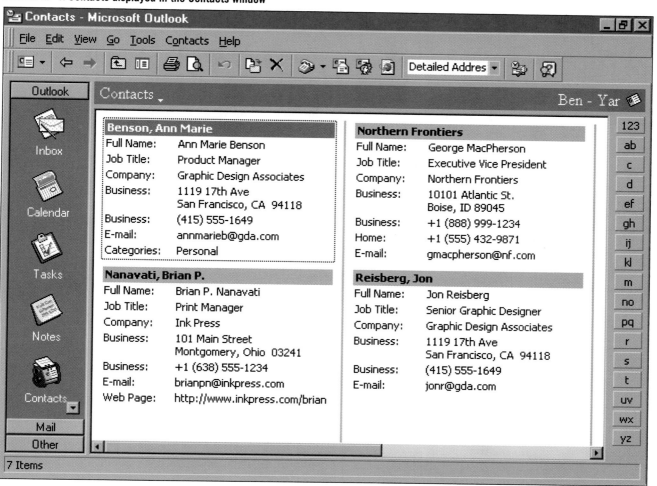

Tracking Your Activities and Files

To help track the information that travels through your personal computer, Microsoft Outlook includes the Journal and files features. **Journal** is uniquely designed to track the histories of your activities on a timeline. Open the Outlook group on the Outlook Bar, then click the Journal folder to open Journal. See Figure AP-5.

Details

Below is a list of Journal's features:

Automatically track your activities

Using Outlook's **AutoJournal** feature, you can have Outlook automatically track your activities with any of the contacts in your Contacts list. Activities such as e-mail messages, faxes, meeting and task requests and responses will be recorded automatically. In addition, you can use the AutoJournal feature to have Outlook automatically track every Microsoft Office document you use. If you use Outlook to telephone a contact, Outlook can track the duration of the call. If you wish to record an activity that does not involve your computer, such as a conversation or hand-written note, simply click the New Journal button ▐▇▾ on the Journal toolbar to manually open a new Journal entry. Once your activities have been recorded, you can organize the entries on the timeline into groups to quickly locate the information you need. For example, Outlook can display the entries by type such as phone calls or meetings so you can quickly tell how many phone calls you made today or how many meetings you attended last week.

Locate your files quickly

Journal also can help you immediately locate files. If you do not remember the path of an Office file you created, only the day on which you created it, you can easily find that entry in the Journal timeline. You can double-click the entry to view the details of the journal entry, or you can specify that the entry be a shortcut to the actual Office document.

Use the files feature to find misplaced files

If you are unable to locate a file, and you did not have Outlook track your work with the file, you can use the **files** features of Microsoft Outlook to locate the file. Open the Other group on the Outlook Bar to access the Files features of Outlook, as shown in Figure AP-6. Using the Files features, you can view files just as you would in Windows Explorer, without having to leave Outlook. However, unlike with Windows Explorer, you can use Outlook to view Office files grouped by Author or program type, and you can sort the list of Office files by such file properties as keywords, author, or number of pages. If you cannot locate your file in the file list, click the Find Items button on the Outlook toolbar to locate any file. Open the Favorites folder on the Outlook Bar to conveniently go to your favorite Web pages without leaving Outlook.

FIGURE AP-5: Journal displaying activities tracked on a timeline

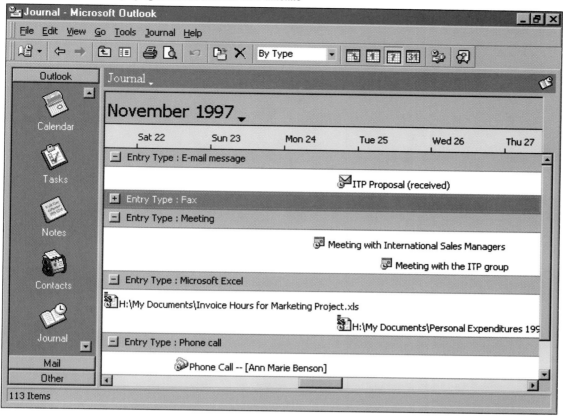

FIGURE AP-6: Outlook displays files grouped by type

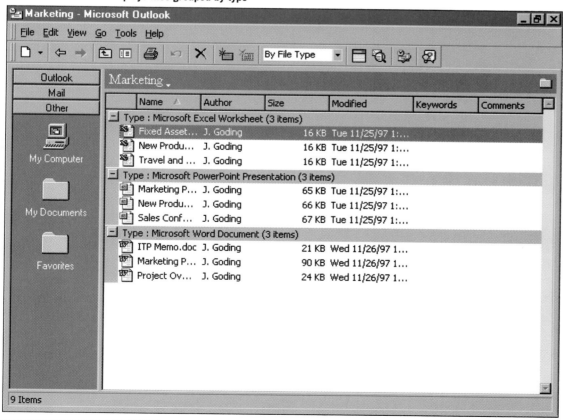

Getting
Started with Internet Explorer 4

Objectives

▶ **Understand Web browsers**
▶ **Start Internet Explorer 4**
▶ **Explore the browser window**
▶ **Open and save a URL**
▶ **Navigate Web pages**
▶ **Get Help**
▶ **Print a Web page**
▶ **Search for information on the Internet**
▶ **Exit Internet Explorer 4**

In this unit, you learn the benefits of the World Wide Web, examine basic features of Internet Explorer 4, and access Web pages. You need to connect to the Internet to complete this unit. If your computer is not connected to the Internet, check with your instructor or technical support person to get connected, or, if necessary, simply read the lessons without completing the steps to learn about using Internet Explorer. Nomad Ltd is a cutting-edge business. Natasha Seyb, a new marketing assistant, is investigating whether Nomad Ltd should expand into bicycle production. She uses Internet Explorer to find information about other cycle shops in the country and to check on possible new sources for bike parts.

Understanding Web Browsers

A **computer network** consists of two or more computers that can share information. The **Internet** is a communications system that connects computers and computer networks located all over the world. Over 40 million computers are currently connected to the Internet through telephone lines, cables, satellites, and other telecommunications media, as depicted in Figure A-1. Through the Internet, these computers can share many types of information, including text, graphics, sounds, videos, and computer programs. Anyone who has access to a computer and a link to the Internet through a computer network or modem can tap into this rich information source. The **World Wide Web** (the Web, WWW) is a part of the Internet containing Web pages or Web documents that are linked together. Web pages contain high-lighted words, phrases, or graphics called **hyperlinks**, or simply **links**, that open other Web pages when you click them. Figure A-2 shows a sample Web page. In addition to displaying other Web pages, a page's links may open graphic files, or they may play sound or video files. **Web browsers** are software programs used to access and display Web pages. Web browsers, such as Microsoft Internet Explorer and Netscape Navigator, make navigating the Web easy by providing a graphical, point-and-click environment. This unit features Internet Explorer 4, a popular browser from Microsoft Corporation. Although you only use the Internet Explorer Web browser in this unit, the Internet Explorer 4 suite contains many other network communications options listed in Table A-1. Natasha realizes many Internet Explorer browser features can benefit her company.

She can:

Display Web pages from all over the world

Natasha can access Web pages for many business purposes, such as checking the pages of other bike shops to see how they market their products.

Use links to move from one Web page to another

From the competing bicycle Web pages Natasha finds, she can jump to more specific information on subsequent Web pages simply by clicking the hyperlinks found on those initial pages.

Play audio and video clips

In addition to text, some links contain graphics that include sound and live action. By accessing a page on European bike races, Natasha can see some short video clips of the bike races as well as hear interviews with the races' winners.

Search the Web for information

Natasha can click a search button on her Web browser to access a list of search programs. These search programs let her look for information on any topic, such as bicycles, on computers throughout the world.

Save a list of her favorite Web pages

Using Internet Explorer, Natasha can save a list of her favorite Web pages. When she finds a particularly helpful bicycle-related page, she can add it to her list and easily return to it later.

Print the text and graphics on Web pages

If Natasha finds some key bicycle-related information or images and wants a hardcopy, she can easily print the entire Web page, including its graphics.

FIGURE A-1: **Internet structure**

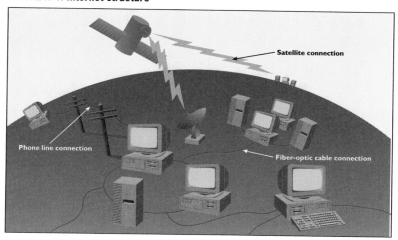

Satellite connection

Phone line connection

Fiber-optic cable connection

FIGURE A-2: **Sample Web page**

Graphic hyperlinks

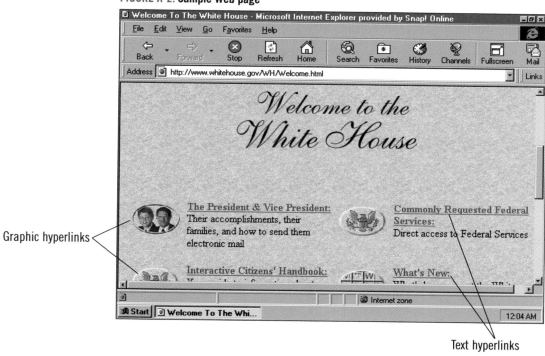

Text hyperlinks

TABLE A-1: **Internet Explorer 4 suite components**

feature	description
Internet Explorer	Lets you view and print Web pages located anywhere on the World Wide Web
FrontPage Express	Provides tools for creating new Web pages and editing existing pages located on your computer
Outlook Express	Lets you read and send e-mail and read and post messages in public newsgroups, or discussions organized around specific topics
NetMeeting	Lets you set up audio and video links to people at different locations for a live discussion
Webcasting	Lets you subscribe to Web pages that are updated on a regular basis, providing information on your specific areas of interest
NetShow Player	Provides tools for creating multimedia presentations that you can easily share with others on the Web

Internet

Internet

Starting Internet Explorer 4

Internet Explorer is a Web browser that can connect you to the Web if you have an Internet connection. When you install Internet Explorer 4, its icon appears on your system's desktop. The exact location of the Internet Explorer icon may vary on different computers. See your instructor or technical support person for assistance if you cannot see the Internet Explorer icon or if you do not have an Internet connection. ◢ Before Natasha can take advantage of the Web's many features, she must start Internet Explorer.

Steps

1. If you connect to the Internet by telephone, follow your normal procedure or your instructor's directions to establish your connection

2. Place the mouse pointer on the Internet Explorer icon. The icon should appear on the left side of your screen, as shown in Figure A-3. If the icon is not visible, click the Start button on the taskbar, point to Programs on the Start menu, point to Internet Explorer on the Programs list, click Internet Explorer, then skip Step 3

Trouble?

It's okay if the Web page on your screen differs from the one shown in Figure A-4. Later in this unit, you learn to change the home page that appears when you first start Internet Explorer.

3. Double-click the Internet Explorer icon
Your Internet Explorer program starts, and an initial Web page appears in your window. See Figure A-4. Continue with the next lesson to view various elements of the browser window.

CLUES TO USE

History of the Internet and the World Wide Web

The Internet has its roots in the United States Department of Defense Advanced Research Projects Agency Network (ARPANET), which was started in 1969. In 1986, the National Science Foundation (NST) formed NSFNET, which replaced ARPANET. NSFNET expanded the foundation of the U.S. portion of the Internet with high-speed, long-distance lines. In 1991, the U.S. Congress further expanded the Internet's capacity and speed and opened it to commercial use. Over 200 countries now have access to the Internet.

The World Wide Web was first created in Switzerland in 1991 to link documents on the Internet. In other words, while you read a document, you may see words or images that you can click to access another document or file. Software programs designed to access the Web (called Web browsers) use common "point-and-click" interfaces. The first graphical Web browser, Mosaic, was introduced at the University of Illinois in 1993. Recently, Microsoft Internet Explorer and Netscape Navigator have become the two most popular Web browsers.

FIGURE A-3: Internet Explorer icon on desktop

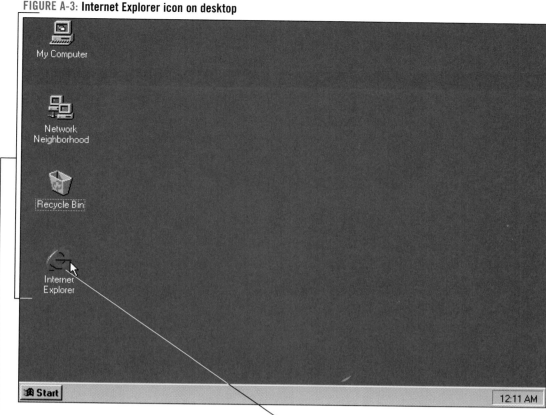

Your icons might differ

Internet Explorer icon

FIGURE A-4: Sample Web page for Microsoft Corporation

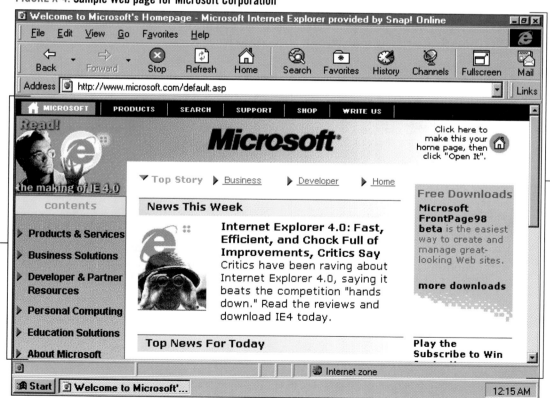

Current Web page displayed (yours may differ)

Internet Explorer browser window

Internet

Exploring the Browser Window

Elements of the Internet Explorer window, shown in Figure A-5, let you view, print, and search for information. Before exploring, or **surfing**, the Web Natasha decides to become familiar with the components of the browser window.

Details

She notes the following features:

 The **title bar** at the top of the page generally displays the name of the Web page.

 The **menu bar** provides access to most browser features through a variety of commands, much like other Windows 95 programs.

Trouble?

Because the toolbar and address bar can be customized, yours may appear differently from those in Figure A-5.

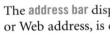 The **toolbar** provides icons for many options, such as changing text size on the screen, moving from one Web page to another, printing Web pages, and searching for information on the Internet. Table A-2 explains these options. Many commonly used commands available on menus are more readily accessed with buttons on the toolbar.

The **address bar** displays the address of the current Web page. The **Uniform Resource Locator (URL)**, or Web address, is contained in the address bar.

 The **status indicator** (the Internet Explorer logo) animates while a new Web page loads.

 The **document window** is the specific area of the browser window where the current Web page appears. You may need to scroll down the page to view its entire contents.

 The **vertical scroll bar** lets you move up or down the current Web page. The **scroll box** indicates your relative position within the Web page.

 The **status bar** displays information about your connection progress when you open new Web pages, including notification that you have connected to another site and the percentage of information transferred. The bar also displays the Web addresses of the links in the document window as you move your mouse pointer over them.

FIGURE A-5: Elements of Internet Explorer window

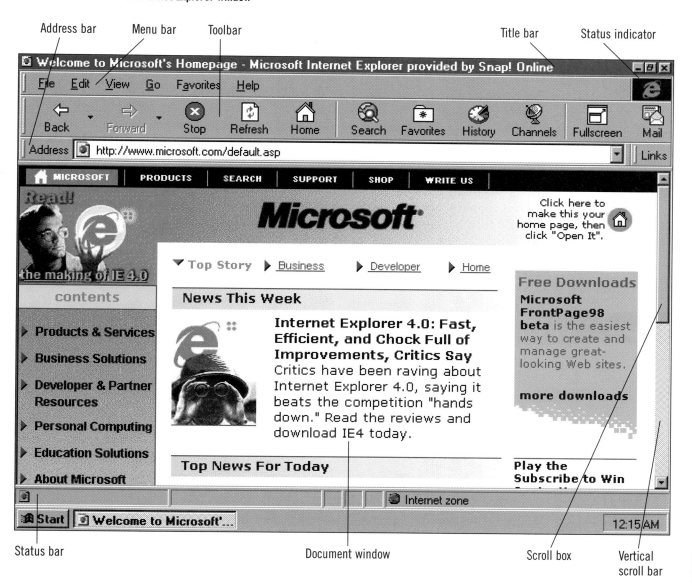

Address bar   Menu bar   Toolbar   Title bar   Status indicator

Status bar   Document window   Scroll box   Vertical scroll bar

TABLE A-2: Toolbar buttons

button	description	button	description
Back	Opens the previous page	Favorites	Opens the Explorer Favorites bar
Forward	Opens the next page	History	Opens the Explorer History bar
Stop	Stops loading the page	Channels	Opens the Explorer Channels bar
Refresh	Refreshes the contents of the current page	Fullscreen	Displays Internet Explorer window without Toolbar and Address bar
Home	Opens the Home page	Mail	Displays options for working with Mail
Search	Open the Explorer Search bar		

Internet

Opening and Saving a URL

The address for a Web page is called a URL. Each Web page has a unique URL beginning with "http" (HyperText Transfer Protocol), followed by a colon, two slashes, and the Web site's name. After the Web site's name, another slash may appear, followed by one or more directory names and a filename. For example, in the address, http://www.course.com/downloads/illustrated/chet/chet.html, the Web site's name is *www.course.com*; a directory at that site is called *downloads/illustrated/chet*; and within the chet directory is the file *chet.html*. The Internet Explorer Favorites feature lets you create a list of Web pages you view most often. To add a Web page to your Favorites list, simply click the Favorites command on the menu bar when the page is visible in your document window, and then click Add to Favorites. After you add a Web page to your Favorites list, you can automatically access that page by clicking Favorites on the menu bar, or clicking the Favorites button on the toolbar and then selecting the page's name. Natasha wants to investigate the Web page for a competitor, Chet's Cycles. She knows that the URL for Chet's Web page is http://www.course.com/downloads/illustrated/chet/chet.html. Natasha wants to add this Web page to her Favorites list so that she can return to the page later without typing its URL.

Steps

1. Click anywhere in the address bar
The current address is highlighted; any text you type replaces it.

2. Type www.course.com/downloads/illustrated/chet/chet.html
Internet Explorer automatically adds "http://" to the beginning of the address you typed, saving you time.

3. Press [Enter]
The status bar displays the connection progress. After a few seconds, the Web page for Chet's Cycles opens in the browser window, as shown in Figure A-6.

4. Click Favorites on the menu bar, click Add to Favorites, if necessary; in the Add Favorite dialog box, type Chet's Cycles if necessary (or another appropriate name), then click OK
The name and URL for Chet's Cycles are added to your list of favorite pages.

5. Click Go on the menu bar, then click Back
The previous Web page reopens in the browser window. In many cases, options on the toolbar are easier to locate and use than selections on the menu bar. For example, you may find it's quicker to simply click the Back button [Back] on the toolbar to return to the previous page rather than access the Back command from the Go menu.

Trouble?
If the Web page for Chet's Cycle's doesn't open, you may have typed the address incorrectly. Repeat Steps 2 and 3. If you still receive an error message, enter one of the URLs listed in Table A-3 instead.

FIGURE A-6: Web page for Chet's Cycles

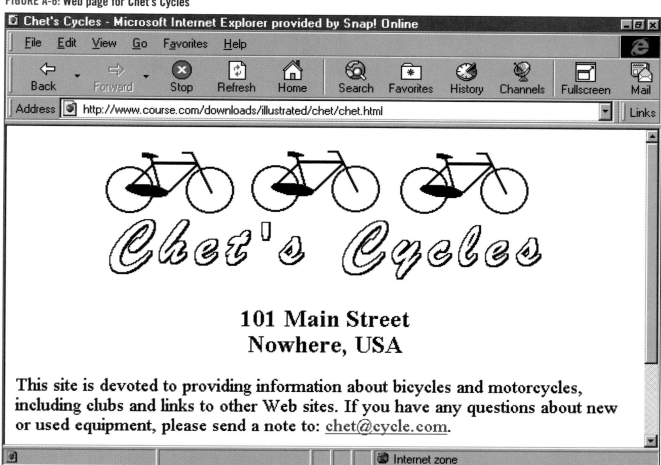

TABLE A-3: URLs of bicycle-related Web sites

name of Website	url
The Bicycle Trader	http://www.bicycletrader.com/
The Cyberider Cycling WWW Site	http://blueridge.databolts.ibm.com/bikes/
McBride Cycle	http://www.mcb-ride.com

Choosing Favorites

When you add a Web page to your Favorites list, returning to the page is much easier. To keep your Favorites list a reasonable length, you should only add pages that you expect to visit several times.

If your Favorites list grows long, you can organize page names in folders. To add a folder to your Favorites list, click Favorites on the menu bar, click Organize Favorites, then click the Create New Folder button.

Internet

Internet

Navigating Web Pages

Web pages can be connected to each other. By clicking a link, you can jump to another location on the same Web page or open a different Web page. You can follow links to obtain more information about a topic by simply clicking the highlighted word or phrase. If you change your mind or the page takes too long to load, you can click the Stop button. While viewing the Web page for Chet's Cycles, Natasha decides to investigate the Cycle Clubs link.

1. Click **Favorites** on the menu bar

2. Click **Chet's Cycles** (or the name you entered in the previous lesson)
   The Web page for Chet's Cycles opens in your browser window.

3. If necessary, click the **vertical scroll bar** to move down the Web page until you see the link <u>Cycle Clubs</u>, then place your mouse pointer on the link
   As shown in Figure A-7 the mouse pointer changes to 🖑 when you move it over an active link. This indicates that the text or graphic is a link.

Trouble?

If you receive an error message, click a different link on the page.

4. Click <u>Cycle Clubs</u>
   The status indicator animates as the new Web page is accessed. The Cycle Club Web page opens in your browser window, as shown in Figure A-8.

5. Click the **Home button** [🏠] on the toolbar
   The initial Web page that opens when you start Internet Explorer reappears in your browser window.

Selecting a Home page

When you click the Home button [🏠], the page that is specified as "home" opens in your document window. When you first install Internet Explorer, the default Home page is a page at the Microsoft Web site. If you want a different page to open each time you start

Internet Explorer and whenever you click the Home button, open that page in the document window, click View on the menu bar, click Internet Options, click the General tab, then click Use Current, then click OK to specify the current page as the Home page.

FIGURE A-7: Hyperlinks on Chet's Cycles Web page

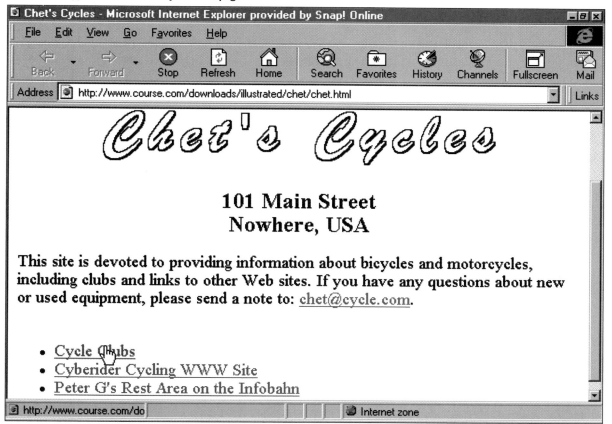

FIGURE A-8: Web page for Cycle Clubs

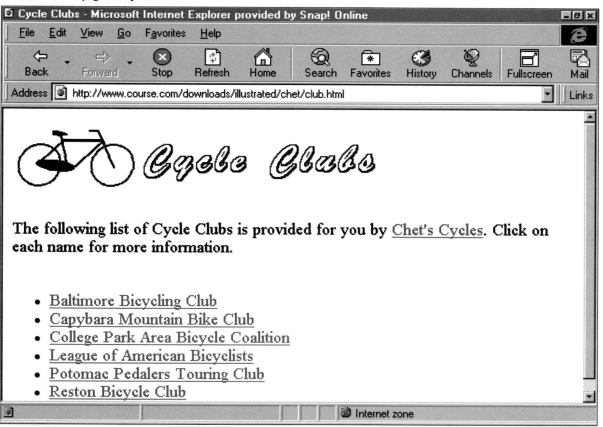

Internet

Getting Help

On its menu bar Internet Explorer provides a Help option with information and instructions on various features and commands. 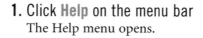 Exploring various Web pages for cycle clubs, Natasha finds one with very small type. She decides to access the Help option to find instructions for increasing the font size of the type.

Steps 1 2 3 4

Trouble?

Don't worry if a different tab is in front.

1. **Click Help on the menu bar**
   The Help menu opens.

2. **Click Contents and Index**
   The Internet Explorer Help dialog box opens as shown in Figure A-9, with the Contents tab in front. Table A-4 explains how each of the three tabs provides a different way to access help information.

3. **Click the Search tab**
   The Search tab lets you search for a specific word or phrase.

4. **In the "Type in the keyword to find" text box, type font sizes, then click List Topics**
   As shown in Figure A-10, a list of relevant topics appears under Topic in the Select Topic to display area.

5. **Under Topic, double-click Displaying text larger or smaller**
   As shown in Figure A-11, text in the right pane of the Internet Explorer Help window provides information on how to change the font size.

6. **Click the Close button in the upper-right corner of the Internet Explorer Help window**
   The Help window closes and the Web page that opens when you start Internet Explorer reappears in your browser window.

TABLE A-4: Help options

tab	function
Contents	Lists categories available in Help
Index	Lists Help topics in alphabetical order and lets you locate specific topics
Search	Helps you locate the topic you need when you enter a keyword or phrase

FIGURE A-9: **Internet Explorer Help dialog box**

Help tabs

Description of Help feature

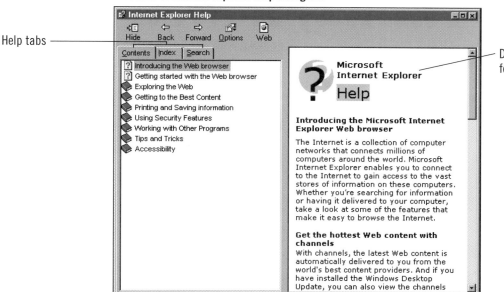

FIGURE A-10: **Search tab**

Keywords

List of topics relevant to keywords

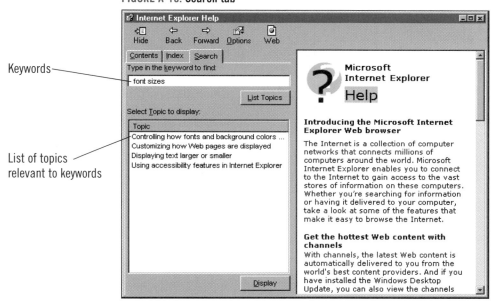

FIGURE A-11: **Help information**

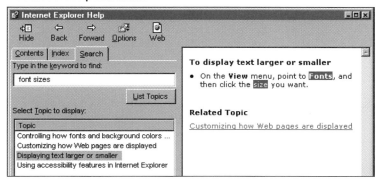

Internet

Internet

Printing a Web Page

You can print the Web page that currently appears in the document window by clicking the Print button on the toolbar. Using the Print dialog box, you can specify such parameters as the number of copies and the page ranges you want to print. When you print a Web page, you print its text and any graphics. Table A-5 explains printing options. ◆ Natasha decides to print two copies of the bicycle Web page: one for her files and the other for her boss.

1. Click the **Back button** twice to return to the Chet's Cycles Page

2. Click **File** on the menu bar, then click **Print**
   The Print dialog box opens, as shown in Figure A-12.

QuickTip

To open the Print dialog box quickly, press [Ctrl][P].

3. Under Copies, click the **up arrow** in the Number of copies text box until the number 2 appears
   The Number of copies text box changes, displaying the number 2 to indicate two copies will be printed.

4. Make sure your computer is connected to a printer that is turned on and contains paper

5. Click **OK**
   The print dialog box closes, and two copies of the current Web page print.

Trouble?

If you are not connected to a printer, or if an error message appears, contact your instructor or technical support person for assistance.

FIGURE A-12: **Print dialog box**

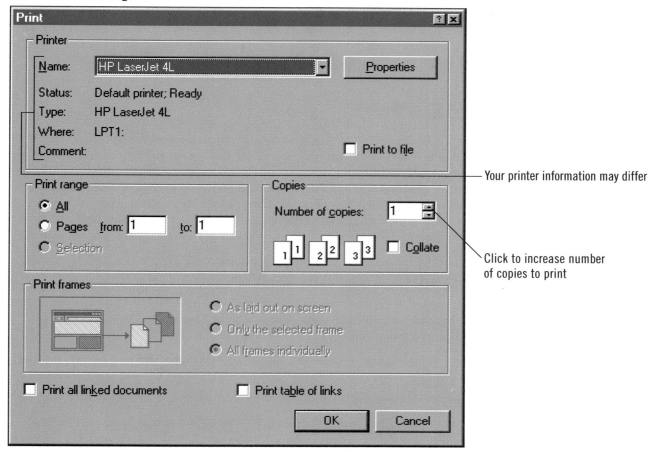

Your printer information may differ

Click to increase number
of copies to print

TABLE A-5: **Printing options**

option	description
Printer	Displays information about the name, status and location of the active printer
Print range	Indicates which pages to print. You can select all or specify a range.
Copies	Indicates the number of copies of each page to print and the sequence of the pages.
Print frames	Allows you to print only the current frame, or to print all frames separately or together
Print all linked documents	Opens and prints each document referenced by a link on the current page
Print table of links	Prints links in a table at the end of the document

Printer properties

If you select Properties from the Print dialog box,   orientation, and other parameters.
you can specify paper size, paper source,

Internet

Internet

Searching for Information on the Internet

Literally millions of Web pages and other information sources are available through the Internet. At times, finding the information you want seems like looking for the proverbial needle in the haystack. Luckily, **search engines** are designed to help you locate useful information. You simply enter a **keyword** or phrase describing the information you want to find, and the search engine provides you with a list of related Web sites. The name of each Web site is a hyperlink; you simply click the link to jump to the corresponding Web page. 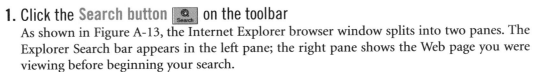 Natasha needs to find information about mopeds. She decides to use Internet Explorer's built-in shortcuts to conduct her search.

 **Steps**

1. **Click the Search button** 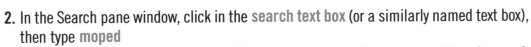 **on the toolbar**
   As shown in Figure A-13, the Internet Explorer browser window splits into two panes. The Explorer Search bar appears in the left pane; the right pane shows the Web page you were viewing before beginning your search.

 Trouble?

It's OK if your search text box or Search button is unnamed.

2. **In the Search pane window, click in the search text box (or a similarly named text box), then type moped**
   Now that you've specified the keyword(s) you want to search for, you can initiate the search

3. **Under the search text box, click the Search button (or a similarly named button)**
   Your search results appear as a list of related Web sites, called **hits**. See Figure A-14. You can click the hyperlink for any sites listed to access more specific information.

4. **Scroll down the hit list, then click a hyperlink of your choice**
   The related page containing more information about mopeds opens in your browser window. When you finish exploring the hyperlinked site, you can continue or end your search.

5. **Click the Back button** , **then click**

CLUES TO USE

Search engines

Many search engines can help you locate information on the Internet, such as Yahoo, Infoseek, Lycos, WebCrawler, and Excite. These search engines routinely use software programs to methodically catalog, or **crawl**, through the entire Internet and create huge databases with links to the Web pages and their URLs. When you enter a keyword or phrase, the search engine looks through the database index for relevant information and displays a list of Web sites.

Each search engine differs slightly in the way it formats information, the number of Internet sites and the amount of text it records in the database, and the frequency with which it updates the database. As you practice searching for information on the Internet, it is best to try several different search engines. Soon you will develop personal favorites and learn which engine works best in various situations.

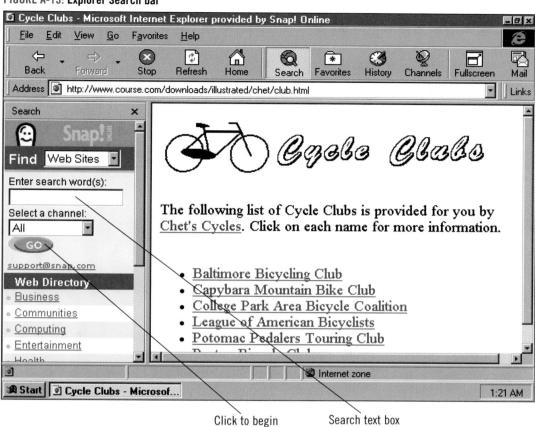

Click to begin
search

Search text box

Click to jump to
other Web sites

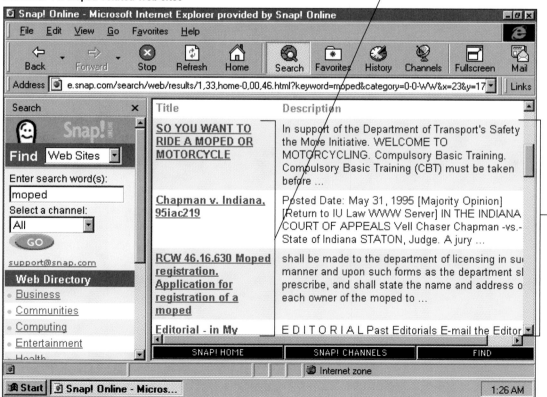

Descriptions of
corresponding Web
sites

Internet

Internet

Exiting Internet Explorer

When you are ready to exit Internet Explorer, you can click the Close button in the upper-right corner of the browser window or select the Close command from the File menu. You do not need to save files before you exit, because all files you view with Internet Explorer are already saved on your computer or another machine connected to the network you are using. ◢━━ Natasha completes her bicycle research on the Web and is ready to exit Internet Explorer.

Steps

1. **Click File on the menu bar**
   The File menu opens, as shown in Figure A-15.

2. **Click Close on the File menu**
   The Internet Explorer browser window closes.

QuickTip

You can also exit from Internet Explorer by clicking the Close button in the upper-right corner of the browser window.

3. **If you connected to the Internet by telephone, follow your normal procedure or your instructor's directions to close your connection**

FIGURE A-15: Internet Explorer with File menu open

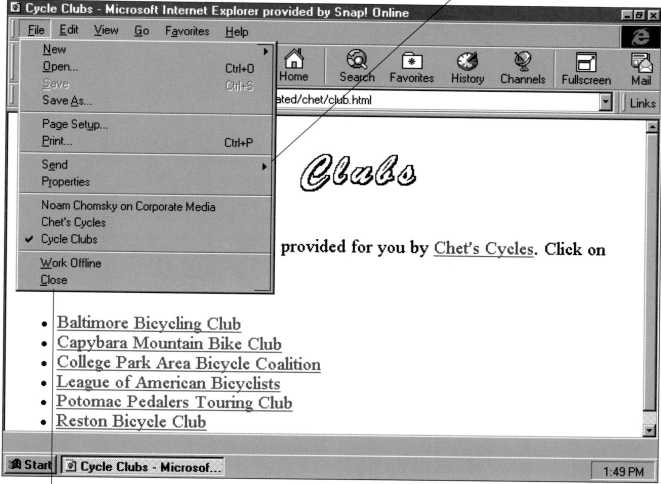

Click to close
Internet Explorer

Saving or sending a Web page

Before you exit from Internet Explorer, you may want to save a copy of the current page or send someone a copy. By selecting Save As on the File menu, you can save the text from the page in a file on your computer. (The graphics will not be saved.) Later, you can open the page in a wordprocessing program such as WordPad. If you want to send the page to someone, point to Send on the File menu, click Page By Email, then type the address of the person you want to receive the page.

Internet

Practice

► Concepts Review

Label each Internet Explorer 4 screen elements indicated in Figure A-16.

FIGURE A-16

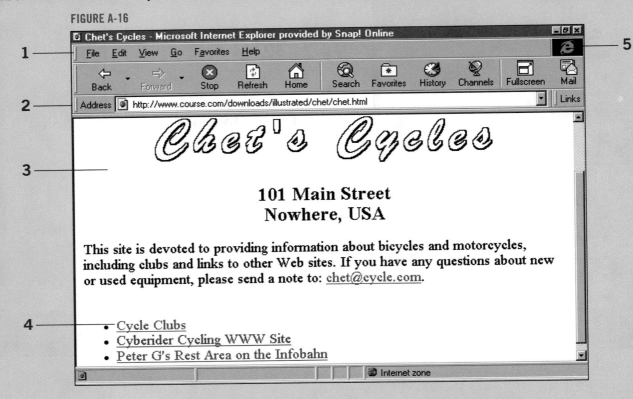

Match each term with the statement that describes its function.

6. Address bar
7. Toolbar
8. Favorites button
9. Status indicator
10. Back button

a. Animates when Internet Explorer loads a page
b. Displays the URL for the current page
c. Provides shortcuts for options on the menu bar
d. Displays a list of selected Web pages
e. Displays the previously viewed page

Select the best answer from the list of choices.

11. Software programs used to access and display Web pages are called
    a. Web sites   c. Web documents
    b. Web windows   d. Web browsers

12. If you want to save the name and URL of a file and return to it later, you can add it to a list called
    a. Favorites   c. Home pages
    b. Bookmarks   d. Preferences

13. An international telecommunications network that consists of hyperlinked documents is called
    a. NSFNET   c. Internet Explorer
    b. Netscape Navigator   d. World Wide Web

14. Where are the icons that perform many common functions, such as printing, located in Internet Explorer?
    a. Address bar   c. Status bar
    b. Toolbar   d. Menu bar

15. Most Web pages are longer than the document window. What feature must you use to view the entire page?
    a. Scroll bar   c. Forward button
    b. Status bar   d. Home button

16. Which of the following is a valid URL?
    a. www.usf.edu/   c. http:/www.usf.edu/
    b. htp://www.usf.edu/   d. http//www.usf.edu/

17. Which icon should you click if you want to stop a Web page that is currently loading on your computer?
    a. [Fullscreen]   c. [Stop]
    b. [Favorites]   d. [Refresh]

18. Highlighted or underlined words with an embedded URL to jump to another location are called
    a. Explorers   c. Web browsers
    b. Favorites   d. Hyperlinks

19. The URL of the current Web page appears in the
    a. Title bar   c. Address bar
    b. Document window   d. Status bar

20. To locate information on a specific topic on the Internet, you can use a
    a. URL locator   c. Favorites list
    b. Web browser   d. Search engine

► Skills Review

1. Start Internet Explorer and explore the browser window.
   a. Make sure your computer is connected to the Internet.
   b. Double-click the Internet Explorer icon.
   c. Identify the toolbar, menu bar, address bar, status bar, status indicator, URL, document window, and scroll bars.
   d. In the toolbar, identify the icons for printing, searching, viewing favorites, changing the font size, and moving to the previous page.

2. Open a URL.
   a. Click in the Address bar, type "www.cnet.com", then press [Enter].
   b. Explore the site using the scroll bars, toolbar, and hyperlinks.

3. Save a URL.
   a. Click the Address bar, type "www.loc.gov", then press [Enter].
   b. Click Favorites on the menu bar, click Add to Favorites, then click OK.
   c. Click the Home button.
   d. Click the Favorites button.
   e. Click "Library of Congress Home Page" to return to that page.
   f. Click the Favorites button again to close the Explorer Favorites bar.

4. Follow links on a Web page.
   a. Click in the Address bar, type "www.sportsline.com", then press [Enter].
   b. Follow the links to investigate the content.
   c. Click the Home button.

5. Get Help.
   a. Click Help on the menu bar.
   b. Click Contents and Index.
   c. Click the Index tab.
   d. Type "search" in the text box at the top of the window.
   e. Scroll down to the entry "searching the Web" in the index list, then double-click it.
   f. In Topics Found dialog box, double-click "Searching the Web."
   g. Click the Close button.

6. Search for information on the Internet.
   a. Click the Search button.
   b. Type a keyword or phrase.
   c. Click Go.
   d. When you finish your search, click the Search button again to close the Explorer Search bar.

7. Print a Web page and exit Internet Explorer.
   a. Click in the Address bar, type "www.whitehouse.gov", then press [Enter].
   b. Print the page.
   c. Click the Close button to exit Internet Explorer.

▶ Independent Challenges

1. You will soon graduate from college with a degree in Business Management. Before entering the workforce, you want to be sure that you are up to date on all advances in your field. You decide that checking the Web will provide the most current information. In addition, you can research potential companies for employment opportunities.

Use Internet Explorer to open the All Business Network Home page at www.all-biz.com. Select a promising site, then click the Print icon to print the page.

2. You leave tomorrow for a business trip to France. You want to be sure that you take the right clothes for the weather and decide that the best place to check weather conditions is the Web. Access one or two of the following weather sites to determine the weather in Paris at this time of year. Use the Print command to print the weather report.

The Weather Channel	www.weather.com
CNN Weather	www.cnn.com/WEATHER
Yahoo Weather	weather.yahoo.com

3. You work at a newspaper company and your manager wants to buy a new desktop computer. She assigns you the task of investigating her options. You decide that using the Web for this research is more expedient than traveling to various computer stores. Access the following computer company Web sites, and print a page from the one or two that you think offer the best deals.

IBM	www.ibm.com
Apple	www.apple.com
Dell	www.dell.com

4. A recent newspaper article you read listed the URLs of some popular search engines. To compare these search engines, create a chart showing the results of searching for the word "floptical." List the search engine and the number of hits in your chart. You should compare the effectiveness of the default browser Internet Explorer uses with the search engines listed below.

Yahoo	www. yahoo.com
Lycos	www.lycos.com
Excite	www.excite.com

Internet

▶ Visual Workshop

You must write a 10-page paper for your history class. You choose the Holocaust as the topic for your paper. Using your favorite Web search engine, find the Web site shown in Figure A-17. (*Hint*: Add quotations marks to your search string, for example: "A Teacher's Guide to the Holocaust".)

FIGURE A-17

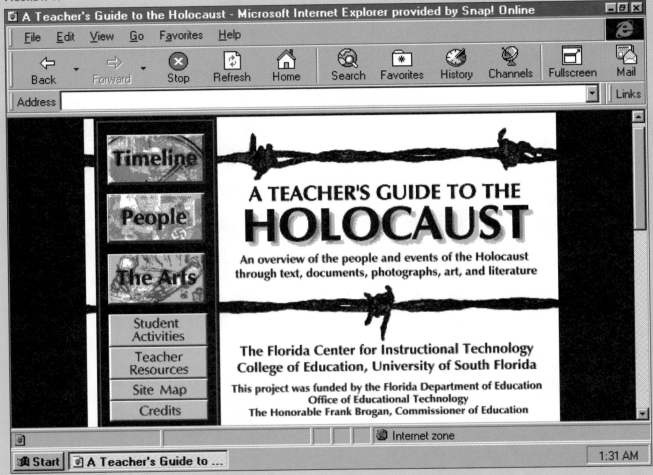

Creating
a Web Publication

Objectives

▶ **Plan Web publication content**
▶ **Create a Web page document**
▶ **Format a Web page**
▶ **Create a Web page from a Word document**
▶ **Create a Web page from an Access object**
▶ **Create a Web page from an Excel file**
▶ **Create Web pages with PowerPoint**
▶ **Add hyperlinks**

Microsoft Office 97 offers features that help you to create your own Web pages either from scratch or by converting existing Office documents to **Hypertext Markup Language (HTML)**. HTML is the language used to describe the content and format of pages on the World Wide Web. ✐ Cleveland Mack works in the Human Resources department at Nomad Ltd. His manager, Becky Riis, asks Cleveland to create a set of Web pages to help new Nomad Ltd employees learn more about the company. The Human Resources department will then **publish,** or make these pages available, on the Nomad Ltd **intranet**—a private network that uses Internet communications technologies—so that all new employees can access them. Cleveland uses Office to create the new Web pages.

Internet

Planning Web Publication Content

As with any other document type, planning your Web pages carefully before creating them is important. This is especially crucial when you are creating a **Web publication**, or a group of associated Web pages focusing on a particular theme or topic. Following a step-by-step process can help you organize tasks logically and also help ensure that you identify and complete necessary tasks. Cleveland decides to use the following plan to create the Web publication for new employees:

Details

 Sketch outlines of the pages

Draw a sketch of how you want each page to look to identify tasks that must be completed. Be sure your sketch shows the links between pages. Cleveland identifies the documents he wants to include in his pages, sketches the layout, and adds notes, as shown in Figure B-1.

For each page, perform the following tasks:

- **Create a new document and enter the page's text, or use a Web page tool to create a page from an existing file**

   Creating a page containing all new text using a word processing program is usually easier. The Word 97 Web Page Wizard simplifies the creation of high-quality Web pages by providing illustrated templates in which you can place text. Additionally, each Office 97 program contains a tool that can automatically create a Web page from a file in that program's format. Cleveland creates a new page in Word and converts several Office documents to HTML files.

- **Format page appearance**

   Special Word 97 features facilitate editing a Web page document, including those documents not created with Word. When you use **Word Web**, the Web page editing feature of Word 97, the Style menu lists acceptable text styles for Web pages. With Word Web, you also can add thematic graphics to your pages easily. To personalize each page further, you may want to add your own images as well. Cleveland uses the Word Web text tools to enhance each page's appearance when he edits it. He also applies a common visual style to his pages and inserts the Nomad Ltd company logo at the top of the **home page** of the Web publication.

- **Use a Web browser**

   View the page in your Web browser window to confirm that it appears as desired. If necessary, use a Web page editor to make corrections. Cleveland views his pages in Internet Explorer to be sure they appear as desired.

 Format hyperlinks

After you finalize the text and graphics for all of your pages, add hyperlinks to each page for referenced pages. Cleveland's sketch indicates that he will create a link on his home page to each associated Web page. He also will create links to other important Nomad Ltd pages at the bottom of the home page, as well as add a link back to the home page on each associated page.

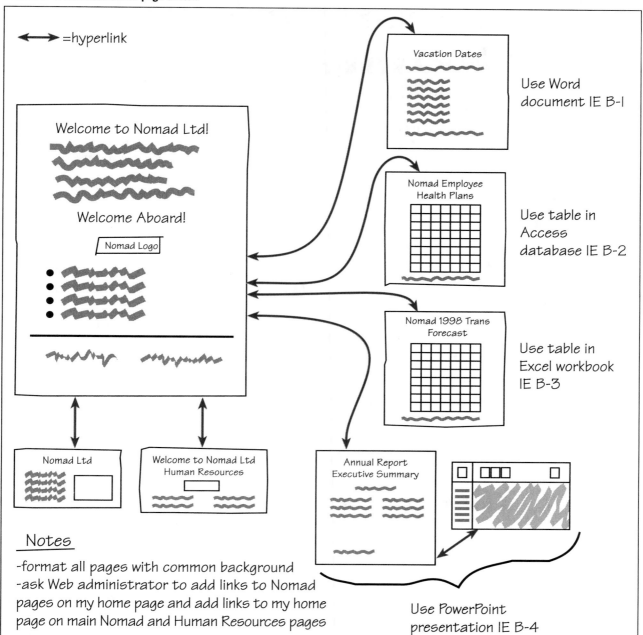

Use Word
document IE B-1

Use table in
Access
database IE B-2

Use table in
Excel workbook
IE B-3

Use PowerPoint
presentation IE B-4

Internet

Creating a Web Page Document

To create a Web page you create a document that uses HTML formatting. HTML places codes, called **tags**, around all elements of your document, which describe how these elements appear when viewed using a Web browser. The Microsoft Office Web tools simplify this process by inserting codes for you. Additionally, the Web Page Wizard in Word includes templates that add thematic formatting and graphics to your Web pages.  Cleveland uses the Web Page Wizard to create the basic structure of his home page.

Steps

1. **Start Word, then make sure the Standard and Formatting toolbars are visible**
   You use the Web Page Wizard to both create and format your new document.

2. **Click File on the menu bar, click New, click the Web Pages tab, then double-click the Web Page Wizard icon**
   The Web Page Wizard dialog box displays a list of templates, as shown in Figure B-2. The Simple Layout style, which is currently selected, previews in the Word document window. Note that some templates are used for specific page types.

3. **Click Next**
   The Web Page Wizard dialog box displays a list of visual style options. You choose a nature theme consistent with Nomad Ltd's company image.

4. **Click Outdoors, then click Finish**
   The Simple Layout template opens in the document window with the Outdoors style, featuring ivy and stones.

5. **Click the Save button** **on the Standard toolbar, type Welcome in the File name text box, select the location of your Student Disk in the Save in list box, then click Save**
   The status bar indicates you saved your file in HTML format, confirming that Word is inserting the HTML tags for you. You begin creating the page by entering your page heading.

6. **Click in the selection bar next to the heading Insert Heading Here, type Welcome to Nomad Ltd!, then repeat this procedure to replace the next paragraph with the text shown in Figure B-3, and the line "Type some text." with the text Welcome Aboard!**
   Now enter the text for the rest of the page.

7. **Select the text Add a list item. next to the first stone bullet but do not select the stone graphic, type List of vacation dates for Nomad employees, then repeat this procedure to enter the text for the remaining bullets shown in Figure B-3**

8. **Press [Pg Down], select the line Type some text, then press [Delete]**
   The blue text in the last line of the page indicates the text is in hyperlink format. Now you type the appropriate text for links to two other Nomad Ltd pages. You will create the actual links later.

9. **Select the text Related Page 1, type Nomad Ltd home page, select the text Related Page 2, type Nomad Ltd Human Resources Department home page, select the text Related Page 3 and the vertical line to the left, then press [Delete]**

Trouble?

You must have the Web Authoring tools installed to complete this unit. If not, contact your instructor or technical support person for assistance.

QuickTip

To add a bullet, place the insertion point at the end of the current bulleted line, then press [Enter].

Time To

✓ Save
✓ Close

FIGURE B-2: Web Page Wizard dialog box

Preview of Simple Layout template

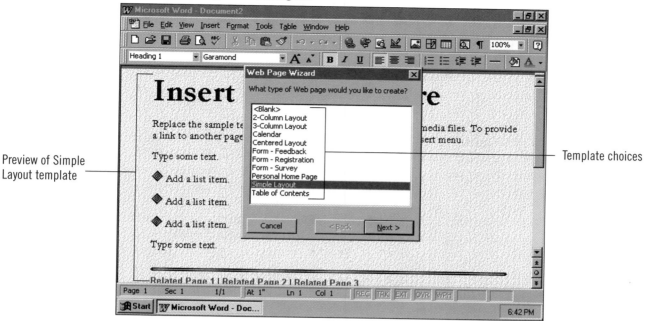

Template choices

FIGURE B-3: Text entered for home page

Heading inserted

Text to replace existing line

Stone bullets

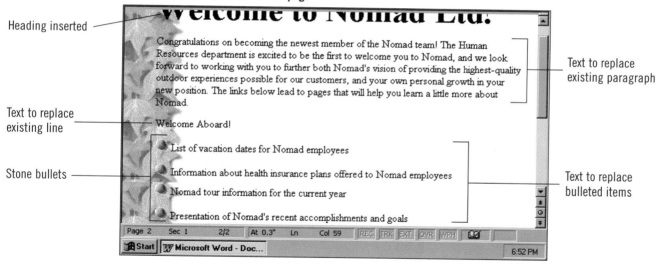

Text to replace existing paragraph

Text to replace bulleted items

Choosing Web page content and style

Before finalizing the appearance of your Web publication, look at existing Web pages. The styles, layouts, and contents of other pages can suggest new ideas about how to present your information. By viewing a wide variety of pages, you also may learn about Web page formatting features that have only recently become available. Remember, however, that a Web publication expresses your company's or your own identity; include personal touches rather than simply copying other pages.

Internet

Formatting a Web Page

In addition to working with Web pages in Word Web, you can also create and edit Web documents in **FrontPage Express**, a program specifically designed for Web page production that is included as part of the Internet Explorer 4 suite. Like Word Web, FrontPage Express—or **FrontPage** for short—includes templates for creating new pages and a collection of tools that let you produce high-quality Web pages and implement the latest HTML features. HTML does not support some formatting options available in standard Office documents, such as the Justify button and the [Tab] key. Instead, Word Web and FrontPage offer other types of tools for formatting Web pages. Table B-1 lists some HTML-specific buttons available on both the FrontPage and Word Web toolbars. 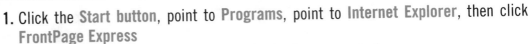 Although Cleveland likes the template and visual style he selected for his Web page, he wants to change some formatting and text layout and add a graphic. He decides to use FrontPage to make these formatting changes.

1. Click the **Start button**, point to **Programs**, point to **Internet Explorer**, then click **FrontPage Express**
   FrontPage opens, displaying a blank page in the document window.

2. Click the **Open button** 📂 on the Standard toolbar, click **Browse** in the Open File dialog box, select the location of your Student Disk in the Look in text box, then open the file **Welcome**

3. Be sure the insertion point is in the heading "Welcome to Nomad Ltd!" at the top of the page, click the **Bulleted List button** 📋 on the Formatting toolbar, then click the **Center button** ≡ on the Formatting toolbar
   With the heading centered, now center the border and hyperlink text.

4. Click in the selection bar next to the text "Welcome Aboard!", click the **Change Style list arrow**, click **H2**, click ≡, press **[Ctrl][End]**, select the **stone border** and the **hyperlink text** at the bottom of the page, click ≡, then click anywhere on the page
   The FrontPage Change Style list contains only styles compatible with HTML. Next, you indent the main paragraph and the list.

5. Use the selection bar to select the entire bulleted list, click the **Increase Indent button** 📑 on the Formatting toolbar, press **[Ctrl][Home]**, click anywhere in the paragraph beginning with "Congratulations...", then click 📑
   The list and paragraph are now indented, as shown in Figure B-4. Next you insert the Nomad Ltd company logo on the Web page.

6. Move the insertion point to the end of the line "Welcome Aboard!", then press **[Enter]**
   This new line will be the location of the graphic file containing the logo.

7. Click the **Insert Image button** 🖼 on the Standard toolbar
   The Image dialog box opens.

Time To

✔ Save
✔ Close FrontPage

8. Click **Browse**, select the location of your Student Disk in the Look in text box, click **Nomad** in the file list, then click **Open**
   The Nomad Ltd logo appears centered in the blank paragraph, as shown in Figure B-5. The final step in the process is to view the page in your browser window to confirm its appearance. However, because your page contains only simple formatting and no advanced elements like tables, FrontPage displays the page exactly as it will appear in your browser window. Therefore, you need not open the page in Internet Explorer.

FIGURE B-4: Heading and list formatted

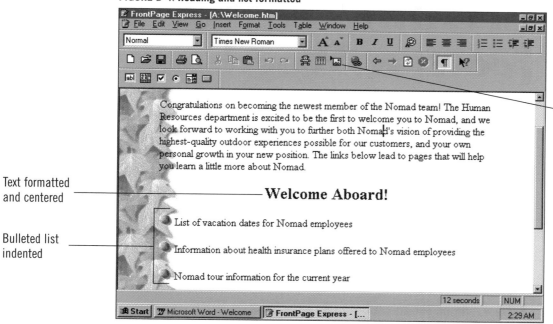

Insert Image button

Text formatted and centered

Bulleted list indented

FIGURE B-5: Completed home page

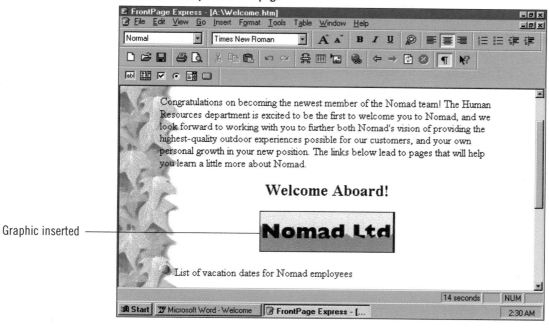

Graphic inserted

TABLE B-1: Formatting buttons for HTML

button	function
A˄	Increases font size for selected text to next-highest HTML-standard size
A˅	Decreases font size for selected text to next-lowest HTML-standard size
🎨	Allows specification of text color and creation of custom colors
🖥	Inserts automated Web page component, such as a Java script, to automatically perform a task
🔄	Refreshes display of current page
🖼	Inserts an existing picture in the active file at the insertion point

Creating a Web Page from a Word Document

In addition to offering tools that help you create new Web pages, Microsoft Office 97 makes creating Web pages from existing files easy. You can use the Web features in Office to convert files from their Office formats to HTML, making them easy to view on the Web. 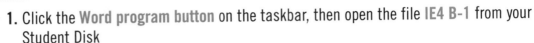 As he noted on his original sketch, Cleveland wants to create Web pages using several existing Office documents. He starts by creating a Web page from a list of company vacation dates stored in a Word file.

 **Steps**

Trouble?

If the file IE4 B-1 does not appear in the file list, change the Files of type list box to display "All files" or "Word Documents."

1. Click the **Word program button** on the taskbar, then open the file **IE4 B-1** from your Student Disk
   The file contains a list of vacation dates for all Nomad Ltd employees.

2. Click **File** on the menu bar, then click **Save as HTML**
   The Save As HTML dialog box opens.

3. Type **Vacation** in the file name text box, select the location of your Student Disk in the Save in list box, then click **Save**
   Word saves a copy of the document in HTML format and switches to Word Web mode. Notice that the formatting toolbar changes to include only those tools compatible with HTML and the document's line spacing increases to reflect HTML styles. Now you can change some page formatting.

Trouble?

"Vacation dates" appears in the title bar because Word automatically uses the page heading as the Web page title instead of the filename.

4. Center the heading **Vacation dates**, press **[Ctrl][End]**, insert a blank line at the end of the document, type **Return to Welcome page**, then indent the list of dates
   You use this new text as a link back to the Web publication's home page. Now add the same outdoor background you used on the home page.

5. Click the **Background button**  on the Formatting toolbar
   Word displays the Background toolbar shown in Figure B-6, which contains a palette of colors that you can click to fill the background of the page in the active document window.

6. Click **Fill Effects**
   The Fill Effects dialog box opens, displaying patterns that you can choose as background for the current page.

7. Click **Other Texture**, then click the **Preview button** if necessary
   The Select Texture dialog box opens, displaying a list of graphic files that contain additional background choices.

Trouble?

If Leaves on the Side is not listed, use the Look in list arrow to open the folder Program Files\Microsoft Office\Office\Web Page Templates\Styles on the drive from which Word is running.

8. Double-click **Leaves on the Side**, then click **OK**
   The leaf border appears on the left edge of the screen, as shown in Figure B-7. It matches the appearance of the Welcome page you created.

9. Click the **Save button** , then close your document

Web page title

Background button

Background toolbar

List indented

Click to see more options

Line spacing increased from original file

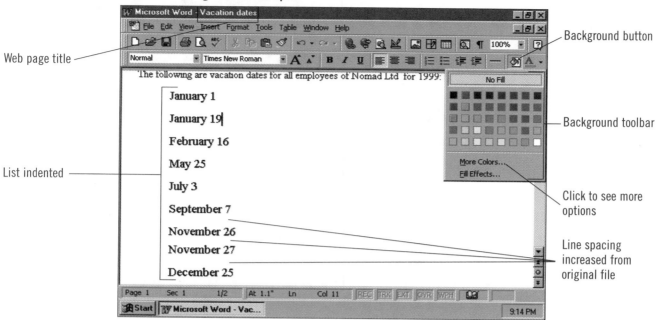

FIGURE B-7: Completed Vacation page

Leaf border added

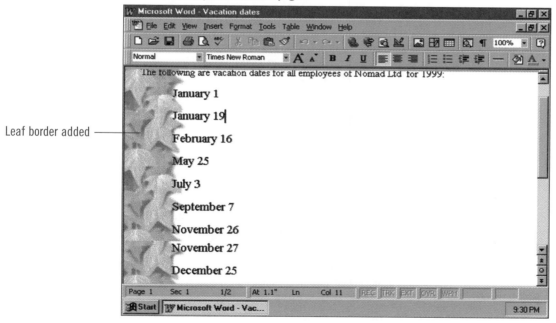

CLUES TO USE

Web browsers and Web page appearance

When you use a browser other than Microsoft Internet Explorer 4, such as Netscape Navigator or Lynx (a text-only browser), remember that the same Web pages' appearance may differ. Depending on your browser's options, you can change settings, such as always using a certain font or selecting a certain window size, that affect the way pages display. Using only the limited style choices Word Web provides is one way to help ensure that your Web page's appearance is consistent as possible in different browser windows.

Internet

Creating a Web Page from an Access Object

Like Word, Access offers a tool for converting existing files to Web pages. The Publish to the Web Wizard creates a separate HTML file from each element of a database that you select. You can use Word to format the resulting file like any other HTML file. ✎ Cleveland wants to create a Web page that contains a table describing various health insurance plans available to Nomad Ltd employees. This information is currently stored in an Access database.

Steps

1. Start Access, open the file IE4 B-2 from the WWWAccess folder on your Student Disk, then open the table Nomad Employee Health Plans in Table view

2. Click File on the menu bar, click Save As HTML, be sure the check box regarding Web publication profiles is empty in the first Publish to the Web Wizard dialog box, then click Next
   The next Publish to the Web Wizard dialog box lets you select elements of the current database from which you want to create your Web page.

3. Click the Tables tab if necessary, click the Nomad Employee Health Plans check box to select it, then click Next
   The Publish to the Web Wizard displays a dialog box for selecting a template.

4. Click Browse, click Stones, click Select, then click Next
   The next Publish to the Web Wizard dialog box offers you a choice between different types of HTML code for your new Web page. Because the original file resides on a local computer rather than on the company Web server, you decide to create a static page.

5. If necessary, click the Static HTML option button to select it, click Next, click Browse, in the Look in text box select the WWWAccess folder on your Student Disk, click Select, be sure the No option button is selected, then click Next
   The next Publish to the Web Wizard dialog box offers you the option of having Access create a home page containing a link to the Web page you are creating.

6. Be sure the Yes check box is empty, click Next, then click Finish
   The Publish to the Web Wizard creates a new Web page and saves it on your Student Disk. The Wizard uses the table's name in the original database as the filename, adding a number to the end in case you create multiple Web pages from the same table. Open your new Web page in Word so that you can edit as necessary.

7. Close Access, open FrontPage Express, then open the file Nomad Employee Health Plans_1 from the WWWAccess folder on your Student Disk
   The Health Plan Web page opens in FrontPage, as shown in Figure B-8. Note that the table contents are not correctly arranged. Advanced Web page features, such as tables, don't always appear correctly in Web page editors. Next you make changes to the Web page that Access created, then check table formatting in Internet Explorer.

8. Scroll to the bottom of the table, select the graphic image below the table on the left side, press [Delete], type Return to Welcome page, save your changes to the Web page, click the Internet Explorer program button on the taskbar, then open the file Nomad Employee Health Plans_1 from the WWWAccess folder on your Student Disk
   The page opens in your Internet Explorer window in the correct format, as shown in Figure B-9.

9. Click the FrontPage Express program button on the taskbar, then exit FrontPage Express

QuickTip
Notice that the Publish to the Web Wizard used the Access object name to create a Web page title, which replaces the filename in the title bar.

FIGURE B-8: Health Plans Web page in FrontPage Express

Web page title

Heading added by Publish to the Web Wizard

Table from Access database

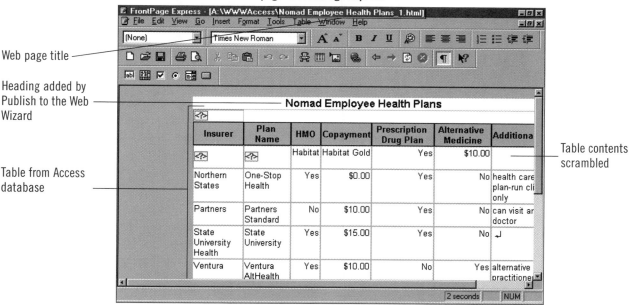

Table contents scrambled

FIGURE B-9: Health Plans Web page in Internet Explorer

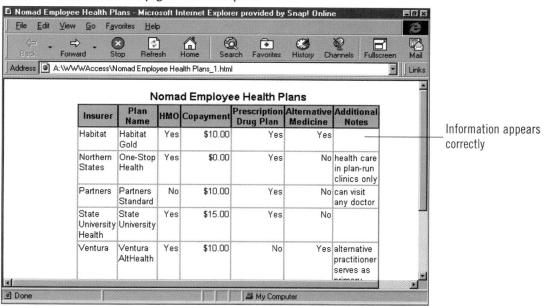

Information appears correctly

Static and dynamic pages

The Web Wizard in Access can create both static and dynamic Web pages. A **static HTML page** contains only the information currently in the table that you are converting. A **dynamic HTML page**, on the other hand, links your Web page to the original database file from which you created it. When you change the original object in the database, the content of a dynamic page changes to reflect your updates, while the contents of a static page will remain unchanged. Use a dynamic Web page if you expect to change your original Access object often. However, to use this feature, you must locate the database file containing the object on the same file server that contains the dynamic Web page.

Internet

Internet

Creating a Web Page from an Excel File

Steps

Like Word and Access, Excel includes a Wizard for creating Web pages; however, this feature is tailored to the Excel environment, letting you select specific ranges in a worksheet as sources for Web pages. Cleveland wants to add a Web page to the Welcome publication that tells new employees about Nomad Ltd's products. He uses Excel's Internet Assistant Wizard to create this page from an Excel workbook that breaks down tours planned for 1999 by quarter and tour type.

1. Start Excel, open the file **IE4 B-3** from your Student Disk, click and drag to select the range **A1...G8**, click **File** on the menu bar, then click **Save as HTML**

The Internet Assistant Wizard – Step 1 of 4 dialog box opens, displaying the address of the range you selected.

2. If necessary, in the Ranges and charts to convert list click **Range "$A$1:$G$8"**, then click **Next**

The next Internet Assistant Wizard dialog box offers you a choice between creating a new HTML file from the selected range or adding this information to an existing Web page file. You create an independent Web page using this information, so you select the first option.

3. If necessary, click the **create an independent HTML document option button** to select it, click **Next**, edit the information in the dialog box to match Figure B-10, then click **Next**

The final Internet Assistant Wizard dialog box contains options for the new Web page's type and location.

4. If necessary click the **Save the result as an HTML file option button** to select it, click **Browse**, type **1999 Tours Forecast** in the File name text box, select the location of your Student Disk in the Save in text box, click **Save**, then click **Finish**

The Internet Assistant Wizard closes after creating and saving your new Web page in the location specified. Now, view and edit your new file.

Trouble?

If the file 1999 Tours Forecast does not appear in the file list, be sure the Files of type list box displays "HTML Document."

5. Close Excel, click **No** if you are asked whether to save changes, click the **Word program button** on the taskbar, then open the file **1999 Tours Forecast** from your Student Disk

The Tours Forecast Web page opens in the Word Web document window, as shown in Figure B-11. You delete the table's top row because it contains a duplicate heading. You also resize the second column to be consistent with the others in the table and add a link to the bottom of the Welcome page.

6. Next to the table's top row, right-click in the **selection bar**, click **Delete Rows**, press and hold **[Shift]** while dragging the right border of the second column left until the column's width is the same as the other columns, release the mouse button and [Shift], press **[Ctrl][End]**, press **[Enter]**, click the Italic button _I_ on the Formatting toolbar, then type **Return to Welcome page**

Now add the same leaf pattern you used on the other Web pages you created.

7. Click the **Background button**, click **Fill Effects**, click **Other Texture**, open the folder **Program Files\Microsoft Office\Office\Web Page Templates\Styles**, double-click **Leaves on the Side**, then click **OK**

8. Save your changes to the Web page, then click the **Web Page Preview button** on the toolbar

The page appears as shown in Figure B-12.

9. Click the **Word program button**, then close the file **1999 Tours Forecast**

FIGURE B-10: Internet Assistant Wizard - Step 3
of 4 dialog box

Enter text as shown ⎯

Check both boxes ⎯

Type your personal
information here

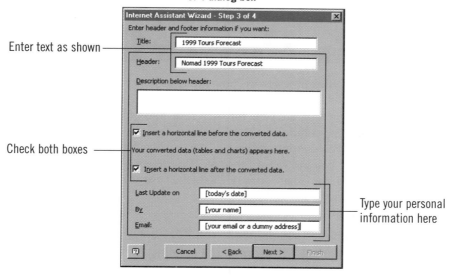

FIGURE B-11: 1999 Tours Forecast in Word Web

Web page title

Heading added by
Internet Assistant
Wizard

Table from Excel
workbook

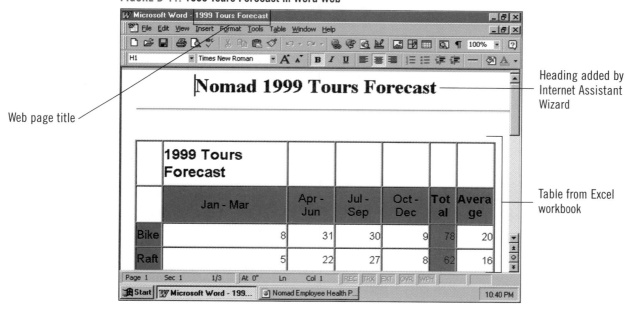

FIGURE B-12: 1999 Tours Forecast in Internet Explorer

Leaf background
added

Top row of table
deleted

Column resized

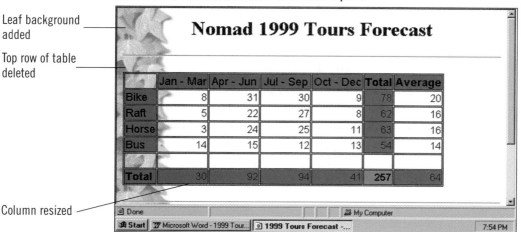

Internet

Creating Web Pages with PowerPoint

Unlike other Office files, PowerPoint presentations contain multiple distinct screens of information. When you convert a PowerPoint presentation to HTML format, the Save as HTML Wizard creates a separate page for each slide and groups the pages together in a folder. When viewing your presentation on the Web, your audience can then navigate through it much like they would in PowerPoint. Cleveland wants to convert a PowerPoint presentation consisting of eight slides to HTML format. The presentation outlines the company's recent accomplishments and immediate goals. He uses the Save as HTML Wizard to create a set of Web pages from this presentation.

Steps

1. **Start PowerPoint, open the file IE4 B-4 from your Student Disk, click File on the menu bar, click Save as HTML, read the opening Wizard screen, click Next, be sure the New layout option button is selected, then click Next**
   The current Wizard screen provides a choice of Web page styles. The browser frames format takes advantage of the frames capability of the newest Web browsers. When a page uses frames, the browser displays different parts the page divided by borders (the frames) to make navigating a group of pages easier for the viewer.

Trouble?

If the Office Assistant opens, click No to close it.

2. **Click the Browser frames option button, click Next, then complete the remaining Save as HTML dialog boxes selecting only the following options: GIF, 640 by 480, 3/4 width of screen, Use browser colors, large square button, your Student Disk, Finish, and Don't Save**
   PowerPoint exports the information in the current presentation in HTML format, creating a title page to serve as a directory of these Web pages. Next, preview the PowerPoint presentation in your browser window.

3. **Click OK in the current PowerPoint dialog box, close PowerPoint without saving changes, click the Word program button on the taskbar if necessary, then open the file index from the folder IE4 B-4 on your Student Disk**
   The Presentation title page that the Wizard created appears in the Word Web document window, as shown in Figure B-13. Now add the text for the link and the leaf background to your Web publication home page.

4. **Press [Ctrl][End], press [Enter], type Return to Welcome page, click the Background button , click Fill Effects, click Other Texture, open the folder Program Files\Microsoft Office\Office\Web Page Templates\Styles, double-click Leaves on the Side, then click OK**
   The title page of the annual report now has a format similar to your other Web pages.

5. **Save your changes to the Web page, click the Web Page Preview button , then click the text Click here to start to begin viewing the presentation**
   Internet Explorer displays the first slide from the presentation, as well as navigation tools for the remaining slides, in frames, as shown in Figure B-14.

QuickTip

To move between presentation pages, use the navigation buttons or the outline.

6. **Experiment with navigating through the slides using both the navigation buttons and the outline, then click the Index button **

7. **Click the Word program button, then close the file index**

FIGURE B-13: Presentation title page in Word Web

FIGURE B-13: **Presentation title page in Word Web**

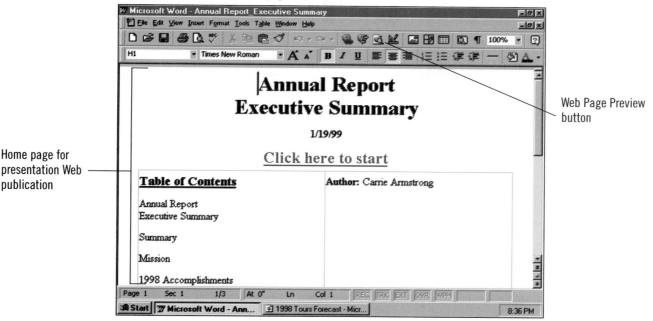

Home page for presentation Web publication

Web Page Preview button

FIGURE B-14: **First slide in frames**

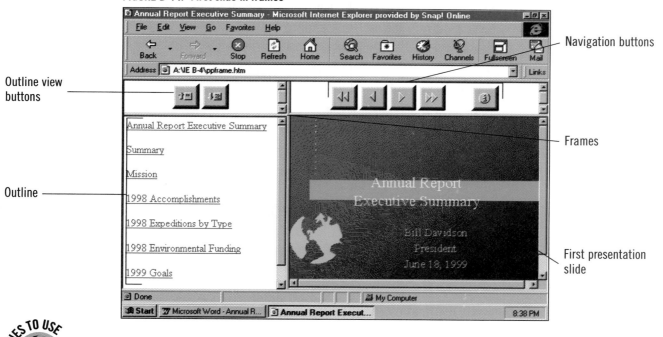

Outline view buttons

Navigation buttons

Frames

Outline

First presentation slide

CLUES TO USE

Using frames

Frames help you navigate a group of associated Web pages. Frame formatting is most useful when you want common navigation elements visible for all the pages. Although frames are convenient, remember that not all Web browsers support them. A popular way to address this problem is to create two versions of a publication—one with frames and one without—and to offer a choice between the two on the publication's home page. If time or resources limit you to one version, however, base your decision on your audience's capabilities. For example, if you create a page for a company intranet and know that every computer has the latest version of a browser installed, adding frames to your publication makes sense. If, however, you create a page for Web publication and want the largest possible audience, choosing frames excludes some users from viewing your document.

Internet

Adding Hyperlinks

After you publish your pages on the Web, you need to add hyperlinks both between publication pages and to other Web pages. This helps your audience to locate the information they want more efficiently. Cleveland's sketch shows links from the home page to each associated page as well as a link back to the home page from each associated page. He also includes links on the home page to take users to other Nomad Ltd pages that they may find useful. Cleveland starts by adding the links to his home page.

1. Using Word, open the file **Welcome** from your Student Disk, then scroll down until all of the bulleted items are visible in the document window if necessary
   Now you create links to the associated pages. You use **relative links**, which provide another page's address in relation to the current page, rather than **absolute links**, which contain only a fixed address. Once created, relative links remain accurate when you publish pages on the Web in their current directory structure.

2. Select the text next to the first bullet but not the bullet itself, then click the **Insert Hyperlink button** 🔳 on the Standard toolbar
   The Insert Hyperlink dialog box opens, as shown in Figure B-15.

3. Click **Browse** next to the Link to file or URL text box, select the location of your Student Disk in the Look in list box, double-click the file **Vacation**, be sure the **Use relative path for hyperlink check box** is selected, then click OK
   The underlined and blue text is the standard hyperlink format.

4. Move the mouse pointer over the linked text
   The mouse pointer changes to 👆. Note that when you place the pointer over the link, Word Web displays the address to which the object is linked right above the object.

5. Repeat Steps 2 and 3 to create relative links for the remaining lines of bulleted text, linking the second line to the file **Nomad Employee Health plans_1**, the third line to **1999 Tours Forecast**, and the fourth line to **index** (located in the folder IE B-4)
   Your final tasks are adding a link to the home page at the bottom of each associated page and checking all of the links you inserted.

6. Click the text **List of vacation dates for Nomad employees**
   The Vacation file opens. Because you followed a link between files on your computer, Word Web displays the Web toolbar, as shown in Figure B-16.

7. Press **[Ctrl][End]**, select the text **Return to Welcome page**, click 🔳, create a relative link to the file **Welcome** on your Student Disk, save the file **Vacation**, then click the new link to return to the Welcome page
   Repeat Steps 6 and 7 to create links to the home page on each remaining associated page

8. Save the file **Welcome**, then close Word and Internet Explorer

QuickTip

Although the link address shows the full pathname, the link remains relative as long as you checked the appropriate box when you created it.

QuickTip

Links work between unpublished documents as well as published Web pages; you can now use the home page to easily open and add links to the remaining documents.

Trouble?

Clicking a link closes the current file and opens the new one.

FIGURE B-15: Insert Hyperlink dialog box

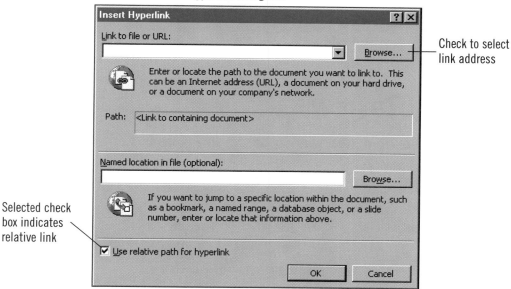

Check to select
link address

Selected check
box indicates
relative link

FIGURE B-16: Vacation file in Word Web window

Web toolbar

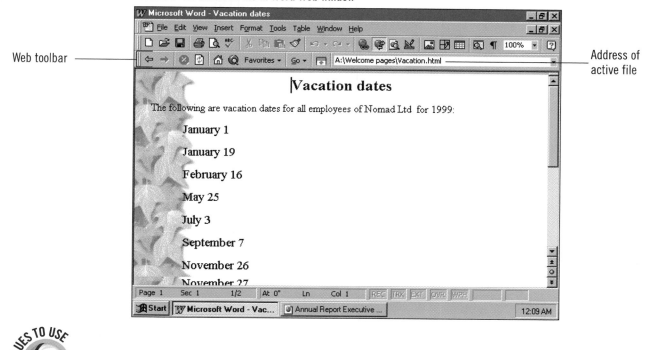

Address of
active file

Publishing your Web publication

Your Web publication is not available to anyone outside your local computer network or workgroup until you publish it, either by placing a copy on the Web or an intranet server. Remember that links you create on your home page are one way: they help users viewing your page to find other interesting pages but do not help users locate your page in the first place. Try the following to advertise your Web publication: ask friends and colleagues to create links to your home page on their pages; ask the administrator of your server to add your homepage to the index of the site's Web pages; or e-mail groups, organizations, or people with Web sites who you think may be interested in your publication. To publish effectively on an intranet, send a memo to employees who you think may be interested in your page or ask the network administrator and the owners of other relevant pages to add links to your publication on their pages.

Internet

Practice

► Concepts Review

Label each element of the Word Web window shown in Figure B-17.

FIGURE B-17

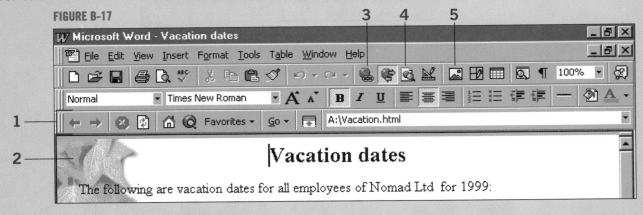

Match each term below with the statement that best describes it.

6. Frames
7. HTML
8. Home page
9. Dynamic page
10. Word Web

a. Language for describing Web page contents and format
b. Page linked to original database file
c. Web page editing tool in Word 97
d. Format creating borders between screen elements
e. First page of a Web publication

Select the best answer from the list of choices.

11. To preview the current Word document in Internet Explorer, click
   a. 🖳
   b. 🖉
   c. 🔍
   d. 🖼

12. Frames are most useful for
   a. navigating a group of associated Web pages.
   b. creating hyperlinks.
   c. formatting headlines.
   d. creating a home page.

13. Web pages that you create are available to users outside your local network
   a. when you save them on your hard drive.
   b. after you format them.
   c. when you place a copy on a Web or intranet server.
   d. only if you use frames.

14. The final step in creating a Web publication is
   a. viewing a page and making final corrections.
   b. formatting hyperlinks.
   c. creating Web pages based on existing files.
   d. creating a home page.

15. Which of these Word Web options does HTML *not* support?
   a.
   b.
   c.
   d. HTML supports all Word Web options.

16. To add a background to a Web page in Word Web,
   a. click , then select an image.
   b. click , then type the address of the image file to use.
   c. display the Web toolbar, type the address of the image file to use in the Address text box, then press [Enter].
   d. click , then select a style or image.

► Skills Review

1. Plan Web publication content.
   a. Sketch an outline of a Web publication for the Nomad Ltd sales department, including a home page, a recent letter sent to customers, a table of contact information for customers, a table of the most recent sales figures, and a presentation on Nomad Ltd's Outback division.
   b. Draw arrows on your sketch indicating hyperlinks between pages in your publication.

2. Create a Web page document.
   a. Start Word, then make sure the Standard and Formatting toolbars are visible.
   b. Click File, click New, click the Web Pages tab, then double-click Web Page Wizard.
   c. Use the Web Page Wizard to create a new document using the Table of Contents template and the Jazzy visual style, then save the document on your Student Disk as "Nomad Ltd Tour Sales Department".
   d. Select the heading, then type "Tour Sales Information".
   e. Replace the paragraph beneath the heading with "Our company vision:", press [Enter], then type, "To provide the highest quality outdoor experiences possibe for our customers".
   f. Replace the next line ("Type some text") with "Use these links to access the latest information about Nomad Ltd Tour Sales:".
   g. Right-click the last "Add a Hyperlink" line, then click Insert Rows to add a fourth row to the table.
   h. Select the table's fourth row, click the Copy button, select the row you just inserted, right-click the selected row, then click Paste Cells.
   i. Select the first line "Add a Hyperlink," then type "Letter accompanying survey sent to past customers".
   j. Repeat Step i to replace the remaining three lines with "Recent tour sales customers", "Most recent sales figures", and "Outback division overview presentation".
   k. Replace the text "New!" next to the first line of the table with "Research".
   l. Replace the three Related Page hyperlinks at the bottom of the page with "Nomad Ltd home page", "Nomad Ltd Sales Dept.", and "Nomad Ltd New Employee Orientation", then save and close your document.

3. Format a Web page.

    a. Start FrontPage Express, then open the file "Nomad Ltd Tour Sales Department" from your Student Disk.

    b. Apply the Heading 3 style to the text "Our company vision:" and center it; apply the Heading 2 style to the company vision statement and center it; click to the left of the O in the line "Our company vision:", press [Enter], then move the insertion point to the blank paragraph you created.

    c. Click the Insert Image button, then insert the Nomad graphic from your Student Disk.

    d. Save the changes to your Web page.

    e. Open Internet Explorer, click File, click Open, click Browse, then open the Nomad Ltd Tour Sales Department file from your Student Disk.

    f. Review the appearance of your Web page in the browser window, click the FrontPage program button, then close FrontPage.

4. Create a Web page from a Word document.

    a. Click the Word program button, then open the file IE4 B-5 from your Student Disk.

    b. Click File, click Save as HTML, then save the file as "Customer Survey Letter".

    c. Delete the three lines for customer address information and the blank paragraph that follows, then delete the text block beginning "Very truly yours," and ending at the end of the document.

    d. Type "Return to Tour Sales home page" at the end of the document.

    e. Apply Heading 2 style to the first line of the document, then center it.

    f. Click the Background button, click Fill Effects, then apply an appropriate background texture or graphic.

    g. Save your changes to the Nomad Ltd Customer Survey Letter page, then close it.

5. Create a Web page from an Access table.

    a. Open the file IE4 B-6 from the appropriate WWWAccess directory on your Student Disk, open the table Customers in Table view, click File, then click Save As HTML.

    b. Be sure the check box for Web publication profiles is empty, then click Next.

    c. Click the Customers check box on the Tables tab to select it, then click Next.

    d. Click Browse, select an appropriate template, click Select, then click Next.

    e. Click the Static HTML option button to select it, click Next, select the WWWAccess folder on your Student Disk, be sure the No option button is selected, then click Next.

    f. Be sure the Yes check box is empty, click Next, then click Finish.

    g. Close Access, start FrontPage Express, then open the file Customers_1 from the WWWAccess folder on your Student Disk.

    h. Scroll to the bottom of the table, click the graphic below the table on the left side, press [Delete], type "Return to Tour Sales home page", then save your changes.

    i. Click the Internet Explorer program button, open your page in Internet Explorer, then inspect your page.

    j. Click the FrontPage Express program button, then close FrontPage Express.

6. Create a Web page from an Excel file.

    a. Start Excel, then open the file IE4 B-7 on your Student Disk.

    b. Select the range A1 to H11, click File, then click Save as HTML.

    c. Be sure Range "$A$1:$H$11" in the Ranges and charts to convert list is selected, click Next, be sure the option button for the create an independent HTML document is selected, then click Next.

    d Enter "1999 Summer Tour Sales" in the Title text box, enter "1999 Summer Sales Figures" in the Header text box, click both check boxes to select them, complete the dialog box, then click Next.

    e. Be sure the Save the result as an HTML file option button is selected, click Browse, type "1999 Sales", select the location of your Student Disk, click Save, then click Finish.

f. Close Excel without saving changes, click the Word program button, then open the file 1999 Sales on your Student Disk. Use the selection bar to select the table's top four rows, right-click the selected area, click Delete Rows, move the insertion point to the end of the document, press [Enter], click the Italic button to remove italic formatting, then type "Return to Tour Sales home page".

g. Click the Background button, click Fill Effects, then apply an appropriate background texture or graphic.

h. Save your changes to the Web page, click the Web Page Preview button, inspect the Web page, use Word to adjust column widths if necessary, save your changes, then click the Web Page Preview button to inspect them.

i. Click the Word program button, then close the file 1999 Sales.

7. Create Web pages with PowerPoint.

a. Start PowerPoint, open the file IE4 B-8 from your Student Disk, then use the slide navigation buttons to page through the presentation quickly.

b. Click File, click Save as HTML, click Next, be sure the New layout option button is selected, then click Next.

c. Click the Browser frames option button, click Next, then complete the remaining Save as HTML dialog boxes, selecting only these options: GIF; 640 by 480; 3/4 width of screen; Use browser colors; circular button; the directory containing your Student Disk; Finish; and Don't Save.

d. Click OK to close the dialog box, close PowerPoint without saving changes, click the Word program button if necessary, then open the file "index" from the folder IE4 B-8 on your Student Disk.

e. Move the insertion point to the end of the file, insert a new paragraph, type Return to Tour Sales home page, then add an appropriate background.

f. Save your changes to the Web page, click the Web Page Preview button, then click the text "Click here to start".

g. Navigate through the slides using the navigation buttons or the outline, click the Index button to return to the title page, click the Word program button, then close the file index.

8. Add hyperlinks.

a. Open the file Nomad Ltd Tour Sales Department from your Student Disk in Word, then scroll down if necessary so the entire table is visible in the document window.

b. Highlight the text for the first hyperlink, "Letter accompanying...", then click the Insert Hyperlink button.

c. Select the file Customer Survey Letter from your Student Disk, be sure the Use relative path button for hyperlink is checked, then click OK.

d. Repeat Steps b and c to create relative links for the remaining cells in the column, linking the text in the second cell to the file Customers_1 from the WWWAccess folder, the text in the third cell to 1999 Summer Tour Sales, and the text in the fourth cell to index (located in the folder IE4 B-8), then save the document.

e. Click the text "Letter accompanying..." Move the insertion point to the end of the file, select the text Return to Nomad Ltd Tour Sales home page, click the Create Hyperlink button, create a relative link to the file Nomad Ltd Tour Sales Department in the appropriate folder on your Student Disk, save the file Customer Survey Letter, then click the new link to return to the Nomad Ltd Tour Sales home page.

f. Repeat Step e to create links to the home page for each remaining associated page.

g. Print the first page of each of your Web pages using Word Web, then close Word and Internet Explorer.

Internet

▶ Independent Challenges

1. You volunteer at the Safe Haven Emergency Shelter for families in crisis. Knowing that you have experience in creating Web publications, staff members mention that they want to put information about their services and resource requests on the Internet and ask you to create pages for them using existing files for their printed materials.

To complete this independent challenge:

1. Sketch the Safe Haven Web publication. In addition to a home page, the publication should include a list of items sought as donations, a table detailing programs the shelter offers, a chart showing last year's income and expenses, and a presentation summarizing the shelter's recent activities and immediate goals. Be sure to include links between pages.

2. Create a home page for Safe Haven using the Word Web Page Wizard. Select the Simple Layout template and the Community visual style. Use "Safe Haven Emergency Shelter" as the heading (decrease the font size to fit on one line, if necessary) and create a brief mission statement or summary of the shelter's function (to help families survive homelessness and domestic violence) to replace the sample paragraph. Replace the first line "Type some text" with "More about us:". Create appropriate text for links to associated pages on the topics Making Donations, Shelter Programs, Financial Report, and Year in Review, deleting other template text as necessary. Replace sample text for the "Related page" hyperlinks with the names of national or local organizations whose missions are similar to Safe Haven's. (Search the WWW to find organization names if necessary.) Save your home page as "Safe Haven" on your Student Disk.

3. Create a Web page from the Word file IE4 B-9 on your Student Disk. Save your file as "Donations", and use the Brick Wall background. Change the appearance of the Web page as necessary, and be sure to insert text at the bottom of the page for a link back to the home page.

4. Create a Web page from the table Programs in the Access database IE4 B-10, located in the WWWAccess folder on your Student Disk. Use the Grayst template, Static HTML, and the Brick Wall background, and save the file on your Student Disk. Use FrontPage Express to delete the graphic in the page's lower-left corner; be sure to insert text for a link to the home page.

5. Create a Web page from the range A1:F20 in the Excel workbook IE4 B-11. Enter an appropriate title and header; include your name, the creation date, and your e-mail address. Save the page as "Financial Report." Use Word Web to add the Brick Wall background, and format the page as necessary. Be sure the page has only one heading; delete table rows if necessary. Be sure to insert text for a link to the home page.

6. Create a Web page from the PowerPoint presentation file IE4 B-12 on your Student Disk. Because you want a wide WWW audience for your publication, use the standard page style rather than browser frames. Select GIF, 640 × 480, 3/4 width of screen, Use browser colors, and the button shape and location of your choice. Add the Brick Wall background to the index page in Word Web, and format the page as necessary, being sure to insert text for a link to the home page.

7. Add link addresses to the bulleted list of links on your home page, then test the links in Word Web while adding return links from each associated page.

8. Print the first page of each of your Web pages using Word Web.

2. You work in the public relations office at Fox Oil Corporation. Recognizing public concern following recent oil spills by other companies, Fox Oil wants to publicize the steps it is taking to guard against oil-tanker spills. Your supervisor asks you to adapt documents created for print and television ad campaigns to create a Web publication for Fox's Internet site.
To complete this independent challenge:

1. Files for adapting include a press release, a table of Fox's oil-spill-prevention programs, a table summarizing recent oil spills by company, and a presentation detailing Fox's oil-spill record and the steps it is taking to ensure that no future spills occur. Sketch how this Web publication should look. Be sure to indicate links between the home page and associated documents.

2. Create a home page for the oil-spill publication. Use an appropriate template and visual style. Enter text for the home page, format it, and save it on your Student Disk. Include text for a link to the Fox Oil corporate home page, and add the Fox company logo, located in the file fox.gif on your Student Disk.

3. Convert the Word document IE4 B-13 on your Student Disk to HTML; add, delete, and format text as necessary; apply a background; make other necessary changes.

4. Convert the table Prevention Programs in the Access database IE4 B-14, located in the WWWAccess folder on your Student Disk, to HTML. Edit the resulting Web page as necessary, apply a background, and make other appropriate changes.

5. Convert the table in the Excel spreadsheet IE4 B-15 on your Student Disk to HTML, using an appropriate template. Edit the resulting Web page as necessary.

6. Convert the PowerPoint presentation IE4 B-16 on your Student Disk to a set of HTML documents. Edit the resulting index page as necessary, apply a background, and make other appropriate changes.

7. Format and test the hyperlinks between pages in your Web publication.

8. Print the first page of each of your Web pages.

▶ Visual Workshop

You are an employee at the Shared Harvest restaurant. The manager wants to post information about the restaurant on a local computer network that publishes Web pages for area groups and businesses. Use Word's Web Page Wizard to create the calendar of daily specials shown in Figure B-18. (*Hint:* you can use a Word template to apply the calendar formatting.) Sketch what a publication for this restaurant should look like, then create an appropriate home page to accompany the calendar. Create at least two other associated Web pages by creating files in Office programs, then converting them to HTML and formatting them. Finally, add links between your pages. Print the first page of each of your Web pages using Word Web.

FIGURE B-18

Shared Harvest Restaurant

June 1999

Daily Specials

Sunday	Monday	Tuesday	Wednesday	Thursday	Friday	Saturday
		1 Shiitake stir-fry	2 Lentil-nut loaf	3 Lasagne	4 Tempeh sloppy joes	5 Tofu scramble
6 Baked tofu with broccoli	7 Vegetable cutlets	8 Lentil-tomato dal	9 Falafel	10 Cashew chili	11 Garlic grilled vegetables	12 Chickpea soufflé
13 Barbecue tempeh burgers	14 Mushroom-barley soup	15 Curried lentils and collards	16 Shiitake stir-fry	17 Lentil-nut loaf	18 Lasagne	19 Tempeh sloppy joes
20 Tofu scramble	21 Baked tofu with broccoli	22 Vegetable cutlets	23 Lentil-tomato dal	24 Falafel	25 Cashew chili	26 Garlic grilled vegetables
27 Chickpea soufflé	28 Barbecue tempeh burgers	29 Mushroom-barley soup	30 Curried lentils and collards			

Join us for lunch or dinner!

Shared Harvest home page

Comparing

Microsoft Windows 95 and Windows 98

Objectives

▶ **Explore the differences between the Windows 95 and Windows 98 desktop**

▶ **Compare the Windows 95 and Windows 98 Start menus**

▶ **Compare mouse operations under Windows 95 and Windows 98**

▶ **Examine Active Desktop capabilities**

▶ **Explore Web view**

In this unit you will be introduced to the Microsoft Windows 98 operating system. If you have already worked with Microsoft Windows 95, you will see many similarities. This introduction will compare and contrast the two operating systems and how you use them. You will learn about changes in the Start menus, desktops, and mouse operations from Windows 95 to Windows 98. You will also become familiar with the new Active Desktop features and Web capabilities of Windows 98.

Upgrading to a New Operating System

If you have worked with computers for very long, you already know that computer owners regularly face the decision to upgrade. **Upgrading** is the process of placing a more recent version of a product onto your computer. Upgrades to **hardware**, the physical components of a computer, occur when a computer user decides to purchase a newer computer or computer component that will add features, space, or speed to his or her computer system.

Software developers upgrade their **software** programs that perform particular tasks for a variety of reasons. Because hardware is constantly changing as new technology emerges, software developers need to ensure that their software takes full advantage of the latest hardware technology. For example, when it became cheaper and easier to expand the amount of memory on personal computers, many software companies developed their software to take advantage of extra memory. Another important reason for software upgrades is usability. Developers are constantly trying to make their software easier to learn and use. For example, when it became clear that people found a graphical interface easy to work with, most software companies provided such an interface to their software. Software upgrades also occur when a new software technology emerges. Developers update their products so they can compete against newer products that use newer technology. For example, with the recent explosion in popularity of the World Wide Web, many software companies hastened to include Web features in their products.

The Microsoft Corporation operating system upgrade from Windows 95 to Windows 98 is a response to these and other upgrade trends. For example, hardware now exists that makes it possible for you to run your computer through your television set, so Windows 98 includes a software accessory, TV Viewer, that lets you use this technology if you have the appropriate hardware. Windows 98 features such as automated disk maintenance are a response to the demand for ease of use. To take advantage of emerging software technology, Microsoft designed Windows 98 around features of the World Wide Web.

The decision to upgrade an operating system can be difficult to make. Upgrades can be expensive. To take full advantage of the Windows 98 upgrade, you might need to purchase new hardware, such as an Internet connection via a modem, a TV tuner card, or additional memory. Some upgrades don't greatly affect how a software product is used, but other upgrades change the interface so significantly that computer owners need to evaluate whether the advantages of the upgrade are greater than the disadvantages of having to learn a practically new product. Users also consider the newness of the technology; some like to wait until the dust settles and the technology is tested and proven before they risk using it on their own computers.

In this tutorial, you'll examine how the upgrade to Windows 98 from Windows 95 affects what you see as you use the interface. This tutorial was developed using a prerelease version of Windows 98, so there might be slight differences between what you see in the figures and what you see in the final product. If you want more information about a feature that seems to be operating differently from what you see here, click the Start button and then click Help. Use the online Help system to learn more about the feature.

The Windows 98 Desktop

When you first turn on your computer, you might not notice much difference between the Windows 95 and Windows 98 desktops. Recall that the **desktop** is the workspace on your screen. Because it's easy to customize the desktop, someone might have changed your desktop so that it looks different from the one shown in the figures in this tutorial. You should, however, be able to locate objects similar to those in the figures. Figure 1 shows the Windows 95 desktop. Remember that you might see additional icons, and your screen might show a different background.

FIGURE 1: Windows 95 desktop

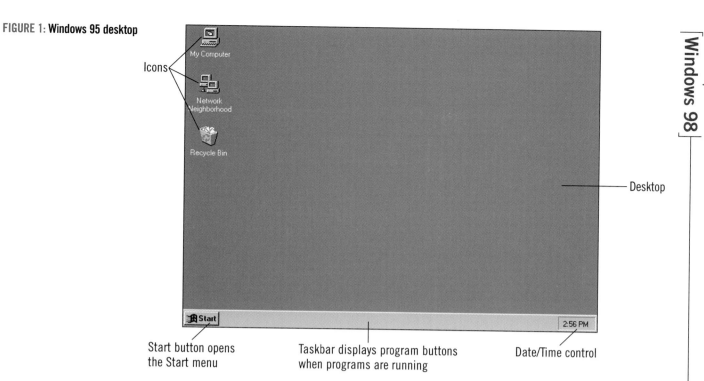

Icons

Desktop

Start button opens
the Start menu

Taskbar displays program buttons
when programs are running

Date/Time control

Figure 2 shows the Windows 98 desktop. Notice that the Start button, taskbar, Date/Time control, and icons all look the same as their Windows 95 counterparts. Your Windows 98 desktop might show additional objects; you'll learn more about these shortly.

FIGURE 2: Windows 98 desktop

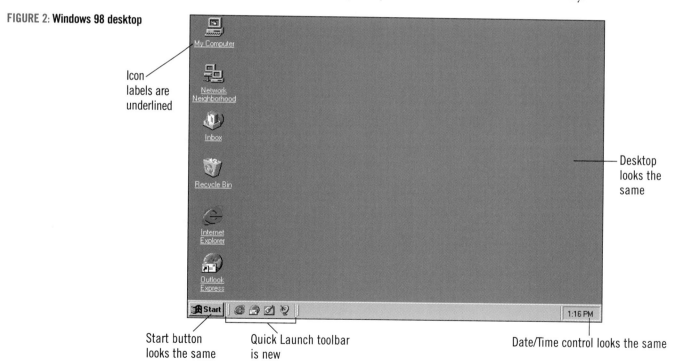

Icon
labels are
underlined

Desktop
looks the
same

Start button
looks the same

Quick Launch toolbar
is new

Date/Time control looks the same

Windows 98

There are really only two visible differences between the basic Windows 95 and Windows 98 desktops:

- Windows 98 includes the Quick Launch toolbar.
- In Windows 98, icon names appear underlined. (Since you can configure Windows 98 to look like Windows 95, icon names might not be underlined.)

If you have access to the Internet and the Web, and if your desktop has been customized, it's possible you'll see additional desktop objects. Windows 98 makes it possible to integrate your Web experience into your desktop, as you'll see shortly.

► Underlined Icon Names

Microsoft has underlined icon names in an attempt to make your experience with the Windows 98 desktop more like your experience with the Web. The **World Wide Web**, or just the **Web**, is a service on the Internet that allows you to view documents on computers around the world. Documents on the Web are called **Web pages**. Web pages contain elements known as **links** that you can select, usually by clicking a mouse, to move to another part of the document or another document altogether. A link can be a word, a phrase, or a graphic image. When a link consists of text, the text link usually appears underlined and in a different color.

To view Web pages, you use a program called a **browser**. When you click a link on a Web page in your browser, you jump to a different location—perhaps to a page stored on another computer, as shown in Figure 3.

FIGURE 3: Clicking Web page links

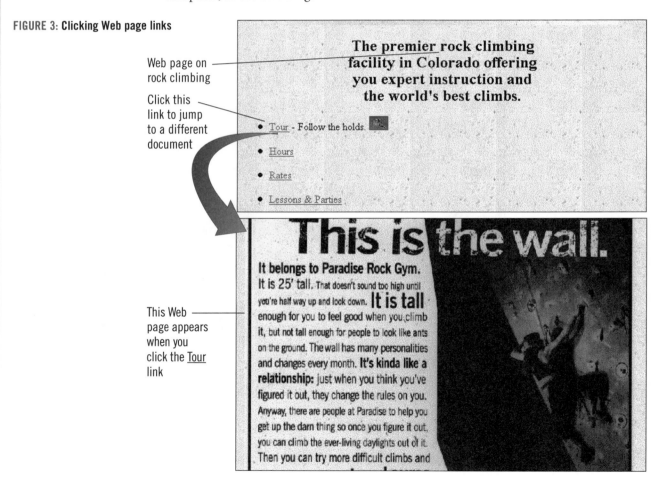

On the Windows 98 desktop, icon labels are underlined to resemble the links you see on Web pages. By attempting to mimic the Web experience, Microsoft is trying to simplify how you interact with your computer. If the actions you take on the desktop are similar to those you take in your browser, you have to learn only one set of techniques.

Thus, when you click one of the icon labels on the Windows 98 desktop, you "jump" to that icon's destination. For example, in Windows 95, to open My Computer, you had to double-click its icon (or click its icon to select it and then press Enter). In Windows 98, however, the My Computer icon label is underlined just like a link. When you point at the icon label, the pointer changes from ↳ to ⌐ₘ, just as it would if you pointed at a link in your browser. When you click the underlined icon label, you "jump" to the My Computer window. The result is the same: The My Computer window opens, but the Windows 98 technique is more like the technique you use on the Web. Figure 4 illustrates this difference.

FIGURE 4: Activating an icon in Windows 95 vs. Windows 98

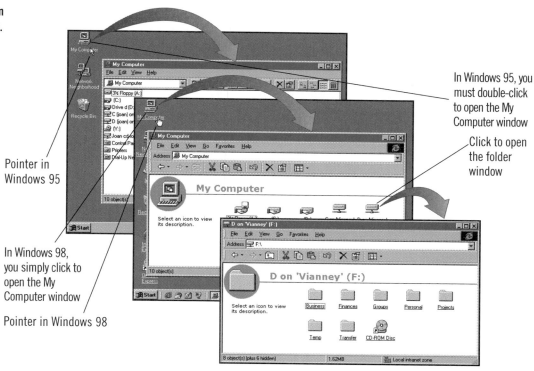

As you work with the Windows 98 operating system, you'll see that underlined text appears not just on the desktop but in numerous places—the My Computer window, the folder windows, and the Windows Explorer window, just to name a few. You can also display Windows 98 icons in the traditional Windows 95 manner: From My Computer, click View, click Folder Options, and then on the General tab, click the Classic style option button.

▶ The Quick Launch Toolbar

The Windows 95 taskbar displays the Start button, buttons that correspond to active programs or open documents, and the tray area that includes the Date/Time control and any other active controls. The Windows 98 taskbar looks the same except for one difference: You can now display toolbars on the taskbar. Figure 5 shows the Windows 95 taskbar, and below it, the Windows 98 taskbar.

FIGURE 5: Taskbars in Windows 95 and Windows 98

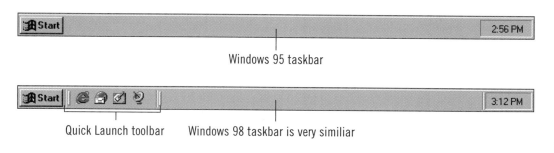

Windows 98

Unless a user has customized his or her taskbar, only the Quick Launch toolbar appears on the Windows 98 taskbar, but you can also display three other taskbar toolbars. Like a toolbar in an application, the taskbar toolbars give you single-click access to common operations. Figure 6 summarizes the Windows 98 taskbar toolbars.

FIGURE 6: Windows 98 taskbar toolbars

toolbar	description
Address	As in a browser, allows you to select or enter an address, such as a URL, to open the browser to that location.
Links	As in a browser, displays buttons for popular Web pages, such as the Microsoft home page. When you click a button on the Links toolbar, your browser opens and displays the location you clicked.
Desktop	Displays a button for each desktop icon on the taskbar.
Quick Launch	Displays buttons for Internet services and for a direct route to the desktop.

The Quick Launch toolbar is the only toolbar to appear by default; the others you can enable by right-clicking the taskbar, pointing at the Toolbars menu option, and clicking the toolbar you want. Figure 7 shows a Windows 98 taskbar with the Address and Links toolbars visible in addition to the Quick Launch toolbar.

FIGURE 7: Windows 98 taskbar with multiple toolbars

Quick Launch toolbar

Address toolbar; if you activate this, your browser will open to the displayed Web page

Links toolbar; if you click one of the Links buttons, that page will open in your browser

Scroll arrow appears when there are additional objects on a toolbar

Figure 8 describes the default buttons on the Quick Launch toolbar.

FIGURE 8: Quick Launch toolbar buttons

icon	name	description
	Launch Internet Explorer Browser	Starts the Internet Explorer browser.
	Launch Outlook Express	Starts Outlook Express, an e-mail tool that comes with the Windows 98 operating system.
	Show Desktop	Minimizes all open windows so you can view the desktop.
	View Channels	Opens the Active Channel Viewer, which makes it easy to subscribe to Web pages.

You can easily customize the taskbar toolbars by adding and removing buttons. Figure 9, for example, shows a taskbar whose Quick Launch toolbar includes buttons for popular applications.

FIGURE 9: Quick Launch toolbar with application buttons

You can place, for example, Office 97 buttons on the Quick Launch toolbar for immediate access to those programs

To add a button to the Windows 98 Quick Launch toolbar, you simply drag the object you want to the toolbar.

The Start Menu

The Windows 98 Start menu looks similar to the Windows 95 Start menu. The only difference is that the Windows 98 Start menu includes a Favorites folder and a Windows Update link to the Microsoft Web site. Figure 10 shows the two Start menus. Again, since you can customize Start menus, yours might look different.

FIGURE 10: **Windows 95 and Windows 98 Start menus**

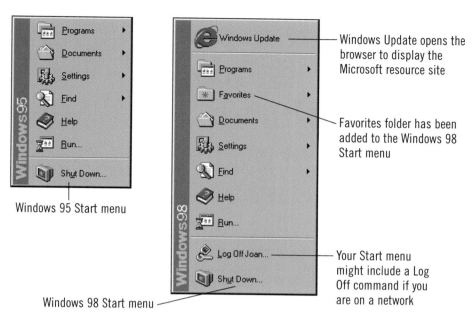

Windows 95 Start menu

Windows Update opens the browser to display the Microsoft resource site

Favorites folder has been added to the Windows 98 Start menu

Windows 98 Start menu

Your Start menu might include a Log Off command if you are on a network

The Favorites folder that Microsoft has added to the Windows 98 Start menu duplicates the Favorites folder in your browser. In your browser, you create a Favorites folder by collecting and saving a list of favorite Web pages. Once a Web page is in your Favorites folder, you can return to it in your browser by simply selecting the page from the folder. By duplicating the browser's list of favorite Web pages on the Windows 98 Start menu, Microsoft allows you to reach your favorite Web pages without having to go through the interim steps of starting your browser and opening the Favorites folder. To view a favorite Web page in Windows 98, you simply click Start, point at the Favorites option, and then click the Web page you want. Your browser launches automatically and connects you directly to that page.

The Windows Update link that appears on the Windows 98 Start menu is a Microsoft resource site on the Web that you connect to by clicking Windows Update on the Start menu. Your browser displays the Windows Update page, which helps you ensure that your system is running the most recent and efficient system software possible.

You might notice one final difference between the Windows 95 and Windows 98 Start menus. If you have more items on your Start menu than can be displayed on the screen, Windows 95 doubles the width of the menu to display the entire list of Start menu objects. Windows 98, however, adds to the bottom of the Start menu an arrow that you can point to see additional objects.

Mouse Operation

You won't notice a difference between how your mouse operates in Office 97 or your other Windows 95 applications when you run them under the Windows 98 operating system. But if you work with certain Windows 98 windows, such as My Computer or Windows Explorer, be aware that Microsoft has simplified the actions you need to take with the mouse.

You've already seen that the icons on your desktop now behave like links and are, therefore, activated with a single-click rather than a double-click. In fact, in Windows 98, single-clicking completely replaces double-clicking on the desktop. In Windows 95, you generally selected an object by clicking it, but in Windows 98, you select an object by simply pointing to it for a moment.

Windows 98

Windows 98 uses the term **hover** to describe pointing to an object, such as an icon, long enough to select it. Passing the pointer over an icon does not select it; you need to hover the pointer over the object long enough for Windows 98 to realize that you mean to select it. Once you've practiced hovering, you'll find it easy. Figure 11 summarizes how mouse functions have changed from Windows 95 to Windows 98.

FIGURE 11: Comparing mouse functions

task	Windows 95	Windows 98
Select	Click	Hover
Open or run	Double-click (or click and press Enter)	Click
Select multiple contiguous objects	Shift+click	Shift+hover
Select multiple noncontiguous objects	Ctrl+click	Ctrl+hover

Changes in mouse operation do not affect Windows 98 dialog boxes: they affect only the desktop, My Computer, Windows Explorer, and similar windows.

Active Desktop

In Windows 95, to experience the Web you generally must first start your browser (although new generations of Internet communications software products are now bypassing the browser and placing Web information directly on the desktop). Users with Web access will find Windows 98 **Active Desktop** technology brings Web content directly to the desktop, without requiring extra communications software, allowing your desktop to act like your personal Web page.

You can enable Active Desktop by right-clicking the desktop and then clicking View As Web Page. Active Desktop integrates your Web experience with the Windows 98 desktop in two primary ways: with background wallpaper and Web components. You can use a Web page as the desktop's background, and you can place Web components (updateable information from the Web) on the desktop.

▶ Using a Web Page as Background Wallpaper

If you've ever worked with the Desktop Properties dialog box in Windows 95 (which you access by right-clicking the desktop and then clicking Properties), you might have experimented with the look of your desktop by changing the color or pattern of the default background wallpaper. Figure 12 shows a Windows 95 desktop that uses the Bubbles wallpaper, along with the dialog box you use to change background wallpaper.

FIGURE 12: Windows 95 desktop with a background wallpaper

Display Properties dialog box allows you to change background wallpaper

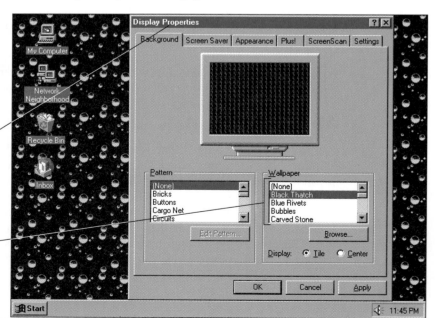

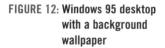

Available wallpaper—all backgrounds in Windows 95 are image files

Windows 95 limited you to using image files as your background wallpaper. Trying to create a desktop background that integrated text and images and other objects was impossible. Windows 98, however, extends your control over your desktop's background by allowing you to use Web pages as wallpaper. To write Web pages, you use a language called **HTML**, which stands for Hypertext Markup Language. HTML uses special codes to describe how the page should appear on the screen. A document created using the HTML language is called an **HTML file** and is saved with the htm or html extension.

Because Windows 98 enables you to use an HTML file as your background wallpaper, your Windows 98 desktop background can feature text, images, links, and multimedia objects. You can use Microsoft Word to save a document as an HTML file; also, you can use the HTML editor, included with Windows 98 FrontPage Express, to create more complex and sophisticated HTML files. Alternatively, you can use the Internet Explorer browser to save an existing Web page as an HTML file that you can then use as your wallpaper. To use a Web page as your wallpaper, right-click the desktop, click Properties, click the Background tab, click the Browse button, locate and select the HTML file you want to use, then click the OK button.

The added control Windows 98 gives you over background wallpaper makes it possible to make the desktop a launch pad for your most important projects. A corporation, for example, might create an HTML file that contains important company information, an updateable company calendar, links to company documents, a sound clip welcoming new employees to the company, and so on.

Figure 13 shows a sample Windows 98 desktop that might appear on the computers of a gift shop chain's main headquarters.

FIGURE 13: Windows 98 desktop with a background HTML file

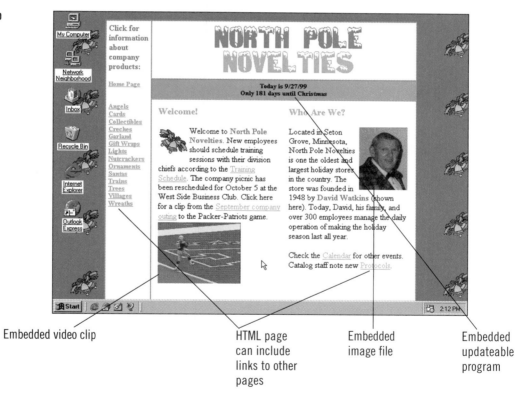

Embedded video clip

HTML page can include links to other pages

Embedded image file

Embedded updateable program

Windows 98

This company created a wallpaper that includes links to product groups, information about the company, a video clip of a recent company outing, and links to current events, company protocols, and training procedures.

► Web Components on the Desktop

In addition to using a Web page as a background, you can also add Web components to the Windows 98 desktop in resizable, moveable windows. A **Web component** is an object on the desktop that you can set to update automatically via your Web connection. For example, you might place a weather map, an investor ticker, or a news component on your desktop. You can schedule when each component will update itself and the information will be delivered to your desktop without your having to look for it.

Windows 95 users can purchase separate software that performs a similar function, such as the Internet Explorer 4.0 browser, Netscape Communicator's Netcaster component, or a product such as PointCast. But with Windows 98, the ability to place updateable Web information on the desktop is actually integrated into the operating system.

Figure 14 shows a Windows 98 desktop with several such Web components.

FIGURE 14: Windows 98 desktop with Web components

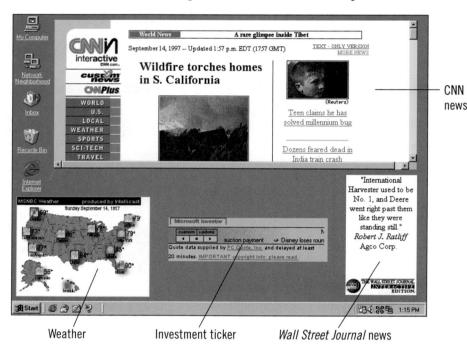

Every morning when this user checks her desktop, each component will have been automatically updated (if, that is, she has set the update schedules that way). The weather map will show the morning's weather instead of weather from the night before, her news service will display the most recent news, and the other Web components will update in a similar fashion. If she wants a more detailed look at, for example, the news, she can select and enlarge one of the Web component windows, as shown in Figure 15.

FIGURE 15: Enlarging a Web component

CNN news Web component is temporarily enlarged

There are three ways to add Web components to the Windows 98 desktop:

 Active Desktop Gallery — Offers a small set of useful Web components, including the weather map, investment ticker, clock, and so on. To access the Active Desktop Gallery, right-click the desktop, point to Active Desktop, and then click Customize my Desktop. A list of current Web components appears on the Web tab of the Display Properties dialog box. To add new ones, click the New button and follow the prompts to locate the Active Desktop Gallery.

 Channel Bar — Lists companies that have agreements with Microsoft to deliver information directly to the desktops of those who subscribe to the Active Channel service. (A site that offers regularly updated information that can be delivered to the desktop on a predetermined schedule is called a **channel**.) When you subscribe to a channel delivery service, you request that information be "broadcast" to you from that channel at whatever schedule you specify. To add a channel from the Channel Bar, you must first enable the Channel Bar from the Web tab of the Display Properties dialog box. Once you can see the Channel Bar, click the channel you want to add. Follow the prompts to add the channel to your list of channels.

You can customize your channel list — Add your own components by connecting to channel sites not necessarily associated with Microsoft and then subscribing to those channels. In most cases, you do this by connecting to the site with your browser. Sites that support channel delivery include a link that asks if you want to subscribe to the site. Click the link and follow the prompts; they vary from site to site.

If any of these components are on your desktop, a rectangular block appears that seems to be a part of the background. When you select that component, however, a window border appears that you can resize and move.

Web View in Explorer Windows

In addition to the Web components that appear on the desktop, the Windows 98 Explorer windows also have changed to extend the Web experience to folder navigation. The term **Explorer windows** is a general term that applies to windows such as Windows Explorer, My Computer, the folder and drive windows, and the Printer window. In other words, any window that displays and allows you to navigate the object hierarchy of your computer is an Explorer window.

With Windows 98 Explorer windows, you can enable **Web view**, which does the following:

- Displays objects on your computer as links
- Allows single-click navigation
- Adds to the window an HTML document with customizable links and information
- Enables you to use the Explorer window as a browser

Figure 16 shows the My Computer window as it looks in Windows 95 and in Windows 98. Below the Windows 98 window is a folder window in Windows 98.

FIGURE 16: My Computer in Windows 95 and Windows 98

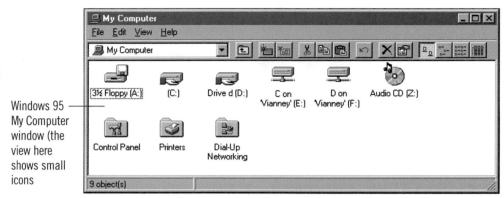

Windows 95 My Computer window (the view here shows small icons

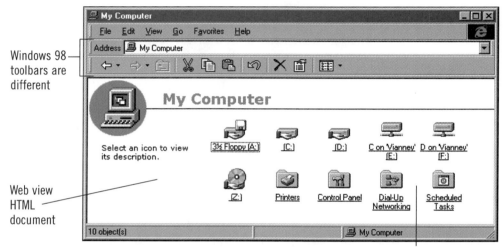

Windows 98 toolbars are different

Web view HTML document

List of objects is the same as in Windows 95, except labels are underlined and perform like links (the view here shows large icons)

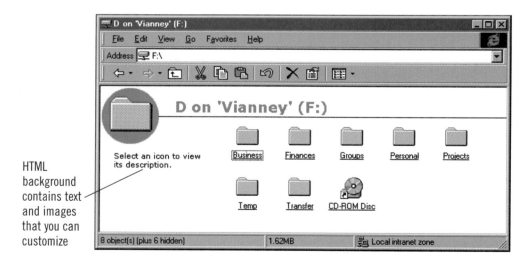

HTML background contains text and images that you can customize

The Windows 95 window shows the familiar object list, but Windows 98 Explorer windows now have HTML documents in the background that you can customize. The ability to customize the Explorer windows by editing their background HTML page makes it easier than ever for you to work efficiently. For example, you could customize a network folder's HTML page so that anyone who accesses that Explorer window sees a description of the folder's contents, links to the most important objects in that window, and links to related objects.

For example, you could customize a network folder containing 1999 corporate reports so that it contains links to corporate reports for 1998 and 1997.

The objects that your computer displays look like the links you see on a Web page. As on the desktop, a single click suffices to open the object. For example, if you click the Floppy (A:) icon, the A: window opens. If you are used to thinking of a link as something that targets an object on the Web, you'll have to expand your vision. In Windows 98, links target any object accessible to your computer—not just Web pages, but also local drives, network folders, and files.

▶ Web View Toolbars

In the Explorer windows, the Windows 95 Standard toolbar has been updated to include buttons that enable you to use the Explorer windows as browsers. The Address toolbar looks like the Address bar in a browser, and the Standard toolbar includes buttons that allow you to navigate through the hierarchy of drives and folders just as you would move through pages on the Web in your browser. Figure 17 first shows the Windows 95 Standard toolbar and then the Windows 98 Address and Standard toolbars on separate lines so you can see all the buttons.

FIGURE 17: My Computer toolbars in Windows 95 and Windows 98

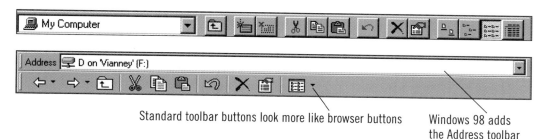

Standard toolbar buttons look more like browser buttons

Windows 98 adds the Address toolbar

As you move from one location on your computer to another, Windows 98 "remembers" where you've been, just as in your browser you can move back to previously viewed Web pages. You can use the navigation buttons to move easily through the hierarchy of your computer's objects. Figure 18 describes the function of each Standard toolbar button.

FIGURE 18: Windows 98 My Computer Standard toolbar buttons

icon	button	description
←	Back	Returns you to the object you were most recently viewing in an Explorer window. If you click the button twice, it returns you to the object you were viewing before that, and so on, until you reach the first object you viewed in the current session. This button is active only when you have viewed more than one object in the current session.
→	Forward	Reverses the effect of the Back button, sending you forward to the object from which you just clicked the Back button. This button is active only when you have used the Back button.
⬆	Up	Moves you up the Explorer hierarchy.
✂	Cut	Cuts the selected object, such as a file or folder, and places it into memory, removing it from the current Explorer window.
📋	Copy	Copies the selected object, such as a file or folder, and places it into memory, leaving the original in the current Explorer window.
📋	Paste	Pastes the object from memory into the current Explorer window.
↩	Undo	Reverses the effect of the previous action.
✕	Delete	Removes the selected object from the current Explorer window without placing it into memory.
📄	Properties	Opens the property sheet for the selected object.
▦	Views	Allows you to choose a view from the standard Windows 95 views: Large Icons, Small Icons, List, and Details.

Now you will look at how the navigation buttons work. Suppose you want to view the contents of a folder on drive A:. You could open My Computer and click the A: icon. The A: Explorer window would open. Then you could click the folder whose contents you want to view. The folder's Explorer window would open. To return to My Computer, you'd simply click the Back button twice.

Additionally, you can display the Links toolbar in Web view. When you click one of the buttons on the Links toolbar, the Explorer window functions just like your browser to display the page you selected.

► Using Windows Explorer to Browse the Web

In both Windows 95 and Windows 98, Windows Explorer displays a hierarchy of objects on your computer. Windows 98 includes the Internet icon 🅔 as one of those objects. You might recognize this icon as the one that appears on the desktop in Windows 95; if you have an Internet service set up on your computer, double-clicking that icon on the Windows 95 desktop starts your browser. In Windows 98, however, when you can click 🅔 in the Windows Explorer window, your browser's home page appears in the Exploring window. Figure 19 shows Windows Explorer with the object hierarchy on the left and a Web page off the Internet on the right.

FIGURE 19: Using Windows Explorer as a browser

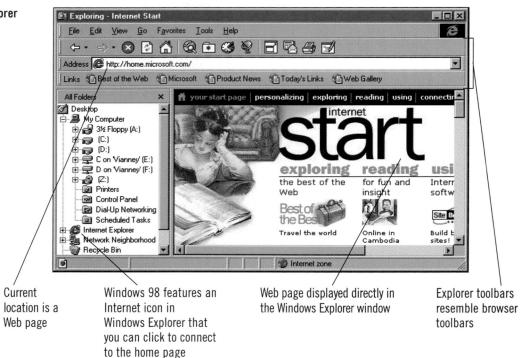

Current location is a Web page

Windows 98 features an Internet icon in Windows Explorer that you can click to connect to the home page

Web page displayed directly in the Windows Explorer window

Explorer toolbars resemble browser toolbars

Notice that when you select a Web page in Windows Explorer, the standard Explorer toolbars and menus are replaced with toolbars and menus that are more browser-oriented. Indeed, you could use Windows Explorer as a Web-browsing tool.

Additional Windows 98 Features

Although this tutorial has focused primarily on how upgrading to Windows 98 affects the way you interact with the operating system, Windows 98 offers many other features that replace or expand Windows 95 functions. There are also a number of completely new features that take the operating system in a new direction. Figure 20 describes some of the most intriguing updated, expanded, or new features. You might not understand the technology behind all these features, but they should give you an idea of what you can do if you are running Windows 98 with the latest hardware.

FIGURE 20: Additional
Windows 98
features

feature	description
Digital Versatile Disc (DVD) support	The successor to CD-ROM disks, DVD stores many times the capacity of a CD-ROM, enough to store full-length digitized movies that you can then view on your monitor or TV screen if you have the appropriate hardware.
Disk space	The space available on your hard disk is limited by the type of file system you use. Windows 95 employed the FAT 16 file system. With Windows 98 FAT 32, you can store up to 30 percent more data on your disk, and you can work with drives that are much larger than those available to FAT 16. The FAT 32 converter utility also makes it easy to upgrade your file system.
Internet communications	Windows 98 ships with Internet Explorer, an Internet communications software suite that offers state-of-the-art integrated browsing, e-mail, newsgroup, Web page editing, and conferencing software—and much more!
Internet Connection Wizard	Establishing a connection to the Internet is much easier with this wizard, which works with your Internet service provider to configure your Internet connection properly.
On-line Help	Information about the Windows 98 operating system now appears as a Web page, and is continually updated by Microsoft. You can access the Windows 98 Help Desk to receive online technical support.
Peripheral device support	Windows 98 supports Universal serial bus (USB) technology, a hardware device that plugs into a single port from which you can run multiple peripheral devices.
Power management	If you own a new PC that supports OnNow hardware technology, your PC will start much more quickly, and you will consume less power if you take advantage of power-down features.
Speed	Windows 98 runs your applications faster, saving you time.
Tune-Up Wizard	In an effort to simplify and streamline your computer maintenance program, the Tune-Up Wizard analyzes your system and helps you schedule maintenance tasks such as defragmentation, disk scan, and tasks. Most of the maintenance tools have also been improved.
TV Viewer	This accessory brings television to the PC—not just regular TV signals, but also content-rich broadcasts that provide interactivity on your TV. For example, a cooking show might include links to recipes that you could download over your TV satellite or cable connection.
Video playback	ActiveMovie expands the multimedia capabilities of your computer, featuring improved video playback.
Windows Update	Accessed directly from the Windows 98 Start menu, this Microsoft site features a service that scans your system and allows you to update it with the most recent software. This site also helps you troubleshoot problems.

When computer owners consider whether or not to upgrade, they review feature lists and comparisons such as the ones you've seen in this tutorial. They then assess their needs and budget to determine whether to make the upgrade.

Now that you've had a chance to explore how Windows 98 changes the operating system landscape, you can see why users must balance the advantages against the sometimes uncertain world of switching to a new operating system and a new way of working with computers. Many users believe, however, that Windows 98 raises personal computing to new heights, and the benefits far outweigh the challenges.

▶ Independent Challenges

1. Based on what you've read in this tutorial, if you were a Windows 95 user, would you make the upgrade to Windows 98? Write a page-long essay that answers this question. In your essay, you'll need to define your computing needs, address how Windows 95 fulfills those needs, and evaluate the degree to which Windows 98 could better meet those needs. Be sure to itemize the features that were most prominent in helping you to make up your mind—either pro or con.

2. Using the resources available to you, either online or through your library, locate information about the release of Windows 98. Computing trade magazines, both hard copy and online, are an excellent source of information about software. Read several articles about Windows 98 and then write a page-long essay that discusses the features that seem most important to those evaluating the software. If you can find reviews of the software, mention the features reviewers had the strongest reaction to, pro or con.

3. Write a single-page essay defending or refuting the following proposition: "Software developers only upgrade their software to make money."

4. Interview three people you know who are well-informed computer users. Ask them how they decide when to upgrade a software product. If they are using a PC with the Windows 3.x, 95, or 98 operating system, ask them why they did or did not upgrade to Windows 98. Write a single-page essay summarizing what you learned about making the decision to upgrade.

5. Based on what you learned about Windows 98 in this tutorial, what Windows 98 features interest you the most? The least? Write two paragraphs describing those features and explaining why you do or do not find them interesting.

6. How has Windows 98 changed the concept of the "home computer"? Research the Windows 98 features that might benefit home users, such as its TV and appliance capabilities, and write two paragraphs summarizing those features and assessing how they could impact home life.

Previewing
Microsoft Office 2000 Professional

Objectives

► **Examine improvements to the installation process**
► **Use personal menus**
► **Use personal toolbars**
► **Learn how to use multiple languages**
► **Explore changes to dialog boxes**
► **Explore changes to switching between open files**
► **Explore changes to other commonly used features**
► **Explore new features of Microsoft Word**
► **Explore new features of Microsoft Excel**
► **Explore new features of Microsoft Access**
► **Explore new features of Microsoft PowerPoint**
► **Examine new online features**

Having learned about Office 97, you are probably curious about Office 2000, the latest version of the Office programs. What are the differences? Why might someone be better off using Office 2000 instead of Office 97? When you hear about new technology, you probably ask yourself questions like these and wonder whether you should upgrade. **Upgrading** is the process of placing a more recent version of a product onto your computer. This unit will introduce you to some of the main differences between Office 97 and Office 2000.

Office

Installing Microsoft Office 2000

Before you can use a software product, you must **install** it on your computer, which involves copying the files from the CDs or floppy disks that make up the software product onto your computer. Most software products will begin the installation process for you when you first insert the CD or floppy disk. Installing Office 2000 will vary according to your computer and network specifics. Be sure to check with your instructor or network administrator before installing any software. The following terms will help take you through the basics of installation.

Details

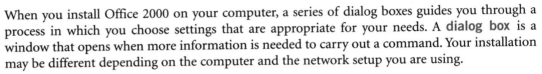

QuickTip

Note that this unit was developed using Office 2000 Professional. Your Office 2000 may contain different features, depending on the edition you purchased. See Table 1 for a list of the available editions of Office 2000 and what comes with each edition. You might also see differences because this unit was developed using a prerelease version of Office 2000.

When you install Office 2000 on your computer, a series of dialog boxes guides you through a process in which you choose settings that are appropriate for your needs. A **dialog box** is a window that opens when more information is needed to carry out a command. Your installation may be different depending on the computer and the network setup you are using.

As you go through these dialog boxes, you'll notice they usually have default settings selected. **Default settings** are options that the software developer selects as the most commonly used, such as installing the spell checker. You can always select something other than the default settings, but you should become familiar with all the program's features before changing them.

In Office 1997 and Office 2000, one of the default settings is to install only the most popular or commonly used programs and components, such as Word. Additional programs and features are installed only when you try to use them for the first time. In Office 97, once you are using the programs, you can't see what additional features could be installed. However, with Office 2000, commands and buttons for features that are not installed still appear in the program window. When you click those commands and buttons, a dialog box opens, prompting you to insert your installation CD. Inserting your installation CD enables you to install the feature immediately, without requiring you to close any open programs. This option is called **Install on first use**. When you install Office 2000, you can accept the default settings for which features are installed. You can also customize the installation by choosing which features you want to install, which you want to install on first use, or which you would like to become unavailable after installation. See Figure B-1.

Personalization is another big benefit of upgrading to Office 2000. By installing features as needed, you end up with a customized set of programs, containing only the standard Microsoft features and the non-standard features that you choose to install. Furthermore, the "Install on first use" feature saves considerable space on your computer's hard drive by not automatically installing all of the Office features.

FIGURE B-1: Selecting which features to install

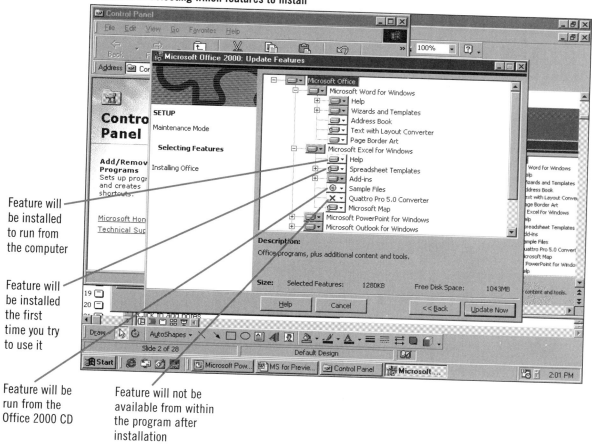

Feature will be installed to run from the computer

Feature will be installed the first time you try to use it

Feature will be run from the Office 2000 CD

Feature will not be available from within the program after installation

TABLE B-1: Editions of Microsoft Office 2000

edition	programs
Standard	Word, Excel, PowerPoint, and Outlook
Small Business	Word, Excel, Outlook, Publisher, and Small Business Tools
Professional	Word, Excel, PowerPoint, Access, Outlook, Publisher, and Small Business Tools
Premium	Professional plus FrontPage and PhotoDraw
Developer	Premium plus tools and documentation for building, managing, and organizing programs

Office

Using Personalized Menus

In each Office program, you can perform tasks using a **menu command** (a word or phrase on a menu that you click to perform a task) or a **toolbar button** (which corresponds to a commonly used menu command). In previous versions of Office, the menus contained and displayed commands for all the installed features. However, as the programs become more powerful, the list of commands gets long and difficult to navigate. For this reason, Microsoft developed "personalized" menus. **Personalized menus** (also referred to as "adaptive," "expanding," "full and short," and "cascading") adapt themselves to fit your work habits. As you work in Office 2000 programs, commands that you use most often are put on the short personal menus. The ones you don't use are hidden, but remain available. You can return your menus to their default settings by resetting your usage data. Resetting usage data erases the record of the commands you have used.

Steps 1 2 3 4

1. Start Word, click Insert on the menu bar to display its short personal menu, compare your screen to Figure B-2
   The commands displayed on your short Insert menu are probably different from those in Figure B-2, which are the default commands. You'll return the menus to their defaults, so the commands you see on your computer will match the figures as you complete these steps.

2. Click Insert on the menu bar again to close the menu

3. Click Tools on the menu bar, click Customize (you might need to pause until the full menu appears to see the command), then click the Options tab in the Customize dialog box

4. Make sure the Menus show recently used commands first check box and the Show full menus after a short delay check box are selected, click the Reset my usage data button, click Yes to confirm that you want to reset the commands, then click the Close button

5. Click Insert on the menu bar again, notice that there is no Bookmark command, then pause until the full Insert menu appears, as shown in Figure B-3
   Notice that the commands from the short menu appear on the regular gray background (sometimes referred to as "3D"), and that the commands belonging to the long menu appear on a lighter gray background ("non 3D").

6. Click Bookmark

7. Click Cancel to close the Bookmark dialog box

8. Click Insert on the menu bar to display the short personal menu
   Notice the Bookmark command now appears on the short personal menu because you used it.

9. Click Insert on the menu bar again to close the menu

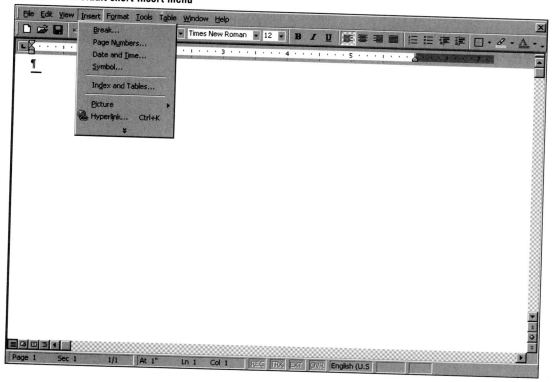

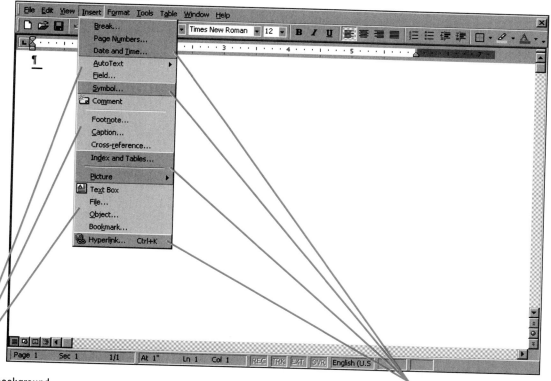

Light gray background indicates commands that are not on the short menu

Regular gray background indicates commands that are on the short menu

Office

Using Personalized Toolbars

In each Office program, the **toolbar buttons** (which correspond to commonly used menu commands) are also used frequently to perform common tasks. As with Office menus, the toolbars display the most commonly used buttons for all the installed features. But, with all the features available in Office 2000 (even those that might not yet be installed), the list of buttons can get lengthy, making it difficult to locate the ones you need. To address this problem, Microsoft developed the same "personalized" menu feature for toolbars. **Personalized toolbars** (also referred to as "adaptive," "expanding," and "full and short") adapt themselves to fit your work habits. When you use an Office 2000 program for the first time, the toolbars display only the most commonly used buttons so that there is less clutter in the program window. To display the hidden buttons on a toolbar, click the More Buttons button ⯈. You can also restore personalized toolbars to their default settings by resetting your usage data.

Steps

1. **Note that the Standard and Formatting toolbars appear side by side below the menu bar, as shown in Figure B-4**
   To learn how you can adjust toolbars to suit your work habits, you'll first set them to make sure they appear on the same row and then you'll reset your usage data so the default buttons are displayed.

2. **Click Tools on the menu bar, click Customize, click the Options tab in the Customize dialog box, click the Standard and Formatting toolbars share one row check box to select it, as shown in Figure B-4, click the Reset my usage data button, click Yes to confirm you want to reset the commands, then click Close**
   Now the Formatting toolbar sits to the right of the Standard toolbar. Notice that you can see some of the Standard toolbar buttons and some of the Formatting toolbar buttons. The rest of the buttons are stored in the More Buttons drop-down list for each toolbar. Your available buttons may be different.

3. **Click the More Buttons button ⯈ at the right side of the Standard toolbar**
   See Figure B-5.

4. **Click the Show/Hide ¶ button ¶**
   Notice that the Show/Hide ¶ button moves to the visible part of the Standard toolbar and the Highlight button ▱▾ on the Formatting toolbar disappears (it moved into the Formatting toolbar's More Buttons list). Your buttons may be different.

5. **Click ¶ again to return the formatting marks to their original setting**

To turn off personalized toolbars

You may find that you like the way the toolbars in Office 2000 change to meet your work habits, or you might prefer to display the toolbars on different rows so that all the buttons are always visible. To display the Standard and Formatting toolbars on separate rows:

1. Click **Tools** on the menu bar, and then click **Customize**.
2. Click the **Options** tab in the Customize dialog box.
3. Click the Standard and Formatting toolbars share one row check box to remove the check mark.
4. Click the **Close** button in the Customize dialog box to close the dialog box.

Similarly, you can turn off the short personal menu by removing the check marks from the Menus show recently used commands first check box and the Show full menus after short delay check box on the Options tab in the Customize dialog box.

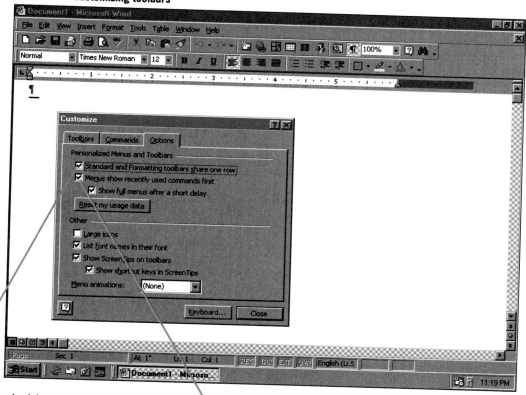

Deselecting this check box
would place the toolbars on
separate rows

Deselecting this check box makes
menus display all the commands
when you first click the menu
name, as in Office 97

FIGURE B-5: **Standard and Formatting toolbars on one row**

Standard
toolbar

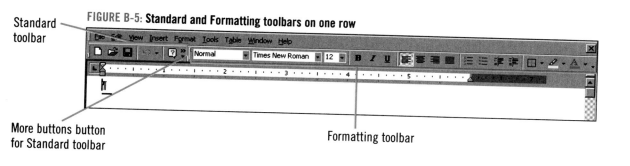

More buttons button
for Standard toolbar

Formatting toolbar

Office

Using Multiple Languages in Office 2000

Our global economy means that many companies do business with clients who speak multiple languages. Microsoft created several different versions of Office 97 to support different languages, but each computer can usually be installed with only one language. With Office 2000, you can change the **interface language**, the language used in command names, dialog boxes, Help, and so on. This is because there is only one **code base** (set of programming instructions) and **executable file** (a file that tells a computer how to perform tasks) for each program, rather than multiple executable files of each program for multiple languages. Figure B-6 shows a German interface. No matter what interface language you choose in Office 2000, you can create and edit documents in any language.

Steps 1 2 3 4

1. Click the Start button on the taskbar, point to Programs, point to Microsoft Office Tools, then click Microsoft Office Language Settings

   The Microsoft Office Language Setting dialog box opens, as shown in Figure B-7.

2. If necessary, click the Enabled Languages tab

   To add a language, click its check box to select it. See Figure B-8.

3. Scroll through the list of languages you can install

   You don't want to install any languages now, so you close the dialog box without making any changes.

4. Click the Cancel button

Menus and toolbars after changing interface language to German

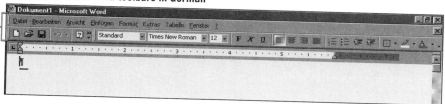

FIGURE B-7: Changing the interface language

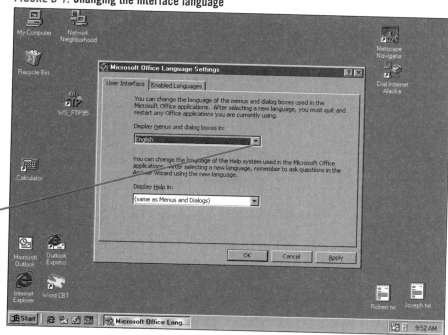

Click to change the interface language

FIGURE B-8: Adding enabled languages

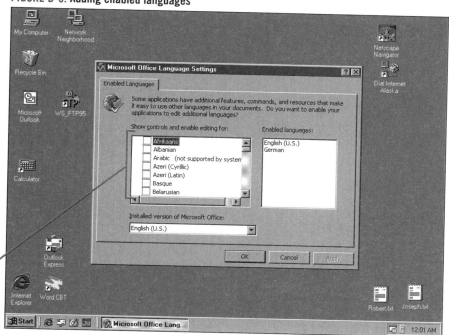

Languages you can enable, thereby gaining access to that language's dictionary, thesaurus, and spelling checker

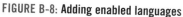

Office

Office

Exploring Changes to Dialog Boxes

In previous versions of Office, commonly used dialog boxes were often awkward to use or unnecessarily complicated to navigate. In Office 2000, Microsoft added features to some of the most often used dialog boxes including the Open, Save, and Save As dialog boxes.

Details

The most obvious dialog box change involves size. In Office 2000, the dialog boxes are bigger, providing more room to display files. This is helpful when you are looking for a certain file and have many files in one location—you can see them all at once rather than having to scroll to see them. See Figures B-9 and B-10 for a comparison of the Open dialog box with the same folder displayed in Excel 97 and Excel 2000.

Second, there is a **Places Bar**, a vertical list of buttons that provides quick access to commonly used folders. See Figure B-10 for a visual representation of the Places Bar and Table B-2, which lists and describes each button found on the Places Bar. In Office 97, you can access the Recent folder, the My Documents folder, the Desktop, and the Favorites folder from these dialog boxes, but it takes several more steps than simply clicking the button on the Places Bar.

A third change to the Open, Save, and Save As dialog boxes is the addition of buttons and commands that make copying, moving, and deleting files right from these dialog boxes much easier. The **Back button** displays the last location you visited, while the new **Delete button** allows you to delete selected files without right-clicking them. The **Search the Web button** starts your browser so that you can find files easily, whether they're located on your computer or on a Web server. See Figure B-10 for the location of these buttons.

TABLE B-2: Places Bar buttons and their functions

button	description
History	Displays the Recent folder, which contains shortcuts to the last 20 locations you visited and files you opened. In Office 97, the Recent list could be only nine files long, it contained shortcuts only to files (not folders or drives), and there was no button to display it easily in the Open, Save, and Save As dialog boxes.
My Documents	Displays the My Documents folder, which is created by Windows and is normally found on the main hard drive of your computer. You can rename and move the folder to make it more useful to you, and those changes will be reflected in the Open, Save, and Save As dialog boxes.
Desktop	Displays the shortcuts found on the Windows desktop. The desktop is actually a folder called Desktop that is created by Windows and is located on your hard drive. Since you can place files and shortcuts to files on the desktop, having quick access to the Desktop folder from the Open, Save, and Save As dialog boxes makes using those files and shortcuts even easier.
Favorites	Displays the items found in the Favorites folder, another folder created by Windows and located on your hard drive. Like the My Documents folder, you can rename and move the Favorites folder to suit your needs, and the changes will be reflected in the Places Bar.
Web Folders	If you have access to a Web server that supports this new feature of Office 2000, you can use this folder to publish files to the Web.

FIGURE B-9: Open dialog box in Excel 97

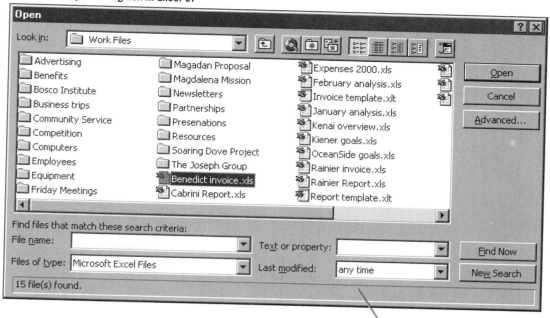

Open dialog box in Excel 97 displaying same folders and files as below; fewer files are visible and there is no Places Bar

FIGURE B-10: Open dialog box in Excel 2000

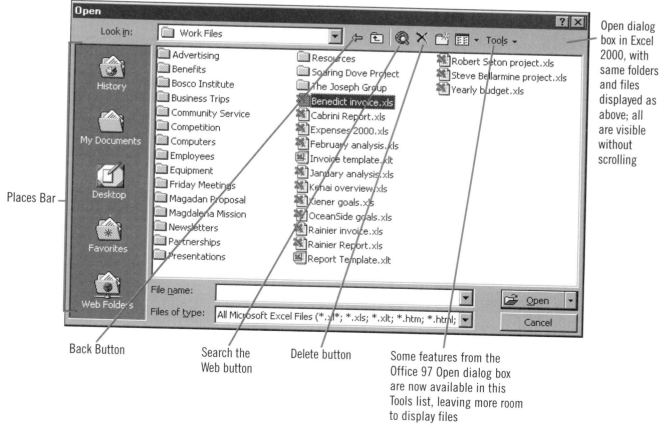

Open dialog box in Excel 2000, with same folders and files displayed as above; all are visible without scrolling

Places Bar

Back Button

Search the Web button

Delete button

Some features from the Office 97 Open dialog box are now available in this Tools list, leaving more room to display files

Office

Exploring Changes to Switching Between Open Files

In previous versions of Office, to switch between two files open in the same program, you click Window on the menu bar, and then click the name of the file you want to switch to. Each open program (not each open file) has a button on the taskbar, so that switching between programs involves a single click, while switching between files takes two or three clicks. In Office 2000, each open file—not just each open program—gets its own button on the taskbar, making it easier to switch between open files created with the same program.

Steps

1. Start Word

2. Type Microsoft Office 2000 in the new document, then save the file as Office 2000 on a blank floppy disk

Trouble?

If your taskbar button lists Word first and the filename second, click Tools on the menu bar, click Options, click the View tab if necessary, and then click the Windows in taskbar check box to select it.

3. Open a new, blank document, type Costs and Benefits of Upgrading, then save the file to the floppy disk as Upgrading

   Notice that there are two buttons in the taskbar, one for each file, and that the filename is listed *before* the program name. See Figure B-11.

4. Leave both files open

CLUES TO USE

If you frequently use many files at once, this new quick file switching feature may make your taskbar too cluttered to find the file you need. Regardless of the version of Office you are using, however, it is a good habit to close files you aren't using because it frees up RAM (memory) for the files and programs that you are using.

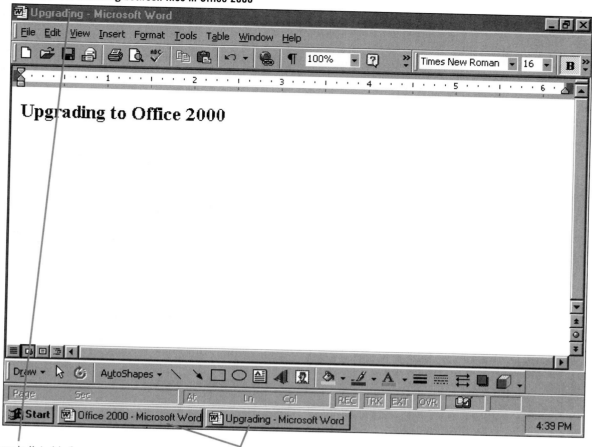

Filename is listed before the program name

Both open files appear as buttons on the taskbar and the filename is listed before the program name

Office

Exploring Changes to Other Commonly Used Features

In earlier versions of Office, some tasks were unnecessarily complicated or repetitive for the user. Microsoft has responded to this user feedback by creating a powerful new Clipboard and improving the Help system and Clip Gallery.

Details

 Using the Office Clipboard

In earlier versions of Office, when you cut or copy data, it is placed on the **Windows Clipboard**, a temporary storage area on your computer's hard drive. The data remains on the Clipboard until you paste it into another location, turn off your computer, or cut or copy other data. In Office 2000, there is also an **Office Clipboard**, a temporary storage area for Office 2000 programs. The Office Clipboard can hold up to 12 selections of data (including data created in other programs and data from the Web), so that you can cut or copy up to 12 different times, without losing your previous selections. You don't have to think about whether your data is placed on the Windows Clipboard or the Office Clipboard, unless your goal is to paste multiple selections into files created with programs other than Office. See Figure B-12.

 Getting Help in Office 2000

Like all Microsoft programs, Office 2000 comes with extensive information on how to use the programs. This information, referred to simply as **Help**, is similar to a huge encyclopedia stored on your computer. The **Office Assistant**, an interactive guide to finding information from the Office Help system, is one of the main ways of getting help in both Office 97 and Office 2000. Microsoft changed the Office Assistant in Office 2000 based on user feedback that the Office Assistant be less obtrusive, but remain readily available; that the user be able to turn it off completely while still having access to all the Help information and features; and that it use as much **natural language**, or words and syntax that people use in everyday usage, as possible. Users also requested a Web-like interface and ready access to Help information on the Web. See Figure B-13.

 Using the Office 2000 Clip Gallery

Clip art, pictures saved as files for use on a computer, has become an integral part of business documents, personal correspondence, and Web pages. The **Clip Gallery**, a program that organizes pictures, sounds, and motion clips (all of which Microsoft refers to as **clips**), has been improved with Office 2000, making it easier to make your documents more dynamic. In Office 97, inserting a clip into a document involved many steps, after which the Clip Gallery automatically closed. With Office 2000, you can drag clips from the Clip Gallery into your Office documents, placing them at the desired location as you drop them into the document. The Clip Gallery remains open until you close it, making it much easier to insert multiple clips. To facilitate dragging and dropping, the new Clip Gallery window can be resized, minimized, and maximized. Another important improvement in the Office 2000 Clip Gallery is that clips are inserted into documents in their original file formats. See Figure B-14.

FIGURE B-12: Clipboard toolbar

Clipboard toolbar displays icons for up to 12 selections

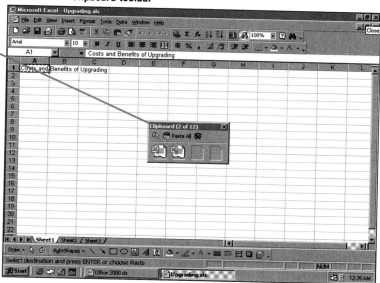

FIGURE B-13: The Office Assistant in Office 2000

New Office Asssistant is smaller, blends into program window better, and presents list of suggested topics in natural language matching the question

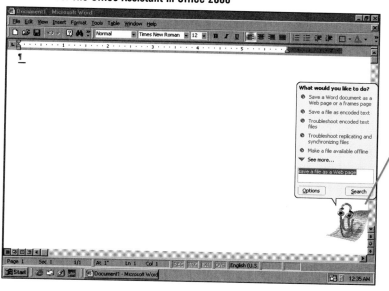

FIGURE B-14: Office 2000 Clip Gallery

New Clip Gallery can be minimized and resized, unlike the Office 97 Clip Gallery

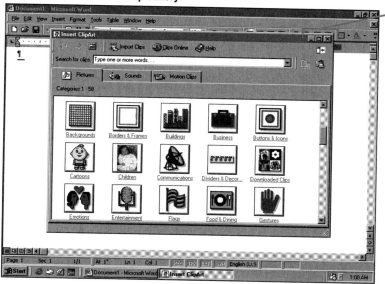

Office

Examining New Online Features

More companies than ever are advertising on the Web, creating their own Web sites, and using intranets and the Internet to communicate. (**Intranets** are private, company-wide, Web-like connections of computers.) More individuals, too, are using the Web. With Office 2000, all of these tasks become even easier than they were before. Enhanced online capabilities are some of the most powerful and beneficial new features of Office 2000 across applications.

Creating and Editing Web Pages with Office 2000

HTML, or HyperText Markup Language, is the computer programming language used to create and display files for use on the Web. You don't need knowledge of HTML, however, to produce Web pages with Office 97 and Office 2000. Once you save files as HTML (the command in Office 97 is "Save as HTML;" the Office 2000 command is "Save as Web Page"), you can **publish** them to the Web, a process that makes the files available to all who have Internet access. Office 97 files sometimes look different in your Web browser than they do in your Office program. Office 2000 solves this problem by making a cleaner conversion possible. Therefore, when you view Office documents on the Web, the transition is almost seamless—almost no features are lost or distorted.

Publishing Files to the Web with Office 2000

When you publish files, you place them on a **Web server**, a computer connected to the Web that stores files for use on the Web. Most Web servers are maintained by **Internet Service Providers** (ISPs), companies that provide access to the Internet, usually for a fee. With Office 2000, when you create a Web page, a folder is automatically created, using the same name as the Web page file. All the files that are part of the Web page are automatically stored in that folder. Each HTML file you create with Office 2000, therefore, has two easily-managed parts: the HTML file and its corresponding folder. See Figure B-15 and B-16.

Using Online Collaboration in Office 2000

Recent changes in Web technology have made it possible to open a document on one computer and, using an Internet connection and a program such as **Microsoft NetMeeting**, display that document on another computer, so that both computer users can view, edit, and comment on the document. NetMeeting has been available for several years, but is now bundled with Office 2000 Professional. Also, commands have been added to each Office 2000 program that allow you to start NetMeeting right from the Office program and to collaborate with other computer users who have NetMeeting, even if they don't have Office. See Figure B-16.

If both users have microphones attached to their computers, they can discuss the document (and any other topics) using live audio, just like a regular telephone conversation. If both users also have video devices attached to their computers, they can see each other as they talk. If your server uses OSE (Office Server Extensions), you can also use the Online Collaboration command to initiate and join **Web discussions**, a series of comments that users add to Office and HTML documents, making creating documents with other users more efficient.

FIGURE B-15: Automatically created folder for files associated with a Web page, as displayed in Windows Explorer

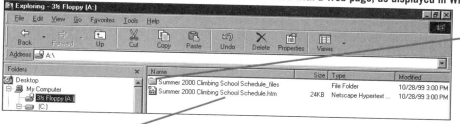

Web page created with Excel 2000

Folder is automatically created (with name to match the Web page) and files associated with the Web page are placed inside

FIGURE B-16: Commands for setting up a NetMeeting conference

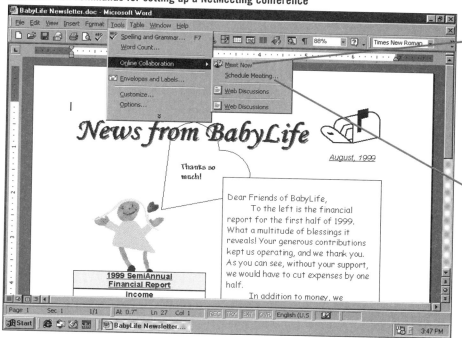

Starts NetMeeting, where you log on to a server and place a call to anyone else running NetMeeting and logged on to that server

Diplays an Outlook e-mail message window where you can select the contact with whom you want to meet and the server you want to use; most of the message is typed for you

CLUES TO USE

Office 2000 Web Folders

If your ISP uses Microsoft's **Office Server Extensions (OSE)**, a set of features and technologies that bridge the gap between Web technology and Office, Windows, and your browser, you can publish files to the Web simply by saving them to your own hard drive or network. This means that you can create, move, delete, and copy HTML files and folders to and from a Web server just as you would to your own hard drive. See Figure B-17. This is possible using a new Office 2000 feature called **Web Folders**, a folder for shortcuts to files on your Web server. The folder is placed on your computer when you install Office 2000.

FIGURE B-17: Adding a Web folder

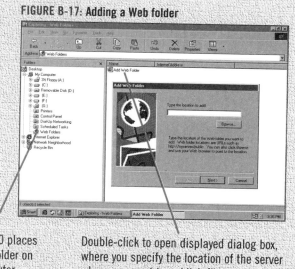

Office 2000 places this new folder on your computer

Double-click to open displayed dialog box, where you specify the location of the server where you want to publish files

Office

Exploring the New Features of Microsoft Word

Microsoft continually tries to improve the overall functionality of how the Office programs work together and individually, and to give each program a wider range of features and greater ease of use. Microsoft Word is the most frequently used of all the office applications. The following is a list of improvements.

Details

 Click and Type

In the Print Layout and Web Layout views, you can position the pointer at any blank location in a document and double-click to position the insertion point there (alignment and blank lines are automatically formatted and inserted).

 Table improvements

You can insert tables as objects so that you can move and resize them as you do other objects. You can also nest tables, one inside the other, wrap text around them, and divide cells into diagonal halves.

 Improved Web authoring tools

Web themes provide consistent formatting and are compatible with FrontPage 2000 (see Figure B-18). Word's rich formatting is not lost when you view Web pages in Internet Explorer 4.0 or higher or in Netscape Navigator, and the Web Page Preview command on the File menu allows you to view a document quickly in your browser.

 Improved spelling checker

Not only does Word's spell checker and AutoCorrect feature catch "hte" and change it to "the," but it also corrects more complex typos, such as correcting "sracastic" to "sarcastic."

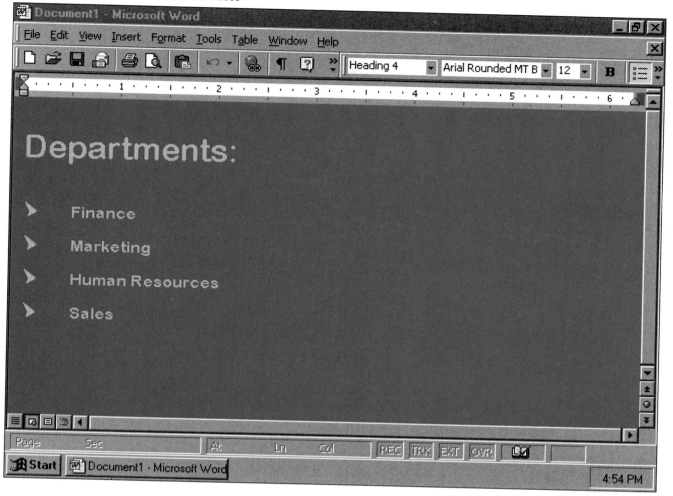

Office

Office

Exploring the New Features of Microsoft Excel

Microsoft continually tries to improve the overall functionality of how the Office programs work together and individually, and to give each program a wider range of features and greater ease of use. Microsoft Excel is the spreadsheet component of the Office applications. The following is a list of improvements.

Details

 Built-in HTML file format for Web pages

This feature, available in all Office programs and discussed earlier ("Exploring New Online Features"), represents an especially significant improvement in Excel. In Office 2000, when you save workbooks as HTML, they retain much more formatting, and you have the option of saving it for viewing only from the browser, or saving it as an interactive Web page (allowing Web users to change cells, charts, or PivotTables).

 Improved PivotTables and charts

You can link a chart to a PivotTable so it will change automatically when you change the PivotTable. You can also work with a pivot chart directly to move fields, create new ones, and more. You can easily format PivotTables by choosing from a dozen preset formats. See Figure B-19.

 Support for the new euro currency

You can display, enter, format and print the euro symbol € and work with values in the euro currency. To type the euro symbol, turn on NumLock, then press Alt+0128.

 Browser Copy and Paste

You can drag table data from an Internet Explorer browser window directly into a spreadsheet, and it will be formatted appropriately.

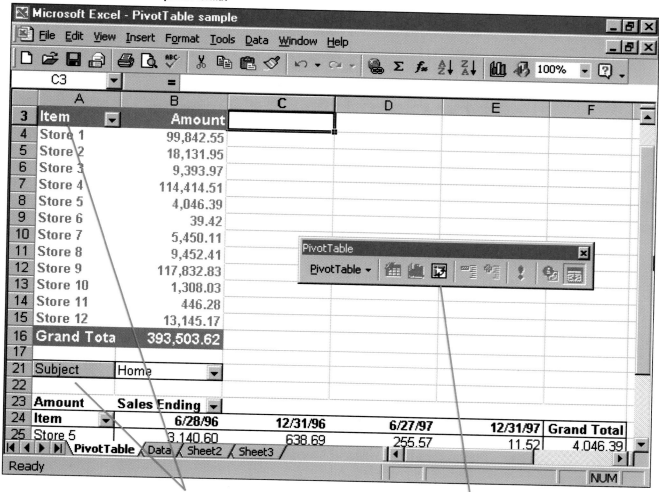

Pivot table buttons that contains
the name of a summarized field
of data

Pivot table toolbar

Office

Exploring the New Features of Microsoft Access

Microsoft continually tries to improve the overall functionality of how the Office programs work together and individually, and to give each program a wider range of features and greater ease of use. Microsoft Access is the database component of the Office applications. The following is a list of improvements.

 Name AutoCorrect

Automatically tracks and updates changes to the names of database objects. This feature is extremely useful in keeping all data up to date and accurate, especially in a large, complicated database.

 Conditional formatting

Enables you to specify formatting features that appear only when certain conditions are met (for example, the records of all clients from Colorado could be shaded green).

 Subdatasheets

Enables you to view and edit related records in tables, queries, or forms from Datasheet view, Query Datasheet view, or Form view. See Figure B-20.

 Data access pages

Enables you to create Web pages in Access to collect data over the Web for an Access or SQL server database.

CourseID	Description	Hours	MOUS	Prereq	Cost
⊞ Access1	Introduction to Access	12	Proficient	Comp1	$200
⊞ Access2	Intermediate Access	24	Expert	Access1	$400
⊞ AccessLab	Access Case Problems	12		Access2	$200
⊟ Comp1	Computer Fundamentals	12			$200

	LogNo	SSN	Attended	Passed
	1	115-77-4444	01/31/2000	☑
	2	134-70-3883	01/31/2000	☑
∗	(AutoNumber)			☐

CourseID	Description	Hours	MOUS	Prereq	Cost
⊞ Excel1	Introduction to Excel	12	Proficient	Comp1	$200
⊞ Excel2	Intermediate Excel	12	Expert	Excel1	$200
⊞ ExcelLab	Excel Case Problems	12		Excel2	$200

Office

Office

Exploring the New Features of Microsoft PowerPoint

Microsoft continually tries to improve the overall functionality of how the Office programs work together and individually and to give each program a wider range of features and greater ease of use. Microsoft PowerPoint is the presentation component of the Office applications. The following is a list of improvements.

 Normal view displays three panes
Normal view displays the current slide, its speaker notes, and an outline of the entire presentation all in the same window, enabling you to work on all aspects of a presentation without switching views. See Figure B-21.

 ScreenSaver can be disabled during a slide show
To prevent slide show interruptions, the ScreenSaver is automatically disabled—even if there is no mouse or keyboard activity for long periods of time.

 Improved Web authoring
Slide shows lose no formatting when displayed in Internet Explorer 4.0 or above.

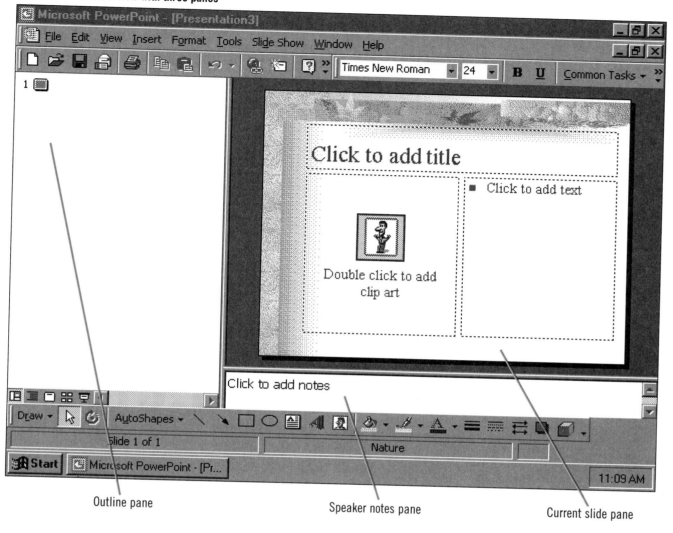

Outline pane   Speaker notes pane   Current slide pane

Preparing
for the Year 2000 Computer Problem

Objectives

► **Understand and assess the Year 2000 computer problem on a PC**

► **Examine how Office 2000 handles the Year 2000 computer problem**

By now you have probably heard much about the Year 2000 computer problem, sometimes referred to as the "millennium bug" or the "Y2K bug" (the Y stands for "year" and the K is an abbreviation for "kilo," a prefix that means "thousand"). The phrase **Year 2000 computer problem** is a catchall term to describe a host of computer difficulties anticipated to occur when we begin the year 2000. This appendix will introduce you to the basics of the Year 2000 computer problem and the steps you can take to protect your own personal computer. In addition, this appendix will examine how the Y2K bug affects Microsoft Office 2000.

Office 2000

Understanding and Assessing the Year 2000 Computer Problem on a PC

The Year 2000 problem is important because computers affect nearly every aspect of most peoples' lives. There are millions of computers in the world, and billions of embedded control systems, which are computers (or electronics devices that function like computers) found inside other products. ECSs can be as small as a chip in a watch or as large as a mainframe computer in an electric plant. Every computer and ECS that we want to ensure works through the turn of the millennium needs to be found, tested, and fixed. The information that follows will help you understand how the Year 2000 computer problem affects our lives and help you prepare your personal computer for the turn of the millennium.

Understanding the Year 2000 Computer Problem

The source of the problem goes back to the 1960s, when software was first being used on a widespread basis and the standards for our current software were developed. Software developers who used two digits in their programs saved companies hundreds of thousands of dollars in memory and hard disk space, both of which were significantly more expensive then than they are now. In the years that followed, hardware prices were slow to drop in relation to other costs, so using two-digit years became standard for the first 20-30 years of the computer era. And because new programs have to be compatible with the old—it is often easier and less expensive to extend, patch, and improve upon old software than it is to buy new—the two-digit standard stuck. There may be two, five, ten, or more components of your computer that are involved in producing accurate time and date results. This means that you may have a difficult time determining exactly what in the computer needs to be fixed. You should not, for example, merely set the date to January 1, 2000 and see what happens; you may lose valuable data, and you won't find the source of the problem. Table AP-1 lists and describes the various parts of a computer that use date and time functions.

TABLE AP-1: **Computer components involved in tracking date and time**

Component	Function
The system clock, or **RTC** (Real Time Clock)	An internal clock on the CMOS (see below) that keeps track of time even when the computer is off. Most RTCs have room for only two digits for the century (80 for 1980, for example), so that the year 2000 (00) may be interpreted as 1900.
CMOS, or Complementary Metal Oxide Semiconductor	The memory chip that contains the RTC. The CMOS chip requires only a trickle of current to maintain its settings, supplied by an onboard battery. The CMOS chip stores the settings unique to each computer, such as the time and date, the hard disk type, and BIOS preferences.
The **BIOS** (Basic Input/Output System)	A small program built into computers that starts when a computer is turned on and that relays information between the hardware and the software
The **operating system**	The program that communicates with the BIOS and runs all the other programs, coordinating the interaction and sharing of a computer's components so that they don't interfere with one another
Programs (also called software or applications)	The lists of instructions that tells a computer how to perform various tasks
Data files	Information a user enters and saves on a computer

Assessing and Fixing Year 2000 Problems on a Personal Computer

The problem is made more complex by the fact that a computer has three main components—hardware, software, and data files—and faulty date references in any one of those can cause a computer to produce inaccurate results or to cease to work entirely. For this reason, you should test your personal computer to see whether it will handle the change to the year 2000 correctly. A personal computer represents a significant investment for most people, and many of us are incredibly dependent on them for communication, record-keeping, and working at home. Tests have revealed that even computers made by the same manufacturer and running the same software will respond to the change to 2000 differently. So even if your computer hardware and/or software vendors claim that their products are free of year 2000 problems, you would be wise to perform a few tests yourself and assess your data files and how you entered dates.

The general steps you should take to get your computer ready for the year 2000 are as follows:

- Back up your data files and make sure you have installation disks for all of your software, including device drivers (software for peripheral devices), and a system disk.

- List the components of your computer that you need to assess (include the processor, the BIOS, hard disks, disk drives, the modem, printers, and fax, as well as your operating system and software programs). List the manufacturer and model names, serial numbers, and other pertinent data (such as processor speed, hard disk capacity, and program versions). You may have to refer to this list if your computer malfunctions after December 31 or while you are performing tests.

- Test each component for year 2000 compliance. The best way to do this is to run a program designed to test various computer components for problems with the year 2000. Many such programs exist, and many, many more are likely to be developed in the middle and later parts of 1999. You can either get such a program free from the Internet or spend between $20 and $40 for one. See Table AP-2.

- Formulate and implement a solution for each component that handles the year 2000 incorrectly. You might need to install a **patch** (an update to a program) that the vendor creates (these are often available on the Web), or you might need to purchase and install new hardware and/or software components. You might also need to re-enter the four-digit dates in all of your data files and enter all new dates with four digits. Note that you will probably have multiple solutions—one for each component that mishandles the year 2000.

- Re-test each component.

The testing and fixing process can be complicated, and it will be different for each computer. You can also find hundreds of books, articles, and Web sites devoted to the topic. See Table AP-2 for a brief list.

Note: You should contact your computer's vendor for information specific to your computer system before you perform any tests.

Office 2000

TABLE AP-2: Resources for assessing and fixing year 2000 problems in a personal computer

URL or book title	Web site creator or book publisher	Description
www.microsoft.com/y2k	Microsoft	Includes a guide to all Microsoft products, a list of frequently asked questions, and compliancy definitions
www.support2000.com	Support2000	Offers help to small business owners who are just getting started on their year 2000 planning.
Know2000	The Year 2000 Group, Inc.	A program that takes you through the process of checking your hardware and software, then prepares a summary and a suggested plan of action. Includes a database of Y2K-readiness reports for more than 3,500 home and small business programs, and a database of hardware vendors.
Norton 2000	Symantec	A program that tests your hardware, software, and data files. It is especially helpful for Excel users, because it analyzes Excel workbooks, makes copies of them, then color-codes and annotates each cell (in the copied files, leaving the originals as they were) to help you find and fix year 2000 problems.
Check 2000 PC	Greenwich Mean Time (1-800-216-5545)	A program that tests and fixes BIOS problems, then tells you which programs and data will be affected by the year 2000. Also helps you prioritize fixing any problems it finds on your PC.
www.y2k.policyworks.gov	U.S. Federal Government	A comprehensive list of vendors and their products, which you can search to determine year 2000 compliance.

Office 2000 and the Year 2000

As you develop your strategy for making sure your computer will work in the next millennium, one component you may decide to upgrade is your programs. The Office 2000 suite of programs is deemed "Year 2000 Compliant," a feature that may save you considerable time, money, and effort. **Y2K compliant** is a term applied to various computer products; it describes a product that the manufacturer says will handle the year 2000 appropriately. However, there is no industry standard that defines "Y2K compliant;" nor is there any regulation that ensures products claiming to be compliant are using the term accurately and consistently. An important benefit of Office 2000 is that it also has new features to help prevent problems caused by the year changing to 2000. Office 2000 has been labeled Y2K compliant by Microsoft, meaning that if the other components in your computer are also compliant, dates will be handled correctly before and after 2000.

 To eliminate confusion about its own products, Microsoft created a strategy containing a statement defining what it means when it calls one of its products "Y2K compliant." They have also created a list of products that are Y2K compliant, those that need patches or service packs in order to become compliant, those that are not compliant, those that have not yet been assessed, and those that will not be tested for compliance. You can read this statement (along with its lengthy disclaimer) and access the list of products and their compliance levels at *http://www.microsoft.com/technet/year2k/*. The site also has general Year 2000 information and links to Web sites that give or sell programs to test your computer.

 Both Office 2000 and Office 97 use 2029 as the pivot year, so if you haven't encountered any problems working in Office 97, you don't have to change any settings when you upgrade to Office 2000. Note that changing the pivot year has nothing to do with what dates you can enter and expect Office 2000 to use accurately. The **pivot year** refers only to the 100-year period for which you can use two-digit dates. You can enter any year you want using four digits. See Figure AP-1.

FIGURE AP-1: Changing the two-digit pivot year

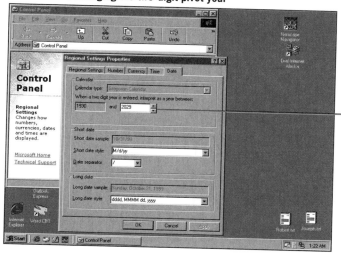

Click up or down list arrow to change pivot year

Now that you've had a chance to explore the new features of Office 2000, you can assess the advantages of upgrading and balance those with your computer needs and your budget. If you do decide to upgrade, you can use this appendix as a resource, along with the powerful Office Help system, to learn how to use the new features, minimizing the time you spend learning and maximizing the time you spend actually using the new features to create effective documents for work and pleasure.

Resources

http://www.microsoft.com/technet/year2k/

http://www.microsoft.com/office/preview/

http://www.cnn.com/TECH/specials/y2k/

JD Consulting: *Year 2000 Personal Computer Fix-It Guide*. Charles River Media, Rockland, MA, 1999.

Yourdon, Edward, and Jennifer Yourdon: *Time Bomb 2000: Revised and Updated*. Prentice Hall, Upper Saddle River, NJ, 1999.

Webster, Bruce. *The Y2K Survival Guide: Getting to, Getting through, and Getting Past the Year 2000 Problem*. Prentice Hall, Upper Saddle River, NJ, 1999.

Index

Access, program improvements, OF B-22

Back button, OF B-10

Buttons
 Back, OF B-10
 Delete, OF B-10
 Desktop, OF B-10
 Favorites, OF B-10
 History, OF B-10
 My Documents, OF B-10
 Search the Web, OF B-10
 Web folders, OF B-10

Clip art, OF B-14

Clip Gallery
 Changes, OF B-14
 Using, OF B-14

Clipboard, Office, OF B-14

Clipboard, Windows OF B-14

Clips, OF B-14

Code base, OF B-8

Default settings, OF B-2

Delete Button, OF B-10

Dialog box, changes, OF B-2

Embedded control systems, OF AP-2

Excel, program improvements, OF B-20

Executable file, OF B-8

Features, selecting which to install, OF B-2

Files, switching between open, OF B-12

Full menus, OF B-4

Help, OF B-14

HTML, OF B-16

Install, OF B-2

Install on first use, OF B-2

Interface language, changing, OF B-8

Internet Service Providers (ISPs), OF B-16

Intranets, OF B-16

Languages, using multiple, OF B-8

Menu command, OF B-4

Microsoft Office editions, OF B-3

Natural language, OF B-14

NetMeeting, OF B-16

Office Assistant, OF B-14

Office Server Extensions (OSEs), OF B-16

Online
 Collaboration, OF B-16
 features, new, OF B-16
 NetMeeting, OF B-16

Open dialog box, OF B-10
 Back button, OF B-10
 Delete button, OF B-10
 Places Bar, OF B-10
 Search the Web button, OF B-10

Pasting, OF B-20

Patch, OF AP-3

Personalization, OF B-2

Personalized menus, OF B-4

Personalized toolbars, OF B-6

Pivot year, OF AP-5

Places Bar, OF B-10

PowerPoint, program improvements, OF B-24

Publish, to the Web, OF B-16
 Formatting discrepancies, OF B-16

Save As dialog box, OF B-10

Save dialog box, OF B-10

Search the Web button, OF B-10

Toolbar buttons, OF B-4

Upgrading, OF B-1

Web Discussions, OF B-16

Web Folders, OF B-16

Web Server, OF B-16

Word, program improvements, OF B-18

Y2K bug, OF AP-1

Y2K compliant, OF AP-3

Year 2000 computer problem, OF AP-1
 Assessing and fixing, OF AP-3
 BIOS, OF AP-4
 CMOS, OF AP-4
 Data files, OF AP-4
 Embedded control systems, OF AP-2
 Operating system, OF AP-4
 PCs, OF AP-3
 Patch, OF AP-3
 Pivot year, OF AP-5
 Programs, OF AP-4
 Resources, OF AP-4
 Understanding, OF AP-2
 Web sites, OF AP-4

Glossary

Word 97

Alignment The horizontal position of text within the width of a line or between tab stops. There are three kinds of alignment in Word.

Application *See* program.

Arrow keys The [↑], [↓], [←], and [→] keys. Used to move the insertion point or to select from a menu or a list of options.

Automatic save A feature that automatically saves document changes in a temporary file at specified intervals. If power to the computer is interrupted, the changes in effect from the last save are retained. Enabled by default, you can turn off this feature by clicking Tools then Options.

AutoCorrect A feature that automatically corrects a misspelled word. Word provides several entries for commonly misspelled words, but you can add your own.

AutoFormat A feature that improves the appearance of a document by applying consistent formatting and styles based on a default document templates or a document template you specify. The AutoFormat feature also adds bullets to lists and symbols for trademarks and copyrights where necessary.

AutoText entry A stored text or graphic you want to use again.

Border A straight vertical or horizontal line between columns in a section, next to or around paragraphs and graphics, or in a table. You can assign a variety of widths to a border. *See also* Rule.

Bullet A small graphic, usually a round or square dot, often used to identify items in a list.

Cell The basic unit of a table, separated by gridlines. In a table, the intersection of a row and a column forms one cell.

Cell reference Identifies a cell's position in a table. Each cell reference contains a letter (A, B, C and so on) to identify its column and a number (1, 2, 3 and so on) to identify its row.

Click To press and release a mouse button in one motion.

Clipboard A temporary storage area for cut or copied text or graphics. You can paste the contents of the Clipboard into any Word document or into a file of another Microsoft Windows application, such as Microsoft Excel. The Clipboard holds the information until you cut or copy another piece of text or a graphic.

Cut To remove selected text or a graphic from a document so you can paste it to another place in the document or to another document. The cut information is placed in a temporary storage area called the Clipboard. The Clipboard holds the information until you cut or copy another piece of text or a graphic.

Default Predefined settings such as page margins, tab spacing, and shortcut key assignments. The default template when you create documents is NORMAL.DOT, whose default settings include margins of 1.25 inches and no indents.

Dialog box A box that displays the available command options for you to review or change.

Document window A rectangular portion of the screen in which you view and edit a document. When you enlarge a document window to maximum size, it shares its borders and title bar with the Word program window.

Drag To hold down the mouse button while moving the mouse.

Drive The mechanism in a computer that read a disk to retrieve and store information. Personal computers often have one hard disk drive labeled C and two drives labeled A and B that read removable floppy disks.

Edit To add, delete, or change text and graphics.

File A document that has been created, then saved, under a unique file name. In Word, all documents and pictures are stored as files.

Folders Subdivisions of a disk that work like a filing system to help you organize files.

Font A name given to a collection of characters (letters, numerals, symbols, and punctuation marks) with a specific design. Arial and Times New Roman are examples of font names.

Font effects Refers to enhanced formatting you can apply to text, such as Shadow, Engraved, all caps, and hidden, among others.

Font size Refers to the physical size of text, measured in points (pts). The bigger the number of points, the larger the font size.

Font style Refers to whether text appears as bold, italicized, or underlined, or any combination of these formats.

Format The way text appears on a page. In Word, a format comes from direct formatting and the application of styles. The four types of formats are character, paragraph, section, and document.

Formatting toolbar A bar that contains buttons and options for the most frequently used formatting commands.

Global template In Word, a template with the file name NORMAL.DOT that contains default menus, AutoCorrect entries, styles and page setup settings. Documents use the global template unless you specify a custom template. *See also* template.

Graphics A picture, chart, or drawing in a document.

Hanging indent A paragraph format in which the first line of a paragraph starts farther left than the subsequent lines.

Horizontal ruler A graphical bar displayed across the top of the document window in all views. You can use the ruler to indent paragraphs, set tab stops, adjust left and right paragraph margins, and change column widths in a table. You can hide this ruler by clicking View then Ruler.

Indent The distance between text boundaries and page margins. Positive indents make the text area narrower than the space between margins. Negative indents allow text to extend into the margins. A paragraph can have left, right, and first-line indents.

Insertion point Vertical blinking line on the Word screen that shows your current location and where text and graphics are inserted. The insertion point also determines where Word will begin an action.

Line break Mark inserted where you want to end one line and start another without starting a new paragraph.

Line spacing The height of a line of text, including extra spacing. Line spacing is often measured in lines or points.

Menu bar Lists the names of the menus that contain Word commands. Click a menu name on the menu bar to display a list of commands.

Non-printing characters Marks displayed on the screen to indicate characters that do not print, such as tab characters or paragraph marks. You can control the display of special characters with the Options command on the Tools menu, and the Show/Hide ¶ button on the ribbon.

Normal view The view you see when you start Word. Normal view is used for most editing and formatting tasks.

Office assistant A feature that appears in a program to offer tips and assistance when you carry out certain tasks or when you type specific phrases. For example, when you type "Dear Ms. So and So:" and press [Enter] you see an office assistant asking if you want help creating a letter. You can work with or without the assistant.

Options The choices available in a dialog box.

Overtype An option for replacing existing characters one by one as you type. You can select overtype by pressing the [Insert] key or by selecting the Overtype option with the Options command on the Tools menu. When you select the Overtype option, the letters "OVR" appear in the status bar at the bottom of the Word window.

Page layout view A view of a document as it will appear when you print it. Items such as headers, footnotes, and framed objects appear in their actual positions, and you can drag them to new positions. You can edit and format text in page layout view.

Paste To insert cut or copied text into a document from the temporary storage area called the Clipboard.

Path Drive, folder, and file name. For example, the complete path for Microsoft Word might be C:\WINWORD\WINWORD.EXE.

Point size A measurement used for the size of text characters. There are 72 points per inch.

Position The specific placement of graphics, tables, and paragraphs on a page. In Word, you can assign items to fixed positions on a page.

Program A software application that performs specific tasks, such as Microsoft Word or Microsoft Excel.

Program window A window that contains the running application. The window displays the menus and provides the workspace for any document used within the application. The application window shares its borders and title bar with document windows that are fully enlarged.

Redo The ability to repeat reversed actions or changes, usually editing or formatting actions. Only reversed changes can be repeated with the redo feature.

Repetitive text Text that you use often in documents.

Resize The ability to change the size of an object (such as framed text or a graphic) by dragging sizing handles located on the sides and corner of the selected object.

Resolution Refers to size of your monitor's screen display. Resolution is measured in pixels, such as a typical resolution is 640 x 480. The illustrations in this book were taken on a computer with these resolution. Because a higher resolution results in more space visible on the screen and smaller text, your screen might not exactly match the illustrations in this book if you are using a higher resolution. You can change the resolution of the monitor using the Control Panel on the Start menu.

Sans serif font A font whose characters do not include serifs; the small strokes at the ends of the characters. Arial is a sans serif font.

Scroll bar A graphical device for moving vertically and horizontally through a document with a mouse. Scroll bars are located at the right and bottom edges of the document window. You can display or hide scroll bars with the Horizontal Scroll Bar and Vertical Scroll Bar check boxes, View options in the Options dialog box (Tools menu).

Selection bar An unmarked column at the left edge of a document window used to select text with the mouse. In a table, each cell has its own selection bar at the left edge of the cell.

Serif font A font that has small strokes at the ends of the characters. Times New Roman and Palatino are serif fonts.

ScreenTip When you move the pointer over a button, the name of the button is displayed and a brief description of its function appears in the status bar.

Shading The background color or pattern behind text or graphics.

Soft return A line break created by pressing [Shift] + [Enter]. This creates a new line without creating a new paragraph.

Spreadsheet program A software program used for calculations and financial analysis.

Standard toolbar The topmost row of buttons that perform some of the most frequently used commands.

Status bar Located at the bottom of the Word window, it displays the current page number and section number, the total number of pages in the document, and the vertical position (in inches) of the insertion point. You also see the status of commands in effect, and the current time. The status bar also displays descriptions of commands and buttons as you move around the window.

Tab stop A measured position for placing and aligning text at a specific place on a line. Word has four kinds of tab stops, left-aligned (the default), centered, right-aligned, and decimal.

Table One or more rows of cells commonly used to display numbers and other items for quick reference and analysis. Items in a table are organized into rows and columns. You can convert text into a table with the Insert Table command on the Table menu.

Template A special kind of document that provides basic tools and text for creating a document. Templates can contain the following elements: styles, AutoText items, macros, customized menu and key assignments, and text or graphics that are the same in different types of document.

Title bar The horizontal bar at the top of a window that displays the name of the document or application that appears in that window. Until you save the document and give it a name, the temporary name for the document is DOCUMENT1.

Toolbar A graphical bar with buttons that perform some of the most common commands in Word, such as opening, copying, and printing files. There are also toolbars that contain buttons related to completing specific tasks in Word. For example, the Formatting toolbar contains common formatting features while the Tables and Borders toolbar contains buttons that are useful when you work in tables or add borders to your document.

Undo The ability to reverse previous actions or changes, usually editing or formatting actions. Actions from the File menu cannot be reversed. You can undo up to 100 previous actions from the time you opened the document.

Vertical alignment The placement of text on a page in relation to the top, bottom, or center of the page.

Vertical ruler A graphical bar displayed at the left edge of the document window in the page layout and print preview views. You can use this ruler to adjust the top and bottom page margins, and change row height in a table.

View A display that shows certain aspects of the document. Word has many views, including: normal, draft, online, outline, page layout, full screen, and print preview.

View buttons Appear in the horizontal scroll bar. Allow you to display the document in one of three views: normal, online, page layout and outline.

Window A rectangular area on the screen in which you view and work on documents.

Wizard An on-line coach you use to create documents. When you use a wizard to create a document, you are asked questions about document preferences, and the wizard creates the document according to your specifications.

Word processing program A software used for creating documents efficiently. Usually includes features beyond simple editing, such as formatting and arranging text and graphics to create attractive documents, as well as the ability to merge documents for form letters and envelopes.

Wordwrap Automatic placement of a word on the next line. When you type text and reach the right margin or indent, Word checks to see if the entire word you type fits on the current line. If not, Word automatically places the entire word on the next line.

WYSIWYG (What You See Is What You Get) application Indicates a document will print with the same formatting that is displayed in the document window.

Glossary

Absolute reference A cell reference that contains a dollar sign before the column letter and/or row number to indicate the absolute, or fixed, contents of specific cells. For example, the formula $A$1+$B$1 calculates only the sum of these specific cells.

Active cell The current location of the cell pointer.

Address The location of a specific cell or range expressed by the coordinates of column and row; for example, A1.

Alignment The horizontal placement of cell contents; for example, left, center, or right.

Anchors Cells listed in a range address. For example, in the formula =SUM(A1:A15), A1 and A15 are anchors.

Area chart A line chart in which each area is given a solid color or pattern to emphasize the relationship between the pieces of charted information.

Argument A value, range of cells, or text used in a macro or function. An argument is enclosed in parentheses; for example, =SUM(A1..B1).

Arithmetic operator A symbol used in formulas, such as + or −.

Attribute The styling features such as bold, italics, and underlining that can be applied to cell contents.

AutoCalculate box The area in the status bar which displays the sum (or function of your choice) of the values in the selected range.

AutoComplete A feature that automatically completes labels entered in adjoining cells in a column.

AutoFill A feature that creates a series of text or numbers when a range is selected using the fill handle.

AutoFit Changes the width a column to accommodate its widest entry.

AutoFormat Preset schemes which can be applied to instantly format a range. Excel comes with sixteen AutoFormats which include colors, fonts, and numeric formatting.

Background color The color applied to the background of a cell.

Bar chart The bar chart displays information as the series of (horizontal) bars.

Border Edges of a selected area of a worksheet. Lines and color can be applied to borders.

Cancel button The X in the formula bar, the Cancel button removes information from the formula bar and restores the previous cell entry.

Cascading menu A subgroup of related commands that display beside a drop-down menu.

Cell The intersection of a column and row.

Cell address Unique location identified by intersecting column and row coordinates.

Cell pointer A highlighted rectangle around a cell that indicates the active cell.

Cell reference The address or name of a specific cell; cell references can be used in formulas and are relative or absolute.

Chart A graphic representation of selected worksheet information. Types include 2-D and 3-D column, bar, pie, area, and line charts.

Chart title The name assigned to a chart.

Chart Wizard A series of dialog boxes which helps create or modify a chart.

Check box A square box in a dialog box that can be clicked to turn an option on or off.

Clear A command used to erase a cell's contents, formatting, or both.

Clipboard A temporary storage area for cut or copied items that are available for pasting.

Close A command that puts a file away but keeps Excel open so that you can continue to work on other workbooks.

Column chart The default chart type in Excel. The column chart displays information as a series of (vertical) columns.

Column selector button The gray box containing the column letter above the column.

Conditional format The format of a cell is based on its value or outcome of a formula.

Confirm button The check mark in the formula bar, the Confirm button is used to confirm an entry.

Control menu box A box in the upper-left corner of a window used to resize or close a window.

Copy A command that copies the selected information and places it on the Clipboard.

Cut A command that removes the contents from a selected area of a worksheet and places them on the Clipboard.

Data marker Visible representation of a data point, such as a bar or pie slice.

Data point Individual piece of data plotted in a chart.

Data series The selected range in a worksheet that Excel converts into a graphic and displays as a chart.

Delete A command that removes cell contents from a worksheet.

Delete records A command that removes records from a list.

Dialog box A window that displays when you choose a command whose name is followed by an ellipsis (...). A dialog box allows you to make selections that determine how the command affects the selected area.

Drop-down menu A group of related commands located under a single word on the menu bar. For example, basic commands (New, Open, Save, Close, and Print) are grouped on the File menu.

Dummy column/row Blank column or row included at the end of a range which enables a formula to adjust when columns or rows are added or deleted.

Edit A change made to the contents of a cell or worksheet.

Electronic spreadsheet A computer program that performs calculations on data and organizes information. A spreadsheet is divided into columns and rows, which form individual cells.

Ellipsis A series of dots (...) indicating that more choices are available through dialog boxes.

Exploding pie slice A slice of a pie chart which has been pulled away from a pie to add emphasis.

Fill Down A command that duplicates the contents of the selected cells in the range selected below the cell pointer.

Fill handle Small square in the lower-right corner of the active cell used to copy cell contents.

Fill Right A command that duplicates the contents of the selected cells in the range selected to the right of the cell pointer.

Find A command used to locate information the user specifies.

Find & Replace A command used to find one set of criteria and replace it with new information.

Floating toolbar A toolbar within its own window; not anchored along an edge of the worksheet.

Folder A section of a disk used to store workbooks, much like a folder in a file cabinet.

Font The typeface used to display information in cells.

Format The appearance of text and numbers, including color, font, attributes, and worksheet defaults. *See also* number format.

Formula A set of instructions that you enter in a cell to perform numeric calculations (adding, multiplying, averaging, etc.); for example, +A1+B1.

Formula bar The area below the menu bar and above the Excel workspace where you enter and edit data in a worksheet cell. The formula bar becomes active when you start typing or editing cell data. The formula bar includes an Enter button and a Cancel button.

Freeze The process of making columns or rows visible.

Function A special predefined formula that provides a shortcut for commonly used calculations; for example, AVERAGE.

Gridlines Horizontal and/or vertical lines within a chart which makes the chart easier to read.

Input Information which produces desired results in a worksheet.

Insertion point Blinking I-beam which appears in the formula bar during entry and editing.

Label Descriptive text or other information that identify the rows and columns of a worksheet. Labels are not included in calculations.

Label prefix A character that identifies an entry as a label and controls the way it is displayed in the cell.

Landscape orientation Printing on a page whose dimensions are 11" (horizontally) by 8½" (vertically).

Launch To open a software program so you can use it.

Legend A key explaining the information represented by colors or patterns in a chart.

Line chart A graph of data that is mapped by a series of lines. Line charts show changes in data or categories of data over time and can be used to document trends.

Menu bar The area under the title bar on a window. The menu bar provides access to most of the application's commands.

Mode indicator A box located at the lower-left corner of the status bar that informs you of the program's status. For example, when Excel is performing a task, the work "Wait" displays.

Mouse pointer A symbol that indicates the current location of the mouse on the desktop. The mouse pointer changes shapes at times; for example, when you insert data, select a range, position a chart, change the size of a window, or select a topic in Help.

Name box The left-most area in the formula bar that shows the name or address of the area currently selected. For example, A1 refers to cell A1 of the current worksheet.

Number format A format applied to values to express numeric concepts, such as currency, date, and percent.

Object A chart or graphic image which can be moved and resized and contains handles when selected.

Office Assistant Animated help assistant that provides tips based on your work habits and lets you ask questions. The Assistant's appearance can be changed and has sounds and animation features.

Open A command that retrieves a workbook from a disk and displays it on the screen.

Order of precedence The order in which Excel calculates parts of a formula: (1) exponents, (2) multiplication and division, and (3) addition and subtraction.

Output The end result of a worksheet.

Pane A column or row which always remains visible.

Paste A command that moves information on the Clipboard to a new location. Excel pastes the formulas, rather than the result unless the Paste Special command is used.

Paste function A series of dialog boxes that lists and describes all Excel functions and assists the user in function creation.

Paste Special A command that enables you to paste formulas as values, styles, or cell contents.

Pie chart A circular chart that displays data as slices of pie. A pie chart is useful for showing the relationship of parts to a whole; pie slices can be extracted for emphasis.

Point A unit of measure used for fonts and row height. One inch equals 72 points.

Print Preview window A window that displays a reduced view of area to be printed.

Program Software, such as Excel or Word, that enables you to perform a certain type of task, such as data calculations or word processing.

Program Manager The main control program of Windows. All Windows applications are started from the Program Manager.

Program Menu The Windows 95 Start menu that lists all the available programs on your computer.

Radio button A circle in a dialog box that can be clicked when only one option can be chosen.

Random Access Memory (RAM) A temporary storage area in a computer that is erased each time the computer is turned off or whenever there is a fluctuation in power. When a program is launched, it is loaded into RAM so you can work with that program.

Range A selected group of adjacent cells.

Range format A format applied to a selected range in a worksheet.

Range name A name applied to a selected range in a worksheet.

Relative cell reference Used to indicate a relative position in the worksheet. This allows you to copy and move formulas from one area to another of the same dimensions. Excel automatically changes the column and row numbers to reflect the new position.

Row height The vertical dimension of a cell.

Row selector button The gray box containing the row number to the left of the row.

Save A command used to save incremental changes to a workbook.

Save As A command used to create a duplicate of the current workbook.

Scroll bars Bars that display on the right and bottom borders of the worksheet window that give you access to information not currently visible in the current worksheet as well as others in the workbook.

Selection handles Small boxes appearing along the corners and sides of charts and graphic images which are used for moving and resizing.

Series of labels Pre-programmed series, such as days of the week and months of the year. Formed by typing the first word of the series, then dragging the fill handle to the desired cell.

Sheet A term used for worksheet.

Sheet tab Indicates the sheets contained in a workbook and their names.

Sheet tab scrolling buttons Enable you to move among sheets within a workbook.

Spell check A command that attempts to match all text in a worksheet with the words in the Excel dictionary.

Status bar Located at the bottom of the Excel window, this area lets you know information about various keys, commands, and processes.

Start To open a software program so you can use it.

Start button The rectangular button at the left end of the taskbar which displays the Windows 95 menus.

Taskbar The gray bar, usually at the bottom of the screen, containing the Start button, as well as program buttons for all programs currently running.

Text annotations Labels added to a chart to draw attention to a particular area.

Text color The color applied to the text within a cell.

Title bar The bar at the top of the window that displays the name given a workbook when it is saved and named.

Tick marks Notations of a scale of measure within a chart axis.

Toggle button A button that can be clicked to turn an option on. Clicking again turns the option off.

Tool A picture on a toolbar that represents a shortcut for performing an Excel task. For example, you can click the Save tool to save a file.

Toolbar An area within the Excel screen which contains tools. Toolbars can be docked against a worksheet edge or can float.

Values Numbers, formulas, or functions used in calculations.

What-if analysis Decision-making feature in which data is changed and automatically recalculated.

Window A framed area of a screen. Each worksheet occupies a window.

Workbook A collection of related worksheets contained within a single file.

Worksheet An electronic spreadsheet containing 256 columns by 16,384 rows.

Worksheet tab A description at the bottom of each worksheet that identified it in a workbook. In an open workbook, move to a worksheet by clicking its tab.

Worksheet window The workbook area in which data is entered.

X-axis The horizontal line in a chart.

X-axis label A label describing the x-axis of a chart.

Y-axis The vertical line in a chart.

Y-axis label A label describing the y-axis of a chart.

Zoom Enables you to focus on a larger or smaller part of the worksheet in print preview.

Excel 97

Glossary

Active cell A selected cell in a Graph datasheet.

Adjustment handle A small diamond positioned next to a resize handle that changes the dimension of an object.

Annotation A freehand drawing on the screen using the Annotation tool. You can annotate only in Slide Show view.

AutoContent wizard Helps you get your presentation started by creating a sample outline using information you provide.

AutoLayout A predesigned slide layout that contains placeholder layouts for titles, main text, clip art, graphs, and charts.

Background The area behind the text and graphics of your slide.

Bullet A small graphic symbol, often used to identify a line of text in a list.

Cell A rectangle in a Graph datasheet where you enter data.

Chart The component of a graph that graphically portrays your Graph datasheet information.

Clip Art Professionally designed pictures that come with PowerPoint.

Color scheme The basic eight colors that make up a PowerPoint presentation. For example, a color scheme has a separate color for text, lines, and background color. You can change the color scheme on any presentation at any time.

Common Tasks toolbar A toolbar that contains buttons for common tasks performed in PowerPoint.

Control boxes The gray boxes located along the left and top of a Graph datasheet.

Crop Hides part of a picture or object using the Cropping tool.

Data label Information that identifies the data in a column or row.

Data series A column or row of the datasheet.

Data series marker Graphical representation of a data series, such as a bar or column.

Datasheet The component of a graph that contains the information you want to display on your Graph chart.

Design Templates Prepared slide designs with formatting and color schemes that you can apply to an open presentation.

Dialog box A box that displays the available command options for you to review or change.

Drive The mechanism in a computer that turns a disk to retrieve and store information. Personal computers often have one hard drive labeled C and two drives labeled A and B that read removable floppy disks.

Drawing toolbar A toolbar that contains buttons that let you create lines and shapes.

Embedded object An object that is created in another application but is stored in PowerPoint. Embedded objects maintain a link to their original application for easy editing.

Folder A subdivision of a disk that works like a filing system to help you organize files.

Formatting toolbar The toolbar that contains buttons for the most frequently used formatting commands, such as font type and size.

Gallery A visual index that stores the PowerPoint clip art into categories.

Graph The datasheet and chart you create to graphically display information.

Grid Evenly spaced horizontal and vertical lines that do not appear on the slide.

Keyword A word you use to quickly find an object.

Main text Sub points or bullet points under a title in Outline view.

Main text placeholder A reserved box on a slide for the main text points.

Master text placeholder The placeholder on the Slide Master that controls the formatting and placement of the Main text placeholder on each slide. If you modify the Master text placeholder, each Main text placeholder is affected in the entire presentation.

Master title placeholder The placeholder on the Slide Master that controls the formatting and placement of the Title placeholder on each slide. If you modify the Master title placeholder, each Title placeholder is affected in the entire presentation.

Menu bar The horizontal bar below the title bar that contains the PowerPoint commands. Click a menu name to display a list of commands.

Object The component you place or draw on a slide. Objects are drawn lines and shapes, text, clip art, imported pictures, and embedded objects.

Office Assistant An animated character that provides online Help.

Organizational chart A diagram of connected boxes that shows reporting structure.

Outline view Displays the titles and main text of all the slides in your presentation.

Outlining toolbar The toolbar that contains buttons for the most used outlining commands, such as moving and indenting text lines.

Placeholder A dashed line box where you place text or objects.

PowerPoint Viewer A special application designed to run a PowerPoint slide show on any compatible computer that does not have PowerPoint installed.

PowerPoint window A window that contains the running PowerPoint application. The PowerPoint window displays the PowerPoint menus, toolbars, and Presentation window.

Presentation graphics application A software program used to organize and present information.

Presentation window The area or "canvas" where you work and view your presentation. You type text and work with objects in the Presentation window.

Scroll To move within a window to see more of the window contents.

Selection box A slanted line border that appears around a text object or placeholder indicating it is ready to accept text.

Sizing handle The small square at each corner of a selected object. Dragging a resize handle resizes the object.

Slide icon A symbol that appears next to a slide in Outline view.

Slide Indicator box A small box that appears when you drag the elevator in Slide and Note Pages view. This box identifies which slide you are on.

Slide miniature A reduced color version of the current slide that appears in a small window.

Stacking order The order in which objects are placed on the slide. The first object placed on the slide is on the bottom while the last object placed on the slide is on the top.

Standard toolbar The row of buttons, or toolbar, that perform the most frequently used commands, such as copy and paste.

Status bar Located at the bottom of the PowerPoint window, it displays messages about what you are doing and seeing in PowerPoint, such as the current slide number or a description of a command or button.

Text box A box within a dialog box where you type information needed to carry out a command.

Text object Any text you create with the Text Tool or enter into a placeholder. Once you enter text into a placeholder, the placeholder becomes a text object.

Text label A text object you create with the Text Tool that does not automatically wrap text inside a box.

Timing The time a slide stays on the screen during a slide show.

PowerPoint 97

Title   The first line or heading in Outline view.

Title bar   The horizontal bar at the top of the window that displays the name of the document or the application.

Title placeholder   A reserved box on a slide for a presentation or slide title.

Title slide   The first slide in your presentation.

Toggle button   A button that turns a feature on and off.

Toolbar   A graphical bar with buttons that performs certain PowerPoint commands, such as opening and saving.

Transition   The effect that moves one slide off the screen and the next slide on the screen during a slide show. Each slide can have its own transition effect.

TrueType font   A font that can be displayed or printed at any size.

Window   A rectangle area on your screen where you view and work on presentations.

Wizard   A guided approach that steps you through a task.

Word processing box   A text object you draw with the Text Tool that automatically wraps text inside a box.

Access 97

AND and OR criteria   Parameters used to qualify records selected in a query or filter. AND is used to narrow the number of selected records, whereas OR is used to broaden the number of selected records.

Ascending order   A sort order in which fields are alphabetized from A to Z.

AutoNumber field   Counts records in a table; this field automatically increases by one to create consecutive, unique numbers.

AutoReport   Button that automatically creates a report that displays all fields in a single-column format.

Bound control   A control on a form that is linked to a specific field in the database. *See also* Control.

Calculated control   A control that has a mathematical expression as its data source.

Cell   The intersection of a column and a row.

Control   A graphical object that consists of the field text and the data in it. Controls are either bound, unbound, or calculated.

Counter field   A field that automatically assigns the next consecutive number each time a record is added.

Criteria   Qualifications that determine whether a record is chosen for a filter or query.

Data   The information contained in a database table.

Database   A collection of data related to a particular topic or purpose.

Database window   The window that opens when you start Access. It provides access to the objects in the database.

Datasheet   A grid in which each record is contained in a row, and field names are listed as column headings. You enter data for a table in the datasheet.

Datasheet View   A window that displays records in a grid format of columns and rows, which you can use to navigate through the records quickly.

Data type   Determines the type of data a field contains, such as text, dates, or numbers.

Descending order   A sort order in which fields are alphabetized from Z to A.

Design View   A window that shows the structure of a table, form, query, or report. You use this view to modify the structure of a table by adding and deleting fields and adding field descriptions and field properties.

Detail   Section of a form that appears on the screen form and displays the fields and data for each record visible in Design View. Detail section also appears in Report Design window, in which you can make modifications to the format of a report.

Dynaset   Collection of records resulting from a query; looks and acts like a table, but is merely a view based on the query.

Expression A mathematical equation created within a form or report's control.

Expression Builder A feature that displays helpful fields and mathematical symbols you use to create expressions.

Field Category of information in a database table, such as a customer's last name.

Field description Optional text that clarifies the purpose or function of a field. The field description appears in the status bar when you enter data.

Field label Describes the contents in a field value text box.

Field properties Information you can define that affects the data entered in a field, such as the number of decimal places in a number. You define field properties in the Design view.

Filter window A window that consists of two areas: the field list on top, containing all the fields in the table, and the filter grid on the bottom, into which fields are dragged and filtering criteria are defined.

Filtering A more complex method of organizing records, in which you define the fields on which the table is sorted.

Form An object used to enter, edit, and display records one at a time.

Form Footer A section of a form that appears at the bottom of each screen form and can contain totals, instructions, or command buttons.

Form Header A section of a form that appears at the beginning of each screen form and can contain a title or logo.

Form View Screen in which table data can be viewed, entered, or changed one record at a time.

Form Wizard A feature that guides you through the process of creating a form by providing sample form layouts and form-specific options.

Function An easy-to-use preprogrammed mathematical equation that can be used in forms and reports to make calculations.

Graphic image Artwork in an electronic format.

Handles Black squares that appear around the perimeter of a control, indicating the control is selected.

Help On-line system that gives you immediate access to definitions, explanations, and useful tips as they related to Access.

Input Materials necessary to produce the results you want.

Label Wizard Allows easy creation of labels using Avery products and table fields.

Mouse pointer An arrow indicating the location of the mouse on the desktop. The mouse pointer changes shape at times, depending on the application and task being executed or performed.

Object The principal component of an Access database. Tables, queries, forms, and reports are all referred to as objects in Access.

Object buttons Buttons on the left side of the database window that allow you to open, create, and modify database components.

Office Assistant Animated help assistant that provides tips based on your work habits and lets you ask questions. The Assistant's appearance can be changed and has sounds and animation features.

Output The desired results of a database, often printed reports or screen forms.

Page Footer Material that appears at the bottom of each page in printed output.

Page Header Material that appears at the top of each page in printed output.

Primary key A field that qualifies each record as unique. If you do not specify a primary key, Access will create one for you.

Print Preview A window that displays a view of how a page will appear when printed.

Property Quality or characteristic of a control that makes data entry more efficient.

Property Sheet A window that displays the control's name and source and that lists the qualities for the selected control that can be edited.

Query A set of qualities, or criteria, that you specify to retrieve certain data from a database. You can save a query to use at a later time.

Query grid Area in which fields and query instructions are contained.

Record A group of related fields, such as all information on a particular customer.

Relational database A database that contains more than one table and allows information within its tables to be shared.

Report An Access object that presents data selected and formatted for printing.

Report Footer Material that appears at the bottom of the last printed page of a report.

Report Header Material that appears at the top of the first printed page of a report.

Report Wizard A feature that guides you through the process of creating a report by providing sample report layouts and options for including specific fields in the report.

Row selector A gray box at the left edge of a datasheet that is used to select an entire row.

Select query A query that created a dynaset in which records are collected and viewed, and can be modified.

Shortcut keys A key or key combination that allows you to select a command without using the menu bar or toolbar.

Sort A feature that organizes records from A to Z or Z to A, based on one or more fields in a table or query.

Source document The document from which information will be copied into the clipboard.

Startup window The window that appears when you start Access; the area from which you carry out database operations.

Status bar A horizontal bar at the bottom of the screen that displays information about commands or actions and descriptions of ToolTips.

Tab order Determines the order in which you advance from one field to the next when you press [Tab] to enter data in a form.

Table A collection of related records in a database.

Table Wizard A feature that guides you through the process of creating a simple table, prompting you to choose from a variety of fields and options.

Toolbar A horizontal bar with buttons that provide access to the most commonly used Access commands.

Unbound control A control that is entirely stored in the design of a form or report. There is no link to data in a table. For example, a title above a group of controls is an unbound control.

Wildcards Symbols that can be used to substitute for characters in text.

Wizard A feature that provides a series of dialog boxes that guide you through the process of creating a table, form, report, query, or other Access object; unique to Microsoft products.

Internet

Glossary

Absolute link A link that contains only a fixed address. *See also* relative link.

Dynamic HTML page A Web page that is linked to the original file from which it was created, allowing it to reflect subsequent changes to that file. *See also* Static HTML page.

Favorites The Internet Explorer feature that allows you to create a list of Web pages you often view.

Frames Web page display format showing different parts of the page divided by borders, making navigating a group of pages easier.

Home page The main page of a Web publication.

Hyperlink A highlighted word, phrase, or graphic that opens another Web page when you click it. Also called a link.

Hypertext Markup Language (HTML) The language used to describe the content and format of pages on the World Wide Web.

Internet A worldwide communications system that connects computer networks from all over the world.

Internet Explorer A popular Web browser from Microsoft that comes with Microsoft Office 97.

Intranet A private network that uses Internet communications technologies.

Key word A word or phrase describing a topic of interest, from which a search engine generates a list of related links.

Link A highlighted word, phrase, or graphic that opens another Web page when you click it. Also called a hyperlink.

Network Two or more computers that can share information.

Publish To make Web pages available to a wide audience on an intranet or on the Internet.

Relative link A link that gives another page's address in relation to the location of the current page. *See also* absolute link.

Search engine An index of information on the Web that provides a list of links related to your topic of interest. *See also* key word.

Static HTML page A Web page containing only the information from which the file was originally created. *See also* dynamic HTML page.

Surf the Web To explore the Web by clicking successive links that interest you.

Tags Formatting codes surrounding each element in an HTML document. Describe how the element should be displayed in a Web browser.

Uniform Resource Locator (URL) The address, or location, of a Web page on the World Wide Web.

Web browser A software program used to access and display Web pages. *See also* Internet Explorer.

Web page A document that is part of the World Wide Web. Also called a Web document.

Web publication A group of associated Web pages dealing with a particular theme or topic.

Word Web The Web editing tool that comes with Word 97.

World Wide Web A part of the Internet that contains Web pages or Web documents that are linked together. Also called the Web, the WWW.

Glossary

Calendar The Outlook tool that allows you to schedule your appointments and events.

Cc: An abbreviation for Carbon Copy or Courtesy Copy, which is a copy of a message you send or receive.

Contacts The Outlook tool that allows you to manage your contacts information.

Deleted Items folder A folder that contains items you have deleted. Deleted items remain in the folder when you exit the Outlook application.

Delivered Report The message you receive informing you that a message you sent has been delivered.

Directory A collection of names to whom you can send messages. The Global Address List and your Personal Address Book are examples of directories.

E-mail A popular abbreviation for electronic mail.

Electronic mail software Software that lets you send and receive electronic messages over a network.

Folder A storage location for items such as the Inbox folder or the Deleted Items folder. You can also create your own folders where you can store messages.

Folder banner The horizontal bar beneath the toolbar that displays the name of the open folder to the left and the icon of the open folder to the right.

Global Address List A list that contains the names of users to whom you can send messages on your electronic mail system.

Importance The priority level you assign to a message, indicated with an icon.

Inbox folder A folder that contains mail messages you have received.

Journal The Outlook tool that tracks the history of your activities on a timeline.

Message A form of communication you send or receive from other electronic mail users.

Message header Identifies the sender of the message, the subject, and the date and time the message was received.

Network A group of computers connected to each other with cables and software to allow users to share applications, disk storage, printers, and send and receive electronic messages from one another.

Notes The Outlook tool that is the electronic equivalent of the popular paper sticky notes.

Outlook Bar Navigation bar on the left side of the Outlook window containing the most frequently used folders arranged into groups.

Personal Address Book A collection of names with whom you frequently communicate using electronic mail.

Personal Distribution List A collection of names to whom you regularly send the same message, listed as one e-mail address in your Personal Address Book.

Re: An abbreviation for reference, which identifies the subject of the message.

Read Report The message you receive informing you that a message you sent has been read.

Tasks The Outlook tool that serves as an electronic to-do list.

TaskPad The portion of the Calendar window that displays the task list from Tasks.

Index

A

absolute cell references
    copying formulas with, EX B-14-15
    defined, EX B-14
absolute hyperlinks, IE B-16
absolute links, IE4 B-16
Access 97, OF A-2
    basics, AC A-1-17
    closing, AC A-16-17
    creating and managing data in, AC B-1-17
    creating Web publications, IE B-10-11
    entering and editing records, AC A-10-11
    exporting tables to Excel, IN B-6-7
    exporting tables to Word, IN B-7
    features, OF A-8-9
    Help, AC A-14-15
    merging data with Word, IN B-2-5
    opening table database in, AC A-8-9
    previewing and printing, AC A-12-13
    starting, AC A-4-5
    startup window, AC A-6-7
Access 97 window
    elements of, AC A-6
    File menu, AC A-7
    viewing, AC A-6-7
Accessories menu, W A-6-7
active cells, EX A-6
    in Microsoft Graph, PP C-6
Active Desktop, W98 8-11
Active Desktop Gallery, W98 11
ActiveMovie, W98 15
active programs, I A-2, I A-3
active window, WD B-7
address bar
    in Internet Explorer 3, IE A-6-7
    Internet Explorer 4, IE4 A-6-7
Address Books, OL A-10, OL A-16-19
Address toolbar, Windows 98, W98 6
Advanced Filter/Sort, AC B-12
Align command, in PowerPoint, PP C-8-9
alignment
    in charts, EX D-13

of fields in reports, AC D-6-7
of labels, EX A-10, EX C-6-7
of multiple program windows, I A-2-3
of objects, PP C-8-9
paragraph, WD C-8-9
with tabs, WD C-6-7
of text, WD A-2
of values, EX A-10
All Fields button, AC C-2
Analyze It with MS Excel, IN B-6
AND criteria, in complex queries, AC B-16, AC B-17
animation effects, for slides, PP C-16-17
Animation tab, Font dialog box, WD C-4
annotation
    of charts, EX D-14-15
    of slides, PP C-12
annotation pen, PP C-12-13
applications, defined, W A-2
Apply Filter button, AC B-12
appointments, managing, OF A-12
area charts, EX D-3
arguments, in functions, EX B-8
arithmetic operators
    in criteria, AC B-16
    in formulas, EX B-6
ARPANET, IE4 A-4
Arrow button, on Drawing toolbar, EX D-14
arrows, for charts, EX D-14-15
ascending sort order, WD D-10, AC B-11-12
asterisk (*) wildcard, in Find command, AC B-9
attributes
    of labels, EX C-6-7
    replacing, PP C-13
    in slides, PP C-12-13
AutoAddress, in Contacts, OL AP-4
AutoComplete feature, WD C-8
AutoContent Wizard, PP A-6-7, PP A-14
    dialog box, PP A-6-7
AutoCorrect, WD A-2, WD A-9, PP C-16-17
    dialog box, PP C-16-17
AutoDial, in Contacts, OL AP-4
AutoFit, EX C-8

AutoFit Selection, IN B-6
AutoForm, AC C-3
AutoFormat, EX C-7
AutoJournal, OL AP-6
AutoLayout, PP B-4-5
    creating slides with, PP B-8-9
    defined, PP B-4
    placeholder types, PP B-9
AutoName, in Contacts, OL AP-4
AutoNumber data type, AC B-7
AutoNumber field, AC A-10
AutoReport, AC D-3
AutoShapes, PP C-4
AutoSum, EX B-8-9
AutoSummarize, WD A-3
AutoText, WD A-3
AutoText entries
    built-in, inserting, WD A-11
    defined, WD A-10
AVERAGE function, EX B-8
Avery labels, printing, AC D-16

B

Back button, IE4 A-8
Background dialog box, PP C-14
backgrounds
    for slides, PP C-14-15
    transparent, PP C-4
    for Web pages, IE4 B-8, IE B-8, IE B-12, IE B-14
background wallpaper, Web pages as, W98 8-10
backups, for databases, AC B-3
bar charts, EX D-3
black and white, viewing presentations in, PP A-17
.bmp format, PP C-5
Bold, Extra, AC C-10
Bold button, WD C-2, WD D-12
    on Formatting toolbar, EX C-6-7
borders, WD C-16-17
    around cells in tables, WD D-2
    creating, WD C-17
    defined, WD C-16
    for tables, IN C-4

Index

for Web pages, IE4 B-6

for worksheets, EX C-12-13

Borders button list arrow, EX C-12

Borders and Shading dialog box, IN C-4-5

bound controls, AC C-4

adding expressions to, AC D-10

browsers. *See* Web browsers

browsing, OF A-14, OF A-15

Build button, AC C-8

built-in AutoText entries, WD A-11

built-in formulas, for table calculations in Word, WD D-8-9

bulleted lists, WD C-14-15

in Outline View, PP B-10-11

slide show animation effects, PP C-16

in Web pages, IE4 B-4, IE4 B-6

bullets, defined, WD C-14

Bullets and Numbering dialog box, WD C-14

►C

calculated controls, AC C-4

calculations

built-in formulas, WD D-8-9

creating, WD D-9

of table data, in Word, WD D-8-9

Calendar, OL AP-2-3

camera icon, WD B-8, WD B-9, PP C-8-9

Cancel button, in Excel, EX B-4

capitalization errors, AutoCorrect for, PP C-16-17

cascading menu, W A-6-7

case-sensitivity, in Uniform Resource Locators (URLs), IE A-8

cell addresses, EX A-6

cell markers, WD D-2

cell pointer, EX A-6

cell references, WD D-9

absolute, EX B-14-15

defined, EX B-6

relative, EX B-12-13

cells

active, EX A-6

borders around, WD D-2

copying contents of, EX B-10-11

defined, OF A-6, EX A-6, PP C-6

editing contents of, EX B-4-5

formatting, EX C-2

in Microsoft Graph, PP C-6

moving contents of, EX B-10

center alignment, WD C-8

Center button, on Formatting toolbar, WD D-12, WD D-16, EX C-6-7

Channel Bar, W98 11

channel list, customizing, W98 11

character spacing, adjusting, WD C-4

Character Spacing tab, WD C-4

Chart AutoLayout, PP C-6

Chart Formatting toolbar, PP C-10

Chart Options dialog box, EX D-10, EX D-11

chart placeholders, PP C-6-7

charts, EX D-1-17

alignment in, EX D-13

arrows for, EX D-14-15

changing appearance of, EX D-10-11

creating, EX A-2, EX D-4-5

customizing, in Microsoft Graph, PP C-11

editing, EX D-8-9

embedding in slides, PP C-6-7, IN C-6-7

enhancing, EX D-12-13

entering and editing data for, PP C-8-9

fonts in, EX D-13

formatting, PP C-10-11

in graph objects, PP C-6-7

gridlines on, EX D-10

moving, EX D-6-7

planning and designing, EX D-2-3

previewing, EX D-16

printing, EX D-16

resizing, EX D-6-7

results of, EX D-3

rotating, EX D-9

selecting ranges for, EX D-4

text annotations for, EX D-14-15

types of, EX D-3, EX D-8-9

value of, EX D-1, EX D-3

X- and Y axis titles, EX D-12-13

Chart toolbar, editing charts with, EX D-8-9

Chart Type, EX D-8, EX D-9

Chart Wizard, EX D-4-5

check boxes, in dialog boxes, W A-13

circles, creating in PowerPoint, PP C-4

clicking, with mouse, W A-4, W A-5

clip art

cropping, PP C-4-5

defined, PP C-2

galleries, PP C-2

importing into Clip Gallery, PP C-3

in presentations, PP C-2-3

previewing, PP C-2

sizing, PP C-2

clip art placeholder, PP C-2

Clipboard

copying information from with Paste Special, I A-6

copying objects to, W B-8-9

copying text with, WD B-6

defined, W B-8

embedding objects from with Paste Special, IN C-7

moving text with, WD B-8

Clip Gallery

dialog box, PP C-3

importing clip art into, PP C-3

opening, PP C-2

Close button, W A-18, W A-19

exiting PowerPoint with, PP A-16-17

exiting Word with, WD A-16

Close command

Internet Explorer 3, IE A-18

Internet Explorer 4, IE4 A-18-19

color

of fonts in slides, PP C-12

in worksheets, EX C-12-13

Color list arrow, for formatting text, WD C-4

color palette, in Paint, W B-4

color presentations, PP B-16, PP B-17

viewing in black and white, PP A-17

Color Scheme dialog box, PP C-14

color schemes, for slides, PP C-14-15

Columnar layout, for forms, AC C-2

column charts, EX D-3

Column command, EX C-8

columns

customizing with Draw Table button, WD D-14-15

distributing evenly, WD D-16

dummy, EX C-11

inserting and deleting, WD D-6-7, EX C-10-11

moving, AC A-10

sorting by, WD D-10-11

sorting by more than one, WD D-11

Column Standard Width dialog box, EX C-8

column width, in worksheets, changing, EX C-8-9

Column Width dialog box, EX C-8

combination charts, EX D-3

command buttons, in dialog boxes, W A-13

Comma Style button, on Formatting toolbar, EX C-2

comments, in slides, PP C-11

Common Tasks toolbar, PowerPoint, PP A-8-9

communications software, Windows 98, W98 15

complex queries, AC B-16-17

conditional formatting, in worksheets, EX C-14-15

Conditional Formatting dialog box, EX C-14-15

Contacts, OF A-12, OF A-13, OL AP-4-5

Contemporary template, PP B-4-5

control headings, AC D-6-7

Control Panel, W A-10-11

controls

    bound, AC C-4

    calculated, AC C-4

    for database forms, AC A-2

    defined, AC C-4

    deleting, AC C-10

    formatting, AC C-10-11

    handles on, AC C-4

    resizing, AC D-8-9

    unbound, AC C-4

Copy button, on Standard toolbar, WD B-6, I A-4

copying

    cell contents, EX B-10-11

    with drag-and-drop, I A-4, I A-5

    files, W B-15

    files, using My Computer, W B-14-15

    formatting, with Format Painter, WD C-2

    formulas with absolute cell references, EX B-14-15

    formulas with relative cell references, EX B-12-13

    text, in Word, WD A-2, WD B-6-7

    Word data into Excel, I A-4-5

CourseHelp, WD B-9

criteria

    AND, in queries, AC B-16, AC B-17

    arithmetic operators in, AC B-16

    for filtering tables, AC B-12

    OR, in queries, AC B-16, AC B-17

cropping, pictures in PowerPoint, PP C-4

Currency data type, AC B-7

Currency Style button, EX C-2

▶ **D**

Custom Animation dialog box, PP C-16-17

Custom Order list box, AC C-6

Cut button, WD B-8

Cut command, W B-15

cutting, files, W B-14, W B-15

database management systems, OF A-2

database objects

    object buttons for, AC A-8-9

    types of, AC A-8

databases, *See also* tables

    backups for, AC B-3

    building, AC B-1-17

    complex queries, AC B-16-17

    creating tables, AC B-4-5

    creating Web pages from, IE4 B-10-11

    defined, OF A-2, AC A-2

    filtering tables, AC B-12-13

    finding records in, AC B-6-7

    input for, AC B-2

    modifying tables, AC B-4-5

    naming, AC B-2

    output of, AC B-2

    planning, AC B-2-3

    simple queries, AC B-14-15

    sorting tables, AC B-10-11

    structure, AC A-3

database software, AC A-2-3

Database toolbar, AC A-8

    commands, AC A-6

data labels, in Microsoft Graph, PP C-6

data markers, in charts, EX D-3

data points, in charts, EX D-3

data series

    in charts, EX D-3

    formatted, in charts, EX D-11

    markers, PP C-6

    in Microsoft Graph, PP C-6

datasheets

    defined, AC A-10

    editing data in, PP C-8-9

    entering data into, AC A-10-11, PP C-8-9

    in graph objects, PP C-6-7

    keystrokes for navigating, AC B-8

    previewing, AC A-12-13

    printing, AC A-12-13

    using magnifier pointer with, AC A-12, AC A-13

Datasheet View, viewing query results in, AC B-14, AC B-15, AC B-16

data source, IN B-2

Data Type list arrow, AC B-6

data types, AC B-2, AC B-6, AC B-7

Date Navigator, in Calendar, OL AP-2

Date/Time data type, AC B-6, AC B-7

Date and Time dialog box, WD A-10

DDE. *See* dynamic link exchange (DDE)

Decimal Places box, in Field Properties, AC B-6

Decrease Decimal button, PP C-10

Deleted Items folder, in Outlook, OL A-14

deleting

    controls, AC C-10

    files, W B-10, W B-18-19

    rows and columns in worksheets, EX C-10-11

    shortcuts, W B-20

    text, WD A-10-11

Demote button, on Outlining toolbar, PP B-10

descending sort order, AC B-11-12

    tables, WD D-10, WD D-11

design templates

    creating, PP B-17

    defined, PP B-1

    for presentations, PP B-4-5, PP B-16

Design View

    adding fields to forms in, AC C-12-13

    Detail section, AC C-4

    Form Footer section, AC C-4

    Form Header section, AC C-4

    modifying tables in, AC B-6-7

    viewing query grid in, AC B-14, AC B-16

Design View button, AC C-4

desktop

    Active Desktop, W98 8-11

    defined, W98 2, W A-2

    elements of, W A-3

    managing files on, W B-20-21

    Web components on, W98 10-11

    Windows 98, W98 2-4

Desktop toolbar, Windows 98, W98 6

Details button, on My Computer toolbar, W B-12, W B-13

Details command, on Control Panel View menu, W A-10, W B-12

Detail section, AC C-4
   in reports, AC D-6
   Units control, AC D-8
dialog boxes, W A-12-13
   defined, W A-12
   typical items, in, W A-13
Digital Versatile Disc (DVD) support, in Windows 98,
   W98 15
dimmed commands, on menus, W A-11
disk space, Windows 98 features, W98 15
Distribute Columns Evenly button, WD D-16
docucentric environment, OF A-3
Document Map, WD A-3
documents
   aligning text with tabs, WD C-6-7
   borders, WD C-16-17
   bulleted lists, WD C-14-15
   closing, WD A-16
   creating with Word, OF A-4-5
   deleting text in, WD A-10-11
   entering text in, WD A-8-9
   formatting, WD C-1-17
   inserting graphics in, OF A-4-5
   inserting text in, WD A-10-11
   numbered lists, WD C-14-15
   opening in Word, WD B-4-5
   paragraph alignment, WD C-8-9
   paragraph indention, WD C-10-11
   paragraph spacing, WD C-12-13
   planning, WD B-2-3
   printing, WD A-16
   Print Preview, WD A-16-17
   replacing text in, WD A-12-13
   saving, WD A-8-9
   saving with new name, WD B-4-5
   shading, WD C-16-17
   special effects in, OF A-4-5
   tone of, WD B-2
document window
   Internet Explorer 3, IE A-6-7
   Internet Explorer 4, IE4 A-6-7
   Word, WD A-6-7
DOS file extension settings, changing, PP A-13
double arrow mouse pointer shape, PP C-4
double-clicking
   with mouse, W A-4, W A-5
   to put Excel in edit mode, EX B-4

drag-and-drop, W A-4, W A-5
   for copying cell contents in worksheets, EX B-10-11
   copying information from source file to target file
     with, I A-4, I A-5
drawing area, in Paint, W B-4
drawing objects
   aligning, PP C-8-9
   creating, PP C-4-5
   editing, PP C-6-7
   grouping, PP C-8-9
   in PowerPoint, PP C-4-5
   of stacking order, PP C-9
Drawing toolbar, EX D-14, PP A-8, PP C-4-5
   buttons, PP C-5
Draw Table button, in Word 97, WD C-16, WD D-14-15
drop shadows, in chart titles, EX D-12
dummy rows and columns, in worksheets, EX C-11
dynamic HTML pages, IE4 B-11, IE B-11
dynamic link exchange (DDE)
   breaking, I A-7
   creating between Excel and Word, I A-6-7
   defined, I A-6
dynamic links, OF A-2

►E

Edit commands, W B-15
editing, documents in Word, WD B-1-17
Edit mode, in Excel, EX B-4-5
electronic mail (e-mail), OF A-2, OF A-12-13
   basics, OL A-2-3
   creating and sending messages, OL A-10-11,
     OL A-18-19
   emoticons in, OL A-9
   etiquette, OL A-3
   folders for, OL A-6-7, OL A-15
   forwarding messages, OL A-12-13
   Inbox management, OL A-14-15
   personal distribution lists, OL A-16-19
   replying to messages, OL A-8-9
   sorting, OL A-14-15
   Tracking Options, OL A-12-13
electronic spreadsheets, defined, EX A-2
ellipsis, on menus, W A-11
e-mail, sending Web pages as, IE4 A-19, IE A-19
embedding
   charts in slides, PP C-6-7
   defined, OF A-2, PP C-6

Excel charts into PowerPoint slides, IN C-6-7
   vs. linking, IN C-8, IN C-9
   using Paste Special, IN C-7
   Word tables into PowerPoint slides, IN C-4-5
emoticons, in e-mail, OL A-9
end-of-row markers, WD D-2
Engraved formatting, WD C-4
equal sign (=), beginning formulas with, EX B-6
Eraser button, WD D-14
Excel 97, OF A-2, *See also* worksheets
   benefits of, EX A-2
   closing, EX A-16-17
   copying Word data into, I A-4-5
   creating dynamic link (DDE) with Word, I A-6-7
   creating Web pages, IE B-12-13
   embedding charts into PowerPoint slides, IN C-6-7
   features, OF A-6-7
   getting started, EX A-1-17
   Help, EX A-14-15
   importing tables from Access, IN B-6-7
   linking worksheets to PowerPoint slides, IN C-8-9
   opening with Word, I A-2-3
   starting, EX A-4-5
   updating linked worksheets, IN C-10-11
   viewing window, EX A-6-7
   window elements, EX A-6-7
exiting
   Access, AC A-16-17
   Excel, EX A-16-17
   Exit command, W A-18
   Word, WD A-16
Explorer windows
   as browsers, W98 13-14
   defined, W98 11
   links in, W98 12-13
   Web view in, W98 11-13
exporting
   PowerPoint presentations to Word, IN C-12-13
   tables, IN B-6-7
Expression Builder, AC C-8-9
expressions
   adding to reports, AC D-10-11
   defined, AC B-16
   in queries, AC B-16-17
Extra Bold, AC C-10

▶ **F**

F1 key, accessing Office Assistant with, AC A-14

Favorites

adding Web pages to, IE4 A-8-9

folders, IE4 A-8

in Windows 98, W98 7

favorites list

Internet Explorer, IE A-8

organizing, IE A-9

field descriptions

adding to tables, AC B-6-7

defined, AC B-6

field label, AC C-4

Field List button, AC C-12

field properties, AC B-6

fields

adding to forms, AC C-12-13

adding to reports, AC D-10

aligning in reports, AC D-6-7

data types, AC B-2

defined, AC A-2

defining in labels, AC D-17

selecting, AC C-4

field value text box, AC C-4

file extension settings, changing in Windows Explorer

Options dialog box, PP A-13

filenames, long, Windows Explorer settings, PP A-13

files

copying, W B-10, W B-15

using My Computer, W B-14-15

cutting, W B-14, W B-15

deleting, W B-10, W B-18-19

on desktop, W B-20-21

finding, W B-10

hierarchy of, W B-10, W B-11

managing, W B-10-11, W B-20-21

moving

among folders, W B-10

using My Computer, W B-14-15

previewing, W B-10, W B-17

renaming, W B-10

using keyboard, W B-16

restoring, W B-18-19

saving, W B-6-7

searching for, by properties, PP C-3

selecting, W B-15

viewing

in My Computer, W B-12-13

in Windows Explorer, W B-16-17

Files feature, for finding misplaced files, OL AP-6

Fill Color button list arrow, on Formatting toolbar,
EX C-12

Fill Color list arrow, PP C-4, IN C-6

Fill Color palette, EX C-13

Fill with Color tool, in Paint, W B-4

Fill Effects dialog box, IE4 B-8, PP C-14, PP C-15,
IE B-8

fill handles

copying formulas with, EX B-12-13, EX B-14

defined, EX B-12

Fill Series command, EX B-12

filter grid, AC B-12, AC B-13

filtering

criteria for, AC B-12

defined, AC B-12

determining when to use, AC B-12

sorting vs., AC B-12

tables, AC B-12-13

Filter window, AC B-12, AC B-13

Find area, of Open dialog box, searching for files in,
PP C-3

Find Clip dialog box, PP C-3

Find command, in Word, WD B-12

Find feature, W B-10

finding

files with Files feature, OL AP-6

records, in tables, AC B-8-9

and replacing text, in Word, WD B-12-13

find records, using wildcards, AC B-9

Find and Replace dialog box, More button, WD B-12

First Line Indent Marker, WD C-10

flipping, objects, PP C-7

floating toolbars, PP A-8

3 1/2 Floppy (A:) icon, W B-12

floppy disks

defined, W B-2

deleting files from, W B-19

formatting, W B-2-3

saving files on, W B-6-7

folder banner, in Outlook, OL A-6-7

folders

creating, W B-10

creating in My Computer, W B-12-13

for e-mail messages, OL A-6-7, OL A-15

Favorites, IE4 A-8

hierarchy of, W B-10, W B-11

moving files among, W B-10

renaming with Windows Explorer, W B-16-17

selecting, W B-15

for shortcuts, W B-20

font color, EX C-12, PP C-12

Font dialog box, WD C-4-5

Animation tab, WD C-4

Font tab, WD C-4-5

font formatting, WD C-1, WD C-2-3

Font list arrow, WD C-2, PP C-12

fonts

attributes, of labels, EX C-6-7

changing, on worksheets, EX C-4-5

in charts, EX D-13

defined, EX C-4

in presentations, PP B-16, PP B-17

selecting, WD C-2-3

serif vs. sans serif, WD C-3

in slides, PP C-12-13

font size, WD C-2, WD C-4, PP C-12

changing, in Internet Explorer 4, IE4 A-12

Font style list, WD C-4

Font tab, Font dialog box, WD C-4-5

Font Weight, displaying, AC C-10

footers, adding to slides, PP B-13

Format Axis dialog box, EX D-13, PP C-10

Format Cells dialog box, EX C-2-3, EX C-4-5, EX C-6-7,
EX C-12

Format Column commands, EX C-8

Format Data Series dialog box, EX D-11, PP C-11

Format dialog box, W B-2-3

Format Painter, WD C-2, EX C-3

formatting

charts, PP C-10-11

conditional, in worksheets, EX C-14-15

controls, AC C-10-11

copying with Format Painter, WD C-2

defined, EX C-2

floppy disks, W B-2-3

fonts and point sizes, EX C-4-5

Index

options, W B-3

tables, WD D-12-13

text in slides, PP C-12-13

values, EX C-2-3

Web pages, IE B-6-7, IE B-8-9

formatting documents, WD A-2, WD C-1-17

borders, WD C-16-17

bulleted lists, WD C-14-15

font effects, WD C-2-5

fonts, WD C-1

numbered lists, WD C-14-15

paragraphs, WD C-1

alignment, WD C-8-9

indention, WD C-10-11

spacing, WD C-12-13

shading, WD C-16-17

text alignment with tabs, WD C-6-7

Formatting toolbar, EX A-6, EX C-2, EX C-6-7, EX C-12

font effects, WD C-2-3

fonts and styles, EX C-5

formatting changes, WD A-6-7, WD C-8, WD C-9

indenting paragraphs, WD C-10-11

Numbering button, WD C-14

Form Design Toolbar, AC C-12

Form Footer section, AC C-4

Form Header section, AC C-4

forms, OF A-8-9

adding fields to, AC C-12-13

adding graphic images to, AC C-14-15

adding records with, AC C-16-17

changing tab order, AC C-6-7

Columnar layout, AC C-2

creating, AC C-1-17

creating with Form Wizard, AC C-2-3

for databases, AC A-2, AC A-3

Expression Builder, AC C-8-9

formatting controls, AC C-10-11

modifying layout, AC C-4-5

saving as reports, AC D-14-15

formula bar, EX A-6, EX B-6

Formula dialog box, WD D-8-9

formulas

with absolute cell references, copying, EX B-14-15

built-in, for table calculations in Word, WD D-8-9

copying with fill handles, EX B-12-13, EX B-14

defined, EX B-6

entering in worksheets, EX B-6-7

inserting and deleting rows and columns and, EX C-10-11

order of precedence in, EX B-7

with relative cell references, copying, EX B-12-13

Form View

adding graphic images to forms, AC C-14

formatting controls, AC C-10-11

forms displayed in, AC C-6, AC C-7

Form Wizard, AC C-2-3

forwarding, e-mail messages, OL A-12-13

frames

in Web pages, IE B-14, IE B-15

printing, IE4 A-15

pros and cons, IE4 B-13

FrontPage Express, formatting Web pages in, IE4 B-6-7

functions

arguments in, EX B-8

defined, EX B-8-9, AC D-10

▶G

galleries, clip art, PP C-2, PP C-3

grammar correction, in Word, WD A-9, WD B-10-11

graphical user interface (GUI), W A-1

graphics, *See also* pictures

adding to forms, OF A-8-9, AC C-14-15

adding to reports, OF A-8-9

common types, AC C-14

formats, in PowerPoint, PP C-5

inserting in documents, OF A-4-5

in presentations, PP B-16, PP B-17

graph objects

defined, PP C-6

embedding in charts, PP C-6-7

green wavy lines

hiding, WD C-2

potential grammatical errors identified by, WD C-9

gridlines, EX D-10

Group command, in PowerPoint, PP C-8-9

Group Header, AC D-6

grouping

defined, AC D-4

objects, PP C-8-9

records in reports, AC D-4-5

Grouping dialog box, AC D-3

groups, of folders, in Outlook, OL A-6-7

▶H

handles

on controls, AC C-4

fill, EX B-12, EX B-14

Hanging Indent Marker, WD C-10

hanging indents

defined, WD C-11

formatting, WD C-11

hard disks, W B-2

hardware upgrades, W98 2

Header and Footer dialog box, for slides, PP B-13

Header row option button, in tables, WD D-10

headers, adding to slides, PP B-13

Help

accessing with right mouse button, IE A-13

Excel, EX A-14-15

Internet Explorer 3, IE A-12-13

Internet Explorer 4, IE4 A-12-13

Office Assistant, WD A-14-15

PowerPoint, PP A-14-15

What's This pointer, WD A-15

Windows 95, W A-16-17

Windows 98, W98 15

Word, WD A-15

Help button (?), W A-17

Help Topics dialog box, W A-17

highlighting attribute, EX C-6

"hits," found by search engines, IE A-17

hits, in Internet searches, IE4 A-16

Home button, IE4 A-10

Internet Explorer, IE A-10

home pages

creating, IE4 B-2

defined, IE B-2

selecting, IE4 A-10

selecting in Internet Explorer, IE A-11

horizontal ruler, in Word program window, WD A-6-7

horizontal scroll bar, W A-14-15

in Word program window, WD A-6-7

hovering, mouse operation, W98 8

HTML

codes, IE4 B-4

defined, IE4 B-1, W98 9, IE A-1

dynamic, IE4 B-11

formatting buttons, IE4 B-7

saving documents in, IE4 B-4

static, IE4 B-11

HTML files, *See also* Web pages; Web publications

defined, W98 9

in Web view, W98 12-13

http (HyperText Transfer Protocol), IE4 A-8, IE A-8

Hyperlink button, IE4 B-16

hyperlinks. *See* links

Hypertext Markup Language (HTML). *See* HTML

►I

icons

defined, W A-1, W A-2

selecting with mouse, W A-4

underlined names, in Windows 98, W98 3, W98 4-5

Image button, on Toolbox toolbar, AC C-14

images, inserting in Web pages, IE4 B-6-7

Import Clips command button, PP C-3

importing, tables, IN B-6-7

Inbox, OF A-12-13

defined, OL A-6-7

managing, OL A-14-15

sorting messages in, OL A-14-15

Inbox folder, OL A-6-7

Increase Indent button, WD C-10, WD C-14

for Web publications, IE B-6

indenting

lists, IE4 B-6

paragraphs, WD C-10-11

indicators, in row selectors, AC B-6

input, for databases, AC B-2

Insert dialog box, EX C-10-11

Insert Hyperlink dialog box, IE4 B-16, IE B-16-17

inserting

links, IE B-16-17

merge fields, IN B-4

objects, PP C-4, IN C-6, IN C-8-9

pictures, AC C-14-15, IE B-6

rows and columns in worksheets, EX C-10-11

slides, PP B-8

tables, WD D-2, WD D-4-5, IN C-4

text, WD A-10-11

insertion point

in cells, EX B-4

defined, WD A-4

in title slides, PP B-6

Insert Merge Field menu button, IN B-4

Insert Microsoft Word Table button, IN C-4

Insert New Slide button, on Standard toolbar, PP B-8

Insert Object dialog box, PP C-4, IN C-6, IN C-8-9

Insert Picture dialog box, AC C-14-15, IE B-6

Insert Table button, on Standard toolbar, WD D-2,
WD D-4-5

Insert Table command, on Table menu, WD D-2

integration, *See also* multitasking

of Access and Excel, exporting tables from Access
to Excel, IN B-6-7

of Access and Word, merging data between,
IN B-2-5

of Excel and PowerPoint

embedding Excel charts into PowerPoint slides,
IN C-6-7

linking Excel worksheets to PowerPoint slides,
IN C-8-9

updating linked Excel worksheets in PowerPoint,
IN C-10-11

of Excel and Word, I A-1-7

copying Word data into Excel, I A-4-5

creating Dynamic Link (DDE) between Word and
Excel, I A-6-7

opening multiple programs, I A-2-3

of PowerPoint and Word

embedding Word tables into PowerPoint slides,
IN C-4-5

exporting PowerPoint presentations to Word,
IN C-12-13

inserting Word documents into PowerPoint
presentations, IN C-2-3

Internet

communications software, Windows 98, W98 15

defined, IE4 A-2, IE A-2, OL A-2

history, IE4 A-4

history of, IE A-3

searching, IE4 A-16-17

Internet Assistant Wizard, IE4 B-12-13, IE B-12-13

Internet Connection Wizard, W98 15

Internet Explorer 3, OF A-2, IE A-1-19

browser window elements, IE A-6-7

defined, IE A-2

dialog box, IE A-12-13

exiting, IE A-18-19

Favorites, IE A-8

features, OF A-14-15

following Web page links, IE A-10-11

Help, IE A-12-13

Home button, IE A-10

Home page, IE A-11

icon, IE A-4, IE A-5

initial page displays, IE A-4, IE A-5

opening and saving URLs in, IE A-8-9

printing Web pages, IE A-14-15

searching the Internet with, IE A-16-17

starting, IE A-4-5

Stop button, IE A-10

Internet Explorer 4

browser window, IE4 A-6-7

capabilities, IE4 A-2

exiting, IE4 A-18-19

Help, IE4 A-12-13

icon, IE4 A-4, IE4 A-5

starting, IE4 A-4-5

suite components, IE4 A-3

Windows 98 features, W98 15

intranets, IE4 B-1, IE B-1

italic text, WD C-2, EX C-6-7, PP C-12

►J

Journal, OF A-12, OL AP-6-7

justification, in Word, WD C-8-9

►K

keyboard shortcuts, W A-11

for tables, AC A-10, AC A-11

keystrokes, for navigating datasheets, AC B-8

keywords, for Internet searches, IE4 A-16, IE A-16

►L

labels

alignment of, EX A-10, EX C-6-7

attributes of, EX C-6-7

creating, AC D-16-17

defined, EX A-10

defining fields in, AC D-17

entering in worksheets, EX A-10-11

truncated, EX A-10

Label Wizard, AC D-16-17

landscape orientation, for charts, EX D-16-17

Large Icons button, on My Computer toolbar, W B-12

Learning Outlook, *See also* Microsoft Outlook
 defined, OL A-1
 starting, OL A-4-5
 window elements, OL A-6-7
left-aligned tab marker, WD C-6, WD C-7
left alignment, WD C-8
Left-handed radio button, W A-12
Left Indent Marker, WD C-10
left tab stop, WD C-6
legends
 for charts, EX D-3, PP C-10
  moving, EX D-6
Letter Wizard, WD A-10
line charts, EX D-3
Line Color list arrow, PP C-4
Linesize box, in Paint, W B-4
line spacing, WD C-12-13
Line Style list arrow, WD C-16
linking
 vs. embedding, IN C-8, IN C-9
 Excel worksheets to PowerPoint slides, IN C-8-9
links, IE4 B-4
 absolute, IE4 B-16, IE B-16
 adding to Web pages, IE4 B-16-17
 breaking, I A-7
 creating, IE4 B-2
 defined, IE4 A-2, W98 4, OF A-14, IE A-2
 dynamic link exchange (DDE), I A-6-7
 in Explorer windows, W98 12-13
 history of, IE A-3
 identified by search engines, IE A-16-17
 navigating Web pages with, IE4 A-10-11
 relative, IE4 B-16, IE B-16
 updating linked objects, IN C-10-11
 in Web pages, IE B-2, IE B-16-17
  following, IE A-10-11
Links dialog box, I A-7, IN C-11
Links toolbar, Windows 98, W98 6
lists
 bulleted, IE4 B-4, IE4 B-6, WD C-14-15
 indenting, IE4 B-6
 numbered, WD C-14-15
 in Web publications, IE B-4
long filenames, Windows Explorer settings, PP A-13
Look in list box, EX A-8
Lookup Wizard data type, AC B-7

▶ M

Magnifier pointer
 using in datasheets, AC A-12, AC A-13
 using in reports, AC D-5
 using in Word, WD B-14
Mail Merge, IN B-2-5
 buttons, IN B-2
 dialog box, IN B-2-3
main document, for Mail Merge, IN B-2, IN B-3
main text, in Outline view, PP B-10-11
main text placeholders, in title slides, PP B-6-7
Major Gridlines checkbox, EX D-10
Maximize button, W A-8, WD A-6, WD B-6, AC A-6
Meeting Planner, in Calendar, OL AP-2
Memo data type, AC B-7
menu bar
 defined, W A-10, EX A-6
 Internet Explorer 4, IE4 A-6-7
 Internet Explorer, IE A-6-7
 Outlook, OL A-6-7
 PowerPoint, PP A-8-9
 sorting with, AC B-12
 Word, WD A-6-7
menus, W A-10-11
 cascading, W A-6-7
 defined, W A-10
 typical items on, W A-11
Merge and Center button, EX C-6-7
Merge to New Document button, IN B-4
merging
 defined, IN B-2
 inserting merge fields, IN B-4-5
 Word and Access files, IN B-2-5
message header, defined, OL A-6-7
message header icons, in Outlook, OL A-7
messages. *See* electronic mail (e-mail)
Microsoft Access dialog box, AC A-4
Microsoft Clip Gallery 3.0 dialog box, PP C-2-3
Microsoft Excel program icon, EX A-4
Microsoft Graph, PP C-6-7
 chart types, PP C-7
 customizing charts in, PP C-11
Microsoft Office 97 Professional
 basics, OF A-1-15
 components, OF A-2-3

 features, OF A-2
Microsoft Office Shortcut bar, OF A-2, OF A-3
Microsoft Outlook, OF A-2, OL A-1-19, *See also*
 Learning Outlook
 Calendar, OL AP-2-3
 Contacts, OL AP-4-5
 creating and sending messages, OL A-10-11
 defined, OL A-1
 e-mail basics, OL A-2-3
 features, OF A-12-13, OL AP-1
 files, OL AP-6
 forwarding messages, OL A-12-13
 Inbox management, OL A-14-15
 Journal, OL AP-6-7
 Learning Outlook, OL A-1, OL A-4-7
 Notes, OL AP-2, OL AP-3
 personal distribution lists, OL A-16-19
 replying to messages, OL A-8-9
 Tasks, OL AP-2-3
Microsoft PowerPoint, on Programs menu, PP A-4-5
Microsoft Windows 95
 closing programs in, W A-18-19
 defined, W A-1
 desktop elements, W A-3
 dialog boxes in, W A-12-13
 file management, W B-10-11
 formatting a floppy disk in, W B-2-3
 getting started, W A-1-19
 Help, W A-16-17
 menus in, W A-10-11
 resizing windows in, W A-8-9
 scroll bars, W A-14-15
 shutting down, W A-18-19
 starting, W A-2-3
 starting programs in, W A-6-7
 toolbars in, W A-10-11
 working with multiple programs in, W B-8-9
Microsoft Windows 98, W98 1-15
 Active Desktop, W98 8-10
 background wallpaper, W98 8-10
 desktop, W98 2-4
 features, W98 15
 mouse operation in, W98 7-8
 Quick Launch toolbar, W98 3, W98 4, W98 5-6
 Start menu, W98 7
 taskbar toolbars, W98 5-6

underlined icon names, W98 3, W98 4-5

updating, W98 15

upgrading to, W98 2

Microsoft Word Mail Merge Wizard dialog box, IN B-2-3

Minimize button, W A-8, I A-2

Modify the table design option button, AC B-4

Mosaic, IE4 A-4, IE A-3

mouse, W A-4-5

clicking with, W A-4, W A-5

double-clicking with, W A-4, W A-5

dragging with, W A-4, W A-5

left button, W A-4

pointing with, W A-4, W A-5

right-clicking, W A-4, W A-5

selecting icons with, W A-4

selecting text with, WD A-13

in Windows 98, W98 7-8

mouse pointer, W A-4

shapes, W A-5, AC C-5, PP B-6

trail, W A-12

Mouse Properties dialog box, W A-12-13

Move Up button, on Outlining toolbar, PP B-10

moving

around worksheets, EX A-11

cell contents, EX B-10

charts, EX D-6-7

columns, AC A-10

files, W B-10, W B-14-15

text in slides, PP C-10-11

text in Word, WD A-2, WD B-8-9

Word data into Excel, I A-4-5

worksheets, EX B-16-17

MS-DOS, W A-3

multiple documents, opening in Word, WD B-6, WD B-7

multiple programs, working with, W B-8-9

multiple worksheets, viewing, EX D-7

multitasking, See also integration

defined, I A-2

opening two programs, I A-2-3

My Computer

copying files using, W B-14-15

creating folders in, W B-12-13

file management with, W B-10-11

formatting a floppy disk with, W B-2-3

icon, W A-2

moving files with, W B-14-15

toolbar, W B-12

viewing files in, W B-12-13

My Computer window, Web view, W98 11, W98 12

▶ N

name box, EX A-6

naming

files, W B-10, W B-16

folders, W B-16-17

worksheets, EX B-16-17

navigation buttons, toolbars, W98 13-14

Netscape Navigator, IE4 A-4

networks, IE A-2, OL A-2

defined, IE4 A-2

New Database button, AC B-4

New Form dialog box, AC C-2-3

New Mail Message button, OL A-10

New Mail Message window, OL A-10-11

New Object button, AC D-2, AC D-12

creating simple forms with, AC C-3

New Personal Distribution List Properties dialog box,
OL A-16-17

New Presentation dialog box, PP B-4, PP B-5

New Record button, AC A-10, AC C-16

New Report dialog box, AC D-2, AC D-13, AC D-16

New Slide dialog box, PP B-8-9

New Task button, in Task, OL AP-2

Next button, for scrolling through e-mail messages,
OL A-8

Next Slide button, PP B-12

nonprinting characters, displaying with Show/Hide
button, WD A-12

Normal View button, WD A-6

Notes, OF A-12, OL AP-2, OL AP-3

Notes Page view, PP A-10-11

entering text in, PP B-12-13

NSFNET, IE4 A-4

Number data type, AC B-6, AC B-7

numbered lists, WD C-14-15

Numbering button, WD C-14

numerical information, aligning with tabs, WD C-6-7

▶ O

object buttons, for database objects, AC A-8-9

objects

aligning, PP C-8-9

copying onto Clipboard, W B-8-9

defined, EX D-6

editing, PP C-6-7

embedding, using Paste Special, IN C-7

flipping, PP C-7

grouping, PP C-8-9

rotating, PP C-7

selecting AutoShapes menu, PP C-4-5

on slides, PP B-6-7

stacking order, PP C-9

Office Assistant, WD A-10, WD A-14-15, AC D-10

changing appearance of, EX A-14, AC A-14

closing, EX A-14

dialog box, EX A-14

in Excel, EX A-14-15

in PowerPoint, PP A-8, PP A-14, PP A-15

in Spelling and Grammar dialog box, WD B-10

Standard toolbar button, AC A-14

using in Access, AC A-14-15

OLE object data type, AC B-7

One Page button, on Print Preview toolbar, WD B-14

online Help. See Help

Open Database dialog box, AC A-8

Open dialog box, EX A-8, EX A-9, PP C-2

Find area, searching for files in, PP C-3

Word, WD B-4, WD B-5

opening documents, WD B-4-5

multiple, WD B-6, WD B-7

operating systems, W A-3

Operator list arrow, EX C-14

operators, arithmetic, EX B-6, AC B-16

Options tab, for sending e-mail messages, OL A-11

Or criteria, in complex queries, AC B-16, AC B-17

order of precedence, in formulas, EX B-7

Outline formatting, WD C-4

outlines, Word, inserting into PowerPoint slide, IN C-2-3

Outline View, PP A-10-11, PP A-12

inserting Word documents into, IN C-2

working in, PP B-10-11

Outlining toolbar, PP B-10

commands, PP B-11

Outlook. See Microsoft Outlook

Outlook Bar, defined, OL A-6-7

output

of databases, AC B-2

of presentations, PP B-2

for worksheets, EX B-2-3

ovals, creating in PowerPoint, PP C-4

OVR indicator, WD A-10

Index

►P

Page Footer, AC D-6

Page Footer section, AC D-2

Page Header, AC D-6

Page Header section, AC D-2

  control headings, AC D-6-7

  Units control, AC D-8

Page Layout View button, WD A-6

Page Setup dialog box, AC A-13

Paint

  creating files, W B-4-5

  saving files, W B-6-7

  toolbox tools, W B-5

  working with WordPad and, W B-8-9

Paragraph dialog box, WD C-9, WD C-10

paragraphs

  alignment, WD C-8-9

  formatting, WD C-1

  indenting, WD C-10-11

  spacing, WD C-12-13

Password box, Outlook, OL A-4

password dialog box, W A-2

passwords, security of, OL A-4, OL A-5

Paste button, on Standard toolbar, WD B-6, WD B-8, I A-4

Paste function

  for entering functions, EX B-8, EX B-9

  in Excel, OF A-6

Paste Special

  creating dynamic link with, I A-6

  embedding objects using, IN C-7

Pattern list arrow, EX C-12

patterns, in worksheets, EX C-12-13

pen, annotation, PP C-12-13

Percent Style button, EX C-2

peripheral device support, Windows 98, W98 15

Personal Address Book, OL A-16-19

Personal Distribution Lists

  creating, OL A-16-17

  sending mail to, OL A-18-19

personal lists, OL A-16

pictures, *See also* graphics

  cropping, PP C-4-5

  defined, PP C-4

  inserting in slides, PP C-4-5

  transparent backgrounds for, PP C-4

Picture toolbar, PP C-4

pie charts, EX D-3, EX D-8

  pulling slice from, EX D-15

placeholders

  AutoLayout types, PP B-9

  charts, PP C-6-7

  clip art, PP C-2

  text, PP B-6-7, PP B-12

planning

  charts, EX D-2-3

  databases, AC B-2-3

  documents, WD B-2-3

  presentations, PP B-2-3

  Web publications, IE B-2-3

pointer trail, mouse, W A-12

pointing, W A-4, W A-5

  specifying cell references with, EX B-6

point size, EX C-4-5

pop-up menus, displaying, W A-4, W A-5

pound sign (#) wildcard, in Find command, AC B-9

PowerPoint 97, OF A-2

  AutoContent Wizard, PP A-6-7

  creating presentations, PP B-1-17

  creating Web pages, IE B-14-15

  drawing in, PP C-4-9

  embedding Excel charts in slides, IN C-6-7

  evaluating presentations, PP B-16-17

  exiting, PP A-16-17

  exporting presentations to Word, IN C-12-13

  features, OF A-10-11, PP A-2-3

  getting starting, PP A-1-17

  Help, PP A-14-15

  inserting Word outlines into slides, IN C-2-3, IN C-4-5

  linking Excel worksheets to slides, IN C-8-9

  modifying presentations, PP C-1-17

  mouse pointer shapes, PP B-6

  Notes Page view, PP B-12-13

  Outline view, PP B-10-11

  output capabilities, PP A-3

  printing files, PP A-16-17

  saving presentations, PP A-12-13

  searching for files, PP C-3

  shortcut, PP A-5

  spell checking, PP B-14-15

  starting, PP A-4-5

  startup dialog box options, PP A-7

  text editing, PP C-10-11

  updating linked Excel worksheets in, IN C-10-11

  uses of, PP A-1

  viewing presentations, PP A-10-11

  views, PP A-8-9

  window elements, PP A-5, PP A-8-9

PowerPoint startup dialog box, PP C-2

PowerPoint Viewer, PP A-2, PP C-13

.PPT extension, PP A-13, PP A-14

precedence, order of, in formulas, EX B-7

Presentation Designs tab, PP B-4

presentation design templates

  consistency and, PP B-16

  creating, PP B-17

  defined, PP B-1

  vs. presentation templates, PP B-4

presentation graphics, OF A-2, PP A-2

presentations, OF A-10-11

  checklist for, PP C-17

  clip art in, PP C-2-3

  creating new slides, PP B-8-9

  creating Web pages from, IE4 B-14-15, IE B-14-15

  design guidelines, PP B-16-17

  determining output type, PP B-2

  determining purpose of, PP B-2

  enhancing, PP C-1-17

  entering slide text, PP B-6-7

  evaluating, PP B-16-17

  exporting to Word, IN C-12-13

  inserting Word outlines into, IN C-2-3

  modifying, PP C-1-17

  planning, PP B-2-3

  printing, PP A-16-17

  saving, PP A-12-13

  slide show commands, PP C-12-13

  speaker's notes for, PP B-12-13

  spell checking, PP B-14-15

  templates for, PP B-4-5

  titles for, PP B-2

  viewing, PP A-10-11

  viewing in black and white, PP A-17

  working in outline view, PP B-10-11

Presentation style screen, PP A-6

presentation templates, vs. presentation design templates, PP B-4

Presentation type screen, PP A-6

Presentation window, PP A-8-9

Preview feature, W B-10

previewing
  charts, EX D-16
  clip art, PP C-2
  datasheets, AC A-12-13
  documents, WD A-16-17, WD B-14-15
  file contents, W B-10
  files, W B-17
  Web pages, IE B-8, IE B-10, IE B-12, IE B-14
  worksheets, EX A-12-13
Previous button, e-mail, OL A-8
Previous Slide button, PP B-10
primary key, AC A-2, AC B-4
Print dialog box, EX A-12-13
  Internet Explorer, IE A-14-15
  options, AC A-12, AC A-13
  Word, WD B-16, WD B-17
printer properties, Internet Explorer 4, IE4 A-15
printing
  charts, EX D-16
  datasheets, AC A-12-13
  documents, WD A-16-17, WD B-16-17
  Help topics, EX A-14
  options, IE4 A-15
  presentations, PP A-16-17
  Web pages, IE4 A-14-15, IE A-14-15
  worksheets, EX A-12-13
Print Preview, WD B-14-15
  charts, EX D-16
  keyboard shortcut, WD B-14
  worksheets, EX A-12
  Zoom, EX A-13, AC D-4
priority level, e-mail, OL A-11, OL A-14, OL A-15
program buttons, active, I A-2, I A-3
programs
  closing, W A-18-19
  defined, W A-2
  running side by side, I A-2-3
  shortcut keys for, I A-3
  starting in Windows 95, W A-6-7
Programs menu, WD A-4
proofreading, documents, WD A-2, WD B-10-11
Properties dialog box, W B-16
Properties Sheet
  Expression Builder, AC C-8-9
  formatting controls with, AC C-10-11
publishing
  defined, IE B-1

Web pages, IE4 B-1
Web publications, IE4 B-17
Publish to the Web Wizard, IE4 B-10, IE B-10-11

▶ Q

queries
  complex, AC B-16-17
  creating reports from, AC D-12-13
  defined, AC A-2
  expressions in, AC B-16-17
  saving, AC B-14, AC B-15, AC B-16, AC B-17
  select, AC B-14-15
  simple, AC B-14-15
Query Design toolbar, AC B-14-15
question mark (?) wildcard, in Find command, AC B-9
Quick Launch toolbar
  buttons, W98 6
  Windows 98, W98 3, W98 4, W98 5-6
Quick View command, W B-17

▶ R

radio buttons, in dialog boxes, W A-13
random access memory (RAM), W B-6
range finder, EX B-14
range names, in workbooks, EX B-5
ranges
  for charts, selecting, EX D-4
  defined, EX A-10, EX B-5
  formatting, EX C-2
  working with, EX B-4-5
recalculation, EX A-2
recipients, for e-mail messages, OL A-10
records
  adding with forms, AC C-16-17
  adding to tables, AC B-8
  editing, AC A-10-11
  entering, AC A-10-11
  finding, AC B-8-9
  grouping in reports, AC D-4-5
rectangles, creating in PowerPoint, PP C-4
Recycle Bin, W B-18
  icon, W A-2
  size of, resetting, W B-18
Redo Typing feature, in Word, WD A-12
red wavy lines
  hiding, WD C-2

indicating spelling errors, WD C-9, PP B-6, PP B-12, PP B-15
Rehearsal dialog box, PP C-15
rehearsing, slide timing, PP C-15
relational databases, AC A-2
relative cell references, copying formulas with, EX B-12-13
relative hyperlinks, IE B-16
relative links, IE4 B-16
Remove Filter button, AC B-12
Remove Single Field button, AC C-2
renaming. See naming
Replace command, PP C-13
Replace dialog box, WD B-12
replacing
  attributes in slides, PP C-13
  text, WD A-12-13, WD B-12-13
  text in slides, PP C-12, PP C-13
replying to e-mail with, OL A-8-9
Report Detail section, AC D-2
Report Footer section, AC D-2, AC D-6
Report Header section, AC D-2, AC D-6
reports, OF A-8-9, AC D-1-17
  adding expressions to, AC D-10-11
  adding fields to, AC D-10
  aligning fields, AC D-6-7
  creating, AC D-1-2
  creating from queries, AC D-12-13
  creating labels, AC D-16-17
  database, AC A-2
  grouping records in, AC D-4-5
  resizing controls, AC D-8-9
  saving forms as, AC D-14-15
  value of, AC D-1
Report Wizard, AC D-2
  dialog box, AC D-2, AC D-12, AC D-13
resizing. See sizing
restoring files, W B-18-19
reviewing documents, WD B-14-15
ribbon objects
  editing, PP C-6-7
  selecting and sizing, PP C-4-5
right-aligned tab marker, WD C-6, WD C-7
right alignment, WD C-8
right-clicking
  to access Internet Explorer Help, IE A-13
  defined, W A-4, W A-5

Index

Right-handed radio button, W A-12

Right Indent Marker, WD C-10

Roman numerals, in numbered lists, WD C-14

rotating
 charts, EX D-9
 objects, PP C-7

Row Height command, EX C-9

rows
 creating, WD D-2
 customizing with Draw Table button, WD D-14-15
 dummy, EX C-11
 height of, WD D-5
 inserting and deleting, WD D-6-7, WD D-14-15,
  EX C-10-11

row selectors, indicators in, AC B-6

► S

sans serif fonts, WD C-3

Save As dialog box
 Excel, EX A-8, EX A-9
 Paint, W B-6
 PowerPoint, PP A-12, PP C-1
 for queries, AC B-14, AC B-15
 in Word, WD A-8, WD A-9, WD B-4

Save As/Export dialog box, for queries, AC B-16,
 AC B-17

Save As Report command, AC D-14-15

Save as type list arrow, W B-6

Save as HTML dialog box, IE4 B-8, IE4 B-10, IE4 B-12,
 IE4 B-14, IE B-8, IE B-10

Save as HTML Wizard, IE B-12, IE B-14-15

Save In list arrow, W B-6

saving
 documents, WD A-8, WD A-9
 documents as HTML, IE4 B-4
 documents with new name, WD B-4-5
 forms as reports, AC D-14-15
 Paint files, W B-6-7
 presentations, PP A-12-13
 queries, AC B-14, AC B-15, AC B-16, AC B-17
 URLs, IE4 A-8-9
 Web pages, IE4 A-19, IE A-19
 workbooks, EX A-8-9

ScreenTips
 customizing, WD A-7
 in Word program window, WD A-6-7

scroll bars, W A-14-15, PP A-9, PP A-10
 Internet Explorer, IE4 A-6-7, IE4 A-10, IE A-6-7
 in Word program window, WD A-6-7

scroll boxes, W A-14-15

scrolling, PowerPoint windows, PP A-9, PP A-10

search engines, IE4 A-16, IE A-16-17

searching
 for files, PP C-3
 the Internet, IE4 A-16-17

selecting
 files and folders, W B-15
 text, WD A-12-13

selection bar, in tables, WD D-7

selection box, around title placeholder, PP B-6

selection handles, in charts, EX D-4

Select Names dialog box, OL A-10, OL A-11

select queries, AC B-14-15

Select Query window, AC B-14-15

Select Texture dialog box, IE4 B-8, IE B-8

sending e-mail messages, OL A-8, OL A-10-11

sensitivity level, for e-mail messages, OL A-11

Sent Items folder, in Outlook, OL A-6-7

Series in Columns command, PP C-8, PP C-9

Series in Rows command, PP C-9

serif fonts, WD C-3

shading
 in documents, WD C-16-17
 in tables, IN C-4

Shading Color list arrow, WD C-16

shadows, drop, in chart titles, EX D-12

sheet tabs, EX A-6

Shortcut bar, OF A-2, OF A-3

shortcut keys, opening programs with, I A-3

shortcuts
 adding to Start menu, W B-21
 creating, W B-20-21
 creating folder for, W B-20
 defined, W B-20, WD A-4
 deleting, W B-20
 double-clicking, WD A-4
 PowerPoint, PP A-5
 Word, WD A-4

Show/Hide button, displaying nonprinting characters
 with, WD A-12

Shrink to Fit button, WD B-14

Sign In dialog box, Outlook, OL A-4, OL A-5

simple queries, AC B-14-15

Single Field button, AC B-4

sizing
 charts, EX D-6-7
 clip art, PP C-2
 controls, AC D-8-9
 windows, W A-8-9

sizing handles
 defined, PP C-4
 selecting objects with, PP C-4

slide headers and footers, PP B-13

slide icons
 creating slides with, PP B-10
 moving, PP B-10

Slide indicator box, PP A-10, PP C-10

Slide Layout dialog box, PP C-2, PP C-6

slide miniatures, PP A-6

slides
 adding and arranging text on, PP C-10-11
 animation effects, PP C-16-17
 annotation, PP C-12
 automatic text correction, PP C-16-17
 backgrounds for, PP C-14-15
 color schemes for, PP C-14-15
 comments in, PP C-11
 creating, PP B-8-9
 cropping pictures on, PP C-4-5
 defined, OF A-10
 embedding charts in, PP C-6-7, IN C-6-7
 entering text on, PP B-6-7
 formatting text in, PP C-12-13
 inserting pictures in, PP C-4-5
 inserting Word outlines into, IN C-4-5
 linking worksheets to, IN C-8-9
 objects on, PP B-6-7
 updating linked worksheets in, IN C-10-11
 uses of, PP A-2

Slide Show menu icon, PP C-12

slide shows
 commands, PP C-12-13
 setting timings and transitions, PP C-14-15
 showing on other computers, PP C-13
 sound effects, PP C-14
 transition effects, PP C-14, PP C-15

Slide Show view, PP A-10-11

Slide Sorter view, PP A-10-11, IN C-10-11
 animation effects in, PP C-16-17
 transition effects in, PP C-14-15

slide timing
 rehearsing, PP C-15
 setting, PP C-14-15
slide transitions, setting, PP C-14-15
Slide view, PP A-6, PP A-10-11
 inserting Word documents into, IN C-2
Small Icons
 Control Panel View menu, W A-10
 My Computer toolbar, W B-12
software upgrades, W98 2
Sort dialog box, WD D-11, IN B-6-7
sorting
 by more than one column, WD D-11
 defined, AC B-11
 filtering vs., AC B-12
 imported tables, IN B-6-7
 Inbox messages, OL A-14-15
 order of, WD D-10, WD D-11
 tables, WD D-10-12, AC B-10-11
 using menu bar, AC B-12
sort order
 ascending, AC B-11-12
 descending, AC B-11-12
 selecting, AC D-4, AC D-5
Sort Order button, AC D-4
sound effects, slide shows, PP C-14
source files
 defined, I A-4
 linking, IN C-8
source programs, IN C-1
spacing
 between lines, WD C-12-13
 between paragraphs, WD C-12-13
speaker's notes, creating, PP B-12-13
special effects, in documents, OF A-4
spell checking
 AutoCorrect, PP C-16-17
 automatic, PP B-15
 documents, OF A-4, WD A-2, WD A-9, WD B-10-11
 modifying, EX C-17
 presentations, PP B-14-15
 worksheets, EX C-16-17
Spelling dialog box, EX C-17, PP B-14-15
Spelling and Grammar dialog box, WD B-10-11
Split Cells dialog box, WD D-16-17
spreadsheets, See also worksheets
 defined, OF A-2

uses of, EX A-3
spreadsheet software, EX A-2-3
squares, creating in PowerPoint, PP C-4
stacking order, of objects, PP C-9
Standard toolbar
 Excel, EX A-6
 PowerPoint, PP A-8-9
 Word, WD A-6-7
Stars and Banners menu, PP C-4
Start button, W A-2, WD A-4, AC A-4, PP A-4-5
Start menu, W A-6-7, EX A-4, EX A-5
 adding shortcuts to, W B-21
 categories, W A-6
 Windows 98, W98 7
static HTML pages, IE4 B-11, IE B-11
status bar
 defined, EX A-6
 Internet Explorer 3, IE A-6-7
 Internet Explorer 4, IE4 A-6-7, IE4 A-8
 Outlook, OL A-6-7
 PowerPoint, PP A-8
 Word, WD A-6-7
status indicator
 Internet Explorer 3, IE A-6-7
 Internet Explorer 4, IE4 A-6-7, IE4 A-10
Stop button, IE4 A-10
 to stop transmission of Web pages, IE A-10
styles, in presentations, PP B-16, PP B-17
Subject box, for e-mail messages, OL A-10
suites, OF A-1
SUM function, EX B-8-9
Summary Info dialog box, EX A-8
Summary Options dialog box, AC D-5
surfing the Web, IE4 A-6, IE A-6

▶ T

Table AutoFormat, WD D-12-13, WD D-16
tables, in Access, See also databases
 adding new records to, AC B-8
 complex queries of, AC B-16-17
 creating, AC B-4-5
 creating manually, AC B-5
 creating with Table Wizard, AC B-4-5
 creating Web pages from, IE B-10-11
 criteria for filtering, AC B-12
 data types in, AC B-6, AC B-7
 defined, AC A-2, AC A-8

entering and editing records in, AC A-10-11
 filtering, AC B-12-13
 finding records in, AC B-8-9
 imported, sorting, IN B-6-7
 importing and exporting, IN B-6-7
 keyboard shortcuts, AC A-10, AC A-11
 modifying, AC B-6-7
 moving columns in, AC A-10
 opening, AC A-8-9, AC B-8
 simple queries of, AC B-14-15
 sorting, AC B-10-11
tables, in Web pages, IE4 B-12-13
tables, in Word, WD A-2, WD D-1-17
 calculating data in, WD D-8-9
 converting text to, WD D-4-5
 creating, WD D-2-3
 customizing with Draw Table button, WD D-14-15
 defined, WD D-1
 embedding into slides, IN C-4-5
 formatting, WD D-12-13
 inserting and deleting rows and columns, WD D-6-7
 modifying, WD C-16-17, WD D-16-17
 selection bar, WD D-7
 sorting information in, WD D-10-11
 uses of, WD D-1
Tables and Borders toolbar, WD C-16-17, WD D-16-17
Table Wizard, AC B-4
tab order
 defined, AC C-6
 on forms, changing, AC C-6-7
Tab Order dialog box, AC C-6, AC C-7
tabs
 aligning text with, WD C-6-7
 in dialog boxes, W A-12
 tab alignment indicators, WD C-6-7
 tab markers, WD C-6-7
 tab stops, creating, modifying, and deleting,
  WD C-6-7
tags
 defined, IE4 B-2
 for Web pages, IE B-4
target files, I A-4
Task, OL AP-2-3
taskbar toolbars, Windows 98, W98 5-6
TaskPad, OL AP-2
task requests, OL AP-2
Tasks, OF A-12

Index

Template option button, PP B-4

templates

for documents, WD B-3

for presentations, PP B-4-5

for Web pages, IE4 B-6

for Web publications, IE B-4

text annotation, for charts, EX D-14-15

Text box button, AC D-10

text boxes, in dialog boxes, W A-13

Text and ClipArt AutoLayout, PP C-2

Text data type, AC B-6, AC B-7

text editing, in PowerPoint, PP C-10-11, PP C-12-13

text placeholders

in Notes Page view, PP B-12

in title slides, PP B-6-7

Thesaurus, WD B-11

three-dimensional charts, EX D-8

rotating, EX D-8

3-D Column Charts, EX D-8

tick marks, in charts, EX D-3

tiling, vertically, I A-2

timing, of slide shows, PP C-14-15

Tip of the Day, I A-2

title bar

defined, EX A-6

Internet Explorer 3, IE A-6-7

Internet Explorer 4, IE4 A-6-7

PowerPoint, PP A-8-9

of windows, W A-8

Word, WD A-6-7

titles

adding to X- and Y-axes of charts, EX D-12-13

in Outline view, PP B-10-11

for presentations, PP B-2

title slides

creating, PP B-4-5

entering slide text, PP B-6-7

text placeholders, PP B-6-7

Title Text Color dialog box, PP C-14, PP C-15

tone, of documents, WD B-2

Toolbar command, W A-10

toolbars, W A-10-11

defined, W A-10

floating, PP A-8

Formatting, EX A-6

Internet Explorer 3, IE A-6-7

Internet Explorer 4, IE4 A-6-7

navigation buttons, W98 13-14

Outlook, OL A-6-7

Standard, EX A-6

Web view, W98 13-14

toolbox buttons, locking, AC C-14

Toolbox toolbar, AC C-4

ToolTips, in Access, AC A-6

Tracking Options, for e-mail messages, OL A-12-13

transition effects, slide shows, PP C-14, PP C-15

transition icon, PP C-14

transparent backgrounds, PP C-4

triangle, on menus, W A-11

truncated labels, EX A-10

Tune-Up Wizard, W98 15

TV Viewer, W98 2, W98 15

2-D Column Charts, EX D-8

typefaces, in presentations, PP B-16, PP B-17

Typing Replaces Selection feature, WD A-12-13

typographical errors, identified and corrected by Word, WD A-9

U

unbound controls, AC C-4

adding expressions to, AC D-10

Underline button, on Formatting toolbar, EX C-6-7

underlined letters, on menus, W A-11

underlined text, in Windows 98, W98 3, W98 4-5

Undo Delete command, W B-18

Undo feature, W B-4, W B-5

Undo Typing button, WD A-12

Uniform Resource Locators (URLs), IE A-6

case-sensitivity, IE A-8

defined, IE4 A-8, IE A-8

opening, IE4 A-8-9

opening and saving, IE A-8-9

saving to Favorites, IE4 A-8-9

Units control

Detail section, AC D-8

Page Header section, AC D-8

Universal serial bus (USB), W98 15

upgrading

defined, W98 2

hardware, W98 2

software, W98 2

Up One Level button, on My Computer toolbar, W B-12

V

values

alignment of, EX A-10

defined, EX A-10

entering in worksheets, EX A-10-11

formatting, EX C-2-3

vertical scroll bar, W A-14-15

Internet Explorer, IE4 A-6-7, IE4 A-10, IE A-6-7

Word, WD A-6-7

video playback, Windows 98, W98 15

view buttons

PowerPoint, PP A-8

Word, WD A-6-7

viewing

files with Windows Explorer, W B-16-17

multiple worksheets, EX D-7

presentations, PP A-10-11

presentations in black and white, PP A-17

View menu, W A-10

View Merged Data button, IN B-4

views, PowerPoint, PP A-8

View as Web Page, W98 8

voting options, for e-mail messages, OL A-11

W

wallpaper, Web pages as, W98 8-10

Web. *See* World Wide Web

Web addresses. *See* Uniform Resource Locators (URLs)

Web browsers, IE4 A-2-3, IE4 A-4, IE A-2-3, *See also*

Internet Explorer 3; Internet Explorer 4

defined, IE4 A-2, W98 4, OF A-14, IE A-2

viewing Web publications in, IE4 B-2

Web page appearance and, IE4 B-9, IE B-9

Windows Explorer as, W98 14

Web components

adding to, W98 11

defined, W98 10

on desktop, W98 10-11

Web documents. *See* Web pages; Web publications

Web Page Preview, IE4 B-12, IE B-8, IE B-10, IE B-12, IE B-14

Web pages, *See also* Web publications

adding to Favorites, IE4 A-8-9, IE A-8

adding links, IE4 B-16-17

appearance in browsers, IE4 B-9

backgrounds, IE4 B-8, IE B-12, IE B-14

as background wallpaper, W98 8-10

creating, IE4 B-4-5

creating from Access objects, IE4 B-10-11, IE B-10-11

creating from Excel files, IE4 B-12-13, IE B-12-13

creating from Word documents, IE4 B-8-9, IE B-8-9

creating with PowerPoint, IE4 B-14-15, IE B-14-15

defined, W98 4, IE A-2

dynamic HTML, IE4 B-11, IE B-11

formatting, IE4 B-6-7, IE B-6-7, IE B-8-9

inserting images, IE4 B-6-7

layout styles, IE4 B-4-5

navigating, IE4 A-10-11

planning, IE4 B-4-5

previewing, IE B-8, IE B-10, IE B-12

printing, IE4 A-14-15, IE A-14-15

saving, IE4 A-19, IE A-19

sending as e-mail, IE4 A-19, IE A-19

static HTML, IE4 B-11, IE B-11

tables in, IE4 B-12-13

templates for, IE4 B-6

Web Page Wizard, IE4 B-2-3, IE B-2, IE B-4-5

templates, IE B-4

Web publications, OF A-14, *See also* Web pages

advertising, IE4 B-17

choosing content and style, IE B-5

creating, IE4 B-1-17, IE B-1-17

defined, IE4 B-2, IE B-2

frames in, IE B-14, IE B-15

hyperlinks in, IE B-16-17

Increase Indent button, IE B-6

Insert Picture button, IE B-6

page appearance formatting, IE4 B-2

planning, IE4 B-2-3, IE B-2-3

publicizing, IE B-17

publishing, IE4 B-1, IE4 B-17, IE B-17

tags, IE B-4

Web view

defined, W98 11

in Explorer windows, W98 11-13

toolbars, W98 13-14

what-if analysis, OF A-6, EX A-2, EX B-15

What's This, WD A-15, PP A-14

wildcards, in Find command, AC B-9

windows

minimizing, I A-2

resizing, W A-8-9

restoring to previous size, W A-8-9

side-by-side alignment, I A-2-3

tiling vertically, I A-2

Windows 95. *See* Microsoft Windows 95

Windows 98. *See* Microsoft Windows 98

Windows Explorer

browsing the Web with, W98 14

file management, W B-10-11

renaming folders, W B-16-17

viewing files, W B-16-17

Windows Explorer Options dialog box, PP A-13

Windows Update link, in Windows 98, W98 7

Wizards, PP A-6

.wmf format, PP C-5

Word 97, OF A-2

closing, WD A-16

copying data into Excel, I A-4-5

copying text, WD B-6-7

creating documents with, OF A-4-5

creating dynamic link (DDE) with Excel, I A-6-7

creating Web pages from, IE4 B-8-9, IE B-8-9

defined, WD A-1

editing and proofing documents, WD B-1-17

embedding tables into slides, IN C-4-5

entering and saving text in documents, WD A-8-9

exporting presentations to, IN C-12-13

features, OF A-4-5, WD A-2-3

finding and replacing text, WD B-12-13

formatting documents, WD C-1-17

getting started, WD A-1-17

grammar correction, WD B-10-11

importing tables from Access, IN B-7

inserting and deleting text, WD A-10-11

inserting outlines into PowerPoint slide, IN C-2-3

merging data with Access, IN B-2-5

moving text, WD B-8-9

Office Assistant, WD A-14-15

opening documents in, WD B-4-5

opening with Excel, I A-2-3

previewing documents, WD B-14-15

printing documents, WD B-16-17

Print Preview, WD A-16-17

saving documents with new name, WD B-4-5

selecting and replacing text, WD A-12-13

shortcut, WD A-4

spell checker, OF A-4

spelling correction, WD B-10-11

starting, WD A-4-5

Table AutoFormat, WD D-12-13

Web Page Wizard, IE B-2

Word 97 program window, WD A-4, WD A-5

viewing, WD A-6-7

Word 97 Web Page Wizard, IE4 B-2

WordPad

shutting down, W A-18

starting, W A-6-7

working with Paint and, W B-8-9

word processing software, OF A-2, WD A-2-3

Word Web, IE4 B-2, IE B-2

word-wrap, WD A-8, WD A-9

workbooks

closing, EX A-16-17

creating Web pages from, IE4 B-12-13

defined, EX A-6

opening, EX A-8-9

range names in, EX B-5

saving, EX A-8-9

Work Disk, W B-2

worksheets

borders in, EX C-12-13

color in, EX C-12-13

column width adjustments, EX C-8-9

conditional formatting, EX C-14-15

creating, OF A-6-7, EX B-2-3

creating Web pages from, IE B-12-13

defined, OF A-6, EX A-2

determining formulas needed for, EX B-2, EX B-3

determining output for, EX B-2-3

dummy rows and columns, EX C-11

editing cell entries, EX B-4-5

entering formulas, EX B-6-7

fonts, EX C-4-5

formatting, EX C-1-17

formatting values, EX C-2-3

functions, EX B-8-9

inserting and deleting rows and columns, EX C-10-11

label attributes and alignments, EX C-6-7

linked, updating, IN C-10-11

linking to PowerPoint slides, IN C-8-9

moving, EX B-16-17

multiple, viewing, EX D-7

naming, EX B-16-17

Index

navigating, EX A-11

patterns in, EX C-12-13

planning and designing, EX B-2-3

point size, EX C-4-5

previewing and printing, EX A-12-13

spell checking, EX C-16-17

working with ranges, EX B-4-5

worksheet window, defined, EX A-6

World Wide Web, *See also* Web pages; Web publications

browsing, OF A-14-15

defined, IE4 A-2, W98 4, IE A-2

following links in, IE A-10-11

history, IE4 A-4, IE A-3

opening and saving URLs, IE A-8-9

printing pages from, IE A-14-15

searching, IE A-16-17

write-protection, W B-2, W B-3

Write-Up dialog box, IN C-12-13

WWW. *See* World Wide Web

► X

X-axis

adding title to, EX D-12-13

in charts, EX D-3

title for, PP C-10

XY (scatter) charts, EX D-3

► Y

Y-axis

adding title to, EX D-12-13

in charts, EX D-3

title for, PP C-10

Yes/No data type, AC B-7

► Z

Z-axis, title for, PP C-10

Zoom, I A-4

box, on Standard toolbar, WD D-2

button, on Print Preview toolbar, AC D-4

list arrow, in Notes Page view, PP B-12

using in Print Preview, EX A-13